Mexico City

John Noble

D0103902

LONELY PLANET PUBLICATIONS
Melbourne • Oakland • London • Paris

Mexico City
2nd edition – September 2000
First published – May 1998

Published by
Lonely Planet Publications Pty Ltd A.C.N. 005 607 983
192 Burwood Rd, Hawthorn, Victoria 3122, Australia

Lonely Planet Offices
Australia PO Box 617, Hawthorn, Victoria 3122
USA 150 Linden St, Oakland, CA 94607
UK 10a Spring Place, London NW5 3BH
France 1 rue du Dahomey, 75011 Paris

Photographs
Most of the images in this guide are available for licensing from
Lonely Planet Images.
email: lpi@lonelyplanet.com.au

Front cover photograph
Fruit cups and church (Paul Edmondson/Tony Stone Images)

ISBN 1 86450 087 5

Printed by SNP Offset (M) Sdn Bhd
Printed in Malaysia

Although the authors
and Lonely Planet try
to make the informa-
tion as accurate as
possible, we accept
no responsibility for
any loss, injury or
inconvenience sus-
tained by anyone
using this book.

Contents

The Author

John Noble

John grew up in the cool, green valley of the River Ribble, England. He escaped intermittently from a career in newspaper journalism by taking lengthy trips to various parts of the globe, one of the first of which included a six-week stay in Mexico City. Since then he has made regular extended visits to the megalopolis, several of them in the course of research for Lonely Planet's *Mexico* guide, of which he has been a co-author since 1987 and coordinating author since 1993. John also wrote the first edition of this Mexico City guide and in between times he has written or cowritten editions of numerous Lonely Planet books including *Spain, Andalucía, Walking in Spain, USSR, Baltic States, Central Asia, Australia, Indonesia, Sri Lanka* and *Russia, Ukraine & Belarus.* John and his wife and fellow author Susan Forsyth and their children Isabella and Jack (all experienced Mexico travelers) currently have home base in southern Spain.

FROM THE AUTHOR

John proffers extra-special thanks to Ron Mader, Danny Schechter, Myra Ingmanson and Anthony Wright for hospitality, introductions, good company and countless invaluable snippets of information and advice. He's also grateful to fellow *Mexico* authors James Lyon, Scott Doggett, Nancy Keller and Michele Matter for facts and comradeship, which benefited this book, too; to senior editor Tom Downs for many qualities including patience; to eagle-eyed editor Rebecca Northen for introducing many good ideas and removing many silly errors; to Tracey Croom, Colin Bishop and the map team for producing some excellent maps from some very complicated instructions; Jen Loy for data on airfares; Elvira and everyone at Hostal Moneda, Mundo Joven, Viajes Educativos and the Casa de los Amigos for varied information and help; all readers of this book's previous edition and of Lonely Planet's *Mexico* who took the trouble to send in news and views on Mexico City; and, not least, Susan for keeping the home fires burning while John raced around Mexico then came home and sat at his keyboard night after night. And *gracias* to chilango band Café Tacuba whose songs always carry him straight to *la gran Tenochtitlán!*

This Book

The 1st edition of *Mexico City* was also researched and written by John Noble.

FROM THE PUBLISHER

This 2nd edition of *Mexico City* was produced in Lonely Planet's Oakland office. The book was edited by Rebecca Northen. Senior editor and all-around cool cat Tom Downs guided the project, with senior editor 'Fancy' Michele Posner deftly stepping in for him when he went off to do some writing. Millions of little questions were answered by the patient Robert Reid, and proofing tasks were shared by Paige Penland and Kevin Anglin. Ken DellaPenta indexed the book.

Lead cartographer Colin Bishop drew and perfected the maps under the gentle watch of senior cartographer Tracey Croom. Some early map drawing was done by Mary Hagemann, and other cartographic efforts included those of Monica Lepe, Eric Thomsen, Andy Rebold, Dion Good, Heather Haskell, Matt DeMartini and Connie Lock.

Book layout was handled by design whiz Margaret Livingston, while Beca Lafore and Rini Keagy designed the cover. Illustrations were drawn by artists Justin Marler, Hannah Reineck, Rini, Beca, Jennifer Steffey, Hugh D'Andrade, Hayden Foell and Lisa Summers, with design efforts overseen by Susan Rimerman.

Foreword

ABOUT LONELY PLANET GUIDEBOOKS

The story begins with a classic travel adventure: Tony and Maureen Wheeler's 1972 journey across Europe and Asia to Australia. Useful information about the overland trail did not exist at that time, so Tony and Maureen published the first Lonely Planet guidebook to meet a growing need.

From a kitchen table, then from a tiny office in Melbourne (Australia), Lonely Planet has become the largest independent travel publisher in the world, an international company with offices in Melbourne, Oakland (USA), London (UK) and Paris (France).

Today Lonely Planet guidebooks cover the globe. There is an ever-growing list of books, and there's information in a variety of forms and media. Some things haven't changed. The main aim is still to help make it possible for adventurous travelers to get out there – to explore and better understand the world.

At Lonely Planet we believe travelers can make a positive contribution to the countries they visit – if they respect their host communities and spend their money wisely. Since 1986 a percentage of the income from each book has been donated to aid projects and human-rights campaigns.

Updates Lonely Planet thoroughly updates each guidebook as often as possible. This usually means there are around two years between editions, although for more unusual or more stable destinations the gap can be longer. Check the imprint page (following the color map at the beginning of the book) for publication dates.

Between editions, up-to-date information is available in two free newsletters – the paper *Planet Talk* and email *Comet* (to subscribe, contact any Lonely Planet office) – and on our website at www.lonelyplanet.com. The *Upgrades* section of the website covers a number of important and volatile destinations and is regularly updated by Lonely Planet authors. *Scoop* covers news and current affairs relevant to travelers. And, lastly, the *Thorn Tree* bulletin board and *Postcards* section of the site carry unverified, but fascinating, reports from travelers.

Correspondence The process of creating new editions begins with the letters, postcards and emails received from travelers. This correspondence often includes suggestions, criticisms and comments about the current editions. Interesting excerpts are immediately passed on via newsletters and the website, and everything goes to our authors to be verified when they're researching on the road. We're keen to get more feedback from organizations or individuals who represent communities visited by travelers.

Lonely Planet gathers information for everyone who's curious about the planet – and especially for those who explore it first-hand. Through guidebooks, phrasebooks, activity guides, maps, literature, newsletters, image library, TV series and website, we act as an information exchange for a worldwide community of travelers.

Research Authors aim to gather sufficient practical information to enable travelers to make informed choices and to make the mechanics of a journey run smoothly. They also research historical and cultural background to help enrich the travel experience and allow travelers to understand and respond appropriately to cultural and environmental issues.

Authors don't stay in every hotel because that would mean spending a couple of months in each medium-size city and, no, they don't eat at every restaurant because that would mean stretching belts beyond capacity. They do visit hotels and restaurants to check standards and prices, but feedback based on readers' direct experiences can be very helpful.

Many of our authors work undercover; others aren't so secretive. None of them accept freebies in exchange for positive write-ups. And none of our guidebooks contain any advertising.

Production Authors submit their raw manuscripts and maps to offices in Australia, the USA, the UK or France. Editors and cartographers – all experienced travelers themselves – then begin the process of assembling the pieces. When the book finally hits the shops, some things are already out of date, we start getting feedback from readers and the process begins again....

WARNING & REQUEST

Things change – prices go up, schedules change, good places go bad and bad places go bankrupt – nothing stays the same. So, if you find things better or worse, recently opened or long since closed, please tell us and help make the next edition even more accurate and useful. We genuinely value all the feedback we receive. Julie Young coordinates a well-traveled team that reads and acknowledges every letter, postcard and email and ensures that every morsel of information finds its way to the appropriate authors, editors and cartographers for verification.

Everyone who writes to us will find their name in the next edition of the appropriate guidebook. They will also receive the latest issue of *Planet Talk*, our quarterly printed newsletter, or *Comet*, our monthly email newsletter. Subscriptions to both newsletters are free. The very best contributions will be rewarded with a free guidebook.

Excerpts from your correspondence may appear in new editions of Lonely Planet guidebooks, the Lonely Planet website, *Planet Talk* or *Comet*, so please let us know if you *don't* want your letter published or your name acknowledged.

Send all correspondence to the Lonely Planet office closest to you:

Australia: PO Box 617, Hawthorn, Victoria 3122
USA: 150 Linden St, Oakland, CA 94607
UK: 10A Spring Place, London NW5 3BH
France: 1 rue du Dahomey, 75011 Paris

Or email us at: talk2us@lonelyplanet.com.au

For news, views and updates, see our website: www.lonelyplanet.com

HOW TO USE A LONELY PLANET GUIDEBOOK

The best way to use a Lonely Planet guidebook is any way you choose. At Lonely Planet, we believe the most memorable travel experiences are often those that are unexpected, and the finest discoveries are those you make yourself. Guidebooks are not intended to be used as if they provided a detailed set of infallible instructions!

Contents All Lonely Planet guidebooks follow the same format. The Facts about the Destination chapters or sections give background information ranging from history to weather. Facts for the Visitor gives practical information on issues like visas and health. Getting There & Away gives a brief starting point for researching travel to and from the destination. Getting Around gives an overview of the transport options available when you arrive.

The peculiar demands of each destination determine how subsequent chapters are broken up, but some things remain constant. We always start with background, then proceed to sights, places to stay, places to eat, entertainment, getting there and away, and getting around information – in that order.

Heading Hierarchy Lonely Planet headings are used in a strict hierarchical structure that can be visualized as a set of Russian dolls. Each heading (and its following text) is encompassed by any preceding heading that is higher on the hierarchical ladder.

Entry Points We do not assume guidebooks will be read from beginning to end, but that people will dip into them. The traditional entry points are the list of contents and the index. In addition, however, some books have a complete list of maps and an index map illustrating map coverage.

There may also be a color map that shows highlights. These highlights are dealt with in greater detail later in the book, along with planning questions. Each chapter covering a geographical region usually begins with a locator map and another list of highlights. Once you find something of interest in a list of highlights, turn to the index.

Maps Maps play a crucial role in Lonely Planet guidebooks and include a huge amount of information. A legend is printed on the back page. We seek to have complete consistency between maps and text, and to have every important place in the text captured on a map. Map key numbers usually start in the top left corner.

Although inclusion in a guidebook usually implies a recommendation, we cannot list every good place. Exclusion does not necessarily imply criticism. In fact, there are a number of reasons why we might exclude a place – sometimes it is simply inappropriate to encourage an influx of travelers.

Introduction

Spread across some 2000 sq km of the Valle de México, 2200m high at the heart of the country it rules, Mexico City is a seething, cosmopolitan megalopolis that is by turns exhilarating and overpowering. All the extremes of Mexico the country are here: one moment the city is glamour, color and music, the next it's drabness, poverty and foul smells. This is a city of Aztec pyramids, colonial palaces, world-renowned cultural treasures, and sprawling slums; of earsplitting traffic and quiet, peaceful plazas; of fine boulevards and potholed slum streets; of gourmet restaurants and greasy taco stands; of huge wealth and miserable poverty; of green parks and brown air.

According to United Nations figures, Mexico City is the world's fourth-biggest city (after Tokyo, São Paulo and New York). But no one really knows how many people live here: most estimates are around 20 million. Despite its obvious environmental and economic problems, Mexico City is a magnet to Mexicans and visitors alike because, with nearly a quarter of the country's population, it far outstrips anywhere else in the country in economic, cultural, intellectual and political importance. Mexico City is home to ex-

citing music, art and club scenes, to an ever-growing and ever more varied range of enjoyable restaurants and to some of the world's most fascinating museums. It's also at the forefront of an exciting current of political change as Mexico attempts to move to more open and more democratic government. As one Mexican acquaintance put it, *'Lo que ocurre en México, ocurre en el DF'* – 'What happens in Mexico, happens in Mexico City.'

Mexico City is known to Mexicans simply as México – pronounced 'MEH-hee-ko.' If they want to distinguish it from Mexico the country, they call it either *la ciudad de México* or *el DF* ('el de EFF-e'). The DF is the Distrito Federal (Federal District) in which half the city, including all its central areas, lies. The outlying – and fastest growing – parts of Mexico City are in the state of México, which rings the Distrito Federal on three sides.

When the street bustle becomes too much, there are plenty of relaxing parks and other retreats surprisingly close to the center. Or you can easily hop on a comfortable bus and get away to one of the many attractive smaller cities, or the spectacular countryside, all within a few hours of the city.

Facts about Mexico City

HISTORY

It's accepted that, barring a few Vikings in the north and conceivably some direct transpacific contact with southeast Asia, the pre-Hispanic inhabitants of the Americas arrived from Siberia. They came in several migrations during the last ice age, between perhaps 60,000 and 8000 BC, crossing land now submerged beneath the Bering Strait.

As early as 10,000 BC, humans and animals were drawn to the shores of a lake, Lago de Texcoco, which covered much of the floor of the Valle de México. Some time after 7500 BC the lake began to shrink and hunting became more difficult, so the inhabitants turned to agriculture. A loose federation of farming villages had evolved around Lago de Texcoco and surrounding pools by approximately 200 BC. Probably the biggest village was Cuicuilco (in the south of modern Mexico City), which was destroyed by a volcanic eruption about 100 AD.

Teotihuacán & Tula

The first major city to arise in the area was Teotihuacán, 25km northeast of the lake (about 50km northeast of the center of present-day Mexico City). Now famed for its huge Pirámide del Sol (Pyramid of the Sun) and Pirámide de la Luna (Pyramid of the Moon), Teotihuacán grew into one of Mexico's biggest pre-Hispanic cities. It had an estimated 125,000 people at its height in the 5th century AD, and controlled probably the biggest of all Mexico's pre-Hispanic empires, which may have reached as far south as modern El Salvador and Honduras.

In the 7th century AD, Teotihuacán was plundered and abandoned. Xochicalco, a hilltop site near modern Cuernavaca, south of Mexico City, became a major power center in central Mexico. Another may have been Cholula, near Puebla, east of Mexico City. But probably the most important was Tula, 65km north of Mexico City, the base of a militaristic kingdom that seems to have dominated central Mexico.

Tula is widely thought to have been the capital of a great empire referred to by later Aztec histories as that of the Toltecs (Artificers). It was abandoned about the start of the 13th century, apparently destroyed by Chichimecs, as the various hordes of northern barbarians who periodically raided central Mexico came to be known. Many later Mexican peoples revered the Toltec era as a golden age.

Rise of the Aztecs

The fall of Tula left a number of small city-states around the Lago de Texcoco to compete for control of the Valle de México, or as it was called then, Anáhuac (Near the Water). The ultimate winners were the Mexica ('meh-SHEE-kah') or Aztecs, a wandering Chichimec tribe from the north or west who were led to the Valle de México by their priests.

The Aztecs had settled on the western shore of the lake, but other valley inhabitants objected to Aztec interference in their relations, and to Aztec practices such as wife-stealing and human sacrifice in order to appease their god, Huizilopochtli. In the early 14th century, fighting as mercenaries for Coxcox, ruler of Culhuacán on the southern shore of the lake, the Aztecs defeated nearby Xochimilco and sent Coxcox 8000 human ears as proof of their victory. Coxcox granted them land and even agreed that they could make his daughter an Aztec goddess. Little did he know what this would entail. As described in *The Course of Mexican History* by Michael Meyer & William Sherman:

... the princess was sacrificed and flayed. When her father attended the banquet in his honor, he was horrified to find that the entertainment included a dancer dressed in the skin of his daughter .... Coxcox raised an army which scattered the barbarians ...

Sometime between 1325 and 1345 the Aztecs, wandering around the swampy

VALLE DE MÉXICO IN THE 15TH CENTURY

The Aztec capital Tenochtitlán stood on an island in Lago de Texcoco, and was linked by causeways to important settlements on the nearby shores. Today the lake has been reduced to five artificial lagoons: the Zócalo, the heart of modern Mexico City, is where the center of Tenochtitlán was, but many other central areas of the city stand on reclaimed land.

Approximate Area of
Mexico City in 1990

TEPOTZOTLÁN •

CUAUTITLÁN •

TEOTIHUACÁN •

ACOLMAN
•

Approximate
Area of
Mexico City
in 1910

*Lago de
Texcoco*

TENAYUCA •

TEXCOCO
•

(Lago de
Texcoco
Today)

AZCAPOTZALCO •

• TEPEYAC

TLACOPAN •

• TLATELOLCO
• TENOCHITITLÁN

CHAPULTEPEC •

*15th-Century
Causeways*

MIXCOAC •

• IZTAPALAPA

COYOACÁN •

• CULHUACÁN

TLALPAN •

*Lago de
Xochimilco*

*Lago de
Chalco*

XOCHIMILCO •

• CHALCO

0   5   10 km
0   3   6 miles

fringes of the lake, finally founded their own town, Tenochtitlán, on an island near the lake's western shore (today the downtown area around Mexico City's main plaza, the Zócalo). The site was chosen, according to legend, because there the Aztecs saw an eagle perched on a cactus and eating a snake – a sign, they believed, that they should stop their wanderings and build a city.

In about 1370 the Aztecs began to serve as mercenaries for Azcapotzalco on the western shore of the lake, the rising star among the rival statelets in the valley. When they finally rebelled against Azcapotzalco, about 1427, they became the greatest power in the valley.

Tenochtitlán & the Aztec Empire

As Tenochtitlán rapidly grew into a sophisticated city-state, the Aztecs' sense of their own importance as the chosen people of the voracious Huizilopochtli grew, too. In the mid-15th century they formed the Triple Alliance with the lakeshore states Texcoco and Tlacopan, to conduct the so-called 'Flowery Wars' against Tlaxcala and Huejotzingo, which lay east of the valley. The purpose was to gain a steady supply of the prisoners needed to sate Huizilopochtli's vast hunger for sacrificial victims, so that the sun would continue to rise each day and floods and famines could be avoided. In four days in 1487, the Aztec king Ahuizotl had no less than 20,000 prisoners sacrificed for the dedication of Tenochtitlán's newly rebuilt main temple, the Templo Mayor.

The Triple Alliance brought most of central Mexico from the Gulf Coast to the Pacific (though not Tlaxcala) under its control, and by the early 16th century the Aztec empire stretched far down into southern Mexico. The total population of its 38 provinces may have been about 5 million.

The Aztecs' prosperity allowed them to develop Tenochtitlán into a large, splendid city on a grid plan, with canals used as thoroughfares. Three main causeways beginning at the central *teocalli* (sacred precinct) crossed the lake from Tenochtitlán to the shore: one ran west to Tlacopan, a second

south to Coyoacán, and the third north to Tepeyac. This was the city that amazed the Spanish when they arrived in 1519, by which time the population of Tenochtitlán and the neighboring Aztec island-city of Tlatelolco was an estimated 200,000 – far bigger than any city in Spain at that time. The population of the whole Valle de México at the time has been estimated at 1.5 million, making it even then one of the world's biggest and most densely populated urban areas.

Aztec Economy & Society

The Aztecs practiced a variety of intensive farming methods using only stone and wooden tools, including irrigation, terracing and lake and swamp reclamation. In the marshier parts of the Valle de México they created raised gardens by piling up vegetation and mud from the lake and stabilizing the resulting plots with willows. These *chinampas* – versions of which can still be seen along the canals at Xochimilco in the south of Mexico City – were highly fertile, giving three or four harvests a year.

But the valley couldn't feed its own growing population: the Aztecs also needed to extract tribute from conquered tribes to supplement their resources – another reason for their rapid imperial expansion in the 15th century. The empire yielded products such as jade, turquoise, cotton, paper, tobacco, rubber, lowland fruits and vegetables, cacao and precious feathers, which were needed for the glorification of the elite and to support the many nonproductive servants of its war-oriented state. At Tenochtitlán's height, its imports included about 7000 tons of maize and 5000 tons of beans a year.

The basic unit of Aztec society was the *calpulli*, consisting of a few dozen to a few hundred extended families, owning land communally. The Aztec king held absolute power but delegated important roles such as priest or tax collector to members of the *pilli* (nobles). Military leaders were usually *tecuhtli*, elite professional soldiers. Another special group was the *pochteca*, militarized merchants who helped extend the empire, brought goods to the capital and organized

Aztec Culture & Religion

Tenochtitlán-Tlatelolco had hundreds of temple complexes. At the city's heart stood the main *teocalli* (sacred precinct) with a double-pyramid temple that was dedicated to Huizilopochtli and the water god, Tláloc. The remains of this temple, the Templo Mayor, can be seen today just off the Zócalo.

Much of Aztec culture was drawn from earlier Mexican civilizations. The Aztecs had writing and bark-paper books, and they observed the heavens for astrological purposes. They measured time both in 'sacred years' composed of 13 periods of 20 days, and in 'vague solar years' of 18 20-day 'months' followed by a special five-day 'portentous' period. The interlocking of these two calendars enabled a date to be located precisely within a period of 52 years called a Calendar Round. A routine of great ceremonies, many of them public, was performed by celibate priests. Typically these would include sacrifices and masked dances or processions enacting myths.

The Aztecs believed they lived in the fifth world, whose four predecessors had all been destroyed by the death of the sun and of humanity. Human sacrifices were designed to keep the sun alive. The Aztecs saw the world as having four directions, 13 heavens and nine hells. Those who died by drowning, leprosy, lightning, gout, dropsy or lung disease went to the idyllic gardens of Tláloc, the god who had killed them; warriors who were sacrificed or died in battle, merchants killed traveling far away, and women who died giving birth to their first child all went to heaven as companions of the sun; everyone else traveled for four years under the northern deserts, in the subterranean abode of the death god Mictlantecuhtli, before reaching the ninth hell where they vanished altogether.

large markets, held daily in big towns. At the bottom of the social chain were pawns (paupers who could sell themselves for a specified period of time), *mayeque* (serfs) and slaves.

The Spanish Conquest

The Aztec empire, and with it nearly 3000 years of ancient Mexican civilization, was shattered in two short years – 1519 to 1521. A tiny group of invaders brought a new religion and reduced the native people to second-class citizens and slaves. So alien to each other were the two sides that each doubted whether the other was human (the Pope gave the Mexicans the benefit of the doubt in 1537).

From this traumatic encounter arose modern Mexico. Most Mexicans, being *mestizo* (of mixed indigenous and European ancestry), are descendants of both cultures. But while Cuauhtémoc, the last Aztec emperor, is now an official Mexican hero, Hernán Cortés, the leader of the Spanish conquistadors, is seen as a villain, and native people who helped him as traitors.

The Spanish had been in the Caribbean since Columbus arrived in 1492. Realizing that they had not reached the East Indies, they began looking for a passage through the land mass to their west but were distracted by tales of gold, silver and a rich empire there.

The successor of King Ahuizotl was Moctezuma II Xocoyotzin, a reflective character who believed – perhaps fatally – that Cortés, who arrived on the Gulf Coast in 1519, might be the feathered serpent god Quetzalcóatl, who according to legend had been driven out of Tula centuries before but had vowed to return one day and reclaim his throne.

Cortés' Expedition In 1518 the Spanish governor of Cuba, Diego Velázquez, asked Hernán Cortés, a colonist on the island, to lead a new expedition westward. As Cortés gathered ships and men, Velázquez became uneasy about the costs and Cortés' loyalty, and tried to cancel the expedition. But Cortés ignored him and set sail on February 15, 1519, with 11 ships, 550 men and 16 horses. The Spaniards landed first at Cozumel off the Yucatán Peninsula then moved round the coast to Tabasco. There they defeated some hostile locals and Cortés gave the first of many lectures to Mexicans on the importance of Christianity and the greatness of King Carlos I of Spain. The locals gave him 20 maidens, among them Doña Marina (La Malinche), who became his interpreter, aide and lover.

The expedition next put in near the site of the city of Veracruz. In Tenochtitlán, Moctezuma began hearing tales of 'towers floating on water' bearing fair-skinned beings. Lightning struck a temple, a comet sailed through the night skies, and a bird 'with a mirror in its head' was brought to Moctezuma, who saw warriors in it. Unsure whether Cortés was the returning Quetzalcóatl or not, Moctezuma tried to discourage him from traveling to Tenochtitlán by sending messages about the difficult terrain and hostile tribes that lay between them.

Cortés apparently then scuttled his ships to prevent his men from retreating and, leaving about 150 men on the coast, set off for Tenochtitlán. On the way, he won over the Tlaxcalans as allies. After an unsuccessful attempt to ambush the Spaniards at Cholula, about 120km east of Tenochtitlán, Moctezuma finally invited Cortés to meet him. The Spaniards and 6000 indigenous allies thus entered Tenochtitlán on November 8, 1519. Cortés was met by Moctezuma, who was carried by nobles in a litter with a canopy of feathers and gold.

The Spaniards were lodged in luxury – as befitted gods – in the palace of Axayacatl, Moctezuma's father. But they were trapped. Some Aztec leaders advised Moctezuma to

...and his lookalike, Cortés

attack them, but Moctezuma hesitated and the Spaniards took *him* hostage instead. Moctezuma told his people he went willingly, but hostility rose in the city, aggravated by the Spaniards' destruction of Aztec idols.

Fall of Tenochtitlán After the Spaniards had been in Tenochtitlán about six months, Moctezuma informed Cortés that another fleet had arrived on the Veracruz coast. This had been sent from Cuba to arrest Cortés. Cortés left 140 Spaniards under Pedro de Alvarado in Tenochtitlán and sped to the coast with his remaining forces. They routed the bigger rival force and most of the defeated men joined Cortés.

Meanwhile, things boiled over in Tenochtitlán. Apparently fearing an attack, Alvarado's men struck first and killed about 200 Aztec nobles trapped in a square during a festival. Cortés and his enlarged force returned to the Aztec capital and were allowed to rejoin their comrades, only to come under fierce attack. Trapped in Axayacatl's palace, Cortés persuaded Moctezuma to try to pacify his people. According to one version, the king went on to the roof to address the crowds but was wounded by missiles and died soon afterwards; other versions say that the Spaniards killed him.

Quetzalcóatl...

The Spaniards fled on the night of June 30, 1520, but several hundred, and thousands of their indigenous allies, were killed on what's known as the Noche Triste (Sad Night). The survivors retreated to Tlaxcala, and prepared for another campaign by building boats in sections that could be carried across the mountains for a waterborne assault on Tenochtitlán. When the 900 Spaniards reentered the Valle de México, they were accompanied by perhaps 100,000 native allies.

Moctezuma had been replaced by his nephew, Cuitláhuac, who then died of smallpox brought to Mexico by a Spanish soldier. Cuitláhuac was succeeded by another nephew, the 18-year-old Cuauhtémoc. The attack started in May 1521. Cortés resorted to razing Tenochtitlán building by building, and by August 13, 1521, the resistance ended. The captured Cuauhtémoc asked Cortés to kill him, but was denied his request.

Capital of Nueva España
Establishing their headquarters at Coyoacán on the southern shore of the Lago de Texcoco, the Spaniards had the ruined Tenochtitlán rebuilt as the capital of Nueva España (New Spain), as the new colony was called. The city's central plaza (today the Zócalo) was laid out next to the former site of the Aztecs' teocalli. Beside the plaza, Cortés had a palace (today the Palacio Nacional) and a cathedral built.

From this capital, the Spanish sent out expeditions to subdue not only the rest of the Aztec empire but also other parts of Mexico and Central America that had not been under Aztec control. By 1600 the territory ruled from Mexico City stretched from what's now northern Mexico to the border of Panama (though in practice Central America was governed separately).

Mexico City developed quickly into a prosperous and beautiful, if somewhat unsanitary, capital. Broad, straight streets and elegant plazas were laid out, and fine buildings constructed to Spanish designs in local materials such as *tezontle*, a light-red, porous volcanic rock that the Aztecs had used for their temples. Hospitals, schools, churches, palaces, parks, a university and even an insane asylum were built. But right up to the late-19th century the city suffered floods caused by the partial destruction in the 1520s of the Aztecs' canals. The Lago de Texcoco often overflowed into the city, damaging streets and buildings, bringing epidemics and forcing the relocation of thousands of people. In 1779-80 nearly 20% of the city's population died of smallpox.

Colonial Government & Society
The Spanish king Carlos I denied Cortés the role of governor of Nueva España, and the crown waged a long, eventually successful struggle through the 16th century to restrict the power of the conquistadors in the colony. (Cortés returned disillusioned to Spain in 1540 and died there in 1547.) In 1527 Carlos I set up Nueva España's first *audiencia*, a high court with government functions. Then in 1535 he appointed Antonio de Mendoza as the colony's first viceroy, his personal representative to govern it. Mendoza, who ruled from Mexico City for 15 years, brought badly needed stability, limited the worst exploitation of indigenous people, encouraged missionary efforts and ensured steady revenue to the Spanish crown.

The conquered peoples declined disastrously, less because of harsh treatment than because of a series of plagues, many of them new diseases brought by the Spaniards, such as smallpox and measles. The native population of the Valle de México shrank, by most estimates, to less than 100,000 within a century of the conquest.

The indigenous people's best allies were some of the monks who started arriving in Nueva España in 1523 to convert them. Many of these were compassionate, brave men; the Franciscan and Dominican orders distinguished themselves by protecting the natives from the colonists' worst excesses. The monks' missionary work also helped extend Spanish control over Mexico. Under the second viceroy, Luis de Velasco, indigenous slavery was abolished in the 1550s. Forced labor continued, however, as indigenous slavery was partly replaced by African slavery.

A person's place in colonial Mexican society was determined by their skin color, parentage and birthplace. Spanish-born colonists – known as *peninsulares* or, derisively, *gachupines* – were few in number but were at the top of the pecking order and considered nobility in Nueva España, however humble their status in Spain.

Next on the ladder were the *criollos*, people born of Spanish parents in Nueva España. By the 18th century some criollos had acquired fortunes in the colony.

Below the criollos were the *mestizos*, people of mixed Spanish and indigenous or African-slave ancestry, and at the bottom of the pile were the remaining indigenous people and the Africans. Though the poor were, in the end, paid for their labor, they were paid very little and many were *peones*, bonded laborers tied by debt to their employers.

Criollo Unrest

The Spanish king Carlos III (1759-88), aware of the threat to Nueva España from British and French expansion farther north, sought to bring his colony under firmer control and improve the flow of funds to the crown. He reorganized the colonial administration and expelled the Jesuits, whom he suspected of disloyalty, from the entire Spanish empire. The Jesuits in Nueva España had played major roles in missionary work, education and administration, and two-thirds of them were criollos.

In 1804 the Spanish crown decreed the transfer of the powerful Catholic Church's many assets in Nueva España to the royal coffers. The church had to call in many debts, which hit criollos hard and created widespread discontent. Then, in 1808, France's Napoleon Bonaparte occupied most of Spain and direct Spanish control over Nueva España evaporated. Rivalry in the colony between peninsulares, who remained loyal to Spain, and criollos, who sought political power commensurate with their economic power, intensified. Criollos began plotting rebellion.

Independence

On September 16, 1810, Miguel Hidalgo, the criollo priest of the town of Dolores (now Dolores Hidalgo), 325km northwest of Mexico City, summoned his parishioners and issued his now-famous call to rebellion, the Grito de Dolores. His exact words have been lost to history, but the gist was:

My children, a new dispensation comes to us this day. Are you ready to receive it? Will you be free? Will you make the effort to recover from the hated Spaniards the lands stolen from your forefathers 300 years ago? We must act at once . . . Long live Our Lady of Guadalupe! Death to bad government!

The rebels quickly took most of the main towns north of Mexico City and on October 30 their army, numbering about 80,000, defeated loyalist forces at Las Cruces outside the capital. But Hidalgo decided against advancing on the city – a mistake that would cost him his life, and Mexico 11 more years of fighting before independence was achieved. In 1813 rebel forces under José María Morelos encircled Mexico City, but the loyalists broke through his lines.

Eventually in 1821 the royalist general Agustín de Iturbide defected during an offensive against the rebel leader Nicolás Guerrero. Iturbide and Guerrero worked out a blueprint for Mexican independence called the Plan de Iguala, which won over all influential sections of society. That same year, the incoming Spanish viceroy agreed to Mexican independence. By then Mexico City had a population of 155,000, which made it the biggest city in the Americas.

Santa Anna

The following decades were particularly confusing on the political front, with Mexico ruled by a long succession of short governments. Interference in politics by ambitious generals and a struggle between pro-reform liberals and anti-reform conservatives were two recurring themes. Between 1833 and 1855, while economic decline and corruption became entrenched, the Mexican presidency changed hands 36 times, with 11 of those terms going to one general, Antonio López de Santa Anna. Santa Anna's main contributions to history were manifestations of his megalomaniac personality. In 1842, he had his amputated, mummified leg (which he lost in an 1838 battle with the French) disinterred and paraded through Mexico City.

Santa Anna is also remembered for losing large chunks of Mexican territory to the USA. Missionaries and a few settlers had, by the early 19th century, brought much of what's now the southern and southwestern USA under the rule – albeit often tenuous – of Mexico City. But in 1836 restless American settlers in Texas declared Texas independent and defeated the army that Santa Anna led against them. In 1845 the US congress voted to annex Texas, while US president Polk demanded even more Mexican territory. This led to the Mexican-American War, in which US troops captured Mexico City after a fierce battle at the Ex-Convento de Churubusco in Coyoacán. The Niños Héroes (Boy Heroes), six Mexican military cadets, made the ultimate sacrifice for their country by wrapping themselves in Mexican flags and leaping to their deaths from the Castillo de Chapultepec, rather than surrender to the invaders.

Santa Anna ceded or sold Texas, New Mexico, Arizona, California, Utah and Colorado to the US in the Treaty of Guadalupe Hidalgo (1848) and the Gadsden Purchase (1853).

Mexico City now had a population of about 170,000 but stretched little more than 2km in any direction from the Zócalo: the site of the Zona Rosa was open country, and the Bosque de Chapultepec, Basílica de Guadalupe, San Ángel and Coyoacán, all well within the city today, were several kilometers outside it.

The French Intervention

The liberal government that finally replaced Santa Anna in 1855 attempted to dismantle Mexico's conservative state and break the economic power of the church, but only succeeded in precipitating the internal War of the Reform (1858-61) between liberals and conservatives. The liberals won, but in 1862 France's Napoleon III decided to invade a weakened Mexico. Despite a May 5th defeat

at Puebla (still celebrated every year as Cinco de Mayo), 130km east of Mexico City, the French occupied Mexico City in 1863. The following year Napoleon installed the Austrian archduke, Maximilian of Hapsburg, as emperor of Mexico. The liberal leader Benito Juárez and his government retreated to the provinces.

Maximilian, aged 32, and his wife, Empress Carlota (24), entered Mexico City on June 12, 1864, and moved into the Castillo de Chapultepec (instead of the Palacio Nacional on the Zócalo, traditional residence of Mexico's heads of state). They had Paseo de la Reforma, still the city's grandest boulevard, laid out to connect Chapultepec with the city center. But their reign was brief. Under pressure from the USA, Napoleon withdrew his troops and in 1867 Maximilian – a noble but naive figure – was defeated and executed by republican forces at Querétaro, 215km northwest of Mexico City. President Juárez set in motion economic and educational changes that included completion of a new railway between Mexico City and Veracruz.

The Porfiriato

Mexico City entered the modern age under the despotic Porfirio Díaz, who ruled Mexico for most of the period from 1877 to 1911. Díaz launched an unprecedented building boom in the city and had additional railways constructed to link the city to the provinces and the USA. As well, some 150km of electric tramways were built to provide urban transport while industry expanded. By 1910 the city had well over 400,000 inhabitants. A drainage canal with two tunnels finally succeeded in drying up a large part of the Lago de Texcoco, allowing the city to expand. Díaz's most famous project was one of his last: El Ángel (The Angel), the monument to Mexico's independence on Paseo de la Reforma.

Díaz kept Mexico free of the wars that had plagued it for over 60 years, but at the price of political repression, foreign ownership of Mexican resources, and appalling conditions for many workers. Wealth became concentrated in the hands of a small minority.

The Revolution

All this led to the Mexican Revolution (1910-20), a confusing sequence of allegiances and conflicts between a spectrum of leaders and their armies, in which successive attempts to create a stable government were wrecked by new outbreaks of devastating fighting. When rebels under Francisco 'Pancho' Villa took Ciudad Juárez on the US border in May 1911, Díaz resigned. The liberal Francisco Madero was elected president in November 1911, but found himself in conflict with more radical leaders, including Emiliano Zapata in the state of Morelos, south of Mexico City, who was fighting for the transfer of land from large estates to the peasants. Other forces of varied political complexions took up local causes elsewhere, and soon all of Mexico was plunged into military chaos.

In February 1913, two conservative leaders – Félix Díaz, nephew of Porfirio, and Bernardo Reyes – were sprung from prison in Mexico City and commenced a counter-revolution based in La Ciudadela, a building 700m south of the Alameda Central (Map 4), which brought 10 days of fierce fighting, the 'Decena Trágica,' to the capital. Thousands were killed or wounded and many buildings were destroyed. The fighting ended only after US ambassador Henry Lane Wilson negotiated for Madero's general, Victoriano Huerta, to switch to the rebel side and help depose Madero. Huerta became president; Madero and his vice president José María Pino Suárez were executed.

The unpopular Huerta himself was soon deposed and the revolution devolved into a confrontation between the liberal 'Constitutionalists,' led by Venustiano Carranza, and the forces led by populist Villa and the radical Zapata. But Villa and Zapata, despite a famous meeting in Mexico City in 1914, never formed a serious alliance and the fighting became increasingly anarchic. Carranza emerged the victor in 1917, but in 1920 former allies including Álvaro Obregón and Plutarco Elías Calles ran him out of office and had him assassinated. The revolutionary decade had devastated the economy – starvation was widespread, including in Mexico City – and an estimated 1.5 to 2 million Mexicans, roughly one-eighth of the country's population, had lost their lives.

Reconstruction & Growth

The 1920s ushered in peace and a modicum of prosperity. The post-revolution minister of education, José Vasconcelos, commissioned Mexico's top artists – notably Diego Rivera, David Alfaro Siqueiros and José Clemente Orozco – to decorate numerous public buildings in Mexico City with large, vivid, semipropagandistic murals on social, political and historical themes. This was the start of a major movement in Mexican art, with a lasting impact on the face of the city.

Progress was halted by the Depression, but afterwards a drive to industrialize attracted more and more money and people to the city; Mexico City's population had passed 1.7 million by 1940. In the '40s and '50s factories and skyscrapers rose almost as quickly as the population, which was growing 7% a year. But the supply of housing, jobs and social services could not keep pace; shantytowns started to appear around the city's fringes, and its modern problems began to take shape.

Political and social reform lagged far behind economic growth. Student-led discontent with the government of President

Emiliano Zapata

Gustavo Díaz Ordaz (1964-70) came to a head as Mexico City prepared to stage the 1968 Olympic Games, the first ever held in a developing country. More than half a million people rallied in the Zócalo on August 27, 1968; in mid-September, troops seized the city's UNAM university campus to break up a student occupation. On October 2, 10 days before the games started, several thousand people gathering in Tlatelolco, north of the city center, were encircled by heavily armed troops and police. To this day, no one is certain how many people died in the ensuing massacre, but most estimates put the number between 300 and 400.

Megalopolis

Mexico City continued to grow at a frightening rate in the 1970s, spreading beyond the Distrito Federal into the state of México and developing some of the world's worst traffic and pollution problems, only partly alleviated by the metro system (opened in 1969) and by more recent attempts to limit motor traffic.

People have continued to pour into Mexico City despite the earthquake on September 19, 1985, which registered more than eight on the Richter scale, killed at least 10,000 people (possibly 20,000), made many tens of thousands homeless and caused more than US$4 billion in damage. The spongy ground on which the city stands and shoddy construction of some buildings, heightened the effects of the quake, in which severe tremors continued for three minutes. Buildings above 18 stories high were less badly damaged than some shorter blocks, apparently because they swayed more slowly, allowing each succeeding tremor to counteract the motion before it reached its fullest extent. Mexico City's people carried out a lot of rescue work without officially organized help, a phenomenon that helped launch a wave of independent popular organizations in the following years, campaigning for human and civil rights, political reform and social justice as never before. The movement became known as 'civil society' and has undoubtedly helped spur the democratic reforms of the 1990s.

Today Mexico City's population is estimated at 18 to 20 million. Efforts to move industry and government jobs away from the capital have so far been limited. Since 1940, Mexico City has multiplied in area more than 10 times, yet it's still one of the world's most crowded metropolitan areas, as well as one of the most polluted.

The poverty that has always coexisted with wealth in Mexico City was worsened by the recession of the mid-1990s. Among the most destitute are the thousands of children (14,000 even on official estimates) who live on the city's streets and sleep in drains, metro ventilation shafts and the like. In 1996 it was estimated that more than one-fifth of people in the Distrito Federal were living on marginal levels of basic subsistence, and another two-thirds were hardly able to cover material necessities. Those figures did not include the outer parts of the city in the state of México, where most of the newer shantytowns lie. One effect of the crisis has been a big rise in crime.

In 1997 the Distrito Federal was permitted for the first time to elect its own head of government, after being ruled by regents appointed directly by the federal government since 1928. The winner was Cuauhtémoc Cárdenas of the center-left PRD party. Cárdenas' stated aims, which showed, if nothing else, the nature of the city's challenges, were to improve public security and public services (especially water), tackle traffic problems and pollution, combat organized crime and police corruption, raise salaries and educational standards and bring down unemployment. When Cárdenas stepped down in 1999 to concentrate on his campaign for the national presidency in 2000, the verdict on his less than two years in office was mixed. He had (probably wisely) offered no grand plan to solve the city's problems, but his administration had appeared well-intentioned and honest, encouraged citizen participation and more open government, and took some measures against crime and corruption in the police force and local government. Whether these would have any deep or enduring effect remained to be seen. Cárdenas was succeeded as DF head of government by Rosario Robles, a woman from the left of the PRD. A new head of government was due to be elected in mid-2000.

GEOGRAPHY

Mexico City lies in the 2240m-high Valle de México, a flat, broad valley ringed by hills and mountains, high in the Cordillera Neovolcánica, the volcanic chain that runs across central Mexico from east to west. The valley is about 60km across from east to west and 30 to 40km from north to south. In the north, west and south the city reaches right up to the surrounding hills. In the east the hills are farther away and the perimeter of the valley is marked by the extinct volcano Iztaccíhuatl and the very much alive Popocatépetl. Once regularly visible from the city, this pair – both over 5000m high – can now only be seen on exceptionally clear days. Here and there the stumps of smaller extinct volcanoes, such as Cerro de la Estrella, rise within the city.

The Lago de Texcoco and the adjoining shallow lakes that filled 1500 sq km of the Valle de México before the Spanish came have nearly all been drained, leaving only a few patches of water east of the city and the canals of Xochimilco in the southeast.

All the central areas of Mexico City are in the Distrito Federal (Federal District). Many of the city's outlying areas – and more than half of its population – are in the state of México, which surrounds the Distrito Federal on three sides.

CLIMATE

The weather is temperate or warm all year, and mainly dry. The chart shows average monthly rainfall and temperatures. It can be cool on winter nights, and afternoon showers are common from June to September.

ECOLOGY & ENVIRONMENT

Mexico City is an ecological tragedy. What was once a beautiful highland valley with abundant water and forests now has some of the least breathable air on the planet and only scattered pockets of greenery. It faces the real prospect of serious water shortages in the not too distant future.

Environmental damage in the Valle de México is actually nothing new. As early as the 15th century, king Nezahualcóyotl of Texcoco, alarmed at the dwindling of the valley's forests, decreed tree cutting in some areas punishable by execution. During the colonial period and 19th century, a few voices were raised against further clearing of forests on the hills around the valley. It was argued that the lack of trees was partly responsible for the floods that periodically inundated the valley. Draining the valley's lakes, however, was seen as the solution to the floods – work on this began in the 17th century and was largely completed by 1900. As a result the city suffered fierce dust storms in the 20th century, though these have been alleviated since the 1970s by the Proyecto Texcoco (see 'An Environmental Success Story').

Mexico City's Air

The city's severe traffic and industrial pollution is intensified by the mountains that ring the Valle de México and prevent air from dispersing, and by the altitude and consequent lack of oxygen (air at high altitudes contains less oxygen than air at sea level). Pollution is at its worst in the cooler months, especially from November to February, when an unpleasant phenomenon called thermal inversion is most likely to happen. Thermal inversion occurs when warmer air passing over the valley stops cooler, polluted air near ground level from rising and dispersing.

At any time, the pollution and altitude may make any visitor feel breathless and tired, or cause a sore throat, headache, runny nose or insomnia. People with serious lung,

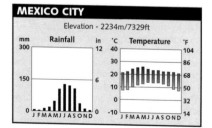

MEXICO CITY

Elevation - 2234m/7329ft

Rainfall — mm 300 / 150 / 0 — in 12 / 6 / 0 — J F M A M J J A S O N D

Temperature — °C 40 / 30 / 20 / 10 / 0 / -10 — °F 104 / 86 / 68 / 50 / 32 / 14 — J F M A M J J A S O N D

heart, asthmatic or respiratory problems are advised to consult a doctor before coming.

Air pollution is blamed for skin problems, nervous disorders, mental retardation, cancer and thousands of premature deaths a year among Mexico City's inhabitants. Estimates of the annual cost of pollution-related disease in the city, in terms of lost wages and costs of medical care, are around US$1 billion.

Industry accounts for some of the air pollution, as does fecal dust from sewerless slums that blows about the city carrying disease, but the major culprit is ozone. Too much ozone causes respiratory and eye problems in humans, and corrodes rubber, paint and plastics. Leaks of unburned LPG (liquefied petroleum gas), used for cooking and heating, play a role in raising ozone levels. But the major ozone producer is generally reckoned to be low-lead gasoline, introduced in 1986 to counter lead pollution, which until then was the city's worst atmospheric contaminant. (By 1985 birds had started falling dead from the city skies, with lethal concentrations of lead and other metals in their bodies.) The reaction between sunlight and combustion residues from low-lead gasoline produces a great deal of ozone.

In an attempt to reduce traffic pollution, many cars in the city have been banned from the streets on one day each week since 1989 in a program called 'Hoy No Circula' (Don't Drive Today). Catalytic converters have been compulsory on all new cars sold in Mexico since the early 1990s. But ozone levels have remained high. Hoy No Circula unwittingly encouraged people to buy or rent extra cars to get around the once-a-week prohibition, and in the program's first year alone, the number of cars in Mexico City grew by 300,000. Today there are around 4 million; the number has doubled since 1980.

The city's average ozone level is almost twice the maximum permitted in the USA and Japan. Ozone concentrations are worst around midday on sunny days and in the southwest of the city, because the prevailing wind is northeasterly.

Air contamination is measured by the Índice Metropolitana de Calidad de Aire (IMECA, Metropolitan Air Quality Index). IMECA assesses five pollutants – ozone, sulphur dioxide, nitrogen dioxide, carbon monoxide and suspended particulate. Readings below 100 are classed as satisfactory (though they wouldn't be considered satisfactory in most other cities in the world), 101 to 200 is 'unsatisfactory,' 201 to 300 is 'bad,' and over 300 'very bad.' In 1994, ozone levels in the southwest of the city were 'unsatisfactory' or worse on 345 days of the year. Ozone readings of over 240 – which occur several times a year – or suspended particle levels of over 175 trigger phase one of the city's environmental contingency plan, which includes the 'Doble Hoy No Circula' (Double Don't Drive Today) rule, which takes more vehicles off the streets. Three successive days of phase one trigger phase two, which immobilizes more vehicles, reduces industrial activity by 30% to 40%, and stops outdoor activities at schools. Phase three, which is rare, stops all industry and permits only emergency traffic.

The News publishes daily air quality reports and forecasts. Hourly reports (from 7 am to 8 pm) are posted on the excellent Mexico City Air Quality Report website (www.sima.com.mx), which also explains in detail, in English and Spanish, how the pollution is measured.

The more exotic remedies suggested for the pollution crisis have included fleets of helicopters to sweep the smog away, and exploding a hole in the ring of mountains around the city, then using giant fans to blow the smog through it. More feasible, perhaps, is the idea of ionizing the air to create winds that would disperse pollution. Large ionizing antennae would alter the rate at which water vapor condenses, releasing heat and therefore creating winds to blow pollution away. This proposal began tests in 1998 and 1999 in the Parque Ecológico de Xochimilco in the southeast of the city: the scientists responsible claimed that it significantly lowered levels of ozone and other pollutants.

An Environmental Success Story

By the 1970s, the Lago de Texcoco, the shallow, salty lake that filled much of the Valle de México in pre-Hispanic times, had been reduced to a small, noxious pond amid an almost desert-like landscape. The shrinking was the result of drainage schemes intended to prevent flooding in Mexico City and to allow the city to expand. Its consequences included regular dust storms that spread disease.

In 1971 a group of concerned scientists led by Dr Nabor Carrillo initiated the Proyecto Texcoco (Texcoco Project) with the aims of combating pollution, recycling wastewater, and improving the desolate appearance of the remaining lake area, east of Mexico City airport and between the city and Texcoco town. Five artificial lakes were built covering a total of 18 sq km. They are fed by rain, two rivers and with purified wastewater from the south and east of Mexico City. The Proyecto Texcoco is one of Mexico's environmental success stories of the late 20th century. Over 140 bird species have been recorded at the lakes, both Mexican residents – from ducks, herons and coots to owls, buzzards, eagles and falcons – and migratory fowl from the US and Canada. The migrants are most numerous in December and January and the largest lake, Lago Nabor Carrillo, has the biggest bird population.

Another part of the project has been the channeling of rain falling on the badly eroded surrounding region to feed the lake and to water millions of newly planted trees.

As you fly into or out of Mexico City airport you may well fly over the new lakes. You pass between them if you travel the Autopista Peñón Texcoco toll road between the city and Texcoco.

Mexico City's Water

Extraction of groundwater makes the city sink steadily, about 6cm a year in the center (where some areas sank 9m in the 20th century) and as much as 15cm to 40cm a year on the city's fringes. Even so, about one-third of the city's water needs to be pumped up at great cost from the Lerma and Cutzamala valleys west and southwest of the Valle de México. Meanwhile the water table is sinking by about 1m a year.

The city uses 300L of water a day per person, much more than some cities in Europe, for instance, even though millions of slum dwellers have no running water in their homes. Inefficient use of water by industry, with very little recycling, is partly to blame.

Only about 7% of wastewater (which includes sewage and industrial effluent) is treated. The Valle de México's streams are, as a result, among the most polluted in the world. Most wastewater, treated or not, eventually leaves the valley northward by a 50km tunnel called the Emisor Central, which leads to the Río Tula, a tributary of the badly polluted Río Pánuco, which enters the Gulf of Mexico at Tampico. The Emisor Central is not big enough to cope with the extra water brought by the rainy season, when backed-up sewage floods some low-lying parts of the valley.

Sinking ground levels break underground pipes, wasting up to a quarter of the city's water supplies and allowing contaminants to enter the supply. Contaminated water supplies spread diseases such as dysentery, typhoid and hepatitis.

GOVERNMENT & POLITICS
National

Mexico the country is a federal republic of 31 states (estados) and one federal district, with the states further divided into 2394 municipalities (municipios). The directly elected president carries out, in theory, laws made by a two-chamber federal congress. The congress has a 500-member lower chamber, the Cámara de Diputados (Chamber of Deputies), and a 128-member upper chamber, the Cámara de Senadores (Senate). Both chambers meet in Mexico City: the Chamber of Deputies in the Palacio Legislativo at Avenida Congreso de la Unión 66, 1.5km east of the Zócalo (Map 4), and the Senate at Xicoténcatl 9, beside the Museo Nacional de Arte (Map 4). The governors and legislatures of Mexico's states are also elected by their citizens, as are the *ayuntamientos* (town councils) that run municipios, and their presidents.

Until 1997 Mexico was effectively a one-party state, that party being the Partido Revolucionario Institucional (PRI, Institutional Revolutionary Party, 'pree'), which dominated political life for most of the 20th century, with presidents ruling in the tradition of strong, centralized leadership going back to Moctezuma. Though the Cámara de Diputados has the power of the purse and weighty powers to oversee the executive, the president's will was rarely denied. The powers of the states, too, were very much subordinate to the federal government, and elections at all levels routinely raised accusations of fraud, bribery, intimidation and violence by the all-conquering PRI.

President Carlos Salinas de Gortari (1988-94) made the first concessions to democratic plurality: during his term, non-PRI governors were allowed to be elected in three Mexican states. But the first real cracks in the PRI monolith opened up as President Ernesto Zedillo (1994-2000) responded to growing dissatisfaction with PRI corruption and economic failure, to mounting clamor in Mexico for real democratic change, and to the pressure from other countries that came with NAFTA, a free trade agreement with the USA and Canada.

Zedillo freed from government control the body that organizes federal elections, the Instituto Federal Electoral (IFE), and let it spend hundreds of millions of dollars to build an electoral apparatus transparent enough to overcome fraud. The first elections under this new regime, in 1997, were for all 500 seats in the Cámara de Diputados and a quarter of the Cámara de Senadores. The elections were not flawless but they were hailed as the freest and fairest in Mexico since 1911, and in an unprecedented outcome, the PRI lost overall control of the Cámara de Diputados, with the center-right Partido de Acción Nacio-

nal (PAN, National Action Party) and the center-left Partido de la Revolución Democrática (PRD, Party of the Democratic Revolution) each winning about a quarter of the seats.

Results of state elections left 10 of Mexico's states under PAN or PRD governorship by the end of 1999.

For the elections to choose Zedillo's successor in July 2000, the PRI's candidate was selected by an unprecedented nationwide primary election in which all registered voters, regardless of party affiliation, were entitled to vote. Around 10 million did, and they chose Francisco Labastida, a former Interior Minister widely thought to be favored by Zedillo and the party reformers. His rivals in 2000, both chosen by primaries restricted to party members, were to be Cuauhtémoc Cárdenas, former Mexico City head of government, for the PRD, and Vicente Fox, former Guanajuato state governor, for the PAN.

City

One of Mexico City's problems is that its governmental system was designed for a place a fraction of its current size. No one foresaw, back in 1854 when the Distrito Federal was given its present 1500-sq-km limits, that the city would burst these bounds. Yet as early as the 1930s the city started to spread into the neighboring state of México. Today 27 of the state of México's

President Zedillo

120 municipios are wholly or partly within the city's sprawl. The Distrito Federal and the state of México are run by completely different administrations – not exactly ideal conditions for planning the megalopolis that straddles their boundaries.

The state of México, with its capital at Toluca, west of Mexico City, is just like the other 30 Mexican states in electing its own governor (since 1999, Arturo Montiel of the PRI) and Cámara de Diputados (state legislatures have no upper house). The Distrito Federal, however, being the nation's capital, has long been treated as a special case. Back in 1917 it was decided that its governor should be appointed by Mexico's president instead of elected. In 1928, all elected local government bodies in the DF were abolished, and the district was placed under the direct control of the national president and his chosen governor, known as the *regente* (regent). The bureaucracy in charge of the city, the Departamento del Distrito Federal, became a department of the national executive government, answerable to the national president.

Over the following decades the only concession to popular democracy came when the Asamblea de Representantes del Distrito Federal (Federal District Assembly of Representatives) was set up in 1989. But this small elected body was given very restricted powers. In 1993 it was renamed the Asamblea Legislativa del Distrito Federal (ALDF) and gained greater powers.

Things changed more radically in 1997 when President Zedillo opened the post of DF governor – henceforth known as *jefe de gobierno* (head of government) or *alcalde* (mayor) – to popular elections. The vote was easily won by Cuauhtémoc Cárdenas of the PRD, son of the 1930s Mexican president Lázaro Cárdenas.

Many people believe Cuauhtémoc Cárdenas would have become national president in 1988 but for a mysterious computer failure during vote-counting after that election. Before the failure Cárdenas was well ahead of the PRI candidate, Carlos Salinas de Gortari; in the end the official figures gave Salinas an easy victory.

In 1997 in Mexico City there were no such shenanigans. Cárdenas won 47% of the votes, against 25% for the PRI candidate Alfredo del Mazo and 15% for the PAN's Carlos Castillo Peraza.

President Zedillo handed over to Cárdenas the right to choose the city's police chief and *procurador de justicia* (attorney general), posts that had previously been in the president's choosing. Nevertheless the federal congress still had to approve any debt issues by the DF and retained the exclusive right to impeach the DF head of government.

When Cárdenas resigned as head of the DF government in October 1999 to concentrate on his bid for the national presidency in 2000, he was replaced by Rosario Robles, a woman from the left wing of the PRD who had previously held the second most important post in the DF government, *secretaría de gobierno*.

At the same time as the 1997 mayoral elections, voting was held for all the seats in the ALDF. The PRD won an absolute majority, 38 of the 66 seats in this previously PRI-dominated body. PRD members want to make the Distrito Federal into Mexico's 32nd state, developing the ALDF into a full Cámara de Diputados. Meanwhile, the ALDF meets in the old Cámara de Diputados building at Donceles and Allende in the Centro Histórico (Map 4).

New elections in July 2000 were scheduled to choose the next DF head of government. Andrés Manuel López Obrador, a former PRD national director, was chosen in 1999 as the PRD's candidate by a vote of party members in the city. The PRI candidate Jesús Silva Herzog, a former Mexican ambassador to the USA, was also chosen in a primary election.

Administratively, the Distrito Federal is subdivided not into municipios but into 16 *delegaciones*. These do not have elected assemblies, though it was planned to reorganize them into nine new areas that would have elected administrations from the year 2000.

ECONOMY

Mexico City is the hub of the Mexican economy. About half the entire country's

Gross Domestic Product (GDP) is produced within 150km of the city. The Distrito Federal alone, with less than half of Mexico City's population, accounts for 24% of the GDP and about the same proportion of Mexico's industrial production, commerce, financial services and restaurant, hotel, transportation and communications businesses. Areas of the city within the neighboring state of México – notably the municipios of Tlalnepantla, Naucalpan, Ecatepec and Cuautitlán Izcalli – produce something like 20% of the country's industrial output.

Mexico City also has the highest cost of living in Mexico and, with under a quarter of the national population, consumes two-thirds of the nation's energy and buys over half its cars and most of its domestic appliances. Heavy subsidies – on transportation, food, health services, education, electricity, garbage collection and water – are needed to keep the place from seizing up. Over half the country's spending on social welfare goes to the capital.

National Resources & Products

Mexico, almost entirely agricultural before the 1910 revolution, is now one of Latin America's most industrialized nations. Manufacturing employs around 18% of the workforce and is responsible for about a quarter of Mexico's GDP and most of its exports. Computers, motor vehicles, pharmaceuticals, processed food, steel, chemicals, paper, textiles and other modern products have joined more traditional sources of income such as sugar, coffee, silver, lead, copper and zinc. Mexico is the world's biggest clothing exporter. Apart from the Mexico City area, the major industrial centers are Guadalajara and Monterrey. Other cities within the triangle formed by these 'big three,' notably Toluca, Guanajuato, Aguascalientes, Querétaro and San Luis Potosí, are also developing, as are the northern border areas, which are the traditional home of *maquiladora* industries and close to that major export market the USA. Maquiladoras are plants (usually foreign-owned) that are allowed to import raw materials, parts and equipment duty-free for processing or assembly by inexpensive Mexican labor. Maquiladoras employ almost 1 million Mexicans.

Among the most important national assets is oil, of which Mexico has the world's eighth largest reserves, concentrated mainly along the Gulf Coast and belonging to a government-owned monopoly, Pemex. Oil and natural gas yield about one-tenth of Mexico's export earnings and one-third of the government's revenues. Mining, the source of most of Mexico's income during the colonial era, remains significant in the northern half of the country, and is currently enjoying a boom. It accounts for about 3% of the GDP. Mexico is still the world's largest silver producer.

Services employ one-third of the workforce. Tourism is one of the most important service industries: some 20 million foreign visitors a year bring in around US$8 billion of foreign exchange (a similar figure to that of petrochemical exports), and the domestic tourism business is three times as big.

The agriculture industry occupies about 25% of Mexico's workers but produces only about 8% of the national product.

Restructuring the Economy

The oil boom of the 1970s encouraged Mexico to undertake ambitious spending projects, piling up a big burden of national debt that could not be paid when revenues slumped in the early 1980s oil bust. In response, particularly from 1988 to 1994 under President Salinas, debt was rescheduled, austerity measures were introduced, and government enterprises from banks and utilities to steel mills were sold off. Private enterprise now dominates the key manufacturing sector. Inflation was cut from well over 100% to less than 10% under Salinas. By the early 1990s Mexico was showing steady growth, and the peso had been stabilized.

NAFTA The key to Salinas' plans was the North American Free Trade Agreement (NAFTA), which took effect on January 1, 1994. Known to Mexicans as the TLC, (Tratado de Libre Comercio), NAFTA is set up to eliminate restrictions on trade and investment between the US, Mexico and Canada gradually over a 15-year period. The hope was that NAFTA would bring Mexico increased employment and growing exports, as well as cheaper imports. Opponents charge that the gap between rich and poor is being widened as new imports damage uncompetitive sectors of the Mexican economy.

Peso Crisis

The peso collapse of 1994-95 happened after Salinas left office but was a consequence of his policies. The foreign investment that had poured into Mexico in the early 1990s slowed to a trickle in 1994, also partly because of political alarms in Mexico, partly because of rising US interest rates, and also due to fears that the peso was overvalued. After Mexico had spent nearly all its foreign reserves in a futile attempt to support the peso, Salinas' successor Ernesto Zedillo had to let the peso float to find its own level. It fell far and fast, and Mexico had to be bailed out by a multibillion-dollar package of emergency credit from the US, Canada and international financial bodies.

The government raised taxes and interest rates, cut spending and announced new privatization. More than 1.5 million people lost their jobs, prices and crime soared, production and standards of living fell, and borrowers went broke. Inflation in 1995 was over 50%. More Mexicans looked to (usually illegal) emigration to the USA as the only way out of poverty.

Roller-coaster Recovery

The government's austerity measures and its successful raising of new capital in private markets, coupled with big help for exports from NAFTA and the cheap peso, began to pull Mexico out of its slump surprisingly quickly. Foreign investment revived, and Mexico repaid most of its emergency debt ahead of schedule. By 1998 production was rising about 6% a year and inflation was down to around 15%. But the peso crisis and resulting recession had slashed Mexicans' average spending power by 50%. One 1997 study concluded that more than one-

fifth of the people in the Distrito Federal were living in extreme poverty, on 'marginal levels of basic subsistence.'

A slump in oil prices in 1998 and the global economic crisis of 1997-98 caused a blip in Mexico's recovery. Even the long-standing government subsidy on tortillas was abolished in 1999, bringing the price of this staple food to nearly double what it was a year before. That year's budget was the strictest in nearly 20 years, but by late 1999 the outlook was brightening quickly. Inflation for the year looked likely to better the government's target of 13% and the crucial US market was growing steadily. Real incomes – allowing for inflation – were starting to rise again, and consumption and production were expected to grow in 2000.

But as the 21st century dawned, Mexicans still had less purchasing power than in 1994. The minimum wage is about US$3.50 a day, which is what many people in unskilled jobs are actually paid, while most workers earn under US$10 a day. Then there are the millions in the so-called informal economy, such as street hawkers and entertainers, home workers, criminals – anybody whose work is not officially registered and who doesn't pay taxes. Perhaps one-third of Mexico's workers are 'informal.' Few of these people scrape together much more than the minimum wage. Meanwhile, Mexico City's growing population adds perhaps an extra 150,000 work seekers every year. According to one report released by the DF government in 1999, nearly half of the city's 15- to 29-year-olds have no work.

POPULATION & PEOPLE

No one really knows how many people there are in Mexico City. Most counts put the population at between 18 and 20 million, about 10 times what it was in 1940.

Mexico's 1995 census counted 8.49 million people, growing by about 45,000 a year, in the Distrito Federal. The rest are in the city's outlying areas in the state of México, where most of its current growth is taking place. The difficulties in assessing the population arise partly from trying to work out where the city begins and ends – as it grows, it absorbs previously separate communities, and which of these are now part of the city is always debatable.

The population density is around 15,000 people per sq km, which is similar to New York and São Paulo, much denser than Paris or London, but less crowded than Calcutta or Hong Kong. Since 1940 Mexico City's population has grown more than twice as fast as that of the country, but the rate has slowed: between 1940 and 1980 the city's growth rate hovered at about 5% a year; in 1999 it was measured at 3.7%. More than half the growth is accounted for by an annual 400,000 migrants from other parts of Mexico, chiefly the poorer southern half of the country.

Unless Mexico City's expansion is somehow halted, there seems nothing to prevent it from merging before long with cities outside the Valle de México such as Toluca, Cuernavaca, Cuautla, Puebla and Tlaxcala, creating a monster megalopolis of perhaps 30 million people.

Ethnicity & Class
Residents of Mexico City are known as *capitalinos* or, less respectfully, *chilangos*. As is the case throughout Mexico, the majority are mestizos, people of mixed ancestry – usually Spanish and indigenous, although African slaves and other Europeans were also elements. If you were to judge Mexico just by watching its television programs, you might think it was populated entirely by people of pure Spanish descent. In fact there are relatively few of these, though they hold many positions of power and influence in Mexican society.

Mexico's indigenous people – *indígenas* or *indios* – are descendants of Mexico's pre-Hispanic peoples who have retained their sense of distinct identity. The 50 or so indigenous cultures that have survived in Mexico – each with their own language but some now with only a few hundred people – have done so largely because of rural isolation. Indigenous people in general remain second-class citizens, often restricted to the worst land or forced to migrate to city slums or the USA in search of work. Their main

wealth is traditional and spiritual, their way of life imbued with communal customs and rituals bound up with nature. But indigenous people who live in Mexico City have more or less abandoned traditional dress and lifestyles. The 1995 census identified only 100,000 people in the Distrito Federal as speakers of indigenous languages, though many more in Mexico City probably still think of themselves as members of one indigenous people or another. The country's largest indigenous group is the Nahua, descendants of the ancient Aztecs. At least 1.7 million Nahuatl speakers are spread around central Mexico.

ARTS
Dance
Indigenous Colorful traditional indigenous dances are an important part of many Mexican regional fiestas. There are hundreds of them, some popular in many parts of the country, others danced only in a single town or village. Many bear traces of pre-Hispanic ritual. Some have evolved from old fertility rites. Others tell stories of Spanish origin. Nearly all require special costumes, sometimes including masks or enormous feathered headdresses.

Since most people in Mexico City have left behind their country roots, such traditional acts are rare. An exception is the *conchero* dance (a recreation of a pre-Hispanic central Mexican dance) performed daily to booming drums by groups in the Zócalo. Excellent performances of traditional dances from around Mexico are staged by the Ballet Folklórico in the Palacio de Bellas Artes (see the Entertainment chapter).

Latin Caribbean and South American dance and dance music – broadly described as *música afroantillana* or *música tropical* – have become highly popular in Mexico. Basically this is tropical-style ballroom dancing, with percussion, guitars and brass providing infectious rhythms. Mexico City has a dozen or more clubs and large dance halls devoted to this scene; aficionados can go to a different hall each night of the week, often featuring big-name bands and performers from the Caribbean and South America (see the Entertainment chapter).

One of the more formal, old-fashioned varieties of Latin dance is **danzón**. Originally from Cuba, danzón is associated particularly with the port city of Veracruz. For danzón, high heels and a dress are de rigueur for women, as is a Panama hat for men. Steps are small, movement is from the hips down, and danzón can be danced only to danzón music.

Cumbia, originally from Colombia but now with its adopted home in Mexico City, has set steps, too, but is livelier, more flirtatious and less structured than danzón; you also move the top half of your body. The music rests on thumping bass lines with an addition of brass, guitars, mandolins and sometimes marimbas (wooden xylophones).

Salsa developed out of the 1950s New York introduction of jazz to cha-cha-cha, rumba and son brought by immigrants from Cuba and Puerto Rico. Musically it boils down to brass (with trumpet solos), piano, percussion, singer and chorus – the dance is a hot one with a lot of exciting turns.

Merengue, mainly from Colombia and Venezuela, is a cumbia/salsa blend with a hopping step: the rhythm catches the shoulders, and the arms go up and down. The music is strong on maracas, and its musicians go for puffed-up sleeves.

Music

In Mexico City live music may start up at any time on streets, plazas or even buses or the metro. The musicians are playing for a living and range from mariachi bands of trumpeters, violinists, guitarists and a singer, all dressed in smart cowboy-like costumes, to ragged lone buskers with out-of-tune guitars and sandpaper voices. **Mariachi** music – perhaps the most 'typical' Mexican music of all – originated in the Guadalajara area. Mexico City's Plaza Garibaldi is one of its main adopted homes.

Mexico has a thriving pop music business. Its outpourings can be heard live at fiestas, nightspots and concerts or bought from music shops or cheap bootleg-tape vendors.

(Ask tape vendors to play cassettes before you buy them, as there are many defective or blank copies.)

See the Entertainment chapter for information on how to find out about live music in Mexico City.

Rock & Pop Mexican rock was pretty raw and basic until the mid-to-late 1980s when a more sophisticated music began to emerge. **El Tri**, still together after more than 30 years, head up the older generation with their still-energetic rock & roll. The '80s changes were spearheaded by mystical Def Leppard-type rockers **Caifanes**, a middle-class Mexico City group typical of the sort of Mexicans exposed earliest to North American and European music. Caifanes are still together under the name **Jaguares**.

Foreign rock acts were not allowed to play live in Mexico until the late '80s. Their arrival greatly broadened rock's appeal. Today Mexico, so close to the big US Hispanic market, is probably the most important hub of Spanish-language rock. Talented and versatile Mexico City bands such as **Café Tacuba** and **Maldita Vecindad** have taken *rock en español* to new heights and new audiences (well beyond Mexico) in the '90s, mixing a huge range of influences – from rock & roll, ska and punk to traditional Mexican son, bolero or mariachi. Four-piece Café Tacuba's exciting handling of so many styles – yet still with their own very strong musical identity – led the *New York Times* to compare their 1994 album *Re* with the Beatles' *White Album*. Their most recent production is the 1999 double album *Revés/YoSoy*.

Top groups from other parts of Mexico include **Maná** from Guadalajara, who are an unashamedly commercial band sounding strongly reminiscent of the Police; Monterrey's politically-minded hip-hop trio **Control Machete**; and the Monterrey twosome **Plastilina Mosh**, a kind of Mexican Beastie Boys whose 1998 debut CD *Aquamosh* was a huge success, selling over 1 million copies.

Meanwhile, romantic balladeer **Luis Miguel** (from Veracruz) is probably the Mexican pop act best known internationally.

If you don't know his voice you will almost certainly have read about his love life.

You have probably also read about **Gloria Trevi**, the controversial 'Mexican Madonna' who vanished in 1998 after Chihuahua authorities ordered the arrest of her and her manager, Sergio Andrade, for the alleged sexual abuse and kidnapping of minors. The story went that the school for young female talent run by Trevi was actually a harem for Andrade. In a saga that gripped Mexico, the pair was on the run for over a year before being arrested in Rio de Janeiro in 2000.

Regional Music The deepest-rooted Mexican folk music is **son**, a broad term covering a range of styles that grew out of the fusion of indigenous, Spanish and African music. Son is essentially played on guitars plus harp or violin, with witty, often improvised lyrics, usually performed for a foot-stamping dance audience. The origin of mariachi music was the son of Jalisco state in western Mexico. Particularly celebrated son musicians include violinist Juan Reynoso from the hot Río Balsas basin southwest of Mexico City; harpist La Negra Graciana from Veracruz, whose son is particularly African- and Cuban-influenced; and Los Camperos de Valles from the Huasteca region in northeast Mexico, a trio composed of a solo violinist and two guitarists who sing falsetto between soaring violin passages. The independent recording label Discos Corasón is doing much to promote son. One place you can buy its CDs is the Tianguis Cultural del Chopo (see Markets in the Shopping chapter).

Ranchera is Mexico's urban 'country music.' Developed in the expanding towns and cities of the 20th century, it's melodramatic with a nostalgia for rural roots: vocalist-and-combo music, sometimes with a mariachi backing. Women such as Eugenia León and men such as Juan Gabriel and Alejandro Fernández are among the leading contemporary ranchera artists.

Norteño is country ballad and dance music, originating in northern Mexico but popular countrywide. Its roots are in *corrido* ballads dealing with Latino/Anglo strife in the borderlands in the 19th century, and themes from the Mexican Revolution. Today's ballads tend to deal with small-time crooks such as drug-runners or *coyotes* trying to survive amid big-time corruption and crime. Norteño *conjuntos* (groups) go for 10-gallon hats; backing for the singer is guitar-based, with accordion, bass and drums. Los Tigres del Norte, the superstars of this genre, added saxophone and absorbed popular cumbia rhythms from Colombia.

Banda is a 1990s development of norteño, substituting large brass sections for guitars and accordion, playing a combination of Latin and traditional Mexican rhythms. Banda del Recodo from Mazatlán are the biggest name in banda. This music also gave birth to an energetic new dance, *la quebradita.*

Grupera, a feebler blend of ranchera, norteño and cumbia, is very popular, especially at fiestas deep in rural Mexico. Límite and Banda Machos are star exponents.

Música Tropical Though originating in the Caribbean and South America, several brands of *música tropical* or *música afroantillana* have become integral parts of the Mexican musical scene. Two types of dance music – danzón, originally from Cuba, and cumbia, from Colombia – both took deeper root in Mexico than in their original homelands (see Dance, earlier in this section). Banda groups play a lot of cumbia, and leading Mexican exponents have included Sonora Dinamita and (before they split in the mid-1990s) Los Bukis, whose *Me Volví a Acordar de Ti* was the biggest selling Mexican recording ever.

Canto Nuevo This name is usually given in Latin America to what's called *nueva canción* in Spain and *nueva trova* in Cuba – troubadour-type folk songs, often with a protest theme and poetic lyrics, typically performed by singer-songwriters *(cantautores)* with a solitary guitar. Fernando Delgadillo and Alberto Escobar are leading exponents, while others such as Betsy Pecanins and the highly versatile Eugenia León have moved on to other styles such as norteño, ranchera and – in Pecanins' case – blues.

Painting

Since pre-Hispanic times there has been no shortage of talented painters in Mexico. Many of these paintings show a particular excitement with bright colors, and Mexico City's many murals and galleries of modern and historic art are among its highlights.

Pre-Hispanic The earliest outstanding Mexican murals are found at Teotihuacán (at its height around the 5th century AD), where the colorful *Paradise of Tláloc* depicts in detail the delights awaiting those who died at the hands of the water god Tláloc.

The people of Cacaxtla near Puebla (650 to 900 AD) also left some vivid murals. The surviving art of the Aztecs (about 1350 to 1521) is more sculpture than painting but some frescos survive. The Maya of southeast Mexico and Guatemala, at their cultural height from about 250 to 900 AD, were ancient Mexico's most artistic people and created some marvelous multicolored murals and pottery.

Colonial Period Mexican art during Spanish rule was heavily Spanish-influenced and chiefly religious in subject – though por-

The Art Scene

In addition to permanent collections, many of Mexico City's art museums show excellent temporary exhibitions. A good place to find out what's on where is the website Arte-México (www.arte-mexico.com), which lists openings and current exhibitions, and has maps showing the locations of about 100 galleries and cultural centers. The website of Conaculta, the Consejo Nacional para la Cultura y las Artes (www.cnca.gob.mx), also has good exhibition listings in its La Cartelera section. For a fuller list of Diego Rivera and Frida Kahlo sites, see 'Diego & Frida' in the Things to See & Do chapter. Here's where to find some of the best art in the city.

Centro Histórico

Catedral Metropolitana – colonial-era paintings by Correa and Cabrera
Museo José Luis Cuevas – Picassos, Rembrandts and work by Cuevas and other contemporary Mexicans
Museo Nacional de Arte – the best place in the city to get an overview of Mexican colonial and 19th-century art
Museo de San Ildefonso – murals by Rivera, Orozco and Siqueiros
Museo de la Secretaría de Hacienda y Crédito Público – Mexican art from Correa to Rivera and Tamayo to contemporary work
Palacio Nacional – Rivera's epic murals on the history of Mexican civilization
Secretaría de Educación Pública – hundreds of mural panels by Rivera and others

Around the Alameda

Museo Mural Diego Rivera – one of Rivera's most famous murals
Palacio de Bellas Artes – outstanding murals by Rivera, Siqueiros, Orozco and Tamayo
Pinacoteca Virreinal de San Diego – big collection of colonial work

Around Plaza de la República

ACE Gallery – one of the city's leading contemporary galleries, linking Mexican and US art
Museo de San Carlos – Goya, Rubens, Van Dyck, Tintoretto, Zurbarán, Ingres and other Europeans

Roma

Galería Nina Menocal – specialist in Latin American art, just one of the prominent galleries in this area which has recently emerged as a contemporary art hub

traits grew in popularity under wealthy patrons later in the period. The Academia de San Carlos, founded in Mexico City in 1783 by Spanish royal decree, had its students learn by copying European masterworks. The 18th-century painters Juan Correa and Miguel Cabrera were leading figures of the era in Mexico. Cabrera in particular had a sureness of touch lacking in the more labored efforts of others.

Independent Mexico Juan Cordero (1824-84) began the modern Mexican mural tradition by expressing historical and philo-sophical ideas on public buildings. The land-scapes of José María Velasco (1840-1912) captured the magical qualities of the country around Mexico City before it was swallowed up by urban growth.

The years before the 1910 revolution saw the beginnings of socially conscious art and of a real break from European traditions. Slums, brothels and indigenous poverty began to appear on canvases. The cartoons and engravings of José Guadalupe Posada (1852-1913), with his characteristic *calavera* (skull) motif, satirized the injustices of the Porfiriato and were aimed at a much wider

The Art Scene

Bosque de Chapultepec
Casa del Lago – interesting temporary exhibitions
Castillo de Chapultepec – murals by Siqueiros, Orozco and O'Gorman
Galería de Arte Mexicano – top-class gallery of modern Mexican art
Museo de Arte Moderno – smaller-scale work by Rivera, Siqueiros, Orozco, Dr Atl, Kahlo, Tamayo, O'Gorman and others
Museo Nacional de Antropología – excellent overview of pre-Hispanic arts, with fine reproductions as well as original works
Museo Rufino Tamayo – international modern art

Polanco
Galería Enrique Guerrero and *Galería López Quiroga* – leading galleries of contemporary Latin American art
Museo Sala de Arte Público David Alfaro Siqueiros – Siqueiros' house and studio

Insurgentes Sur
Polifórum Cultural Siqueiros – Siqueiros' last, enormous mural best seen in a sound-and-light show with recorded narration by Siqueiros

San Ángel
Museo de Arte Carrillo Gil – smaller-scale work by Rivera, Siqueiros, Orozco and some big foreign names
Museo Casa Estudio Diego Rivera y Frida Kahlo – the famous couple's 1930s home
Museo Soumaya – 70 sculptures by Auguste Rodin, Tamayo murals and Mexican colonial art

Ciudad Universitaria
Ciudad Universitaria – 1950s mosaics and murals by Rivera, O'Gorman, Siqueiros, Francisco Eppens and José Chávez Morado

Coyoacán
Museo Frida Kahlo – Kahlo's house
Anahuacalli – Rivera's collection of pre-Hispanic art and studies for his own murals

Xochimilco & Around
Museo Dolores Olmedo Patiño – excellent collection of Riveras and a room of Kahlos

audience than most earlier Mexican art. At a show marking the 1910 centenary of the independence movement, Gerardo Murillo (1875-1964), who took the name Dr Atl (from a word meaning 'water' in Náhuatl, the language of the Aztecs and their modern descendants the Nahua), displayed some scandalously orgiastic paintings.

The Muralists Immediately after the revolution, in the 1920s, education minister José Vasconcelos commissioned leading young artists to paint a series of murals on public buildings to spread awareness of Mexican history and culture and impel social and technological change. The trio of great muralists were Diego Rivera (1885-1957), David Alfaro Siqueiros (1896-1974), and José Clemente Orozco (1883-1949).

Rivera's work carried a clear left-wing message, emphasizing past oppression suffered by indigenous people and peasants. He had an intense interest in native Mexico and tried hard to pull together the country's indigenous and Spanish roots into one national identity. Typically, his murals are colorful, crowded tableaux depicting historical people and events or symbolic scenes of Mexican life, with a simple, clear-cut moral message. They're realistic, if not always lifelike. To appreciate them you need a bit of knowledge of Mexican history and, preferably, an explanation of the details.

Siqueiros, who fought on the Constitutionalist side in the revolution (while Rivera was in Europe), remained a political activist afterwards, spending time in jail as a result, and leading an attempt to kill Leon Trotsky in Mexico City in 1940. His murals lack Rivera's detailed realism but convey a more clearly Marxist message through dramatic, symbolic depictions of concepts like the oppressed and the people, and grotesque caricatures of the oppressors.

Orozco was less of a propagandist. He conveyed emotion, character and atmosphere, and focused more on the universal human condition than on historical or political specifics. More of a pessimist than Rivera or Siqueiros, by the 1930s Orozco

The Dream Team: David Alfaro Siqueiros, Diego Rivera and José Clemente Orozco

Part of Diego Rivera's *Mexico Through the Centuries* mural at the Palacio Nacional

RICHARD I'ANSON

More stunning Rivera artwork at the Museo Dolores Olmedo Patiño

STUART WASSERMAN

Diego Rivera mural, Palacio Nacional

Detail of mural by Orozco, Casa de Azulejos

An untitled Rivera mural splashes across the Teatro Insurgentes.

grew disillusioned with the revolution. Some of his most powerful works, such as those in the Palacio de Bellas Artes in Mexico City, depict oppressive scenes of degradation, violence or injustice but do not offer any simplistic political solution.

Rivera, Siqueiros and Orozco were also great artists on a smaller scale. A number of their portraits, drawings and other works can be seen in various art museums in Mexico City.

The mural movement continued well after WWII. Rufino Tamayo (1899-1991), from Oaxaca, was relatively unconcerned with politics and history but absorbed by abstract and mythological scenes and effects of color. Juan O'Gorman (1905-81), a Mexican of Irish ancestry, was even more realistic and detailed than Rivera. His mosaic on the Biblioteca Central at Mexico City's Ciudad Universitaria is probably his best-known work, though atypical of his usual style.

Other 20th-Century Artists Mexico City-born Frida Kahlo (1907-54), physically crippled by an accident and mentally tormented in her tempestuous marriage to Diego Rivera, painted anguished, penetrating self-portraits and grotesque, surreal images that expressed her left-wing views and externalized her inner tumult. After several decades of being seen as an interesting oddball, Kahlo suddenly seemed to strike an international chord in the 1980s, almost overnight becoming hugely popular and as renowned as Rivera. Frida fans, by the way, will enjoy The Original Frida Kahlo Home Page (www.cascade.net/kahlo).

Since WWII, Mexican artists have moved away from muralism, which they saw as too didactic and too obsessed with *mexicanidad* (Mexicanness). They opened Mexico up to world trends such as abstract expressionism, op art and performance art. The Museo José Luis Cuevas in Mexico City's Centro Histórico was founded by, and named for, one of the leaders of this movement. Today the city has an increasingly exciting contemporary art scene. The Roma and Polanco districts are home to many of the most progressive galleries.

Architecture & Sculpture

Architecture and sculpture are inextricably intertwined in Mexico. In the pre-Hispanic, Spanish and modern Mexican traditions, carving and molding have been integrated into building designs or used as features of architectural spaces, while buildings have often been conceived as pieces of large-scale sculpture.

Pre-Hispanic The ancient civilizations of Mexico produced some of the most spectacular architecture ever built. At sites near Mexico City such as Teotihuacán, Tula and Cacaxtla, you can still see fairly intact, large sections of pre-Hispanic cities. Their ceremonial centers, used by the religious and political elite, were designed to impress with their great stone pyramids and palaces. Pyramids usually functioned as the bases for small shrines on their summits. Three of the biggest pyramids in the world – the Great Pyramid of Cholula near Puebla, and the Pirámide del Sol and Pirámide de la Luna at Teotihuacán – are within easy reach of Mexico City.

There were many differences in style between pre-Hispanic civilizations: while Teotihuacán and Aztec buildings were relatively simple, designed to awe by their grand scale, the Maya in Mexico's southeast paid more attention to aesthetic detail and created countless beautiful stone carvings. The Toltecs' fearsome, militaristic style of carving is exhibited at their presumed capital Tula. Aztec sculpture reflects the harsh Aztec worldview, with many carvings of skulls and complicated, symbolic representations of gods. Earlier, the Olmecs of the Gulf Coast (about 1200 to 600 BC) had produced perhaps the most remarkable pre-Hispanic stone sculpture to be found. Most awesome are the huge 'Olmec heads,' which combine the features of human babies and jaguars.

Teotihuacán's typical *talud-tablero* building style, in which pyramids and other structures were constructed with alternating sloping (talud) and upright (tablero) sections, was copied by several later Mexican cultures.

Substantial remains of pre-Hispanic cere-monial centers can be seen at the Templo Mayor, off the Zócalo, and elsewhere in the city at Tlatelolco, Cuicuilco, Tenayuca and Santa Cecilia Acatitlán. But the most im-pressive sites in the region are outside the city at such places as Tula, Cacaxtla and, supremely, Teotihuacán. The city's Museo Nacional de Antropología has fine pre-His-panic sculpture, and models and full and partial replicas of buildings.

Colonial Period One of the Spaniards' first preoccupations was replacing pagan temples with Christian churches. Mexico City's cathedral stands on part of the site of the Aztecs' teocalli, or main sacred precinct.

Many of the fine mansions, churches and plazas that are today oases of beauty and tranquility amid Mexico City's bustle were created during the 300 years of Spanish rule. Most were designed in basic Spanish styles, but with unique local variations. We owe to this period the lovely courtyards of such buildings as the Museo de la Secretaría de Hacienda y Crédito Público, the Museo Na-cional de las Culturas, the Museo Franz Mayer, the Palacio de Iturbide and the San Ángel Inn.

The influence of indigenous artisans is seen in churches and monasteries, particu-larly the elaborate altarpieces, sculpted walls and ceilings that overflow with tiny details.

Renaissance This style dominated in the 16th and early 17th centuries. It emphasized ancient Greek and Roman ideals of harmony and proportion: columns and shapes like the square and circle predomi-nated.

The usual Renaissance style in Mexico was **plateresque**, a name derived from *platero* (silversmith), because its decoration resembled the ornamentation that went into silverwork. Plateresque was commonly used on façades, particularly church doorways, which had round arches bordered by classi-cal columns and stone sculpture. Puebla's Templo de San Francisco and the church of the Ex-Convento Domínico de la Natividad in Tepoztlán are fine examples.

A later, more austere Renaissance style was called **Herreresque** after the Spanish ar-chitect Juan de Herrera. The Mexico City and Puebla cathedrals both mingle Renais-sance and baroque styles.

The influence of the **Muslims**, who had ruled much of Spain until the 15th century, was also carried to Mexico. The 49 domes of the Capilla Real in Cholula almost resemble a mosque.

Baroque This style, which reached Mexico in the early 17th century, was a reaction against the strictness of Renaissance styles, combining classical influences with other el-ements and aiming for dramatic effect rather than pure proportion. Curves, color, contrasts of light and dark, and increasingly elaborate decoration were among its hall-marks. Painting and sculpture were inte-grated with architecture for added elaborate effect – most notably in ornate, often enor-mous altarpieces.

Mexico City's more restrained baroque buildings include the Iglesia de Santo Domingo and the Palacio de Iturbide in the Centro Histórico, the Templo de Santiago at Tlatelolco, and the Antigua Basílica de Guadalupe. The Altar de los Reyes in the Catedral Metropolitana is an extravagant piece of baroque carving.

Mexican baroque reached its final form, **Churrigueresque**, between 1730 and 1780. Named after a Barcelona carver and archi-tect, José Benito de Churriguera, this was characterized by riotous surface ornamenta-tion with a characteristic 'top-heavy' effect. Outstanding Churrigueresque stone carving appears on churches such as the Sagrario Metropolitano and Templo de la Santísima in Mexico City, the Templo La Valenciana in Guanajuato and Santa Prisca in Taxco. This last has several notable Churrigueresque al-tarpieces.

Mexican indigenous artisans added a pro-fusion of detailed sculpture in stone and colored stucco to some baroque buildings. Among their most exuberant works are the Capilla del Rosario in the Templo de Santo Domingo, Puebla, the nearby village church of Tonantzintla, and the Templo de la

Tercera Orden de San Francisco in Cuernavaca. Arabic influence continued with the popularity of colored tiles *(azulejos)* on the outside of buildings, notably on Mexico City's Casa de Azulejos and many buildings in and around Puebla.

Neoclassic This style was another return to Greek and Roman ideals. In Mexico it lasted from about 1780 to 1830. Spanish-born Manuel Tolsá (1757-1816) was the most prominent neoclassical architect and sculptor. His outstanding works in Mexico City include the dome and clock tower of the Catedral Metropolitana, the Colegio de Minería, and the equestrian statue *El Caballito* outside the Museo Nacional de Arte. Another fine building in neoclassical style is the Alhóndiga de Granaditas in Guanajuato.

Independent Mexico In the 19th and 20th centuries, Mexico turned to revivals of many earlier styles, and many buildings copied French or Italian modes. The marble Palacio de Bellas Artes is one of the finest buildings from this era. The beautiful Correo Mayor (Central Post Office) and the Museo Nacional de Arte were built in the style of Italian Renaissance palaces. The 1910 Monumento a la Revolución (El Ángel) on Paseo de la Reforma is kind of neo-neoclassical.

After the revolution of 1910-21, **art deco** appeared in buildings such as the Lotería Nacional and Frontón México. Later, architects attempted to return to pre-Hispanic roots in the search for a national identity. This trend was known as **Toltecism** and many public buildings exhibit the heaviness of Aztec or Toltec monuments. It culminated in Mexico City's UNAM university campus of the early 1950s, where many buildings are covered with colorful murals.

Since the 1960s, Mexico City's major prestige buildings have mainly adopted international modern styles and materials, but with some impressive results, made the more dramatic in some cases by the use of bright colors. The 1960s Museo Nacional de Antropología and the 1970s Basílica de Guadalupe, both by Pedro Ramírez Vásquez,

and the 1990s Centro Nacional de las Artes in Coyoacán and Centro Bursátil (Stock Exchange, on Paseo de la Reforma), are some of the most imaginative and striking modern constructions you'll see anywhere.

Literature
Apart from pre-Hispanic poems and histories that have survived in inscriptions and codices (books painted on skin or bark paper), perhaps the first book that can be considered Mexican is *History of the Conquest of New Spain* by Bernal Díaz del Castillo – an eyewitness account of the Spanish arrival by one of Cortés' lieutenants.

An interesting counterpoint to Díaz is provided in *The Broken Spears*, edited by Miguel León-Portilla. This is a collection of Aztec accounts of the conquest, some of them written as soon as seven years after the fall of Tenochtitlán. Several of them are translations of codices.

Mexico's most internationally known novelist is probably Carlos Fuentes, and one of his most highly regarded novels is his first, *Where the Air is Clear* (1958). It traces the lives of various Mexico City dwellers through the decades after the Mexican Revolution as part of his critique of the upheaval and its aftermath. Fuentes' *Aura*, also set in the city, is a short, magical book with one of the most stunning endings of any novel.

Octavio Paz (1914-98), poet, essayist and winner of the 1990 Nobel Prize in literature, wrote perhaps the most probing examination of Mexico's myths and the Mexican character in *The Labyrinth of Solitude* (1950). Paz's *The Other Mexico: Critique of the Pyramid* is a shorter book – published in 1972 in the aftermath of the 1968 Tlatelolco massacre – which assesses the lingering influence of the savage Aztec worldview.

For information on non-Mexican writing about Mexico City, see Books in the Facts for the Visitor chapter.

SOCIETY & CONDUCT
Despite strong currents of machismo and nationalism, Mexicans are in general very

friendly, humorous, and helpful to visitors. Even if you don't speak much Spanish, any attempts – however rudimentary – will be welcomed.

Traditional Culture

Traditional culture is strong in Mexico. The Catholic religion – with its calendar of saint's days and major festivals such as Semana Santa (Holy Week), El Día de los Muertos (Day of the Dead, November 2), El Día de la Virgen de Guadalupe (December 12) and Christmas – is one deep-rooted source of tradition. These events inspire people to gather for the same processions and rituals, dance the same costumed dances, and create the same kind of special festival handicrafts as part of traditions that go back hundreds of years.

Another vital thread of tradition is that of the country's many surviving indigenous peoples. Some of these peoples' entire ways of life – from their colorful traditional costumes and crafts to their agricultural calendars as well as their communalist social organization – are governed by customs that are still in varying degrees pre-Hispanic. Such phenomena are much less apparent in Mexico City than in rural regions, however.

Many Mexican traditions interweave indigenous and Hispanic influences. The Día de los Muertos, for instance, is All Souls' Day in Catholic terms yet is celebrated with strong overtones of ancestor worship.

The faith that so many Mexicans have in traditional medicine – a mixture of charms, chants, herbs, candles and incense – is further evidence of the strength of pre-Hispanic tradition.

You'll find more information on aspects of Mexican traditional culture in sections of this book under Music, Dance and Religion in this chapter, Public Holidays & Special Events in the Facts for the Visitor chapter, and the Artesanías section of the Shopping chapter.

The Family & Machismo Traditional family ties remain very strong in Mexico. Despite tensions, family loyalty is strong. One European who lived in Mexico for years commented that Mexicans rarely reveal their true selves outside the family. An invitation to a Mexican home is quite an honor for an outsider; as a guest you'll probably be treated royally and will enter a part of real Mexico to which few outsiders are admitted.

Not unconnected with Mexican family dynamics is the phenomenon of machismo, an exaggerated masculinity aimed at impressing other males as well as women. Its manifestations range from aggressive driving and the carrying of weapons to heavy drinking.

The macho image may have roots in Mexico's often violent past and seems to hinge on a curious network of family relationships. Since it's not uncommon for Mexican husbands to have extramarital affairs, wives in response lavish affection on their sons, who end up idolizing their mothers and, unable to find similar perfection in a wife, philander in their turn …. The strong mother-son bond also means that it's crucial for a Mexican wife to get along with her mother-in-law. And while the virtue of daughters and sisters has to be protected at all costs, other women – including foreign tourists without male companions – may be seen as 'fair game' by Mexican men.

The other side of the machismo coin is women who emphasize their femininity. Such stereotyping, however, is not universal and is under pressure from more modern influences. The women's movement has made some advances since it began in the 1970s as a small middle-class affair, but abortion, for instance, remains illegal in most cases.

Dos & Don'ts

Language difficulties may be the biggest barrier to friendly contact with Mexicans: some people are shy or will ignore you because they don't imagine a conversation is possible; just a few words of Spanish will often bring smiles and warmth, probably followed by questions. Most tourists and travelers in Mexico are assumed until it's proven otherwise to be citizens of the USA.

Some indigenous peoples have learned to mistrust outsiders after five centuries of ex-

What's in a Name?

You may soon notice that there's something not quite straightforward about Mexican names. María García and Pedro Blanco present no problem – but what to make of Alicia López López, Francisco Sánchez G, or Isabel Romero de Colón?

Basically a Mexican of either sex has three names: a given name *(nombre)*, and two surnames *(apellidos)*. The first of the surnames is the person's father's first surname. The second surname is the mother's first surname. So Isabel, the daughter of Antonio Romero Echeverría and Patricia Ruiz Álvarez, is Isabel Romero Ruiz. Women don't necessarily change their names at all when they marry, but may use their husband's first surname (preceded by *de)* after their own. So if Señorita Isabel Romero Ruiz married Pedro Colón Villalobos, she could call herself Señora Isabel Romero de Colón.

In practice, many people don't bother with their second surname, or occasionally just shorten it to an initial – so Francisco Sánchez Guerrero could be simply Francisco (or Señor) Sánchez, or maybe Francisco Sánchez G. On the other hand, if the first surname is a particularly common one (such as García, Fernández, López or González), a person is more likely to keep the second one in use, too – as was the case with the 20th-century Mexican presidents Adolfo López Mateos and José López Portillo. Some such people may even, when a short version of their name is wanted, use only the second surname. A case in point was the famous 19th-century bungler Antonio López de Santa Anna, who is always known as Santa Anna.

Sometimes things are complicated a little by a person having two given names – for example José Antonio Vázquez Perico. In such cases they are often called by both given names together – but either one on its own may also be used!

Further confusion may be added by diminutives or nicknames, which are very common. Diminutives are usually formed just by sticking *ita* on the end of a woman's name (eg, Juanita for Juana) or *ito* on a man's (eg, Pablito for Pablo). The following are some of the more common nicknames:

For women
Bety – Beatriz or Elisabeth
Chabe or Chabela – Isabel
Chela – Graciela
Chole – Soledad
Concha – Concepción
Lola – Dolores
Lupe – Guadalupe
Malu – María Luisa
Mayte – María Teresa
Tere – Teresa

For men
Beto – Alberto or Roberto
Chuy – Jesús
Manolo – Manuel
Nacho – Ignacio
Neto – Ernesto
Paco or Pancho – Francisco
Pepe – José
Toño – Antonio

ploitation. They don't like being gawked at by tourists and can be very sensitive about cameras: if in doubt about whether it's OK to take a photo, always ask first.

In general, it's recommended for women to dress conservatively in Mexico City and other cities. In off-the-beaten-track places avoid shorts, sleeveless tops, etc. Everyone should lean toward the more respectful end of the dress spectrum when planning to visit churches.

Nationalism

Most Mexicans are fiercely proud of their country at the same time as they despair of it ever being governed adequately. Their independent-mindedness has roots in Mexico's 11-year war for independence from Spain in the early 19th century and subsequent struggles against US and French invaders. Any threat of foreign economic domination – as many Mexicans fear will result from NAFTA – is resented. The classic

Mexican attitude toward the US is a combination of the envy and resentment that a poor neighbor feels for a rich one. The word *gringo*, incidentally, isn't exactly a compliment, but it's not necessarily an insult either: it's often simply an un-value-laden synonym for 'American,' 'citizen of the USA.'

Time

The fabled Mexican attitude toward time – *'mañana, mañana . . . '* – has probably become legendary simply by contrast with the USA. But it's still true – though less so in Mexico City and other big cities – that the urgency Europeans, Americans and Canadians are used to is often lacking. Mexicans tend to value *simpatía* (congeniality) over promptness. If something is really worth doing, it gets done. If not, it can wait. Life should not be a succession of pressures and deadlines. According to many Mexicans, life in the 'businesslike' cultures has been de-sympathized. You may come away from Mexico convinced that the Mexicans are right!

Treatment of Animals

As in most countries where humans may not have enough to eat, animals in Mexico are rarely mollycoddled in the way they often are in wealthier societies. In general Mexicans view animals in terms of their direct practical use – as food, as beasts of burden and in the case of some wild animals, despite protective legislation, as sources of money that they or their hides, shells, feathers or eggs will fetch if sold. Mexicans may be less sensitive about animal welfare than some other cultures but they don't in general wantonly mistreat animals. Bullfighting and cockfighting, it may be argued, are evidence to the contrary – but such is the weight of tradition, ritual and the preparation surrounding these activities, especially bullfighting, that you could hardly expect a Mexican to think of them as anything other than sport, or even art.

RELIGION
Roman Catholicism

About 90% of Mexicans profess Catholicism. Though its grip over emerging generations today is perhaps marginally less strong than over their predecessors, Catholicism's dominance is remarkable considering the rocky history that the Catholic Church has had in Mexico, particularly in the last two centuries.

The church was present in Mexico from the very first days of the Spanish conquest. Until independence it remained the second most important institution after the crown's representatives, and was really the only unifying force in Mexican society. Almost everyone belonged to the church because, spirituality aside, it was the principal provider of social services and education. No doubt the presence of the Inquisition (Mexico's first heretic-burning took place in 1539) also encouraged any doubters to stay within the fold.

The bottom line was money and property, both of which the church was amassing faster than the generals and political bosses. The 1917 Mexican constitution prevented the church from owning property or running schools or newspapers, and banned clergy from wearing clerical garb or speaking out on government policies and decisions. In practice most of these provisions ceased to be enforced in the second half of the 20th century, and in the early 1990s President Salinas had them removed from the constitution and established diplomatic relations with the Vatican.

The Mexican Catholic Church is one of Latin America's more conservative. Few of its leaders get involved with political issues like human rights and poverty.

The church's most binding symbol is the dark-skinned Virgin of Guadalupe *(Nuestra Señora de Guadalupe)*, a manifestation of the Virgin Mary that appeared to a native Mexican in 1531 on the Cerro de Tepeyac in what's now the north of Mexico City. The Guadalupe Virgin became a crucial link between Catholic and indigenous spirituality and, as Mexico grew into a mestizo society, she became the most potent symbol of Mexican Catholicism. Today she is the country's patron; her blue-cloaked image is ubiquitous; her name is invoked in religious ceremonies, political speeches and literature; and the Basílica de Guadalupe is Mexico's most revered shrine.

Other Christians

Around 5% of Mexicans profess other varieties of Christianity. One group includes the Methodist, Baptist, Presbyterian and Anglican Churches, set up by American missionaries in the 19th century. The other group results from a new wave of evangelical American missionaries in the 20th century, who have made most of their converts among rural and indigenous peoples.

Indigenous Religion

The missionaries of the 16th and 17th centuries won the indigenous people over to Catholicism as much by grafting it onto pre-Hispanic religions as by deeper conversion. Often old gods were simply identified with Christian saints and old festivals continued to be celebrated, little changed, on the nearest saint's day. Acceptance of the new religion was greatly helped by the appearance of the Virgin of Guadalupe in 1531.

Today indigenous Christianity is still fused with more ancient beliefs. In some remote regions of Mexico, Christianity is a veneer at most. The Huichol people of Jalisco, for instance, have two Christs but neither is a major deity. More important is Nakawé, the fertility goddess.

Even among the more orthodox Christian indigenous peoples it is not uncommon

for spring saints' festivals, or the pre-Lent carnival, to be accompanied by remnants of fertility rites. The famous Totonac voladores (see 'Voladores' in the Things to See & Do chapter) enact one such ritual.

Judaism

Jews make up just 0.1% of Mexico's population. Most of them live in the state of México and Mexico City, where there are several synagogues.

LANGUAGE

The predominant language of Mexico is Spanish. Mexican Spanish is unlike Castilian Spanish, the language of Spain, in two respects: in Mexico, the Castilian lisp has more or less disappeared, and numerous indigenous words have been adopted.

In Mexico City and in other cities, towns and larger villages you can almost always find someone who speaks at least some English. All the same, it is still advantageous and courteous to know at least a few words and phrases of Spanish. The response you get will generally be more positive if you attempt to speak it.

About 50 indigenous languages are spoken by 7 million or more people in Mexico, of whom about 15% – nearly all outside Mexico City – don't speak Spanish.

For a selection of useful Spanish words and phrases, and a guide to pronunciation, see the Language chapter at the end of the book.

Facts for the Visitor

WHEN TO GO

The climate at this altitude is temperate year round, though it occasionally gets a bit chilly at night from November to February. These are also the months when thermal inversion (see Ecology & Environment in the Facts about Mexico City chapter) is most likely to occur, so air pollution tends to be at its worst. April is one of the best months in Mexico City, with nice temperatures and lovely lilac-colored jacaranda blossom all around. The city bustles year round, though the holiday periods of Christmas-New Year and Semana Santa (the week before Easter Sunday and the couple of days after it) are not good times to get much business done here. Many Mexicans also take holidays in July or August.

ORIENTATION

Mexico City's hundreds of *colonias* (neighborhoods) sprawl across the ancient bed of the Lago de Texcoco and beyond. Though this vast urban expanse is daunting at first, most of what's important to the majority of visitors lies in a relatively limited, well-defined and easily traversed central area.

Centro Histórico

The historic heart of the city is the wide plaza known as El Zócalo (Ⓜ Zócalo). It is surrounded by the Palacio Nacional (the presidential palace), the cathedral, and the excavated site of the Templo Mayor, which is the main temple of Aztec Tenochtitlán. The Zócalo and the surrounding neighborhood are known as the Centro Histórico (Historic Center) and are full of notable old buildings, interesting museums and other sights. North, west and south of the Zócalo are many good and mainly economical hotels and restaurants.

Alameda Central

Avenida Madero (for eastbound traffic) and Avenida Cinco de Mayo (or 5 de Mayo, for westbound traffic) link the Zócalo with the verdant park named the Alameda Central, eight blocks to the west (Ⓜ Bellas Artes). On the east side of the Alameda stands the magnificent Palacio de Bellas Artes. The landmark building, the Torre Latinoamericana (Latin American Tower), pierces the sky a block south of the Bellas Artes, beside one of the city's main north-south arterial roads, the Eje Central Lázaro Cárdenas.

Plaza de la República

Some 750m west of the Alameda across Paseo de la Reforma is Plaza de la República, marked by the somber, domed, art deco-style Monumento a la Revolución. This is a fairly quiet, mostly residential area with many budget and mid-range hotels (Ⓜ Revolución).

Paseo de la Reforma

Mexico City's grandest boulevard runs for several kilometers across the city's heart, connecting the Alameda to the Zona Rosa

CHARLOTTE HINDLE

What's green and white and red by the pole?

and the Bosque de Chapultepec (Maps 4, 5, 6 and 8). Major hotels, embassies, office buildings and banks rise along it, and streets branching off have a number of important commercial and business addresses as well. Landmark *glorietas* (traffic circles) along Reforma are marked with statues, including those commemorating Cristóbal Colón (Christopher Columbus); Cuauhtémoc, the last Aztec emperor (at the intersection with Avenida Insurgentes); and Mexican independence (the Monumento a la Independencia, or *El Ángel*).

Zona Rosa

The Zona Rosa (Pink Zone; **Ⓜ** Insurgentes) is a shopping, eating, hotel and nightlife district anchored on the Monumento a la Independencia and bounded by Paseo de la Reforma on the north, Avenida Insurgentes on the east and Avenida Chapultepec on the south.

Condesa & Roma

These two middle-class colonias just south of the Zona Rosa have lots of good places to eat and some interesting entertainment venues.

Bosque de Chapultepec

The Wood of Chapultepec, generally known to gringos as Chapultepec Park, is to the west of the aforementioned districts. A large expanse of trees, gardens and lakes, it is Mexico City's 'lungs,' and holds many of the city's major museums, including the renowned Museo Nacional de Antropología and the Museo Nacional de Historia (**Ⓜ** Chapultepec or Auditorio).

Polanco

Polanco, north of the Bosque de Chapultepec, is an upper-middle-class area with a lot of embassies and expensive restaurants and a cluster of the city's top hotels (**Ⓜ** Audotorio or Polanco).

North of the Center

Five kilometers north of the Alameda Central is the Terminal Norte, the largest of the city's four major bus terminals (**Ⓜ** Auto-

---

Shantytowns

Not surprisingly, you won't find Mexico City's notorious shantytowns near popular areas like the Zócalo or the Zona Rosa. They're on the city's fringes, many of them in the state of México, where most of the city's current expansion is taking place. You may glimpse some as you enter or leave by road, but most of the main roads are lined by established communities. In addition, many of the oldest shantytowns – such as the vast Ciudad Nezahualcóyotl ('Neza,' east of the airport and north of the Puebla road), which is home to well over a million people – are no longer really even shantytowns. One reason is that they have succeeded in gaining services such as running water and electricity. Another is that many of their inhabitants have earned enough money to build themselves relatively comfortable homes.

---

buses del Norte; Map 1). Six kilometers north of the Zócalo is the Basílica de Guadalupe (**Ⓜ** La Villa-Basílica; Map 3), Mexico's most revered shrine.

South of the Center

Avenida Insurgentes, the city's major north-south axis, intersects with Paseo de la Reforma, connecting it to most points of interest in the south. It's straight as an arrow for many kilometers and straddled by mostly middle-class areas with a lot of restaurants and businesses.

Five to 10km south of Reforma are the atmospheric former colonial villages of San Ángel (**Ⓜ** M A de Quevedo) and Coyoacán (**Ⓜ** Viveros, Coyoacán or General Anaya), and the vast campus of the Universidad Nacional Autónoma de México (UNAM, National University of Mexico; **Ⓜ** Copilco or Universidad; Map 11). Also down in this area is the Terminal Sur, which is the southernmost intercity bus station (**Ⓜ** Tasqueña; Map 9). In the far southeast of the city are the canals and gardens of Xochimilco.

The Eje System

Besides their regular names, many major streets in Mexico City are termed *Eje* (Axis). The Eje system superimposes a grid of priority roads on this sprawling city's maze of smaller streets, which makes driving easier and quicker. The key north-south Eje Central Lázaro Cárdenas, running all the way from Coyoacán in the south to Tenayuca in the north, passes just east of the Alameda Central.

Major north-south roads to the west of the Eje Central are termed Eje 1 Poniente (West), Eje 2 Poniente, etc, and major north-south roads east of the Eje Central are called Eje 1 Oriente (East), Eje 2 Oriente and so on. Eje 1 Poniente is also called Guerrero, Rosales and Bucareli as it passes through the central area; Eje 2 Poniente is Avenida Florencia and Monterrey; Eje 1 Oriente is Alcocer and Anillo de Circunvalación; Eje 2 Oriente is Avenida Congreso de la Unión.

The same goes for major east-west roads to the north and south of the Alameda Central and the Zócalo: Rayón is Eje 1 Norte, and Fray Servando Teresa de Mier is Eje 1 Sur.

Finding an Address

Some major streets, such as Avenida Insurgentes, keep the same name for many kilometers, but the names – and numbering systems – of many lesser streets change every few blocks. In some neighborhoods, street names concentrate on a particular subject, such as famous writers, rivers or Mexican states. Many of the streets near the Zócalo are named for Latin American countries; Zona Rosa streets are named for European cities.

Street addresses normally include the name of a colonia. Another term you may come across is *Local* (sometimes abbreviated to *Loc*), which refers to a particular office or shop number in a mall. Often the easiest way to find an address is by asking where it is in relation to the nearest metro station.

MAPS

Maps handed out by Mexico City's tourist offices are currently pretty basic. You can find better ones in many bookstores (including those in Sanborns chain stores and top-end hotels) and at the shops of INEGI (the Instituto Nacional de Estadística, Geografía e Informática, or National Institute of Statistics, Geography & Information Technology). INEGI has map shops at Local 61 in the airport and at Baja California 272 in Colonia Condesa, on the corner of Culiacán (Ⓜ Chilpancingo). Another convenient map outlet is at Local (Office) CC23, Glorieta Insurgentes, just outside Insurgentes metro station (Map 6). This shop sells INEGI's large-scale series of 1:50,000 (1cm:500m) maps covering the whole of Mexico, plus a variety of other maps of Mexico City, Mexico, Mexican states and other Mexican cities. It's open 8 am to 8 pm Monday to Friday, 8.30 am to 4 pm Saturday. Photocopies of 1:50,000 sheets cost US$1.50 each.

Among the best maps of Mexico City is the *Guía Roji Ciudad de México* street atlas (US$8.50), which has comprehensive indexes of streets and colonias and is updated annually. It's fairly easy to find in Mexico City, but harder elsewhere. The Adventurous Traveler Bookstore (www.adventuroustraveler.com) is an Internet source worth checking.

TOURIST OFFICES
Local Tourist Offices

Mexico City has three tourist information offices in central areas. None of them has a great deal of free printed material, but they willingly answer questions and usually at least one staff member in each can speak English.

The tourist office of SECTUR, the national tourism ministry (☎ 5-250-01-23, 800-903-92-00), is inconveniently located for most visitors. It is at Avenida Presidente Masaryk 172, on the corner of Hegel in Polanco, about 600m north of the Museo Nacional de Antropología (Ⓜ Polanco). It has multilingual staff who willingly answer queries on Mexico City and the rest of the country and can provide computer printouts on some specific subjects.

SECTUR's two phone lines are staffed 24 hours, seven days a week, to provide tourist information and help with tourist problems and emergencies. The office itself is open 8 am to 6 pm Monday to Friday, 10 am to 3 pm Saturday.

Easier to reach is the Oficina de Turismo de la Ciudad de México (☎ 5-525-93-80), Amberes 54, at Londres in the Zona Rosa (Ⓜ Insurgentes), providing information on Mexico City only. It's open 9 am to 8 pm daily.

The Cámara Nacional de Comercio de la Ciudad de México (Mexico City National Chamber of Commerce), Paseo de la Reforma 42 between Avenida Juárez and Guerra (Ⓜ Juárez; Map 5), also has a tourist office (☎ 5-592-26-77 ext 1015) providing information on the city only. It's on the 4th floor of the building, open 9 am to 2 pm and 3 to 6 pm Monday to Friday.

Other tourist offices are in the southern suburbs of San Ángel, Coyoacán and Xochimilco (see those sections in the Things to See & Do chapter) and at the airport and the Terminal Norte bus station (see the Getting There & Away chapter).

Tourist Offices Abroad
In the USA or Canada you can call ☎ 800-446-3942 for Mexican tourist information. You can also contact the following Mexican Government Tourist Offices:

Chicago
(☎ 312-606-9252)
300 N Michigan Ave, 4th floor, 60601

Houston
(☎ 713-780-8395)
1400 W Office Drive, 77042

Los Angeles
(☎ 213-351-2076)
2401 W 6th St, 5th floor, 90057

Miami
(☎ 305-718-4091)
1200 NW 78th Ave No 208, 33126-1817

Montreal
(☎ 514-871-1052)
1 Place Ville Marie, Suite 1931, H3B 2C3

New York
(☎ 212-821-0304)
21 E 63rd St, 3rd floor, 10021

Toronto
(☎ 416-925-2753)
2 Bloor St W, Suite 1502, M4W 3E2

Vancouver
(☎ 604-669-2845)
999 W Hastings St, Suite 1110

There are the following Mexican Government Tourism Offices in other countries:

Argentina
(☎ 01-328-9970)
Avenida Santa Fe 920, 1059 Buenos Aires

France
(☎ 01 42 61 51 80)
4 rue Notre Dame des Victoires, 75002 Paris

Germany
(☎ 069-253-509)
Wiesenhuettenplatz 26, D60329
Frankfurt-am-Main

Italy
(☎ 06-487-2182)
Via Barberini 3, 00187 Rome

Spain
(☎ 91-561-18-27)
Calle Velázquez 126, Madrid 28006

UK
(☎ 020-7734-1058)
60-61 Trafalgar Square, 3rd floor,
London WC2N 5DS

DOCUMENTS
Visitors to Mexico should have a valid passport. Some nationalities have to obtain visas, but many nationalities require only an easily obtained document such as the FMT (tourist card) or the FMN or FMVC for business travelers (see the following sections). Travelers under 18 who are not accompanied by *both* parents must have special documentation – see Consent Form for Minors under Travel Permits in this section.

Since regulations sometimes change, it is wise to confirm them at a Mexican Government Tourism Office or Mexican embassy or consulate before your trip. Several Mexican embassies and consulates, and foreign embassies in Mexico, have websites with useful information on tourist permits, visas, travel with minors and so on (see 'Embassy & Consulate Internet Sites') but they don't all agree with each other, so you should back up any Internet findings with some phone calls. The Lonely Planet website (www.lonelyplanet.com) has links to updated visa information.

Passport

Though it's not recommended, US citizens can enter Mexico as tourists without a passport if they have official photo identification such as a driver's license, plus some proof of their citizenship, such as a birth certificate certified by the issuing agency or their original certificate of naturalization (not a copy). Citizens of other nationalities who are permanent residents in the United States have to present their passport and Permanent Resident Alien card.

Canadian tourists may enter Mexico with official photo identification plus proof of citizenship, such as a birth certificate or notarized affidavit of it. Naturalized Canadian citizens, however, require a valid passport.

In any case it is best to take your passport, because officials are used to passports and may delay those with other documents. This applies to US and Canadian officials as well as to Mexican officials: the only proof of citizenship recognized by US or Canadian immigration is a passport or (for nonnaturalized citizens) a certified copy of your birth certificate. In Mexico you will often need your passport when you change money.

Tourists from other countries need to show a passport that will be valid for at least six months after they arrive in Mexico.

Mexicans with dual nationality must carry proof of both their citizenships and must identify themselves as Mexican when entering or leaving Mexico. They are considered Mexican by the Mexican authorities but are not subject to compulsory military service.

Visas

In addition to any Mexican requirements (see Tourists and Business Travelers, below), non-US citizens passing through the USA on the way to or from Mexico, or visiting Mexico from the USA with plans to return, should check their US visa requirements beforehand.

Tourists Citizens of the USA, Canada, EU countries, Australia, New Zealand, Norway, Switzerland, Iceland, Israel, Japan, Argentina and Chile are among those who do *not* require visas to enter Mexico as tourists. But they must obtain a Mexican government FMT (tourist card) – see Travel Permits, below.

Countries whose nationals *do* need visas to visit Mexico as tourists include South Africa, Brazil and most eastern European nations – check well ahead of travel with your local Mexican embassy or consulate.

Business Travelers Travelers on business, company transferees and some others going to Mexico for work purposes, of many nationalities, can spend up to 30 days in Mexico with easily obtained FMN or FMVC documentation (see Travel Permits, below). Those who want to stay in Mexico more than 30 days, or who don't qualify for an FMN or FMVC, must obtain an FM3 visa, which is valid for multiple entries for up to one year. An FM3 can be obtained in advance at a Mexican consulate, or you can replace an FMN or FMVC with an FM3 in Mexico at the Instituto Nacional de Migración (INM, National Immigration Institute) – see FMT Extensions & Lost FMTs, below, for locations of INM offices in Mexico City. The broad categories of people to whom FM3s are available are business visitors, investors, people coming to Mexico to fill a salaried position, technicians, scientists and professionals. Procedures and fees vary according to the category, your nationality and where you are applying.

The FM3 can be renewed for four one-year periods. If you plan to find work in Mexico, see the Work section at the end of this chapter for more on obtaining an FM3 for that situation.

Travel Permits

FMT Tourists must obtain a Forma Migratoria para Turista (FMT), often called the 'tourist card' or *'tarjeta de turista.'* This is a small paper document that must be stamped by Mexican immigration when you enter Mexico and which you must keep until you leave. It is available free of charge at official border crossings, international airports and ports, and often from airlines, travel agencies, Mexican consulates and Mexican Government Tourism Offices. At the US-Mexico border you won't usually be given one automatically – you have to ask for it.

At many US-Mexico border crossings you don't *have* to get the card stamped at the border itself. The Instituto Nacional de Migración has control points on the highways 20km to 30km farther into Mexico where it's also possible to do it – but it's advisable to do it at the border, in case difficulties crop up elsewhere.

One section of the card – to be filled in by the immigration officer – deals with the length of your stay in Mexico. You may be asked a couple of questions about how long you want to stay and what you'll be doing, but normally you will be given the maximum 180 days if you ask for it. It's always advisable to put down more days than you think you'll need, in case you are delayed or change your plans.

Look after your tourist card, as it will probably be checked when you leave the country.

Nonimmigrant Fee Since 1999, all foreign tourists (of any age) visiting Mexico have been charged a fee of 150 pesos (about US$15) called the Derecho para No Inmigrante (DNI, Nonimmigrant Fee).

If you enter Mexico by air, the fee is included in the price of your ticket. If you enter by land you must pay the fee at a branch of any of 27 Mexican banks listed on the back of your FMT before you check in at an airport to fly out of Mexico or before you pass an INM highway checkpoint approaching the border. It makes sense to get the job done as soon as possible, and at least some Mexican border posts have on-the-spot bank offices where you can do so.

When paying, you need to present your FMT, which will be stamped to prove that you have paid. This will probably be checked when you leave the country. Tourists only have to pay the fee once in any 180-day period. You are entitled to leave and reenter Mexico as many times as you like within 180 days without paying again. If you are going to return within the 180-day period, retain your stamped FMT when you leave Mexico.

FMT Extensions & Lost FMTs If for some reason the number of days given on your FMT is less than the 180-day maximum, its validity may be extended one or more times, at no cost, up to the maximum. To get a card extended you have to apply to the INM, which has offices in many towns and cities. The procedure is free and usually accomplished in a few minutes; you'll need your passport, FMT, photocopies of the important pages of these documents, and – at some offices – evidence of 'sufficient funds.' A major credit card is usually OK for the latter, or an amount in traveler's checks, which could vary from US$100 to US$1000 depending on the office you are dealing with. It's advisable to phone first to ask.

Most INM offices will not extend a card until a few days before it is due to expire – don't bother trying earlier.

In Mexico City the INM has offices at Avenida Chapultepec 284, in the Zona Rosa (☎ 5-626-72-00) and at Homero 1832, in Polanco (☎ 5-387-24-00). Both are open 9 am to 1 pm Monday to Friday. The Avenida Chapultepec office is just outside Insurgentes metro station.

If you lose your FMT or need further information, contact the SECTUR tourist office (☎ 5-250-01-23, 800-903-92-00) or your embassy or consulate. Your embassy or consulate may be able to give you a letter enabling you to leave Mexico without your card, or at least an official note to take to your local INM office, which will have to issue a duplicate.

FMN & FMVC The regulations for business travelers entering Mexico were simplified in the 1990s but are still complicated and subject to revisions. You should contact a Mexican consulate well in advance of travel to discuss your particular situation. Contracts or other legal documents signed in Mexico by people who do not have the proper migratory status may not be considered legally binding.

US & Canadian Citizens Under NAFTA regulations, four categories of US and Canadian citizens can visit Mexico for up to 30 days with an FMN (Forma Migratoria de Negocios) form, easily obtained from Mexican consulates in the US and Canada, Mexican immigration officials on arrival in the country or through airlines. The four categories are:

- Business visitors – people engaged in activities such as research, marketing, sales, distribution and after-sales services
- Traders and investors – people engaged in commercial transactions or negotiations, or establishing, developing or administering investments
- Transferees – employees of US or Canadian companies sent to perform managerial or specialist activities in a subsidiary or affiliate
- Professionals – scientists, doctors, dentists, professors and others classified as professionals by NAFTA: they may need to present an official license known as a *cédula profesional*, issued by Mexico's Secretaría de Educación Publica (Secretariat of Public Education), in order to obtain an FMN

The FMN is free. To get it, you will need to show your passport or other proof of citizenship (see Passport, earlier in this section). A letter from your company stating the purpose of your trip and that your expenses and income will be paid from outside Mexico is useful to have but it is not usually required. You must hand your FMN in to Mexican immigration officials when you leave the country, unless you intend to return to Mexico before your 30 days expires, in which case you can keep it. If you come back after the 30 days is up, you can get another 30-day FMN.

If you wish to stay in Mexico more than 30 days, or you do not qualify for an FMN, you must obtain an FM3 visa (see Visas, earlier).

Other Nationalities For those from many other countries, including Britain, Ireland, France, Germany, most other western European countries, Australia, New Zealand, South Africa, Argentina, Brazil, Chile, Uruguay and Israel, the FMVC (Forma Migratoria Visitante y Consejero) is good for multiple visits during a 30-day period by business visitors, technicians, and individuals sent by their companies to work in Mexico. It can be obtained through a Mexican consulate or (in the case of most of the above nationalities) at immigration on arrival in Mexico. You may need to show a letter from your company stating the purpose of your trip and that your expenses and income will be paid from outside Mexico.

For stays of more than 30 days, an FM3 visa must be obtained (see Visas, earlier in this section).

Nonimmigrant Fee People traveling on FMN or FMVC forms must pay the 150-peso Nonimmigrant Fee (see Nonimmigrant Fee under FMT, earlier). The regulations are the same as for tourists except that the validity of the fee is 30 days, the same as that of the FMN or FMVC.

Consent Form for Minors Each year numerous parents try to run away from the USA or Canada to Mexico with their children to escape the legal machinations of the children's other parent. To prevent this, minors (people under 18) entering Mexico without one or both of their parents may be – and often are – required to show a notarized consent form, signed by the absent parent or parents, giving permission for the young traveler to enter Mexico. A form for this purpose is available from Mexican consulates. In the case of divorced parents, a custody document may be acceptable instead. If one or both parents is dead, or the traveler has only one legal parent, a notarized statement saying so may be required.

These rules are aimed primarily at Americans and Canadians but apparently apply to all nationalities. Procedures vary from country to country and you should contact a Mexican consulate to find out exactly what you need to do.

Travel Insurance
A travel insurance policy to cover theft, loss (including plane tickets), delay or cancellation of flights and medical problems is a good idea. It's also a good idea to buy insurance as early as possible. If you buy it the week before you fly, you may find, for

example, that you're not covered for delays to your flight caused by strikes.

If you suffer some serious medical problem, you may want to find a private hospital or fly out for treatment. Travel insurance can cover those costs. Some US health insurance policies stay in effect, at least for a limited time, if you travel abroad, but it's worth checking exactly what you'll be covered for in Mexico. For people whose medical insurance or national health systems don't extend to Mexico – which includes most non-Americans – a travel policy is advisable.

You may prefer a policy that pays doctors or hospitals directly rather than requiring you to pay on the spot and claim later. If you have to claim later, make sure you keep all documentation. Some policies ask you to call back (reverse charges) to a center in your home country, where an immediate assessment of your problem is made.

A wide variety of policies is available, so check the small print. Some policies specifically exclude 'dangerous activities,' which can include scuba diving and motorcycling. A locally acquired motorcycle license is not valid under some policies. Check that the policy covers ambulances and an emergency flight home.

Hostel, Student, Youth & Teacher Cards

Take your hostel card along if you have one, but it's not worth getting one just for a short visit to Mexico City. If you find that you need it, you can buy one when you get here (see below). An HI (Hostelling International) card or a membership card of a national youth hostel association will save you paying US$2 for 'welcome stamps' for your first six nights at youth hostels in the REMAJ group, and may bring you a US$1 discount in AMAJ group hostels (see the Places to Stay chapter).

The ISIC student card, the GO25 card for any traveler aged 12 to 25, and the ITIC card for teachers can all help you obtain reduced-price air tickets to or from Mexico at student and youth-oriented travel agencies (see Travel Agencies in the Getting There &

Away chapter). In Mexico, notices at museums, archaeological sites and so on usually state that reduced entry prices for students are only for those with Mexican credentials, but in practice the ISIC will sometimes get you a reduction. It may also get you discounts on some bus tickets and in a few hostel-type accommodations. The GO25 and ITIC are less recognized in Mexico, but worth taking along if you have them.

Mundo Joven, at the Casa de Francia, Havre 15, Zona Rosa (☎ 5-525-04-07) and at Insurgentes Sur 1510, Local D (☎ 5-661-32-33; Map 6), can issue ISIC, ITIC and GO25 cards for US$12.50 and HI cards for US$24. For the first two you need a card or letter from your college showing that you are a full-time student or teacher. For a GO25 (for which you have to be under 26) or HI card you just need your passport. The Insurgentes office is the headquarters and is just south of Avenida Río Mixcoac. You can get there on a 'San Ángel' pesero (small bus) southbound from Insurgentes metro.

Viajes Educativos (☎ 5-661-42-35), Local B10, Insurgentes Sur 421 (entrance on Aguascalientes just north of Chilpancingo metro; Map 7) can issue ISIC and HI cards.

Driver's License & Permits

If you're thinking of renting a vehicle in Mexico, take your driver's license and a major credit card. For more on rentals, and information on the paperwork involved in taking your own vehicle into Mexico, see the Getting There & Away chapter.

Photocopies

All important documents (passport data pages and visa pages, birth certificate, vehicle papers, credit or bank cards, insurance papers, air tickets, driver's license, traveler's check receipts or serial numbers, etc) should be photocopied before you leave home. Leave one set of copies with someone at home and keep another with you, separate from the original documents. When you get to Mexico, add a photocopy of your FMT, FMN or FMVC and, if you're driving, vehicle import papers.

It's also a good idea to store details of your vital travel documents in Lonely Planet's free online Travel Vault in case you lose the photocopies or can't be bothered with them. Your password-protected Travel Vault is accessible online from anywhere in the world; you can create it at the eKno website (www.ekno.lonelyplanet.com).

EMBASSIES & CONSULATES
Mexican Embassies & Consulates

Unless otherwise noted, details are for embassies or their consular sections.

Argentina
(☎ 01-821-7172)
Larrea 1230, 1117 Buenos Aires

Australia
(☎ 02-6273-3905)
14 Perth Ave, Yarralumla, Canberra, ACT 2600
Consulate: (☎ 02-9326-1311)
Level 1, 135-153 New South Head Rd, Edgecliff, Sydney, NSW 2027

Belize
(☎ 02-30-193/194)
20 North Park St, Fort George Area, Belize City

Brazil
(☎ 061-244-1011)
SES Av das Nacoes Lote 18, 70412-900 Brasilia

Canada
(☎ 613-233-8988/6665)
45 O'Connor St, Suite 1500, Ottawa, Ontario K1P 1A4
Consulate: (☎ 514-288-2502)
2000 rue Mansfield, Suite 1015, Montreal, PQ H3A 2Z7
Consulate: (☎ 416-368-2875)
Commerce Court West, 199 Bay St, Suite 4440, Toronto, ON M5L 1E9
Consulate: (☎ 604-684-1859)
810-1130 West Pender St, Vancouver, BC V6E 4A4

Costa Rica
(☎ 225-4430)
Avenida 7a No 1371, San José

El Salvador
(☎ 243-0445)
Circunvalación y Pasaje No 12, Colonia San Benito, San Salvador

France
(☎ 01 53 70 27 40)
9 rue de Longchamps, 75116 Paris
Consulate: (☎ 01 42 61 51 80)
4 rue Notre Dame des Victories, 75002 Paris

Germany
(☎ 0228-914-8620)
Adenauerallee 100, 53113 Bonn
Consulate: (☎ 030-324-9047)
Kurfurstendamm 72, 10709 Berlin
Consulate: (☎ 069-299-8750)
Hochstrasse 35-37, 60330 Frankfurt-am-Main

Guatemala
(☎ 333-7254)
Edificio Centro Ejecutivo, 15ª Calle No 3-20, 7º Nivel, Zona 10, Guatemala City
Consulate: (☎ 331-8165)
13a Calle No 7-30, Zona 9, Guatemala City
Consulate: (☎ 763-1312)
9a Avenida No 6-19, Zona 1, Quetzaltenango

Honduras
(☎ 32-0138)
Avenida República de México 2402, Colonia Palmira, Tegucigalpa

Ireland
(☎ 01-260-0699)
43 Ailesbury Rd, Ballsbridge, Dublin 4

Italy
(☎ 06-440-2309)
Via Lazzaro Spallanzani 16, 00161 Rome
Consulate: (☎ 02-7602-0541)
Via Cappuccini 4, 20122 Milan

Netherlands
(☎ 070-360-2900)
Nassauplein 17, 2585 EB The Hague

New Zealand
(☎ 04-472-5555)
8th floor, 111-115 Customhouse Quay, Wellington

Nicaragua
(☎ 0-278-1860)
Carretera a Masaya Km 4.5, 25 varas arriba (next to Optica Matamoros), Altamira, Managua

South Africa
(☎ 12-342-6190)
Southern Life Plaza, 1st floor, CNR Schoeman & Festival Streets, Hatfield, 0083 Pretoria

Spain
(☎ 91-369-2814)
Carrera de San Jerónimo 46, 28014 Madrid
Consulate: (☎ 93-201-1822)
Avinguda Diagonal 626, 08021 Barcelona
Consulate: (☎ 95-456-3944)
Calle San Roque 6, 41001 Sevilla

UK
(☎ 020-7235-6393)
8 Halkin St, London SW1X 7DW

USA
(☎ 202-728-1694)
1911 Pennsylvania Ave NW,

Washington DC 20006
Consulate: (☎ 202-736-1000)
2827 16th St NW, Washington DC 20009

Mexican Consulates in the USA

There are consulates in many US cities, particularly in the border states (for the embassy and consulate in Washington, DC, see above):

Arizona
Douglas: (☎ 520-364-3107)
1201 F Ave, 85607
Nogales: (☎ 520-287-2521)
571 N Grand Ave, 85621
Phoenix: (☎ 602-242-7398)
1990 West Camelback Rd, Suite 110, 85015
Tucson: (☎ 520-882-5595)
553 S Stone Ave, 85701

California
Calexico: (☎ 760-357-3863)
331 West 2nd St, 92231
Fresno: (☎ 209-233-3065)
830 Van Ness Ave, 93721
Los Angeles: (☎ 213-351-6800)
2401 West 6th St, 90057
Sacramento: (☎ 916-441-2987)
1010 8th St, 95814
San Bernardino: (☎ 909-889-9837)
532 North D St, 92401
San Diego: (☎ 619-231-9741)
1549 India St, 92101
San Francisco: (☎ 415-392-6576)
870 Market St, Suite 528, 94102
San Jose: (☎ 408-294-8334)
380 North 1st St, Suite 192, 95112

Colorado
Denver: (☎ 303-331-1110)
48 Steele St, 80206

Florida
Miami: (☎ 305-716-4979)
1200 NW 78th Ave, Suite 200, 33126
Orlando: (☎ 407-422-0514)
100 Washington St, 32801

Georgia
Atlanta: (☎ 404-266-2233)
2600 Apple Valley Road, 30319

Illinois
Chicago: (☎ 312-855-1380)
300 North Michigan Ave, 2nd floor, 60601

Louisiana
New Orleans: (☎ 504-522-3596)
World Trade Center Building, 2 Canal St, Suite 840, 70130

Massachusetts
Boston: (☎ 617-426-4942)
20 Park Plaza, 5th floor, Suite 506, 02116

Michigan
Detroit: (☎ 313-567-7709)
600 Renaissance Center, Suite 1510, 48243

Missouri
St Louis: (☎ 314-436-3426)
1015 Locust St, Suite 922, 63101

New Mexico
Albuquerque: (☎ 505-247-2139)
400 Gold SW, Suite 100, 87102

New York
New York: (☎ 212-217-6400)
27 East 39th St, 10016

Oregon
Portland: (☎ 503-274-1442)
1234 SW Morrison St, 97205

Pennsylvania
Philadelphia: (☎ 215-922-4262)
111 S Independence Mall East, Bourse Building, Suite 310, 19106

Texas
Austin: (☎ 512-478-9031)
200 East 6th St, Suite 200, 78701
Brownsville: (☎ 956-542-5182)
724 E Elizabeth St, 78520
Corpus Christi: (☎ 512-882-3375)
800 North Shoreline Boulevard, Suite 410 North Tower, 78401
Dallas: (☎ 214-630-1604)
8855 N Stemmons Freeway, 75247
Del Rio: (☎ 830-775-2352)
2398 Spur 239, South Park Plaza, 78840
Eagle Pass: (☎ 830-773-9255)
140 Adams St, 78852
El Paso: (☎ 915-533-3644)
910 East San Antonio St, 79901
Houston: (☎ 713-271-6800)
10103 Fondren Rd, Suite 555, 77096
Laredo: (☎ 956-723-0990)
1612 Farragut St, 78040
McAllen: (☎ 956-686-4684)
600 South Broadway Ave, 78501
Midland: (☎ 915-687-2334)
511 W Ohio, Suite 121, 79701
San Antonio: (☎ 210-227-9145)
127 Navarro St, 78205

Utah
Salt Lake City: (☎ 801-521-8502)
230 West 400 North, 2nd floor, 84101

Washington state
Seattle: (☎ 206-448-6819)
2132 3rd Ave, 98121

Embassy Websites

Many Mexican embassies and consulates and foreign embassies in Mexico City have websites. Links to most of them can be found on http://mexico.web.com.mx/mx/embajadas .html. Two particularly useful sites, with tourist information and data on Mexican visas and tourist permits, are those of the Mexican embassy in Washington DC (www.embassyofmexico.org) and also the Mexican Consulate in New York (www .quicklink.com/mexico).

Embassies in Mexico City

All foreign embassies in Mexico are in Mexico City. The following is a selective list. They often keep limited business hours – usually something like 9 or 10 am to 1 or 2 pm Monday to Friday – and may close on both Mexican and their own national holidays. Many provide 24-hour emergency telephone contact. If you're visiting your embassy, it's best to call ahead to check hours and confirm that the address you're heading for is the right one for the service you want. The following addresses include the colonias (neighborhoods) in which the embassies are located, and any convenient metro stations.

It's important to realize what your embassy can and can't do. Generally speaking, it won't be much help in emergencies if the trouble you're in is remotely your own fault. Remember that you are bound by the laws of the country you are in. Your embassy will not be sympathetic if you end up in jail after committing a crime locally, even if such actions are legal in your own country.

In genuine emergencies you might get some assistance, but only if other channels have been exhausted. For example, if you need to get home urgently, a free ticket home is exceedingly unlikely – the embassy would expect you to have insurance. If you have all your money and documents stolen, it might assist in getting a new passport, but a loan for onward travel is out of the question.

Argentina
(☎ 5-520-94-32)
Boulevard Manuel Ávila Camacho 1, 7th floor, Lomas de Chapultepec

Australia
(☎ 5-531-52-25; Australians needing out-of-hours assistance can call reverse-charges the Australian number ☎ 61-2-6261-1446)
Rubén Darío 55, Polanco – open 8:30 am to 2 pm Monday to Friday, 3 to 5 pm Monday to Thursday (Ⓜ Polanco or Auditorio)

Belize
(☎ 5-520-12-74)
Bernardo de Gálvez 215, Lomas de Chapultepec

Brazil
(☎ 5-202-75-00)
Lope de Armendáriz 130, Lomas de Chapultepec

Canada
(☎ 5-724-79-00)
Schiller 529, Polanco, 400m north of the Museo Nacional de Antropología – open 9 am to 1 pm and 2 to 5 pm Monday to Friday (Ⓜ Polanco)

Chile
(☎ 5-520-00-25)
Montes Urales 460, Lomas de Chapultepec

Cuba
(☎ 5-280-80-39)
Avenida Presidente Masaryk 554, Polanco (Ⓜ Polanco)

France
(☎ 5-282-97-00)
Lafontaine 32, Polanco – open 9 am to 1 pm Monday to Friday (Ⓜ Auditorio)

Germany
(☎ 5-283-22-00)
Lord Byron 737, Polanco – open 9 am to noon Monday to Friday (Ⓜ Polanco)

Guatemala
(☎ 5-540-75-20)
Avenida Explanada 1025, Lomas de Chapultepec

Italy
(☎ 5-596-36-55)
Paseo de las Palmas 1994, Lomas de Chapultepec

Netherlands
(☎ 5-258-99-21 or ☎ 5-505-07-52 for emergencies)
Avenida Vasco de Quiroga 3000, 7° piso, Santa Fe – open 8.30 am to 4 pm Monday to Friday

New Zealand
(☎ 5-281-54-86)
Lagrange 103, 10° piso, Los Morales (Map 8)

Spain
(☎ 5-282-22-71)
Galileo 114, Polanco (Ⓜ Polanco)

UK

(☎ 5-207-20-89)
Río Lerma 71, Colonia Cuauhtémoc, north of the Monumento a la Independencia – open 8.30 am to 3.30 pm Monday to Friday; consular section at rear (Río Usumacinta 30) – open 9 am to 2 pm Monday to Friday (⊕ Insurgentes; Map 6)

USA

(☎ 5-209-91-00, always attended)
Paseo de la Reforma 305, Cuauhtémoc, not far from the Monumento a la Independencia – open 9 am to 5 pm Monday to Friday, closed on Mexican and US holidays (⊕ Insurgentes; Map 6)

CUSTOMS

Things that visitors are allowed to bring into Mexico duty-free include items for personal use such as clothing, footwear and toiletries; medicine for personal use, with prescription in the case of psychotropic substances (medicines that can alter perception or behavior); one still or video or movie camera; up to 12 rolls of film or videocassette reels; one portable computer; and, if you're 18 or older, 3L of wine, beer or liquor and 400 cigarettes. These limits are not always applied very strictly.

The normal customs inspection routine when you enter Mexico is to complete a customs declaration form (which lists duty-free allowances), then choose between going through a goods-to-declare channel or a nothing-to-declare channel. Those declaring items have their belongings searched, and duty is collected. Those not declaring items have to pass a full-size traffic signal. The signal responds randomly: a green light lets you pass without inspection, a red light means your baggage will be searched.

MONEY
Currency

Mexico's currency is the peso. The peso is divided into 100 centavos. Coins come in denominations of five, 10, 20 and 50 centavos and one, two, five, 10, 20 and 50 pesos. There are notes of 10, 20, 50, 100, 200 and 500 pesos.

The $ sign is used to refer to pesos in Mexico. The designations 'N$,' 'NP' (both for nuevos pesos) and 'MN' *(moneda nacional)* all refer to pesos. Prices quoted in US dollars will normally be written 'US$5,' '$5 Dlls' or '5 USD' to avoid misunderstanding.

Coins and notes minted between 1993 and 1995 bear the wording *nuevos pesos* (new pesos), or the abbreviation N$. They are worth exactly the same as more recent coins and notes which simply say *pesos* or $.

Since the peso's exchange value is unpredictable, prices in this book are given in US dollar equivalents.

Exchange Rates

The peso has been reasonably stable since the currency crisis of 1994-95, when it lost 60% of its value in three months. Exchange rates as this book went to press were as follows:

country	unit		pesos
Australia	A$1	=	5.66
Belize	BZ$1	=	4.66
Canada	C$1	=	6.34
European Union	€$1	=	9.07
France	FF1	=	1.38
Germany	DM1	=	4.64
Guatemala	Q1	=	1.21
Japan	1¥	=	0.09
New Zealand	NZ$1	=	4.50
UK	UK£1	=	14.70
USA	US$1	=	9.33

Exchanging Money

The easiest form of money to have in Mexico City is a major international credit card or debit card. Cards such as Visa, American Express and MasterCard (Eurocard, Access) are accepted by many hotels, restaurants and shops, and by virtually all airlines, car rental companies and travel agents.

Equally convenient, you can use major credit cards and some bank cards, such as those on the Cirrus and Plus systems, to withdraw cash pesos from ATMs (bank cash machines, which are plentiful) and over the counter at banks. ATMs are generally the easiest source of cash. Despite the handling fee that may be charged to your account, you win by using ATMs because you get a good exchange rate and avoid the commission you would pay when changing cash or traveler's checks.

Mexican banks call their ATMs by a variety of names – usually something like *caja permanente* or *cajero automático*. Each ATM displays the cards it will accept.

To guard against robbery when using ATMs, try to use them during working hours and choose ones that are securely located inside a bank building, rather than ones open to the street or enclosed only by glass.

Traveler's Checks & Cash Even if you have a credit card or bank card, as a backup it's still a good idea to take along some major-brand traveler's checks (best denominated in US dollars), or – less desirable for security reasons – cash US dollars. If you don't have a credit or bank card, use US-dollar traveler's checks. American Express is a good brand to have because it's recognized everywhere, which can prevent delays. American Express in Mexico City (☎ 5-207-72-82) is on the edge of the Zona Rosa at Paseo de la Reforma 234, on the corner of Havre (Ⓜ Insurgentes). It's open 9 am to 6 pm Monday to Friday, 9 am to 1 pm Saturday. You can change American Express traveler's checks here: when we last checked the rate was better than in most other places. The office also has other financial and card services, a travel bureau and a mail pick-up desk. It maintains a 24-hour hot line (☎ 5-326-27-00) for lost American Express traveler's checks and cards; you can call collect from anywhere in Mexico.

You can change travelers checks and currency denominated in major non-US currencies (especially Canadian dollars) fairly easily in Mexico City.

Banks & Casas de Cambio You can change money in banks or at *casas de cambio* (exchange houses; often single-window kiosks). Mexico City has many of each, with the greatest concentrations on Paseo de la Reforma between the Monumento a Cristóbal Colón and the Monumento a la Independencia. The Zona Rosa has numerous casas de cambio.

Banks – mostly open 9 am to 5 pm Monday to Friday – go through a more time-consuming procedure than casas de cambio. But casas de cambio may not accept traveler's checks, something that happens rarely in banks. If you have any trouble finding a place to change money, particularly on Saturday or Sunday, you can try a hotel – though the exchange rate won't be the best.

Exchange rates vary a little from one bank or casa de cambio to another. Different rates are also often posted for cash *(efectivo)* and traveler's checks *(documento)*.

The two blocks of Londres between Génova and Florencia in the Zona Rosa have many casas de cambio, and the airport terminal has several, some of them open 24 hours. The following useful casas de cambio offer good rates for cash and traveler's checks with exceptions noted:

Centro Histórico

Cambios Exchange – on Avenida Madero between Mata and Condesa, open 10 am to 7 pm daily

Casa de Cambio Plus – on Avenida Juárez facing the Alameda Central, open 9 am to 4 pm Monday to Friday

Zona Rosa

Casa de Cambio Bancomer – Avenida Florencia 6 at Reforma, open 9 am to 12.30 pm and 1 to 5 pm Monday to Friday, 10 am to 2 pm Saturday – reasonable rates for US dollar cash and traveler's checks

Casa de Cambio Tíber – a short distance north of the Zona Rosa at Río Tíber 112, open 8.30 am to 5 pm Monday to Friday, 8.30 am to 2 pm Saturday (Map 6)

Impulsora Cambiaria – Belgrado 1 at Reforma, open 8.30 am to 5 pm Monday to Friday, 8.30 am to 2 pm Saturday – reasonable rates

Money Exchange – at Paseo de la Reforma and Lancaster, on the southwest side of the Monumento a la Independencia traffic circle, open 9 am to 4 pm Monday to Friday – good rates for cash and American Express traveler's checks, or Liverpool 162, open 9 am to 8 pm Monday to Saturday – reasonable rates for cash, poor rates for traveler's checks

International Transfers

If you need money wired to you, an easy and quick method is the Western Union 'Dinero en Minutos' (Money in Minutes) service. This is offered by several shops and offices in Mexico City, all identified by black-and-yellow signs bearing the words 'Western Union' and 'Dinero en Minutos.' Among them are the following:

Central de Telégrafos
Tacuba 8, Centro Histórico, open 9 am to 10 pm Monday to Friday, 9 am to 8.30 pm Saturday, 9 am to 4.30 pm Sunday (Ⓜ Allende)

Telecomm
Insurgentes 114, 1½ blocks north of Reforma, open 8 am to 8 pm Monday to Friday, 9 am to noon Saturday (nearest Ⓜ Revolución; Map 5)

Elektra electrical-goods stores
Pino Suárez at El Salvador, three blocks south of the Zócalo, Centro Histórico, open 9 am to 9 pm daily (Ⓜ Pino Suárez)
Balderas 62, two blocks south of the Alameda Central, same hours (Ⓜ Juárez)
East side of Insurgentes Sur, same hours (two blocks south of Ⓜ Insurgentes; Map 7)

The person sending you the money pays it at their Western Union branch, along with a fee and details of who is to receive it and where. When you go to pick it up, take photo identification. Western Union has offices worldwide: information is available on ☎ 5-721-30-80 or ☎ 5-546-73-61 in Mexico City, ☎ 800-325-6000 in the USA, or on the Internet at www.westernunion.com.

Security

Ideally, when you're out and about, carry only the money you'll need that day. Leave the rest in the safe *(caja fuerte)* in your room or at your hotel reception. If there isn't a safe you have to decide whether it's better to carry your funds with you or try to secret them in your room. Baggage that you can lock up is an advantage for this. It's also a good idea to divide your funds into several stashes in different places. See Dangers & Annoyances, later in this chapter, for more tips on safeguarding money.

Costs

A single budget traveler, staying in budget accommodations and eating two meals a day in restaurants, can expect to pay between US$12 to US$25 a day for those basics. Add

in other costs (such as snacks, soft drinks, entry to museums), and you'll spend more like US$20 to US$35. If there are two or more of you sharing a room, costs per person come down considerably. Double rooms are often only a dollar or two more than singles, and triples or quadruples are available in many hotels for only slightly more than doubles.

In the middle range you can live well in Mexico City for US$30 to US$50 per person per day. Two people can easily find a clean, modern room with private bath and TV for US$20 to US$35, and have the rest for food, admission fees, transportation and incidentals.

At the top of the scale, a few hotels charge more than US$300 for a room, and there are restaurants where you can pay US$50 or more per person. But you can also stay at very comfortable hotels for under US$100 a double, and eat very well for US$20 to US$50 per person per day.

These estimated figures do not include extra expenses like travel outside Mexico City, car rental, or any shopping you do.

Tipping & Bargaining

In general, workers in small, cheap restaurants don't expect much in the way of tips, while those in expensive establishments expect you to be lavish in your largesse. Tipping in top-end places is up to American levels of 15%; elsewhere, 10% is usually sufficient. If you stay a few days in one hotel, you should leave up to 10% of your room

costs for the people who have kept your room clean (assuming they *have*). A porter in a mid-range hotel would be happy with US$1 for carrying two bags. Taxi drivers don't generally expect tips unless they provide some special service.

Goods in shops have fixed prices. In markets, some items do as well, but for others bargaining is expected, and you may pay much more than the going price if you accept the first price quoted.

Taxes

Mexico's *Impuesto de Valor Agregado* (Value-Added Tax), abbreviated IVA ('EE-bah'), is levied at 15%. By law the tax must be included in virtually any price quoted to you; it should not be added afterwards. Signs in shops and notices on restaurant menus often state *'IVA incluido.'* Occasionally they state instead that IVA must be added to the quoted prices, which is fine as long as it is noted up front.

The *Impuesto Sobre Hospedaje* (ISH, 'ee-ESS-e-AH-che,' Lodging Tax) is levied on the price of hotel rooms. Each Mexican state sets its own level of ISH: in Mexico City it's 2%.

Most budget and mid-range accommodations include both IVA and ISH in quoted prices (though it's sometimes worth checking). But in top-end hotels a price may often be given as, say, 'US$100 *más impuestos*' ('plus taxes'), in which case you must add 17% to the figure. If in doubt, you can ask *'¿Están incluidos los impuestos?'* ('Are taxes included?').

Prices in this book all, to the best of our knowledge, include IVA and ISH.

See the Getting There & Away chapter for details of taxes on air travel, and Travel Permits in the Documents section, earlier in this chapter, for details of the Nonimmigrant Fee of 150 pesos required of by all foreign visitors.

POST & COMMUNICATIONS
Postal Rates

An airmail letter or postcard weighing up to 20g costs US$0.45 to the US or Canada, US$0.55 to Europe and US$0.60 to Aus-

tralasia. Items weighing between 20g and 50g cost US$0.75, US$0.85 and US$1 respectively.

Sending Mail

The Correo Mayor (Central Post Office) of Mexico City is on Eje Central Lázaro Cárdenas at Tacuba, across the road from the Palacio de Bellas Artes (Ⓜ Bellas Artes; Map 4). The stamp windows in the Correo Mayor, marked '*Estampillas*,' are open 9 am to 9 pm Monday to Friday, 9 am to 7 pm Saturday, and 9 am to noon Sunday. For information, go to window No 16 or 49. For philatelic sales, go to window No 45. Upstairs is a postal museum, open 9 am to 6 pm Monday to Friday, 10 am to 2 pm Saturday and Sunday.

Other post offices in the city are typically open 8 am to 7 pm Monday to Friday and 9 am to 1 pm Saturday. A partial list follows:

Zócalo – inside at Plaza de la Constitución 7 (opposite the west side of the Zócalo; Ⓜ Zócalo)

Near Plaza de la República – corner of Mariscal and Arriaga (Ⓜ Revolución)

Plaza Colón – Reforma at Ramírez, open 9 am to 7 pm Monday to Friday, 9 am to 5 pm Saturday (Ⓜ Revolución)

Zona Rosa – corner of Varsovia and Londres, open 8 am to 7 pm Monday to Friday, 9 am to 1 pm Saturday (Ⓜ Insurgentes or Sevilla)

Delivery times for mail from Mexico are elastic. Packages sometimes go missing. If you are sending something by airmail, be sure to clearly mark it 'Vía Aérea.' Registered *(certificado* or *registrado)* service helps ensure delivery and costs just US$0.80 extra for international mail. An airmail letter from Mexico to the US or Canada may take from four to 14 days. Mail to Europe may take between one and three weeks, while to Australasia it might be a month or more. The Mexpost express mail service, available at window No 44 at the Correo Mayor, supposedly takes three working days to anywhere in the world: charges for up to 500g are US$12 to the US or Canada or US$15.50 to Europe.

If sending a package internationally from Mexico, you have to be prepared to open it for customs inspection at the post office – take packing materials with you, or don't seal it until you get there.

Courier Services Expensive international courier services, such as United Parcel Service (UPS), FedEx and DHL are other alternatives for speedy delivery. Packages weighing up to 500g cost about US$20 to the US or Canada or US$25 to Europe. They will usually pick up from wherever you are staying at no extra cost. Offices include the following:

DHL (☎ 5-345-70-00), Avenida Madero 70, Centro Histórico, open 9 am to 6 pm Monday to Friday; Reforma 76 at Versalles, Colonia Juárez, open 9 am to 11 pm Monday to Friday, 9 am to 4 pm Saturday; Niza 5, Zona Rosa, open 9 am to 6.30 pm Monday to Friday.

FedEx (☎ 5-228-99-04), Reforma 308, open 9 am to 7 pm Monday to Friday, 9 am to 1.30 pm Saturday (Map 6); also in the Centro Comercial Plaza Inn, Insurgentes Sur 1971, San Ángel, and in Plaza Polanco, Balmes 11, Colonia Los Morales (Map 8).

UPS (☎ 5-228-79-00), Reforma 404 (Map 6).

Receiving Mail

If you're on a short trip to Mexico City and nowhere else, it's not worth having any mail sent to you there. Delivery times for inbound mail are similar to those for outbound mail (see Sending Mail, earlier in this section).

You can receive letters and packages at the Correo Mayor if they're addressed as follows:

Albert JONES (last name in capitals)
Lista de Correos
Oficina Central de Correos
México 06002 DF
MEXICO

When such mail reaches the post office, the name of the addressee is placed on an alphabetical list. To claim your mail, take your passport or other identification to window No 3 in the Correo Mayor, which is open 8 am to 8 pm Monday to Friday, 9 am to 5 pm Saturday, 9 am to 1 pm Sunday. There's no charge. If you can, check the list yourself

because your mail may be listed under your first name instead of your last. Lista de Correos mail may be returned to sender if it has not been collected within 10 days of arrival. If you think you're going to pick mail up more than 10 days after it has arrived, have senders put 'Poste Restante' instead of 'Lista de Correos' in the address. Poste Restante, also at window No 3, may hold mail for up to a month, but no list of what has been received is posted. Again, there's no charge for collection.

American Express If you carry an American Express card or American Express traveler's checks, you can use their office (see Traveler's Checks & Cash in the Money section, earlier in this chapter) as your mailing address in Mexico City. Have mail addressed like this:

Lucy CHANG (last name in capitals)
Client Mail
American Express
Paseo de la Reforma 234
México 06600 DF
MEXICO

The office holds mail for about one month before returning it to sender.

Telephone

Local calls are cheap. International calls can be expensive, but needn't be if you call from the right place at the right time.

You can place a call from three main types of place. Cheapest is normally a public pay phone. A bit more expensive is a *caseta de teléfono* or *caseta telefónica* – a call station, maybe in a shop or restaurant, where an on-the-spot operator connects the call for you and you take it in a booth. The third option is to call from your hotel, but hotels can – and do – charge what they like for this service. It's nearly always cheaper to go elsewhere.

Public Pay Phones There are thousands of pay phones on the streets of Mexico City and at the airport and bus terminals. Most work OK. Pay phones are operated by a number of different companies: the most

Mexico's Area Code & Phone Number Changes

The country code for Mexico is still 52. All of Mexico's area codes were being modified in 1999-2000, however, altering local phone numbers in the process. In the case of Mexico City, the single-digit area code has simply been added to the beginning of all local numbers. In most cases, however, two- or three-digit area codes are being reduced to the first digit with the excess digits shifted to the front of all local numbers. For example, the area code for the town of Tlaxcala used to be 246, and all Tlaxcala phone numbers had five digits. Now the Tlaxcala area code is 2 and all phone numbers have seven digits, starting with 46.

Until 1999, Mexico City had the area code 5 and all Mexico City numbers had seven digits. Now Mexico City has no area code and all its phone numbers have eight digits, starting with 5. You now use the same eight-digit number whether you are calling locally from within the city or calling long-distance. The difference is that when calling long-distance you need to use the appropriate prefixes (see the Prefixes, Codes & Costs table in the text).

The only other cities in Mexico without area codes will be Guadalajara and Monterrey, both of which were due to switch from their previous one-digit area codes (3 for Guadalajara, 8 for Monterrey) in late 2000. All other places will end up with one-digit area codes and seven-digit phone numbers.

In practice the changes make no difference to what you dial on a long-distance call, but they do make a difference to what you dial on local calls.

These changes were being made gradually by groups of towns and cities through 1999 and 2000.

---

common, and most reliable on costs, are those marked with the name of the country's biggest phone company, Telmex.

Telmex pay phones work on *tarjetas telefónicas* or *tarjetas Ladatel* (phone cards), which come in denominations of 30, 50 or 100 pesos (about US$3, US$5 and US$10). These cards are sold at many kiosks and shops around the city – look for the blue-and-yellow sign reading *'De Venta Aquí Ladatel.'* 'Ladatel' means *teléfono de larga distancia* (long distance telephone), but these phones work for both local and long-distance calls.

Casetas de Teléfono These can be more expensive than Telmex pay phones, but not always, and you don't need a phone card to use them and they eliminate street noise. Many have off-peak discounts, for instance 50% off domestic long-distance calls and 33% off international calls at night and for much of the weekend.

Casetas usually have a telephone symbol outside, or signs saying 'teléfono,' 'Lada' or 'Larga Distancia.'

Prefixes, Codes & Costs When dialing a call yourself in Mexico, you need to know what *prefijo* (prefix) and *claves* (country or area codes) to put before the number. Mexican area codes and phone numbers were all being changed in 1999-2000 (see 'Mexico's Area Code and Phone Number Changes').

The following table approximates the cost per minute of a telephone call from a Telmex pay phone, using AC for area code, and CC for country code. Note that, in some cases, there may not be an area code:

call	prefix & codes	approximate cost in US dollars
Local	None	0.05
Nat'l	01+AC	0.40
Int'l	00+CC+AC	1.25 (USA/Canada) 2.50 (Europe/Australasia)

So if you're in Mexico City and you want to call the Mexico City number 5-876-54-32, just dial 5-876-54-32. To call from Mexico City to the Oaxaca number 517-65-43, dial 01, then the Oaxaca area code 9, then 517-

65-43. To call from Oaxaca to the Mexico City number 5-876-54-32, you just dial 01 then 5-876-54-32, as Mexico City has no area code.

To call the New York City number 212-987-6543 from Mexico, dial 00, then the US country code 1, then the area code 212, then 987-6543. Other country codes include: Canada, 1; UK, 44; Australia, 61; New Zealand, 64; France, 33; Germany, 49; Italy, 39; Spain, 34; Guatemala, 502; Belize, 501; and Argentina, 54.

To dial the Mexico City number 5-876-54-32 from another country, dial the international access code, then the Mexico country code (52), then 5-876-54-32.

If you need to speak to a domestic operator in Mexico, call ☎ 020; for an international operator, call ☎ 090. For Mexican directory information, call ☎ 040.

Mexican toll-free numbers – ☎ 800 followed by seven digits – always require the 01 prefix. You can call these numbers from Telmex pay phones without inserting a telephone card.

Most United States and Canadian toll-free numbers are ☎ 800 or 888 followed by seven digits. The majority can be called from either of the two countries. Some can also be reached from Mexico (dial 001 before 800) but you will probably have to pay for the call.

North American Calling Cards If you have an AT&T, MCI or Sprint calling card, or a Canadian calling card, you can use it for calls from Mexico to the USA or Canada by dialing the access numbers listed below. Before traveling to Mexico you can check with your phone company about costs and exactly what procedures you will have to follow. Normally, after dialing the access number you have to either enter your calling card number or follow a series of voice prompts or operator instructions to complete the call:

AT&T	☎ 001-800-462-4240
MCI	☎ 001-800-674-7000
Sprint	☎ 001-800-877-8000
AT&T Canada	☎ 001-800-123-0201
Bell Canada	☎ 001-800-010-1990

If you get an operator who asks for your Visa or MasterCard number instead of your calling card number, or says the service is unavailable, hang up right away. There are various scams out there in which calls are rerouted to super-expensive credit-card phone services.

International Calling Cards There's a wide range of international calling cards. Lonely Planet's eKno Communication Card provides budget international calls, a range of messaging services, free email and travel information. You can join online at www.ekno.lonelyplanet.com or by phone from Mexico by dialing the eKno access number (☎ 001-800-514-0287).

Collect Calls A *llamada por cobrar* (collect call) can cost the receiving party much more than it would if *they* call *you*. This means you may prefer to find a phone where you can receive an incoming call, then pay for a quick call to the other party to ask them to call you back.

If you do need to make a collect call, you can do so from pay phones without a card. Call an operator on ☎ 020 for domestic calls, or ☎ 090 for international calls, or use a Home Country Direct service (see below). Mexican international operators can usually speak English.

Some telephone casetas and hotels will make collect calls for you, but they usually charge for the service.

Home Country Direct This service allows you to make an international collect call via an operator in the country you're calling and is available for several countries. You can get information on Home Direct services from your phone company before you leave for Mexico, and you can make the calls from pay phones without a card.

For Home Direct calls to the USA through AT&T, MCI or Sprint, and to Canada via AT&T Canada or Bell Canada, dial the numbers given above under North American Calling Cards. Mexican international operators may be able to tell you access numbers for other countries. The

Mexican term for Home Country Direct is *País Directo*.

Fax

You can send faxes from the Central de Telégrafos, Tacuba 8, from 9 am to 10 pm Monday to Friday, 9 am to 8.30 pm Saturday, 9 am to 4.30 pm Sunday (Ⓜ Bellas Artes). One page to the USA or Canada costs about US$2. Many telephone casetas, shops and businesses also offer public fax service, including at the airport and long-distance bus stations – look for *'fax'* or *'fax público'* signs.

Email & Internet Access

For those traveling with their own computers, CompuServe (www.compuserve.com) has nodes (local access numbers) in Mexico City (currently ☎ 5-262-00-00, 5-262-45-00 for V90/ISDN) and in seven other Mexican cities, and one toll-free node (☎ 800-720-00-00) that you can access from anywhere in the country. America Online (www.aol.com) has 10 AOL Globalnet nodes around Mexico. The Mexico City node is currently at ☎ 5-628-93-93.

Some hotel rooms in Mexico have direct-dial phones and phone sockets that allow you to unplug the phone and insert a phone jack that runs directly to your computer. Some top-end hotels geared to business travelers have extra sockets specifically for this purpose. At least 14 top-end hotels in Mexico City also have business centers with modern communications facilities.

In less advanced hotels you may be confronted with switchboard phone systems and/or room phones with a cord running directly into the wall, both of which make it impossible to go online from your room. In such cases you can ask to borrow reception's fax line for a couple of minutes.

When traveling with a computer, remember that the voltage abroad may vary from that at home, risking damage to your equipment. The best investment is a universal AC adapter for your appliance. Your PC-card modem may or may not work outside your home country – the safest option is to buy a reputable 'global' modem before you leave home, or buy a local PC-card modem if you're spending an extended time in any one country. Telephone sockets can differ from country to country, so ensure that you have at least a US RJ-11 telephone adapter that works with your modem. You can almost always find an adapter that will convert from RJ-11 to the local variety. For more information on traveling with a portable computer, see www.teleadapt.com.

If you aren't carrying a computer you can still access the Internet and use web-based email services such as Yahoo! Mail (www.yahoo.com) or Hotmail (www.hotmail .com) at numerous cybercafés or other public Internet services in Mexico City. Prices in the following listings are for an hour online; most places have lower rates for less time.

Centro Histórico

Centro de Estudios Superiores Lafoel (☎ 5-512-35-84), Donceles 80, open 10 am to 8 pm Monday to Friday (US$4)

NETFM (☎ 5-510-96-73), Plaza de la Computación y Electrónica, Eje Central Lázaro Cárdenas 54, open 10 am to 8 pm Monday to Saturday, noon to 5 pm Sunday (US$3.50)

Ultra Byte, on Uruguay east of Restaurante Danubio (US$3.25)

Plaza de la República Area

Sala Internet, Bucareli 8 in *El Universal* newspaper office (take photo ID to enter building), open 10 am to 3 pm and 4 to 7 pm Monday to Friday (free; maximum 1½ hours)

Zona Rosa

Café Internet, Hamburgo east of Florencia, open 10 am to 10 pm Monday to Saturday (US$3); food and drinks service

Java Chat, Génova 44K, open 9 am to 11 pm Monday to Friday, 10 am to 11 pm Saturday and Sunday (US$3.75); free coffee and soft drinks

Other Areas

Coffee Net (☎ 5-286-71-04), Nuevo León 104B, Condesa, open 10 am to 10 pm Monday to Saturday (US$3); pleasant environment, drinks available

Escape Cibercafé (☎ 5-550-76-84), Avenida La Paz 23, San Ángel

Internet Station, Arquímedes 130, Polanco

Some websites with listings of Mexican cybercafés include www.netcafeguide.com, www.planeta.com and www.amcc.org.mx.

INTERNET RESOURCES
The World Wide Web is a rich resource for travelers. You can research your trip, hunt down bargain airfares, book hotels, check on weather conditions or chat with locals and other travelers about the best places to visit (or avoid!). In addition to the listings below, websites dealing with specific Mexico City places or topics are recommended throughout the book.

Lonely Planet
There are few better places to start your web explorations than the Lonely Planet website (www.lonelyplanet.com). Here you'll find succinct summaries on traveling to most places on earth, postcards from other travelers, and the Thorn Tree bulletin board where you can ask questions before you go or dispense advice when you get back. You can also find travel news, updates to many of our most popular guidebooks, and the sub-WWWay section, which links you to the most useful travel resources elsewhere on the Internet.

Mexico City Sites
One of the better broad visitor's introductions on the Internet is Mexico City Virtual Guide (www.mexicocity.com.mx/mexcity .html), with material on sights, hotels and restaurants (mainly top end), a good reading list and some interesting links. The Spanish-language version has more information than the English one.

The Distrito Federal tourism department's site (www.mexicocity.gob.mx) has exhaustive listings of museums and galleries and what's on in them, as well as contact details for countless hotels, restaurants, travel agencies and transportation companies – but for the moment it's all in Spanish.

Tiempo Libre magazine's site (www.tiempolibre.com.mx) has heaps of useful information, and not just about the current week's entertainment in Mexico City, covered by the magazine itself. It includes links to the websites of many of the city's museums and has archives with the best collection of Mexico City restaurant reviews you'll likely find – all in Spanish, of course.

Readers of Spanish who would like to know what the DF government is up to can have a look at its interesting official site, www.df.gob.mx.

Other Mexico Sites
Mexico Online (www.mexonline.com) and Mexico Connect (http://mexconnect.com) both combine news and message/discussion centers with a wide variety of other content and links: Mexico Online is good for, among other things, travel, politics, Mexican soccer and baseball, culture and organizations (government and otherwise); turn to Mexico Connect for matters of food, practical information for living in Mexico, art and history.

The Mexico section of Eco Travels in Latin America (www.planeta.com) is a marvelous resource for anyone interested in travel or the environment in Mexico. You'll find articles, lists and links covering birds, butterflies, books, language schools, cybercafés, protected areas, environmental organizations and lots more on this constantly growing site, hosted by a dedicated Mexico City-based American, Ron Mader.

Mexico (http://mexico-travel.com), the official site of SECTUR, Mexico's Ministry of Tourism, contains a lot of interesting stuff, but updating has been meager since the site was launched in 1996.

Mexico Channel (www.trace-sc.com) is a truly impressive collection of Mexico links in fields as diverse as politics, sports, music, airlines and Chiapas.

BOOKS
Mexico City has many bookstores, and several of them stock a fair range of English-language titles – see the Shopping chapter for recommendations. But of the books mentioned below, only the Mexican-published ones are more or less sure to be available. If there's any particular book you must have, it's wise to try to obtain it before coming. For information on Mexican literature, see the Arts section in the Facts about

Mexico City chapter; for useful business publications, see the Doing Business section, later in this chapter.

Many books are published in several editions by different publishers in different countries. As a result, a book might be a hardcover rarity in one country while it's readily available in paperback in another. Fortunately, bookstores and libraries can search by title or author, so your local bookstore or library is the best place to find out about the availability of the following recommendations.

Lonely Planet

A handy companion for anyone visiting Mexico City is Lonely Planet's *Latin American Spanish Phrasebook*, which contains practical, up-to-date words and expressions in Latin American Spanish. For those traveling more widely in Mexico, Lonely Planet's *Mexico* has over 1000 pages of practical advice and lively background covering the whole country from Tijuana to the Guatemalan border.

Lonely Planet's *World Food Mexico* is an intimate, full-color guide to exploring Mexico and its cuisine. This book covers every food or drink situation the traveler could encounter and plots the evolution of Mexican cuisine. Its language section includes a definitive culinary dictionary and useful phrases to help you on your eating adventure.

Guidebooks

Several useful series of straightforward guides to single archaeological sites and museums are fairly widely available in Mexico City. The INAH-SALVAT *Official Guide* booklets cost US$4 to US$5. Also useful, and a little cheaper, is the *Easy Guide* series by Richard Bloomgarden. Those with an interest in pre-Hispanic sites might also dig out C Bruce Hunter's *A Guide to Ancient Mexican Ruins*, which has maps and details of all the main central Mexican sites.

An excellent book for those keen to experience Mexico's natural wonders is Ron Mader's *Mexico – Adventures in Nature*, with practical information on visiting some

60 sites of natural interest all around Mexico, from a very ecologically aware perspective. *Mexico's Volcanoes* by RJ Secor covers routes up the main peaks of Mexico's central volcanic belt.

Blue Guide Mexico by John Collis and David M Jones is a comprehensive, authoritative guide to the country's archaeology, architecture and art.

History & Society

La Capital – The Biography of Mexico City by Jonathan Kandell is a very lively account of the city's story, from the geological upheaval that created the Valle de México to the late 1980s. It focuses on the lives of the many weird and wonderful characters in the city's history as well as the issues, 'isms' and acronyms.

Michael C Meyer & William L Sherman's *The Course of Mexican History*, one of the best general accounts of Mexican history and society as a whole, has plenty about Mexico City to help you see the capital in a wider context. It concentrates chiefly on the period since the Spanish conquest.

Pre-Hispanic Civilizations Michael D Coe's *Mexico* and Nigel Davies' *The Ancient Kingdoms of Mexico* are two of the best books on the pre-Hispanic cultures of central Mexico. Both are scholarly but readable (and not overlong), and have diagrams, illustrations, plans and maps complementing the text. *The Daily Life of the Aztecs* by Jacques Soustelle (1962) is a classic on its subject. Also good are *The Aztecs* by Richard F Townsend (1992) and *The Aztecs – Rise and Fall of an Empire* by Serge Gruzinski (1987).

Spanish Conquest & Colonial Era William Henry Prescott's mammoth *History of the Conquest of Mexico* remains a classic, though published in 1843 by an author who never went to Mexico. Only with Hugh Thomas' *Conquest: Montezuma, Cortes & The Fall of Old Mexico* did the 20th century produce an equivalent tome. Thomas' book, the product of meticulous research, was published in Britain as *The Conquest of*

Mexico (1993). Charles Gibson's *The Aztecs Under Spanish Rule* (1964) is an authoritative book on the colonial period.

Modern Times *Urban Leviathan – Mexico City in the 20th Century* by Diane E Davis is a detailed treatment of the city's politics, economy and society since the Porfiriato.

Distant Neighbors by Alan Riding, first published in 1984, remains a good introduction to modern Mexico and its love-hate relationship with the United States. In Britain it's published as *Mexico, Inside the Volcano*. *The Mexicans* by Patrick Oster is a sort of microcosmic counterpart to *Distant Neighbors*, focusing on the lives of 20 individual Mexico City residents.

Environment

Defending the Land of the Jaguar by Lane Simonian (1995) is the absorbing story of Mexico's long, if weak, tradition of conservation, from pre-Hispanic forest laws in the Valle de México to the modern environmental movement.

Joel Simon's compelling and alarming *Endangered Mexico: An Environment on the Edge* (1997) tells of modern Mexico's environmental crises and its politics with the benefit of a lot of first-hand journalistic research. The Mexico City area provides a good deal of the subject matter for both books.

You'll also find plenty on the city's environment in the Kandell and Davis books mentioned earlier.

Art, Architecture & Crafts

The Art of Mesoamerica by Mary Ellen Miller, in the Thames & Hudson World of Art series, is a good survey of pre-Hispanic art and architecture. On colonial architecture, the most important work is George Kubler's 1948 *Mexican Architecture of the Sixteenth Century*.

Good books on Mexico's great 20th-century artists include Diego Rivera's autobiography *My Art, My Life*; Patrick Marnham's 1998 biography of Rivera, *Dreaming with His Eyes Open*; *Frida: A Biography of Frida Kahlo* by Hayden Herrera; *Frida Kahlo*, another biography, by Malka Drucker; and *The Mexican Muralists* by Alma M Reed.

Mexico City bookstores are full of beautifully illustrated coffee-table books in English on Mexican arts, archaeology and anthropology. One such book is *Mask Arts of Mexico*, by Ruth D Lechuga and Chloe Sayer, a finely illustrated work by two experts in the field. Sayer has also written two fascinating books tracing the evolution of crafts from pre-Hispanic times to the present, with dozens of beautiful photos. *Arts & Crafts of Mexico* is a wide-ranging overview, while *Mexican Textiles* (originally published in Britain as *Mexican Costume)* is a comprehensive treatment of its absorbing topic, with a wealth of detail about Mexican life.

Booklets Published in Mexico

Mexican publisher Minutiae Mexicana produces a range of interesting booklets including *A Guide to Mexican Witchcraft, The Aztecs Then and Now, A Guide to Mexican Ceramics* and even *A Guide to Tequila, Mezcal & Pulque*. They're widely available at about US$5 each.

A similar Mexican series with many titles in English is Panorama.

NEWSPAPERS & MAGAZINES

Mexico City's long-established English-language daily newspaper, *The News*, is sold at many downtown and Zona Rosa newsstands, as well as by several of the bookstores mentioned in the Shopping chapter. The paper covers the main items of Mexican and foreign news, has long stock exchange listings and a few interesting Mexico features, and will keep you in touch with US, Canadian and European sports. Extracts from its current day's print issue are on the Internet at www.novedades.com.mx/the-news.htm.

The essential Spanish-language directory for entertainment in Mexico City is the weekly magazine *Tiempo Libre* – see the Entertainment chapter.

Some US, Canadian and European newspapers and magazines are sold at hotel newsstands and at the bookstores mentioned in the Shopping chapter. La Casa de la Prensa, with branches in the Zona Rosa at Avenida Florencia 59 (Ⓜ Insurgentes) and Hamburgo 141, sells major British and American newspapers and magazines, plus a few French and German ones. The Florencia branch is open 8 am to 10 pm Monday to Friday, 8 am to 4 pm Saturday and Sunday; the Hamburgo branch is open 8 am to 10 pm Monday to Saturday, 8 am to 9 pm Sunday. La Torre del Papel, Mata 6A, Centro Histórico, sells US and British newspapers, at best same-day and previous-day respectively. La Bouquinerie in the Casa de Francia, Havre 15, Zona Rosa, sells one-day-old French newspapers.

Those who read Spanish have a huge choice of newspapers and magazines. *La Crónica* is a good Mexico City-focused daily and *La Jornada* is a national daily with a nonestablishment viewpoint; it covers a lot of stories other papers don't. Both have good websites: www.cronica.com.mx and http://unam.netgate.net/jornada.

RADIO & TV

Mexican TV is dominated by Televisa, the biggest TV company in the Spanish-speaking world, which runs four of the six main national channels – Nos 2 *('El Canal de las Estrellas')*, 4, 5 and 9. Its rival, TV Azteca, has two main channels – Azteca Siete (7) and Azteca Trece (13). Mexican airtime is devoted mainly to ads, low-budget *telenovelas* (soap operas), soccer, game/chat/variety shows, movies and comedy. Nudity, graphic violence and offensive language are pretty much kept off the screen.

Better than the commercial channels are Once TV (Eleven TV), run by Mexico City's Instituto Politécnico Nacional, with intelligent travel, documentary and interview programs and movies, and Canal 22, a culture channel from Conaculta, the National Culture & Arts Council.

You'll find at least a few cable and satellite channels in many mid-range and top-end hotel rooms. The main cable providers are Multivisión and Cablevision: at our last check, both rivals offered the Cartoon Network, MTV and ESPN; Cablevision also had CNN in English, Fox Sports, and the r son channel (No 17), devoted to Mexican, Caribbean and Latin music.

The News and several Mexican newspapers publish full TV schedules.

Mexico City has about 60 AM and FM radio stations, most commercial, including many owned by Televisa. In the evening you may be able to pick up US stations on the AM (medium wave) band.

If you have a shortwave radio you can try to pick up the BBC World Service on 15.22 MHz from 11 am to 2 pm GMT, 17.84 MHz from 2 to 5 pm GMT, or 6.175 MHz from 4.30 pm to 8 am GMT.

PHOTOGRAPHY & VIDEO
Film & Equipment

Camera and film processing shops, pharmacies and some hotels all sell film. Most types of film are readily available (with the exception of Kodachrome slide film). A 36-exposure 100-ASA print film generally costs US$5 to US$6. Film being sold at lower prices may be outdated. If the date on the box is obscured by a price sticker, look under the sticker. Avoid film from sun-exposed shop windows.

If your camera breaks down, you should be able to get it repaired inexpensively. Many shops around the corner of Brasil and Donceles in the Centro Histórico sell film and cameras and do processing and camera repairs

Nearly all video tapes on sale in Mexico (like the rest of the Americas) use the NTSC image registration system. This is incompatible with the PAL system common in most of Western Europe and Australia and the SECAM system used in France. NTSC videos won't give a picture on a machine that lacks NTSC capability.

Technical Tips

Mexico City is full of colorful scenes that make great photos. You'll get better results if you take pictures in the morning or afternoon rather than at midday, when the bright sun bleaches out colors and contrast. Smog and haze are less of a problem early in the morning and on weekends (especially Sundays). Wide-angle and zoom lenses are useful.

Photographing People
Be sensitive about photographing people; if in doubt, ask first. It's not a good idea to photograph soldiers.

Airport Security
To avoid any risk of damage by airport x-ray machines, carry your film in a lead-lined pouch or have it hand-inspected.

TIME
Mexico City – like all the rest of Mexico except a few western states – is on Hora del Centro (Central Time), which is the same as US Central Time. This is GMT minus six hours, and GMT minus five hours during daylight saving time *(horario de verano)*, which runs from the first Sunday in April to the last Sunday in October.

ELECTRICITY
Voltages & Cycles
Electrical current in Mexico is the same as in the USA and Canada: 110V, 60 cycles. Don't use European or Australian 220-240V appliances without a transformer (which will be built into an adjustable appliance).

Plugs & Sockets
Though most plugs and sockets are the same as in the US, Mexico actually has three different types of electrical socket: older ones with two equally sized flat slots, newer ones with two flat slots of different sizes, and a few with a round hole for a grounding (earth) pin. If the plug on your appliance doesn't fit your Mexican socket, the best thing to do is to get an adapter. Mexican electrical goods shops have a variety of adapters and extensions that should solve the problem.

WEIGHTS & MEASURES
Mexico uses the metric system. For conversion between metric and US or Imperial measures, see the inside back cover of this book.

LAUNDRY
The following three laundries all charge US$2.50 to US$3 for you to wash and dry 3kg, or US$4 to US$5 for a 3kg service wash:

Lavandería Automática Édison, Édison 91 between Iglesias and Arriaga near Plaza de la República, open 10 am to 7 pm Monday to Friday, 10 am to 6 pm Saturday (Ⓜ Revolución)

Lavandería Las Artes, Antonio Caso 82 near the Jardín del Arte, Colonia San Rafael, open 9 am to 7.30 pm Monday to Friday, 9 am to 8 pm Saturday

Lavandería Automática, Río Danubio 119B, not far north of the Zona Rosa, open 8.15 am to 6 pm Monday to Friday, 8.15 am to 5 pm Saturday (Map 6)

The following are two reliable dry cleaners where you'll pay around US$2 for a pair of trousers, or US$4 for a two-piece suit:

Dryclean USA, Paseo de la Reforma 32, open 8 am to 7 pm Monday to Friday, 10 am to 2 pm Saturday (Map 5)

Jiffy ('HEE-fee') on the corner of Río Tíber and Río Lerma, two blocks north of the Monumento a la Independencia (Map 6)

TOILETS
Public toilets are virtually nonexistent, but museums, restaurants and cafés nearly always have toilets. They may not have toilet paper, however – it's worth carrying a little of your own. If there's a bin beside the toilet, put paper and feminine articles in it to avoid overloading Mexico City's drains.

LEFT LUGGAGE
The airport and the four long-distance bus terminals all have luggage lockers or checkrooms (see the Getting There & Away chapter). Some places to stay can hold luggage for you, sometimes for a small fee.

HEALTH
Predeparture Planning
Insurance Mexican medical treatment is generally inexpensive for common diseases and minor treatment, but if you suffer some serious disease or injury you may want to visit a private hospital or fly out of the

country for treatment. Travel insurance can cover the costs of this (see Travel Insurance in the Documents section, earlier in this chapter).

Medical Kit It's always a good idea to travel with a small first aid kit. Items it might contain include: antihistamine (eg, Benadryl), useful as a decongestant for colds and allergies, or to ease the itch from insect bites; Lomotil or Imodium to control diarrhea; prochlorperazine (eg, Stemetil) or metaclopramide (eg, Maxalon) for nausea and vomiting; rehydration mixture for severe diarrhea (particularly important for children); antiseptic such as povidone-iodine (eg, Betadine) for cuts and scrapes; scissors, tweezers and a thermometer (but note that mercury thermometers are prohibited by airlines); bandages and Band-Aids; and a couple of syringes, in case you need injections and are dubious about medical hygiene (ask your doctor for a note explaining why they have been prescribed).

Don't forget an adequate supply of any medication you're already taking: the prescription may be difficult to match in Mexico.

Altitude & Pollution Mexico City's air pollution, at its worst from November to February, may aggravate allergies, asthma, hypertension, or heart, lung or breathing problems. If you have any such problems to a significant extent, you should consult your doctor before visiting Mexico City.

The altitude, dryness and pollution can cause a sore throat, runny nose or eyes, lightheadedness, insomnia, slight headaches, or shortness of breath in anyone, especially at first.

Medical Information Services For advice on immunizations or other matters, talk to your doctor or an appropriate information service. In the USA, you can call the Centers for Disease Control & Prevention's (CDC's) international travelers' hot line at ☎ 877-394-8747. In Canada information is available from Health Canada (☎ 613-957-8739). In the UK, you can obtain a free printed health brief for any country by calling MASTA (Medical Advisory Services for Travellers Abroad) on ☎ 0906-8-224100. In Australia, call the Australian Government Health Service, or consult a clinic such as the Travellers Medical & Vaccination Centre (TMVC, ☎ 1300-658844), which has 19 clinics in Australia and New Zealand.

There are a number of excellent travel health sites on the Internet. The Lonely Planet website has links to the CDC, MASTA and TMVC (which offers online personal travel health reports).

Immunizations Discuss your requirements with your doctor: a lot depends on where you are going and what you'll be doing. Plan ahead for vaccinations: some of them require more than one injection, while some should not be given together. It's recommended that you seek medical advice at least six weeks before travel.

It's always a good idea to be up to date on tetanus, typhoid, diphtheria and measles. In addition, you may want to have a vaccination against hepatitis A or B. The CDC recommends hepatitis B vaccine for all infants and for children age 11 or 12 who did not receive it as an infant.

Mexico requires travelers arriving from areas infected with yellow fever (which are all in Africa or tropical South America) to have had yellow fever vaccination and to carry a yellow fever certificate. Discuss this with a doctor if necessary.

Basic Rules

Mexico City's booming population and sinking infrastructure are a couple of the factors that have combined to create serious sanitation problems. Studies have been done, but for the time being these rules are followed by many locals and travelers should heed their example.

Food Vegetables and fruit should be washed with purified water or peeled where possible. Beware of ice cream that might have melted and refrozen: if there's any doubt, steer well clear. Shellfish such as mussels, oysters and clams should be avoided, as should undercooked meat, particularly in the form of mince. Steaming does not make shellfish safe for eating.

If a place looks clean and well run and the vendor looks clean and healthy, then the food is probably safe. The food in busy restaurants is cooked and eaten quite quickly with little standing around, and it is probably not reheated.

Water The number-one rule is *be careful of the water*, especially of ice. Reputable brands of bottled water or soft drinks are generally fine, but only use water from containers with a serrated seal – not tops or corks.

Many Mexican hotels have large bottles of purified water from which you can fill your water bottle or canteen. Inexpensive purified water *(agua purificada)* is available from supermarkets, grocery shops and liquor stores.

Heat Mexico City does not get nearly as hot as some of Mexico's low-lying coastal areas, but it may still be hotter than where you have come from. You can avoid heat problems by drinking plenty of fluids and generally not overdoing things. Take time to acclimatize, avoiding excessive alcohol and strenuous activity when you first arrive.

Medical Problems & Treatment

Mexico City – at least the parts where most visitors go – is not an especially unhealthy place. Diseases spread by contaminated food or water are perhaps the biggest risk, but even traveler's diarrhea is less likely here than in remoter parts of Mexico. You can minimize the danger by following the basic rules about food and water, above.

If you do come down with a serious illness, be careful to find a competent doctor, and don't be afraid to get second opinions. You may want to telephone your doctor at home as well. Self-diagnosis and treatment can be risky, so you should always seek medical help. Correct diagnosis is vital.

Medical Services For recommendation of a doctor, dentist or hospital, you can call your embassy or SECTUR's 24-hour telephone help-line (☎ 5-250-01-23). Most major hotels have a doctor available. A private doctor's consultation will generally cost between US$25 and US$40, and doctors usually require immediate cash payment. Most hospitals also have to be paid at the time of service, but they are generally inexpensive for common ailments such as diarrhea, minor injury or surgery like stitches. Some facilities may accept credit cards.

In some serious cases it may be best to fly home for treatment. Adequate travel insurance will certainly prove its worth if you have to do this.

One of the best hospitals in all Mexico is the Hospital ABC (American British Cowdray Hospital, ☎ 5-230-80-00) at Calle Sur 136 No 116, just south of Avenida Observatorio in Colonia Las Américas, south of the Bosque de Chapultepec. The hospital has an outpatient section and many of the staff speak English. But fees can be steep so adequate medical insurance is a big help – the hospital will give receipts. (Nearest Ⓜ Observatorio, about 1km southeast; Map 1.)

The Hospital Español (Spanish Hospital, ☎ 5-203-38-90), Avenida Ejército Nacional 613, Polanco, also has a good reputation.

The Centro Médico, which is on Avenida Cuauhtémoc, about 3km south of the Alameda Central, is a very large public medical center with a general hospital and various specialist units. Costs here are likely to be low. Its Hospital General section is at Avenida Cuauhtémoc and Dr Márquez (Ⓜ Hospital General; Map 7).

For an ambulance, you can call the Cruz Roja (Red Cross, ☎ 5-557-57-57), or the general emergency numbers – ☎ 060 and ☎ 080 – for ambulance, fire and police.

You can buy many medicines at pharmacies. The 100-plus branches of the Sanborns chain store have pharmacies, which are among the best in the city.

Infectious Diseases

Diarrhea Simple things such as a change of water, food or climate can cause a mild bout of diarrhea – known informally among travelers in Mexico as Montezuma's Revenge or *turista* – but a few rushed toilet trips with no other symptoms are not indicative of a major problem.

Dehydration is the main danger with any diarrhea, particularly in children and the elderly. Under all circumstances, *fluid replacement* (at least equal to the volume lost) is the most important thing to remember. Weak black tea with a little sugar, soda water, or soft drinks allowed to go flat and diluted 50% with clean water are all good. With severe diarrhea, a rehydrating solution is preferable to replace minerals and salts lost. Commercially available oral rehydration salts (ORS) are very useful; add them to boiled or bottled water. In an emergency, you can make a solution of six teaspoons of sugar and a half teaspoon of salt to a liter of boiled or bottled water. You need to drink at least the same volume of fluid that you are losing in bowel movements and vomiting. Urine is the best guide to the adequacy of replacement – if you have small amounts of concentrated urine, you need to drink more. Keep drinking small amounts often. Stick to a bland diet as you recover.

Lomotil or Imodium bring relief from the symptoms but do not cure the problem. Only use these drugs if you do not have access to toilets – if you *must* travel. Lomotil and Imodium are not recommended for children under 12. Do not use these drugs in cases of a high fever or severe dehydration.

In certain situations, antibiotics may be required: diarrhea with blood or mucus (dysentery), any fever, watery diarrhea with fever and lethargy, persistent diarrhea that doesn't improve after 48 hours, and severe diarrhea. In these situations, gut-paralyzing drugs such as Imodium or Lomotil should be avoided.

Seek urgent medical help if you suspect dysentery, as a stool test is necessary to diagnose what kind you have. Where this is not possible, the recommended drugs for bacterial diarrhea (the most likely cause of severe diarrhea in travelers) are norfloxacin (400mg twice daily for three days) or ciprofloxacin (500mg twice daily for five days). These are not recommended for children or pregnant women. The drug of choice for children would be co-trimoxazole (Bactrim, Septrin or Resprim), with dosage dependent on weight. A five-day course is given. Ampicillin or amoxycillin may be given in pregnancy, but medical care is necessary.

Amoebic Dysentery This is characterized by a gradual onset of low-grade diarrhea, often with blood and mucus. Cramping abdominal pain and vomiting are less likely than in other types of diarrhea, and fever may not be present. It will persist until treated and can recur and cause other health problems.

Giardiasis The parasite causing this intestinal disorder, another type of diarrhea, is present in contaminated water. Symptoms are stomach cramps, nausea, a bloated stomach, watery, foul-smelling diarrhea and frequent gas. Giardiasis can appear several weeks after you have been exposed to the parasite. Symptoms may disappear for a few days and then return; this can go on for several weeks. Tinidazole, known as Fasigyn, or metronidazole (Flagyl) are the recommended drugs.

Cholera This is the worst of the watery diarrheas, and medical help should be sought. Though Mexico suffers occasional cholera epidemics, the risk of getting cholera in Mexico City is minimal if you follow the basic rules for food and water mentioned earlier. Outbreaks of cholera are generally widely reported, so avoid such problem areas. *Fluid replacement is the most vital treatment* – the risk of dehydration is severe, as you may lose up to 20L a day. If there is an unavoidable delay in getting to a hospital, then begin taking tetracycline.

Typhoid Typhoid fever is a dangerous gut infection caused by contaminated water and food. Medical help must be sought. It's much less of a risk in Mexico City than in rural areas of Mexico.

Early symptoms are headache, body aches and a fever that rises a little each day until it is around 40°C (104°F) or more. The victim's pulse is often slow relative to the degree of fever present – unlike a normal fever, in which the pulse increases. There may also be vomiting, abdominal pain, diarrhea or constipation.

In the second week, the high fever and slow pulse continue and a few pink spots may appear on the body; trembling, delirium, weakness, weight loss and dehydration may occur. Complications such as pneumonia, perforated bowel or meningitis may occur.

Hepatitis Hepatitis is a general term for inflammation of the liver. It is common worldwide. Symptoms are fever, chills, headache, fatigue, feelings of weakness, and aches and pains, followed by loss of appetite, nausea, vomiting, abdominal pain, dark urine, light-colored feces and jaundiced (yellow) skin. The whites of the eyes may turn yellow. **Hepatitis A** is transmitted by contaminated food and drinking water. Victims need medical advice but there is not much you can do apart from rest, drink lots of fluids, eat lightly and avoid fatty foods. People who have had hepatitis should avoid alcohol for some time after the illness, as the liver needs time to recover.

Hepatitis E is transmitted in the same way, and can be very serious in pregnant women.

Incidence of **Hepatitis B** is low in Mexico. It is spread through contact with infected blood, blood products or body fluids – for example, through sexual contact, unsterilized needles and blood transfusions, body-piercing, tattooing, having a shave, or contact with blood via small breaks in the skin. Symptoms of type B may be more severe and may lead to long-term problems. **Hepatitis D** is spread in the same way, but the risk is mainly from shared needles.

Hepatitis C can lead to chronic liver disease. The virus is spread by contact with blood, usually via contaminated transfusions or shared needles. Avoiding these is the only means of prevention.

Tetanus Tetanus occurs when a wound is infected by a germ that lives in soil and in the feces of horses and other animals. It enters the body via breaks in the skin. All wounds should be cleaned promptly and adequately and an antiseptic cream or solution applied. Use antibiotics if the wound becomes hot or throbs or pus is seen. The first symptom may be discomfort in swallowing, or stiffening of the jaw and neck; this is followed by painful convulsions of the jaw and whole body. The disease can be fatal.

Rabies This is a fatal viral infection. Many animals can be infected (such as dogs, cats, bats and monkeys), and it is their saliva that is infectious. Any bite, scratch or even lick from a warm-blooded, furry animal should be cleaned immediately and thoroughly. Scrub with soap and running water, and then apply alcohol or iodine solution. Medical help should be sought promptly to receive a course of injections to prevent the onset of symptoms and death.

Insect-Borne Diseases

Protecting yourself against insect bites will help to prevent these diseases. Travelers are especially advised to prevent mosquito bites at all times. In general, mosquitoes in Mexico are most bothersome from dusk to dawn and during the rainy season (May to October in most places). The main messages are as follows:

- Wear light-colored clothing.
- Wear long pants and long-sleeve shirts.
- Use mosquito repellents containing the compound DEET on exposed areas (prolonged overuse of DEET may be harmful, especially to children, but its use is considered preferable to being bitten by disease-transmitting mosquitoes).
- Avoid highly scented perfumes or aftershaves.

Malaria Malaria is not a risk in Mexico City or any of the places covered in this book's Excursions chapter.

Dengue Fever No preventative drug exists for this mosquito-spread disease, which can be fatal in children. A sudden onset of fever, headaches and severe joint and muscle pains are the first signs before a rash develops. Recovery may be prolonged.

Sexually Transmitted Diseases

Gonorrhea, herpes and syphilis are among these diseases; sores, blisters or rashes around the genitals, and discharges or pain when urinating, are common symptoms. Syphilis symptoms eventually disappear completely, but the disease continues and can cause severe problems in later years. While abstinence from sexual contact is the only 100% effective prevention of STDs, using condoms is also effective. Gonorrhea and syphilis are treated with antibiotics. Each STD requires specific antibiotics. No cures exist for herpes or HIV/AIDS.

HIV & AIDS

HIV, human immunodeficiency virus, causes AIDS, acquired immune deficiency syndrome *(SIDA, síndrome de inmunodeficiencia adquirida)*, which is a fatal disease. Nearly 40,000 AIDS cases had been recorded in Mexico by 1999. Any exposure to blood, blood products or body fluids may put you at risk. The disease is often transmitted through sexual contact or contaminated needles – vaccinations, acupuncture, tattooing and body-piercing can be potentially as dangerous as intravenous drug use. HIV/AIDS can also be spread through transfusions of infected blood; some developing countries cannot afford to screen blood used for transfusions. If you do need an injection, ask to see the syringe unwrapped in front of you, or take a needle and syringe pack with you. Fear of HIV infection should never preclude treatment for serious medical conditions, however.

Women's Health

Antibiotic use, synthetic underwear, sweating and contraceptive pills can lead to fungal vaginal infections in hot climates. Wearing loose-fitting clothes and cotton underwear will help prevent these infections.

Fungal infections, characterized by a rash, itch and discharge, can be treated with a vinegar or lemon-juice douche or with yogurt. Nystatin, miconazole or clotrimazole pessaries or vaginal cream are the usual treatments.

Sexually transmitted diseases are a major cause of vaginal problems. Symptoms include a smelly discharge, painful intercourse and sometimes a burning sensation when urinating. Sexual partners must also be treated. Medical attention should be sought. Remember that in addition to these diseases, HIV or hepatitis B can also be acquired from sexual contact. Besides abstinence, the best thing is to practice safe sex using condoms.

Pregnancy Some vaccinations normally used to prevent serious diseases are not recommended during pregnancy, making travel to some places inadvisable. Some diseases are much more serious for pregnant women (and may increase the risk of a stillborn child).

Most miscarriages occur during the first three months of pregnancy. Miscarriage is not uncommon, and it can occasionally lead to severe bleeding. The last three months of pregnancy should also be spent within reasonable distance of good medical care. A baby born as early as 24 weeks stands a chance of survival, but only in a good modern hospital. Pregnant women should avoid all unnecessary medication; vaccinations and malarial prophylactics should still be taken where needed. Additional care should be taken to prevent illness, and particular attention should be paid to diet and nutrition.

WOMEN TRAVELERS

In the land that invented machismo, women have to make some concessions to local custom, but don't let that put you off. In general, Mexicans are great believers in the differences between – rather than the equality of – the sexes. Lone women have to expect a few catcalls and attempts by men to chat them up. The best way to discourage unwanted attention is to avoid eye contact and, if possible, ignore the attention altogether. Otherwise use a cool but polite initial response and a consistent, firm 'No.' Dressing conservatively will spare you a lot of hassle, and a wedding ring and talk of your husband may help, too.

It's inadvisable to put yourself in peril by doing things Mexican women would not do, such as challenging a man's masculinity, drinking in a cantina or going alone to isolated places. If you do find yourself in a potentially dangerous situation, try to get to a well-lit, crowded area where other women are present. Always be aware of your surroundings and walk purposefully; if you don't seem like an easy target, most predators will look elsewhere. Consider taking a self-defense course before you travel.

GAY & LESBIAN TRAVELERS

Though it might ostensibly be one of the world's more heterosexual countries, Mexico is more broad-minded than visitors might expect. Gay bashing isn't unknown to Mexico, however, so gay couples would be wise to keep displays of affection behind closed doors. Mexico City has one of the country's more active scenes (see the Entertainment chapter). A good source of information on the Internet is The Gay Mexico Network (www.gaymexico.net).

The annual *Damron Women's Traveller*, with listings for lesbians, and *Damron Address Book*, for men, are both published by Damron Company of San Francisco, USA. *Men's Travel in Your Pocket*, *Women's Travel in Your Pocket* and *Gay Travel A to Z* (for men and women), all published by Ferrari Publications, and *Gay Mexico: The Men of Mexico* by Eduardo David are also useful. They can be obtained at any good bookstore, including on the Internet.

DISABLED TRAVELERS

Mexico doesn't yet make very many concessions to the disabled, though some hotels and restaurants (mostly toward the top end of the market) and public buildings are starting to provide wheelchair access *(acceso para silla de ruedas)*. Mobility is easiest in the more expensive hotels. Public transportation is mainly hopeless. Flying and taxi or car are easiest. *Tiempo Libre* magazine and the Ticketmaster website provide some information on wheelchair access for entertainment venues (see the Entertainment chapter).

Mobility International USA (☎ 541-343-1284, www.miusa.org), PO Box 10767, Eugene, OR 97440, USA, runs exchange programs in Mexico and publishes *A World of Options: A Guide to International Educational Exchange, Community Service & Travel for People with Disabilities*. In Europe, Mobility International is at Boulevard Baudouin 18, Brussels B-1000, Belgium (☎ 02-201 5608, mobint@arcadis.be).

The Council on International Educational Exchange (see Volunteer Work, at the end of this chapter) can help disabled people interested in working, studying or volunteering outside their home countries.

Twin Peaks Press (☎ 360-694-2462, www.pacifier.com/~twinpeak), PO Box 129, Vancouver, WA 98666-0129, USA, publishes and sells many books for disabled travelers.

An excellent website for disabled travelers to check is www.access-able.com.

SENIOR TRAVELERS

The American Association of Retired Persons (AARP, ☎ 800-424-3410, www.aarp .org), 601 E St NW, Washington, DC 20049, USA, is an advocacy and service group for Americans 50 years and older and a good resource for travel bargains. Membership for one/three years is US$8/20.

If you have a membership in the National Council of Senior Citizens (☎ 301-578-8800, www.aoa.dhhs.gov/AOA/dir/149.html), 8403 Colesville Road, Suite 1200, Silver Spring, MD 20910, USA, you'll have access to discount information and travel-related advice.

Grand Circle Travel (☎ 800-597-3644, www.gct.com), 347 Congress St, Boston, MA 02210, USA, offers escorted tours and travel information for seniors in a variety of formats.

MEXICO CITY FOR CHILDREN

Mexicans, as a rule, like children. Any child whose hair is less than jet black will be called *güera* (blonde) if she's a girl, *güero* if he's a boy. Children are welcome at all kinds of accommodations, and in virtually every café and restaurant.

Children are likely to be excited and stimulated by the sights and bustle of Mexico City, but they may feel the effects of the altitude, pollution, noise and heat more than grownups do. They need time to acclimatize. Take care to replace fluids if a child gets diarrhea (see the Health section, earlier in this chapter), and be prepared for minor effects brought on by change of diet or water, or disrupted sleeping patterns.

Diapers (nappies) are widely available and you shouldn't have too much trouble finding creams, lotions or baby foods. But it's wise to bring a few supplies to start you off, plus any medicines that you rely on.

If your kids don't take to typical Mexican food, there are plenty of restaurants serving up 'international-style' food to satisfy them.

Many hotels above the budget category can provide a baby sitter *(niñera)* if the grownups want to go out on their own.

Most airlines allow children under two to travel for 10% of the adult fare, and those between two and 12 usually pay 67%.

Lonely Planet's *Travel with Children*, by Maureen Wheeler, has lots of practical advice on its subject, and firsthand stories from many Lonely Planet authors and others who have traveled with children.

Things to See & Do

The first place to head for when seeking diversion for children is definitely the **Bosque de Chapultepec**, with its woodlands, open spaces, lakes and a whole series of child-friendly attractions. In the park's first section are the Centro de Convivencia Infantil (an adventure playground for smaller children) and a large zoo. In the second section you'll find the marvelous hands-on children's museum, Papalote Museo del Niño, plus two sets of fairground rides, one of them specifically for children. In the third section are Atlantis, an aquatic park with dolphin and sea lion shows, trained birds and more, and El Rollo, with waterslides, tunnels and a wave pool.

Another enjoyable outing is a ride on the canals of **Xochimilco**.

Out in the southwest of the city on Carretera Picacho-Ajusco is **Reino Aventura**, claiming to be the biggest amusement park in Latin America, with dozens more rides. Scientifically inclined kids will probably enjoy **Universum**, a hands-on science museum in the Ciudad Universitaria. For a change of temperature, try **ice-skating** at Pista de Hielo San Jerónimo.

On top of all this, Mexico City offers a huge range of **theater, music, puppet shows, dance performances** and other entertainment specifically for children. The what's-on magazine *Tiempo Libre* has several pages of listings every week in its *Niños* section. (The Spanish word for puppets, by the way, is *títeres*.)

Some kids' **movies** shown in Mexico City cinemas are in their original language with Spanish subtitles *(subtítulos)*; others are dubbed into Spanish *(doblado en español)*. The only way to find out is to ask the cinema.

You'll find more detail on all these things in the Things to See & Do and Entertainment chapters.

LIBRARIES

There are several useful foreign-run libraries in Mexico City including the following:

Biblioteca Benjamín Franklin (Benjamin Franklin Library, ☎ 5-211-00-42), Londres 16, west of Berlin, is run by the US embassy. A wide range of books about Mexico is available, plus English-language periodicals. You must be 20 or over to use the library, and to borrow books you need the signature support of a Mexican registered voter. It's open 3 to 7.30 pm Monday and Friday, 10 am to 3 pm Tuesday to Thursday (Ⓜ Cuauhtémoc; Map 5).

Canadian Embassy Library (☎ 5-724-79-00), Schiller 529, Polanco, in the embassy, has a wide selection of Canadian books and periodicals in English and French. Hours are 9 am to 12.30 pm Monday to Friday (Ⓜ Polanco).

Casa de Francia (☎ 5-511-31-51), Havre 15, Zona Rosa, has a good computer-equipped French library, open 10 am to 8 pm Monday to Saturday (Ⓜ Insurgentes).

Consejo Británico (British Council, ☎ 5-566-61-44), Antonio Caso 127, has a library with lots of books and magazines in English, plus British newspapers a couple of weeks old. Membership, allowing people living in Mexico City to borrow books, costs US$5.50. Hours are 8.30 am to 7.30 pm Monday to Friday, 10 am to 1 pm Saturday (Ⓜ San Cosme; Map 5).

Instituto Goethe (☎ 5-207-04-87), Tonalá 43, Colonia Roma, has a German library open 9 am to 1 pm and 4 to 7.30 pm Tuesday to Thursday, 10 am to 2 pm Saturday (Ⓜ Insurgentes).

The national library is the Biblioteca de México in La Ciudadela, a historic colonial building on Plaza José María Morelos (near Ⓜ Balderas; Map 4).

UNIVERSITIES

Mexico City is home to the Universidad Nacional Autónoma de Mexico (UNAM, National Autonomous University of Mexico), the biggest university in Latin America, and to several private universities, some of which have overtaken UNAM in academic prestige in recent years. See the Things to See & Do chapter for some information on courses in Spanish and other subjects at Mexico City universities, and on the Ciudad Universitaria (University City), UNAM's main campus, which is the site of some spectacular architecture (Ⓜ Copilco or Universidad; Map 11).

CULTURAL CENTERS

The Consejo Británico and Instituto Goethe (see Libraries, above) and the Institut Français d'Amérique Latine (☎ 5-566-07-77) at Río Nazas 43 (Ⓜ San Cosme or Insurgentes; Map 5) all put on films, exhibitions, concerts and other events from their home countries. The Casa de Francia (see Libraries) has a French bookstore and café and an exhibition hall.

DANGERS & ANNOYANCES

The economic recession of the mid-1990s catalyzed a big increase in crime in Mexico City, with foreigners among the juicier and often easier targets for pickpockets, purse snatchers, thieves and armed robbers. By 1999 the city authorities were claiming that their efforts to crack down on crime were starting to succeed. True or not, far too many violent incidents have happened in Mexico City (including assaults *by* the police) for anyone to deny the risks, and foreigners are often the victims. But there's no need to walk in fear whenever you step outside your hotel: a few basic precautions greatly reduce any dangers.

Official information can make Mexico sound more alarming than it really is, but for a variety of useful tips on travel to Mexico, including potential risks, you can contact your country's foreign affairs department, by telephone or on the Internet: Australia (☎ 02-6261-3305, www.dfat.gov.au); Canada (☎ 613-944-6788, 800-267-6788, www.dfait-maeci.gc.ca); UK (☎ 020-7238-4503, www.fco.gov.uk); USA (☎ 202-647-5225, http://travel.state.gov). If you're already in Mexico, you can contact your embassy.

Mexico City's metro, buses, *peseros* (minibuses), bus stops and markets are favorite haunts of pickpockets and thieves, particularly when crowded. Taxis are now even more notorious for armed robberies. The riskiest time is after dark and the riskiest places are those where foreigners most often go. These include central metro stations and places such as the Bosque de Chapultepec, the Museo Nacional de Antropología area, the Zona Rosa, the Polanco restaurant area, and the area around the US embassy. Steer clear of empty streets after dark.

Robbery or mugging is more likely in less crowded places, such as empty pedestrian underpasses or quiet streets at night. Resistance to robbers may be met with violence. They may force you to remove your money belt or neck-strap pouch, watch, rings etc. They may be armed. Usually they will not harm you: what they want is your money, fast. But in some cases robbers have beaten victims, or forced them to drink large amounts of alcohol, to extract credit or bank card personal numbers.

Mexico City's police are certainly not always to be trusted. On average they earn around US$350 a month and they often have to pay some of this to their superiors as a kind of protection money. So it's hardly surprising that many of them rely on *mordidas* (small bribes) from the public to supplement their earnings. Worse, police are sometimes the criminals. In one incident in

1998, a 27-year-old American was kidnapped by police, driven around for several hours, robbed of his money and ATM cards so that the police could withdraw his money from ATMs, and forced to drink alcohol. Abandoned in his car near the entrance to the Bosque de Chapultepec, he choked on his own vomit and died. The incident did lead to the arrests of several police and ex-police who were allegedly part of a gang that perpetrated this and many similar crimes.

Pickpockets

Pickpockets often work in teams: one or two of them may grab your bag or camera (or your arm or leg), and while you're trying to get it free another will pick your pocket. Or one may 'drop' something as a crowd jostles onto a bus or a metro car, and as he 'looks for it,' a pocket will be picked or a bag slashed or taken in the jostling. Pickpockets often carry razor blades with which they slit pockets, bags or straps. The operative principle is to outnumber you, confuse you, and to get you off balance. If your valuables are *underneath* your clothing, your chances of losing them are greatly reduced.

Taxi Crime

In 1999 the US State Department warned: 'Robbery assaults on passengers in taxis are frequent and violent, with passengers subjected to beating, shootings and sexual assault.' Ask any foreigner living in Mexico City: if it hasn't happened to them, it has happened to someone they know. Many victims had hailed a cab on the street and were attacked or robbed by armed accomplices of the driver. The State Department specifically warned against taking taxis parked outside the Palacio de Bellas Artes, in front of nightclubs or restaurants, or cruising anywhere in the city.

At the airport, use only the official yellow 'Transportación Terrestre' airport cabs (see the Getting Around chapter). Elsewhere in the city, you can telephone (or get your hotel or restaurant to call for you) a radio taxi or a *sitio* (taxi stand): ask the dispatcher for the driver's name and the cab's license plate number. These cabs are more expensive than ordinary cruising *(libre)* street cabs, but the extra money buys you security. Sitio cabs have the letter S at the start of their license plate and an orange stripe along the bottom of the plate. Cruising taxis have the letter L and a green stripe.

Cab firms are listed under *'Sitios de Automóviles'* in the telephone yellow pages. Hotels and restaurants will nearly always be able to call a reliable cab for you. Radio taxi firms include the following:

Servitaxis (☎ 5-516-60-20)
Sitio 101 (☎ 5-566-00-77, 5-566-72-66)
Super Sitio 160 (☎ 5-271-91-46, 5-271-90-58)
Taxi-Mex (☎ 5-538-14-40, 5-519-76-90)
Taxi Radio Mex (☎ 5-584-05-71, 5-574-45-96)

If you *must* hail a cab on the street – and it's much better never to do so – check that the cab has license plates and that the number on them matches the number painted on the bodywork. Also check the *carta de identificación*, an ID card, which should be displayed visibly inside the cab, to see that the driver matches the photo. If a cab does not pass these tests, do not get into it.

Do not travel alone by taxi after dark, and do not carry ATM cards, credit cards or large amounts of cash. It's fairly common for robbers to force hijack victims to tour the city and withdraw cash from ATMs. If you become a robbery victim, surrender your valuables. They are not worth risking injury or death for.

For more information on taxis, see the Getting Around chapter.

Metro

Using the metro only at less busy times enables you to find a less crowded car (at one end of the train), where thieves will find it harder to get close to you without being noticed (but avoid near-empty cars). During peak hours (roughly 7.30 to 10 am and 5 to 7 pm) all trains and buses in the central area are packed tight, which suits pickpockets. Hold on to any belongings tightly. Our advice is to avoid getting on or off or changing trains at Hidalgo station, where pickpockets and bag snatchers often wait for foreigners and follow them on to crowded trains. If you're on a train that's going through Hidalgo, use only the last cars, so that thieves waiting in the station are less likely to spot you.

Lost & Found If you've lost something on the metro, you can try calling ☎ 5-627-46-43. If it's something that 10 million other people wouldn't want, there's a chance you just might find it there.

Precautions

To minimize risk of losing your possessions in Mexico City, follow these general precautions without fail.

• Unless you have immediate need of them, leave most of your cash, traveler's checks, passport, jewelry, air tickets, credit cards, watch (and perhaps your camera) in a sealed, signed envelope in your hotel's safe. Virtually all hotels except the very cheapest provide safekeeping for guests' valuables.

• Leaving valuables in a locked suitcase in your hotel room is often safer than carrying them on the streets.

• If you have to carry valuables on the streets, keep them in a moneybelt, shoulder wallet, or a pouch on a string around your neck, *underneath your clothing*. Visible round-the-waist moneybelts ('fanny packs,' 'bum bags') are an invitation for thieves, and an easy target. You can carry a small amount of ready money in a pocket.

• Walk with purpose and be alert to people around you, such as people who are walking close to you or toward you for no obvious reason. Try to keep clear of crushes at bus stops, metro stations, etc.

• Don't keep money (cash or plastic), purses or bags in open view any longer than you have to. At ticket counters in bus stations and airports, keep your bag between your feet, particularly when you're busy with a ticket agent.

• Use ATMs only in secure locations, not those open to the street.

• If you participate in any Mexican festivities (rallies or celebrations in the Zócalo, etc) be aware that half the pickpockets in the city will be there, too.

• Do not drive alone at night in Mexico City.

• Do not leave anything even vaguely valuable-looking visible in a parked vehicle.

• Perhaps most important, don't risk injury by resisting robbers.

EMERGENCIES

SECTUR (☎ 5-250-01-23, 800-903-92-00), the national tourism ministry, is available by phone 24 hours a day to help tourists with problems and emergencies.

The Procuraduría General de Justicia del Distrito Federal (Federal District Attorney General) maintains mobile tourist assistance units to go to the aid of visitors who are victims or witnesses of crime. Call ☎ 061 for help on the spot from these police units.

The general emergency numbers for fire, police and ambulance are ☎ 060 and ☎ 080.

See the following section, Legal Matters, for information on reporting crimes.

LEGAL MATTERS

Mexico's legal system is based on the Napoleonic Code, which presumes guilt until innocence is proven. All drivers involved in a road accident that involves injuries, for instance, are likely to be detained until blame is established (see Accidents in the Car & Motorcycle section in the Getting

There & Away chapter for more on that topic).

If arrested, you have the right to call your embassy, which should at the least be able to provide information on lawyers who speak your language and to contact your family or friends at home.

The SECTUR tourist office (☎ 5-250-01-23, 800-903-92-00) can provide information on laws protecting visitors 24 hours, seven days a week, by telephone. The Procuraduría General de Justicia del Distrito Federal maintains police offices to aid tourists with legal questions and problems. One office (☎ 5-625-70-07, 5-625-81-53) – always open, with English-speaking staff available – is at Avenida Florencia 20 in the Zona Rosa (Ⓜ Insurgentes). Another is at the Terminal Sur de Autobuses.

In any case of trouble with the police, it would be useful if you could manage to note the officer's number, name (most wear nameplates), department and/or vehicle number. Contact the Protección Legal al Turista (Legal Protection for Tourists) section at SECTUR if you wish to make an official complaint.

Reporting Crimes

If you become the victim of a crime, you may want to seek your embassy's and SECTUR's help or advice. There may be little to gain from going to the police unless you have been injured or physically mistreated during the crime, or feel that the gravity of an offense is such that the authorities ought to know about it, or if you need a police statement to present to your insurance company.

You can report crimes by calling ☎ 061 for a mobile tourist assistance unit of the Procuraduría General de Justicia del Distrito Federal (see the Emergency section, above) or by going to one of the Procuraduría's offices (see the Legal Matters section, above). These services will take you to a doctor or hospital if you're injured in an assault. If you go to a different police station and your Spanish is poor, take a more fluent speaker. Also take your passport and tourist card, if you still have them.

If you just want to report a theft for insurance purposes, say you want to *'poner una acta de un robo'* (make a record of a robbery). This should make clear that you merely want a piece of paper and aren't going to ask the police to do anything inconvenient like recover your goods. You should get the required piece of paper without too much trouble.

BUSINESS HOURS

Government offices are typically open Monday to Friday from 8 or 9 am to 2 or 3 pm. They may also work from 5 to 8 or 9 pm, but are often not open to the public at these times. Most other offices are open Monday to Friday from 9 am to 6 or 7 pm, with a lunch break from 2 to 3 or 4 pm. Those with tourist or leisure-related business might open some of Saturday, too.

Most museums have one closing day a week, often Monday. On Sundays nearly all museums and archaeological sites are free, and the major ones can get very crowded.

PUBLIC HOLIDAYS

Christmas/New Year and Semana Santa (Holy Week, the week leading up to Easter) are the chief Mexican holiday periods. There's little point scheduling a business trip to the city between about December 20 and January 4, or during Semana Santa or the couple of days after Easter. Many Mexicans also take holidays in July or August.

Banks, post offices, other offices and many shops are closed on the following days:

January 1
Año Nuevo – New Year's Day

February 5
Día de la Constitución – Constitution Day

February 24
Día de la Bandera – Day of the (national) Flag

March 21
Día de Nacimiento de Benito Juárez – Anniversary of the birth of the 19th-century president Benito Juárez

May 1
Día del Trabajo – Labor Day; a big unionists' gathering in the Zócalo in the morning, and parades around the city

May 5

Cinco de Mayo – anniversary of Mexico's 1862 victory over the French at Puebla

September 16

Día de la Independencia – commemoration of the start of Mexico's war for independence from Spain; military parade from the Zócalo to the Monumento a la Independencia (El Ángel) – also see September 15 in the next section

October 12

Día de la Raza – commemorating Columbus' discovery of the New World, and the founding of the Mexican (mestizo) people

November 20

Día de la Revolución – anniversary of the Mexican Revolution of 1910; a parade starts from the Zócalo in the morning

December 25

Día de Navidad – Christmas Day; the Christmas feast traditionally takes place in the early hours of December 25, after midnight mass; for the couple of weeks beforehand, the Alameda Central is ringed with brightly lit fairy-tale castles and polar grottoes, where children pose for photos with Santa Clauses and their reindeer

SPECIAL EVENTS

Though not official holidays, some of the following are among the most important festivals in Mexico City's calendar. Many offices and businesses close.

January 6

Día de los Reyes Magos – Three Kings' Day (Epiphany); Mexican children traditionally receive gifts this day, rather than at Christmas (but some get two lots of presents!); between Christmas and January 6, the Santa Clauses around the Alameda Central (see December 25, above) are replaced by the Three Kings, who are equally popular and look, if anything, even more ill at ease: families flock in and hosts of stalls selling anything from tacos to music tapes pop up, too.

March

Festival del Centro Histórico – this excellent three-week program of classical and popular music, dance, exhibitions and other cultural events, with top-class Mexican and international performers, takes place in numerous picturesque and historic plazas, palaces, theaters and archaeological sites in the Centro Histórico and Alameda area; check the festival's website (www.festival.org.mx) for schedule details and performers.

March or April

Semana Santa – Holy Week, starting on Palm Sunday (Domingo de Ramos); closures are usually from Good Friday (Viernes Santo) to Easter Sunday (Domingo de Resurrección or Domingo de Pascua); most of Mexico seems to be on the move at this time

May 10

Día de la Madre – Mothers' Day

A Vivid Production

The most evocative events of Semana Santa in Mexico City are in the humble district of Iztapalapa, about 9km southeast of the Zócalo (Ⓜ Iztapalapa; Map 1). Thousands of locals take part in realistic scenes from the Passion and death of Christ, watched by up to 4 million spectators. The Iztapalapa rituals began as a form of thanksgiving after the end of a cholera epidemic in 1833.

Palm Sunday sees the triumphal entry into Jerusalem, and on Holy Thursday the betrayal by Judas and the Last Supper are played out in the plaza of Iztapalapa. The most emotive scenes, however, begin at noon on Good Friday, in the plaza. Christ is sentenced by Pontius Pilate, beaten, and has a crown of thorns placed on his head (drawing real blood!), then he carries his 90kg cross 4km up Cerro de la Estrella, the hill rising to the south, which has been a site of religious ritual since pre-Hispanic times. Thousands of barefoot penitents, with their own crosses and crowns of thorns, follow him up the hill. Once atop the hill, Christ is tied to the cross and 'crucified.' Judas hangs himself beside Jesus, after which, Christ is carried down the hill and taken away to a hospital.

The young people who take on these intense roles are chosen carefully – and must meet some strict conditions. The part of Mary must be played by a virgin. The role of Christ has to be played by a young, locally born man with some physical resemblance to the usual image of Jesus, who is strong enough to endure the ordeal, and – who has never had a girlfriend.

September 15

On the eve of the Día de la Independencia (see previous section), thousands of people gather in the Zócalo to hear the president of Mexico recite a version of the *Grito de Dolores* (Cry of Dolores) from the central balcony of the Palacio Nacional at 11 pm. The Grito was priest Miguel Hidalgo's famous rallying call to rebellion against the Spanish, made in the town of Dolores Hidalgo on September 16, 1810. The president then rings the ceremonial Bell of Dolores, and there's lots of cheering, fireworks and throwing of confetti and flour-filled eggs. If you go, leave valuables and good clothes at the hotel.

November 1

Día de Todos los Santos – All Saints' Day

November 2

Día de los Muertos – Day of the Dead; Mexico's most characteristic fiesta; the souls of the dead are believed to return to earth this day. Families build altars in homes and visit graveyards to commune with their dead on the preceding night and the day itself, taking garlands, gifts of the dead one's favorite foods and so forth. A happy atmosphere prevails. The souls of dead children, called Angelitos because they are believed to have automatically become angels, are celebrated the previous day, All Saints' Day. The events have roots in pre-Hispanic ancestor worship. Sweets resembling human skeletons and skulls are sold in almost every market.

December 12

Día de Nuestra Señora de Guadalupe – Day of Our Lady of Guadalupe, Mexico's national patron, the manifestation of the Virgin Mary who appeared to an indigenous Mexican, Juan Diego, on the hill Cerro del Tepeyac in 1531. From December 3 onward, ever-growing crowds flood toward the Basílica de Guadalupe (Map 3), at the foot of the hill. Vendors sell a special Virgin-shaped corn cake called *la gordita de la Virgen*. On December 11 and 12 groups of brightly costumed indigenous dancers and musicians from all over Mexico perform in an uninterrupted sequence on the basilica's large plaza for two days. The numbers of pilgrims reach their millions by December 12, when religious services go on in the basilica almost round the clock.

December 31

New Year's Eve is at least a half-day holiday for many people.

DOING BUSINESS

Though Guadalajara, Monterrey and other cities, especially in the north, are significant industrial centers, Mexico City is the hub of Mexico's economy and Mexican business. Not only is half the country's Gross Domestic Product (GDP) produced within 150km of the city; it's also the headquarters of a high proportion of the country's major businesses and national organizations, not to mention the entire federal government.

Mexican Business Culture

The single most important key to business success in Mexico is to develop personal rapport with the Mexicans you're dealing with. It's often said that business deals in Mexico are only made between friends, and the social side of business is very important. So you need to take time to get to know people as individuals, and let them get to know you, too. With a few introductions (which are important) to start you off, whole networks of friendships can become fairly quickly accessible.

The (extended) family is crucially important in Mexican society – social life tends to be family-based, and many companies (including some of the very biggest) are family-run. Inquiries about an associate's family go down well – as do comments indicating a genuine interest in and enjoyment of Mexico's culture, beauty, history and so on. Small talk is the norm before you get down to business on any occasion.

Long business breakfasts and lunches, and drinks in some of the city's classier bars, are times for getting to know colleagues. Actual business is more likely to get discussed over breakfast than lunch.

Using some Spanish, however minimal your knowledge of it, shows courtesy and is appreciated. Increasing numbers of educated Mexicans speak English, but most important business is conducted in Spanish. You'll need an interpreter if your grasp of the language is not adequate.

You can expect the Mexican younger generation in particular to match Americans in education, business skills and technological sophistication. Mobile phones and email are commonplace.

But be prepared for business negotiations to take longer than you may be used to at home. Mexicans will want to get to know you before getting down to serious business. Meetings can go on a long time, most deadlines are considered flexible, and you may find that decisions can only be made when the head of the company is available. Red tape can certainly be a big frustration. All you can do is find out what all the regulations are, and comply with them however long it takes.

Mexicans tend to avoid direct differences of opinion and direct criticism or confrontation. They don't like to say 'no,' so you have to learn to judge the amount of real commitment in a 'yes,' and when and when not to apply tactful pressure. Dealing with problems requires patience and a constructive approach.

Mexican business is still pretty much a man's world. Women are making some progress, but the top jobs are nearly always held by men.

Etiquette Mexicans attach a lot of importance to professional titles such as Licenciado/a (a lawyer or a person with a liberal arts degree), Ingeniero/a (an engineering graduate), Arquitecto/a (an architecture graduate), or Doctor/a (medical doctor or PhD holder). People will often be introduced to you with such titles, and you should use them – not just Señor, Señora or Señorita – when addressing them subsequently (until you get on to more familiar terms). For more on the tricky subject of Mexican names, see 'What's in a Name?' in the Facts about Mexico City chapter.

Business cards are used extensively. It's a good idea to have the information in Spanish on one side and English on the other.

Manners and appearance count for a lot. Hand-shaking on introduction, and on arrival and departure, is customary. Businessmen normally wear suits, and businesswomen well-tailored, conservative styles. It's better to be overdressed than underdressed.

It pays to make appointments well in advance, then confirm them at least once by phone – and to be on time for them. Mexicans may not like being kept waiting by a foreigner. Choose a hotel that's convenient for where you will be going, and allow for traffic delays.

On the other hand, it's rude to arrive on time for social occasions. If you are invited to a Mexican home, it's an honor. Bring a gift. Gestures such as sending birthday presents or Christmas cards are also valued.

Also see Society & Conduct in the Facts about Mexico City chapter.

Office Zones

Because of traffic problems, considering location is at least as important as internal conditions when you are looking for office space in Mexico City. One attractive office area, amid desirable residential districts, is Polanco. Rental costs there in 1998 were averaging about US$17 per sq meter a month. More economical office areas (US$12 to US$16) are Paseo de la Reforma between Avenida Insurgentes and the Bosque de Chapultepec (popular with banks, financial companies and multinationals), the Periférico Sur (industrial corporations) and Avenida Insurgentes Sur. More expensive (US$22 to US$25) are Lomas de Chapultepec, west of the Bosque de Chapultepec, and Bosques de las Lomas and Santa Fé, both in the west of the city near the point where Paseo de la Reforma and Avenida Constituyentes meet and become the main road to Toluca.

Useful Organizations in Mexico City

Embassies are usually more than willing to help their country's businesspeople. For example the Commercial Service at the US embassy (USCS, ☎ 5-209-91-00, fax 5-207-89-38), Paseo de la Reforma 305, Colonia Cuauhtémoc, México 06500 DF (Map 6), can provide counseling, market information, contacts and more for businesspeople from the US.

A number of foreign chambers of commerce in Mexico City work to provide information and contacts and generally promote trade and investment between their countries and Mexico. One particularly helpful one is the American Chamber of Commerce of Mexico (☎ 5-724-38-00, fax 5-724-38-24, www.amcham.com.mx), at Lucerna 78, Colonia Juárez, México 06600 DF. Its 2700 member companies are 55% Mexican, 38% from the US and 7% from other countries. Its Infocenter, which has a great deal of useful information about companies, contacts, organizations, laws, taxes, trade shows and statistics, offers its services to nonmembers on a commercial basis. It's open 9 am to 5 pm Monday to Friday. Take along your passport or other photo ID.

The US-Mexico Chamber of Commerce (Cámara de Comercio México-Estados Unidos, ☎ 5-286-15-55, fax 5-557-99-21) represents nearly 1000 businesses on both sides of the border. It has offices at Miguel de Cervantes Saavedra 376, Colonia Irrigación, México 11500 DF, and in Monterrey, Guadalajara and 12 US cities.

Many US states have their own trade offices in Mexico City, offering information and help to importers and exporters – the American Chamber of Commerce of Mexico can provide contact details.

Other useful foreign and international organizations in Mexico City include the following:

American Business Information Center (ABIC, ☎ 5-140-26-50, fax 5-566-11-15), Liverpool 31, Colonia Juárez, México 06600 DF

British Chamber of Commerce (☎ 5-256-09-01, fax 5-211-54-51, britcham@infoabc.com), Río de la Plata 30, Colonia Cuauhtémoc, México 06500 DF (Map 6)

Canadian Chamber of Commerce (☎ 5-545-39-97, fax 5-255-44-68, cdnchmbr@data.net.mx), Cantú 11, Colonia Anzures, México 11590 DF (Map 8)

Interamerican Development Bank (☎ 5-580-18-63, fax 5-580-60-83, www.iadb.org), Horacio 1855, Colonia Los Morales Polanco, México 11510 DF

International Monetary Fund (IMF, ☎ 5-237-24-56, fax 5-237-24-55, www.imf.org), Avenida Cinco de Mayo 20, Colonia Centro, México 06059 DF

Japanese Chamber of Commerce (☎ 5-514-34-10, fax 5-207-71-16, camjap@planet.com.mx), Sevilla 9, Zona Rosa, México 06600 DF (Map 6)

NAFTA Secretariat, Mexican Section (☎ 5-629-96-30, fax 5-629-96-37, www.nafta-sec-alena.org), Boulevard López Mateos 3025, Colonia Héroes de Padierna, México 10700 DF

United States Hispanic Chamber of Commerce (☎ 5-709-22-81, fax 5-709-11-77, www.ushcc.com), Balderas 144, Colonia Centro, México 06079 DF

US Trade Center (☎ 5-140-26-00, fax 5-566-11-15), Liverpool 31, Colonia Juárez, México 06600 DF

World Bank (☎ 5-480-42-00, fax 5-480-42-22, www.worldbank.org), Insurgentes Sur 1650, Colonia San José Insurgentes, México 03900 DF

Mexican Chambers of Commerce The dozens of Mexican national chambers represent everything from candy manufacturers to mining and electronics companies. All are based in Mexico City. The following organizations can provide useful information:

Cámara Nacional de Comercio de la Ciudad de México, Servicios y Turismo (CANACO, National Chamber of Commerce of Mexico City, Services & Tourism, ☎ 5-592-03-71, fax 5-703-29-58, www.ccmexico.com.mx), Paseo de la Reforma 42, Colonia Centro, México 06048 DF, has a membership of 41,000 commercial businesses in the Distrito Federal, and can provide information on trade opportunities and economic data (Map 5).

Cámara Nacional de la Industria de la Transformación (CANACINTRA, National Chamber of Manufacturing Industry, ☎ 5-563-34-00, fax 5-598-80-44, www.canacintra.org.mx), San Antonio 256, Colonia Nápoles, México 03849 DF, represents industry and has a membership of 87,000 manufacturers throughout Mexico; it can provide information to foreign businesspeople.

Confederación Nacional de Cámaras Industriales (CONCAMIN, National Confederation of Industrial Chambers, ☎ 5-566-78-22, fax 5-535-68-71, www.concamin.org.mx), at Manuel María Contreras 133, Colonia Cuauhtémoc, México 06500 DF, is an umbrella organization for 67 national, regional and state chambers and 23 industry associations; it has an information center involved in promoting international trade, which nonmembers can use free of charge (Map 5).

Mexican Secretariats Mexican national government departments are known as *secretarías*. Each usually comprises a number of *subsecretarías*, which in turn are composed of *direcciones generales* (general offices) with specific functions. Subsecretarías and direcciones generales may not be located in the same building as their parent divisions.

The Secretaría de Comercio y Fomento Industrial (Secretariat of Commerce & Industrial Development, SECOFI, ☎ 5-729-92-43, fax 5-729-93-20, www.secofi.gob.mx), Reyes 30, Colonia Condesa, México 06170 DF, handles international trade matters. Its subsecretarías include the following:

Subsecretaría de Negociaciones Comerciales Internacionales (Undersecretariat for International Trade Negotiations, ☎ 5-729-91-01, fax 5-729-93-07) implements laws and regulations established by international trade agreements, and has direcciones generales covering, among other things, supervision of laws on foreign trade, authorization of foreign investment, and economic negotiations with European and South American countries.

Subsecretaría de Normatividad y Servicios a la Industria y al Comercio Exterior (Undersecretariat of Standards & Services for Industry & Foreign Trade, ☎ 5-729-92-67, fax 5-729-93-22) provides information on tariffs, and has direcciones generales covering official standards, NAFTA antidumping and anti-subsidy laws, and permits and authorizations for imports, exports and maquiladoras.

Subsecretaría de Promoción de la Industria y el Comercio Exterior (Undersecretariat for Promotion of Industry & Foreign Trade, ☎ 5-229-65-61, fax 5-229-65-68) deals with registration of foreign investors and permits for certain imports, and has direcciones generales covering, among other things, promotion of industry, exports and foreign investment, and regional development.

Any company wishing to operate in Mexico has to register with the Secretaría de Hacienda y Crédito Público (Secretariat of Finance & Public Credit, SHCP, ☎ 5-518-54-20, fax 5-510-37-96, www.shcp.gob.mx), Palacio Nacional, Colonia Centro, México 06066 DF. 'Hacienda' regulates imports, exports, customs, mining and property laws. Its subsecretarías include the following:

Subsecretaría de Hacienda y Crédito Público (Undersecretariat of Finance & Public Credit, ☎ 5-687-41-74, fax 5-687-28-81) implements global financial development programs, monitors international private debt, and has direcciones generales dealing with, among other things, banks and financial institutions.

Subsecretaría de Ingresos (Undersecretariat of Revenues, ☎ 5-512-61-78, fax 5-228-28-80) deals with policy on ports, airports and tax declarations, and has direcciones generales dealing with, among other things, government revenue policies, ports, airports, customs laws and border development programs.

Other important secretariats include:

Secretaría de Comunicaciones y Transportes (SCT, Secretariat of Communications & Transportation, ☎ 5-519-74-56, fax 5-519-06-92, www.sct.gob.mx), Avenida Universidad y Xola, Cuerpo C, Colonia Narvarte, México 03028 DF

Secretaría de Energía (Secretariat of Energy, ☎ 5-448-60-00, fax 5-448-60-64, www.energia.gob.mx), Avenida Insurgentes Sur 890, Colonia Del Valle, México 03100 DF

Secretaría de Gobernación (Secretariat of Internal Affairs, ☎ 5-566-02-45, fax 5-546-53-50, www.gobernacion.gob.mx), Bucareli 99, Colonia Juárez, México 06699 DF

Secretaría del Medio Ambiente, Recursos Naturales y Pesca (SEMARNAP, Secretariat of Environment, Natural Resources & Fisheries, ☎ 5-628-06-02, fax 5-628-06-43, www.semarnap.gob.mx), Anillo Periférico Sur 4209, Colonia Jardines en la Montaña, México 14210 DF

Secretaría de Relaciones Exteriores (Secretariat of Foreign Affairs, ☎ 5-782-35-82, fax 5-782-41-09, www.sre.gob.mx), Ricardo Flores Magón 2, Ala A, Nivel 4, Colonia Guerrero, México 06595 DF

Secretaría del Trabajo y Previsión Social (Secretariat of Labor & Social Welfare, ☎ 5-645-55-91, fax 5-545-55-94, www.stps.gob.mx), Periférico Sur 4271, Edificio A, Colonia Fuentes del Pedregal, México 14149 DF

Secretaría de Turismo (SECTUR, Secretariat of Tourism, ☎ 5-250-82-06, fax 5-250-44-06, http://mexico-travel.com), at Avenida Presidente Masaryk 172, Colonia Polanco, México 11587 DF

Other Mexican Organizations

The Mexican Investment Board (MIB, Consejo Mexicano de Inversión, ☎ 5-202-78-04, fax 5-202-79-25, www.mib.org.mx), Paseo de la Reforma 915, Colonia Lomas de Chapultepec, México 11000 DF, is funded jointly by the public and private sectors to help foreign investors in Mexico. It has good leverage with government and business and can help with viability studies.

The Mexico City head of government's office (☎ 5-522-28-55, fax 5-510-07-71, www.df.gob.mx) and the headquarters of the city's bureaucracy are on the south side of the Zócalo at Plaza de la Constitución y 20 de Noviembre, Colonia Centro, México 06068 DF.

The following organizations are mostly *entidades paraestatales* (state-dependent organizations):

Asociación Mexicana de Promotores de Ferias, Exhibiciones y Convenciones (AMPROFEC, Mexican Trade Show, Exhibition & Convention Promoters Association, ☎/fax 5-592-57-85, infor@ amprofec.com.org.mx), Atenas 21, Colonia Juárez, México 06600 DF

Banco Nacional de Comercio Exterior (BAN-COMEXT, the National Foreign Trade Bank, ☎ 5-227-90-00, fax 5-652-94-08, http://mexico .businessline.gob.mx), at Periférico Sur 433, in Colonia Jardines en la Montaña, México 14210 DF

Comisión Federal de Electricidad (CFE, Federal Electricity Commission, ☎ 5-207-37-04, fax 5-553-64-24, www.cfe.gob.mx), Rodano 14, Colonia Cuauhtémoc, México 06598 DF

Ferrocarriles Nacionales de México (FNM, Mexican National Railways, ☎ 5-547-79-20, fax 5-547-09-59), Jesús García Corona 140, Colonia Buena Vista, México 06358 DF

Fondo de Inversión en Infraestructura (FINFRA, Investment in Infrastructure Fund, ☎ 5-723-60-10, fax 5-723-61-14, 74174.2071@compuserve .com), Teyocotitla 100, Colonia Florida, México 01030 DF

Nacional Financiera (NAFIN, National Development Bank, ☎ 5-325-60-00, fax 5-661-72-96, www.nafin.gob.mx), Avenida Insurgentes Sur 1971, Torre 4, Colonia Guadalupe Inn, México 01020 DF

Petróleos Mexicanos (PEMEX, Mexican Petroleum, ☎ 5-250-34-57, fax 5-625-43-85, www.pemex .com.mx), Avenida Marina Nacional 329, Torre Ejecutiva, Colonia Huasteca, México 11311 DF

Puertos Mexicanos (Mexican Ports, ☎ 5-605-29-98, fax 5-605-39-87), Municipio Libre 377, Ala A, Colonia Santa Cruz Atoyac, México 03310 DF

Useful Organizations in the USA & Canada

These include:

Association of American Chambers of Commerce in Latin America (AACCLA, ☎ 202-463-5485, fax 202-463-3126, www.aaccla.org), 1615 H St NW, Washington, DC 20062-2000

Export/Import Bank of the United States (US Ex-Im Bank, ☎ 202-565-3946, fax 202-565-3380, http://206.3.143.3), 811 Vermont Ave NW, Washington, DC 20571

NAFTA Secretariat, Canadian Section (☎ 613-992-9388, fax 613-992-9392, www.nafta-sec-alena .org), Royal Bank Center, 90 Sparks St, Suite 705, Ottawa, ON K1P5B4

NAFTA Secretariat, USA Section (☎ 202-482-5438, fax 202-482-0148, www.nafta-sec-alena .org), 14th St & Constitution Ave NW, Washington, DC 20230

North American Development Bank (NadBank, ☎ 210-231-8000, fax 210-231-6232, www.nadbank .org), 203 South St Mary's, Suite 300, San Antonio, TX 78205

Trade Commission of Mexico (BANCOMEXT Representative Office in New York, ☎ 212-826-2978, fax 212-826-2979, http://mexico.businessline .gob.mx), 375 Park Ave, 19th floor, New York, NY 10152 – BANCOMEXT has 36 other trade offices in other US, Canadian and world cities (see Investment Environment, below)

United States Hispanic Chamber of Commerce (☎ 202-842-1212, fax 202-842-3221, www.ushcc .com), 1019 19th St NW, Suite 200, Washington, DC 20036

US-Mexico Chamber of Commerce (☎ 202-371-8680, fax 202-371-8686, www.usmcoc.org), 1300 Pennsylvania Ave NW, Suite 270, Washington, DC 20004

US Trade & Development Agency (☎ 703-875-4357, fax 703-875-4009, www.tda.gov), 1621 N Kent St, Suite 200, Arlington, VA 22209

Investment Environment

Deregulation, privatization, industrial modernization, increased competition, rising productivity and greater openness to international trade have all been among the consistent thrusts of Mexico's governments for a decade or more. The country has for a long time had labor costs that are considered low by American or European standards. It also has a relatively well-educated workforce: more than 60% of urban workers have completed at least high school. The recession of the mid-1990s has made the country more productive and competitive than it had been in the past.

Trade NAFTA, the North American Free Trade Agreement, took effect in 1994, creating a free-trade area between Mexico, the US and Canada. NAFTA immediately exempted close to 80% of Mexican exports to the US and Canada from tariffs; further trade barriers are being eliminated step by step up to the year 2008. Mexico-US trade, in both directions, has already grown rapidly, even though Mexico's mid-1990s devaluation and recession slowed imports of consumer goods. Total US-Mexico trade was approaching US$200 billion a year by 2000, double what it had been in 1994. In 1997 Mexico overtook Japan as the US's second-biggest export market (after Canada). Nearly half of US exports to Mexico come from Texas.

Some 80% of Mexico's imports are intermediate goods such as parts, supplies and raw materials for industry, with capital goods such as manufacturing equipment accounting for another 12%. The most important imports include electrical parts; motors, parts and assembly materials for motor vehicles; data processing machines and parts; TV and radio receivers and transmitters; and paper and cardboard. Nearly all materials for making chemical products, textiles, footwear, and electrical and electronic components in Mexico are imported from the USA.

Mexico's main manufacturing exports are motor vehicles, motors and parts, electrical parts, cables, data processing machines and textiles.

The Mexican businesses that have done best in the post-1995 recovery tend to be large, to have already invested in modernizing their operations, and to be geared to exports.

Mexico also has free-trade agreements with Colombia, Venezuela, Bolivia, Costa Rica, Nicaragua and Chile, and an agreement with the European Union (EU) was due to take effect in mid-2000. Mexico is working toward the creation of the Free Trade Area of the Americas encompassing all 34 countries of the western hemisphere.

Mexico is a member of the Organisation for Economic Co-operation and Development (OECD), the World Trade Organization (WTO, formerly GATT) and the Asian-Pacific Economic Cooperation (APEC).

Maquiladoras Close to a quarter of Mexico's industry is in the more than 3000 maquiladora plants, employing about a million people, mainly near the US border. These are mostly foreign- (usually US-) owned plants in which the owner imports the equipment, raw materials and parts duty-free under bond, for assembly or finishing. Until 1994, all maquiladora products had to be exported to the country of origin. Since then, maquiladoras have been allowed to sell a steadily increasing percentage of their production in Mexico, and by 2001 there will be no limit on sales in Mexico.

Foreign Investment Following a series of reforms, foreign ownership is now permitted in most business activities. The main exceptions are areas reserved for the Mexican state (including oil and hydrocarbons, basic petrochemicals, electricity and nuclear energy) or to Mexican investors (including domestic land transportation, gasoline retailing, and radio and non-cable TV services). In some activities, such as airlines, forestry, cable TV, telephone services and port administration, a company's foreign stockholding is limited to 49%. In others, such as railroads, cellular telephony and some aspects of the oil and gas industry, permission to exceed 49% is needed from the Comisión Nacional de Inversiones Extranjeras (CNIE, National Foreign Investment Commission).

Of existing foreign direct investment in Mexico, the US accounts for about 60%, and Europe for 23%. Britain is the leading European investor. In 1998, foreign direct investment was around US$10 billion, with 62% going into the manufacturing industry and 18% into retail and wholesale trade.

Taxes There is a key distinction between doing business *with* Mexico from another country, and doing business *in* Mexico by setting up a 'permanent establishment' in

Mexico. Doing business *with* Mexico avoids many of the taxes and regulatory consequences of doing business *in* Mexico. Tax treaties between Mexico and the US, Canada and many European countries narrow the definition of 'permanent establishment.' Foreign companies use three main vehicles to conduct business in Mexico without setting up a 'permanent establishment.' They include commercial intermediaries, distributorship agreements, and technology licensing. Companies doing business *in* Mexico pay 32% corporate income tax and 1.8% corporate assets tax.

Finance The Mexican banking system went through a severe crisis and costly government bailout after the 1994 devaluation. Credit from Mexican domestic banks was sharply curtailed, and Mexican banks afterwards preferred to lend to large corporations. The banks were hit hard again by the 1998 financial crisis and one of the country's biggest banks, Banca Serfin, went under in 1999. Interest rates have fallen, from around 50% (short-term) in late 1995 to 17% in late 1999, but Mexican banks are still relatively reluctant lenders. Until new legislation is passed, they have little comeback against defaulters. NAFTA has, however, brought a big increase in the number of foreign banks operating in Mexico. Legislation in 1995 permitted foreign institutions to acquire majority stakes in all but three of Mexico's largest financial institutions.

The country's two development banks, Nacional Financiera (NAFIN) and the Banco Nacional de Comercio Exterior (BANCOMEXT), provide finance and other services for small and medium-sized Mexican firms that help the economy modernize and compete. BANCOMEXT has a network of business centers in Mexico and trade offices in the US, Canada and many countries in Europe, Latin America, the Caribbean and Asia. The Fondo de Inversión en Infraestructura (FINFRA) provides financing for infrastructure projects. Other sources of finance include the World Bank, the Interamerican Development Bank, the North American Development Bank, the Export/Import Bank of the United States, and the US Trade & Development Agency.

Trade Exhibitions

Trade exhibitions are a big business in Mexico and can be a major help to companies wanting to establish themselves there. The US Trade Center (☎ 5-140-26-00, fax 5-566-11-15), part of the US Department of Commerce, is a popular trade show organization for US businesses. The Asociación Mexicana de Promotores de Ferias, Exhibiciones y Convenciones (☎/fax 5-592-57-85, infor@ amprofec.com.org.mx) organizes shows in Mexico City. Many others are held at the Cintermex exhibition center in Monterrey.

Services

Many of Mexico City's top hotels are well appointed for business travelers. At least 14 of them have business centers equipped with computers, fax machines, photocopiers, secretarial help and conference rooms. Some can also provide translators and rent computers. Several hotels have special executive floors with big rooms, private lounges, and so on, and reduced corporate rates are available at many.

Foreign chambers of commerce and embassies can usually help organize translating and interpreting services.

Publications

The American Chamber of Commerce of Mexico (see Useful Organizations in Mexico City, earlier in this chapter) produces and sells several extremely informative publications including *Guide to Mexico for Business*, an annual introduction to the Mexican business scene; *Markets in Mexico: Location and Logistics*; and *Bu$iness Mexico*, a monthly magazine. Another good monthly magazine is *MB* (formerly *Mexico Business*) – for information visit its website, www.mexicobusiness.com.

Other useful introductions to the business scene in Mexico include *Doing Business in Mexico*, published by Price Waterhouse (☎ 5-722-17-00, fax 5-286-62-48), Río de la

Plata 48, Colonia Cuauhtémoc, México 06500 DF; and *Mexico Business Opportunities & Legal Framework*, published by Goodrich, Riquelme y Asociados (☎ 5-533-00-40), Paseo de la Reforma 265, Colonia Cuauhtémoc, México 06500 DF.

Internet Sites

Apart from the Internet sites already mentioned in this section, many of which have useful links, the site of the Mexican consulate in New York (www.quicklink.com/mexico) provides Mexican economic indicators and links to the sites of some Mexican financial institutions; Mexico Online has links to about a dozen sources of NAFTA information at www.mexonline.com/nafta.htm; and the Mexico Information Center for North America website (www.mexicotrade.com) provides a wide-ranging information service from BANCOMEXT.

WORK

Mexico has high unemployment and people who enter Mexico as tourists are not legally allowed to take jobs. The many expats working in Mexico have usually been posted there by their companies with all the right papers.

It's not completely unknown, however, for foreigners in Mexico to be given work by local employers. The most common avenue is language-teaching work in language schools, high schools *(preparatorias)* or universities, or personal tutoring. Mexico City is the best place in the country to get such work. The pay is low but you can live on it.

The News and the telephone yellow pages are sources of job opportunities. Ads in *The News* for work in Mexico City quote pay rates of US$6 to US$10 an hour. Positions in high schools or universities are more likely to become available with the beginning of each new term – contact institutions that offer bilingual programs or classes in English; for universities, arrange an appointment with the director of the language department. Language schools tend to offer short courses, so teaching opportunities with them come up more often and your commit-

ment is for a shorter time, but they may pay less than high schools and universities.

For teaching work it's certainly helpful to know at least a little Spanish, even though some institutes insist that only English be spoken in class.

A foreigner working in Mexico normally needs an FM3 visa, but a school may pay a foreign teacher in the form of a scholarship *(beca)*, and thus circumvent the law, or the school's administration will procure the appropriate papers. Just so you don't embark on the FM3 process lightly, a summary of the requirements for getting an FM3 follows.

FM3 Visa

The most important document for those intending to work in Mexico is the FM3 visa. Procedures for obtaining this are rather fluid but at the time of writing. To get an FM3 in Mexico you must submit the following, along with any fee required, to an office of the Instituto Nacional de Migración (INM – see the Travel Permits section, earlier in this chapter, for locations of its Mexico City offices):

- FMT (tourist card) or business traveler's FMN or FMVC (see Travel Permits, earlier)
- A copy of your birth certificate stamped by the Mexican consulate nearest your place of birth (you can get this done by mail, but call ahead to check the costs and procedural details)
- A copy of a professional certificate or academic degree appropriate to the kind of work you intend to do in Mexico, stamped by the Mexican consulate nearest the place where you obtained the certificate or degree
- Your passport
- A written job offer on the offering company's letterhead, including your name as it appears on your passport, and specifying the position you'll hold, the date you will start, and the salary you'll be paid, signed by a representative of the institution whose name appears on the Acta Constitutiva de la Institución (see below), with a photocopy of that representative's identification
- Notarized copy of the Acta Constitutiva de la Institución of the company offering you a job – this is the company's permit to do business in Mexico, and if you find out at a late stage in the proceedings that the company hasn't got one, you will

have wasted a whole lot of time, effort and probably money

- Ultima Declaración de Impuestos de la Institución – the company's most recent quarterly tax declaration, which it might choose to submit direct to the INM itself
- Eight passport-size photographs (not Polaroids) of you: four facing the camera, four in profile, with forehead and ears clearly visible

It's also possible to obtain an FM3 from a Mexican consulate outside Mexico. Requirements are similar but you won't need to show an FMT, FMN or FMVC.

Volunteer Work

The website of the International Study & Travel Center (☎ 612-626-4782, fax 612-626-0979, www.istc.umn.edu), 94 Blegen Hall, 269 19th Ave S, Minneapolis, MN 55455, USA, has a Volunteer Work database with many possibilities in Mexico. The Council on International Educational Exchange (☎ 212-822-2600, 888-268-6245, www.ciee.org), 205 E 42nd St, New York, NY 10017, USA, also has information on volunteer programs in Mexico.

The Casa de los Amigos (see the Places to Stay chapter) has files on volunteer opportunities in Latin America and can place fluent Spanish-speaking volunteers on projects in Mexico City focusing on issues such as education, street children, AIDS, refugees or democratic struggle. Most openings are for full-time work of six months or longer.

Getting There & Away

Most international visitors to Mexico City arrive by air. However you are traveling, give serious thought to taking out travel insurance and buying it as early as possible. If you buy it the week before you fly, you may find, for example, that you're not covered for delays to your flight caused by strikes. See Travel Insurance in the Documents section of the Facts for the Visitor chapter for more on insurance.

The peak travel periods of Semana Santa (Easter Week) and Christmas/New Year are hectic and heavily booked throughout Mexico: try to book transportation in advance for these periods.

AIR

The cost of flying to Mexico City depends on a few things. Those include the time of year (it's generally higher at Christmas/New Year and during summer holidays), how long you're staying (usually the longer the more

Warning

The information in this chapter is particularly vulnerable to change: Prices for international travel are volatile, routes are introduced and canceled, schedules change, special deals come and go, and rules and visa requirements are amended. Airlines and governments seem to take a perverse pleasure in making price structures and regulations as complicated as possible. You should check directly with the airline or a travel agent to make sure you understand how a fare (and ticket you may buy) works. In addition, the travel industry is highly competitive and there are many lurks and perks.

The upshot of this is that you should get opinions, quotes and advice from as many airlines and travel agents as possible before you part with your hard-earned cash. The details given in this chapter should be regarded as pointers and are not a substitute for your own careful, up-to-date research.

expensive), and whether or not you have access to discount or advance-purchase fares or special offers. The cheapest tickets often have to be bought months in advance. Airlines are a good source of information on routes, timetables and standard fares, but they don't usually sell the cheapest tickets, so consult travel agents or the Internet.

Some agencies specialize in officially or unofficially discounted air tickets. In the USA, the cheapest fares are available through 'consolidators.' In the UK, there are unbonded agencies known as bucket shops. Their tickets often cost less than advance-purchase fares. Most discount agencies are well established and honorable, but unscrupulous agents might take your money and disappear before issuing a ticket, or issue an unusable ticket. Check carefully before handing over your money and confirm the reservation directly with the airline.

Charter flights can offer cheap deals, too, and some agencies specialize in these. The dates of charter flights are fixed.

The Internet can be a useful source of cheap-fare quotes and bookings. In addition to the sites mentioned in following sections, Lonely Planet's website (www.lonelyplanet .com) has links to several useful pages. Most airlines have their own websites with online ticket sales, sometimes discounted for online customers. You'll find links to 500 or so airline websites on http://dir.yahoo.com/ business_and_economy/companies/travel/ airlines. To buy a ticket on the Internet you need to use a credit card.

Fares given in this book are a guide only; they are approximate and based on the rates advertised at research time. Quoted airfares do not imply a recommendation for the carrier.

Departure Tax

A departure tax equivalent to about US$17 is levied on international flights from Mexico. If you buy your ticket in Mexico,

Air Travel Glossary

Baggage Allowance This will be written on your ticket and usually includes one 20kg item to go in the hold, plus one item of hand luggage.

Bucket Shops These are unbonded travel agencies specializing in discounted airline tickets.

Cancellation Penalties If you have to cancel or change a discounted ticket, there are often heavy penalties involved; insurance can sometimes be taken out against these penalties. Some airlines impose penalties on regular tickets as well, particularly against 'no-show' passengers.

Check-In Airlines ask you to check in a certain time ahead of the flight departure (usually one to two hours on international flights). If you fail to check in on time and the flight is overbooked, the airline can cancel your booking and give your seat to somebody else.

Confirmation Having a ticket written out with the flight and date you want doesn't mean you have a seat until the agent has checked with the airline that your status is 'OK' or confirmed. Meanwhile you could just be 'on request.'

Consolidator This is the US equivalent of a bucket shop: a consolidator buys seats in bulk from airlines at considerable discounts and resells them to the public through travel agents or newspaper or magazine ads.

ITX An ITX, or 'independent inclusive tour excursion,' is often available on tickets to popular holiday destinations. Officially, it's a package deal combined with hotel accommodations, but many agents will sell you one of these for the flight only and give you phony hotel vouchers in the unlikely event that you're challenged at the airport.

Lost Tickets If you lose your airline ticket, an airline will usually treat it like a traveler's check and, after inquiries, issue you another one. Legally, however, an airline is entitled to treat it like cash: If you lose it, it's gone forever. Take good care of your tickets.

No-Shows These are passengers who fail to show up for their flight. Full-fare passengers who fail to turn up are sometimes entitled to travel on a later flight. The rest are penalized (see Cancellation Penalties).

On Request This is an unconfirmed booking for a flight.

Open-Jaw Tickets These are return tickets on which you fly to one place but return from another. If available, these can save you backtracking to your arrival point.

Overbooking Airlines hate to fly with empty seats, and because every flight has some passengers who fail to show up, airlines often book more passengers than they have seats. Usually excess passengers make up for the no-shows, but occasionally somebody gets bumped. Guess who it's most likely to be? The passengers who check in late.

Reconfirmation At least 72 hours prior to departure time of an onward or return flight, you must contact the airline and 'reconfirm' that you intend to be on the flight. If you don't do this, the airline can delete your name from the passenger list and you could lose your seat.

Restrictions Discounted tickets often have various restrictions on them – such as advance payment, minimum and maximum periods you must be away (for example, a minimum of two weeks or a maximum of one year) and penalties for changing the tickets.

Round-the-World tickets RTW tickets give you a limited period (usually a year) in which to circumnavigate the globe. You can go anywhere the carrying airlines go, as long as you don't backtrack. The number of stopovers or total number of separate flights is decided before you set off, and they usually cost a bit more than a basic return flight.

Stand-By This is a discounted ticket on which you fly only if there is a seat free at the last moment. Stand-by fares are usually available only on domestic routes.

Travel Periods Ticket prices vary with the time of year. There is a low (off-peak) season and a high (peak) season, and often a low-shoulder season and a high-shoulder season as well. Usually the fare depends on your outward flight. If you depart in the high season and return in the low season, you pay the high-season fare.

this tax (and the 15% consumer tax IVA) will be included in your ticket cost; if you buy it outside Mexico, it may or may not be. The letters XD on your ticket show that the tax has been paid. If not, you have to pay in cash at the airport check-in.

Taxes on domestic flights are IVA and an airport tax of about US$12.50 called TUA. In Mexico, both are normally included in quoted fares and paid when you buy the ticket. If you buy the ticket outside Mexico, TUA will not be included and you will have to pay it at check-in.

Other Parts of Mexico

All sizable cities in Mexico, and many smaller ones, have passenger airports, and nearly all of these have regular (usually daily) flights to/from Mexico City. Aeroméxico and Mexicana are the country's two largest airlines. The larger minor airlines serving Mexico City include (with areas or cities of Mexico that they fly to):

Aero California	North, West, Baja California
Aerocaribe	Gulf Coast, South, Southeast
Aerolíneas Internacionales	Center, North
Aerolitoral	Center, West, North, Baja California
Aeromar	West, Monterrey
Aviacsa	Guadalajara, Monterrey, Tijuana, Oaxaca, Southeast

Most of the above airlines are included in travel agents' computerized reservation systems both in Mexico and abroad.

Aerolitoral and Aeromar are feeder airlines for Aeroméxico and normally share its ticket offices and booking networks. A similar arrangement applies to Aerocaribe, Aerocozumel and Mexicana.

Fares Depending what fare you get, flying can be a good value for the money, especially considering the long bus trip that may be the alternative. Fares can vary considerably between airlines, and may also depend on whether you fly at a busy or quiet time of the day, week or year, and how far ahead you book and pay. High season is generally

---

TAESA

The airline TAESA was suspended by the Mexican government in 1999 following a crash of one of its planes in central Mexico in which 18 people died. TAESA was told it must meet 69 conditions – including addressing problems of insufficient financial resources, inadequate staffing and use of outdated manuals – before it could fly again. If the airline does not resume operations, many TAESA routes are likely to be taken over by other airlines.

July and August, and from mid-December to about January 10. For the cheapest fares, you usually have to pay for the ticket a few days ahead of time and you may have to fly late in the evening. Aeroméxico and Mexicana (theoretically competitors, however, both government-controlled until such time as the government sells its stakes) work in tandem. They have identical fare structures, but cheaper fares may be offered by other airlines. Roundtrip fares are often simply twice the price of oneways, but some cheaper advance-payment deals exist.

The following are some examples of the cheapest one-way low-season Aeroméxico/Mexicana fares from Mexico City, including taxes:

destination	fare
Acapulco	US$113
Cancún	US$235
Guadalajara	US$161
Mérida	US$128
Monterrey	US$141
Oaxaca	US$108
Puerto Vallarta	US$157
Tijuana	US$143
Zacatecas	US$115

The USA

The airlines with the most service from the USA to Mexico City include Alaska,

America West, American, Continental, Delta, Northwest, TWA, United, and the two main Mexican airlines, Aeroméxico and Mexicana. You can get direct flights to Mexico City from at least the following cities: Atlanta, Chicago, Dallas/Fort Worth, Denver, Detroit, Houston, Las Vegas, Los Angeles, Miami, New York, Oakland, Orlando, Phoenix, San Antonio, San Diego, San Francisco, San Jose and Washington. There are one-stop connecting flights from many others.

Three Internet sites worth checking for fares are Travelocity (www.travelocity.com), Flifo (www.flifo.com) and Expedia (http://expedia.msn.com). Some good fares are also offered by well-known student travel agencies, such as Council Travel (www.ciee.org) and STA Travel (www.statravel.com), with branches in many major cities. You don't necessarily have to be student to use these agencies.

Consolidators buy seats in bulk from airlines at considerable discounts and resell them to the public, usually through travel agents, but sometimes directly through newspaper and magazine ads. You can ask your travel agent about buying a consolidator ticket, or look for the consolidator ads in the travel section of the newspaper (they're the ones with tables of destinations, fares and toll-free numbers to call).

The Sunday editions of the *San Francisco Chronicle-Examiner*, *New York Times* and *Los Angeles Times* usually advertise cheap flights to Mexico City. Free papers such as New York's *Village Voice* and the Bay Area's *Express* and *San Francisco Bay Guardian* are also good places to look.

The following are some typical examples of roundtrip full and discounted fares to Mexico City at a week's notice in low season:

from	full/discounted fare
Chicago	US$450/360
Dallas/Fort Worth	US$560/360
Los Angeles	US$450/370
Miami	US$530/390
New York	US$600/400

Another possibility is a package-tour flight. Check newspaper travel ads and call a package tour agent, and ask if you can buy 'air only' (just the roundtrip air transportation, not the hotel or other features). This is often possible, and usually cheaper than buying a discounted roundtrip ticket.

Canada

Canadian Airlines, Air Canada and Mexicana all fly nonstop between Toronto and Mexico City, and there are many possible routings with a transfer in the US on these and US airlines. Low-season roundtrip fares start around C$650, but C$750 to C$900 is more likely. From Montreal, there are sometimes direct flights but you'll probably have to transfer at Toronto or a US airport. Low-season roundtrip fares from Montreal start around C$1050. Japan Airlines flies nonstop between Vancouver and Mexico City but with other carriers you'll be changing planes in the US. Roundtrip fares from Vancouver are from about C$1000.

Internet sites to check include Travelocity (www.travelocity.com), Flifo (www.flifo .com) and Expedia (http://expedia.msn .com). Some good fares are offered by well-known student travel agencies, all with branches in major cities, such as Travel CUTS (www.travelcuts.com) and STA Travel (www.statravel.com).

Australia & New Zealand

There are no direct flights from Australia or New Zealand to Mexico. The cheapest way to get there is usually via the USA (normally Los Angeles). Other routes go through Japan or South America with airlines such as Aerolíneas Argentinas. From Sydney/Melbourne to Mexico City via Los Angeles, typical low/high-season roundtrip fares are around A$2000/2300. Check US visa requirements if you're traveling via the USA.

STA Travel (www.statravel.com) and Flight Centre (☎ 13-18-66, www.flightcentre.com.au) are major dealers in cheap airfares in Australia and New Zealand, with offices in numerous main towns and cities. You could also check Internet sites such as www.travel.com.au, and travel agents' ads in the yellow pages and in newspapers.

The UK

British Airways flies nonstop to/from London. Roundtrip fares start at about UK£350. It's often equally cheap to fly with European or US airlines via Europe or the US. On a normal roundtrip ticket, you can often change the date of the return leg, subject to seat availability, at little or no cost – it's worth checking on this before you buy the ticket. If you're traveling via the USA, also remember to check US visa requirements.

For cheap tickets, try Internet sites such as Cheap Tickets (www.cheaptickets.com), Ebookers (www.ebookers.com) or Flifo (www.flifo.com), or pick up a good weekend newspaper travel section, such as the *Sunday Times* or Saturday's *Independent*, or look in *Time Out* or other London magazines. If a travel agent is registered with the ABTA (Association of British Travel Agents), as most are, ABTA will guarantee a refund or an alternative if the agent goes out of business after you have paid for your flight.

Reputable agencies offering good-value fares include Journey Latin America (☎ 020-8747 3108, www.journeylatinamerica.co.uk), 12 & 13 Heathfield Terrace, Chiswick, London W4 4JE; ưsit CAMPUS (☎ 0870-240-1010, www.campustravel.co.uk), at 52 Grosvenor Gardens, London SW1W 0AG; STA Travel (☎ 020-7581-4132, www.statravel.com), 86 Old Brompton Rd, London SW7 3LQ; and Trailfinders (☎ 020-7938-3939, www.trailfinder.com), 194 Kensington High St, London W8 7RG. All of these travel agencies have branches in many other cities, as well.

Continental Europe

Airlines flying nonstop to Mexico City include Aeroméxico from Madrid and Paris, Air France from Paris, Iberia from Madrid, KLM from Amsterdam and Lufthansa from Frankfurt. US airlines will have you changing planes in the US, as may tickets with alliance partners such as KLM and Northwest.

Roundtrip fare from most cities in western Europe to Mexico City start around US$500 to US$600. If you're traveling via the USA, remember to check US visa requirements.

An Internet site worth checking for flights from Europe is www.etn.nl. International student/youth travel agencies with branches in many countries, and usually with good fares for everybody, include STA Travel (www.statravel.com), Council Travel (www.ciee.org), and ưsit CAMPUS (www.campustravel.co.uk) as well as Kilroy Travels (www.kilroytravels.com). Other agencies specializing in cheap tickets and/or youth/student travel include the following:

France – Nouvelles Frontières (☎ 08 03 33 33 33, www.nouvelles-frontieres.com), Minitel 3615 NF, specializes in discount long-distance flights; has dozens of offices around France.

Germany – Cheap flights are advertised in the Berlin magazines *Zitty* and *Tip*. Agents include Alternativ Tours (☎ 030-8 81 20 89), Wilmersdorfer Strasse 94, Wilmersdorf, Berlin; and Atlas Reisewelt in many cities.

Italy – CTS (☎ 06-462 04 31, www.cts.it), Via Genova 16, off Via Nazionale, Rome, has branches all over Italy.

Netherlands – NBBS Reizen (☎ 020-624 09 89), Rokin 66, Amsterdam; Malibu Travel (☎ 020-626 32 20), Prinsengracht 230, Amsterdam

Spain – Halcón Viajes (902-300 600, www.g-air-europa.es), with over 500 branches around Spain, is reliable and has respectable fares. For youth and student fares try TIVE (☎ 91 347 77 88) at Calle José Ortega y Gasset 71, Madrid, and in 40 other cities.

Central & South America & the Caribbean

From Havana, Cuba, you can fly into Mexico City on Mexicana. Mexicana flies from Central American capitals, as do airlines such as Guatemala's Aviateca, TACA of El Salvador and Panama's COPA. Carriers between South America and Mexico City include Mexicana, Aeroméxico, COPA from Lima and Quito, Brazil's Varig and Aerolíneas Argentinas. Regular fares start at around US$500 from Caracas, US$550 from Lima, US$800 from São Paulo and

Airline Offices

If you need to buy an air ticket in Mexico City, a visit to a couple of the city's many travel agencies *(agencias de viajes)* is a good way of finding a suitable ticket. Some useful agencies are mentioned in this chapter's Travel Agencies section, or you could ask at your hotel for a full-service agency.

The following are the Mexico City offices of major domestic and international airlines:

Aero California
(☎ 5-207-13-92) Paseo de la Reforma 332

Aerocaribe
(☎ 5-448-30-00) Xola 535, Piso 28,
Colonia del Valle, or through Mexicana

Aerolíneas Argentinas
(☎ 5-130-30-30) Paseo de la Reforma 24

Aerolíneas Internacionales
(☎ 5-543-12-23) Beistegui 815,
Colonia Del Valle

Aerolitoral
same as Aeroméxico

Aeromar
(☎ 5-627-02-07) Airport

Aeroméxico
(central ☎ 5-133-40-00) Paseo de la
Reforma 80, Paseo de la Reforma 445 and
12 other offices around the city

Air France
(☎ 5-627-60-60) Poe 90, Polanco

Air New Zealand
(☎ 5-208-15-17) Río Nilo 80,
Colonia Cuauhtémoc

Alaska Airlines
(☎ 5-208-38-12) Hamburgo 213,
10th floor, Zona Rosa

Alitalia
(☎ 5-533-55-90) Río Tiber 103, 6th floor,
Colonia Cuauhtémoc

Allegro
(☎ 5-564-15-32) Baja California 128,
Colonia Roma Sur

America West
(☎ 5-514-01-94) Río Tíber 103, 6th floor,
Colonia Cuauhtémoc

American Airlines
(☎ 5-209-14-00) Paseo de la Reforma 300

US$900 from Buenos Aires. One-way and roundtrip fares are much the same. Asatej Group (www.asatej.org), with offices in nine Argentine cities and in Santiago de Chile and Montevideo, offers some interesting student/youth fares – for instance, US$500 to US$600 roundtrip from Buenos Aires.

Airports

Aeropuerto Internacional Benito Juárez (☎ 5-571-36-00), 6km east of the Zócalo, is Mexico City's only passenger airport (Terminal Aérea; Map 1).

The single terminal is divided into six *salas* (halls): Sala A – domestic arrivals; Sala B – check-in for Aeroméxico, Mexicana and Aero California, Aeromar and some other domestic departures, and the entrance to the Marriott Hotel; Sala C – check-in for Aviacsa and Aerolíneas Internacionales;

Sala D – check-in for some other domestic airlines; Sala E – international arrivals; Sala F – international check-in and the Hilton hotel.

The terminal has hosts of shops and facilities, including good bookstores such as those of INAH (the Instituto Nacional de Antropología e Historia) in Sala A and Conaculta (covering art, history and literature) in Sala C. There are many bank branches and casas de cambio where you can change money: Tamize in Sala E is one casa de cambio that stays open 24 hours. You can also obtain pesos from numerous ATMs.

The airport has plenty of pay phones and telephone casetas (call stations), plus shops selling cards for the pay phones (look for blue-and-yellow *'De Venta Aquí Ladatel'* signs). In Salas A and E you'll find 24-hour luggage lockers (US$3 for up to 24 hours)

Airline Offices

Aviacsa /Aeroexo
(☎ 5-716-90-04) Airport

Aviateca
(☎ 5-211-66-04) Paseo de la Reforma 509

British Airways
(☎ 5-387-03-00) Balmes 8,
Colonia Los Morales

Canadian Airlines
(☎ 5-208-18-83) Paseo de la Reforma 385,
14th floor

Continental Airlines
(☎ 5-283-55-00) Andrés Bello 45, Polanco

Cubana
(☎ 5-250-63-55) Temístocles 246, Polanco

Delta Air Lines
(☎ 5-279-09-09) Horacio 1855, Polanco

Iberia
(☎ 5-130-30-30) Paseo de la Reforma 24

Japan Airlines
(☎ 5-533-55-15) Paseo de la Reforma 295

KLM
(☎ 5-202-44-44) Paseo de las Palmas 735,
7th floor, Lomas de Chapultepec

LACSA
(☎ 5-211-66-04) Paseo de la Reforma 509

Lufthansa
(☎ 5-230-00-00) Paseo de las Palmas 239,
Lomas de Chapultepec

Mexicana
(☎ 5-448-09-90) Avenida Juárez 82 at
Balderas, Paseo de la Reforma 312 at
Amberes, and 17 other offices around the
city

Northwest Airlines
(☎ 5-202-44-44) Paseo de las Palmas 735,
7th floor, Lomas de Chapultepec

Qantas
(☎ 5-387-03-00) Balmes 8,
Colonia Los Morales

TAESA
(☎ 5-227-07-00) Paseo de la Reforma 30

United Airlines
(☎ 5-627-02-22) Hamburgo 213,
Zona Rosa

---

and car rental agencies. Sala A has a tourist information office (☎ 5-762-67-73), open 9 am to 8.30 pm daily (it will book hotel rooms for you), and post and telegraph offices.

BUS
Other Parts of Mexico

Mexico has a good intercity road and bus network. There are direct buses – often frequent – between Mexico City and every other sizable city in the country, including main towns on the US border. Fares typically run US$3 to US$4 per hour of travel (60km to 80km) on deluxe or 1st-class buses. There are, for instance, about 50 buses a day from Tijuana (42 hours, US$115 to US$125), 25 from Ciudad Juárez (24 hours, US$85 to US$95), at least 100 from Guadalajara (seven to eight hours, US$30 to US$40), and 30-odd each from Monterrey (11 hours,

US$50 to US$65) and Oaxaca (6½ hours, US$20 to US$33).

Classes Intercity buses vary enormously from comfortable, nonstop, air-conditioned deluxe services to secondhand, 2nd-class buses with broken seats and broken springs. For larger cities and for runs of more than a couple of hours, buses are nearly always in reasonable condition. Terms such as *de lujo* (deluxe) and *primera clase* (1st-class) can cover quite a wide range of comfort and price, depending on the bus company, but all of them offer some combination of features such as extra legroom, reclining seats, aircon (it helps to have a sweater or jacket handy), toilets (though not always toilet paper), drinks, snacks and videos. The most luxurious and most expensive lines, such as ETN, UNO and Turistar Ejecutivo, are sometimes regarded as a class of their own, *ejecutivo* (executive). Some *segunda clase* (2nd-class) buses are almost as quick and comfortable as 1st-class buses; others are uncomfortable and considerably slower because they'll stop anywhere for someone to get on or off.

Types of Service The best bus services are usually *sin escalas* or *sin parada* (nonstop), *directo* (very few stops), or *express* (few or no stops). An *ordinario* is a 2nd-class bus that stops wherever passengers want to get on or off. A *local* is a bus starting its journey at the bus station you're in. It will usually leave on time. A *de paso* bus, by contrast, is one that started somewhere else, may be late, and may or may not have seats available. Fortunately, all buses from Mexico City's four long-distance terminals are *locales*.

Safety There's a small risk of highway robbery on intercity routes. Buses are occasionally held up by bandits or robbed by people who board as passengers. The best way to avoid this risk is to travel only by daylight and use buses that take toll highways – deluxe and 1st-class buses usually do, where they exist; 2nd-class buses don't.

Mexico City Bus Terminals Mexico City has four main long-distance bus terminals, basically serving the four points of the compass: Terminal Norte (north), Terminal Oriente (called TAPO; east), Terminal Sur (south) and Terminal Poniente (west) – see Map 1 (Map 9 for Terminal Sur). All have luggage checkrooms *(guarderías)* or lockers, toilets, pay phones or casetas where you can make local or long-distance calls, post and fax offices, and cafeterias.

Unless you're going on a long trip (more than five hours), you can just go to the bus station, buy your ticket and go. For longer trips, buy your ticket in advance. Turismo Zócalo (☎ 5-510-92-19), at Carranza 67 in the Centro Histórico, sells tickets for the deluxe ETN, UNO and ADO GL services, which could save you an extra trip out to one of the bus stations. In the bus stations, bus lines have schedules posted at their ticket desks, but these aren't always comprehensive. For detail on bus services to places of interest near Mexico City, see the relevant sections of the Excursions chapter.

Most deluxe and 1st-class companies have computerized ticket systems that enable you to select your seat from an on-screen diagram. Try to avoid the back of the bus, which is where the toilets are and which tends to give a bumpier ride.

Many bus companies don't allow big baggage, such as backpacks or suitcases, to be carried in the passenger compartment. Some require you to check in luggage at their counter at least 30 minutes before departure. We suggest that you keep your valuables on your person in a money belt or pouch.

Terminal Norte The Terminal Central Autobuses del Norte (☎ 5-587-52-00), Avenida de los Cien Metros 4907, is about 5km north of the Zócalo (Ⓜ Autobuses del Norte). It's the largest of the four terminals and its name has many variations, including Autobuses del Norte, Central del Norte, Central Camionera del Norte, Camiones Norte or just CN. It serves places north of Mexico City (including cities on the US border), plus some to the west, including Guadalajara, Puerto Vallarta and Colima.

Over 30 different bus companies run services from the terminal. Deluxe and 1st-class ticket counters are mostly in the southern half of the building (to the right as you enter from the street), 2nd-class counters are mostly in the northern half.

There are luggage guarderías at the far south end of the terminal and in the central passage. The one at the south end is always open. Both charge US$1 to US$2 per item per 24 hours, depending on size. Don't leave valuables in your bags.

Near the middle of the main concourse are a Distrito Federal tourist information module (☎ 5-587-15-52), open 9 am to 4 pm Monday to Friday, a Banorte ATM and a casa de cambio with poor rates.

Terminal Oriente (TAPO) The Terminal de Autobuses de Pasajeros de Oriente (☎ 5-762-

59-77), usually known by its acronym TAPO, is at Calzada Zaragoza 200, at the intersection with Avenida Eduardo Molina, about 2km east of the Zócalo (Ⓜ San Lázaro). This is the terminal for buses serving destinations east and southeast of Mexico City such as Puebla, Veracruz, Oaxaca and the Yucatán Peninsula.

There's a Banamex ATM, giving cash on Visa, Cirrus, MasterCard and Plus System cards, in the passage between the metro and the terminal's circular main hall. Luggage lockers are underneath the ticket hall of the Estrella Roja bus company.

Terminal Sur The Terminal Central de Autobuses del Sur (☎ 5-689-97-95), at Avenida Tasqueña 1320, 10km south of the Zócalo (Ⓜ Tasqueña), is busy with services to Tepoztlán, Cuernavaca, Taxco and a few other southward destinations including Acapulco and Zihuatanejo. It has no money-changing facilities.

Terminal Poniente The Terminal Poniente de Autobuses (☎ 5-271-45-19), on Avenida Sur 122 at Avenida Río Tacubaya, is 8km southwest of the Zócalo (Ⓜ Observatorio). This is the terminal for very frequent shuttle services to nearby Toluca and for most other westbound buses. It has no money-changing facilities.

The USA

Since 1997 buses have been permitted to travel between cities in the US and Mexican interiors. Previously they had to terminate at frontier towns.

Companies such as Autobuses Americanos (☎ 800-784-8333 in the US) and El Expreso (☎ 713-650-6565 in the US) link US cities including Houston, Dallas, Austin, San Antonio and Chicago with central and northern Mexican cities including Mexico City. From Mexico City's Terminal Norte, the 1st-class ADO line runs daily buses to McAllen and Brownsville, Texas, for US$50. Services are developing with new companies and routes emerging.

Where there's no direct bus, the straightforward alternative is to get one to the US/

Mexico border then another on from there. Greyhound (☎ 800-231-2222 in the US, www.greyhound.com), Autobuses Americanos and others will carry you from US cities to cities on both sides of the frontier. If you get a bus to a city on the US side, it's usually easy to cross the border by foot, taxi or local bus. Greyhound fares include Los Angeles-Tijuana for US$15, Houston-Reynosa for US$25 and Los Angeles-El Paso for US$45.

Main Mexican border cities such as Tijuana, Mexicali, Nogales, Ciudad Juárez, Nuevo Laredo, Reynosa and Matamoros all have many daily bus departures to the capital. Services between the northeast border and Mexico City take around 15 hours for approximately US$50 to US$70. Buses to/from the northwest take twice as long (or more), and cost approximately double.

Guatemala & Belize

From Guatemala you must first get to a town inside Mexico, such as Tapachula, Comitán or San Cristóbal de Las Casas, from which there are direct buses to Mexico City. Normally this means changing buses at the border, but there are also daily direct buses from Guatemala City to Tapachula by Transportes Galgos, (☎ 253-4868), at 7ª Avenida 19-44, Zona 1, Guatemala City.

From Belize City there are frequent buses to Chetumal in Mexico, where you can get a direct bus to Mexico City.

TRAIN
Other Parts of Mexico

Mexico's passenger train system, in decline for decades, almost ground to a complete halt in the late 1990s after the government decided to sell off as much of the rail network as possible. The private companies that bought railroads simply stopped running many passenger trains because they were so unprofitable.

The few trains that still run are mostly one-class only, offering a seat but no air-conditioning, no food, no drinks and no sleeper cars. The only trains still serving Mexico City at the time of this writing were to/from Querétaro, San Miguel de Allende, San Luis Potosí and Saltillo (US$18.50) three times weekly; and to/from Orizaba, Córdoba and Veracruz (US$6.50) twice daily. These trains cost less than half the price of a 1st-class bus, and take about twice as long even when they run on time.

You can call Ferrocarriles Nacionales de México (FNM, Mexican National Railways) at Mexico City's Estación Buenavista (Buenavista Station) on ☎ 5-547-10-84 or ☎ 5-547-10-97 for information. There's usually an English-speaker available. The station is a cavernous building at Insurgentes Norte and Mosqueta (Eje 1 Norte), 1.2km north of Plaza de la República (Map 1).

The Ferrocarriles de México website (www.ferrocarriles.com) has passenger train schedules but is not official.

The USA

Taking a train to the Mexican border may not be much cheaper than flying when you add in meals and other expenses. Compared to buses, trains tend to be a little slower, a little cheaper, and less frequent. Amtrak (☎ 800-872-7245 in the US, www.amtrak.com) serves three US cities from which access to Mexico is easy: from San Diego, California, cross to Tijuana; from El Paso, Texas, cross to Ciudad Juárez; from Del Rio, Texas, cross to Ciudad Acuña. From San Antonio, Texas, you can take a bus to the border at Eagle Pass and cross to Piedras Negras, or continue to Laredo and cross to Nuevo Laredo. Los Angeles to El Paso, for example, takes 15 hours for US$179. Chicago-El Paso takes 48 hours for US$213.

Once across the border, don't waste too much time looking for another train. At the time of writing the only border town with passenger train service was Piedras Negras, from which a train departs on Tuesday, Thursday and Saturday at 7.30 am for the nine-hour trip to Saltillo (US$8.50). After a night in Saltillo (provided they haven't changed the schedule or canceled the train altogether) you could get a train to Mexico City. You would reach the capital, if lucky, about 36 hours after leaving Piedras Negras.

CAR & MOTORCYCLE

Driving in Mexico is on the right. To drive here requires a bit of Spanish, basic mechanical aptitude and reserves of patience. You should also note warnings about risk areas for highway robbery (see Dangers & Annoyances in the Facts for the Visitor chapter for numbers you can call for advice) and avoid intercity driving at night. See 'Driving Restrictions' in the Getting Around chapter for details of Mexico City's antipollution program, which bans almost every vehicle from being driven in the city at least one day each week.

Mexicans on the whole drive as sensibly as people anywhere. Density of traffic, poor surfaces, and frequent hazards such as potholes, speed bumps, animals, bicycles and children all help to keep speeds down.

The best makes of car to drive in Mexico are Volkswagen, Nissan/Datsun, Chrysler, General Motors and Ford, because they have manufacturing or assembly plants in Mexico, and dealers in most big Mexican towns. Big cars are unwieldy on narrow roads and streets, and a sedan with a trunk (boot) provides safer, more discreet storage than a station wagon or a hatchback. You should carry as many spare parts as you can manage. Spare fuel filters are very useful. Tires (including spare), shock absorbers and suspension should be in good condition. For security, have at least something to secure the steering wheel such as 'The Club'; consider installing a kill switch.

Motorcycling in Mexico is not for the faint-hearted, and mechanics are hard to come by. Generally, the only parts you'll find will be for Kawasaki, Honda and Suzuki bikes.

Two useful websites for people driving in or to Mexico are www.mexicomike.com and www.sanbornsinsurance.com.

Other Parts of Mexico

Mexican highways, even some toll highways, are not up to the US, Canadian or European standards. Still, the main roads are serviceable and fairly fast when traffic is not heavy. Most big cities can be bypassed. The major highways fanning out from Mexico City –

most with at least some toll sections – are 57/57D north to Querétaro, San Luis Potosí and Monterrey, with 45D branching west at Querétaro to León, Aguascalientes, Zacatecas and beyond; 150D east to Veracruz and Puebla (with branches to Oaxaca and Villahermosa); 95D south to Cuernavaca and Acapulco, with a branch to Taxco; and 15 and 15D west to Toluca and Guadalajara.

Driving at night is dangerous – unlit vehicles, rocks, people and livestock on the roads are common. Hijackings and robberies do occur. It's not generally safe to pull over and sleep in your parked vehicle – you should plan to reach accommodations well before nightfall. Especially on roads heading south from the US border, be prepared for drug and weapon searches by the army or police.

Traffic laws, including speed limits, rarely seem to be enforced on the highways. In cities, you'll want to obey the laws strictly so as not to give the police an excuse to hit you with a 'fine' payable on the spot. Speed limits are usually 100km/hour on highways and 30km/hour or 40km/hour in towns and cities.

In towns and cities you must be especially wary of *Alto* (Stop) signs, *topes* (speed bumps) and potholes. They are often not where you'd expect, and missing one can cost you in traffic fines or car damage.

Fuel All gasoline *(gasolina)* and diesel in Mexico is sold by the government's monopoly, Pemex (Petróleos Mexicanos), for cash (no credit cards). Most towns have a Pemex station and they are pretty common along most major roads.

The gasoline on sale is all unleaded *(sin plomo)*. There are two varieties: Magna Sin, equivalent to US regular unleaded, and Premium, equivalent to US 'super unleaded.' At 1999 rates Magna Sin cost about US$0.45 a liter (US$1.75 a US gallon), and Premium about US$0.50. Diesel fuel is also widely available, at a little under US$0.40 a liter. Regular Mexican diesel has a higher sulfur content than US diesel, but there is a new 'Diesel Sin' with less sulfur than before. If diesel drivers change their oil and filter

about every 3500km, they should have no problems.

All stations have pump attendants (who expect tips), but they aren't always trustworthy. Check that the pump registers zero pesos to start, and afterwards be quick to check that you have been given the amount you requested.

Toll Roads Mexico has more than 6000km of toll roads *(autopistas)*, which usually have four lanes. They are generally in much better condition and a lot quicker than the alternative free roads. They also have a reputation for being safer from highway robbery. Some are run by the federal government, and others by private concessions. *Cuotas* (tolls) vary from highway to highway: on average you pay about US$1 for every 10km to 20km.

Maps It pays to get the best road maps you can. The Mexican *Guía Roji Por Las Carreteras de México* road atlas is an excellent investment. In Mexico you can find it at decent bookstores and some city newsstands (US$6). It's updated annually and keeps tabs on new highways. The *Guía Verdi México Atlas de Carreteras* is similar. The 'Travelogs' that Sanborn's Insurance supplies free to its customers – sort of mile-by-mile companions for the driver – are very detailed and can be quite useful.

Parking It's difficult to park in Mexican cities. If a vehicle is parked illegally, inspectors may remove its license plates *(placadas)* and the owner will have to go to the municipal office, *tránsito* headquarters or a police station and pay a fine to get them back. It's inadvisable to park in the street overnight, and many cheap city hotels don't provide parking. Sometimes you can leave a car out front and the night porter will keep an eye on it. Usually you have to use a commercial *estacionamiento* (parking lot), which might cost US$4 or US$5 overnight.

If you're just overnighting and moving on in the morning, you can often find decent motels on highways just outside cities. These have easy parking.

Motorcycle Hazards Certain aspects of Mexican roads make them more hazardous for bikers than for drivers. They include poor signage of road or lane closures, lots of dogs on the roads, debris, deep potholes, vehicles without taillights, and lack of highway lighting.

Breakdown Assistance The Mexican tourism ministry, SECTUR, maintains teams of *Ángeles Verdes* (Green Angels) – bilingual mechanics in green uniforms and green trucks who patrol major stretches of highway daily during daylight hours searching for motorists in trouble. They make minor repairs, replace small parts, provide fuel and oil, and arrange towing and other assistance by radio if necessary. Service is free; parts, gasoline and oil are provided at cost. If you are near a telephone when your car has problems, you can contact them on their 24-hour hot line in Mexico City, ☎ 5-250-82-21, or through the national 24-hour tourist assistance numbers in Mexico City (☎ 5-250-01-23, 800-903-92-00).

Most serious mechanical problems can be fixed efficiently and inexpensively by mechanics in towns and cities as long as the parts are available.

Accidents Under Mexico's legal system, all drivers involved in a road accident are detained and their vehicles impounded while responsibility is assessed. For minor accidents, drivers will probably be released if they have insurance to cover any damage they may have caused. But the culpable driver's vehicle may remain impounded until damages are paid. If the accident causes injury or death, the responsible driver will be jailed until he or she guarantees restitution to the victims and payment of any fines. Determining responsibility *could* take weeks or even months. (Don't be surprised if Mexican drivers *don't* stop after accidents, they often don't.)

Your embassy can only give limited help (see Legal Matters in the Facts for the Visitor chapter). Adequate insurance coverage is the only real protection in this type of situation.

Rental Car rental in Mexico is expensive by US standards, but can be worthwhile if you want to visit several places in a short time. It's not worth it just for getting around Mexico City, unless you are familiar with the streets and have a healthy reserve of stamina and patience.

Renters must have a valid driver's license (your license from home is OK), passport and major credit card, and are usually required to be at least 23 (sometimes 25) years old. Sometimes age 21 is acceptable, but you may have to pay more. You should get a signed rental agreement and read its small print.

In addition to the basic daily or weekly rental rate, you must pay for insurance, tax and fuel. Check just what the insurance covers. Most agencies offer a choice between a per-kilometer deal or unlimited kilometers. The latter is usually preferable if you intend to do some hard driving.

Many car rental companies, including the big international names, have offices at the Mexico City airport and in or near the Zona Rosa; ask at any of the large hotels there. Any hotel except the very cheapest can put you in touch with a rental agent (who may be the hotel owner's brother-in-law). Sometimes it's necessary to book a couple of days ahead.

Prices vary quite a lot between agencies. The seemingly better deals offered by some small ones should be compared carefully with a larger chain before you take the plunge. One Mexico City firm offering good rates is Casanova Chapultepec (☎ 5-514-04-49), at Avenida Chapultepec 442 on the fringe of the Zona Rosa, with VW Sedans – the cheapest cars available from most firms – for US$30 a day including tax, insurance and unlimited kilometers (minimum two days, book one day ahead). A VW Golf on the same terms is US$38. Grey Line (☎ 5-208-11-63), at Londres 166, Zona Rosa, advertises cars from US$199 a week plus insurance and tax. International firms generally charge about double those kind of rates. You can book cars in Mexico through the large international agencies in other countries. This may sometimes get you lower

Rooftops of the Basílica de Nuestra Señora de Guadalupe

Religious artifacts inside the Basílica de Guadalupe of...guess who?

Sparkling El Ángel

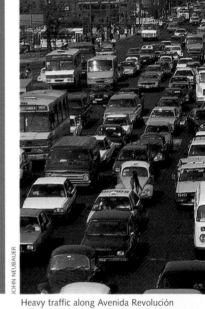

Heavy traffic along Avenida Revolución

Just a little juxtaposition on Paseo de la Reforma in the Zona Rosa

rates. Here's contact information for some major firms operating in Mexico:

Avis (☎ 800-230-4898 in the USA, ☎ 800-288-88-88 in Mexico) www.avis.com

Budget (☎ 800-472-3325 in the USA, ☎ 800-700-17-00 in Mexico) www.drivebudget.com

Dollar (☎ 800-300-3665 in the USA) www.dollar.com

Europcar (☎ 800-003-95-00 in Mexico) www.europcar.com

Hertz (☎ 800-654-3001 in the USA,☎ 800-709-50-00 in Mexico) www2.hertz.com

Thrifty (☎ 800-847-4389 in the USA,☎ 800-021-22-77 in Mexico) www.thrifty.com

The USA

Depending where you start, driving from the US border to Mexico City takes between 14 and 42 hours *without stops*. So it's not for those in a hurry. But if you have a bit of time, it can be an enjoyable way of traveling, especially if there's more than one of you. The major routes from the border to Mexico City are:

From Nogales (opposite Nogales, Arizona) via Mazatlán and Guadalajara (2230km, about 31 hours nonstop)

From Ciudad Juárez (opposite El Paso, Texas) via Chihuahua, Ciudad Jiménez, Torreón, Zacatecas, Aguascalientes, León and Querétaro (1840km, 22 hours nonstop)

From Nuevo Laredo (opposite Laredo, Texas) via Monterrey, Saltillo, San Luis Potosí and Querétaro (1160km, 14 hours nonstop)

From Matamoros (opposite Brownsville, Texas) via Soto La Marina, Tampico and Pachuca (1010km, 15 hours nonstop)

The border crossing points at Nogales/Nogales, El Paso/Ciudad Juárez, Laredo/Nuevo Laredo and Brownsville/Matamoros are all open 24 hours.

In the US or from Internet booksellers you may come across the *Guía Roji Por Las Carreteras de México* road atlas (see Maps under Other Parts of Mexico, earlier in this section) for around US$15.

Paperwork The rules for taking a vehicle into Mexico change from time to time. You can check with the American Automobile Association (AAA), a Mexican consulate, a Mexican Government Tourist Office or the toll-free information number ☎ 800-446-3942 in the USA.

Motor Insurance It is very foolish to drive in Mexico without Mexican liability insurance. If you are involved in an accident, you can be jailed and have your vehicle impounded while responsibility is assessed – or, if you are to blame for an accident causing injury or death, until you guarantee restitution to the victims and payment of any fines. This could take weeks or months. A valid Mexican insurance policy is regarded as a guarantee that restitution will be paid, and it will expedite release of the driver. Mexican law recognizes only Mexican *seguro* (car insurance), so a US or Canadian policy won't help.

Mexican insurance is sold in US towns near the Mexican border. At the busiest border-crossing points (including Nogales, Ciudad Juárez, Nuevo Laredo and Matamoros), there are insurance offices open 24 hours a day. Some deals are better than others. Two organizations worth looking into are the American Automobile Association (AAA, www.aaa.com) and Sanborn's (☎ 800-222-0158, www.sanbornsinsurance.com), both offer lots of useful travel information as well. There are also many other organizations. Short-term insurance is about US$6 a day for full coverage on a car worth US$5000; there are big discounts for longer periods of time.

Driver's License To drive a motor vehicle in Mexico, you need a valid driver's license from your home country.

Vehicle Permit To import a vehicle, you must get the important *permiso de importación temporal de vehículos* (temporary import permit for vehicles) at the *aduana* (customs) office at a border crossing.

In addition to a passport or proof of US or Canadian citizenship, the person importing the vehicle will need originals and at least one photocopy of each of the following documents, which must all be in his/her own name (people at the office may make photocopies for a small fee):

- tourist card (go to *migración* before you go to the aduana)
- certificate of title for the vehicle
- current registration card or notice
- driver's license (see above)
- either a valid international credit card (such as Visa, MasterCard or American Express) issued by a non-Mexican bank or cash to pay a very large bond (see below)

If the vehicle is not fully paid for, you need a notarized letter from the lender authorizing its use in Mexico for a specified period. If the vehicle is leased or rented, bring the original contract (plus a copy), which must be in the name of the person importing the car, and a notarized letter from the rental firm authorizing the driver to take it into Mexico. Note that few US rental firms allow this.

One person cannot bring in two vehicles. If you have a motorcycle attached to your car, you'll need another adult traveling with you to obtain a permit for the motorcycle, and he/she will need to have all the right papers for it. If the motorcycle is registered in your name, you'll need a notarized affidavit authorizing the other person to take it into Mexico. A special permit is needed for vehicles weighing more than 3000kg (about 3.3 US tons).

At the border there will be a building with a parking area for vehicles awaiting

Bonds For All?

In December 1999 Mexico briefly required all drivers of US-registered cars to pay a refundable deposit (bond) of up to US$800 by credit card or cash to obtain the vehicle permit. This regulation, intended to reduce illegal vehicle imports from the US by Mexicans, provoked such fierce opposition that it was abandoned almost immediately – but it is conceivable that something like it may be introduced in the future.

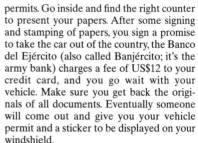

permits. Go inside and find the right counter to present your papers. After some signing and stamping of papers, you sign a promise to take the car out of the country, the Banco del Ejército (also called Banjército; it's the army bank) charges a fee of US$12 to your credit card, and you go wait with your vehicle. Make sure you get back the originals of all documents. Eventually someone will come out and give you your vehicle permit and a sticker to be displayed on your windshield.

If you don't have an international credit card, you will have to deposit a cash bond with the Banco del Ejército or an authorized Mexican *afianzadora* (bonding company). The required bond amounts for medium or small cars range from about US$500 for vehicles over 15 years old to around US$6000 for a vehicle up to two years old. There may be taxes and very hefty processing fees to pay, too. The bond should be refunded when the vehicle finally leaves Mexico and the temporary import permit is canceled. If you plan to leave Mexico at a different border crossing, make sure the bonding company will give you a refund there. There are offices for Banco del Ejército and authorized Mexican bonding companies at or near all the major border points.

Your vehicle permit entitles you to take the vehicle in and out of Mexico for the period shown on your tourist card. If the car is still in Mexico after that time, the aduana may start charging fines to your credit card and the car can be confiscated. The permit allows the vehicle to be driven by the owner's spouse or adult children or by other people if the owner is in the vehicle.

When you leave Mexico for the last time, you must have the permit canceled by the Mexican authorities. An official may do this as you enter the border zone, usually 20 to 30km before the border itself. If not, you'll have to find the right official at the border crossing. If you leave Mexico without having the permit canceled, once the permit expires the authorities may assume you've left the vehicle in the country illegally and start charging fines to your credit card.

Only the owner may take the vehicle out of Mexico. If the vehicle is wrecked completely, you must obtain permission to leave it in the country from either the Registro Federal de Vehículos (Federal Registry of Vehicles) in Mexico City or a Hacienda (Treasury Department) office in another city; your insurance company can help with this.

Guatemala & Belize

The most frequently used border crossings between Guatemala and Mexico are La Mesilla/Ciudad Cuauhtémoc on the Pan-American Highway, between Huehuetenango, Guatemala, and San Cristóbal de Las Casas, Mexico, and Ciudad Tecún Umán/Ciudad Hidalgo and El Carmen/Talismán, both between Quetzaltenango, Guatemala and Tapachula, Mexico.

The main border crossing between Belize and Mexico is Santa Elena/Subteniente López between Corozal, Belize, and Chetumal, Mexico.

Drivers entering Mexico from the south must go through the same procedures as those entering from the USA.

HITCHHIKING

Hitchhiking is never entirely safe in any country in the world, and we don't recommend it. Travelers who decide to hitch should understand that they are taking a small but potentially serious risk. People who do choose to hitch will be safer if they travel in pairs and let someone know where they are planning to go. A woman alone certainly should not hitchhike in Mexico, and two women alone are not advised to do so either.

Very few people hitchhike long distances in Mexico.

TRAVEL AGENCIES

Mexico City has hundreds of travel agencies. Many hotels above the budget bracket have their own travel agent's desk.

Mundo Joven at the Casa de Francia, Havre 15, Zona Rosa (☎ 5-525-04-07) and at Insurgentes Sur 1510, Local D (☎ 5-661-32-33; Map 6), specializes in cheap youth,

student and teachers' travel tickets, and has interesting fares for domestic and one-way international flights from Mexico City.

Other youth/student travel agencies are Viajes Educativos (☎ 5-661-42-35), Local B10, Insurgentes Sur 421 (entrance on Aguascalientes just north of Chilpancingo metro; Map 7), which can change dates on student and youth air tickets; and Cosmo Educación at Local 9, Avenida La Paz 58, San Ángel (☎ 5-550-33-73; Map 10) and at France 17A, Polanco (☎ 5-282-10-21; Map 8).

Two agencies well worth trying if you're looking for reasonably priced air tickets are Tony Pérez (☎ 5-533-11-48), Río Volga 1 at Río Danubio, behind the María Isabel-Sheraton Hotel (Map 6) and Viajes Universales (☎ 5-512-71-20), 3rd floor, Bucareli 12 (Map 5).

ORGANIZED TOURS

Few tour companies offer guided trips focused exclusively on Mexico City. Those listed below are among those that can organize customized trips, or give the city and surrounding areas a decent showing in tours that also cover other parts of Mexico.

Friendly Holidays (☎ 800-221-9748), 1983 Marcus Ave, Suite C130, Lake Success, NY 11042, USA

Fun World Travel (☎ 305-442-2434, 800-462-2434), 1000 Ponce de León Blvd, Suite 101, Coral Gables, FL 33134, USA – 10-day 'Aztecs & Mayans' tour spends three to four days in and around Mexico City before flying off to Guatemala and Cancún.

Journey Latin America (☎ 020-8747 8315, www .journeylatinamerica.co.uk), 12 & 13 Heathfield Terrace, Chiswick, London W4 4JE, UK – varied Mexican itineraries for groups and individuals often include Mexico City.

Sanborn's Viva Tours (☎ 210-682-9872, 800-395-8482), 2015 South 10th St, McAllen TX 78503 – week-long coach tours for seniors, focusing on Mexico City and San Miguel de Allende for around US$400 to US$500 from Texas.

Sunny Land Tours (☎ 800-783-7839, www.gorp .com/sunnyland), 166 Main St, Hackensack, NJ 07601, USA – nine-day 'Colonial Cities Grand Tour' covers Mexico City, San Miguel de Allende, Guanajuato, Guadalajara, Morelia and other destinations for around US$2200 from the USA.

Ecotours

If you're looking for a guided adventure or ecotourism trip elsewhere in Mexico, a good place to start checking for information is Ecogrupos de México (☎ 5-522-58-21, 5-522-58-03) at Hostal Moneda, Moneda 8, just off the Zócalo (see the Places to Stay chapter; Map 4). Ecogrupos offers a wide range of trips, from white-water rafting in Veracruz state to whale-watching off Baja California.

Trips with Río y Montaña Expediciones (☎ 5-520-20-41, www.rioymontana.com), Prado Norte 450, Lomas de Chapultepec, Mexico City, receive good reports: rafting, climbing, mountain biking and hiking are their stocks in trade.

AMTAVE (Asociación Mexicana de Turismo de Aventura y Ecoturismo, ☎ 5-663-53-81, info@amtave.com) at Avenida del Parque 22, Colonia Tlacopac, San Ángel, can supply information on 50-odd Mexican adventure tourism and ecotourism firms: you can contact them for a brochure or visit their website (www.amtave.com). The Eco Travels in Latin America website (www.planeta.com) is also a good source of information on active tourism.

Getting Around

Mexico City has a good, cheap, easy-to-use metro (underground railway). *Peseros* (small buses, also called *microbuses* or *micros*), buses and trolley buses ply all main routes and are cheap and useful. Taxis are plentiful but there's a significant danger of becoming an assault victim in many of them. Indeed, high levels of crime make some precautions advisable on all Mexico City transport – for important tips please see Dangers & Annoyances in the Facts for the Visitor chapter, and relevant sections in this chapter.

TO/FROM THE AIRPORT

Unless you are renting a car, use a taxi or the metro to travel to and from the airport. No bus or pesero runs directly between the airport and the city center.

Metro

Officially, you're not supposed to travel on the metro with anything larger than a shoulder bag – and at busy times the crowds make it inadvisable in any case. However, this rule is often not enforced at quieter times, especially before 7 am, after 9 pm and on Sunday.

The airport metro station is Terminal Aérea on *línea* (line) 5. It's 200m from the airport terminal building: leave the terminal by the exit at the end of Sala A (the domestic flight arrivals area) and continue walking in the same direction until you see the metro logo, which is a stylized 'M,' and the steps down to the station. One ticket costs US$0.15. To get to the hotel areas in the Centro Histórico and near the Alameda Central and Plaza de la República, follow signs for 'Dirección Pantitlán.' At Pantitlán station, you have to change trains: follow signs for 'Dirección Tacubaya' (línea 9). Change trains again at Chabacano, where you follow signs for 'Dirección Cuatro Caminos' (línea 2), which takes you to the Zócalo, Allende, Bellas Artes, Hidalgo and Revolución stations (but note the warning about Hidalgo in the Dangers & Annoy-

ances section in the Facts for the Visitor chapter).

Taxi

Comfortable 'Transportación Terrestre' taxis from the airport give good, safe service and are controlled by a fixed-price ticket system.

At least three kiosks in the terminal sell Transportación Terrestre tickets: one is in the international baggage collection area, one is in Sala E (the international flight arrivals area), and another is in Sala A (domestic arrivals). Maps on display near the kiosks divide the city into *zonas* (zones) that determine the fare from the airport. You can choose between *ordinario* and more expensive *ejecutivo* cabs. The Zócalo is in zona 2 (US$6.50/8.50 for ordinario/ejecutivo), the Alameda Central is in zona 3 (US$8/10) and the Zona Rosa is in zona 4 (US$9.50/11.50). One ticket is valid for up to four people and whatever luggage will fit in the trunk of the cab. If you simply mention a landmark such as 'Zócalo' or 'Plaza de la República' to the ticket clerk, you should receive a ticket for the correct zone – but it's advisable to check the map and count your change, as rip-offs are not unknown. Walk to the taxi stand outside and hand the ticket to the driver. (Porters may want to take your ticket and your luggage the few steps to the taxi, and will then importune you for a tip.) During the ride the driver might ask if you have a reservation for the hotel you have asked to be taken to. Even if you haven't, it's probably better to answer 'Yes.' Otherwise you might be subject to an insistent campaign to persuade you to go to some hotel that will pay the driver a commission for bringing you. At the end of a trip the driver is not supposed to expect a tip.

Ordinary street taxis can be picked up on busy Boulevard Puerto Aéreo, just beyond the metro station. They're cheaper than Transportación Terrestre cabs but not worth the security risk.

To go *to* the airport by taxi, get your hotel to book you a safe cab (see the Taxi section later in this chapter). This should cost approximately US$6 from the Zócalo area, US$9 from the Plaza de la República area, US$12 from the Zona Rosa and US$13 from Polanco.

TO/FROM THE BUS TERMINALS

The metro is the fastest and cheapest way to get to any of the city's four long-distance bus terminals, but the prohibition against luggage bigger than a shoulder bag may prevent you from using it. Each bus terminal is also reachable by city bus, pesero and/or trolley bus. Ticket-taxi systems operate for trips from the bus terminals to other places in the city: these *taxis autorizados* are cheaper than those from the airport, with fares similar to those of street taxis. If you want to travel *to* one of the bus terminals by taxi, get your hotel to call a safe one for you – it will cost around US$7 from the Centro Histórico or Plaza de la República area to the Terminal Norte.

Terminal Norte

Metro The metro station (on línea 5) outside the front door is named Autobuses del Norte, but on some maps it's marked Central Autobuses del Norte, or Autobuses Norte, or just 'TAN' (for 'Terminal de Autobuses del Norte'). To get to the city center, enter the metro station and follow signs for 'Dirección Pantitlán,' then change at La Raza, or at Consulado then Candelaria (at La Raza, you must walk for seven or eight minutes).

Taxi The terminal's Taxi Autorizado kiosk is in the central passageway: a cab for one to four people to Plaza de la República, Alameda, Zócalo or Terminal Oriente (TAPO), all in zona 3, costs US$3.50 (add US$1 to fares between 10 pm and 6 am).

Pesero, Bus & Trolley Bus You can also reach the center by pesero, bus or trolley bus. Trolley buses that are marked 'Eje Central,' 'Tasqueña,' 'Terminal Sur' or 'Central Camionera del Sur' waiting in front of the terminal head south along Eje Central Lázaro Cárdenas. They go within one block of the Alameda Central and six blocks from the Zócalo, and terminate at the Terminal Sur (Southern Bus Station) at Tasqueña, some 15km from the Terminal Norte. Fare is US$0.15. For peseros or buses going downtown, cross under the road via the underpass. Vehicles heading for central areas include those marked 'M(etro) Insurgentes,' 'M(etro) Revolución,' 'M(etro) Hidalgo' or 'M(etro) Bellas Artes.'

To reach the Terminal Norte from central areas, peseros, trolley buses and buses, head north on Eje Central at Donceles, one block north of the Palacio de Bellas Artes. Take one that's marked with some variation of the terminal's name such as 'Central Camionera Norte,' 'Central Norte,' 'Terminal Norte' or 'Central Camionera.' On Avenida Insurgentes, anywhere north of Insurgentes metro station, take a northbound 'Central Camionera' or 'Central Norte' bus or pesero.

Terminal Oriente (TAPO)

Metro TAPO is next door to San Lázaro metro station.

Taxi The taxi autorizado fare to the Zócalo (zona 1) is US$2.25; to the Alameda or Plaza de la República (zona 2) it's US$2.50; to the Zona Rosa (zona 3), US$3.50. Add US$1 between 10.30 pm and 6.30 am.

Pesero & Bus For peseros or city buses from TAPO, follow the signs to Calle Eduardo Molina: the bus stop is on the road outside. Peseros marked 'Zócalo' or 'Alameda' run to the city center, passing a few blocks north of the Zócalo.

To get to TAPO from central parts of the city, you can take a 'M(etro) San Lázaro' pesero on Arriaga at Mariscal, near Plaza de la República, or heading east on Donceles, north of the Zócalo. Or take a 'Santa Martha' bus from the west side of Trujano near the Alameda Central, every 20 to 30 minutes.

Terminal Sur

Metro Tasqueña metro station is a two-minute walk through a crowded hawkers' market from the Terminal Sur.

Taxi A taxi autorizado from Terminal Sur costs US$4.50 to the Zona Rosa, Alameda or Zócalo (zona 4); and to the streets north of Plaza de la República (zona 5), US$5.25. Add US$1 between 10 pm and 6 am.

Pesero, Bus & Trolley Bus 'Eje Central' and 'Central Camionera Norte' trolley buses run north from Terminal Sur along Eje Central Lázaro Cárdenas to the Palacio de Bellas Artes in the city center, then to the Terminal Norte. Walk to the left from Terminal Sur's main exit; you'll find the trolley buses waiting on the far side of the main road.

Heading south from the city center to Terminal Sur, trolley buses are marked with various combinations of 'Eje Central,' 'Tasqueña,' 'Taxqueña,' 'Autobuses Sur,' 'Terminal Sur' or 'Central Camionera del Sur.' You can pick them up one block north of the Palacio de Bellas Artes, on the Eje Central at Santa Veracruz. From San Ángel or Coyoacán, you can take a 'M(etro) Tasqueña' pesero or bus east on Avenida Miguel Ángel de Quevedo.

Terminal Poniente

Observatorio metro station is a couple of minutes' walk from the terminal. A taxi ticket to the Zona Rosa costs US$3.50, to the Zócalo US$4.25.

TO/FROM THE TRAIN STATION

The new Buenavista metro station, on línea B, is just outside the Estación Buenavista train station.

If you want a cab you'll have to run the risk of going outside the station and getting one on the forecourt or the street.

Many peseros and buses run along Avenida Insurgentes right past Estación Buenavista. To catch them, turn to the right outside the station and cross to the far side of Insurgentes. Ones marked 'M(etro) Insurgentes' run as far as Insurgentes metro station, which is at the intersection of Insurgentes and Avenida Chapultepec, 1km south of Paseo de la Reforma; ones marked 'San Ángel' continue to the southern suburb of that name. The 'M(etro) Insurgentes' express bus makes only a few stops, including Ribera de San Cosme (close to Plaza de la República) and Sullivan (just north of Insurgentes' intersection with Reforma).

To reach Estación Buenavista from central areas of the city, there are many buses and peseros going north on Avenida Insurgentes. Any marked 'Buenavista,' 'Central Camionera,' 'Central Norte,' 'M(etro) La Raza' or 'M(etro) Indios Verdes' will do. As you head north on Insurgentes, look for a large Suburbia store on the right and get off at the next stop. The station is topped with the words 'Ferrocarriles Nacionales de México.'

METRO

Mexico City's metro system offers the quickest and most crowded way to get around the city. The fare is US$0.15 a ride, including transfers.

About 4.7 million people ride the metro on an average weekday, making it the world's third-busiest underground railway, after Moscow's and Tokyo's. It has 162 stations and 191km of track on 11 lines *(líneas)*. An extension of the newest line, Línea B, was due to open in 2000.

The stations are generally clean and well organized, but often crowded, sometimes fearfully so. The cars at the ends of trains are usually the least crowded. The platforms can become alarmingly packed with passengers during the morning and evening rush hours (roughly from 7.30 to 10 am and 5 to 7 pm). At these times certain cars on some trains are reserved for women and children. Boarding for these is done through special *'Solo Mujeres y Niños'* lanes.

The best times to ride the metro are late morning, in the evening and Sunday.

From Monday to Friday, trains start at 5 am and end their final runs at 1 am; on Saturday trains run between 6 am and 2 am; on Sunday, 7 am and 1 am.

With such crowded conditions, it's not surprising that pickpocketing is common and that luggage bigger than a shoulder bag is not allowed. Be careful with your belongings. Hidalgo station is particularly notorious for thefts.

The metro is easy to use. Signs in stations reading 'Dirección Pantitlán,' 'Dirección Universidad' and so on name the stations at the end of the metro lines. Check a map for the *dirección* you want. Buy a *boleto* (ticket) – or several at once to save queuing next time – at the booth, feed it into the turnstile, and you're on your way.

When changing trains, look for *'Correspondencia'* (Transfer) signs.

If you've lost something on the metro, you can try calling ☎ 5-627-46-43.

PESERO, BUS & TROLLEY BUS

About 2.5 million people use Mexico City's thousands of peseros (also called *microbuses, micros* or *minibuses*) and buses daily; they run from about 5 am to midnight. They are most crowded from about 7.30 to 10 am and 5 to 7 pm. During other hours, the routes of most use to visitors are not too crowded.

Peseros are usually gray-and-green minibuses, but occasionally, in outer suburbs, they're Volkswagen Combi-type vehicles. They run along fixed routes, often starting or ending at metro stations, and will stop to pick up or drop off at virtually any street corner. Route information is displayed on the front of vehicles, often painted in random order on the windshield. Fares are US$0.20 for trips of up to 5km, US$0.25 for 5km to 12km, and US$0.35 for more than 12km. Add 20% between 10 pm and 6 am.

Municipally-operated full-size buses are gradually replacing peseros, which are privately owned, on many routes. Buses, and the few trolley bus services, make fewer stops than peseros; fares are US$0.20 or so. There are a few express buses, which stop only every kilometer or so.

Information on services to specific places around the city is given in the relevant sections of this book.

TAXI

Please read first the section on Taxi Crime under Dangers & Annoyances in the Facts for the Visitor chapter.

Mexico City has several classes of taxi. Cheapest – but in the recent wave of taxi crime the most dangerous – are the normal street cabs: mostly Volkswagen Beetles, but also small Nissans and other Japanese models. These have registration numbers beginning with the letter L (for *libre*, free) and a green stripe along the bottom of the license plate. Larger and more expensive, but safer, are radio taxis, Transportación Terrestre cabs from the airport, and *sitio* (taxi stand) cars, which have license plates beginning with S and bearing an orange stripe.

In cruising cabs, fares are computed by digital meter *(taxímetro)*. At this writing,

they should start with 5 pesos (US$0.50) on the meter. The total cost of a 3 or 4km ride in moderate traffic – from the Zócalo to the Zona Rosa, for instance – should be about US$1.50. Between 10 pm and 6 am, 20% is added to fares.

A radio or sitio cab costs three or four times as much, but it can't be emphasized enough that the extra cost brings a degree of security you could never have by taking a cruising cab.

You need not tip taxi drivers unless they have provided some special service.

CAR & MOTORCYCLE

Driving yourself around Mexico City is not recommended, unless you are familiar with the streets and have a healthy reserve of stamina and patience. Traffic is often very dense and impatient, one-way systems frustrating, signposting less-than-perfect and lane maneuvers tricky.

If you're traveling through Mexico by car, try to pick a hotel that has off-street parking (many above the budget bracket do). Otherwise use a supervised *estacionamiento público* (public parking lot) where your car will be safe. There are several of these in the streets south of Avenida Madero in the Centro Histórico, charging around US$1 an hour, and others south of the Alameda Central charging US$0.50 to US$0.75 an hour.

Don't drive alone at night in Mexico City. People who have done so have been hijacked, robbed and/or assaulted.

Many hotels catering to business travelers can arrange rentals of cars with bilingual drivers, on a daily basis if desired.

See Car & Motorcycle in the Getting There & Away chapter for further information on driving in Mexico.

Driving Restrictions

As part of its efforts to combat pollution, Mexico City operates an *'Hoy No Circula'* ('Don't Drive Today') program banning many vehicles, no matter where they are registered, from being driven in the city between 5 am and 10 pm on one day each week. The major exceptions are cars of 1993 model or

Have Bra, Can Bust

One hazard those who do drive in Mexico City will hopefully now be spared is the bogus traffic fine or bribe, extracted by traffic cops as a routine means of increasing their miserly salaries. In 1999, the city police chief Alejandro Gertz banned male traffic police from levying fines for motoring infractions in the Distrito Federal. Only the city's 64 female traffic officers were allowed to continue doing so. The anti-corruption measure was based on the theory that since women are not often the main household breadwinners, they will feel less pressure to supplement their earnings illegally.

newer (supposedly less polluting), which have a *calcomanía de verificación* (verification hologram sticker) numbered 0. This sticker, obtained under the city's notoriously corrupt vehicle pollution assessment system, exempts the vehicle from the Hoy No Circula provisions.

For other vehicles, including foreign-registered ones, the last digit of the registration number determines the day when they cannot circulate. Any car may operate on Saturday and Sunday:

day	prohibited last digits
Monday	5, 6
Tuesday	7, 8
Wednesday	3, 4
Thursday	1, 2
Friday	9, 0 & 'Permisos'*

* 'Permisos' are vehicles with a *permiso provisional de circulación* (provisional circulation permit).

Several times a year, when ozone readings in the city top 240 IMECA points (see Ecology & Environment in the Facts about Mexico City chapter), phase one of the city's environmental contingency plan comes into action, with a *'Doble Hoy No Circula'* ('Double Don't Drive Today') rule. This affects vehicles with verification hologram No 2 (the most polluting vehicles). Of these, all with license plates ending in an even number (and all permisos) are banned on the first day, and those ending in an odd number are banned the next. If phase one lasts into a third day, it automatically becomes phase two, in which all hologram No 2 vehicles and permisos are banned from the streets.

Cars with hologram No 1 (intermediate polluters) follow the simple Hoy No Circula restrictions all the time, even during contingency phases one and two.Further information on the driving restriction program is available on ☎ 5-526-95-63 or the website www.sima.com.mx.

WALKING

Your feet are often the best means of moving short distances around the city. If you do a lot of walking soon after arrival, however, the altitude will probably tire you quite quickly.

For security reasons don't walk down empty, dark streets at night. And obvious though it may sound, look both ways when you cross a street: some one-way streets have bus lanes running counter to the flow of the rest of the traffic, and on some divided streets traffic runs in the same direction on both sides.

ORGANIZED TOURS

Many travel agencies, including those in most top-end and mid-range hotels, can book you on bus tours within and outside the city, with English-language guides. A half-day whirl around the Zócalo area and the Museo Nacional de Antropología costs around US$25. Full-day city tours cost around US$40. The international tour company Gray Line (☎ 5-514-30-80), Hamburgo 182B in the Zona Rosa, is one well-established agency offering such tours. A local alternative (no relation) is Grey Line (☎ 5-208-11-63), at Londres 166, also in the Zona Rosa.

Many agencies also offer bus excursions farther afield. A typical day trip to Cuernavaca and Taxco, or to Puebla, costs around US$35, while a two-day outing to Cuernavaca and Taxco approaches US$100, and two days to San Miguel de Allende, Guanajuato and Querétaro is over US$200.

See Organized Tours in the Getting There & Away chapter for information on some firms who can take you on more adventurous trips outside the city.

Things to See & Do

HIGHLIGHTS

If you have time for only one sightseeing outing in Mexico City, you can hardly beat the **Museo Nacional de Antropología** (National Anthropology Museum), a treasure house of Mexican archaeological marvels that is one of the best museums of its kind in the world. The museum stands in the woodland expanse in the midst of the city, the **Bosque de Chapultepec**, which has many other attractions, including the **Museo Nacional de Historia** (National History Museum), **Museo de Arte Moderno** (Modern Art Museum), and the excellent children's museum **Papalote Museo del Niño**.

Also near the top of your list should be the **Centro Histórico** (Historic Center), a bustling area that is still the heart of the city, packed with fine colonial buildings and historic sites. Its nerve center is the **Zócalo**, one of the world's biggest city plazas, which is surrounded by the **Palacio Nacional** (the presidential palace), the **Catedral Metropolitana** (the city's cathedral) and the excavated **Templo Mayor**, the main temple of Aztec Tenochtitlán. The **Museo Nacional de Arte** (National Art Museum) is one of the best of several good museums in the Centro Histórico, while the panoramas from the modern **Torre Latinoamericana** skyscraper are tremendous.

West of the Centro Histórico is the **Alameda Central**, a leafy city center park surrounded by fine buildings and good museums. Highlights among these are the **Palacio de Bellas Artes** (Palace of Fine Arts), an early-20th-century marble concert hall and arts center, which houses some of the city's finest art by the great Mexican muralists, and the **Museo Mural Diego Rivera**, with a single outstanding mural by the greatest of them all, Diego Rivera.

One of the most enjoyable ventures outside the central area is to the southern suburbs **Coyoacán** and **San Ángel**, once separate villages. They're vibrant with weekend markets and contemporary entertainment,

and full of colonial charm and memories of Diego Rivera and Frida Kahlo, who lived here (you can visit their old homes). Today San Ángel is a well-heeled residential area, while Coyoacán has more of a bohemian atmosphere. A couple of kilometers south of San Ángel are the spectacular 1950s buildings of the **Ciudad Universitaria** (University City), Latin America's biggest university.

In the southeast of the city, a gondola ride along the ancient canals of **Xochimilco** is fun and can be combined with a visit to the beautiful **Museo Dolores Olmedo Patiño**, with its superb Diego Rivera collection.

For unique insight into Mexican Catholicism, head north of the center to the **Basílica de Guadalupe**, the country's most revered shrine, always thronged with worshippers and pilgrims.

Also try to find time to wander through some of the city's many fascinating **markets**, which sell everything from wonderful handicrafts and rare music recordings to everyday needs like shoes, furniture and food.

Mexico City on Foot

Altitude, pollution and noise can make walking in Mexico City tiring, especially for new arrivals. But for explorations of limited areas, your feet are often the best means of getting around. The walking tours suggested in some sections of this chapter are intended as fairly brief introductions to those areas of the city. You'll probably want to stop for a closer look at some of the sights along the way, and you'll almost certainly want to avail yourself of some of the places to eat and drink, too.

For walks away from the city's hustle and bustle, see the Cerro de la Estrella section in this chapter and the Desierto de los Leones, La Marquesa & Ajusco section in the Excursions chapter.

CENTRO HISTÓRICO

An excellent place to start your exploration of the city is where it began. The area known as the Centro Histórico (Historic Center) focuses on the large downtown plaza known as El Zócalo and stretches for several blocks in all directions from there. To the west it reaches almost as far as the Alameda Central.

The Centro Histórico is full of historic sites and buildings from the Aztec and colonial eras, contains some of the city's finest art and architecture, and is home to several absorbing museums. More than 1500 of its buildings are classified as historic or artistic monuments and it is on the Unesco World Heritage list. It also vibrates with modern-day street life and nightlife, and is a convenient area to stay in, with a range of hotels in all price categories except the very highest.

It was around the start of the 20th century that the wealthy of Mexico City started building new mansions outside the city's historic center. New middle-class suburbs such as Juárez, Cuauhtémoc, Roma and Condesa started appearing to the west and southwest. In the 1930s and '40s the Centro Histórico was still the commercial, political and intellectual center of Mexico City and Mexico the country. Many faculties of the city's university were still situated here. But by the 1980s much of the Centro had become very rundown, with many of its former mansions turned into overcrowded housing for the poor or simply abandoned.

Since then the city center has received a major, ongoing spruce-up to make it better fit its image as the hub of a proud nation. Streets have been pedestrianized, residential buildings have been rehabilitated, attractive new museums have opened, and glossy eateries and fashionable bars and stores have appeared. In the late 1990s, many of the thousands of street vendors earning a crust by operating small sidewalk stalls in the center were finally – after years of controversy, protests and sometimes riots – persuaded to relocate to other parts of the city.

Sunday is a particularly good day to explore this innermost part of the city. Traffic and street crowds are thinner, a relaxed atmosphere prevails, and museums are free.

Walking Tour

For an introductory exploration of the Centro Histórico, the **Zócalo** is certainly the place to start. Check the important sites around it – Palacio Nacional, Catedral Metropolitana, Templo Mayor. Then maybe make a detour north along **Argentina** and west on **Venezuela** to **Plaza Santo Domingo**, before returning south to the Zócalo and heading off west along one of the center's most important streets, **Avenida Madero**. Madero is dotted with fine buildings such as the **Palacio de Iturbide** and the **Casa de Azulejos** (a nice place to take refreshments) and ends at the **Torre Latinoamericana**, where you can take the elevator up to the 43rd floor for some marvelous panoramas.

Then you could stroll up Condesa, the street on the west side of the Casa de Azulejos, to Tacuba, to admire the handsome surrounds of the **Museo Nacional de Arte** and the beautiful **Correo Mayor** (main post office). Finally you could adjourn to relax in the **Alameda Central**, a little farther west (covered in the Alameda Central & Around section, later in this chapter), or return to the Zócalo along either **Avenida Cinco de Mayo**, another key artery of the Centro Histórico, or shoe-shop-lined **Calle 16 de Septiembre**, a good example of one of the more commercial streets south of Avenida Madero.

El Zócalo

The heart of Mexico City is the Plaza de la Constitución, more commonly known as the Zócalo (**Ⓜ** Zócalo).

The Spanish word *zócalo*, which means plinth or stone base, was adopted in 1843 when a monument to independence was constructed only as far as the base. The plinth is long gone but the name remains and has been adopted informally by a lot of other Mexican cities and towns for their main plazas.

The Aztec sacred precinct known as the Teocalli, which was the center of Tenochtitlán (and indeed of the entire Aztec universe), lay immediately to the north and northeast of the Zócalo. Today, *conchero* dancers remind everyone of this heritage with daily get-togethers in the Zócalo to carry out a sort of pre-Hispanic aerobics to the rhythm of booming drums, dressed in feathered headdresses and anklets and bracelets made of shells *(conchas)*.

In the 1520s, Cortés had the plaza paved with stones from the ruins of the Teocalli and nearby Aztec buildings. Until the early 20th century, the Zócalo was more often a maze of market stalls and narrow passageways than an open plaza. With each side measuring over 200m, it's one of the world's largest city plazas. (A fine way to get a sense of its size is to visit one of the upper-story restaurants overlooking it – see 'Square Meals' in the Places to Eat chapter.)

The Zócalo is also the home of the powers-that-be in Mexico City. On its east side is the Palacio Nacional, on the north, the Catedral Metropolitana, on the south, the Gobierno del Distrito Federal (Government of the DF), housed in two buildings built in 1532 and rebuilt in the 17th century. This makes the plaza a place for political protesters to make their points – it's often dotted with their makeshift camps.

The huge Mexican flag flying in the middle of the Zócalo is ceremonially lowered by soldiers of the Mexican army at 6 pm daily – at times with some difficulty – and carried into the Palacio Nacional.

Palacio Nacional

Home to the offices of the president of Mexico, the Federal Treasury, the National Archives, and dramatic murals by Diego Rivera, the National Palace fills the entire east side of the Zócalo. You need to bring your passport if you want to see the inside of the palace and its murals.

The first palace on this spot was built of tezontle, the local volcanic stone, by the Aztec emperor Moctezuma II in the early 16th century. Cortés had the palace destroyed in 1521 and rebuilt with a large courtyard so he could entertain visitors with Nueva España's first recorded bullfights. The palace remained in Cortés' family until the

king of Spain bought it in 1562 to house the viceroys of Nueva España. It was destroyed during riots in 1692, rebuilt again and continued to be used as the viceregal residence until Mexican independence in the 1820s.

As you face the palace you see three portals. On the right (south) is the guarded entrance for the president of Mexico and other officials. High above the center door hangs the **Campana de Dolores** (Bell of Dolores), which was rung in the town of Dolores Hidalgo by Padre Miguel Hidalgo in 1810 to signal the start of the Mexican War of Independence, and later moved to this place of honor in Mexico City. The bell is rung by the president of Mexico during the independence anniversary celebrations on September 15.

Enter the palace through the center door, where you must show your passport. Colorful **Diego Rivera murals** around the courtyard present Rivera's view of the history of Mexican civilization from the pre-Hispanic plumed serpent god, Quetzalcóatl, to the 1910 revolution. The murals are open for public viewing 9 am to 5 pm daily (free).

The murals above the main staircase were painted between 1929 and 1935. The main, largest work here is one of Rivera's masterpieces, *México a Través de los Siglos (Mexico Through the Centuries)*, which shows just about every major event and personage in modern Mexican history from Cortés' conquest of the Aztecs at bottom center to the Mexican Revolution at top center. Between these two is the eagle-on-cactus symbol of Aztec Tenochtitlán, which figures even today on the Mexican national flag. Portrayed on the right wall of the stairs is the ancient god Quetzalcóatl, as an antecedent to the Spanish-influenced centuries, along with other aspects of pre-Hispanic belief and life. On the left wall Karl Marx presides over what Rivera no doubt believed to be the logical outcome of the colonial and bourgeois eras, *La Lucha de Clases (Class War)*.

The unfinished series of frescos around the walkway level with the top of the staircase was painted by Rivera between 1945 and 1951. They show a sequence of pre-Hispanic cultures – Tenochtitlán, then the Tarascos of Michoacán, the Zapotecs and Mixtecs of Oaxaca, the peoples of Veracruz, and the Huastecs of the northeast. The Huastec panel emphasizes the theme of maize-growing and is followed by panels on two other plants of great importance in pre-Hispanic Mexico, the cacao (source of chocolate) and maguey (from which the drink *pulque* was made). Finally we see the arrival of Cortés – portrayed as a grotesque, knobby-kneed simpleton – in Veracruz in 1519.

A brief multilingual guide booklet to the murals is sold (together with a set of postcards) for US$3.50 at the foot of the main stairs.

The third (north) door of the palace leads to a courtyard where the **Recinto de Homenaje a Benito Juárez** (Place of Homage to Benito Juárez) is located. Juárez, one of Mexico's most respected heroes, was born into poverty in the state of Oaxaca, but rose to lead the reform movement in the 1850s and the fight against the French invaders in the 1860s. He served as president until his death in 1872. This exhibit includes various personal effects and displays on his life and times.

Catedral Metropolitana

The Metropolitan Cathedral, on the north side of the Zócalo, was built between 1573 and 1813. Though its inside is disfigured by scaffolding as builders struggle to arrest its uneven descent into the soft ground below, the cathedral is still impressive. Its size alone – 109m by 59m – is evidence of its importance among Mexican churches. Extraction of groundwater – the source of two-thirds of Mexico City's water – has greatly accelerated the subsidence.

The existing building replaced an earlier cathedral, built between 1524 and 1532 on the southern part of the present cathedral site. In Aztec times the Teocalli's main *tzompantli* (rack for the skulls of sacrifice victims) stood on part of the cathedral site. Cortés reportedly found more than 136,000 skulls of sacrificial victims here and nearby.

Exterior With a three-naved basilica design of vaults on semicircular arches, the cathe-

Benito Juárez

dral was built to resemble those in the Spanish cities of Toledo and Granada. Parts were added or replaced over the years, and as a result the cathedral is a compendium of the architectural styles of colonial Mexico. The grand portals facing the Zócalo were built in the 17th century in baroque style. They have two levels of columns and marble panels with bas-reliefs. The central panel shows the Assumption of the Virgin Mary, to whom the cathedral is dedicated; the west panel represents the entrusting of the keys of the church to St Peter; and the east panel shows the Ship of the Church.

The tall north portals facing Guatemala are older, dating from 1615, and are in pure Renaissance style.

The upper levels of the towers, with their unique bell-shaped tops, were not added until the end of the 18th century. The exterior was finally completed in 1813 when architect Manuel Tolsá added the clock tower topped by statues of Faith, Hope and Charity, and a great central dome, all in neoclassical style, to create some unity and balance.

Interior The cathedral has a central nave and two side naves lined by 14 richly decorated chapels. Much of the interior is a forest of scaffolding. A plumb line hanging from the dome above the central nave graphically demonstrates the building's subsidence problem.

The cathedral's chief artistic treasure is the Altar de los Reyes (Altar of the Kings), behind the main altar, a masterly exercise in controlled elaboration and a high point of baroque style in Mexico. Created between 1718 and 1735, it's made of carved wood covered in gold foil. At the cathedral's southwest corner, the eye-catching Capilla de los Santos Ángeles y Arcángeles (Chapel of the Holy Angels & Archangels) is another exquisite example of baroque sculpture and painting, with a huge main altarpiece and two smaller altarpieces decorated by the 18th-century painter Juan Correa. Four oval paintings by another leading 18th-century Mexican artist, Miguel Cabrera, grace the cathedral's side entrances.

A lot of other artwork in the cathedral was damaged or destroyed in a 1967 fire. The intricately carved late-17th-century wooden choir stalls by Juan de Rojas, and the huge gilded Altar de Perdón (Altar of Forgiveness), all in the central nave, have been restored, and work continues.

Sagrario Metropolitano Adjoining the east side of the cathedral is the 18th-century sacristy, built to house the archives and vestments of the archbishop. Its exterior is a superb example of the ultradecorative Churrigueresque style. It's not open to visitors.

Templo Mayor

The main *teocalli* (sacred precinct) of Aztec Tenochtitlán, demolished by the Spaniards in the 1520s, stood on the approximately 500-sq-meter site now occupied by the cathedral and the blocks to its north and east. Archaeologists established the location of the teocalli's Templo Mayor (Great Temple) in the first half of the 20th century. But the decision to excavate it, with the demolition of colonial buildings that this entailed, wasn't made until 1978 after electrical workers digging northeast of the cathedral happened upon an 8-ton stone-disk carving of the Aztec goddess Coyolxauhqui, She of Bells on Her Cheek. The Templo Mayor is thought to be on the exact spot where the Aztecs saw their symbolic eagle with a snake in its beak, perched on a cactus – still the symbol of Mexico today.

RICHARD I'ANSON

The Catedral Metropolitana

Aztecs believed the spot was, literally, the center of the universe.

The entrance is just east of the cathedral, on pedestrianized Seminario. On your way from the Zócalo stop at the Fuente de Tenochtitlán,the fountain on the east side of the cathedral. In the pool is a brass model of the ancient island city of Tenochtitlán and the causeways that linked it to the lakeshore.

A walkway around the site reveals the temple's multiple layers of construction. There's plenty of explanatory material, though all in Spanish. Like many other sacred buildings in Tenochtitlán, the temple, first begun in 1375, was rebuilt several times – partly because of land subsidence and partly to express the growing glory of the Aztecs. Each rebuilding was bigger than the one before and was accompanied by the sacrifice of captured warriors. In 1487 these rituals were performed at a frenzied pace to rededicate the temple after one major reconstruction. Michael Meyer and William Sherman write in *The Course of Mexican History*:

In a ceremony lasting four days sacrificial victims taken during campaigns were formed in four columns, each stretching three miles. At least twenty thousand human hearts were torn out to please the god . . . . In the frenzy of this ghastly pageant, the priests were finally overcome by exhaustion.

What we see today are sections of several of the temple's different phases, though hardly anything is left of the seventh and final version, built about 1502 and seen by the Spanish conquistadors. A replica of the Coyolxauhqui stone lies near the west side of the site. At the center of the site is an early platform dating from about 1400. On the southern half of this, a sacrificial stone stands in front of a shrine to Huizilopochtli, the Aztec god to whom human sacrifices were made to ensure that the sun would continue to rise. On the northern half is a chac-mool figure in front of a shrine to the water god Tláloc. This platform was built when the Aztecs were not yet the chief power in the Valle de México. By the time the Spanish arrived, a 40m-high double pyramid towered above this spot,

with steep twin stairways climbing to shrines to the same two gods.

Elsewhere in the site don't miss the late-15th-century stone replica of a tzompantli, carved with 240 stone skulls, and the mid-15th-century Recinto de los Guerreros Águila (Sanctuary of the Eagle Warriors, an elite band of Aztec fighters), decorated with colored bas-reliefs of military processions.

A little bookstore next to the ticket office sells publications about the Templo Mayor and other Mexican archaeological and anthropological topics: *The Great Temple and the Aztec Gods* in the Minutiae Mexicana series is a good little guide to the Templo Mayor and its background.

The site (☎ 5-542-06-06) is open 9 am to 5 pm Tuesday to Sunday (US$2 including entrance to the Museo del Templo Mayor; free on Sunday).

Museo del Templo Mayor The excellent museum in the northeast part of the Templo Mayor site houses artifacts from the site and gives a good overview (in Spanish) of Aztec civilization. Pride of place is given to the great wheel-like stone of Coyolxauhqui. She is shown decapitated – the result of her murder by Huizilopochtli, her brother, who also killed his 400 brothers en route to becoming top god. Other outstanding exhibits include a mask of jade and obsidian, full-size terracotta eagle warriors, and a model of the Templo Mayor. The following is an outline of the exhibit rooms:

Sala 1: Antecedentes – the early days of Tenochtitlán

Sala 2: Coyolxauhqui, Ritual y Sacrificio – Aztec beliefs and practices of war and human sacrifice

Sala 3: Tributo y Comercio – Aztec government and trade

Sala 4: Huizilopochtli – lord of the Templo Mayor and demander of sacrifices

Sala 5: Tláloc – the water and fertility god

Sala 6: Flora y Fauna – plants and animals of the Aztecs and their empire

Sala 7: Agricultura – the chinampa system and its products

Sala 8: Arqueología Histórica – archaeological finds from the post-conquest era

Calle Moneda

As you walk back toward the Zócalo from the Templo Mayor, Moneda is the first street on your left. Many of its buildings are made of tezontle. The streets off the east side of the Zócalo are a commercial area, but lacks the glitz of the west side.

The **Museo de la Secretaría de Hacienda y Crédito Público** (Museum of the Secretariat of Finance & Public Credit, ☎ 5-228-12-45), Moneda 4, houses a good collection of Mexican art, from 18th-century master Juan Correa to 20th-century giants Diego Rivera, Rufino Tamayo and Antonio Ruiz, plus interesting contemporary work. The setting is a colonial-era archbishop's palace that has two lovely, peaceful, stone-columned courtyards adding to its attraction. In Aztec times this site was part of the teocalli (see Templo Mayor, above), and a pyramid dedicated to the god Tezcatlipoca, lord of the underworld and protector of warriors, stood here. Some Aztec remnants are visible on the ground floor. The museum is open 10 am to 5 pm Tuesday to Sunday (US$0.80, free on Sunday).

The **Museo Nacional de las Culturas** (National Museum of Cultures, ☎ 5-512-74-52), Moneda 13, in a fine courtyarded building constructed in 1567 as the colonial mint, has a collection of exhibits showing the art, dress and handicrafts of several world cultures. Hours are 9.30 am to 5.45 pm Tuesday to Sunday (free).

A block farther east then a few steps north is a former convent housing the **Museo José Luis Cuevas** (☎ 5-542-89-59), Academia 13, founded by Cuevas, a leading modern Mexican artist. The collection includes engravings by Picasso, sketches and drawings by Rembrandt, and work by Cuevas himself and artists of the 'Generación de la Ruptura' (Generation of the Break) of the past 20 years. Hours are 10 am to 5.30 pm Tuesday to Sunday (US$0.50, free on Sunday).

The fine Churrigueresque **Templo de la Santísima** (Church of the Holy Sacrament) is three blocks east of the Museo Nacional de las Culturas, at the corner of Moneda and Santísima. The profusion of ornamental sculpture on the façade – including ghostly busts of the 12 apostles and a representation of Christ with his head in God's lap – is the main reason to visit this church. Most of the carving was done by Lorenzo Rodríguez between 1755 and 1783.

Nacional Monte de Piedad

Facing the west side of the cathedral on the corner of Avenida Cinco de Mayo is Mexico's national pawnshop, founded in 1775. As one of the world's largest second-hand shops, it's worth a look – who knows, you may pick up a bargain. Housed in a large, dark building, it's open 8.30 am to 6 pm Monday to Friday, 8.30 am to 3 pm Saturday. The site was once occupied by the Palacio de Axayacatl, where Cortés and his companions were first lodged by Moctezuma II in 1519.

Plaza Santo Domingo

This plaza, two blocks north of the cathedral on the corner of Brasil and Cuba, is a less formal affair than the Zócalo. Modern-day scribes, with typewriters and antique printing machines, work beneath the **Portal de Evangelistas** along its west side.

At the north end of the plaza is the pink stone **Iglesia de Santo Domingo**, dating from 1736, a beautiful piece of baroque architecture, decorated on its east side with carved stone figures of Santo Domingo (Saint Dominic) and San Francisco (Saint Francis). Below the figures, the arms of both saints are symbolically entwined as if to convey a unity of purpose in their lives. The front or southern façade is equally beautiful, with 12 columns around the main entrance. Between the columns are statues of San Francisco and San Agustín, and in the center at the top is a bas-relief of the Assumption. The monastery that once adjoined the church was destroyed during the mid-19th-century anticlerical movement.

On the corner of Brasil and Venezuela, opposite the church, is the Palacio de la Escuela de Medicina, a fine courtyarded building constructed in the 18th century as the headquarters of the Inquisition in Mexico. It houses the interesting **Museo de** la **Medicina Mexicana** whose displays range from a model of a *baño de temazcal* – a kind of pre-Hispanic sauna used for spiritual purification – to collections of plants used in modern folk medicine, and a reconstruction of a 19th-century pharmacy. It's open 10 am to 6 pm daily (free).

Murals

In addition to the Palacio Nacional, other buildings near the Zócalo hold important works by Diego Rivera, and by other great Mexican muralists including José Clemente Orozco and David Alfaro Siqueiros.

The **Secretaría de Educación Pública** (☎ 5-329-68-60) is at Argentina 28, 3½ blocks north of the Zócalo. The building – originally a convent – now houses government offices. The two front courtyards are lined with 120 fresco panels done by Rivera and assistants in the 1920s. Helpfully, each panel is labeled. The paintings range over a host of subjects covering the lives, traditions, struggles and expectations of the Mexican people. On the ground floor of both courtyards themes include industry, agriculture, class struggle and artisan and festival scenes. On the middle floor of both courtyards, black-and-white murals painted by Rivera's assistants cover science, work and the coats of arms of the Mexican states. The top floor of the first courtyard is shared between Mexican heroes such as Emiliano Zapata and the Aztec king Cuauhtémoc and panels on themes such as brotherhood, women and the arts. On the top floor of the second courtyard, scenes of capitalist decadence are juxtaposed with proletarian and agrarian revolution – Frida Kahlo can be spotted in the panel called *En El Arsenal*. Through the Pasaje Maestros Mexicanos is the building's rear courtyard whose staircase is adorned with *Patricios y Patricidas* by Siqueiros and others. The Secretaría de Educación Pública is open 9 am to 5 or 6 pm Monday to Friday (free). Sometimes the attendants ask for ID, so it's best to take your passport.

From there, walk 1½ blocks back toward the Zócalo along Argentina, turn east into Sierra to the **Museo de San Ildefonso** (☎ 5-789-25-05), half a block along at Sierra 16.

Constructed in the 16th century as the Jesuit college of San Ildefonso, the beautiful building was remodeled in Churrigueresque style in the 18th century. From 1867 to 1978 it served as the Escuela Nacional Preparatoria, a prestigious training college for teachers. From 1923 to 1933, Rivera, Orozco, Siqueiros and others were brought in to adorn it with murals. Most of the work in the main patio and on the grand staircase is by Orozco, inspired by the Mexican Revolution (recently ended at the time). Some very interesting temporary exhibitions are staged in the building. The amphitheater, off the lobby, holds a gigantic Creation mural by Rivera. The museum is open 11 am to 6 pm daily except Monday (US$2, free on Tuesday).

Three blocks south (through the Zócalo), on the corner of Pino Suárez and Corregidora, is the **Suprema Corte de Justicia**, Mexico's Supreme Court. It houses four big murals on the theme of justice, painted here by Orozco during WWII. At the time of writing the building was only open for pre-arranged group visits.

Sculpture

Opposite the Supreme Court, on the west side of Pino Suárez, is a sculpture showing the Aztecs' legendary discovery of an eagle eating a snake atop a cactus. The sculpture demonstrates the continuing importance of pre-Hispanic, particularly Aztec, roots in Mexico's modern national consciousness.

Palacio de Iturbide

The beautiful baroque façade of the Iturbide Palace rises at Avenida Madero 17, 5½ blocks west of the Zócalo. Built between 1779 and 1785 for colonial nobility, it was claimed in 1821 by General Agustín Iturbide, a hero of the Mexican struggle for independence from Spain. The general responded favorably to a crowd that gathered in front of the palace in 1822 beseeching him to be their emperor (Iturbide is thought to have instigated the gathering himself). Iturbide proclaimed himself Emperor Agustín I but reigned over Mexico for less than a year, abdicating in 1823 after General

Santa Anna announced the birth of the Mexican republic.

The palace was restored in 1972 and now houses the Fomento Cultural Banamex (the cultural promotion section of the bank Banamex). Some excellent art and craft exhibitions are hung in the fine courtyard and several of the rooms. Hours are usually 10 am to 7 pm daily (free).

Casa de Azulejos

A block west of the Palacio de Iturbide, between Avenida Madero to Avenida Cinco de Mayo, stands one of the city's gems. The Casa de Azulejos (House of Tiles, ☎ 5-510-96-13) dates from 1596, when it was built for the Marqués del Valle de Orizaba. Although the superb tile work that has adorned the outside walls since the 18th century is in Puebla style, it's said that most of the tiles were actually produced in China and shipped to Mexico on the Manila *naos* (Spanish galleons used up to the early 19th century).

The building now houses the Sanborns Casa de Azulejos store and restaurants and is a good place to buy a newspaper or have refreshments. The main restaurant (see the Places to Eat chapter) is set in a lovely courtyard with a Moorish-style fountain. The staircase on the north side of the restaurant is decorated with a 1925 mural by Orozco.

Torre Latinoamericana

The Latin American Tower (☎ 5-510-42-84), the landmark 1950s skyscraper on the corner of Avenida Madero and Eje Central Lázaro Cárdenas, has an observation deck and café on its 43rd and 44th floors. The views are spectacular, smog permitting. If it's a day when you can see hills outside the city from street level, it'll be a good day to go up the tower. In the ground-floor lobby near the elevators, check out the aerial-view print depicting Mexico City in 1856, a tiny fraction of the city's present size. Tickets are sold at the street-level entrance on the Eje Central side of the building. The tower is open 9.30 am to 10.30 pm every day (US$3).

It also boasts the 'highest aquarium in the world' on the 38th floor (2358m above sea level), open 10 am to 10 pm daily (US$2.25).

Museo Nacional de Arte

The National Museum of Art (☎ 5-512-32-24), Tacuba 8, contains exclusively Mexican work. You'll recognize the building by the distinctive bronze equestrian statue in front, of the Spanish king Carlos IV (who reigned from 1788 to 1808) by the sculptor and architect Manuel Tolsá. Called *El Caballito* (The Little Horse), it originally stood in the Zócalo but was moved here in 1852. Note that the name refers to the horse, not the rider, who reigned shortly before Mexico gained its independence. A sign points out that the statue is preserved as a work of art (and not, it's implied, out of respect for the king).

The museum – once the Communications Ministry – was built at the turn of the 20th century in the style of an Italian Renaissance palace. A grand marble staircase greets you as you enter. The collections represent every style and school of Mexican art. The work of José María Velasco, depicting Mexico City and the countryside in the late 19th and early 20th centuries, is a chief highlight. Velasco's landscapes show the Lago de Texcoco still filling half the Valle de México, and Guadalupe and Chapultepec far outside the city.

Other collections include 17th-century religious paintings by Antonio Rodríguez, Juan Correa and José de Ibarra; 18th- and 19th-century sculptures; some portraits by Antonio Poblano; prints of skeletal figures sweeping streets; and anonymous paintings with social and political themes. The museum's hours are 10 am to 5.30 pm Tuesday to Sunday (US$2, free on Sunday). It's two blocks north of Avenida Madero, along Mata or Condesa – the streets either side of the Casa de Azulejos.

Colegio de Minería

Across the street from the Museo Nacional de Arte is the College of Mining, at Tacuba 5, a beautiful neoclassical building designed by Manuel Tolsá and built between 1797 and

1813. Four meteorites found in Mexico are on display in the entrance, echoing the time when this first engineering school in the Americas was the center of Mexican mining activity. The building is now used by the UNAM engineering faculty and related organizations. It's open 8.30 am to 9 pm Monday to Friday (free).

Jardín de la Triple Alianza & Museo del Ejército y Fuerza Aérea

The tiny Garden of the Triple Alliance – so small you can't actually set foot in it – on the corner of Tacuba and Mata, opposite the Museo Nacional de Arte, has striking relief sculptures of the three kings who set up the 15th-century Triple Alliance: Izcoatl of Tenochtitlán, Nezahualcóyotl of Texcoco, and Totoquihuatzin of Tlacopan. Just down Mata is the Museo del Ejército y Fuerza Aérea (Army & Air Force Museum), with weapons and historic documents, open 10 am to 6 pm Tuesday to Saturday, 10 am to 4 pm Sunday (free).

Correo Mayor

Certainly worth a look while you're in this bit of the city, even if you have no mail to send or collect, is the Main Post Office on Tacuba at Eje Central Lázaro Cárdenas. It's a beautiful early-20th-century building in the style of an Italian Renaissance palace. It was designed by the Italian Adamo Boari, who was also responsible for the first phase of work on the Palacio de Bellas Artes across the road.

Cámara de Senadores & Asamblea Legislativa

The upper house of Mexico's federal congress, the Cámara de Senadores, meets in a building on Xicoténcatl, the pedestrian street on the east side of the Museo Nacional de Arte. It's usually in session from September to December. The Distrito Federal's elected assembly, the Asamblea Legislativa del Distrito Federal (ALDF), uses the old Cámara de Diputados building around the corner at Donceles and Allende. The Cámara de Diputados itself, the lower house

of the federal congress, now uses the modern Palacio Legislativo on Avenida Congreso de la Unión, about 2km east of the Zócalo. It, too, is in session from September to December.

ALAMEDA CENTRAL & AROUND

A little less than 1km west of the Zócalo is the pretty Alameda Central, Mexico City's largest downtown park. In the surrounding streets are some of the city's most interesting buildings and museums.

Bellas Artes and Hidalgo metro stations are at the northeast and northwest corners of the Alameda respectively. You can also reach the Alameda from the Zócalo area on a 'M(etro) Chapultepec,' 'M(etro) Hidalgo' or 'M(etro) Auditorio' pesero westbound on Avenida Cinco de Mayo.

Alameda Central

What is now a pleasant, verdant park was once an Aztec marketplace. In early colonial times, it became the site of the Catholic Church's *autos da fé*, where heretics were sentenced and often burned or hanged. Then in 1592 Viceroy Luis de Velasco decided the growing city needed a pleasant area of pathways, fountains and trees, and ordered the Alameda to be created. It took its name from the poplar trees *(álamos)* with which it was planted. By the late 19th century the park was dotted with European-style statuary, a bandstand was the venue for free concerts, and gas lamps provided illumination at night. Today, the Alameda is a popular, easily accessible refuge from the city streets. It's particularly busy on Sunday, when food and hawkers' stalls set up and you may catch a rock or salsa band playing open-air.

On the south side of the Alameda, facing Avenida Juárez, is the **Hemiciclo a Juárez,** a gleaming white semicircle of marble columns about a regally seated statue of Benito Juárez (1806-72). Born a poor Zapotec villager in the state of Oaxaca, Juárez – one of Mexico's most respected heroes – rose to become national president and victor over the armies of Maximilian of Hapsburg.

Palacio de Bellas Artes

This splendid white-marble concert hall and arts center (☎ 5-521-92-51), commissioned by President Porfirio Díaz, dominates the east end of the Alameda. Construction of the Palace of Fine Arts began in 1904 under the Italian Adamo Boari, architect of the nearby Correo Mayor, who favored neoclassical and art nouveau styles. It was supposed to be completed by 1910 for the grandiose centennial celebration of Mexican independence. But the heavy marble shell of the building began to sink into the spongy subsoil, and work was halted. Then came the Mexican Revolution, which delayed completion until 1934. Architect Federico Mariscal finished the interior with new designs reflecting the art deco style of the 1920s and '30s.

The palace houses some of Mexico's finest murals, which dominate immense wall spaces on the second and third levels. If you can understand some Spanish, the printed interpretations alongside them add greatly to their interest.

On the second level are two large, striking, early 1950s works by Rufino Tamayo: *México de Hoy* (Mexico Today) at the west end, and *Nacimiento de la Nacionalidad* (Birth of Nationality), a symbolic depiction of the creation of the Mexican mestizo identity, at the east end.

At the west end of the third level is Diego Rivera's famous *El Hombre, Contralor del Universo* (Man, Controller of the Universe), which was first commissioned for the Rockefeller Center in New York. The Rockefeller family had the original destroyed because of its anticapitalist themes, but Rivera recreated it even more dramatically here in 1934. Capitalism, with accompanying sickness, death, wars and a presiding Jehovah/Jupiter figure, is shown on the left; socialism, with health and peace and a decapitated Caesar, is on the right. Lenses in the center project images of the cosmos and the microscopic world, suggesting the power that science gives humanity to determine its own destiny – a recurring Rivera theme.

Artwork on the north side of the third level includes David Alfaro Siqueiros' three-part *La Nueva Democracia* (New Democ-

racy), painted in 1944-45, and Rivera's four-part *Carnaval de la Vida Mexicana* (Carnival of Mexican Life), from 1936. At the east end of this level is José Clemente Orozco's eye-catching *La Katharsis* (Catharsis), from 1934-35. Contradictory 'natural' and 'social' poles of human nature are symbolized by naked and clothed figures fighting each other. Scenes of violence, depravity and degradation result from this conflict, but a giant bonfire threatens to consume all and provide a spiritual rebirth.

Siqueiros' *Apoteosis y Resurección de Cuauhtémoc* (Deification & Resurrection of Cuauhtémoc), painted in 1950-51, occupies the south side of the third level. Cuauhté-moc (the last Aztec king) is shown on the left being tortured by Spanish conquistadors, and on the right rising again to lead the oppressed peoples of the Third World.

Another highlight of the palace is the beautiful stained-glass stage curtain in the theater, depicting the highlands of Mexico, based on a design by Mexican painter Gerardo Murillo ('Dr Atl'). Tiffany Studios of New York assembled the curtain from almost a million pieces of colored glass. It's normally lit up for public viewing on Sunday mornings and just before performances (☎ 5-529-93-20 for times).

You can view the murals and look around the palacio 10 am to 6 pm Tuesday to Sunday (US$2.50, free on Sunday). The palacio also stages some top-class temporary art exhibitions and is home to the Ballet Folklórico, a dazzling spectacle of Mexican music and dance – see the Entertainment chapter for more on this and other events here. A good bookstore and an elegant café are on the premises, too.

Museo Franz Mayer

The Franz Mayer Museum (☎ 5-518-22-65), Avenida Hidalgo 45, is a sumptuous, once-private collection of mainly Mexican art and crafts, housed in the lovely 16th-century Hospital de San Juan de Dios, on the little Plaza de Santa Veracruz opposite the north side of the Alameda. This oasis of calm and beauty is the fruit of the efforts of Franz Mayer, who was born in Mannheim,

Germany, in 1882. He moved to Mexico, became a citizen, earned the name 'Don Pancho,' and amassed a collection of mainly Mexican and European sculpture, painting, silver, textiles, ceramics and furniture masterpieces – among them a superb collection of Talavera ceramics from Puebla. The collection of sculpture also includes some very fine pieces.

The way into the main part of the museum is to the right as you enter. To the left is a lovely colonial garden courtyard. The suite of rooms on the courtyard's west side is done in antique furnishings and is very fine, especially the lovely chapel. On the north side is the delightful Cafetería del Claustro (see the Places to Eat chapter). The museum is open 10 am to 5 pm Tuesday to Sunday (US$1.50, free on Tuesday).

Museo de la Estampa & Iglesia de la Santa Veracruz

Also on Plaza de Santa Veracruz is the Museum of Engraving (☎ 5-521-22-44), at Avenida Hidalgo 39. It has a permanent collection of engravings, lithographs and other graphic art by top Mexican artists, as well as the tools of these techniques and temporary graphics exhibits. Hours are 10 am to 6 pm, Tuesday to Sunday (US$1).

The Iglesia de la Santa Veracruz, next door, leans noticeably as a result of land subsidence. It dates from 1730 and is one of the city's most harmonious baroque constructions. Inside is the tomb of neoclassical architect and sculptor Manuel Tolsá.

Pinacoteca Virreinal

At Dr Mora 7, facing the west side of the Alameda, is the Viceregal Picture Gallery (☎ 5-510-27-93), a former church and monastery that is home to a collection of 16th- to 19th-century baroque and religious paintings. A contemporary mural by Federico Cantú is also displayed. It's open 9 am to 5 pm Tuesday to Sunday (US$1, free on Sunday).

Museo Mural Diego Rivera

Among Diego Rivera's most famous murals is *Sueño de una Tarde Dominical en la Alameda* (Dream of a Sunday Afternoon in the Alameda), a large work, 15m long by 4m high, painted in 1947. The museum housing this work (☎ 5-510-23-29) is just west of the Alameda, fronting the Jardín de la Solidaridad. It was built in 1986 specifically to house this one mural – which had stood in the Hotel del Prado, nearby on the south side of Avenida Juárez, until the hotel was badly damaged in the 1985 earthquake.

In the mural, the artist imagines many of the figures who walked in the city from colonial times onward, among them Hernán Cortés, Benito Juárez, Santa Anna, Emperor Maximilian, Porfirio Díaz, and Francisco Madero and his nemesis, General Victoriano Huerta. All are grouped around a skeleton dressed in prerevolutionary lady's garb. Rivera himself (as a pug-faced child) and his artist wife, Frida Kahlo, appear next to the skeleton.

Charts in English and Spanish identify all the characters. Photos and other material on Rivera's life and work add to the interest, and the museum also has space for temporary exhibitions. It's open 10 am to 6 pm Tuesday to Sunday (US$1).

Jardín de la Solidaridad

The little park-like plaza in front of the Museo Mural Diego Rivera is the Solidarity Garden, created in 1986 on the site of the old Hotel Regis, to commemorate the struggle of Mexico City's residents to rebuild their city after the earthquake of 1985. People gather here to play and watch open-air chess.

La Ciudadela

About 700m south of the Alameda, near Balderas metro station, is the Citadel, a large colonial building now housing the **Biblioteca de México** (Library of Mexico). It was from their base here in February 1913, during the Mexican Revolution, that supporters of the ousted dictatorial president Porfirio Díaz waged bloody street battles that resulted in the deposition and execution of President Francisco Madero. Nearby is a handicrafts market – see the Shopping chapter.

AROUND PLAZA DE LA REPÚBLICA

This plaza, 600m west of the Alameda Central, is dominated by the huge, domed Monumento a la Revolución. It's the hub of an area with a few interesting sites and many cheap and mid-range places to stay. Revolución metro station is close.

Monumento a la Revolución

Begun in the early 1900s under Porfirio Díaz, this structure was originally meant to be a meeting chamber for senators and deputies, but construction (not to mention Díaz's term as president) was interrupted by the revolution. It was modified and given its present role as the Monument to the Revolution in the 1930s: the tombs of the revolutionary and postrevolutionary heroes Pancho Villa, Francisco Madero, Venustiano Carranza, Plutarco Elías Calles and Lázaro Cárdenas are inside its wide pillars (not open to the public).

Beneath the monument lies the interesting little **Museo Nacional de la Revolución** (☎ 5-546-21-15), with exhibits on the revolution and the decades leading up to it. Evocative photos and old newsreels help convey the feeling of the period. You enter from the northeast quarter of the garden around the monument. It's open 9 am to 5 pm Tuesday to Saturday, 9 am to 3 pm Sunday (US$0.50, free on Sunday).

Frontón México

On the north side of Plaza de la República is the Frontón México, Mexico City's grand art deco arena for the sport of jai alai. See the Entertainment chapter for more on jai alai and the Frontón.

Museo de San Carlos

The Museum of San Carlos (☎ 5-566-85-22), Puente de Alvarado 50 at Ramos Arizpe, has a fine collection of European art. It's housed in a mansion designed for the Conde (Count) de Buenavista by Manuel Tolsá in the late 18th century. Later home to often-elected president (and victor at the Alamo) Santa Anna, the mansion subsequently became a cigar factory, then headquarters of the national lottery and later a school, before its present incarnation as an art museum (since 1968). The museum's permanent collection of European paintings from the 14th to 20th centuries includes works by Goya, Rubens, Van Dyck, Tintoretto, Zurbarán and Ingres. Good temporary exhibitions are also staged here. Hours are 10 am to 6 pm Wednesday to Monday (US$2, free on Sunday).

Iglesia y Panteón de San Fernando

North of Puente de Alvarado on Plaza de San Fernando stands the handsome 18th-century baroque Church of San Fernando, with finely carved doors and an impressive altar. Next door is the Panteón de San Fernando, a cemetery containing the tombs of illustrious 19th-century Mexicans such as Benito Juárez, Vicente Guerrero, Ignacio Zaragoza and Melchor Ocampo. The cemetery is open 8 am to 3 pm daily.

Lotería Nacional

Mexico's lottery is a national passion, and the tall art deco tower on the west side of Paseo de la Reforma opposite Avenida Juárez is the game's headquarters. Walk into the building and up the stairs almost any Monday, Tuesday or Friday after 7.30 pm, take a seat in the cozy auditorium, and at exactly 8 pm the *sorteo*, the ceremony of picking the winning numbers, begins. Cylindrical cages spew out numbered wooden balls, which are plucked out by uniformed pages who announce the winning numbers and amounts. Admission is free (Ⓜ Hidalgo).

From the steps of the lottery building you can't help but notice one of the city's most striking modern sculptures, in front of the Torre Caballito office building across the street. It's a huge golden-yellow affair by Sebastián, representing a horse head in memory of the statue *El Caballito*, which used to stand here but is now in front of the Museo Nacional de Arte.

Museo Universitario del Chopo

This northern outpost of UNAM, at Dr González Martínez 10 (☎ 5-535-22-88),

La Lotería

Anyone can play the lottery in Mexico. Odds are about the same as anywhere, but buying a ticket enables you to at least fantasize for a day or two about what you would do with US$3 million. Retire to Mexico? Travel the world for a few decades? Give it to charity? Buy a lifetime supply of Bohemia lager? Not unlike lottery players elsewhere, Mexicans resort to all sorts of calculations, hunches and superstitions to decide which numbers may be lucky.

Tickets are sold all over Mexico by street vendors and at kiosks. Normally they cost US$0.60, US$1 or US$1.50 and each ticket is for a particular draw *(sorteo)* on a specific date. Prizes range from around US$600 to more than US$3 million. The winning numbers are posted at ticket sales points, but since the ticket numbering system is a bit complicated, get a ticket seller or someone else who understands it to check your ticket against the list of winners. Each draw usually has several series of tickets, each of which gets a share of the many prizes.

Added spice is provided by regular *zodiaco* draws, where each ticket bears a sign of the zodiac as well as a number. Then four times a year – including at Christmas – there are *sorteos especiales*, with tickets costing up to five times as much as usual, and prizes similarly higher. Other draws may be suspended for a couple of weeks beforehand to ensure good sales for the big one.

Profits from the lottery go to government charity projects. Good luck!

Found in garbage

stages varied music and dance performances and avant-garde art shows, in an unusual early-20th-century iron-and-glass building. Its basic hours are 10 am to 2 pm and 3 to 7 pm Tuesday to Sunday (US$0.60, free on Tuesday).

ACE Gallery

This gallery (☎ 5-546-90-01), at Pimentel 3, is one of Mexico City's leading contemporary art spaces. Opened in 1997, it provides a strong link between Mexican and US art (there are other ACE Galeries in New York and Los Angeles). It's open 10 am to 7 pm Monday to Saturday.

PASEO DE LA REFORMA & ZONA ROSA

Paseo de la Reforma, Mexico City's main boulevard and one of its status addresses, runs southwest from the Alameda Central down through the Bosque de Chapultepec. It's said that Emperor Maximilian of Hapsburg laid out the boulevard to connect his palace on Chapultepec Hill with the older section of the city. He could look eastward straight along it from his bedroom, and ride it across open countryside to work in the Palacio Nacional on the Zócalo.

Most visitors to Mexico City pass along Reforma at some stage, or call at one of the banks, shops, hotels, restaurants or embassies on or near it. The Zona Rosa (Pink Zone), a restaurant, hotel, shopping and entertainment district, lies on the south side of Reforma west of Avenida Insurgentes, roughly 2km from the Alameda Central.

Many modern skyscrapers have now joined the older buildings on Reforma. The Paseo is also dotted with noteworthy pieces of sculpture and art (Maps 5 & 6). A few blocks due south of Plaza de la República on Reforma is the **Glorieta Cristóbal Colón** traffic circle, with a statue of Christopher Columbus at its center, done by French sculptor Charles Cordier in 1877. About 600m farther southwest, in the main hall of the Bital bank building at Reforma 156, is a large fresco painted in 1965 by Juan O'Gorman.

The busy intersection of Reforma and Avenida Insurgentes is marked by the **Mon-**

umento a **Cuauhtémoc**, the last Aztec emperor. Two blocks northwest of this intersection is the **Jardín del Arte**, a sliver of shady park that becomes an interesting open-air artists' bazaar from 10 am to 4 pm on Sunday. Come for a stroll and a browse, if not to buy.

The most striking of the modern buildings on Reforma is the **Centro Bursátil**, an arrow of reflecting glass at Reforma 255, 600m southwest of Insurgentes. It's the home of the Bolsa Mexicana de Valores, Mexico City's stock exchange.

The Zona Rosa, glossy, sometimes sleazy, is an integral piece of the Mexico City jigsaw puzzle, and people-watching from its sidewalk cafés reveals fascinating variety among the passing parade of pedestrians. For details of how to spend money here, see the Places to Stay, Places to Eat, Entertainment and Shopping chapters.

On the northwest flank of the Zona Rosa, at Reforma's intersection with Avenida Río Tíber and Avenida Florencia, stands the symbol of Mexico City, the 36m-high **Monumento a la Independencia**, topped by a gilded statue of winged Victory, called by locals simply El Ángel. The statue, by sculptor Antonio Rivas Mercado, was inaugurated in 1910, just as the Mexican Revolution got under way. Sculptures around the base are of women personifying Law, Justice, War and Peace, and of Mexican independence heroes such as Miguel Hidalgo, Vicente Guerrero and José María Morelos. Inside the monument – and only opened to the public since 1997 – are displayed the skulls of Hidalgo and his fellow rebels Ignacio Allende, Juan Aldama and Mariano Jiménez, and caskets containing the ashes or remains of Morelos, Guerrero and others. The heads of Hidalgo, Allende, Aldama and Jiménez were those which from 1811 to 1821 hung in cages outside the Alhóndiga de Granaditas in Guanajuato as a Spanish 'lesson' to rebels. The Monumento a la Independencia is open 9 am to 6 pm daily (free).

A few blocks farther west, at the intersection of Reforma and Sevilla, is **La Diana Cazadora** (Diana the Huntress), a 1942 bronze statue of ancient Rome's hunting goddess by Juan Fernando Olaguíbel. Southwest of here, Reforma is lined mostly with large, impersonal, modern office buildings until you reach the Bosque de Chapultepec. The road continues westward through the park to become the start of the main road to Toluca.

Getting There & Away

Hidalgo metro station is on Reforma at the Alameda Central; Insurgentes station is at the southern tip of the Zona Rosa, 500m south of Reforma; and Chapultepec station is just south of Reforma at the east end of the Bosque de Chapultepec.

The westbound 'M(etro) Chapultepec,' 'Reforma' and 'M(etro) Auditorio' peseros on Avenida Cinco de Mayo go along Reforma to the Bosque de Chapultepec, but not frequently: if you get fed up of waiting, you can take the metro, or walk to Reforma and catch another pesero there. Any 'M(etro) Auditorio,' 'Reforma Km 13' or 'Km 15.5 por Reforma' pesero or bus heading southwest on Reforma will continue along Reforma through the Bosque de Chapultepec.

In the opposite direction, 'Zócalo' peseros heading east on Reforma will take you to the Zócalo. 'M(etro) Hidalgo,' 'M(etro) Garibaldi,' 'M(etro) Villa,' 'M(etro) La Villa' and 'M(etro) Indios Verdes' peseros and buses all head northeast up Reforma to the Alameda Central or beyond.

CONDESA & ROMA

Condesa is a fashionable but relaxed neighborhood south of the Zona Rosa. It lacks major sights but does have a couple of pleasant parks, some attractive architecture, and a huge number of good, informal restaurants and coffee bars. It's worth a wander if you're looking for some place off the tourist trail. Many buildings have prettily carved stone doorways and window frames, a product of the baroque-influenced neocolonial trend of the 1930s and '40s.

A main focus is the peaceful, beautifully kept **Parque México**, full of trees, well-maintained paths, benches with cute little roofs, and signs exhorting everyone to demonstrate their eco-consciousness and treat their parque nicely. Amsterdam, which runs in an oval loop one block outside the park's perimeter, was originally a horse-race track. When the track was handed over to developers in 1924, it was stipulated that a certain area inside it must be kept green – hence Parque México. **Parque España**, two blocks northwest, has a children's fun fair and is a bit more frenetic.

Parque México is a 500m walk north from Chilpancingo metro station, or a 1km walk south from Sevilla station – or you can get a pesero south on Avenida Insurgentes from Insurgentes metro station to the intersection with Michoacán (there's a Woolworth store on the corner), and walk two blocks west to the park.

The main cluster of typical Condesa bistro-type eateries (see the Places to Eat chapter) is about 500m west of Parque México, with Patriotismo and Juanacatlán metro stations also within walking distance.

To the north and east Condesa runs into Colonia Roma, which, like Condesa, was founded as a middle-class suburb in the early 20th century. (Both would be good, though increasingly expensive, places to find an apartment if you're planning to live in Mexico City today.) Roma is another tranquil neighborhood with a high proportion of the city's fashionable art galleries. The Galería Nina Menocal (☎ 5-564-72-09) at Zacatecas 93, specializes in contemporary Latin American art. It's open 10 am to 7 pm Monday to Friday, 10 am to 2 pm Saturday. Roma's main boulevard is leafy Obregón where at No 99, the Centro de Cultura Casa Lamm (☎ 5-514-48-99), in a handsome Porfiriato-era building, contains an excellent culturally-oriented bookshop and exhibition rooms. More galleries are found on and around nearby Colima and Plaza Río de Janeiro – the Arte-México website (www .arte-mexico.com) is a good place to find out what's on where.

BOSQUE DE CHAPULTEPEC

According to legend, one of the last kings of the Toltecs took refuge in the Chapultepec woods after fleeing from Tula. Later, Chapultepec hill itself (the name means Hill of Grasshoppers in Nahuatl, the Aztec language) served as a refuge for the wandering Aztecs and then as a fortress for Moctezuma I (1440-69) before becoming a summer residence for Aztec nobles. In the 15th century Nezahualcóyotl, the ruler of nearby Texcoco, gave his sanction for the area to be made a forest reserve. At that time Chapultepec was still separated from Tenochtitlán, the site of modern downtown Mexico City, by the waters of the Lago de Texcoco.

The Bosque de Chapultepec has remained Mexico City's largest park to this day. It now covers more than 4 sq km and has lakes, several excellent museums and a large zoo. It has also remained an abode of Mexico's high and mighty. It contains both the current presidential residence, Los Pinos, and a former imperial and presidential palace, the Castillo de Chapultepec. The park attracts thousands of visitors daily, and is particularly popular on Sunday when vendors line its main paths and throngs of families come to picnic, relax and crowd into the museums.

The park is divided into three sections. Many of the major attractions are in the

JOHN NOBLE

NEZAHUALCOYOTL

eastern or first section (1ª sección), which is the biggest and open 5 am to 4.30 pm daily except Monday. The second section (2ª sección), to the west, is divided from the first by two big north-south roads, Calzada Molino del Rey and Boulevard López Mateos. The third section (3ª sección) is almost 2km southwest of the second along Avenida Constituyentes, past the large Panteón Civil de Dolores cemetery.

The museums in the park generally offer free admission on Sunday and holidays.

Walking Tour

A good route around the first section of the park starts by going from Chapultepec metro station to the **Monumento a los Niños Héroes** and the nearby **Museo de Arte Moderno**, about a five-minute walk. Next go up to the **Castillo de Chapultepec** for a panorama of the park (or take the road-train if you want to save your legs), then descend and head west to the **Lago de Chapultepec**, where you might find an interesting exhibition at the Casa del Lago. The **zoo** is close by here. If you're heading for the Museo Nacional de Antropología or Museo Rufino Tamayo you can now walk a short distance north and cross Reforma (watch the traffic!). If not, stroll south through the park and return around the south side of the castle.

Monumento a los Niños Héroes

The six columns of the Monument to the Boy Heroes, near Chapultepec metro station, mark the main entrance to the park. Vaguely resembling sprigs of asparagus, the pillars commemorate six brave cadets at the national military academy, which was once housed in the Castillo de Chapultepec. On September 13, 1847, when invading American troops reached Mexico City, the six cadets, having defended their school as long as they could, wrapped themselves in Mexican flags and leapt to their deaths rather than surrender. An annual ceremony on the date honors their heroism.

Castillo de Chapultepec

Part of the castle on Chapultepec Hill was built in 1785 as a residence for the viceroys of Nueva España. The building was converted into a military academy in 1843. When Emperor Maximilian and Empress Carlota arrived in 1864, they refurbished the castle as their main residence. After their fall, the castle remained a residence for Mexico's presidents until 1940, when President Lázaro Cárdenas converted it into the **Museo Nacional de Historia** (National History Museum, ☎ 5-286-07-00).

Today two floors of exhibits chronicle the rise and fall of colonial Nueva España, the establishment of independent Mexico, Porfirio Díaz's dictatorship, and then the Mexican Revolution. Several of the 1st-floor rooms are decorated with impressive murals on historical themes by leading 20th-century Mexican artists. The various murals include Juan O'Gorman's *Retablo de la Independencia* (Thanksgiving Panel for Independence) in room 5, José Clemente Orozco's *La Reforma y la Caída del Imperio* (The Reform and Fall of the Empire) in room 7, O'Gorman's *Sufragio Efectivo No Reelección* (Genuine Suffrage – No Re-election) and *El Feudalismo Porfiriato* (Porfirian Feudalism) in room 11, and David Alfaro Siqueiros' *Del Porfirismo a la Revolución* (From Porfirism to the Revolution) in room 13.

Don't miss the rooms entered from a garden walkway around the east end of the castle – this is the portion where Maximilian and Carlota lived, and is furnished in period style, including Carlota's marble bath. Above the rooms, but reached by a staircase at the side of the building, are Porfirio Díaz's sumptuous rooms, flanking a patio with expansive views.

The museum is open from 9 am to 5 pm Tuesday to Sunday (last tickets are sold at 4 pm). Recently, entry was free as half the castle was closed for maintenance work. Previous to that, admission was US$2. To reach the castle, walk up the road that curves up the right-hand side of the hill behind the Monumento a los Niños Héroes. Alternatively, a little road-train runs up this road every 10 minutes or so while the castle is open. The cost of the train ride is US$0.30 roundtrip.

Museo del Caracol

From the Castillo de Chapultepec, the Museo del Caracol (☎ 5-553-62-85) is just a short distance back down the approach road. Shaped somewhat like a snail shell *(caracol)*, this is officially a 'Galería de Historia' on the subject of *la lucha del pueblo mexicano por su libertad* (the Mexican people's struggle for its liberty). Displays cover social and political life from Spanish colonial days, the divisions of Nueva España in the 18th century, Miguel Hidalgo's leadership in the struggle for independence, and Francisco Madero's leadership in the revolution. The self-guided tour ends in a circular hall that contains only one item – the 1917 Constitution of Mexico. It's open 9 am to 5 pm Tuesday to Sunday (US$1).

Museo de Arte Moderno

The two rounded buildings of the Museum of Modern Art (☎ 5-211-83-31) stand in their own sculpture garden just northwest of the Monumento a los Niños Héroes. The museum's permanent collection is of work by Mexico's most famous 20th-century artists, including Dr Atl, Rivera, Siqueiros, Orozco, O'Gorman, Frida Kahlo and Rufino Tamayo. In contrast to the large murals for which many of these artists are best known, some of their more intimate works, such as portraits, are shown here. In addition, temporary exhibitions by prominent artists from Mexico and abroad are always being held. Hours are 10 am to 6 pm Tuesday to Sunday (US$1.50). The entrance is on the north side of the museum, facing Paseo de la Reforma.

Centro de Convivencia Infantil

West of the Museo de Arte Moderno, this is a kind of adventure playground for children, with aerial walkways, slides, swings, monkeys, an aviary, domestic animals, face painting, a large model of King Kong and more. A sign at the entrance bans adults unless they are accompanied by children. It's open 10 am to 4.15 pm Wednesday to Sunday (free).

Lago de Chapultepec

West of the Centro de Convivencia Infantil is Lago de Chapultepec, on which you can row a rented boat. On the west side of the lake is the **Casa del Lago** (☎ 5-553-63-18), a 19th-century mansion now functioning as a cultural center of UNAM. It stages exhibitions, concerts, kids' activities, plays, dance performances and films.

Parque Zoológico de Chapultepec

The first zoo in Chapultepec – and the Americas – is said to have been established by King Nezahualcóyotl, well before the Spanish arrived. In 1975 a gift from China brought pandas. Completely rebuilt in the mid-1990s at a cost of US$30 million, the Chapultepec Zoo (☎ 5-553-62-29) is a mainly open-air place with a decent representation of the world's creatures kept in relatively large enclosures, divided into zones according to their natural habitat. Something went horribly wrong at the zoo in 1998, when almost 400 of its 1800 animals – including a polar bear, three tigresses and a giraffe – died in nine months. It was hoped that a new director appointed in 1999 would improve matters.

The four pandas apparently don't like bright sun and normally two of them are outdoors and two indoors at any one time. You're not allowed to eat or drink inside the zoo except in the snack bar area, where food is not too expensive (pizzas from US$1.50, for example). The zoo is open 9 am to 4 pm Tuesday to Sunday (free).

Museo Nacional de Antropología

The National Museum of Anthropology (☎ 5-553-63-81) is one of the finest museums of its kind in the world, and ranks among Mexico City's not-to-be-missed attractions. It's a huge, fascinating museum, with more than most people can absorb (without brain strain) in a single visit. A good plan is to concentrate on the regions of Mexico that you plan to visit or have visited, with a quick look at some of the other eye-catching exhibits. Highlights are the Sala Teotihuacana, Sala Mexica, Sala Golfo de México and Sala Maya, with the Sala Tolteca and Sala Oaxaca close runners-up. All of the labeling is in Spanish, but some of the spectacular exhibits justify a visit even if you can't decipher a single word.

The spacious museum building, constructed in the 1960s, is the work of Mexican architect Pedro Ramírez Vásquez. Its long, rectangular courtyard is flanked on three sides by the museum's two-story display halls, with over 1km of hallways. An immense umbrella-like stone fountain rises from the center of the courtyard.

The museum's ground-floor halls are dedicated to Mexican societies and civilizations before the Spanish conquest. Rooms on the upper level cover the way modern Mexico's indigenous peoples, the direct descendants of those pre-Hispanic civilizations, live today. With a few exceptions, each ethnological section upstairs covers the same territory as the archaeological exhibit below it, so you can see the great Mayan city of Palenque as it was in the 7th century AD, then go upstairs and see how Mayan people live today. Here's a brief guide to the regions and archaeological sites covered on the ground floor, in counterclockwise order around the courtyard:

Introducción a la Antropología – The exhibits introduce the studies of anthropology, ethnology and pre-Hispanic culture in general.

Sala Orígenes – The Origins Room shows evidence of the first people in this hemisphere, explaining their arrival from Asia, and shows findings from central Mexico and displays on the beginnings of agriculture.

On display at the Museum of Anthropology

JOHN BORTHWICK

Sala Preclásica – The preclassic period lasted from about 1500 BC to 250 AD. The exhibits highlight the transition from a nomadic hunting life to a more settled life of farming in Mexico around 1000 BC.

Sala Teotihuacana – The Teotihuacán Room has models of the awesome city of Teotihuacán, near Mexico City, plus many artifacts. A highlight is the full-size replica of part of the Templo de Quetzalcóatl, showing its original colors.

Sala Tolteca – This hall covers the important cultures of central Mexico between about 650 and 1250 AD and is named after one of the most important of these, the Toltecs. Exhibits include a huge stone statue from Tula of the god Quetzalcóatl.

Sala Mexica – At the west end of the courtyard is the hall devoted to the Mexica, or Aztecs. Come here to see the famous sun (or 'calendar') stone, with the face of the sun god Tonatiuh at the center of a web of symbols representing the five worlds, the four directions, the 20 days and more; the statue of Coatlicue ('She of the Skirt of Snakes'), the mother of the Aztec gods, found – like the sun stone – beneath the Zócalo in 1790; a replica of a carved-stone tzompantli (skull rack); an 'aerial view' painting of Tenochtitlán, the Aztecs' island capital; and other graphic evidence of this awesome culture.

Sala Oaxaca – In the southern state of Oaxaca, artistic heights were reached by the Zapotecs (about 300 BC to 700 AD) and the Mixtecs (about 1200 to 1500 AD). Two tombs from the great hilltop site of Monte Albán are reproduced full-size here.

Sala Golfo de México – Important ancient civilizations along the coast of the Gulf of Mexico included the Olmec, Classic Veracruz, Totonac and Huastec. This hall contains very fine stone carvings, including two awesome Olmec heads.

Sala Maya – The Maya Room has wonderful exhibits not only from southeast Mexico, but also from Guatemala, Belize and Honduras. The full-scale model of the tomb of King Pakal, discovered deep in the Temple of the Inscriptions at Palenque, is breathtaking. On the outside patio are replicas of the famous wall paintings of Bonampak and of Edificio II at Hochob in Campeche, constructed as a giant mask of the Mayan rain god Chac.

Cafetería – Just past the Maya Room is a flight of stairs down to the museum's cafeteria (see the Places to Eat chapter).

Sala Norte – The Northern Mexico room covers Casas Grandes (Paquimé) and other cultures

Voladores

Several times a day, in a clearing in the park about 100m in front of the entrance of the Museo Nacional de Antropología, Totonacs from the Mexican state of Veracruz carry out a spectacular performance called the Voladores (Fliers).

The Voladores is in effect a kind of slow-motion quadruple bungee jump and it can induce vertigo even in watchers firmly planted on the ground. It starts with five men in colorful costumes climbing to the top of a 20m-high pole. Four of them sit on the edges of a small square wooden frame atop the pole, fasten long ropes to it and to themselves, and then rotate the frame to twist the ropes around the pole. The fifth man dances, bangs a drum and plays a whistle while standing on a tiny platform above them.

Suddenly he stops and the others launch themselves backwards into the air. Upside down, arms outstretched, they revolve gracefully around the pole and descend slowly to the ground as their ropes unwind.

This is in fact an ancient ceremony, packed with symbolism. One interpretation is that it's a fertility rite and the fliers are macaw-men who make invocations to the four corners of the universe before falling to the ground, bringing with them the sun and rain. It is also said that each of the four fliers circles the pole 13 times, giving a total of 52 revolutions, which is not only the number of weeks in the modern year but was an important number in pre-Hispanic Mexico, which had two calendars. One corresponded to the 365-day solar year, the other to a ritual year of 260 days – with a day in one calendar coinciding with a day in the other calendar every 52 solar years.

One of the fliers, or an assistant, collects money from onlookers. In a way it's sad to see a sacred act turned into show business, but the feat is dangerous and spectacular, and most of Mexico's indigenous peoples need every peso they can get.

RICHARD I'ANSON

from the dry north. Similarities to the native cultures of the American Southwest can be seen.

Sala Occidente – The Western Mexico room deals with the cultures of Nayarit, Jalisco, Michoacán, Colima and Guerrero states, chief among them the Tarascos of Michoacán, who were one of the few peoples able to repel the invading Aztecs.

The museum is open 9 am to 7 pm Tuesday to Sunday (US$2.50, plus US$1 if you bring a camera – no flash allowed – and US$3 for a video camera). The museum stands in an extension of the Bosque de Chapultepec, on the north side of Paseo de la Reforma.

Museo Rufino Tamayo

The Rufino Tamayo Museum (☎ 5-286-65-99), a multilevel concrete and glass structure about 250m east of the Museo Nacional de Antropología, was built to house the fine collection of international modern art donated by Tamayo and his wife, Olga, to the people of Mexico. Over 150 artists including Pablo Picasso, Andy Warhol, Francis Bacon, Robert Motherwell and Tamayo himself are represented in the permanent collection, but you may find that their works have all been put away to make room for a temporary exhibition or two. The museum is open 10 am to 5.45 pm Tuesday to Sunday (US$1.50).

Galería de Arte Mexicano

This gallery (☎ 5-273-12-61), at Rebollar 43, Colonia San Miguel Chapultepec, just south of the park, is one of the oldest in the country and stages some top-class exhibitions of Mexican art. It's open 10 am to 7 pm Monday to Friday, 10 am to 2 pm Saturday (near Ⓜ Constituyentes).

Segunda (2ª) Sección

The second section of the Bosque de Chapultepec lies west of Boulevard López Mateos.

One highlight here is **La Feria** (☎ 5-230-21-12), a large amusement park with some hair-raising rides, open 11 am to 7 pm Tuesday to Friday, 10 am to 9 pm Saturday and Sunday. A US$7.50 ticket includes most rides; a US$1.50 children's ticket gives them 22 rides or games.

Another highlight is **Papalote Museo del Niño** (☎ 5-160-60-60), a hands-on children's museum that will be a surefire hit with the kids. Activities range from a tunnel slide and a conventional playground to giant soap-bubble making and all manner of technical/scientific gadget-games. Everything is attended by young, child-friendly supervisors and you can be sure that your kids will not want to leave. Hours are 9 am to 1 pm and 2 to 6 pm Monday to Friday during school terms; 10 am to 2 pm and 3 to 7 pm on Saturday, Sunday and holidays and during school vacations. During school vacations Papalote is also open 7.30 to 11.30 pm Thursday to Saturday. Each four-hour session costs US$4 for adults, US$3 for seniors over 60 and children aged two to 11. Papalote also has an IMAX big-screen cinema, shops and places to eat and drink.

Also in Chapultepec's Segunda Sección you'll find two lakes, some large fountains, a handful of restaurants, the **Juegos Mecánicos Infantiles** (amusement rides for kids), the **Museo Tecnológico** (☎ 5-516-09-64), which focuses on electricity, transportation and basic scientific principles and also has a computer workshop (9 am to 5 pm Tuesday to Sunday, free), and the **Museo de Historia Natural** (☎ 5-515-22-22), a set of low, colored domes with exhibits that concentrate on the evolution of the planet and its species (10 am to 5 pm Tuesday to Sunday, US$1).

Panteón Civil de Dolores

Chapultepec's second and third sections are divided by a huge cemetery, the Panteón Civil de Dolores. Near its main entrance on Avenida Constituyentes, the Rotonda de los Hombres Ilustres (Rotunda of Illustrious Men) contains the mortal remains of numerous celebrated Mexicans including the artists Diego Rivera, José Clemente Orozco and Dr Atl (Gerardo Murillo). The *panteón* is open 6 am to 6 pm daily (see Map 1 for the rotonda).

Tercera (3ª) Sección

The main attractions in Chapultepec's third section are water related. **Atlantis** (☎ 5-277-75-83) is a marine park with dolphin, sea lion, pirate, cowboy and trained-bird shows and a 'marine cave museum,' all of which are included in the basic entrance fee of US$2.50. Another US$0.80 buys you more spectacles and rides. **El Rollo** acuatic park (☎ 5-515-13-85) has water slides and tunnels, a wave pool and other places to make a splash, for US$6 per adult and US$2.50 per child between 0.90m and 1.20m tall (shorter children enter free). Opening hours at both seem to change often, so you should call or check with a tourist office. At our last check, both opened on Saturday, Sunday, public holidays and school vacations only, from around 11 am to 6 pm. Both are near the park's entrance on Avenida Constituyentes (Map 1).

Getting There & Away

1ª Sección Chapultepec metro station is at the east end of the first section of the Bosque de Chapultepec, not far from the

Monumento a los Niños Héroes and the Castillo de Chapultepec. Auditorio metro station is at the northwest corner of the first section, 500m west of the Museo Nacional de Antropología.

From the Zócalo area, you can also reach the first section by taking a 'M(etro) Chapultepec' or 'M(etro) Auditorio' pesero westbound on Avenida Cinco de Mayo. From anywhere on Paseo de la Reforma west of the Alameda Central, peseros and buses that are labeled 'M(etro) Chapultepec,' 'M(etro) Auditorio,' 'Km 15.5 por Reforma' or 'Reforma Km 13' will reach Chapultepec metro station, and all except 'M(etro) Chapultepec' vehicles will cross the first section of the park on Paseo de la Reforma: you can get off right outside the Museo Nacional de Antropología (but watch out for pickpockets).

Returning downtown, 'Zócalo' peseros heading east on Reforma will take you to the Zócalo. Any 'M(etro) Hidalgo,' 'M(etro) Garibaldi,' 'M(etro) Villa,' 'M(etro) La Villa' and 'M(etro) Indios Verdes' pesero or bus, from Chapultepec metro station or heading east on Reforma, will go along Reforma at least as far as Hidalgo metro station.

2ª Sección Constituyentes metro station is near the southern edge of the second section. From the station walk up to Avenida Constituyentes, turn left, cross Constituyentes by a footbridge and turn left along a short street to Boulevard López Mateos. Cross this by another footbridge, which brings you down by an entrance to the park.

3ª Sección To reach the third section or the Panteón de Dolores, take a pesero or combi from Chapultepec metro station saying 'Panteón Dolores, Atlantis, Rollo' or 'Panteón Dolores, Hacienda.' These run along Avenida Constituyentes to the park entrance.

POLANCO

In this affluent residential quarter north of the Bosque de Chapultepec, the streets are named after writers and scientists and the spring blossoms are even more of a treat than elsewhere in the city. Polanco contains lots of restaurants, art galleries, embassies, expensive hotels and shops, and the SECTUR tourist office (see the Facts for the Visitor chapter). Much of the architecture is in the appealing neocolonial style of the 1930s and '40s, with stone carved into all sorts of pretty curves and frills around doors and windows. An outstanding example of the genre is Casa Domit at Castelar and Calderón de la Barca facing Parque Lincoln.

You could visit Polanco before or after the Museo Nacional de Antropología, which is close by. There's a market area along Virgilio, north of Parque Lincoln.

Museo Sala de Arte Público David Alfaro Siqueiros

Shortly before his death in 1974, Siqueiros donated his house and studio, at Tres Picos 29, to the government for use as a museum (☎ 5-545-59-52). His private papers and photographs, along with a lot of his art, are on display. It's open 10 am to 6 pm Tuesday to Sunday (US$1, free on Sunday; ⓜ Auditorio or Polanco).

Art Galleries

Two leading Polanco galleries, both dedicated to contemporary Latin American art, are **Galería Enrique Guerrero** (☎ 5-280-29-41) at Horacio 1549A and **Galería López Quiroga** (☎ 5-280-62-18) at Avenida Presidente Masaryk 379. Both are open at least 11 am to 2 pm and 4 to 7 pm Monday to Friday, 11 am to 2 pm Saturday.

LOMAS DE CHAPULTEPEC

West of the Bosque de Chapultepec is Lomas de Chapultepec, one of Mexico City's wealthiest residential areas, full of large houses protected by high walls, a few of which are embassies. You can take a quick tour of the area by boarding a pesero or bus marked 'Km 15.5 por Palmas,' 'Palmas Km 13' or 'Santa Fe x Palmas' at Chapultepec metro station or westbound on Paseo de la Reforma. The vehicle will go along Paseo de las Palmas, the main boulevard of Lomas de Chapultepec, before reemerging on Paseo de la Reforma, 4 or 5km west of the Bosque

The Monumento a la Revolución now contains the tombs of revolutionary heroes.

Hemiciclo a Juárez on the Alameda Central honoring revered hero Benito Juárez

CHARLOTTE HINDLE

Fountain in courtyard of Palacio Nacional

RICHARD I'ANSON

Colonial building facade, now a bank

RICHARD NEBESKY

Statues front the Palacio de Bellas Artes.

RICHARD I'ANSON

Detail on domed church roof

de Chapultepec. Here you can take a 'M(etro) Auditorio' or 'M(etro) Chapultepec' bus or pesero back toward the city center (Map 8).

TLATELOLCO

About 2km north of the Alameda Central up Eje Central Lázaro Cárdenas (Map 1) is the **Plaza de las Tres Culturas** (Plaza of the Three Cultures), so called because it symbolizes the fusion of pre-Hispanic and Spanish roots into the modern Mexican mestizo identity. The Aztec pyramids of Tlatelolco, the 17th-century Spanish Templo de Santiago, and the modern Secretaría de Relaciones Exteriores (Foreign Ministry) building on the plaza's south side represent the three cultures.

Founded by Aztecs in the 14th century as a separate dynasty from Tenochtitlán, on what was then a separate island in Lago de Texcoco, Tlatelolco was annexed by Tenochtitlán in 1473. In pre-Hispanic times it was the scene of the largest market in the Valle de México. The market is described in great detail in Bernal Díaz del Castillo's *History of the Conquest of New Spain*. Spaniards who were under Cortés defeated Tlatelolco's Aztec defenders, led by Cuauhtémoc, here in 1521. An inscription about that battle in the plaza today translates: 'This was neither victory nor defeat. It was the sad birth of the mestizo people that is Mexico today.'

Tlatelolco is also a symbol of more modern troubles. On October 2, 1968, 300 to 400 people (by most estimates) among a crowd of political protesters were massacred by government forces on the eve of the Olympic Games, held in Mexico City. And in 1985, the area suffered some of the worst damage and casualties in the Mexico City earthquake when apartment blocks collapsed, killing hundreds.

Today the plaza is a calm oasis amid the hurly-burly of the city, but haunted by echoes of its somber history. You can view the ruins of Tlatelolco's main pyramid-temple and other Aztec buildings from a walkway around them. The Spanish, recognizing the religious significance of the place, built a monastery here and then, in 1609, the Templo de Santiago, which still stands today. Santiago (St James) is Spain's patron saint, and his aid was no doubt considered to have been crucial in the victory over the Aztecs. Just inside the main (west) doors of the church is the baptismal font of Juan Diego (see the Basílica de Guadalupe section, following). Outside the north wall of the church stands a monument to the victims of the 1968 massacre, erected in 1993. The full truth about the massacre has never come out: the traces were hastily cleaned away, and Mexican schoolbooks still do not refer to it.

You can catch northbound 'Eje Central, Central Camionera, Tenayuca' peseros or buses on Eje Central Lázaro Cárdenas at Donceles, one block north of the Palacio de Bellas Artes; they pass right by the Plaza de las Tres Culturas. Alternatively, take the metro to Tlatelolco station, exit onto busy Manuel González, and turn right. Walk to the first major intersection (Avenida Lázaro Cárdenas), turn right, and you'll soon see the plaza on the far (east) side of the road – 900m from the metro station.

LA VILLA DE GUADALUPE

On December 9, 1531, an indigenous Christian convert named Juan Diego, standing on the Cerro del Tepeyac (Tepeyac Hill), site of an old Aztec shrine about 6km north of the Zócalo, saw a vision of a beautiful lady in a blue mantle trimmed with gold. He told the local priest that he had seen the Virgin Mary, but the priest didn't believe him. Juan returned to the hill, saw the vision again, and an image of the lady was miraculously emblazoned on his cloak. Eventually the church authorities believed his story, and a cult grew up around the place.

Over the following centuries Nuestra Señora de Guadalupe (Our Lady of Guadalupe), as this manifestation of the Virgin came to be known, would receive the credit for all manner of miracles, hugely aiding the acceptance of Catholicism by indigenous Mexicans. In 1737, after she had extinguished a typhoid outbreak in Mexico City, she was officially declared the Patrona Principal (Principal Patroness) of Nueva

Nuestra Señora de Guadalupe

Mother, here?') – were those uttered, according to legend, by the Virgin to calm Juan Diego's fears when she appeared to him.

The rear of the **Antigua Basílica de Guadalupe** (old basilica) is now the **Museo de la Basílica de Guadalupe** (☎ 5-577-60-22), with a fine collection of *retablos* (small tin panels painted by pilgrims in thanks for miracles), plus plenty of colonial religious art. It's open 10 am to 6 pm Tuesday to Sunday (US$0.30). Immediately to the right (east) of the Antigua Basílica is the red-domed 18th-century **Capilla Capuchinas**, the church of a convent that once stood here.

Stairs behind the Antigua Basílica climb about 100m to the hilltop **Capilla del Cerrito** (Hill Chapel), on the spot where Juan Diego saw his vision. From here, stairs lead down the east side of the hill to the **Jardín del**

España. Today her image is seen throughout the country, attracting thousands of pilgrims daily to the Cerro del Tepeyac – and millions on the days leading up to her feast day, December 12. See Public Holidays & Special Events in the Facts for the Visitor chapter for more on these festivities.

The pilgrims' main goal is the modern **Basílica de Nuestra Señora de Guadalupe** (Map 3), at the foot of the Cerro del Tepeyac. Some pilgrims travel the last meters to this church on their knees. By the 1970s the old yellow-domed basilica here, built around 1700, was being swamped by the numbers of worshippers and was leaning alarmingly as it slowly sank into the ground it stood on. A new basilica was built next door. Designed by Pedro Ramírez Vásquez, architect of the Museo Nacional de Antropología, it's a vast, rounded, open-plan structure able to hold thousands of worshippers. The sound of so many people singing together is quite thrilling. The Virgin's image hangs above the main altar, with moving walkways beneath it to bring visitors as close as possible.

The words inscribed here – '*¿No estoy Yo aquí que soy tu Madre?*' ('Am not I, your

Retablos

An engaging Mexican folk-art custom is the practice of adorning the sanctuaries of specially revered saints or holy images with *retablos*, small paintings giving thanks for miracles or answered prayers. Typically done on small sheets of tin, but sometimes on glass, wood or cardboard, retablos depict these miracles in touchingly literal painted images. They may show a cyclist's hair's-breadth escape from a hurtling bus, a sailor escaping a sinking ship, or an invalid rising from a sickbed, beside a representation of the saint and a brief message along the lines of 'Thanks to San Miguel for curing my rheumatism – María González, June 6, 1995.' In Mexico City, the Antigua Basílica de Guadalupe and the Museo Frida Kahlo at Coyoacán both have fascinating collections of retablos.

Somewhat confusingly, the word *retablo* also means altarpiece – a more official form of thanksgiving to God or saints. Many churches in Mexico City, as throughout Mexico, have huge and gloriously elaborate altarpieces, often carved and covered in gold and a variety of paintings.

Tepeyac (Tepeyac Garden), where the modern monument *La Ofrenda* (The Offering) shows the Virgin of Guadalupe receiving gifts from indigenous Mexicans and a Spanish priest. Two streams meet at the Virgin's feet, symbolizing the union of the Aztec people and the Spanish Christian mission. From the Jardín del Tepeyac a path leads back to the main plaza, reentering it in front of the 17th-century **Capilla de Indios** (Chapel of Indians), next to the place where, according to legend, Juan Diego lived from 1531 to his death in 1548.

An easy way to reach the Basílica de Guadalupe is to take the metro to La Villa-Basílica station, then follow the crowds two blocks north along Calzada de Guadalupe. You can also reach the metro station by taking any 'M(etro) La Villa' pesero or bus running northeast on Paseo de la Reforma from central areas of the city. A 'M(etro) Hidalgo' or 'M(etro) Chapultepec' pesero or bus heading south down Calzada de los Misterios, a block west of Calzada de Guadalupe, will return you downtown.

TENAYUCA & SANTA CECILIA ACATITLÁN

These two sites of lesser Aztec ruins in the north of the city might appeal not only to archaeology enthusiasts but also to anyone who enjoys discovering calm and beautiful nooks amid the modern urban sprawl. You can visit both in a half-day trip from the city center.

Tenayuca (☎ 5-391-07-80) is 11 km north-northwest of the Zócalo. Settled by Chichimecs in about the 13th century, it was later ruled by the Aztecs, and the double-staircase pyramid they left is a smaller version of the now-ruined one that stood in the Templo Mayor. As at the Templo Mayor, each staircase was topped by a temple – one dedicated to the water god Tláloc, the other probably dedicated to the Aztec tribal god Huizilopochtli. Striking serpent sculptures, possibly pre-Aztec, surround three sides of its base (imagine what they looked like when they were painted bright red, yellow and green!). A small museum holds artifacts, diagrams and models.

The site is open 10 am to 4.45 pm daily except Monday (US$1.50, free on Sunday and holidays). To get there you can take a northbound 'Tenayuca' pesero on the Eje Central Lázaro Cárdenas at Donceles (one block north of the Palacio de Bellas Artes), or from the Plaza de las Tres Culturas. You need to get off at the intersection of Avenida Acueducto de Tenayuca and Cuauhtémoc, half an hour from the Bellas Artes in moderate traffic (there are traffic signals at the corner; if in doubt ask the driver or fellow passengers for the *pirámide de Tenayuca*). Walk north (to the right) along Cuauhtémoc and you'll see the pyramid beside a park after a couple of blocks.

Santa Cecilia Acatitlán, 2 kilometers north of Tenayuca, is a small but fine pyramid topped with a temple (both reconstructed) dedicated to the gods Tláloc and Huizilopochtli. It stands in pleasant, leafy grounds behind the pretty, 16th-century Parroquia Santa Cecilia, some of whose stone came from the original pyramid. Access to the pyramid is through the Plazuela & Museo Hurtado, with a small collection of pre-Hispanic sculpture – open 10 am to 5 pm Tuesday to Sunday (US$1.75, free Sunday and holidays). You can reach Santa Cecilia by taking a pesero or bus that's headed north up Carretera Tenayuca Santa Cecilia, north of the Tenayuca pyramid. Get off at Calle Pirámide de Tula and walk a few blocks east to the church. You'll probably need to ask for directions – the people at Tenayuca will get you started.

AVENIDA INSURGENTES

Avenida Insurgentes, the longest street in Mexico City, runs from La Villa de Guadalupe in the north to beyond Cuicuilco in the south. Its southern section, Avenida Insurgentes Sur, lined with many restaurants and brightly lit at night, passes a few places of interest between Paseo de la Reforma and the attractive suburb of San Ángel. 'San Ángel' peseros and buses southbound on Insurgentes, from anywhere at least as far north as Estación Buenavista, will take you to these places. Returning north, 'M(etro) Indios Verdes' and 'M(etro) La Raza' buses and peseros travel far up Insurgentes to the north of the city; 'M(etro) Insurgentes' vehicles go to Insurgentes metro station, 1km south of Paseo de la Reforma.

Polifórum Cultural Siqueiros

The bizarre Siqueiros Polifórum (☎ 5-536-45-20, www.polyforum.com.mx), at Insurgentes Sur 701, at the corner of Filadelfia, 4.5km south of Paseo de la Reforma, was designed by muralist Siqueiros and opened in 1971. The 12-sided exterior of the building (which is an arts center and theater) is covered with murals: the atom as the triumph of peace over destruction and dramas of love during the Spanish conquest, among other subjects.

The wall backing Insurgentes shows five leaders of the Mexican artistic resurgence of the late 19th century and the 20th century: Diego Rivera, José Clemente Orozco, the cartoonist and printmaker José Guadalupe Posada, the engraver Leopoldo Méndez, and Dr Atl. Inside, the ground floor houses contemporary art exhibitions, while the auditorium upstairs is covered with Siqueiros' enormous last mural, *La Marcha de la Humanidad en la Tierra hacia el Cosmos* (The March of Humanity on Earth toward the Cosmos). Grand in scale and concept – it took six years and a team of 50 to finish – the mural is meant to be seen from a rotating, tilting central platform in a sound-and-light show. These 25-minute shows currently happen, with recorded narration by Siqueiros, at 11.30 am and 12.45 and 5 pm on Saturday and Sunday (US$3). The center is open for general visits 9 am to 7 pm daily (US$1).

The 50-story World Trade Center – originally destined to be a hotel before funding ran out – towers behind the Polifórum.

Ciudad de los Deportes & Parque Hundido

'Sport City,' 1.5km south of the Polifórum, consists of two things: the Monumental Plaza México, Mexico City's major bullring, (one of the largest in the world, with 48,000 seats), and the 65,000-capacity Estadio Azul, which is home to the Cruz Azul soccer team.

Holbein leads a few blocks west from Insurgentes Sur to both places. See the Entertainment chapter for information on events here.

One fairly easy way to reach the Ciudad de los Deportes is to ride the metro to San Antonio station on línea 7, take the Avenida San Antonio exit, turn right and walk about 10 minutes, crossing the broad Avenida Revolución and Avenida Patriotismo en route.

Parque Luis Urbina, also called the Parque Hundido (Sunken Garden), 500m south along Insurgentes Sur from the Ciudad de los Deportes, is a leafy park containing 51 copies of well-known pre-Hispanic Mexican works of art.

Also within a few minutes' walk are the Fonart crafts store (see the Shopping chapter) and the rock music venue Rockotitlán (see the Entertainment chapter).

SAN ÁNGEL

Sixty years ago San Ángel ('sahn-AHN-hell'), 8.5km south of Paseo de la Reforma, was a village separated from Mexico City by open fields. Today it's one of the city's more charming and affluent suburbs, with quiet, cobbled streets lined by both old colonial houses and expensive modern ones. San Ángel is best known for its weekly arts and crafts market, the Bazar Sábado (Saturday Bazaar; see the Shopping chapter), but there's plenty to do on other days as well (except perhaps on Monday, when the museums are closed).

The two main roads through San Ángel are Avenida Insurgentes Sur, which runs north-south through the eastern side of the suburb, and Avenida Revolución, which parallels Insurgentes about 200m to the west.

Tourist information is available at the Casa de la Cultura (☎ 5-616-12-54) at the corner of Avenida Revolución and Madero, 9 am to 8 pm daily.

Walking Tour

From the pesero terminus on Dr Gálvez, a nice approach to San Ángel's attractions is to walk out on to Insurgentes, head north, and take the second left, Monasterio, a little lane winding through to the **Templo &**

Museo del Carmen. From here, cross Avenida Revolución to Plaza del Carmen – busy with artists and their art on Saturdays – and head up to Plaza San Jacinto. After a browse and maybe a bite or a drink here, walk northwest through the narrow lanes to the San Ángel Inn – another fine spot for a pause in your travels – and the Museo Casa Estudio Diego Rivera y Frida Kahlo. Then head back east to Plaza del Carmen or Plaza San Jacinto and wind up your tour with a visit to Plaza Loreto (to the south) or to Parque de la Bombilla and lovely little Plaza San Sebastián Chimalistac, to the east. From this last, you can drop into the Gandhi bookstore/café then depart from the MA de Quevedo metro station.

Templo & Museo del Carmen

The tile-domed church and museum (☎ 5-550-48-96) of El Carmen are at Avenida Revolución 4. The cool, peaceful church was built between 1615 and 1617 to the designs of Andrés de San Miguel, a Carmelite monk. The museum occupies the former monastic quarters to one side of the church and is mainly devoted to colonial-era furniture and religious art – but its big tourist attraction is the mummified bodies in the crypt, which are thought to be 18th-century monks, nuns and gentry. You can also walk out into the pretty garden, once much bigger, which was a source for cuttings and seeds sent all over colonial Mexico. The museum is open 10 am to 5 pm Tuesday to Sunday (US$1.75, free on Sunday).

Plaza San Jacinto

Every Saturday the Bazar Sábado brings a festive atmosphere, masses of color, and crowds of people to San Ángel's pretty little Plaza San Jacinto. To reach it, walk uphill on Madero (southwest from Avenida Revolución).

The main building of the Bazar Sábado is Plaza San Jacinto 11, on the north side of the square. This house served as quarters for invading forces from the US in 1847 and from France in 1863. A plaque on one of the buildings on the west side of the plaza, however, commemorates 71 soldiers of the Irish Battalion of St Patrick who were hung after helping the Mexicans resist the US invasion. The Irish were originally fighting in the American forces but thought the US cause was so unjust that they switched sides.

The 16th-century Iglesia de San Jacinto, off the west side of the plaza, is entered from a peaceful rear garden where you can take refuge from the crowded market areas. The Museo Casa del Risco (☎ 5-616-27-11) is on the north side of the plaza at No 15, in an 18th-century mansion that has two courtyards with beautiful tiled fountains. The museum has a hall for temporary exhibitions on the ground floor, and upstairs, a permanent exhibition of 14th- to 19th-century European and 17th- to 19th-century Mexican art. It's open 10 am to 5 pm daily, except Monday (free).

Museo Casa Estudio Diego Rivera y Frida Kahlo

A 10-minute walk northwest of Plaza San Jacinto, at Calle Diego Rivera 2 on the corner of Altavista, is the Diego Rivera & Frida Kahlo Studio Museum (☎ 5-550-11-89). The famous artist pair lived in this 1930s avant-garde abode – designed for them by Juan O'Gorman, with separate houses for each – from 1934 to 1940, when they divorced. They remarried again soon afterwards, but Kahlo then returned to her house in Coyoacán while Rivera stayed on here until his death in 1957 (see 'Diego & Frida'). Rivera's house (the pink one) has an upstairs studio. The museum has only a few examples of his art, and none of Kahlo's, but contains a lot of memorabilia including Rivera's collection of Judas figures, personally commissioned from expert artisans.

It's open 10 am to 6 pm daily, except Monday (US$1, free Sunday). To get here from Plaza San Jacinto, walk west along Juárez, then north on Reina and take the second street on the left (Lazcano). Along the way you pass through an area of old colonial villas, side by side with a few expensive modern houses. At the end of Lazcano you'll see the San Ángel Inn restaurant on the other side of the main road, Avenida Altavista. The museum is just past the San

Ángel Inn across the corner of Calle Diego Rivera.

You can reach the museum and San Ángel Inn (see below) from Avenida Revolución on a 'Tetelpan' pesero traveling west along Avenida Altavista.

San Ángel Inn

The San Ángel Inn is in the 18th-century ex-Hacienda de Goicoechea, once the home of the marquises of Selva Nevada and the counts of Pinillos, with a beautiful verdant courtyard, a fountain, a chapel and colonial gardens. If your budget won't run to a meal here (see the Places to Eat chapter), you can still stroll in the gardens and perhaps have a drink in the cocktail bar. See Museo Casa Estudio Diego Rivera y Frida Kahlo, above, for how to get here.

Museo de Arte Carrillo Gil

The Carrillo Gil Art Museum (☎ 5-550-62-89), Avenida Revolución 1608, has a permanent collection of art by Mexican artists of the first rank, with many works by Rivera, Siqueiros and Orozco (including some of Orozco's grotesque, satirical early drawings and watercolors). The museum also includes engravings and prints by such as Klee, Rouault, Braque and Kandinsky, plus often excellent temporary exhibits. Hours are 10 am to 6 pm Tuesday to Sunday (US$1, free on Sunday). In the basement is a pleasant bookstore/café.

To reach the museum from Plaza San Jacinto, walk down to Avenida Revolución, then go two blocks north. From the San Ángel Inn, you could take any bus or pesero heading east down Avenida Altavista, and get out at Avenida Revolución.

Plaza Loreto & Plaza Opción

Plaza Loreto, between Altamirano and Río de la Magdalena, a 600m walk south of Plaza San Jacinto, is Mexico City's most attractive mall, converted from an old paper factory a few years ago. Several patios and courtyards are set between the brick buildings and it's a lot more than just a place to shop. You'll find a mini-amphitheater for the performing arts, two multi-screen cinemas (one of them, Cin-

emanía, devoted to classic and art-house movies and endowed with a nice little lobby bar), one of the city's top cabaret clubs (La Planta de Luz), a variety of eateries, and the excellent **Museo Soumaya** (☎ 5-616-37-31). The Soumaya houses one of the world's three major collections – 70 pieces – of the sculpture of Frenchman Auguste Rodin (1840-1917), including such celebrated works as *The Kiss* and *The Thinker*. It also possesses work by Rodin's contemporaries Degas, Matisse and Renoir, collections of Mexican portraiture and colonial art, and murals by Rufino Tamayo. The Soumaya is open 10.30 am to 6.30 pm Thursday to Monday, 10.30 am to 8.30 pm Wednesday (US$1, free on Monday).

The neighboring Plaza Opción is a more straightforward mall but contains the unusual Modern Art Café (see the Places to Eat chapter) and a couple of popular nightspots (see the Entertainment chapter).

Parque de la Bombilla

This pleasant park lies just east of Avenida Insurgentes, along the south side of Avenida La Paz. The **Monumento a Álvaro Obregón**, near the Insurgentes end of the park, commemorates the Mexican revolutionary and president who was assassinated on this spot during a banquet in 1928, soon after he had been elected to a second presidential term. Obregón's killer was a young Christian fanatic, José de León Toral, who was involved in the Cristero rebellion against the government's anti-Church policies. Just beyond the far (east) end of the park is the lovely, tranquil little **Plaza San Sebastián Chimalistac**, surrounded by colonial houses and with a beautiful little 16th-century stone chapel, the **Capilla de San Sebastián Mártir**.

Getting There & Away

An easy way to reach San Ángel from central Mexico City is to take a 'San Ángel' pesero or bus south on Insurgentes, from Insurgentes metro station or anywhere as far north as Estación Buenavista. Most end on Dr Gálvez between Avenida Insurgentes and Avenida Revolución.

Alternatively, take the metro to either Viveros or MA de Quevedo station, then walk (20 to 30 minutes) or board a 'San Ángel' pesero or bus at either place. The Gandhi bookstore (see the Places to Eat and Shopping chapters) is one block toward San Ángel from the Quevedo station.

Returning north to the city center, 'M(etro) Indios Verdes' and 'M(etro) La Raza' buses and peseros run all the way up Insurgentes to the northern part of the city; 'M(etro) Insurgentes' vehicles go to Insurgentes metro station. A good place to catch any of these is the corner of Insurgentes and Avenida La Paz.

Returning to the metro stations, 'M(etro) Viveros' peseros head east on Avenida Robles, and 'M(etro) Tasqueña' peseros and buses heading east on Avenida MA de Quevedo go to MA de Quevedo metro station.

To Coyoacán, get a 'M(etro) Tasqueña' pesero or bus, which will take you to the corner of Carrillo Puerto (2.5km), from where you can walk five blocks north to the Jardín del Centenario.

CIUDAD UNIVERSITARIA

University City, on the east side of Avenida Insurgentes 2km south of San Ángel, is the main campus of Latin America's biggest university, the Universidad Nacional Autónoma de México (UNAM), and one of the nation's architectural showpieces.

The first university in the Americas was founded in Mexico City in 1553 but was closed in 1865. The new Universidad Nacional de México opened in 1910, with the word Autónoma being added to its title in 1929. After it had functioned for a few decades in buildings elsewhere in the city, the purpose-built Ciudad Universitaria was constructed (between 1950 and 1954) by a team of 150 young architects, sculptors and technicians headed by José García Villagrán, Mario Pani and Enrique del Moral. It stands on part of a vast dried-up lava field called El Pedregal.

The university is a monument both to national pride, with its buildings covered in optimistic murals linking Mexican and global themes, and to an idealistic education system in which almost anyone is entitled to university tuition.

UNAM has 270,000 students and 30,000 teachers. It has often been a center of political dissent, most notably prior to the 1968 Olympics, held in Mexico City, when protests culminated in the tragic massacre at Tlatelolco (see the Tlatelolco section, earlier in this chapter). In 1999-2000 the university was closed by a student strike for 9½ months (see 'The UNAM Strike').

In normal times during the school semesters, the campus is busy with student life; out of term, when its libraries, faculties and cafés are closed, it's very quiet but still open to visitors.

The campus is divided into two main parts. Most of the faculty buildings are scattered over an area about 1 km square at the north end. The second section, about 2km farther south, includes the Centro Cultural Universitario. Student cafés in the Facultad de Economía and the Unidad Posgrado, both off the east end of the Jardín Central in the northern section, and in the Centro Cultural Universitario, are open to visitors during semesters.

Northern Section

As you enter the northern part of the campus from Insurgentes, it's easy to spot the **Biblioteca Central** (Central Library) – 10 floors high, almost windowless, and covered on every side with colorful, complicatedly symbolic mosaics by Juan O'Gorman. The south wall, with two prominent circles toward the top, covers colonial times. The theme of the north wall is Aztec culture. The east wall shows the creation of modern Mexico, including the revolution, and the west wall represents Mexico in more recent times.

La Rectoría, the Rectorate administration building southwest of the library, at the top (west) end of the wide, grassy Jardín Central, has a spectacular 3-D Siqueiros mosaic on its south wall, showing students urged on by the people.

The building south of La Rectoría contains the campus's Librería Central (Central Bookstore), and the **Museo Universitario de**

The UNAM Strike

The strike at UNAM began on April 20, 1999 as a protest against a proposed rise in tuition fees from a token US$0.02 a semester to an average US$65. The university authorities soon abandoned the planned fee increase, but the strikers had by then developed other demands such as the reinstatement of automatic admission to UNAM from its affiliated high schools (a practice scrapped in 1997) and a far-reaching reorganization of the university. The strike also became a wider protest against the Zedillo government's international free-market economic policies, which, many Mexicans argue, set the poor at a disadvantage.

Eventually support for the strike waned, with its leadership increasingly in the hands of radicals. After violent clashes elsewhere in Mexico City that involved UNAM strikers in early 2000, police retook the occupied UNAM campus on February 6. It was a testament to the scars left on the national psyche by the 1968 Tlatelolco massacre that the government had refrained so long from taking any decisive action, and that when it did so, the police carried no firearms and no one was injured.

The strike did further damage to UNAM's already battered academic reputation. Though most recent Mexican presidents and most leading contemporary Mexican politicians, for example, are UNAM graduates, in recent years UNAM has struggled to compete academically with increasingly prestigious Mexican private universities. During the strike numbers of students abandoned UNAM to study elsewhere. Ironically, the proposed tuition hike would have helped improve facilities at UNAM.

Ciencias y Artes (University Sciences & Arts Museum, ☎ 5-622-04-00), open 10 am to 8 pm Monday to Friday, 10 am to 6 pm Saturday and Sunday (US$0.60), with contemporary art and interactive scientific displays.

The **Auditorio Alfonso Caso**, at the bottom (east) end of the Jardín Central, has on its north end a mural by José Chávez Morado showing the conquest of energy. Humanity progresses from the shadow of a primitive jaguar god to the use of fire and then the atom, before emerging into an ethereal, apparently female, future. The east side of the same building depicts a progression from primitive agriculture to modern science.

A little farther east, on the west wall of the **Facultad de Medicina**, a mosaic in Italian stone by Francisco Eppens interprets the themes of life and death in Mexican terms. The central mask has a Spanish profile on the left, an indigenous one on the right, together making up a mestizo face in the middle. An ear of maize and symbols of Aztec and Mayan gods represent the forces of life and death.

Estadio Olímpico

The Olympic Stadium, on the west side of Insurgentes opposite the northern part of the campus, is designed to resemble a rather elliptical volcano cone and is made almost entirely of volcanic rock. It can hold 80,000 people. A Diego Rivera sports-themed mosaic surmounts its main entrance. The stadium is home to the UNAM soccer team, Las Pumas. You can peep inside when it's closed by going to Gate 38, at the south end.

Southern Section

The **Centro Cultural Universitario** (University Cultural Center) is the focus of the southern part of the campus. To reach it take a bus or pesero south on Insurgentes to the second footbridge south of the Estadio Olímpico, then walk the short distance into the campus. Go down the steps behind Rufino Tamayo's tall black sculpture, *La Universidad Germen de Humanismo y Sabiduría* (The University, Seed of Humanism and Wisdom). You'll find the Sala Nezahualcóyotl, one of Mexico City's main concert halls, down here on the left, and a collection of theaters, cinemas and smaller concert halls to the right. Nearby is **Universum** (☎ 5-622-72-87), a hands-on children's science museum, open 9 am to 5 pm Monday to Friday, 10 am to 5 pm Saturday and Sunday (US$2).

The large **Unidad Bibliográfica** (Bibliographic Unit), which houses part of Mexico's National Library, is about 200m north of the Centro Cultural. About 300m northeast of the Unidad Bibliográfica is the **Espacio Escultórico** (Sculptural Space), focused on a work by Mathias Goeritz that few can explain, but that most people agree is striking. It consists of concrete shapes about a round platform, set on a bare lava bed.

Getting There & Away

Any pesero or bus marked 'Villa Olímpica,' 'Perisur' or 'Cuicuilco' traveling south on Avenida Insurgentes from Paseo de la Reforma or San Ángel will take you to the Ciudad Universitaria. If you're north of San Ángel and none of these shows up, take one marked 'San Ángel' and change to another vehicle in San Ángel (on Avenida Insurgentes or at the pesero terminal on Dr Gálvez).

For the northern part of the campus, get off at the first yellow footbridge crossing Insurgentes, a little over 1km from San Ángel, just before the Estadio Olímpico. For the southern part of the campus, get off at the third yellow footbridge from San Ángel (second after the Estadio Olímpico).

From the Centro Histórico, 'CU' peseros run south on Bolívar at Uruguay.

Returning north, 'San Ángel,' 'M(etro) Insurgentes,' 'M(etro) Indios Verdes' and 'M(etro) La Raza' buses or peseros take you along Insurgentes as far as their respective destinations.

Copilco metro station is near the northeast edge of the campus, 1km east of the Biblioteca Central.

CUICUILCO

The early **archaeological site** of Cuicuilco is set just back from the east side of Avenida Insurgentes, just over 1km south of the southern section of the Ciudad Universitaria. The Villa Olímpica (the Olympic Village for the 1968 games), now turned into housing, is on the west side of Insurgentes opposite the site.

Cuicuilco was probably the biggest settlement in the Valle de México from approximately 600 to 200 BC. At this time the Valle de México was something of a backwater, but Cuicuilco is estimated to have had a population of 20,000, and traces of a street layout have been found. It was still occupied when it was buried by the eruption of Xitle volcano, to the south, around 100 AD.

The site and its museum (☎ 5-606-97-58), in an area now called the Parque Ecológico Cuicuilco, are open 9 am to 5 pm daily (free). The main structure is the Pirámide de Cuicuilco, a round, tiered pyramid, 118m wide and 23m high, which you can see as you approach from Insurgentes. A 10m layer of lava has been removed from its lower levels. Atop the pyramid are the remains of an altar. The pyramid shows that Cuicuilco must have been a ceremonial center of an organized, priest-dominated society. Earlier temples in the Valle de México were thatch-roofed affairs on low earth mounds.

Just south of the site is the Cuicuilco branch of the **Museo Soumaya** (☎ 5-223-17-46), Insurgentes Sur 3500, showing temporary expositions, often interesting ones. It's open 10.30 am to 6.30 pm daily, except Wednesday (free). Behind the museum is one of the city's newest and glossiest shopping malls, **Plaza Cuicuilco**.

To reach the Cuicuilco archaeological site, take a 'Cuicuilco,' 'Ajusco,' 'Plaza Cuicuilco' or 'Villa Olímpica' pesero or bus south on Insurgentes from San Ángel or the Ciudad Universitaria, and get off immediately after going under the Anillo Periférico ring road. Returning north, catch a 'San Ángel' or 'M(etro) Insurgentes' vehicle.

REINO AVENTURA

Out in the southwest of the city, 1.4km south of the Anillo Periférico ring road, is Reino Aventura (☎ 5-728-72-00, 5-645-44-57), Carretera Picacho-Ajusco 1500, claiming to be the biggest amusement park in Latin America. It has a dolphinarium, rides, shows, concerts and restaurants. Different areas of the park represent different parts of the world, including Morocco, Switzerland and Polynesia.

Check current hours before going: it's normally open 10 am to 7 pm Friday to Sunday, but may open daily during school holidays. A standard ticket giving entry to many attractions is US$8. 'Reino Aventura' peseros leave from several metro stations including Universidad and MA de Quevedo (Map 1).

COYOACÁN

About 10km south of downtown Mexico City, Coyoacán ('Place of Coyotes' in the Aztec language, Nahuatl) was Cortés' base after the fall of Tenochtitlán. At that time it was on the southern shore of Lago de Texcoco. It remained a small town outside Mexico City until the urban sprawl reached it about 50 years ago. Close to the university and once home to Leon Trotsky and Frida Kahlo (whose old houses are now fascinating museums), it still has its own identity, with narrow colonial-era streets, plazas, cafés and a bohemian atmosphere. Assorted musicians, mime artists and craft markets draw large, relaxed crowds from all walks of life to Coyoacán's central plazas, Plaza Hidalgo and Jardín del Centenario, especially on Saturdays and Sundays.

There's a helpful tourist information office (☎ 5-659-22-56 ext 181), open 9 am to 8 pm daily, in the Casa de Cortés at Plaza Hidalgo 1.

Walking Tour

A pleasant way to approach Coyoacán is from Viveros metro station via the **Viveros de Coyoacán** plant nurseries, a swath of greenery popular with joggers that's about 1km west of Coyoacán's central plazas. You can stroll here any day between 6 am and 6 pm for free. To get here from Viveros metro station, walk south along Avenida Universidad, then take the first street on the left, Pérez Valenzuela. An entrance to the Viveros de Coyoacán is a short distance along Pérez Valenzuela, on the left.

A block south from the southeast corner of the Viveros is the pretty little **Plaza Santa Catarina**. On the plaza's east side is a small church, and on the west side a couple of cafés. The 700m walk east from here along **Avenida Sosa** to Coyoacán's central plazas takes you past 16th- and 17th-century houses, though most are hidden behind high walls.

After you've taken in the adjoining central plazas, **Jardín del Centenario** and **Plaza Hidalgo**, you'll probably want to head north to the **Museo Frida Kahlo** and/or the **Museo Léon Trotsky**, but you might detour first to **Plaza de la Conchita**. From the Kahlo or Trotsky museums, you could head a block or two south to Xicoténcatl, then walk east along this fairly quiet street to the **Ex-Convento de Churubusco** and/or the **Centro Nacional de las Artes**, before catching the metro at General Anaya station.

Plaza Hidalgo & Jardín del Centenario

The focus of Coyoacán life and the scene of most of the area's weekend fun, are its twin central plazas. The eastern Plaza Hidalgo has a statue of Miguel Hidalgo, the western Jardín del Centenario is surrounded by attractive cafés and centers on a fountain with a coyote sculpture, which is a symbol of Coyoacán. Calle Aguayo/Carrillo Puerto divides the two plazas.

The Coyoacán tourist office is housed in the former Coyoacán town hall (Ayuntamiento), also called the **Casa de Cortés**, on the north side of Plaza Hidalgo. It's said that on this spot the Spanish tortured the defeated Aztec king Cuauhtémoc to try to make him reveal the whereabouts of treasure. The existing 18th-century building was the headquarters of the Marquesado del Valle de Oaxaca, the Cortés family's lands in Mexico, which included Coyoacán. Above the entrance is the coat of arms bestowed on Coyoacán by King Carlos IV of Spain.

The **Parroquia de San Juan Bautista**, Coyoacán's parish church and the adjacent ex-monastery, both on the south side of Plaza Hidalgo, were built for Dominican monks in the 16th century. Half a block east of Plaza Hidalgo is the **Museo Nacional de Culturas Populares** (☎ 5-554-89-68), Avenida

Hidalgo 289, which has good temporary exhibitions on popular cultural forms like *lucha libre* (a kind of wrestling; see the Entertainment chapter), *nacimientos* (nativity models) and circuses. It's open 10 am to 6 pm Tuesday to Sunday (usually free).

Plaza de la Conchita

Formally called Plaza de la Concepción, this peaceful little square is two blocks southeast of Plaza Hidalgo, along Higuera. The red house on the corner of Higuera (not open to the public) is the 'Casa Colorada.' Cortés is said to have built it for La Malinche, his Mexican interpreter and mistress, and to have had his Spanish wife, Catalina Juárez de Marcaida, murdered there. On the east side of the plaza stands a pretty, little 18th-century baroque chapel, the Capilla de la Conchita.

East of Plaza de la Conchita is the Jardín Frida Kahlo, a park with a statue of the artist atop a pyramidal base in pre-Hispanic style.

Museo Frida Kahlo

The 'Blue House' (☎ 5-554-59-99), Londres 247 on the corner of Allende, six blocks north of Plaza Hidalgo, was the long-time home of artist Frida Kahlo, who was born here in 1907 and also lived here for her last 13 years, 1941-54. See 'Diego & Frida' for more on her life.

Kahlo and her husband Diego Rivera were part of a glamorous but far from harmonious leftist intellectual circle (which included, in the 1930s, Leon Trotsky). The house is littered with mementos of the artistic and revolutionary couple, and contains some of their artwork. You'll also see pre-Hispanic objects and Mexican crafts they collected, as well as art by José María Velasco, Marcel Duchamp, José Clemente Orozco, Paul Klee and others.

The Kahlo art on show is mostly lesser works, but it still expresses the anguish of her existence: one painting called *El Marxismo Dará la Salud* (Marxism Will Give Health) shows her casting away her crutches. In the upstairs studio an unfinished portrait of Stalin, who became a Kahlo hero after Rivera had fallen out with Trotsky,

stands before a poignantly positioned wheelchair. The folk art collection includes Mexican regional costumes worn by Kahlo, and Rivera's collection of small retablo paintings done by Mexicans to give thanks for miracles.

The house and its garden are open 10 am to 5.45 pm Tuesday to Sunday (US$2). Guided tours in English are given every half-hour from 3 to 4.30 pm on Saturday and 11 am to 3.30 pm on Sunday. In the garden are a small café and a small bookshop.

Museo Léon Trotsky

After losing to Stalin in the Soviet power struggle that followed Lenin's death, Leon Trotsky was expelled from that country in 1929. Condemned to death in absentia, in 1937 he found refuge in Mexico under President Lázaro Cárdenas, thanks to the support of Diego Rivera and Frida Kahlo. At first Trotsky and his wife, Natalia, lived in Kahlo's 'Blue House,' but after falling out with Rivera (see 'Diego & Frida') in May 1939, they moved a few streets away to this house at Viena 45, which is now a museum (☎ 5-554-06-87).

The place has been left pretty much as it was on the day in 1940 when a Stalin agent finally caught up with Trotsky and killed him here. High walls and watchtowers – once occupied by armed guards – surround the house and small garden. These defenses were built after a first attempt on Trotsky's life on May 24, 1940, when 20 attackers led by the Mexican artist David Alfaro Siqueiros (then a member of the Mexican Communist Party) pumped bullets into the house. Trotsky and Natalia survived by hiding under their bedroom furniture. The bullet holes remain.

The final, fatal attack took place in Trotsky's study. The assassin had several identities but is usually known as Ramón Mercader, a Catalan. He had managed to become the lover of Trotsky's secretary and had gained the confidence of the household. On August 20, 1940, he went to Trotsky at his desk, and asked him to look at an article he had written. Mercader then pulled an ice pick from under his coat and smashed it into

Diego & Frida

Diego Rivera, born in Guanajuato in 1886, first met Frida Kahlo, 21 years his junior, in the early 1920s. He was working at Mexico City's prestigious Escuela Nacional Preparatoria (National Preparatory School), which she was attending. Rivera was already a socialist and at the forefront of Mexican art; his commission for a mural at the school was the first of many major, semipropagandistic murals on public buildings that he would execute over the next 30 years. Rivera was also already an inveterate womanizer: he had fathered children by two Russian women in Europe and in 1922 he married Lupe Marín in Mexico. She bore him two more children before their marriage broke up in 1928.

Kahlo, born in Coyoacán in 1907, had contracted polio at the age of six, which left her right leg permanently thinner than her left. At school she was a tomboyish character. In 1925 she was horribly injured in a bus accident that left her with multiple fractures in her back and right leg, plus broken ribs and a broken collarbone and pelvis. She made a miraculous recovery but suffered much pain thereafter and underwent many operations. It was during convalescence from her accident that she began painting. Pain, both physical and emotional, was to be a dominating theme of her art.

Kahlo and Rivera both moved in left-wing artistic circles and met again in 1928 at a party given by the photographer Tina Modotti. 'I did not know it then, but Frida had already become the most important fact in my life,' Rivera later wrote. They married the following year. The liaison, which has been described as a union between an elephant and a dove (he was big and fat, she short and thin), was always a passionate, stormy, love-hate affair. Rivera wrote: 'If I ever loved a woman, the more I loved her, the more I wanted to hurt her. Frida was only the most obvious victim of this disgusting trait.' Both had many extramarital affairs; Kahlo was bisexual and her beauty and unconventional behavior – she drank tequila, swore, told dirty jokes and held wild parties – fascinated many people.

In 1934 the pair, after a spell in the USA, moved into a new home built for them by Juan O'Gorman in San Ángel, merely a village at that time. The place had a separate house for each of them. In 1937 the exiled Russian revolutionary Leon Trotsky arrived in Mexico with his wife Natalia, after Rivera had persuaded President Lázaro Cárdenas to allow them refuge. The Trotskys moved into the 'Blue House,' Kahlo's birthplace in Coyoacán. In 1938 the French surrealist poet André Breton and his wife Jacqueline came to Mexico too, and moved in with Kahlo and Rivera at the San Ángel house. Rivera, Kahlo, the Trotskys and the Bretons all socialized and traveled together in Mexico, and Kahlo and Leon Trotsky wound up having an affair. Rivera quarreled with Trotsky and in 1939 the Trotskys moved to a different house in Coyoacán.

The following year Rivera and Kahlo divorced. Rivera went to San Francisco. Soon afterward, Trotsky was assassinated at his Coyoacán home. Kahlo and Rivera remarried in San Francisco but, back in Mexico, she moved into the Blue House while he stayed at San Ángel – a state of affairs that endured for the rest of their lives, though their relationship endured too. Kahlo remained Rivera's most trusted critic, Rivera was Kahlo's biggest fan.

Kahlo had only one exhibition in Mexico in her lifetime, in 1953. She arrived at the opening on a stretcher. Rivera said of the exhibition: 'Anyone who attended it could not but marvel at her great talent.' Later that year Kahlo's lower right leg was amputated because of gangrene. She died in 1954. Her last public appearance was with Rivera at a demonstration against CIA intervention in Guatemala. The final words in her diary were: 'I hope the leaving is joyful and I hope never to return.' Rivera called the day of her death 'the most tragic day of my life . . . too late I realized that the most wonderful part of my life had been my love for Frida.'

In 1955 Rivera married Emma Hurtado, his agent since 1946. He died in 1957.

Diego & Frida

Kahlo & Rivera Sites There's much more of his work than hers on view in and around Mexico City – partly because he was a more prolific, public and versatile artist, partly because some of her best work is in private collections or other countries. The sections of this or the Excursions chapter in which each site is covered are in parentheses at the end of each entry below:

Anahuacalli – fortress-like museum designed by Rivera to house his pre-Hispanic art collection (Coyoacán)

Estadio Olímpico – Rivera mosaic (Ciudad Universitaria)

Museo de Arte Carrillo Gil – includes Rivera work (San Ángel)

Museo de Arte Moderno – includes works by Kahlo and Rivera (Bosque de Chapultepec)

Museo y Casa de Diego Rivera – Rivera's birthplace, with some 70 of his paintings and sketches (Excursions: Guanajuato)

Museo Casa Estudio Diego Rivera y Frida Kahlo – the double house built for them by Juan O'Gorman (San Ángel)

Museo Dolores Olmedo Patiño – 137 Rivera works and a room of Kahlos in the excellent collection of a Rivera associate (Xochimilco & Around)

Museo Frida Kahlo – the 'Blue House' where Kahlo was born and died (Coyoacán)

Museo Mural Diego Rivera – Rivera's mural *Sueño de una Tarde Dominical en la Alameda* (Alameda Central & Around)

Museo Robert Brady – Kahlo paintings (Excursions: Cuernavaca)

Museo de San Ildefonso – the former Escuela Nacional Preparatoria; mural by Rivera (Centro Histórico)

Museo de la Secretaría de Hacienda y Crédito Público – includes works by Rivera (Centro Histórico)

Palacio de Bellas Artes – 1930s Rivera murals including *El Hombre, Contralor del Universo* (Alameda Central & Around)

Palacio de Cortés – 1920s Rivera mural of scenes from the Spanish conquest to the 1910 Revolution (Excursions: Cuernavaca)

Palacio Nacional – Rivera's mural interpretation of the history of Mexican civilization (Centro Histórico)

Secretaría de Educación Pública – 235 mural panels painted by Rivera in the 1920s (Centro Histórico)

Universidad Autónoma de Chapingo – Rivera's masterpieces, on agricultural and fertility themes, in the Capilla Diego Rivera (Excursions: Texcoco)

Trotsky's demise

the back of Trotsky's skull. Trotsky died the next day; Mercader was arrested and spent 20 years in prison. Books and magazines on Trotsky's desk and in bookcases give an intriguing glimpse of the great revolutionary's preoccupations.

Displays in outbuildings show photos of Trotsky's time in Mexico, plus biographical notes (in Spanish) and memorabilia such as a pair of Trotsky's trademark small, round spectacles. The garden contains a tomb, designed by Juan O'Gorman, that holds Trotskys' ashes.

Hours are 10 am to 5 pm Tuesday to Sunday (US$1, half-price for ISIC cardholders). To enter the museum go to its northern entrance at Avenida Río Churubusco 410, near the corner of Morelos.

Ex-Convento de Churubusco

Less than 1.5km east of the Museo León Trotsky stands the 17th-century former Monastery of Churubusco, scene of one of Mexico's heroic military defeats. It's on Calle 20 de Agosto, a block east of Avenida División del Norte along Xicoténcatl.

On August 20, 1847, an invading US army was advancing on Mexico City from Veracruz. Mexicans who had fortified the old monastery fought until they ran out of ammunition and were finally beaten only after hand-to-hand fighting. General Pedro Anaya, asked by US general David Twiggs to surrender his ammunition, is said to have answered: 'If there was any, you wouldn't be

here.' Cannon and memorials outside the monastery recall these events.

The monastery's church, on its west side, still functions, but most of the monastery is occupied by the interesting **Museo Nacional de las Intervenciones** (National Interventions Museum, ☎ 5-604-06-99). Displays include an American map showing operations in 1847 (note how far outside the city Churubusco was then), and material on the French occupation in the 1860s and the plot by US ambassador Henry Lane Wilson to bring down the Madero government in 1913. It's open 9 am to 6 pm Tuesday to Sunday (US$1.50). Some parts of the peaceful old monastery gardens are also open.

You can reach Churubusco on an eastbound 'M(etro) Gral Anaya' pesero – catch it on Xicoténcatl at Allende, a few blocks north of Coyoacán's Plaza Hidalgo. Alternatively, it's about a 500m walk from General Anaya metro station.

Centro Nacional de las Artes

The National Arts Center (☎ 5-420-45-09), on Avenida Río Churubusco just east of Calzada de Tlalpan, is a modern hothouse of the arts. It's home to the Auditorio Blas Galindo, the Teatro de las Artes and two other theaters, the national music conservatory and schools of theater, dance, cinema, painting, sculpture and engraving. Even if you're not here for a performance, it's still interesting to stroll through the grounds amid the modern architecture and browse the center's excellent bookshop and art materials shop (Ⓜ General Anaya or Ermita).

Anahuacalli

This dramatic museum (☎ 5-617-37-97), at Calle del Museo 150, 3.5km south of central Coyoacán, was designed by Diego Rivera to house his own excellent collection of pre-Hispanic art. It also contains one of his studios and some of his own work.

The fortresslike building is made of dark volcanic stone and incorporates stylistic features from many pre-Hispanic cultures. Its name means House of Anáhuac (Anáhuac was the Aztec name for the Valle de México). An inscription over the door reads:

'To return to the people the artistic inheritance I was able to redeem from their ancestors.' If the air is clear, the view over the city from the roof is great.

The archaeological exhibits are mostly pottery and stone figures, chosen primarily for their artistic qualities. Among Rivera's own art, the most interesting are studies for major murals, like *El Hombre en el Cruce de los Caminos* (Man at the Crossroads) whose final version, *El Hombre, Contralor del Universo*, is in Mexico City's Palacio de Bellas Artes. The Anahuacalli is open 10 am to 6 pm daily except Monday (US$1; Map 1).

To get there from Coyoacán, catch a 'Villa Coapa' pesero south on Tres Cruces. This will eventually travel south on Avenida División del Norte. Three kilometers from Coyoacán, get off at Calle del Museo (there are traffic lights and a church at the intersection), and walk 600m southwest along Calle del Museo, curving to the left at first, then going slightly uphill. Returning northward, take a 'M(etro) División del Norte' pesero or bus along Avenida División del Norte: you can get off at Calle General Anaya and walk into central Coyoacán if you wish.

From central Mexico City you can take the metro to Tasqueña, then the Tren Ligero (streetcar, US$0.20) from the Tasqueña metro station to Xotepingo. Follow 'Salida a Museo' signs at Xotepingo station and go three short blocks west along Xotepingo to the traffic lights at Avenida División del Norte. Then continue ahead along Calle del Museo for 600m, as described in the previous paragraph.

Getting There & Away

The nearest metro stations to Coyoacán are Viveros, Coyoacán and General Anaya, all 1.5 to 2km away. If you don't fancy a walk (or a taxi) from Viveros station, walk south to Pérez Valenzuela and catch an eastbound 'M(etro) Gral Anaya' pesero to Allende; or from Coyoacán station take a 'Coyoacán' pesero going southeast on Avenida México. Many peseros and buses go to central Coyoacán from General Anaya station, too.

For the return trip to these metro stations from central Coyoacán, 'M(etro) Viveros' peseros go west on Malitzin from Allende, 'M(etro) Coyoacán' peseros run north on Aguayo, and 'M(etro) Gral Anaya' peseros head east on Xicoténcatl from Allende.

If you prefer to travel by surface from the city center, 'Coyoacán' peseros run south on Bucareli from Paseo de la Reforma, a couple of blocks west of the Alameda Central.

To reach San Ángel from Coyoacán, 'San Ángel' peseros and/or buses head west on Malitzin from Allende, west on Avenida MA de Quevedo, five blocks south of Plaza Hidalgo, or south on Avenida Universidad from Viveros metro station. A taxi is about US$1. To reach the Ciudad Universitaria, take a 'M(etro) Copilco' pesero west on Malitzin from Allende.

CERRO DE LA ESTRELLA

When you've had enough of the Mexico City streets and crowds, a nice thing to do (in daylight) is to hop on the metro to Iztapalapa station and take a walk up Cerro de la Estrella, an extinct volcanic cone about 12km southeast of downtown. The upper part of the hill is covered in eucalyptus trees, and around the base of the summit is a circular road affording fine 360-degree views. It's instructive to remind yourself that most of the area between here and the city center used to be a lake. You should allow yourself two hours for the walk to the top and back to the metro station at a not-too-strenuous pace.

In Aztec times Cerro de la Estrella, then called Huizachtépetl, was the site of important ceremonies and sacrifices connected with the Aztec new year (in spring). Every 52 years priests here had the responsibility of keeping the world going by lighting a sacred flame to inaugurate a new 52-year cycle of life. Today, the reenactment of the Crucifixion during Iztapalapa's Semana Santa rituals takes place on the hill (see 'A Vivid Production' in the Facts for the Visitor chapter). During December, in a sort of pre-Hispanic revivalist celebration, the people of Iztapalapa make a torch-lit procession up the hill and sing and dance in pre-Hispanic mode on the top.

To get up the hill, turn left out of the entrance of Iztapalapa station, then take the first street on the left, E Corona. At the end of E Corona turn left along the busy, wide street Ermita Iztapalapa. After 350m (35m after a footbridge) turn up to the right on Estrella and follow this street up through semi-open areas to the hill. Just below the start of the wooded slopes, the **Museo Fuego Nuevo** (Museum of the New Flame, ☎ 5-686-94-43) has material on the geology and vegetation of the area as well as its pre-Hispanic importance. It's open 10 am to 2 pm Tuesday to Friday, 10 am to 4 pm Saturday and Sunday (US$0.10; Map 1).

XOCHIMILCO & AROUND

About 20km south of downtown Mexico City, the urban sprawl is strung with a network of canals lined by gardens and agricultural plots, some with houses and their patches of waterside lawn. These are the so-called 'floating gardens' of Xochimilco ('so-chi-MEEL-co'), survivors of the chinampas where the Aztecs grew much of their food. A gondola trip along the canals is an enjoyable, if not often tranquil, experience. Not far from Xochimilco is one of the city's best art museums, the Museo Dolores Olmedo Patiño, and the enjoyable Parque Ecológico de Xochimilco.

Museo Dolores Olmedo Patiño

Opened in 1994 a little over 2km west of Xochimilco, the Dolores Olmedo Patiño Museum (☎ 5-555-08-91), Avenida México 5843, has arguably the biggest and most important Diego Rivera collection of all. It's a fascinating place, set in a peaceful 16th-century hacienda with extensive gardens.

As a rich socialite, Señora Olmedo, who still lives in part of the mansion, was one of Rivera's leading patrons, amassing a large collection of his art, which late in life she decided to put on public display. The museum's 137 Rivera works – oils, watercolors, drawings and lithographs – are drawn from many periods of his life, including Cubist works from 1916, paintings done in Russia in 1956, and 20 sunsets painted on the balcony of Dolores Olmedo's house in

Acapulco. They're displayed together with a fine collection of pre-Hispanic pottery figures and metalwork, as well as memorabilia.

The museum also has a room of Frida Kahlo paintings, including an especially anguished self-portrait depicting her spine as a stone column broken in several places. Elsewhere in the museum you'll find Emperor Maximilian's 365-piece silverware set and an impressive and colorful collection of Mexican folk art.

The museum is open 10 am to 6 pm daily except Monday (US$1). As you cross the gardens from the entrance to the main building, you may spot some of Señora Olmedo's *xoloitzcuintles*, hairless dogs of a pre-Hispanic breed that is now almost extinct.

Getting There & Away Take the metro to Tasqueña, then the Tren Ligero (streetcar, US$0.20) from Tasqueña metro station to La Noria. Leaving La Noria station, turn left at the top of the steps, walk down to the street and continue ahead to an intersection with a footbridge over it. Here make a sharp left – almost doubling back on your path – onto Antiguo Camino Xochimilco. The museum is 300m down this street, just past the first intersection. Altogether the trip is about one hour from the city center.

Xochimilco

The name Xochimilco means 'Place where Flowers Grow' in Nahuatl. Pre-Hispanic inhabitants piled up vegetation and lake mud here in the shallow waters of Lago de Xochimilco, a southern offshoot of Lago de Texcoco, to make fertile gardens called chinampas. These became one of the economic bases of the Aztec empire. As the chinampas proliferated, much of the lake was transformed into a series of canals. About 180km of these canals remain today, some now running between gardens and homes with pretty patches of waterside lawn, others bordering surviving chinampas.

An environmental recovery program since 1989 has eliminated a lot of the pollution that urban sprawl had brought to this corner of the city, and the canals of Xochimilco remain one of Mexico City's favorite places for a bit of fun and relaxation. You can choose between several places to board your boat. Xochimilco also boasts a beautiful church, a bustling daily market and its own archaeological museum. It has its own tourist information office too (☎ 5-676-08-10), at Pino 36, just off the central plaza – open 9 am to 9 pm daily (to 8 pm Sundays).

The **Mercado de Xochimilco** occupies the two blocks south of the central plaza and the pink-painted **Parroquia de San Bernardino de Siena**, Xochimilco's 16th-century church, is on the east side of the plaza. The church's elaborate, gold-painted retablo dates from 1590. You can enter the church and its pretty churchyard from 7 am to 1 pm and 4.30 to 8 pm daily.

Most people board their *trajinera* (gondola) at one of the *embarcaderos* (boat landings) near the center of Xochimilco (see map). Hundreds of colorful trajineras, each punted along by one person with a pole, wait to cruise the canals with parties of merrymakers. There are even waterborne mariachi and marimba bands, photographers, and hawkers of food, drink and handicrafts.

On weekends, especially Sundays, a fiesta atmosphere takes over as the town and waterways of Xochimilco become jammed with people arranging boats, cruising the canals or trying to talk you into buying something. If you fancy a more relaxed atmosphere, come on a weekday, when visitors and hawkers are far fewer.

Official prices for the boats are posted up at the embarcaderos and you needn't pay more, though boatmen or touts may try to persuade you to do so. At most of the embarcaderos a four-person boat (yellow roof) is US$5 an hour; an eight-person boat (red), US$6; a 12-person boat (blue), US$8; and a 16-person boat (green), US$10. On Saturdays, Sundays and holidays, 60-person *lanchas* (motor boats) charging only US$0.50 a person depart from the Salitre and Caltongo embarcaderos.

Fixed prices for food, drink and even music on the waterways are also posted at the embarcaderos – one tune costs US$1.50

on marimbas but US$3.50 from mariachis! You can get a taste of Xochimilco in one hour, but it's worth going for longer; you can go farther and see more, and you get a proper chance to relax.

The **Museo Arqueológico de Xochimilco** (☎ 5-641-68-47) is at the corner of Avenida Tenochtitlán and La Planta, 4km southeast of central Xochimilco. Displays recreate the life of pre-Hispanic Xochimilco and exhibit artifacts of Aztec, Teotihuacán and Olmec influence. It's open 10 am to 5 pm Tuesday to Sunday (free).

Getting There & Away To reach central Xochimilco, take the metro to Tasqueña station, then take the Tren Ligero (streetcar, US$0.20), which starts there, to its last stop, Embarcadero. From Embarcadero station, walk to the left (north) along Avenida Morelos to the market, plaza and church. Five embarcaderos are within 500m of the plaza.

Alternatively, 'Xochimilco' buses and peseros run from outside Tasqueña metro station. It's about 45 minutes from Tasqueña to Xochimilco either way. The last Tren Ligero back to Tasqueña leaves Embarcadero station about 11 pm.

To reach the Nativitas and Zacapa embarcaderos, some 2km southeast of central Xochimilco, board a 'Galeana' pesero southbound on Ramírez del Castillo, a block west of the plaza. This or a 'Tulyehualco' pesero from the same place will take you to the Museo Arqueológico.

Parque Ecológico de Xochimilco

About 3km north of downtown Xochimilco, this 2-sq-km park (☎ 5-673-80-61) contains canals, lakes, ponds, pathways, an incipient botanical garden, demonstration chinampas and a large number and variety of water birds. It's truly surprising to see so many herons, ducks, moorhens, egrets and other fowl within the confines of Mexico City. Though it's enjoyable to walk round the park's pathways, you can also see it by bicycle (US$0.70 for 30 minutes), pedal boat or trajinera. A Centro de Información has displays on the park's plants and birds. The one drawback at this early stage in the park's history – it was founded in the early 1990s – is the lack of mature trees for shade. In summer the park is open 9 am to 7 pm Tuesday to Sunday, in winter it's open (same days) 10 am to 6pm (US$1.50).

On the north side of the Periférico ring road, opposite the park, is a smaller, less interesting section of the Parque Ecológico and a large flower, plant and vegetable market, the Mercado de Flores, Plantas y Hortalizas.

Just west of the park – but a 2km walk from the entrance – is the Embarcadero Cuemanco, the best place to take a trajinera if you want to see the genuine chinampas of northern Xochimilco.

Getting There & Away To reach Parque Ecológico de Xochimilco, take a 'Tlahuac' pesero northbound from the corner of Calzada de Tlalpan and Ciclistas, outside General Anaya metro station. The route is circuitous but after 20 to 30 minutes the pesero will be heading east along the busy Periférico ring road, with the park's Lago Huetzalin on your right and the tentlike roofs of the Mercado de Flores, Plantas y Hortalizas on your left. The park entrance is beside a blue footbridge with blue-and-red spiral towers near each end.

Coming to the park from central Xochimilco, you could take a 'M(etro) Tasqueña' pesero north on Prolongación División del Norte as far as the Periférico, then a 'Canal de Chalco' pesero east along the Periférico to the park.

Leaving the park, cross the footbridge to the westbound bus stop on the north side of the Periférico. 'M(etro) CU' and 'M(etro) Tasqueña' peseros or buses will take you to Universidad and Tasqueña stations respectively, and 'Perisur' peseros will take you to the Periférico's intersection with Prolongación División del Norte, where you can catch a southbound 'Xochimilco' pesero to central Xochimilco.

ICE SKATING

The Pista de Hielo San Jerónimo ice rink (☎ 5-683-19-29) is at Avenida Contreras 300

in Colonia San Jerónimo Lídice, 2.5km west of the Ciudad Universitaria. It's open 11 am to 8 pm Tuesday to Sunday, but closes 3 to 5 pm on Tuesday and 3 to 4 pm Wednesday and Thursday. Cost is US$3 an hour or US$4 for a day including hire of skates. You can get there by a 'Contreras' pesero from Copilco metro station: get off at the Glorieta San Jerónimo intersection on the Periférico ring road (Map 1).

COURSES

Studying in Mexico City can be a great way to meet people and get an inside angle on local life, as well as to learn something.

Language & Culture

The United States International University (☎ 5-264-21-87, fax 5-264-21-88, www .usiumexico.edu), Obregón 110, in attractive Colonia Roma, is a small private university with well-qualified staff. It offers a one-week (15 hours) Spanish course, focusing on survival Spanish and Mexican Spanish, starting every Monday (US$85). It also does a five-week intensive Spanish-language summer course with cultural components for US$1400, including accommodation and two meals a day. For information, call, fax or write USIU-Mexico, Obregón 110, Colonia Roma, México DF 06700, Mexico. This university also puts on a variety of other events and activities, such as guided cultural tours and open lectures and seminars, many of which can be joined on a one-event basis. It's worth popping by to see what's coming up if you're in the city for more than a few days (Map 7).

The Centro de Enseñanza Para Extranjeros (CEPE, Foreigners' Teaching Center, ☎ 5-622-24-70, fax 5-616-26-72, cepe@ servidor.unam.mx) at UNAM offers six-week intensive courses in Spanish language and Latin American culture, five times a year. Classes cater to both beginners and others. Though classes can be quite large, the courses have received good reports from students we have met. For US$265 (US$375 for summer courses, June to August), you get three or more hours in the classroom, five days a week. UNAM offers other courses in Latin American culture, history and society. For more information call or write CEPE (Avenida Universidad 3002, Ciudad Universitaria, 04510 México DF, Mexico), or visit the UNAM website (http://serpiente.dgsca.unam.mx).

Cities outside Mexico City, such as Cuernavaca, Guadalajara, Guanajuato, San Miguel de Allende, Oaxaca and Morelia, are actually more popular places for studying Spanish and have many language schools. You'll find information on many of them in Lonely Planet's *Mexico* guide. Further information about Spanish-language programs in Mexico is available on the Eco Travels in Latin America website (www .planeta.com) and from the National Registration Center for Study Abroad (☎ 414-278-0631, www.nrcsa.com), PO Box 1393, Milwaukee, WI 53201, USA; the Council on International Educational Exchange (☎ 888-268-6245, www.ciee.org), 205 E 42nd St, New York, NY 10017, USA; and the Institute of International Education, at 809 United Nations Plaza, New York, NY 10017, USA, or Londres 16 (☎ 5-211-00-42, www.iie.org), Colonia Juárez, Mexico City. The Institute of International Education publishes *Spanish Study in Mexico*, profiling 43 Spanish-language schools in Mexico, as well as *An International Student's Guide to Mexican Universities*.

Social Issues

The Casa de los Amigos (see the Places to Stay chapter) holds open seminars several times a year – usually lasting four to seven days. Topics include social issues like women, children and health in Mexico, Mexico City's environment and urban popular movements. The seminars include visits to local service organizations, work on community projects, lectures, discussions and group reflection. The fee of around US$50 a day includes lodging and most meals. You don't need to speak Spanish to participate.

Places to Stay

Mexico City has a full range of accommodations, from basic but centrally located hotels and hostels (up to about US$20 for a typical double room) through comfortable mid-range hotels (US$20 to US$60 a double) to a wide range of top-end hotels costing from US$60 up to the sky. In general, the best cheap and moderately priced rooms are near the Zócalo, Alameda Central and Plaza de la República; luxury hotels are mostly in the Zona Rosa, along Paseo de la Reforma, and in the Polanco district.

Note that the Spanish term *cuarto sencillo*, which translates literally as 'single room,' usually means a room with one bed, which is often a *cama matrimonial* (double bed). One person can usually occupy such a room for a lower price than two people. A *cuarto doble* is usually a room with two beds, both often matrimonial. Prices given for 'singles' and 'doubles' in this section are prices for one person and two people respectively and do not refer to the number of beds. But where two prices are given for doubles, the lower is for a one-bed room, the higher for a two-bed room.

Many hotels have rooms for three, four or five people that cost little more than doubles.

A few expensive hotels offer discounts on weekends and/or commercial or corporate rates for business travelers, but there is very little seasonal variation in room rates.

Budget hotel rooms have private bathrooms unless otherwise mentioned. Many also have TV and carafes or bottles of purified water.

Mid-range places provide comfortable and attractive (if sometimes small) rooms in well-located modern or colonial buildings. All rooms have private bathroom (usually with shower, sometimes also with tub) and color TV.

Top-end accommodations range from comfortable medium-sized, tourist-oriented hotels, some with rooms for well under US$100, to modern luxury high-rises geared

Mexico City Hostels

Since 1998 a handful of hostels aimed at international travelers has finally opened in Mexico City, providing an alternative to the budget and mid-range hotel options that were traditionally the general recourse for backpackers.

Some hostels are small, simple budget places but two of them – Hostal Moneda and Hostel Catedral – present a serious challenge to mid-range downtown hotels.

Some hostels are grouped in small Mexican chains affiliated with – though not full members of – Hostelling International (HI, the former International Youth Hostel Federation). One chain is REMAJ (Red Mexicana de Alojamiento para Jóvenes, Mexican Young People's Lodging Network, ☎ 5-662-82-44, fax 5-663-15-56), run by the youth/student travel agency Mundo Joven at Insurgentes Sur 1510D, México DF 03920 (Mexico City). REMAJ's website is www .hostellingmexico.com; you can book for any REMAJ hostel by emailing hostellingmexico@remaj.com.

To stay in a REMAJ hostel you either need an HI membership card (or membership card from your home-country youth hostel organization), or you must buy 'welcome stamps' for US$2 a night (in addition to the nightly hostel charge). After six nights, the card on which you stick the welcome stamps becomes equivalent to an HI card.

The other chain is AMAJ (Asociación Mexicana de Albergues Juveniles, Mexican Youth Hostels Association). It's run by another Mexico City-based youth/student travel agency, Viajes Educativos (☎ 5-661-42-35, fax 5-661-42-35, tourjoven@infosel.net.mx), Local B10, Insurgentes Sur 421, Colonia Hipódromo Condesa, México DF 06170. The AMAJ website is at www.hostels.com.mx. Hostel cards are not needed in AMAJ hostels.

toward international business travelers where the standard rate for the least expensive rooms may be over US$300. For hotels in the Best Western group, you can call ☎ 800-528-1234 in the USA and Canada for reservations.

Hotels are described here in rough order of preference, with your budget always in mind.

CENTRO HISTÓRICO
Budget
Most of the suitable places in this most central area are on Avenida Cinco de Mayo and other streets west of the Zócalo. Hot water supplies are erratic in some.

Hostels The *Pensión del Centro (☎ 5-512-08-32, pensiondf@yahoo.com, Cuba 74, apartment 203)*, at the corner of Chile, is a small (14-bunk), clean, friendly backpacker hostel run by two Mexican brothers. The cost, including self-service breakfast, is US$8 the first night and US$6.50 thereafter (US$7 and US$6 respectively with an ISIC or GO25 card). The hostel has an equipped guest kitchen and Internet access at US$3 per half hour. It's part of the HI-affiliated AMAJ group (Ⓜ Allende).

Dormitory accommodations at *Hostal Moneda* (see Mid-Range, below) also fall into the budget price category.

Hotels Popular with budget travelers because of its convenient location, comfy if old-fashioned rooms, and decent, moderately priced restaurant is the *Hotel Isabel (☎ 5-518-12-13, fax 5-521-12-33, Isabel la Católica 63)*, at El Salvador. All rooms have TV and some rooms are very large; those overlooking the street are noisy but brighter. Singles/doubles cost US$13/15, or US$8/9 on the upper floors with shared bathroom and in some cases good views (Ⓜ Isabel la Católica).

Hotel Juárez (☎ 5-512-69-29, 1a Cerrada de Cinco de Mayo 17) has 39 rooms on a quiet side street off Avenida Cinco de Mayo, only 1½ blocks west of the Zócalo. It's simple but very clean and presentable, with an excellent location, 24-hour hot water, a

fountain in the little courtyard, and low prices (US$8 a single, US$8.50 or US$9 a double). Rooms all have TV but only a few have windows. Those fronting the street can be noisy owing to trucks loading and unloading crates of drinks in the night. The Juárez is a popular place but if you're there by 2 pm you should get a room (Ⓜ Zócalo or Allende).

Hotel Habana (☎ 5-518-15-89, Cuba 77) is an excellent value. Its 40 clean, decent-sized rooms, painted a variety of pastel shades and with TVs and good, tiled bathrooms cost US$11 a single, US$11 or US$16 a double. Four people sharing two double beds pay US$18 (Ⓜ Allende).

Hotel San Antonio (☎ 5-512-99-06, 2ª Cerrada de Cinco de Mayo 29) is just south of the Hotel Juárez across Avenida Cinco de Mayo, on the corresponding side street. All the 40 small, clean rooms have TVs, and it's quiet and convenient. Rooms are US$9 for a single or double. Those on the street side are brighter (Ⓜ Zócalo or Allende).

Hotel Principal (☎ 5-521-13-33, Bolívar 29), between Avenida Madero and 16 de Septiembre, is a friendly place with most rooms opening onto a plant-draped central hall (though lacking exterior windows). Singles/doubles with shared bathrooms are US$6/7. With private bathroom, TV and safe it's US$12 a single, and US$14 or US$16 for doubles. The twin rooms are quite large (Ⓜ Allende or Zócalo).

Hotel Zamora (☎ 5-512-82-45, Avenida Cinco de Mayo 50), between La Palma and Isabel la Católica, has absolutely no frills. Some rooms are dark, but it's clean and friendly, with low prices, hot showers and a safe. Singles and one-bed doubles are US$6.50 with shared bathrooms, US$9 with private bathroom; two-bed doubles are US$10 with shared bathrooms, US$13.50 with private bathroom (Ⓜ Allende or Zócalo).

Hotel Buenos Aires (☎ 5-518-21-04, Motolinía 21) also has good prices: rooms with shared bathrooms are US$7, singles/doubles with private bathroom and TV are US$8/9 (US$10 for twin-bed doubles). Rooms are plain but clean and adequate, and the management is friendly (Ⓜ Allende).

The **Hotel Washington** (☎ 5-512-35-02, *Avenida Cinco de Mayo 54)*, at La Palma, near the aforementioned Hotel Zamora, has small but adequate rooms with TV. Singles are US$12, doubles US$13 or US$15 (Ⓜ Allende or Zócalo).

Hotel Lafayette (☎ 5-521-96-40, *Motolinía 40)*, near 16 de Septiembre, looks like a secondhand-plastic-sofa showroom as you enter, but in fact is a hotel popular with Mexican families. Rooms are quite big, slightly worn but clean enough, with TV and private bathroom, and the staff are friendly. The cost is US$8 or US$9 a single, US$10 or US$12 a double (Ⓜ Zócalo).

DH Lawrence once stayed at the **Hotel Montecarlo** (☎ 5-518-14-18, *fax 5-510-00-81, Uruguay 69)*. Though renovated and clean, it's rather dark and echoing. But its closeness to the Zócalo and its prices – US$8/9 for singles/doubles with shared bathrooms, US$10/11 with private bathroom – make it worth considering (Ⓜ Zócalo).

Hotel Roble (☎ 5-522-78-30, *fax 5-522-80-83, Uruguay 109)* is two blocks south of the Zócalo. Used mostly by Mexicans with dealings in the nearby shops and markets, it's at the top end of the budget range, with good rooms at US$15 for a single or US$17 or US$19.50 for a double. The rooms are reasonably sized and clean, with TVs. A bright, busy restaurant adjoins the hotel (Ⓜ Zócalo or Pino Suárez).

Hotel Azores (☎ 5-521-52-20, *Brasil 25)* has around 100 rooms with bath at US$11 a single, US$12 or US$15 a double. They're a little tired but adequate, with 32-channel cable TV (Ⓜ Zócalo or Allende).

Mid-Range

Hostels A stone's throw from the Zócalo, **Hostal Moneda** (☎ 5-522-58-03, *☎/fax 5-522-58-21, Moneda 8)*, a member of the AMAJ hostel group, opened in early 2000. It has 94 beds in double and triple rooms and six-person dormitories, all with private bath, at US$8 to US$12 per person including breakfast. A kitchen, roof garden, a 'downtown backpackers' café,' areas for TV, Internet and laundry, and recycling and energy-conserving technologies are all part of the

project. The hostel plans to offer an airport shuttle service, a range of English-language city tours (including bicycle tours and nightlife tours), and ecotourism ventures outside the city. For more information or online bookings, go to www.hostalmoneda .com.mx (Ⓜ Zócalo).

Almost as close to the Zócalo is the 209-bunk **Hostel Catedral** (☎ 5-662-82-44, *fax 5-663-15-56, Guatemala 4)*, which also opened in early 2000, charging US$19 per person to hostel card holders. Rooms hold from three to 10 people. The hostel, open 24 hours, is the flagship of the HI-affiliated hostel group REMAJ, and incorporates a restaurant, guest kitchen, Internet center, laundry, pool table and travel agency (Ⓜ Zócalo).

Hotels Handily located at the corner of Avenida Cinco de Mayo, the **Hotel Gillow** (☎ 5-518-14-40, *fax 5-512-20-78, Isabel la Católica 17)* has a pleasant, leafy lobby and clean, cheerful, up-to-date rooms. Singles are US$25, doubles US$29 or US$35. The hotel has a moderately priced restaurant, too (Ⓜ Allende).

Hotel Canadá (☎ 5-518-21-06, *fax 5-521-93-10, Avenida Cinco de Mayo 47)*, east of Isabel la Católica, is bright, modern and tidy, and the location is excellent, though the 100 rooms are mostly modestly sized and exterior ones get some street noise. They cost US$20 or US$22 a single, US$22 or US$24 a double, and all have safes and bottled drinking water (Ⓜ Allende).

Hotel Catedral (☎ 5-518-52-32, *fax 5-512-43-44, Donceles 95)*, just around the corner from the Templo Mayor and a block north of the cathedral, is shiny and bright, with efficient staff and a reasonable restaurant off the lobby. The 120 rooms are well kept, pleasant and comfortable at US$24.50 a single, US$30 or US$35 a double. There's a roof terrace with good views, and parking nearby (Ⓜ Zócalo).

Hotel Capitol (☎ 5-512-04-60, *fax 5-521-11-49, reserv@hotelcapitol.com.mx, Uruguay 12)* is close to the Torre Latinoamericana. Rooms, mostly around a central hall with a fountain, are modern and pleasant, and cost US$21.50 a single, US$27 to US$32 a double (the most expensive are suites with Jacuzzi; Ⓜ San Juan de Letrán).

Hotel El Salvador (☎ 5-521-12-47, fax 5-521-21-60, hsmexico@spin.com.mx, El Salvador 16) offers clean, modern rooms, all with exterior or interior windows, at US$19/25 a single/double. It has a reasonable restaurant, too (Ⓜ San Juan de Letrán).

Top End

The 124-room ***Gran Hotel Ciudad de México*** (☎ 5-510-40-40, fax 5-512-20-85, 16 de Septiembre 82), just off the Zócalo, is a feast of century-old Mexican art nouveau and eclecticism. Sit on one of the plush settees in the spacious lobby, listen to the songbirds in the large cages, and watch the open ironwork elevator glide toward a brilliant canopy of stained glass high above you. The large, comfortable rooms cost US$101 for a standard single or double, US$123 for executive rooms, and US$134 to US$156 for suites. Buffet breakfasts are a specialty of the hotel's restaurants: see 'Square Meals' and the Centro Histórico Mid-Range section in the Places to Eat chapter (Ⓜ Zócalo).

The ***Holiday Inn Select*** (☎ 5-521-21-21, fax 5-521-21-22, Avenida Cinco de Mayo 61) is a 110-room recent addition to the Centro Histórico, with a prime site just across the street from the Catedral Metropolitana. The rooms – modern, pleasant and comfortable, without being huge – cost US$82 single or double. The rooftop restaurant has marvelous views (Ⓜ Zócalo).

The long-established ***Hotel Majestic*** (☎ 5-521-86-00, fax 5-512-62-62, majestic@ supernet.com.mx, Avenida Madero 73), on the west side of the Zócalo, has lots of colorful tiles in the lobby, and a few rooms (the more expensive ones) overlooking the vast plaza. Avoid the rooms facing Madero (too noisy) and around the inner glass-floored courtyard (unless you don't mind people looking through your windows). Rates are US$100 a room and US$176 or US$235 a suite, single or double. The 7th-floor café/restaurant has a good view over the Zócalo. This is a Best Western hotel (Ⓜ Zócalo).

Hotel Ritz (☎ 5-518-13-40, fax 5-518-34-66, hritz@ekonom.com, Avenida Madero 30), 3½ blocks west of the Zócalo, caters to business travelers and North American tour groups, offering 120 comfortable rooms with mini-bars at US$71 a single or double. It has a restaurant and a good little bar with live piano music. It's another Best Western hotel (Ⓜ Allende).

ALAMEDA CENTRAL & NEARBY

This area is convenient if mostly drab.

Budget

Hotel Del Valle (☎ 5-521-80-67, Independencia 35), just a block south of the Alameda, is a friendly sort of place whose medium-sized, slightly worn rooms have TVs and are reasonably priced at US$10 for singles, US$10 or US$12 for doubles (Ⓜ San Juan de Letrán or Juárez).

Hotel San Diego (☎ 5-521-60-10, Moya 98), 5½ blocks south of the Alameda, is a bit far from the action, but offers good value. The 87 spacious modern rooms boast satellite TV, tiled bathrooms, and prices of US$10 or US$11 a single, US$14 a double. The hotel has a good restaurant, bar and garage (Ⓜ Salto del Agua).

One block north of the Alameda, ***Hotel Hidalgo*** (☎ 5-521-87-71, Santa Veracruz 37) is on a fairly grungy street, but the 100 rooms are modern and excellent. The hotel has a restaurant and garage. Singles/doubles are US$17/20 (Ⓜ Bellas Artes).

Mid-Range

The ***Hotel Bamer*** (☎ 5-521-90-60, fax 5-510-17-93, Avenida Juárez 52) faces the Alameda, and many of its 111 comfortable, air-conditioned, mostly very large rooms have fantastic views of the park. Singles/doubles cost US$33/38. A few smaller rooms at the sides, without Alameda views or bathtub (but with shower), cost US$23 single or double. The ground-floor cafeteria serves good breakfasts for US$2 to US$3, and four-course lunches for US$2.75 to US$5 (Ⓜ Bellas Artes).

In the streets south of the Alameda are a few good, modernized hotels. ***Hotel Fleming***

(☎ 5-510-45-30, fax 5-512-02-84, Revillagigedo 35), 2½ blocks from the Alameda, has 100 comfortable rooms with large, tiled bathrooms; some on the higher floors have great views. Singles are US$24, doubles US$27 or US$30. The hotel has a nice restaurant and parking is provided (Ⓜ Juárez).

Hotel Marlowe (☎ 5-521-95-40, fax 5-518-68-62, Independencia 17) is just one short block from the Alameda. It's bright and comfortable, and the 120 rooms are pleasant, tasteful and quite big. Singles are US$23, doubles US$27 or US$29 (Ⓜ San Juan de Letrán).

Hotel Metropol (☎ 5-510-86-60, fax 5-512-12-73, Moya 39), south of Independencia, was totally modernized in 1991. Rooms, though not enormous, are pleasant and comfortable and have safes. They're on the expensive side at US$38/43 for singles/doubles, but the location, just over a block from the Alameda, is good. The hotel has a decent restaurant serving a buffet breakfast for US$5 (Ⓜ Juárez or Hidalgo).

Top End

Facing the north side of the Alameda Central, *Hotel de Cortés (☎ 5-518-21-81, fax 5-512-18-63, Avenida Hidalgo 85)*, has a somewhat forbidding façade of dark tezontle stone, but inside is a charming small colonial courtyard hotel. Built in 1780 as a hospice for Augustinian friars, it now has modern and comfortable rooms with TVs and small windows that look out on the courtyard. Noise can be a problem, though. Singles/doubles are US$82/94; suites cost from US$153. The courtyard restaurant stages a nightly marimba and traditional dance show. It's yet another Best Western hotel (Ⓜ Hidalgo).

NEAR PLAZA DE LA REPÚBLICA

This area, about 1km west of the Alameda, is slightly less convenient, but prices are good and the neighborhood, though drab, is quiet and residential with an amiable feel. The nearest metro station, unless specified, is Revolución; walk east from the station along Puente de Alvarado, then turn right (south) on Arriaga or Ramos Arizpe.

Budget

The hostel *Casa de los Amigos (☎ 5-705-05-21, fax 5-705-07-71, amigos@laneta.apc.org, Mariscal 132)* is a Quaker center involved in community service and education projects in Mexico City (see Work in the Facts for the Visitor chapter and Courses in the Things to See & Do chapter). It offers lodging to people who are interested in participating in its community or who are involved in some way with social concerns, such as by doing research or community service in Mexico. The minimum stay for first-time visitors is four nights and the Casa requires the completion of a questionnaire before accepting bookings. The questionnaire and bookings can be done by email. If you fit the bill, it's a good place for meeting people with an informed interest in Mexico and Central America.

Facilities include a kitchen, information files on volunteer opportunities and language schools, and a library that was once the studio of artist José Clemente Orozco. A US$1.50 breakfast is served Monday to Friday. There's room for 40 people in single-sex dormitories and private rooms. Suggested donations are US$7 for a dorm bed; US$7 or US$7.50 for singles with shared bath; US$11.50 for doubles also with shared bath; and US$13.50 for doubles with private bath. Alcohol and smoking are prohibited in the building.

The small *Hotel Ibiza (☎ 5-566-81-55, Arriaga 22)*, at Édison, is a good value. Nice, clean little singles/doubles, with bright bedspreads and TV, are US$8/10.

For a bit more comfort, a good bet is the *Hotel Édison (☎ 5-566-09-33, Édison 106)*. It has 45 pleasant, clean rooms around a small, plant-filled courtyard, costing US$15 for singles, US$17 or US$19 for doubles. There's a garage, and a bakery just across the street.

Hotel Carlton (☎ 5-566-29-11, Mariscal 32B), at Ramos Arizpe, is a long-time budget travelers' favorite and has started a long-overdue refurbishment. The rooms are carpeted, have TVs, and are vaguely cozy at US$10/11 for a modernized single/double, US$9/10 unmodernized. The hotel has an economical restaurant (four-course comida

US$1.75). It faces Plaza Buenavista, a quiet little square where a few prostitutes look for work.

Hotel Oxford (☎ 5-566-05-00, Mariscal 67), also on Plaza Buenavista, is still awaiting refurbishment – the carpets don't appear to have been washed for a decade – but it has large singles and doubles with TV for US$7 to US$10. Rooms higher up overlook the plaza.

Hotel Frimont (☎ 5-705-41-69, Terán 35), 250m east of Plaza de la República, is a good value with 100 clean, carpeted, decent-sized rooms costing US$15.50 a single, US$17 or US$19.50 a double, and an inexpensive restaurant.

Hotel Texas (☎ 5-705-57-82, fax 5-566-97-24, Mariscal 129), near Arriaga, has helpful staff and 60 cozy, clean rooms with free bottled drinking water. Singles are US$15, doubles US$17.50 or US$19.50, and the hotel has a garage.

Mid-Range

A good value is the **Hotel Mayaland** (☎ 5-566-60-66, fax 5-535-12-73, Antonio Caso 23). The 100 rooms are small but clean and pleasing, with air-con, drinking water and about 100 TV channels. Cost is US$26 for singles, US$28 or US$33 for doubles; there's a decent little restaurant, and parking is available.

The 200-room **Palace Hotel** (☎ 5-566-24-00, fax 5-535-75-20, Ramírez 7) always has lots of bustle in its lobby as guests arrive and depart. The comfortable rooms, some recently modernized, cost US$24 or US$30 for singles, US$27 or US$34 for doubles. More expensive suites and rooms hold up to six people, and there's a restaurant, bar and garage. The similarly-priced **Hotel Corinto** (☎ 5-566-65-55, fax 5-546-68-88, Ignacio Vallarta 24) is sleek and polished with a good restaurant and bar, helpful staff and even a small rooftop pool. The 155 rooms, though small, are comfortable, quiet and air-conditioned.

Service is quiet and polished at the **Hotel Regente** (☎ 5-566-89-33, fax 5-592-57-94, Paris 9), which offers 138 clean, small, comfortable rooms and suites costing US$32 to US$42 a single, US$36 to US$43 a double. The hotel's Restaurant Korinto serves a good US$4 lunch. Parking is available.

North of Plaza de la República, the recently upgraded, 45-room **Hotel New York** (☎ 5-566-97-00, Édison 45) has bright, comfy rooms of reasonable size for US$25 a single, US$33 or US$42 a double, and a nice little restaurant.

Hotel Jena (☎ 5-566-02-77, fax 5-566-04-55, Terán 12), at Mariscal, is a modern, gleaming building with a posh feel. Its 120-plus rooms are ultra-clean and among the most luxurious in the middle range. Singles are US$35, doubles US$38 or US$41. There's a piano bar and a slightly pricey restaurant (Ⓜ Hidalgo).

A little out of the way to the north is the good-value **Hotel Lepanto** (☎ 5-703-39-65, fax 5-535-00-70, Guerrero 90). Good-sized, bright, modern rooms with TV and bath cost US$22 a single, US$27 or US$32 a double. The hotel has a decent restaurant and amiable staff (Ⓜ Guerrero or Hidalgo).

Top End

Between Plaza de la República and Paseo de la Reforma, the **Hotel Casa Blanca** (☎ 5-705-13-00, 800-972-2162 in the USA and Canada, fax 5-705-41-97, Lafragua 7) offers 300 comfy singles/doubles with multi-channel TVs, safes, phones, air-con and heat for US$67/82. Service is good and the hotel has two restaurants and three bars (one on the roof).

Several mainly business-oriented hotels on Reforma itself provide a convenient location between the Alameda and Zona Rosa.

The 76-room **Hotel Imperial** (☎ 5-705-49-11, fax 5-703-31-22, Reforma 64) is a restored early-20th-century building that was the US embassy until the 1950s. Sizable standard rooms are US$93 single or double; deluxe quarters are US$144.

Hotel Sevilla Palace (☎ 5-566-88-77, 800-732-9488 in the USA and Canada, fax 5-535-38-42, Reforma 105) is comfortable, with helpful service and good, modern rooms at the reasonable price of US$115 single or double; suites are US$272. The hotel has a restaurant, a piano bar and a heated top-floor pool. Customers are mostly business-people, who can obtain discounts through the hotel's 'Plan Empresarial.'

The *Fiesta Americana* (☎ *5-705-15-15, 800-343-7821 in the USA, fax 5-705-13-13, Reforma 80)*, is a 26-story, 610-room slab towering over the Glorieta Cristóbal Colón. It boasts, among other things, assorted restaurants and bars, a fitness center, executive floors and a business center with meeting rooms, modern computers, fax machines and audiovisual equipment. Stylish singles/doubles – many with superb views – are US$151/166.

Hotel Crowne Plaza (☎ *5-128-50-00, 800-227-6963 in the USA and Canada, fax 5-128-50-50, Reforma 1)* is a 490-room luxury business-oriented hotel. Service is smooth, just like the glass elevators gliding up and down the high atrium lobby. Standard rooms are US$217, suites from US$293. There are executive floors with fax machines in the rooms, an excellent business center with 2000 sq meters of meeting space, banquet rooms and two restaurants (Ⓜ Hidalgo).

SAN RAFAEL & JUÁREZ

A handful of hotels are located near the Jardín del Arte, a small park between Plaza de la República and the Zona Rosa, not far from the Reforma/Insurgentes intersection. Another pair of mid-range options stands just southeast of that intersection. No metro station is very convenient, but buses and peseros pass nearby on Insurgentes and Reforma (Map 5).

Budget

Facing the north side of the park is *Hotel Compostela* (☎ *5-566-07-33, fax 5-566-26-71, Sulivan 35)*, at Serapio Rendón, with small-ish but pleasant rooms at US$15 for singles, US$17.50 or US$19 for doubles.

Mid-Range

Just 1½ blocks southwest of the Jardín del Arte is *Hotel María Cristina* (☎ *5-703-12-12, fax 5-592-34-47, Río Lerma 31)*, a colonial-style gem. It has 150 comfy rooms, small manicured lawns, baronial public rooms, and

a patio with a fountain. Singles/doubles are US$43/47, suites cost US$54 and up. There's a fine medium-priced restaurant, a bar and parking. The hotel is popular with Mexican businesspeople, families, and foreign tourists, so you should book in advance if you can.

Hotel Mallorca (☎ *5-566-48-33, Serapio Rendón 119)*, half a block north of the park, has clean, pleasant, carpeted rooms with singles at US$19 and doubles from US$21. It's popular with Mexican couples and families. The *'doble chico'* and *'doble grande'* doubles (US$23 and US$25) are large; parking is available.

Hotel Sevilla (☎ /fax *5-566-18-66, Serapio Rendón 124)* has a *sección tradicional* with decent enough rooms costing from US$19 to US$25 single or double, and a nicer *sección nueva*, with some rooms overlooking the park, for US$36 to US$46 single or double. Rooms are mostly moderately sized. The hotel also has a shop, travel agency, restaurant and parking.

Hotel El Ejecutivo (☎ *5-566-65-65, fax 5-705-54-76, ejecutivo@netfm.com.mx, Viena 8)*, southeast of the Jardín del Arte, is a 12-story hotel where pleasant singles/doubles/triples with floor-to-ceiling windows cost US$34/38/42.

Mi Casa (☎ *5-566-67-11, fax 5-566-60-10, General Prim 106)*, around the corner from the Hotel El Ejecutivo, has 27 comfortable suites. Each has twin beds, a sitting room, bathroom and fully equipped kitchen at a reasonable US$35/40 for singles/doubles.

ZONA ROSA & NEARBY

The nearest metro station, unless stated otherwise, is Insurgentes.

Mid-Range

Accommodations right in the posh Zona Rosa are expensive, but there are one or two good mid-range places on the fringes.

A 500m walk north from the heart of the Zona Rosa, in a quieter neighborhood, is *Casa González* (☎ *5-514-33-02, fax 5-511-07-02, Río Sena 69)*. Two beautiful houses set in small plots of lawn have been converted into lovely guestrooms. It's an exceptional place run by a charming family, perfect for those staying more than one or two nights. It's also a good value at US$25 to US$35 a single or US$29 to US$35 a double (plus one double at US$57.50 and a family room at US$57.50 for four or US$69 for five). Good home-cooked meals are available in the pretty dining room. They may have parking. Reserve in advance if you can. No sign marks the houses, and the gate is kept locked: ring the bell to enter.

Hotel Bristol *(☎ /fax 5-208-17-17, Plaza Necaxa 17)*, half a block north of the Casa González, offers a fairly good value with air-conditioned singles/doubles for US$44/51 interior or US$47/54 exterior, and suites from US$53/61. The rooms are pleasant if not huge, with cable TV, and the hotel has a restaurant and parking. It has just 148 rooms and suites and is often full of business travelers during the week, so it's worth booking ahead.

Top End

For quick reference, these hotels are divided into those where a typical double room costs less or more than US$175.

Less than US$175 The **Calinda Geneve & Spa** *(☎ 5-211-00-71, 800-900-00-00, fax 5-208-74-22, Londres 130)* is the dowager of Zona Rosa hotels, older than most but well kept. It has a formal colonial lobby from which you can walk into a glass-canopied Sanborns restaurant or, at the other end, the popular Café Jardín (see the Places to Eat chapter). The 320 rooms are pleasant, with a bit of period style, air-con, mini-bar and cable TV, and cost US$115 a single or double. The Calinda also boasts a business center and a spa with gym, steam bath, sauna and massage.

Hotel Plaza Florencia *(☎ 5-211-00-64, fax 5-511-15-42, Avenida Florencia 61)* is a pleasant, modern hotel, with 142 tasteful – though not huge – rooms all with one or two double beds, air-con, mini-bar and cable TV. Standard rooms are US$130 for one to four people, better ones go up to US$160. There's a restaurant, too.

Hotel Internacional Havre *(☎ 5-211-00-82, fax 5-533-12-84, Havre 21)* has just 48 big and comfy rooms with nice furniture and TVs, and fine views from the top floors. Singles/doubles are US$71/78. Management is helpful and the hotel offers free guarded parking and a restaurant.

The 326-room **Hotel Aristos** *(☎ 5-211-01-12, fax 5-514-44-73, Reforma 276)* is on the corner of the popular restaurant street Copenhague. Rooms are not huge, but are comfortable and pleasant enough. The hotel sports two restaurants, a bar with mariachis, and two nightclubs. The regular room price is US$117 single or double, but promotional deals often cut that by half.

Hotel Royal *(☎ 5-228-99-18, fax 5-514-33-30, royalzrr@netfm.com.mx, Amberes 78)* is a tall, modern hotel well located in the Zona Rosa, with a celebrated Basque restaurant (see the Places to Eat chapter) as well as bars, a café and a health club. The 162 rooms cost US$129.

A few blocks east, but still well situated in Colonia Juárez, the modern **Hotel Misión Zona Rosa** *(☎ 5-533-05-35, fax 5-207-47-25, Nápoles 62)* has just 50 clean and tasteful small suites at US$106 single or double. Ones with double bed also enjoy a small sitting area. All rooms have air-con, cable TV, safe and mini-bar. The hotel has a nice little restaurant, too (Map 6).

San Marino Hotel-Suites *(☎ 5-525-48-86, fax 5-511-78-00, Río Tíber 107)*, two blocks north of the Monumento a la Independencia (El Ángel), is well kept and offers good suites with equipped kitchenettes and cable TVs for US$158 to US$197, single or double. Continental breakfast is included, and it has a restaurant and parking lot as well.

More than US$175 The trendy **Hotel Marco Polo** *(☎ 5-511-18-39, fax 5-533-37-27, marcopolo@data.net.mx, Amberes 27)* attracts mainly foreign customers from the art and business worlds. Its 60-odd sound-proofed, stylishly modern rooms cost US$164/188 a single/double. Some floors are non-smoking.

María Isabel-Sheraton Hotel *(☎ 5-207-39-33, 800-325-3535 in the USA and Canada, fax 5-207-06-84, Paseo de la Reforma 325)*, at the Monumento a la Independencia, is one of the area's older hotels (1962). As attractive and solidly comfortable as ever, it has spacious public rooms, excellent food and drink, nightly mariachi entertainment in the very popular Bar Jorongo (cover US$6), and all the services of a top-class hotel, including pool, fitness center, medical center and two lighted tennis courts. The 755 rooms and suites offer safes and all the comforts. A reasonably sized standard room costs US$234 single or double.

Hotel Marquis Reforma (☎ 5-211-36-00, fax 5-211-55-61, Paseo de la Reforma 465), at Río de la Plata, opened in 1991 with design and decor that draw from the city's rich art deco heritage and update it for the 21st century. It's one of the city's few top-end hotels that's not part of an international chain. It has lots of colored marble, well-trained multilingual staff and facilities such as an outdoor spa with whirlpool baths. The 98 deluxe rooms cost US$293 and the 110 lavish suites are from US$387. A modern business center offers multilingual translation services, conference rooms and Internet access (Ⓜ Sevilla).

Hotel Century (☎ 5-726-99-11, fax 5-525-74-75, Liverpool 152) is a dramatic high-rise with 142 small, pastel-colored, air-conditioned rooms in modern style with sunken marble bathtubs and curved balconies. They cost US$183 single or double. The hotel has all the services – cable TVs and safes in rooms, bars, restaurants, rooftop pool, business center and garage.

Hotel Krystal Rosa (☎ 5-228-99-28, 800-231-9860 in the USA and Canada, fax 5-511-34-90, Liverpool 155) is a glitzy place with a white marble lobby floor, 302 plush rooms – many with good city views – a heated swimming pool, gym, Japanese and international restaurants, evening jazz in the lobby, a business center, convention/banquet facilities and so on. Standard rooms are US$199, single or double.

Hotel Westin Galería Plaza (☎ 5-230-17-17, fax 5-207-58-67, Hamburgo 195) is a classy, comfortable hotel boasting restaurants with a reputation for good, varied cuisine. Its 439 air-conditioned rooms are

US$246 a single or double, half-price on Friday, Saturday and Sunday nights. On the executive floor some rooms are equipped with laser printers and fax machines. The hotel features at least three restaurants and three bars, a business center, and meeting and banquet rooms.

The *Four Seasons Hotel* (☎ 5-230-18-18, fax 5-230-18-08, Reforma 500), at Burdeos, was added to the ranks of Mexico City's top hotels in 1994. Smaller than some, it has an elegant, refined atmosphere. Most of the 240 spacious rooms overlook a handsome interior garden-courtyard. Singles/doubles cost from US$280/315 to US$410/445, the most expensive being deluxe with balcony or terrace. Suites start at US$450. Most of the hotel's customers are business travelers and it has a business center, athletic club and plenty of meeting space (Ⓜ Sevilla).

CONDESA & ROMA

These fashionable, mainly middle-class residential *colonias* south of the Zona Rosa make a welcome tranquil change from the parts of the city more frequented by visitors.

Budget

The pleasant *Home Hostel* (☎/fax 5-511-26-98, hostelhome@yahoo.com, Tabasco 303) opened in 1999 on a quiet, leafy street 700m southwest of Insurgentes metro. It accommodates 20 people at US$8 each (plus US$2 if you need to buy 'welcome stamps' – see 'Mexico City Hostels') in four separate-sex bunk rooms. Facilities include a kitchen and TV/sitting room. Home Hostel is in the REMAJ hostel group. Any pesero heading south on Avenida Insurgentes from Insurgentes metro will take you to the corner of Tabasco.

On the verge of opening when we checked was *Café Dadá* (☎ 5-511-10-05, Insurgentes Sur 226), 2½ blocks south of Insurgentes metro. It will offer bunks for about 40 people in four rooms, plus three showers and three toilets, and the initial price was likely to be US$5 including breakfast. Also on the premises is a café-cum-art gallery, and informal musical evenings were planned.

The **Hotel Saratoga** (☎ 5-564-82-33, Obregón 38), east of Insurgentes on Roma's main avenue, has regular singles/doubles for US$12.50/16, or king size for US$16/20 (Ⓜ Niños Héroes or Insurgentes).

Mid-Range

The **Hotel Parque Ensenada** (☎ 5-208-00-52, fax 5-208-04-76, Obregón 13) offers nice, modern singles/doubles with cable TV, servibar, safe and fan for US$34/38, and suites from US$45. It's on Roma's main street and some rooms overlook the Jardín Pushkin. The hotel has a Wings restaurant (Ⓜ Niños Héroes).

Hotel Milán (☎ 5-584-02-22, fax 5-584-06-96, Obregón 94) has rooms for US$24/26 (king size US$26/28), plus a restaurant and garage (Ⓜ Niños Héroes or Insurgentes).

The **Hotel Roosevelt** (☎ 5-208-68-13, fax 5-533-16-60, Insurgentes Sur 287) offers 75 rooms with cable TV and double bed at US$25 for a single or double (US$28 king size). Insurgentes metro is 900m north – there are frequent peseros that run up and down Insurgentes Sur.

Top End

The elegant **La Casona** (☎ 5-286-30-01, fax 5-211-08-71, casona@data.net.mx, Durango 280) is a small hotel set in a modernized early-20th-century mansion. The comfy, tastefully and individually decorated rooms cost US$144 a single or double, including continental breakfast, and there's a reasonably priced little restaurant, business center and gym. It's very popular, so you should definitely book ahead (Ⓜ Sevilla).

POLANCO

The Polanco area, just north of the Bosque de Chapultepec, within walking distance of the Museo Nacional de Antropología, has some of the city's best hotels, mostly geared to, and used by, international business travelers. The nearest metro, unless stated otherwise, is Auditorio.

Top End

The most economical option in this area is the 72-room **Hotel Polanco** (☎/fax 5-280-80-

82, Poe 8). Comfy little singles/doubles cost US$62/65 and the hotel has a restaurant.

The **Camino Real México** (☎ 5-203-21-21, 800-722-6466 in the USA and Canada, fax 5-250-68-97, Calzada General Escobedo 700) has bold modern architecture with patios, ponds and colored concrete, dotted with work by noted contemporary artists. The 713 rooms can be a mite garish but are suitably equipped and comfy; Sunday to Thursday they cost from US$244 single or double, but on Friday and Saturday they're only US$117 including breakfast. The hotel also boasts Fouquet's de Paris and two other restaurants, six bars, pools, tennis courts, a gym, an executive lounge, and very ample meeting, convention and banqueting facilities (nearest Ⓜ Chapultepec).

The following three hotels are all highrises, standing in a row along Campos Elíseos.

The 38-story, 744-room **Hotel Nikko México** (☎ 5-280-11-11, 800-645-5687 in the USA and Canada, fax 5-280-91-91, nikkosal@nikko.com.mx, Campos Elíseos 204) blends modern luxury with Japanese traditions of service in a dramatically designed building. The hotel features a formal French restaurant and two Japanese restaurants, as well as three tennis courts, a domed and heated swimming pool, a gym, special executive floors, a modern business center with a video conference link, and plenty of convention, meeting and banquet space. Very comfortable standard rooms, all with safes and marble bathrooms, are US$328 single or double but discounts may be available Friday to Sunday nights. Suites (with fax) are from US$410. Facilities for the disabled are good here.

The 659-room **Hotel Presidente Inter-Continental** (☎ 5-327-77-00, 800-327-02-00 in the USA and Canada, fax 5-327-77-37, Campos Elíseos 218), next door to the Nikko, is also in contemporary style, full of luxurious touches. Rooms are US$375 (US$410 on the business floor), and suites range upward from US$626. The hotel features six varied high-quality restaurants, including the French Maxim's de Paris, the Italian Alfredo di Roma and an 'English

Ready for Take-Off

If a quick getaway is a priority, you have your pick of at least five airport hotels (Map 1).

The **Mexico City Airport Hilton** (☎ 5-133-05-05, fax 5-133-05-00) is right inside the airport, with its entrance in the international check-in area, Sala F. It has 129 well-equipped rooms at US$164 single or double, plus a continental restaurant, gym and business center.

Almost as close to check-in is the **Mexico City Airport Marriott Hotel** (☎ 5-230-05-05, fax 5-230-05-66, Puerto México 80), reached by a walkway from the airport's Sala B. It's bigger, with 600 rooms and suites, similarly well equipped, and has lots of facilities including pool, spa, business center and three eateries, as well as live music in the lobby. Rooms are US$164 single or double.

The **Aeropuerto Plaza Mexico City Hotel** (☎ 5-785-85-22, 800-343-7824 in the USA, Boulevard Puerto Aéreo 502) is almost across the street from the terminal building, but as it's a busy street, complicated by flyovers, the hotel runs a free airport shuttle. The 310 rooms and suites, on just three stories, cost from US$105 single or double. Facilities include pool, gym, restaurant, business center, and meeting and convention rooms.

Hotel JR Plaza (☎ 5-785-20-00, fax 5-784-32-21, jr@netfm.com.mx, Boulevard Puerto Aéreo 390) is also just a stone's throw from the airport and, again, offers free transportation to/from the terminal. It has 124 attractive rooms and suites from US$71, two bars, a disco and a restaurant.

Hotel Aeropuerto (☎ 5-785-58-51, fax 5-784-13-29, Boulevard Puerto Aéreo 380) is marginally farther from the airport doors – about 500m – and the cheapest option, with rooms at US$25 (one bed) or US$32 (two beds). It too has a restaurant, but it doesn't offer free airport transportation. On foot, leave the airport by the doors at the end of Sala F, walk to the Terminal Aérea metro station and head to the left along the road.

tearoom.' Business facilities include one of the city's biggest hotel business centers, and a whole floor of modern conference, meeting and banquet facilities.

A couple of doors along Campos Elíseos is the 312-room **JW Marriott Hotel** (☎ 5-282-88-88, fax 5-288-88-11, Andrés Bello 29). It's the youngest on the block, having opened in 1996. Though new, it's in a more traditional style and full of the expected top-end touches. The 312 rooms and suites cost from US$280 single or double (from US$210 including breakfast on Friday and Saturday nights). The hotel has a staffed business center with up-to-date computers, plus meeting facilities, non-smoking and executive floors, an open-air heated pool and a health club.

In contrast to the above-mentioned hotels – in size, at least – is the **Casa Vieja** (☎ 5-282-00-67, fax 5-281-37-80, casaviej@mail.internet.com.mx, Eugenio Sue 45). This beautiful, small, colonial-style hotel/residence opened in 1993, and has just 10 suites, each individually decorated and equipped with a safe, fax, video, stereo system, Jacuzzi, steam bath and full kitchen. Superbly decorated with fine Mexican art, crafts and antiques, the Casa Vieja is just the place for affluent business travelers in search of a quiet, personal touch. Rates per suite range from US$293 to US$837 per night, including continental breakfast.

NEAR ESTACIÓN BUENAVISTA

Standing opposite the west side of Buenavista train station is the **Hotel Pontevedra** (☎ 5-541-31-60, Insurgentes Norte 226). Clean and decently priced, it has good singles for US$10, doubles from US$10 to US$20, and a big garage. You can use buses and peseros on Insurgentes for transportation (Ⓜ Buenavista; Map 1).

NEAR TERMINAL NORTE

The **Hotel Brasilia** (☎ 5-587-85-77, Avenida de los Cien Metros 4823) is a five- to eight-minute walk south of the Terminal Norte bus station; turn left out of the terminal's front door. The hotel has 200 decent rooms from US$16 to US$24, single or double, plus a restaurant and bar ( Autobuses del Norte; Map 1).

NEAR CUICUILCO

The **Radisson Paraiso Hotel** (☎ 5-606-42-11, fax 5-606-40-06, radven@netfm.com.mx, Cúspide 53) stands in Colonia Parque del Pedregal directly across the Periférico Sur from the Perisur shopping center. Its huge atrium lobby is brightened by hundreds of potted plants draped from balconies. The 236 air-conditioned rooms are US$176 single or double. Public transportation is limited to peseros and buses along the Periférico and Insurgentes, which intersects the Periférico just east of the hotel.

COYOACÁN

Accommodations in this attractive area are disappointingly scarce.

Convenient for the Terminal Sur bus station, **Hotel Montreal** (☎ 5-689-00-11, Calzada de Tlalpan 2073) has comfortable rooms with air-con and TV for US$18 a double (Tasqueña).

The **Hotel Cibeles** (☎ 5-672-22-44, fax 5-539-01-50, Calzada de Tlalpan 1507) offers comfy rooms with cable TV and king-size beds for US$24 single or double, and two-bed doubles for US$34 to US$40. It has a decent medium-priced restaurant. There is a metro station almost at the hotel's doorstep (Ermita).

Places to Eat

This cosmopolitan capital has eateries for all tastes and budgets, with plenty of European, American, Argentine, vegetarian and even Middle Eastern, Japanese and Chinese restaurants in addition to Mexican. Some of the best places are very cheap, while some of the more expensive options are well worth the extra expenditure. In the few restaurants we describe as formal, men should wear a jacket and tie, and women should choose something commensurate. Phone numbers are given for places where reservations are advisable.

The city's very cheapest food is served up at the thousands of street stands selling all manner of hot and cold food and drinks. At these places you can often get a taco or a glass of orange juice for under US$0.20. Quite a few are very popular and well patronized but, because of the temporary nature of many of them, and the dubious hygiene of some, we only mention a couple here – it's really a matter of personal judgment. Those with a lot of customers are likely to be the best and safest.

The cheapest sit-down meals are offered by the comedores found in many markets. You sit on benches at long tables and the food is prepared in front of you. It's usually typical local fare, and at good comedores it's like home cooking. It's best to go at lunchtime, when ingredients are fresher, and pick a comedor that's busy, as this should mean it's good.

Few supermarkets exist in the central areas of the city that most visitors frequent. But there are quite a lot of small grocery stores selling a variable range of foods, and plenty of bakeries. Most Mexicans do a lot of their food shopping at markets, which sell fresh fruit, vegetables, meat, seafood, tortillas, cheese, bread rolls and much more. See Markets in the Around the Alameda Central section, later in this chapter, for information on the Mercado San Juan, one of the best.

FOOD

Mexican food is enormously varied and full of subtle surprises.

Staples

Mexicans eat three meals a day: breakfast *(desayuno)*, lunch *(comida)* and supper *(cena)*. Each meal includes one or more of three national staples: *tortillas*, *frijoles* and *chiles*.

Tortillas are thin round patties of pressed corn *(maíz)* or wheat-flour *(harina)* dough cooked on griddles. They can be wrapped around or served under any type of food.

Frijoles are beans, eaten boiled, fried or refried, in soups, on tortillas, or with just about anything.

Chiles are spicy-hot chili peppers that come in dozens of varieties and are consumed in hundreds of ways. If you are unsure about your tolerance for hot chilies, ask if they are *dulce* (sweet), *picante* (spicy-hot) or *muy picante* (very spicy-hot).

Breakfast

The simplest *desayuno* (breakfast) is coffee or tea and *pan dulce* (sweet rolls), a basket of which is set on the table; you pay for the number consumed. Many restaurants offer combination breakfasts for about US$1.50 to US$3.50, typically composed of *jugo de fruta* (fruit juice), *café* (coffee), *bolillo* (bread roll) or *pan tostado* (toast) with *mantequilla* (butter) and *mermelada* (jam), and *huevos* (eggs), which are served in a variety of ways:

huevos pasados por agua – lightly boiled eggs (too lightly for many visitors' tastes)
huevos cocidos – harder-boiled eggs
huevos fritos (con jamón/tocino) – fried eggs (with ham/bacon)
huevos a la mexicana – eggs scrambled with tomatoes, chilies and onions (representing the red, green and white of the Mexican flag)

huevos motuleños – tortilla topped with slices of ham, fried eggs, cheese, peas and tomato sauce

huevos rancheros – fried eggs on tortillas, covered in salsa

huevos revueltos – scrambled eggs

Mexicans often eat hunks of meat for breakfast, while in many places frequented by travelers, granola, fruit salad *(ensalada de frutas)*, porridge *(avena)* and corn flakes are available, too.

Lunch & Dinner

La comida, the biggest meal of the day, is usually served between 1 and 3 or 4 pm. Most restaurants offer not only à la carte fare but also special fixed-price menus called *comida*

Little Whims

Antojitos – literally 'little whims' – are traditional Mexican snacks or light dishes. On some menus they're listed as *especialidades mexicanas* or *platillos mexicanos*.

Some antojitos are actually small meals in themselves. They can be eaten any time, and either on their own or as part of a larger meal. There are many, many varieties, but here are some of the more common ones:

burrita – flour tortilla folded over a filling of ham and cheese, heated a little to make the cheese melt

burrito – any combination of beans, cheese, meat, chicken or seafood seasoned with salsa or chili and wrapped in a flour tortilla

chilaquiles – fried tortilla chips with scrambled eggs or sauce, often with grated cheese on top

chiles rellenos – chilies stuffed with cheese, meat or other foods, deep fried and baked in sauce

empanada – small pastry with savory or sweet filling

enchilada – ingredients similar to those used in burritos and tacos, rolled up in a tortilla, dipped in sauce and then baked or partly fried; *enchiladas Suizas* (Swiss enchiladas) come smothered in a blanket of creamy sauce

enfrijolada – soft tortilla in a frijole sauce with cheese and onion on top

entomatada – soft tortilla in a tomato sauce with cheese and onion on top

gordita – fried maize dough filled with refried beans and topped with cream, cheese and lettuce

guacamole – mashed avocados mixed with onion, chili, lemon, tomato and other ingredients

quesadilla – flour tortilla topped or filled with cheese and occasionally other ingredients, then heated

queso fundido – melted cheese served with tortillas

sincronizada – a lightly grilled or fried flour-tortilla 'sandwich,' usually with a ham and cheese filling

sope – thick patty of corn dough lightly grilled then served with salsa verde or salsa roja and frijoles, onion and cheese

taco – the número uno Mexican snack: soft corn tortilla wrapped or folded around the same fillings as a burrito

tamal – corn dough stuffed with meat, beans, chilies or nothing at all, wrapped in corn husks or banana leaves and then steamed

torta – Mexican-style sandwich in a bread roll

tostada – thin tortilla fried until crisp that may be eaten as a nibble while you're waiting for the rest of a meal, or can be topped with meat or cheese, tomatoes, beans and lettuce

corrida, cubierto or *menú del día*. These constitute the best food bargains, because you get several courses (often with some choice) for much less than such a meal would cost à la carte. Prices typically range from US$1.50 or less at a market *comedor* (eating stall) for a simple meal of soup, a meat dish, rice and coffee, to US$10 or more for elaborate repasts beginning with oyster stew and finishing with *profiteroles*. Typically, however, you'll get four or five courses for US$2.50 to US$4.50. Drinks usually cost extra.

La cena, the evening meal, is usually lighter than the comida. Fixed-price value-for-money dinners are rarely offered.

Fruit

As you'd expect of a tropical country, the range of fruit *(frutas)* is large.

chabacano – apricot
coco – coconut
durazno – peach
ensalada de frutas – plain mixed seasonal fruits
fresa – strawberry or other berry
guayaba – guava (yellow ones are better than pink ones)
higo – fig
limón – lime or lemon
mamey – sweet orange tropical fruit
mango – mango
manzana – apple
melón – melon
naranja – orange
papaya – papaya
pera – pear
piña – pineapple
plátano – banana
tomate or *tomatillo* – green tomato-like fruit used to make salsa verde
toronja – grapefruit
tuna – nopal (prickly-pear) cactus fruit
uva – grape
zapote – sweet fruit of chicle tree, best liquefied with, say, orange juice or Kahlúa

Vegetables

Legumbres (pulses or legumes), *verduras* (greens) and *hortalizas* (other vegetables) are usually mixed into salads *(ensaladas)*, soups and sauces, or used as garnishes. But there are still plenty of options for vegetarians, and Mexico City has a number of good vegetarian restaurants.

aguacate – avocado
betabel – beet
calabaza – squash or pumpkin
cebolla – onion
champiñones – mushrooms
chícharos – peas
col – cabbage
coliflor – cauliflower
ejotes – green beans
elote – corn on the cob; commonly served from steaming bins on street carts
ensalada verde – green salad
espárragos – asparagus
espinacas – spinach
frijoles – beans, usually black
huitlacoche – a mold that grows on maize; considered a delicacy since Aztec times
jitomate – tomato (not to be confused with *tomate* – see Fruit, earlier)
lechuga – lettuce
lentejas – lentils
nopales – green prickly pear cactus paddles
papas – potatoes
papas fritas – French fries (chips)
pepino – cucumber
zanahoria – carrot

Soup

Mexicans eat many soups *(sopas)* made from meat, vegetables and seafood, including:

caldo – broth *(caldo tlalpeño* is a hearty chicken, vegetable and chili variety)
gazpacho – chilled vegetable soup spiced with hot chilies
menudo – tripe soup made with the spiced entrails of various four-legged creatures
pozole – rich, spicy stew of hominy (large maize kernels) with meat and vegetables

Note that *sopa de arroz* is not soup at all but rice pilaf.

Seafood

Fish *(pescado)* is often eaten as a *filete* (fillet), *frito* (fried whole fish) or *al mojo de ajo* (fried in butter and garlic). Shellfish *(mariscos)* come in many varieties. Seafood *cócteles* (cocktails) are popular, but be cautious about eating uncooked seafood such as *ceviche*, the popular concoction of raw fish, shrimp, etc, marinated in lime juice and mixed with onions, chilies, garlic and tomatoes. Some other ways of preparing fish and seafood are listed under Cuts & Preparation, below.

almejas – clams
atún – tuna
calamar – squid
camarones – shrimp or prawns
cangrejo – large crab
caracol – snail
huachinango – red snapper
jaiba – small crab
langosta – lobster
langostinos – crayfish or large prawns
mojarra – perch
ostiones – oysters
pez espada – swordfish
pulpo – octopus
robalo – sea bass
salmón (ahumado) – (smoked) salmon
tiburón – shark
trucha – trout

Meat & Poultry

Meat and poultry are usually listed separately as *Carnes* and *Aves* on Mexican menus. Carne is likely to be beef *(res, bistec, bisteck or bistec/bisteck de res)* unless otherwise specified, but *cordero* (lamb), *jamón* (ham) and *tocino* (bacon) are also often eaten. Poultry is most often *pollo* (chicken) or *pavo* (turkey). Other meats you may be offered include the following:

cabrito – kid (young goat)
carnero – mutton
cerdo – pork
conejo – rabbit
faisán – pheasant or turkey
guajolote – turkey
pato – duck
puerco – pork
ternera – veal
venado – deer (venison)

Cuts & Preparation Mexican cooks have devised infinite ways of cutting and preparing their meat. *Mole*, a sauce made from chilies and other ingredients, is often served over chicken or turkey. *Mole poblano* – Puebla-style mole – is especially delicious: its many ingredients include bitter chocolate and hot chilies.

Cecina is thin-sliced beef that's soaked in lemon or orange and salt, then grilled. *Pibil* is a method of preparing meat – usually *cochinita* (suckling pig) or *pollo* (chicken) – by flavoring it with ingredients such as garlic, pepper, chili, oregano and orange juice, then baking it. It's best baked the traditional way – in a pit in the ground called a *pib*. *Mixiotes* is a stew of sliced lamb. A *birria* is a stew or broth of kid or mutton with chopped onion.

Chiles en nogada are large green chilies stuffed with meat and fruit, covered with a creamy white walnut sauce and sprinkled with red pomegranate seeds. Like huevos a la mexicana, the colors are those of the Mexican flag.

Other cuts and preparations include the following:

adobado – marinated, seasoned and dried
ahumado – smoked
alambre – shish kebab, 'en brochette'
a la parrilla – grilled, perhaps over charcoal
a la plancha – 'planked,' grilled on a hot plate
a la tampiqueña – 'Tampico style': sautéed, thinly sliced meat, officially also marinated in garlic, oil and oregano
a la veracruzana – 'Veracruz style': topped with tomato, olive and onion sauce
al carbón – charcoal-grilled
al horno – baked
al mojo de ajo – in garlic sauce
al pastor – 'shepherd-style': roasted on a stake or spit
arrachera – skirt steak (from diaphragm muscles)
asado – roasted
barbacoa – literally 'barbecued,' but meat is covered and placed under hot coals
bien cocido – well done
carnitas – deep-fried pork

chicharrón – deep-fried pork rind; pigskin cracklings
chorizo – spicy pork sausage
chuleta – chop (such as a lamb chop)
cocido – boiled
costillas – ribs
empanizado – breaded
filete – fillet of fish or meat
frito – fried
hamburguesa – hamburger
hígado – liver
lengua – tongue
lomo – loin
milanesa – breaded (Italian-style)
patas – trotters (feet)
pechuga – chicken breast
pierna – leg
poco cocido – rare
salchicha – spicy pork sausage

Desserts

Most desserts *(postres)* are small afterthoughts to a meal.

arroz con leche – rice pudding
crepa – crêpe, thin pancake
flan – custard; crème caramel
galleta – cookie/biscuit
gelatina – Jello, gelatin or jelly
helado – ice cream
nieve – sorbet
pastel – pastry or cake
pay – fruit pie

Other Foods

The following are some other food words you may find useful:

aceite – oil
aceitunas – olives
arroz – rice
azúcar – sugar
bocadillo – sandwich, often in a long roll (see *sandwich* at end of list)
catsup – ketchup; US-style spiced tomato sauce
chipotles – chilies dried, then fermented in vinegar; many Mexicans feel a meal is not complete without them
cilantro – fresh coriander leaf
crema – cream

entremeses – hors d'oeuvres
mantequilla – butter
margarina – margarine
pan (integral) – (whole-grain) bread
pimienta – pepper
queso – cheese
sal – salt
salsa roja/verde – red/green condiment sauce made with chilies, onions, tomato, lemon or lime juice and spices
sandwich – toasted sandwich

At the Table

Note that *el menú* can mean either the menu, or the special set-price meal of the day. If you want the menu, ask for *la carta* or *la lista*, or you may inadvertently order a set-price meal.

copa – wineglass
cuchara – spoon
cuchillo – knife
cuenta – check (bill)
mesero/a – waiter
plato – plate
propina – tip
servilleta – napkin
taza – cup
tenedor – fork
vaso – glass

DRINKS

Don't drink any water *(agua)* unless you know it has been purified or boiled (see Health in the Facts for the Visitor chapter). You can buy bottles of inexpensive purified or mineral water in many shops.

Nonalcoholic Drinks

Tea & Coffee Ordinary Mexican *café*, grown mostly near Córdoba and Orizaba or in Chiapas, is flavorful but often served weak. Those addicted to stronger caffeine shots should ask for 'Nescafé,' which refers to any instant coffee (see list below) – unless you're lucky enough to be in one of the real coffeehouses that are now appearing. A few of these serve Mexican organic coffee.

Tea in Mexico, invariably from bags, is a profound disappointment to any real tea drinker.

café americano – black coffee

café con leche – half coffee, half hot milk

café con crema – coffee, with cream served separately

café solo – black coffee

Nescafé – any instant coffee *(agua para Nescafé* is a cup of boiled water presented with a jar of instant coffee)

té de manzanilla – chamomile tea

té negro – black tea, to which you can add milk *(leche)* if you wish

Fruit & Vegetable Drinks Pure fresh juices *(jugos)* are readily available from street-side stalls and juice bars, where the fruit is normally squeezed before your eyes. All fruits and a few of the squeezable vegetables are used.

Licuados are blends of fruit or juice with water and sugar. *Licuados con leche* use milk instead of water. Possible additions include raw egg, ice and flavorings such as vanilla or nutmeg. The delicious combinations are practically limitless. In Mexico City's juice bars you can expect the water used in drinks to be purified – but don't assume the same for street stalls.

Aguas de fruta (also called *aguas frescas* or *aguas preparadas)* are made by mixing fruit juice, or a syrup made from mashed grains or seeds, with sugar and water. You will usually see them in big glass jars on the counters of juice stands.

Refrescos Mexico has some interesting and tasty local varieties of *refrescos*, which are bottled or canned soft drinks. Sidral and Manzanita are two reasonable apple-flavored fizzy drinks. A nonalcoholic bottled variety of sangría (see Wine, later in this section) also exists.

Many brands of mineral water *(agua mineral)* are bottled from Mexican springs – Tehuacán and Garci Crespo are two of the best, and refreshing flavored versions, as well as plain bubbly, can sometimes be obtained.

Alcoholic Drinks

Mexico produces a fascinating variety of intoxicating drinks from grapes, grains and cacti. Foreign liquors are widely available, as well.

Mezcal, Tequila & Pulque Mezcal can be made from the sap of several species of the maguey plant, a spray of long, thick spikes sticking out of the ground. Tequila is a type of mezcal made only from the maguey *Agave tequilana weber* (blue agave), grown in Jalisco and a few other Mexican states. The production method for both is similar except that for mezcal, the chopped-up core *(piña)* of the plant is baked, whereas for tequila it's steamed. The final product – after fermentation, often with sugar cane added – is a clear liquid (sometimes artificially tinted and flavored) that is at its most potent as tequila.

Tequila comes in several varieties, and which is best is a matter of personal opinion. The longer the aging, however, the smoother the drink and the higher the price. *Blanco* (white) tequila is not aged, and no colors or flavors are added. 'Gold' tequila is white tequila with caramel added. *Tequila reposado* ('rested tequila') has been aged at least two months in oak barrels and flavoring and coloring agents usually have been added. *Añejo* (aged) tequila has spent at

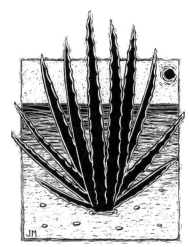

Maguey plant

How to Drink Tequila Like a Pro

There's almost as much mystique about drinking tequila or mezcal as there is about the Japanese tea ceremony. Some insist that if you don't want to look silly you must:

1) lick the back of your hand and sprinkle salt on it
2) lick the salt
3) down the shot *(trago)* in one gulp
4) suck on a wedge of lime
5) lick more salt
6) if you're drinking mezcal, eat the worm when the bottle is finished

In fact, Mexicans may equally well suck a lime *before* downing the shot instead of after it. Nor is there any law whatsoever against savoring tequila or mezcal in a much more measured manner like, say, a glass of brandy. Some real tequila aficionados argue that a quality tequila is wasted if thrown back in one shot.

least one year in oak barrels, and coloring and flavoring agents usually have been added. A repugnant worm *(gusano)* is added to each bottle of mezcal (but not tequila).

A fine place to sample a couple of tequilas in Mexico City is La Casa de las Sirenas on Guatemala, just off the Zócalo. This combined restaurant and bar offers over 250 varieties of the drink.

For foreigners not used to the potency of straight tequila, Mexican bartenders invented the margarita, a concoction of tequila, lime juice and liqueur served in a salt-rimmed glass. Sangrita is a sweet, nonalcoholic drink made with tomato, citrus, chili and spice that's often downed as a tequila chaser.

Pulque is a cheap drink derived directly from the sap of the maguey. It's much less potent than tequila or mezcal. The foamy, milky, slightly sour liquid spoils quickly and thus cannot easily be bottled and shipped. Most pulque is produced around Mexico City and it is served generally in male-dominated, working-class *pulquerías*.

Beer Breweries were established in Mexico by German immigrants in the late 19th century. Mexico's several large brewing companies now produce more than 25 brands of beer *(cerveza)*, many of which are excellent. Each major company has a premium beer, such as Bohemia or Corona de Barril (usually served in bottles); several standard beers such as Carta Blanca, Superior and Dos Equis; and 'popular' brands such as Corona, Tecate and Modelo. All are blond lagers meant to be served chilled – it's a good idea to ask for *una cerveza fría* (a cold beer). Each of the large companies also produces a dark *(oscura)* beer such as Negra Modelo or Dos Equis Oscura. You can find nearly every Mexican beer at the amiable Salón Corona at Bolívar 24 in the Centro Histórico.

Wine Wine is far less popular than beer and tequila, and home-grown wines are usually the cheapest on any Mexican restaurant's wine list, but the country's few large wine growers, all from around Ensenada in Baja California, produce some quite drinkable vintages.

Pedro Domecq, which also owns Sauza, one of the two big tequila firms, has the highest profile. Its Cabernet Sauvignon XA, costing US$15 to US$20 a bottle in most restaurants, is probably the most popular Mexican red. Its Zinfandel XA is of similar quality. Domecq's Calafia and Los Reyes reds and whites cost a little over half that.

The top three wineries in quality are generally considered to be Chateau Camou, Bodegas de Santo Tomás and Monte Xanic. The very best wines fetch US$60 a bottle in upmarket restaurants.

American and even European wine is also available in many top-end restaurants.

Wine mixed with fruit juice, brandy, sugar and a couple of other ingredients makes the tasty *sangría*.

CENTRO HISTÓRICO
Budget
Restaurants Open 24 hours a day, *Café El Popular (Avenida Cinco de Mayo 52)*, just 1½ blocks west of the Zócalo, is a good neighborhood place with tightly packed tables. They serve good breakfasts (fruit, eggs, frijoles, roll and coffee for US$2), and all sorts of other food, from enchiladas and salads to a quarter chicken with mole or carne asada a la tampiqueña, all between US$1.75 and US$3.25. Good, strong café con leche is US$0.70. A second branch of *Café El Popular (Avenida Cinco de Mayo 10)* has the same menu, more space and bright yellow plastic furnishings.

Café La Blanca (Avenida Cinco de Mayo 40), west of Isabel la Católica, is big, always busy, and good for people-watching over a café con leche (US$1). Prices are not the lowest, but you can have their three-course lunch for US$3.75 or four courses for US$4.50.

A good place to start the day is *Los Bisquets Bisquets Obregón*, a good little chain eatery with branches at *(Madero 29* and *Tacuba 85)*, open 7.30 to 10.30 am daily – see 'Chain Restaurants.'

At *La Casa del Pavo (Motolinía 40A)*, three blocks west of the Zócalo, chefs in white aprons slice roast turkeys all day long and serve them up at low prices. The four-course comida corrida offers good value at US$2.50, and there are turkey tacos and tortas, too.

Taco Inn (☎ 5-512-26-11), on Plaza Tolsá outside the Museo Nacional de Arte, is a branch of one of the city's best inexpensive chain eateries (see 'Chain Restaurants') – and they deliver.

Taquería Tlaquepaque (Isabel la Católica 16) is a good solution to late-night hunger. Three tasty tacos will cost you anywhere between US$0.50 and US$2.50 depending on what's in them. It's open 7 am to 3 am Monday to Saturday, to 1 am Sunday night. *Tacos Beguis (Isabel la Católica 8)*, just up the street, is another decent *taquería*: most varieties are US$0.40, but you can have five tacos al pastor (with char-grilled beef) for US$1.50 – or three tacos of bisteck or chuleta with cheese for US$2.

The continental-style *Bertico Café (Avenida Madero 66)*, less than a block from the Zócalo, serves pasta dishes for US$4, baguettes for US$2.25, and good coffee.

Potzollcalli, on Cinco de Mayo just east of Motolinía, is one in a chain of clean, bright and good Mexican restaurants (see 'Chain Restaurants'). Monday to Friday it serves a four-course comida for US$2.50. It's open daily from breakfast to late.

Rincón Mexicano (Uruguay 27) and *Antojitos Tere (Uruguay 29)*, both west of Bolívar, are tiny hole-in-the-wall eateries with home cooking and very low prices. A set lunch at both places costs just US$1.50. They're open daily except Sunday, closing at 6 pm.

Don't ignore hotel restaurants. The Hotel Isabel's *Restaurant Isabel (Isabel la Católica 63)* does breakfasts and lunches for US$2.25 to US$3.50, decent-value two-course dinners for US$3.25 to US$4.50, and a wide range of reasonably-priced á la carte fare. At the Hotel Roble's popular *Restaurante-Bar Maple (Uruguay 109)*, a four-course lunch costs US$3 or US$3.50.

Best ice cream in the Centro Histórico? Try *Santa Clara (Carranza 37)*, where many excellent flavors cost US$0.90 for a standard serve.

Vegetarian & Juice Bars Up a flight of stairs west of La Palma you'll find *Restaurante El Vegetariano (Avenida Madero 56)*. Don't be put off by the unimpressive entrance: upstairs are three busy, high-ceilinged rooms where a pianist plunks out old favorites as you dine. The food is tasty, filling and an excellent value: three- and

Chain Restaurants

Mexico City is liberally provided with modern Mexican chain restaurants whose predictable food is a sound fallback if you fancy somewhere reliable, if not often inspired, to eat. Many of these places are very popular with locals and visitors alike and all are moderately priced if not exactly bargain-basement.

Numerous branches of **VIPS** and **Sanborns**, with both Mexican and international food, can be found in the more affluent and touristed parts of the city. At both places, salads, antojitos and toasted sandwiches cost around US$2.50 to US$4.50, with main dishes costing around US$4 to US$6. **Wings** and **El Portón** are less common, but similar, chains.

A bit more Mexican and more culinarily interesting are the chains Taco Inn, Los Bisquets Bisquets Obregón and Potzollcalli.

Taco Inn, taking its name from the southern colonia of Guadalupe Inn where it was founded, has cheery branches all over the city, all offering over 30 taco choices from US$1.50 to US$3.25 each. The Hawaiiano Inn (four tacos with beef, pineapple, cheese and ham) at US$2.75 is a good, filling option. There's a three-taco *vegetariano* option for US$2. Whatever your choice, there's a range of six or seven salsas and other condiments to go with it.

Los Bisquets Bisquets Obregón takes its name from the tasty *bisquets* (scones) that are one of its specialties. Its range is wide. Combination breakfasts include coffee, juice, bread roll and a pan dulce, as well as a main egg or meat dish, for US$3.50 to US$4.50. At lunchtime a two-course comida with a drink costs the same. Toasted sandwiches and antojitos are US$1 to US$4, chicken and meat dishes US$3.50 to US$4.25.

The bright **Potzollcalli** serves specialties like *taquiza mixta* (five types of taco with rice, US$4.75), chicken or meat grills around US$5, and pozole at US$2.50 to US$4.

Sushi Itto is a widespread, no-fuss chain of little Japanese eateries with moderately priced sushi and sashimi and combination meals from US$7 to US$10.

More familiar names are here, too. Incurable **McDonald's** addicts can sate themselves on soggy burgers and twiglike fries at Avenida Madero 39 near the Zócalo, and on Génova in the Zona Rosa. **Pizza Hut**, on La Palma just south of Avenida Cinco de Mayo, and on Niza in the Zona Rosa, does its pizzas from US$5.50 to US$8. You'll find **KFC** at the corner of Avenida Madero and Isabel la Católica in the Centro Histórico and again on Génova in the Zona Rosa – where it also rubs shoulders with those other old buddies **Dunkin' Donuts** and **Burger King**.

four-course lunches go for US$3 and US$3.25. Breakfasts and à la carte main dishes are around US$2. It's open 8.30 am to 6.30 pm daily except Sunday. El Vegetariano has been going since 1942, and has a more modern, street-level branch at Mata 13 a few blocks away.

Another low-price veggie option is **Comedor Vegetariano (Motolinía 31)**, founded in 1937 and serving up a good US$2.50 comida from 1 to 5 pm daily. A sample menu is vegetable salad or soup; broad beans with mole or rice with carrot; lentil croquettes or vegetarian enchiladas; and dessert. Salads and à la carte main dishes are around US$2 to US$2.50. The entrance is beside Cafetería Teká Fe: go inside and up the stairs to the right.

Jugos Canadá on Avenida Cinco de Mayo at 2a Cerrada de Cinco de Mayo, is good to pop into for a refreshing pure fruit juice, licuado or fruit salad. A big orange or carrot juice, squeezed before your eyes, is US$0.80. A *cóctel biónico*, which combines five fruit juices, condensed milk, granola and cocoa, costs US$1.25.

Super Soya (16 de Septiembre 79), opposite the Gran Hotel Ciudad de México, is in a similar vein, more dedicated to fruit than soya. An array of gaudy-colored signs lists all the varieties of juice, licuado, fruit salad, torta and taco they can manage. Once you've worked out what's what, you could make a meal of it by starting with a plate of pear, cream, cereal and honey (US$1.25), followed by a couple of vegetarian tacos at US$0.50 each, or a torta at US$0.90, and wash it all down with a Dracula – mixed beetroot, pineapple, celery and orange juice (US$1). You can choose a stool at the juice bar or a table. It's open 9 am to 9.30 pm Monday to Saturday, 11 am to 8 pm Sunday. Another branch *(Bolívar 31)* does a veggie menú del día for US$1.75.

Coffee For quick caffeine, pop into *The Coffee Factory* on Madero, just east of Sanborns Casa de Azulejos. Americano or espresso costs US$1, cappuccino or café au lait US$1.75. It's open 8 am to 8 pm Monday to Friday, 9 am to 8 pm Saturday, 10 am to 7 pm Sunday. Another good coffee stop is the tiny *Café del Centro*, almost opposite the Hotel Catedral on Donceles. Here espresso costs just US$0.50 to US$0.90, and café con leche US$1. It offers good inexpensive cakes, muffins and burritos, too.

Bakeries & Pastry Shops Good snacks or light breakfast fare can always be bought at *pastelerías* (pastry shops). You enter the pastelería, take a tray and tongs, fill the tray with what you like, and an attendant will price and bag it.

At *El Molino (16 de Septiembre 37)*, open from 7.30 am daily, you can sit down and have coffee and a croissant or Danish pastry for US$0.70. Another bakery with a café section is *La Vasconia (Tacuba 73)*, at La Palma.

Pastelería Ideal (16 de Septiembre 14), west of Gante, looks fancy and has a huge variety but its prices are reasonable. Simpler breads and pastries are at the back. Upstairs, Mexico's most glorious array of wedding cakes is on offer: this is the place if you need a US$300, 70kg, multistory gâteau for your nuptials. There's no coffee bar, however.

Mid-Range

Café de Tacuba (☎ 5-518-49-50, Tacuba 28), just west of Allende metro station, is a gem

of old-time Mexico City, opened in 1912. Colored tiles, stained glass, brass lamps and oil paintings set the mood. The cuisine is traditional Mexican and delicious. The five-course set-price lunch is US$8 (plus drinks). À la carte main dishes are US$4.50 to US$8.75. It's open 8 am to 11.30 pm daily.

The restaurants in *Sanborns Casa de Azulejos (Avenida Madero 4)* are worth a visit just to see the 16th-century tile-bedecked building housing them (see the Things to See & Do chapter). The main restaurant is in a covered courtyard around a Moorish fountain, with odd murals of mythical landscapes. The food is Mexican and good, if not exceptional, at about US$2.50 to US$4.50 for *platillos mexicanos* and US$5 to US$6 per main dish. The ground-floor lunch counter in the northwest corner of the building, and another restaurant above it, have similar prices but less atmosphere. One or all eating areas are open from 7 am to 1 am.

La Esquina del Pibe (Bolívar 51), at Uruguay, is a busy Argentine grill house, one of the more economical of this popular type of establishment. The set lunch is US$5.25, and à la carte grill dishes cost US$6 to US$10.50. Four people can get a combined mixed grill for either US$18.50 or US$30. It's open 1 to 11 pm daily (to 8 pm on Sunday).

Restaurante Danubio (☎ 5-512-09-76, Uruguay 3), at Eje Central Lázaro Cárdenas, is a city tradition. It's been here, specializing in seafood, since the 1930s, and still does it well. The huge and excellent six-course set-price lunch – including fish *and* meat courses – costs US$7.50. À la carte fish main courses are mostly around US$6 to US$8.50. Lobster and crayfish are the specialties, but prices for them are stratospheric. The Danubio is open 1 to 10 pm daily, but you'll be lucky to get a table for Sunday lunch.

Several hotels have good-value restaurants. A bright, popular one is at the *Hotel Catedral (Donceles 95)*, a block north of the cathedral, with breakfasts from US$1.75 to US$3.25 and set-price lunches for US$4.50 and US$5.75. At the *Hotel Gillow (Isabel la Católica 17)*, set breakfasts are US$2 to

Square Meals: Food with a Zócalo View

Two average sort of eateries at the northwest corner of the Zócalo have sidewalk tables that are good for watching the city in action. **Shakey's Pizza y Pollo** does pizzas (US$4.25 to US$8.75 for the smallest size), chicken nuggets and so on. **Flash Taco** offers Mexican and Tex-Mex staples (two tacos US$0.90 to US$2.75, fajitas US$3.75).

For a truly marvelous view, head up to the **Restaurante El Campanario/Cafetería El Invernadero** *(5 de Mayo 61)* on the roof of the Holiday Inn Select hotel, almost within touching distance of the Catedral Metropolitana's bells and with a magnificent panorama over the Zócalo and much of the rest of the city. They serve a buffet breakfast for US$6.50. Later in the day, most main dishes are US$5 to US$7. You can also enjoy the view just for the price of a drink.

Restaurante Terraza *(Avenida Madero 73)* overlooks the Zócalo from the 7th floor of the Hotel Majestic. The daily buffet breakfast is US$7, and Monday to Friday there's a set lunch for US$5.50 (Saturday and Sunday it's a buffet lunch for US$10.50). You can have something lighter or à la carte if you wish.

Cafetería Mirador *(16 de Septiembre 82)*, on the top floor of the Gran Hotel Ciudad de México, has a small terrace with a great view over the Zócalo. Buffet breakfast is US$6.

La Casa de las Sirenas *(Guatemala 32)*, in a 17th-century house just behind the cathedral, serves up excellent *alta cocina Mexicana* (Mexican haute cuisine) on its terrace, which has views of the Zócalo, Palacio Nacional and Templo Mayor. Soups and salads are good here: a tasty choice is the US$3 sopa de cilantro, made with small squashes, coriander leaves, cheese and cream. Meat, seafood and poultry main dishes are mostly US$7.50 to US$11 – try *suprema de ave Doña Tessie* (chicken breast with shrimp mousse) for $7.50. You could finish off with a crêpe for US$5. To drink – well, the Sirenas offers over 250 varieties of tequila, costing from US$2 to US$13.50 a shot, in the restaurant or in the Salones Tequila on lower floors. It's open 8 am to 11 pm Monday to Saturday, 8 am to 7 pm Sunday.

The amiable **Restaurante México Viejo** *(Tacuba 87)*, facing the Catedral Metropolitana on the corner of Monte de Piedad, sports bright blue tablecloths and sepia photos of old Mexico City, and serves up decent Mexican and international food, from fettuccine Montezuma (pasta with a huitlacoche sauce, US$3.50) to steaks (around US$7); there's also a four-course *menú ejecutivo* lunch for US$5.50. It's open 8 am to 9 pm Monday to Saturday, 10 am to 6 pm Sunday.

US$5, the menú del día US$4 or US$5.50, and individual main dishes US$2.75 to US$8. Live jarocho (Veracruz) music and a folkloric dance show are included in the US$8.50 price of the buffet breakfast at the Gran Hotel Ciudad de México's **Restaurante del Centro** *(16 de Septiembre 82)*.

Top End

Six blocks northwest of the Zócalo, **Hostería de Santo Domingo** *(Belisario Domínguez 72)* is small but intense. Handicrafts crowd the walls and ceiling, while good and unusual regional cooking – including chiles en nogada year-round – fills the menu and the customers. A typical three-course à la carte meal costs about US$12, though you could eat for US$8 or so. If you want somewhere atmospheric, this is it. It's open 9 am to 10.30 pm Monday to Saturday, 9 am to 9 pm Sunday. A pianist or a trio plays from 3 pm.

Los Girasoles *(☎ 5-510-06-30)*, on Plaza Tolsá beside Tacuba in front of the Museo Nacional de Arte, is one of the best of the 1990s wave of restaurants specializing in *alta cocina mexicana* (Mexican haute cuisine). Recipes are either traditional or innovative but all have a very Mexican flavor. You might start with *crema de tres quesos* (three-cheese soup) and follow up with *Sábados 1 a 3* (Sonora ranch-style beef medallions with chipotle) or a Baja California-style shrimp and bacon stew. Starters and soups are mostly US$3.50 to US$6.50, main courses US$6 to US$9.50. Los Girasoles is open 1.30 pm to midnight Monday to Saturday, 1.30 to 4 pm Sunday. It has pleasant outside tables as well as indoor seating.

AROUND THE ALAMEDA CENTRAL
Budget
Restaurants One of the prettiest, most peaceful restaurants in the city is the *Cafetería del Claustro* (Cloister Café) *(Avenida Hidalgo 45)*, in the Museo Franz Mayer opposite the north side of the Alameda. The museum and café are open 10 am to 5 pm Tuesday to Sunday: if you only want to visit the café you need a US$0.50 ticket. Marble-top tables are set in the lovely courtyard, with taped baroque music setting the mood. The self-service food includes sandwiches, salads, quiche and excellent cakes for US$1 to US$1.50, and coffee, juices and yogurt from US$0.60 to US$1.

Café Trevi on Dr Mora, facing the west side of the Alameda, is a good, popular Italian and Mexican restaurant, open 8 am to 11.30 pm daily. It serves breakfasts till noon for US$1.70 to US$2.50, and its six-course set-price daily meal costs just US$2.50. Pasta dishes and one-person pizzas range from US$1.75 to US$4. Photos show the rubble to which the Trevi was reduced by the 1985 earthquake.

One block south of the southeast corner of the Alameda, a group of bright, inexpensive eateries cluster around the intersection of Independencia and López. The pick of the bunch is clean, bustling *Taquería Tlaquepaque (Independencia 4)*, where bow-tied waiters serve up several dozen types of taco, priced at US$0.90 to US$3.25 for three. The chuletas, nopales y queso variety (chopped pork, cactus tips and cheese), at the top of the price range, are delicious. *Fonda Santa Rita*, a few doors west, is also popular – most tacos are US$0.25 to US$0.35 each, or you could go for pechuga (chicken breast) with mole poblano and rice

(US$2.50). *La Pizza* on the corner of Independencia and López serves reasonable one-person pizzas and pasta dishes for US$1.75 to US$3.

Restaurante Continental (Independencia 72), a block south of the Alameda, is a straightforward and popular place with bright-red plastic seats and orange table-cloths, serving up a big range of Mexican and international standards. Options include antojitos, pasta and pizza, as well as meat, fish and seafood main dishes, all between US$2.50 and US$5.50. It's open 7 am to midnight daily.

For a taste of lingering Spanish influence in Mexico, you can't beat a helping of *churros y chocolate*. Churros are long, thin, deep-fried doughnuts, just *made* to be dipped in a cup of thick hot chocolate. A fine spot for this experience is *Churrería El Moro (San Juan de Letrán 42)*, 2½ blocks south of the Torre Latinoamericana, where chocolate with four churros sets you back US$2. It's always open and often busy in the wee hours with people winding down after a night on the town.

Vegetarian The *Centro Naturista de México (Dolores 10B)*, half a block south of the Alameda, is a health food shop with a vegetarian restaurant serving lunches of soup, two main courses, salad, bread, tortillas and dessert for US$2, or an all-you-can-eat buffet for US$2.50, from 12.30 to 7 pm daily.

Markets The best and freshest produce in the city is generally agreed to be at the *Mercado San Juan* on Pugibet west of Plaza de San Juan, 500m south of the Alameda Central. It's open 8 am to 5 pm Monday to Saturday, 8 am to 4 pm Sunday and holidays. Here you'll find rarities such as tofu, and *chapulines* (grasshoppers) from Oaxaca, as well as good fruit, vegetables, cheese, meat and fish (Map 4).

Mid-Range
The elegant *Café del Palacio*, inside the Palacio de Bellas Artes, serves salads for US$4 to US$5.50 and tempting *empareda-dos* (sandwiches), with fillings such as

smoked salmon, smoked turkey, cream cheese and *jamón serrano* (cured ham), for US$4 to US$7.

Mexico City has a small Chinatown centered on Dolores south of the Alameda. One of the best restaurants here is the small **Hong King** *(Dolores 25)*, with set meals from US$4.50 to US$9 per person (minimum two people) and menus in Chinese, Spanish and English. Most à la carte dishes cost between US$3.25 and US$6, though some vegetarian offerings are under US$3. It's open 12.30 pm to 11 pm every day.

NEAR PLAZA DE LA REPÚBLICA

Several small, homey, neighborhood restaurants are to be found here.

Budget

It doesn't look like much from the outside, but **Restaurante Samy** *(Mariscal 42)* is clean and pleasant, offering fixed-price breakfasts for US$1 to US$2, and a four-course comida corrida for US$2.25.

Restaurant Cahuich *(Ramos Arizpe 30)*, at Édison, is a good, clean little place where a breakfast of juice, eggs and coffee, or a comida corrida, will set you back about US$2.50. There's well-priced à la carte fare, too, and it's open 8 am to 1 am daily.

Another pair of decent basic eateries faces each other across the corner of Iglesias and Mariscal. **Super Cocina Los Arcos** *(Iglesias 26)* can prepare bistec several ways for US$1.50 to US$2.50, three tacos for US$2, breakfasts for US$1.50 to US$2, and tortas, eggs, juices, licuados and other staples. Across the corner, **El Tigre** serves tasty hot tortas with fillings of ham, egg, cheese and so on for US$0.90 to US$1.50, as well as tacos, sincronizadas, juices and licuados.

Potzollcalli, on Arriaga just south of Puente de Alvarado, is a branch of the popular Mexican chain eatery – see 'Chain Restaurants.'

A great place for a quick lunch is the **seafood cocktail stand** on Emparán just north of Édison. It has stood here daily except Sunday since at least the mid-1980s and includes many besuited office workers among its regular customers. A *mediano*

(medium-size) prawn or crab cocktail at US$2.50 is filling. Even bigger ones are US$4.50. The neighboring stand serves good tortas for US$0.60 to US$1.25.

Café Vendôme *(Reforma 92)* is a straightforward eatery near the big Fiesta Americana hotel that pleases local office folk with its US$3.50 comida corrida.

The large **Café La Habana** *(Morelos 62)*, at Bucareli, 500m southeast of Plaza de la República, is worth the walk for its good, strong coffee or four-course 'lunch comercial' at US$3.25. It's open 8 am to midnight every day. Journalists and staff from nearby newspaper offices are among the clientele.

Mid-Range

About 100m south of Plaza de la República on Ramírez, next door to a branch of VIPS, **Tacos El Caminero** is a busy, slightly upscale taquería doling out servings of three good tacos for US$2.25, or six for US$3.75. El Caminero's hours are 10 am to 1 am Monday to Friday, 1 pm to 1 am Saturday, 1 pm to 11 pm Sunday.

Toks *(Reforma 108)* is a big, clean, modern and efficient place serving gringo and Mexican food. Though all meals are served, it's the US$5.50 all-you-can-eat lunch buffet, served till 5.30 pm, that pulls people in. There's also a breakfast buffet for US$4.25, set meals from US$3.50 to US$4.75, and à la carte fare, too. It's open 7 am to midnight Monday to Friday, 8 am to midnight Saturday, and 8 am to 7 pm Sunday. Nearby, **Wings** *(Reforma 106)* is in similar vein, with a breakfast buffet for US$4.75 (US$5.50 on Saturday and Sunday), and a Monday-to-Friday lunch buffet for US$6.25.

NEAR THE JARDÍN DEL ARTE
Budget

Little **Restaurante Nucleo** *(Río Lerma 7A)* is packed every weekday lunchtime with local office and shop staff enjoying its simple but excellent-value three-course comidas. For US$2.25 you get soup, rice and a choice of tasty main dishes such as chicken in mole poblano or tuna-stuffed avocado. For an extra US$0.50 the main-course choice extends to several more options. The Nucleo also serves economical breakfasts, and good juices and licuados for US$0.50 to US$0.80. It's open 7.30 am to 5 pm Monday to Friday, 7.30 am to 1 pm Saturday (Map 5).

Café Gran Premio on Antonio Caso at Sadi Carnot is a good, straightforward coffeehouse where a large café con leche or cappuccino is only US$1, an espresso US$0.75. It serves cakes and ice cream, too (Map 5).

ZONA ROSA & AROUND

The Zona Rosa is packed with places to eat and drink. Some streets are closed to traffic, making the sidewalk cafés more pleasant.

Budget

The cheapest meals are at the *Mercado Insurgentes*, on Londres. One corner of this crafts market is given over to market comedores serving up hot lunches daily to customers who sit on benches in front of the cooks and their stoves. You'll find many of the same typical Mexican dishes here as you would in restaurants, at much lower prices – around US$1.75 for a comida corrida at most of them. Pick one that's busy.

A bit farther west along Londres are the area's most economical restaurants, the best of them packed with customers at lunchtime. *Ricocina (Londres 168)* does three-course comidas including drinks for US$3 to US$3.50, and breakfasts such as juice, coffee and eggs/hot cakes/French toast for US$2.25. The four-course, US$3 comida at *La Beatricita (Londres 190D)* includes drinks.

A very cheap comida is served at the nameless little *comedor* beside the Java Chat cybercafé in an alley off Génova. Three courses here will cost you US$1.50.

Taco Inn (Hamburgo 96) is an excellent choice for a good, quick taco (see 'Chain Restaurants').

Inside Plaza La Rosa, a shopping arcade between Hamburgo and Londres just west of Génova, is a small fast-food hall where you order from a choice of counters, then eat at central tables shared by all. You could go for three meat tacos (US$1.25 to US$1.75) from *El Mariachi Tacos*, salads from US$1.75 to US$3 at *Los Bisquets Bisquets Obregón*, Argentine grilled meats from US$4 at *Massangui*, or a serving of *camarones empanizados* (breadcrumbed prawns, US$4) at *Oscar's Seafood*.

On the corner of Génova and Hamburgo is delicious *Häagen-Dazs* ice cream.

Mid-Range

Restaurants Perennially popular *Konditori (Génova 61)* serves a mixture of Italian, Scandinavian and Mexican fare in its elegant small dining rooms and spacious sidewalk café. The latter is a fine place to observe the passing parade on the Zona Rosa's busiest pedestrian street. Pasta or good crepa dishes cost around US$4, meat or fish US$5.50 to US$7. Coffee is US$1.20, and the Konditori also serves good cakes and pastries. It's open 8 am to 11.30 pm daily.

Parri Pollo Restaurante (Hamburgo 154) is a busy, barn-like grill house serving grilled beef, pork and chicken in various ways, from tacos to steaks or whole birds. Chefs tend the grill and waiters scurry about. You can get three tacos for US$2, but you're likely to spend US$5.50 or more on a main course and a drink. Hours are 9 am to 1 am Monday to Thursday, 8 am to 3 am Friday and Saturday, 9 am to midnight Sunday.

If Japanese food is your fancy, try *Sushi Itto (Hamburgo 141)*, a popular little chain eatery (see 'Chain Restaurants').

The pleasant, modern *Café Jardín (Londres 130)*, attached to the Calinda Geneve & Spa hotel, does a reasonable-value US$6 buffet lunch, as well as à la carte fare from burgers and enchiladas around US$4 to meat or fish from US$5 to US$6.

Copenhague is a short street lined with bustling mid-range and upscale eateries. *Freedom (Copenhague 25)* is both a lively bar (see the Entertainment chapter) and a restaurant doing good US-style and Tex-Mex fare like barbecued ribs, nachos, pasta, burgers, salads and chicken. Most main dishes are between US$5 and US$8. Also good and popular are the *Mesón del Perro Andaluz (☎ 5-514-74-80, Copenhague 26)*, serving meat and seafood – with some

Spanish dishes as the name suggests – on the east side of the street, and, opposite, *El Perro d'Enfrente* (☎ 5-511-89-37), with Italian food. Main dishes at both are mostly between US$6.50 and US$7.50. Pasta and pizza at the d'Enfrente are a little cheaper.

Yuppie's Sports Café (Génova 34), at Hamburgo, is a sort of American-style lounge/café/bar where – so long as you can cope with the place's name and being frisked at the door – you can watch TV, look at baseball photos, and eat salads for US$3.50 to US$4.75, burgers and pizzas for around US$5, or steaks from US$9.50.

The Hotel Marco Polo's *Il Caffe Milano (Amberes 27)* lethargically serves up good Italian food amid stylish Italian design, with some sidewalk tables. You pay US$4 to US$7 for pasta, US$7 to US$8 for meat or seafood main dishes.

The *Carrousel Internacional (Niza 33)* is a lively bar/restaurant with mariachis singing energetically most of the time. Come for spaghetti or a salad (around US$4) or a grill or fish (US$6 to US$8). Or, just have a drink and enjoy the music. It's open 11.30 am to midnight daily.

Chalet Suizo (Niza 37) has dependably good food well-served in mock Swiss rusticity. They have fondues (US$6 to US$9 per person), pasta plates at US$4.50, and a range of meat dishes between US$5.50 and US$9, including duck in orange sauce. Full meals will cost around US$8 to US$14. It's open noon to midnight daily.

Across the street, *Luaú (Niza 38)* is a Chinese-Polynesian fantasy with fountains and miniature gardens. The best bargains are the set-price Cantonese meals at US$5.50 to US$14 per person. Hours are noon to 11 pm Monday to Thursday, noon to midnight Friday and Saturday, noon to 10 pm Sunday.

At *Focolare* (☎ 5-207-80-55, *Hamburgo 87*) you can dine while watching a colorful spectacle of Mexican folk dance and song in a large, brightly decorated dining hall, for a cover charge of US$4 per person Monday to Wednesday, US$6 Thursday to Saturday. Classic Mexican dishes such as cochinita pibil and mole poblano line up alongside more standard fare on the menu. Most main

dishes cost US$6 to US$9; starters and soups are in the US$3 to US$5 range.

East of the Zona Rosa on Marsella at Dinamarca, the popular Argentine grill *Restaurant El Asado Argentino* does grills from US$6 to US$12, and pasta around US$4 to US$6.

Vegetarian The good *Restaurante Vegetariano Yug (Varsovia 3)*, just south of Reforma, does a lunch buffet upstairs for US$4 from 1 to 5 pm daily, and daily four-course comidas corridas downstairs, with good whole-wheat bread, for a little less. À la carte fare is served, too. The clientele is mostly local office workers. It's open 7 am to 10 pm Monday to Friday, 8.30 am to 8 pm Saturday, 1 to 8 pm Sunday.

A couple of blocks north of the Zona Rosa, *Restaurante Vegetariano Las Fuentes (Río Pánuco 127)* is big, leafy and attractive, serving tasty food in large portions. Full meals of soup, salad bar, main course and a drink cost US$7.25; big breakfasts are US$4.25. Wine and beer are served, too. It's open 8 am to 6 pm daily.

Coffee, Tea & Sweets At *Auseba (Hamburgo 159B)* there are glass counters filled with enticing cakes and other sweet offerings, and large windows for watching Hamburgo go by. Most cakes and pastries are around US$2, but you can get a *pan danés* (Danish pastry) for US$0.70. Tea and coffee are between US$1.25 and US$1.75.

Handy to pop into for good coffee and cakes is the *Coffee House (Londres 106)*, just east of Génova. Espresso is US$0.90, cappuccino and caffe latte are US$1.50, and slices of good cheesecake run from US$2.

Top End

The *Angus Butcher House* (☎ 5-207-68-80, *Copenhague 31)*, on the corner of Hamburgo, serves fine steaks that cost anywhere from US$9 to US$27, and it's always packed. It has a good outdoor area under an awning as well as indoor tables. It's open daily from 1 pm to 1 am.

Restaurante Passy (☎ 5-208-20-87, *Amberes 10)* is one of the city's most polished restaurants. Formal, quiet, and popular with businesspeople and the well-heeled in general, it has a pleasant conservatorylike area, as well as tables in elegant interior rooms. Cuisine is a mix of international and Mexican: you could start with Brazilian palm hearts (US$4) or Parma ham with melon (US$7.50), then go for beef bourguignon or *lomo adobado de Tepatitlán* (a Mexican pork loin dish), both at US$9. It's open 1 to 10 pm daily except Sunday.

Harry's Bar (Liverpool 155) – the entrance is around the corner on Amberes – is a bright grill/steakhouse-style place popular with gringos and Mexicans. TV screens show sports most of the time. Steaks, chicken and seafood are mostly US$7 or US$8. It's open daily except Sunday. In the same chain and also popular is *Anderson's de Reforma (Reforma 382)* at Oxford, open daily. The many varieties of steak and seafood go for US$8 and up; chicken and pork are a bit cheaper. Both these places impose a cover charge of US$1.25.

The *Ile de France* (☎ 5-230-17-17, Hamburgo 195), in the Hotel Westin Galería Plaza, is one of the Zona Rosa's very best hotel restaurants, a gourmet French affair with roast beef a specialty. It's open 1.30 pm to midnight Monday to Friday, 7 pm to midnight Saturday.

Restaurante Tezka (☎ 5-228-99-18, Amberes 78), in the Hotel Royal, is the creation of Juan Mari Arzak, perhaps the most celebrated chef in the Basque town of San Sebastián, which few would argue has the best food in Spain. Arzak visits Mexico City every six months to supervise the Tezka and try out new recipes. Expect to spend US$50 a head on dinner.

The formal *Restaurant Champs Elysées* (☎ 5-533-36-98, Reforma 316) is part Frenchowned and has been serving very fine French fare since the 1960s. Just two courses will cost you at least US$13 but more likely US$30 to US$35 (for, say, palm hearts with Roquefort dressing followed by grilled snapper with mustard sauce or rib-eye steak in red wine sauce). Special main dishes like lobster or sole are almost US$50. Choice French wines and a good cheese board are part of the scene, too. The main dining room has views along Reforma to the Independence Monument, and on the ground floor is an elegant little bar and a small gourmet grocery. It's open 1 to 11 pm Monday to Saturday.

One of the city's best sophisticated and formal restaurants lies 1½ blocks from the Zona Rosa, just north of Reforma. This is the French *Les Moustaches* (☎ 5-533-33-90, Río Sena 88), where starters cost from US$4.50 up to *pâté de foie gras* at around US$17. Main courses – chicken, duck, meat and fish – are from US$8.50 to about US$17. For dessert, tempting crêpes and soufflés are around US$5. Many tables are on an elegant greenery-filled patio and there's discreet music while you dine. It's open 1 pm to midnight daily, except Sunday.

Also a short distance north of the Zona Rosa is one of the city's best Japanese restaurants: *Fuji* (☎ 5-514-68-14, Río Pánuco 128). This is an unpretentious place with quality food at fair prices. One specialty is the great variety of excellent freshly prepared sushi. Another is *teppanyaki* – from chicken at US$8 to mixed seafood prepared at your table with seven different vegetables (US$16). Traditional sashimi (fish or steak) or tempura costs from US$6. To sample a variety of dishes, order the *Fuji teishoku* (US$13), a meal of about 10 dishes. Fuji is open 1 to 10.30 pm Monday to Saturday, 1 to 6 pm Sunday.

The *Hotel Marquis Reforma (Reforma 465)* serves a top-class Sunday brunch for US$17, and also houses the expensive and classy Belgian *Restaurant La Jolla*.

CONDESA

This relaxed, fashionable and agreeable neighborhood 1 to 2km south of the Zona Rosa has since the mid-1990s become the hub of the Mexico City eating-out scene. Its leafy streets have sprouted dozens of informal, bistro-style restaurants and good cafés, many with sidewalk tables. Cuisines from many parts of the globe are represented here, especially those of Europe and the Middle East. A new eatery seems to open every week. In fact there are so many good places here that you're really spoiled for choice, which helps keep prices moderate. The following are just a few suggestions of spots to head for.

Mid-Range

The heart of the Condesa scene is the intersection of Michoacán, Vicente Suárez and Atlixco, 500m west of Parque México. One of the longest-established places here is *Fonda Garufa (Michoacán 91)*, which serves up a big range of good pasta, vegetarian brochettes and salads for US$3 to US$4.50, plus seafood and other grills. It's open 1 pm to midnight Monday to Wednesday, 1 pm to 1 am Thursday to Saturday, 1 to 11 pm Sunday.

The immensely popular *Mama Rosa's (Atlixco 105)*, on the same intersection, serves almost everything from wood-oven pizzas, chicken and meat – all around US$6 to US$8.50 – to pasta and salads for less and seafood for mostly a bit more. Go by about 8 pm to ensure a table for dinner. *Café La Gloria (Vicente Suárez 41)*, also on the same intersection, cooks up French, Italian, Japanese and other fare, with pasta and salads around US$4, and chicken, fish or meat for US$5.50 to US$8.50. *Creperie de la Paix*, also here, is very popular for its variety of sweet and savory crêpes from US$2.50 to US$4. It serves salads, pasta and meat filetes, too. The busy *La Buena Tierra (Atlixco 94)* characterizes its food as '*gastronómica natural*', but it's not just vegetarian. Specialties include whole wheat focaccia (US$2.50), baguettes (US$3.50 to US$4.50), lots of salads (US$1.75 to US$3.50) and pita-bread tacos (US$3 to US$3.50). For starters (US$2 to US$4), try smoked marlin or *arroz buena tierra* (whole grain rice with vegetables, fruit and curry). Pasta, fish and chicken main dishes cost from US$3.50 to US$7. Big, exotic juice drinks are concocted, too, for around US$2 – some with ginseng. The *Cafecito* across the street is a place to see and be seen – and leave your fancy motorbike parked outside – while sipping a cup of good coffee.

El Zorzal (☎ 5-553-51-81) on Vicente Suárez just east of Michoacán serves up classic Argentine steaks; you'll spend US$10 to US$15 on a full meal with drinks. *Café La Selva (Vicente Suárez 38)*, in the same block, brews good organic coffee from the southern Mexican state of Chiapas, produced by a grouping of small-scale indigenous coffee growers. Just east of Tamaulipas, Algerian *Le Cous-Coussier (Michoacán 74)* specializes (naturally) in good couscous, at US$5 to US$6.

La Casa de las Empanadas, half a block west of Vicente Suárez along Michoacán, is popular for its Argentine-style *empanada* turnovers with vegetarian, cheese or meat fillings for US$1.50 to US$2, and pizzas cooked over a wood fire (US$6 to US$7). Its *chimichurri* seasoning (an Argentine parsley and olive oil concoction) is a treat, too.

To the south, *La Condesa del Mar*, on Campeche at Michoacán, does fine fish. *El Tizoncito (Tamaulipas 122)* serves up delicious tacos al pastor till 3.30 am for around US$0.80 each, with fillings such as fish, prawns and chicken. Half a block north on Tamaulipas is the Japanese deli *Sushi Shalala*.

Northward, *Il Principio (Montes de Oca 17)*, at Tamaulipas, is good for varied Mediterranean food – from lentil soup with banana at US$2.25 or salads for US$4, to fish, chicken, meat or pasta from US$4 to US$6 or risotto for US$7 or US$8. It's open 1.30 pm to 12.30 or 1.30 am daily. *Il Mangiare (Tamaulipas 55A)*, on the same intersection, offers tasty *paninos* (short baguettes with olive oil, not butter) for US$5 to US$10. The *cubano*, with a ham, turkey and manchego cheese filling, is a good choice. Pasta, salads, meat, fish and chicken go for US$4.50 to US$9. Portions are not big, though.

Amar Kemel (Montes de Oca 43) serves generous quantities of excellent Middle Eastern food. Falafel, kofta kebabs, tabuli and hummus are all priced between US$3 and US$5, and there are *kepe* (ground beef), rice, fish and chicken dishes, too. For a selection of varied starters with pita bread, ask for the *messe*. Hours are 1.30 to 11 pm Monday to Wednesday, 1.30 pm to midnight Thursday to Saturday, 1.30 to 8 pm Sunday. *Otro Mundo (Atlixco 38)*, at Escutia, does tasty Basque fish and meat grills from US$6 (closed Monday).

Tierra Gaucha (Montes de Oca 18) is a little less expensive than other Condesa Argentine steak houses – US$6 to US$9 for steaks and other meats. *Il Caffe della Luna*, a block farther north on Tamaulipas, is a trendy little coffee-and-cakes spot, with cappuccino for US$1.50.

To the east, nearer Parque México, *La Casbah (Amsterdam 194)*, at Chilpancingo, cooks up good Moroccan fare, including couscous for US$5 to US$9 or a three-course Moroccan meal for US$8. *Restaurant Specia (Amsterdam 241)* is one of Condesa's more expensive and smarter spots, but its Polish food – unique in the city? – is worth a bit of a splash. Salads are around US$6, main courses US$8.50 to US$10. Try the *pieczen baranis*, a roast-lamb dish. *Toma 5 (Amsterdam at Sonora)* does good toasted tortas for US$2, four tacos for US$2.50, and alambres for US$4 to US$5.50. It's a good spot for the end of a night out, as it stays open from 11 am to 6 am daily. You'll get excellent ice cream at *Tepoznieves* on Michoacán just east of Parque México, and some of the city's best tacos at *El Greco* on Michoacán just east of Nuevo León.

Another good place for a coffee or something light to eat is *El Péndulo (Nuevo León 115)*, which is combined with a bookstore and music store that often stages live music Friday or Saturday evening.

ROMA
Mid-Range
Colonia Roma's main avenue, Obregón, is dotted with cafés and restaurants including a branch of the good *Los Bisquets Bisquets Obregón*. *Café d'Carlo (Orizaba 87)*, nearby, is a good coffee stop. *Restaurant Miguel (☎ 5-574-14-35, Córdoba 226)* has been preparing delicious, spicy Middle Eastern meals for longer than most eateries in Roma or Condesa have existed. The *plato especial árabe*, for about US$8, is a good choice, and a veggie version is available. Kepe (ground beef) is another specialty, with dishes for US$4 and US$5.

BOSQUE DE CHAPULTEPEC
Budget
The primera (1a) sección of the park has lots of snack and drink stalls and even a few makeshift sit-down comedores. The cheap food nearest to the Museo Nacional de Antropología is at *Rincón Seco*, also called *Café Capuchino*, beside Calzada Gandhi 100m north of the museum entrance. It's a basic, open-air eatery with tortas at US$1, or meat, salad and fries for US$2.50.

Mid-Range
The reasonable cafeteria inside the *Museo Nacional de Antropología* opens the same hours as the museum (9 am to 7 pm Tuesday to Sunday). The lunch buffet is US$7 (not including drinks), and individual Mexican and international main dishes are mostly between US$4 and US$7.

Top End
The segunda (2ª) sección of Chapultepec is home to three good Mexican/international restaurants with lovely lakeside locations. The *Café del Bosque* beside the smaller lake, Lago Menor, in the southern part of the park, does big buffets at breakfast (US$10) and lunch (US$13.50), Tuesday to Saturday. *Meridiem Restaurante*, at the north end of the fountain-embellished Lago Mayor, is particularly popular for its Saturday and Sunday buffets (breakfast US$10 and lunch US$13.50) but it's open 8 am to 11 pm daily (to 6 pm Sunday). The *Restaurante del Lago (☎ 5-515-95-85)*, also on the Lago Mayor, is a refined place with Mexican and European haute cuisine and a fine wine list, plus a tobacco room and nightclub. You'll pay around US$25 to US$30 for dinner with drinks. It's open 1.30 to 11 pm Monday to Saturday, 11.30 am to 5 pm Sunday.

POLANCO
Affluent Polanco is home to lots of mid-range and expensive restaurants.

Mid-Range
If you fancy something meaty, a good, fairly economical choice is *La Parrilla*

Suiza, on the traffic circle at Avenida Presidente Masaryk and Arquímedes, 600m northwest of the Museo Nacional de Antropología. It gets packed at lunchtime, when it serves an economical comida for US$2.50. Mixed grills go for US$6 and tacos for US$1.50 to US$2.50, and there's lots of stuff at in-between prices. It's open noon to 2 am Monday to Thursday, noon to 3 am Friday and Saturday, noon to midnight Sunday.

Café de Tacuba (Newton 88), northeast of Arquímedes, is a pleasant little place with colored windows, a beamed ceiling and a bit of character, serving Mexican and international fare. Polanco metro station is 2½ blocks away. Set-price lunches cost US$4 or US$7. Good breakfasts are served, too.

Popular *El Farolito (Newton 130)* serves up excellent tacos al carbón. They're on the costly side at US$1.50 to US$3 each – but fillings are fairly generous. Non-meateaters could go for the cheese varieties. El Farolito stays open till 2 am (3 am on Friday and Saturday nights).

For other moderately priced fare in Polanco, head for Avenida Presidente Masaryk, between Dumas and France, where a string of sidewalk cafés lines the south side of the street. Among them is *Klein's (Masaryk 360B)*, serving hot and cold tortas from US$2, antojitos at US$2.50 to US$7.50, and meat or chicken dishes for US$5 to US$7. Just east of Klein's are *Taconova* with tacos from US$0.60 apiece and tortas from US$2; *TNu3 ('Te Nutré' – 'I will feed you')* with salads, spaghetti, antojitos and sandwiches all between US$2.50 and US$5, and fish and chicken a bit dearer; and the popular *Garabatos (Masaryk 350)*, with deli sandwiches for US$5 to US$7, salads and antojitos for less.

Not far away is a busy branch of Condesa's popular *La Buena Tierra (Masaryk 393)*, in Plaza Mazarik; open 7 am to 11 pm daily. It's easiest entered from the France side of the building. *Mezzanotte (☎ 5-282-01-30, Masaryk 407)*, upstairs in the neighboring mall, Plaza Zentro, is a thriving Italian restaurant that also becomes a New York-style dance club Thursday to Saturday

nights. Many main dishes are under US$8. You need to book ahead.

Another successful Condesa restaurant with a Polanco branch is *Creperie de la Paix (France 79)*, serving, among other things, sweet and savory crêpes.

A very popular Italian spot a few blocks farther east on Avenida Presidente Masaryk is *Il Mercato (Masaryk 214)*, in the Plazza Magna building. This restaurant is hung Adriatic-style with strings of garlic and herbs. Salads are around US$4, pizza and pasta US$5 to US$7.50, fish and meat are more, and there's lots of wine to choose from.

The *Kings Pub (Arquímedes 31)* serves up good steaks for US$8-plus, and pasta and salads around US$4. Surroundings are vaguely reminiscent of a traditional English pub, with coats of arms, stained glass, and the like.

Capuccinos coffeehouse on Wilde gets packed with a younger, less-affluent crowd than most Polanco spots: coffee starts at US$1.75, and salads, antojitos and sandwiches go for US$4 or so.

Top End

Cozy and popular, *Cambalache (☎ 5-280-20-80, Arquímedes 85)*, just north of Avenida Presidente Masaryk, is an Argentine steak house, serving up great steaks from US$10.50 to US$12.50, chicken from US$8.50 and pasta around US$5.50. The wine list is ample. It's open 1 pm to 1 am daily.

Dominique, on Campos Elíseos at Dumas, offers very tempting French-Caribbean food, full of tropical fruits and vegetables, fish and juicy meat, with a spicy oriental and/or classical French touch. Most main dishes cost US$7 to US$12. The formal and popular *La Gran Casona (☎ 5-280-78-33, Dumas 4)* offers original Mexican cuisine of tip-top quality in an elegant hacienda-style setting. Starters are around US$5 to US$10, main dishes US$10 to US$15. It's open noon to midnight daily. The *Crab House (☎ 5-280-66-99, Verne 3)*, around the corner, has an elevated dining room bustling with people tucking into crabs from US$8 to US$30, or fish, prawns and other fare from US$8 to US$12.

Polanco's main drag, Avenida Presidente Masaryk, offers a few top-end choices. *La Valentina* (☎ 5-282-22-97, Masaryk 393), upstairs in Plaza Mazarik, does a very successful *nouvelle* version of Mexican cuisine, with soups, starters and salads from US$3 to US$8, and meat and seafood mains from US$10 to US$12. It's semiformal (jacket and tie not *required*) and it's open 1 pm to 1 am daily. Reservations are essential.

The *Parador de Manolo* (☎ 5-281-13-57, Masaryk 433) serves good Spanish food in European brasserie-style surroundings. Starters and soups range from US$3 to US$7, fish and meat courses from US$8 to US$12. *Jamón serrano* (cured ham), *calamares fritos* (fried squid) and *crepas de flor de calabaza al gratin* (pumpkin-flower crêpes) are all recommended. It's open 1.30 pm to 2 am Monday to Saturday, 1.30 pm to 5 pm Sunday. The Manolo has a tapas bar, too.

Several upmarket restaurants populate Moliere just south of Avenida Presidente Masaryk. *Isadora* (☎ 5-280-15-86, Moliere 50) is an outstanding restaurant with some of the most original and exciting recipes in the country. The menu changes every season: on our visit, delicious options included a starter of Roquefort mousse with nuts and apples and a main course of grilled duck with tamarind sauce and glacé apple. Three courses with drinks will cost you around US$25 to US$30. Isadora is semiformal like La Valentina, above; hours are 1.30 to 5 and 8 to 10.30 pm Monday to Saturday.

La Hacienda de los Morales (☎ 5-281-45-54, Vázquez de Mella 525) is about 1.5km northwest of the middle of Polanco, just south of Avenida Ejército Nacional. It's easiest to go by taxi. Once a grand country hacienda, it's now surrounded by the city, which makes the spacious rooms and pretty gardens all the more appealing. Excellent Mexican, American and European dishes – including some particularly good fish choices – are served in numerous dining rooms by experienced waiters. A three-course

meal with drinks will cost around US$25 to US$40. Reservations are advisable and dress is formal for dinner (though not for lunch). It's open 1 pm to 1 am daily.

A little farther north on Vázquez de Mella, at Homero, is *La Destilería* (☎ 5-395-49-71), a relaxed eatery with indoor and a few outdoor tables that also styles itself a 'museo de tequila,' thanks to a decor of tequila-related artifacts, murals and plaques and over 100 varieties of the national drink on sale. The food is mostly Mexican: fish, seafood, steak and chicken main dishes go for US$7 to US$13. It's open 1 pm to 1 am Monday to Saturday, 1 to 6 pm Sunday. *Ruth's Chris Steak House* (☎ 5-395-51-35, Edificio Corporativo Polanco, Balmes 8), nearby, serves 'serious' US steaks for US$20 to US$45 in a relaxed yet elegant setting. It has a bar and a few outdoor as well as indoor tables. It's open 1.30 to 11 pm Monday to Saturday, 1.30 to 6 pm Sunday. Enter from the south side of the building facing Homero.

Polanco's luxury hotels contain some of the city's best restaurants. Among them are three French highlights, all open Monday to Saturday: *Maxim's de Paris* (☎ 5-327-77-00, Campos Elíseos 218), at the Hotel Presidente Inter-Continental, which has a dinner-dance Friday and Saturday nights; *Les Célébrités* (☎ 5-280-11-11, Campos Elíseos 204) at the Hotel Nikko México; and *Fouquet's de Paris* (☎ 5-203-21-21, Calzada General Escobedo 700) at the Camino Real México. All are formal, with reservations recommended, and dinner at any of them runs US$30 to US$50 (maybe more at Maxim's). The Presidente Inter-Continental also boasts the top-notch Italian *Alfredo di Roma* (☎ 5-327-77-00), perhaps marginally less expensive.

NEAR ESTACIÓN BUENAVISTA

Across Mosqueta in front of the train station, a good chain restaurant, *El Portón*, serves Mexican food at moderate prices including breakfasts or light dishes for US$2.25 to US$3.75 and main dishes for US$3.50 to US$6.50). It's open 7 am to midnight every day (Map 1).

SAN ÁNGEL
Budget

The nameless little *comedor* on the east side of Plaza San Jacinto, next to Restaurante La Vuelta, offers a good comida corrida for US$2, and on weekends great *caldo de camarón* (prawn soup) for US$2.50/3.75 small/large. *Crêperie du Soleil*, on Madero near Plaza del Carmen, does tempting crepas (sweet US$1 to US$2; savory US$2.50 to US$3.50), tortas and coffee.

The *Museo de Arte Carrillo Gil (Avenida Revolución 1608)*, has a pleasant basement café and bookstore, with reasonably priced snacks and drinks and quiet classical music in the background. It's open 10 am to 6 pm daily except Monday. If you wish, you can visit the café and bookstore without paying to enter the museum.

San Ángel's most famous bookstore-café is *Gandhi (Avenida MA de Quevedo 128 to 132)*, 400m east of Parque de la Bombilla. Customers linger over coffee, snacks, books, newspapers and chess in this haunt of Mexico City intelligentsia. It's open 9 am to 11 pm Monday to Friday, 10 am to 10 pm Saturday and Sunday (Ⓜ MA de Quevedo one block away).

The attractive Plaza Loreto mall, between Altamirano and Río de la Magdalena, has a few inexpensive options including a *food court* with a branch of *Taco Inn*, as well as sushi, *tamal*, crêpe and burger counters.

Mid-Range

The Indian restaurant *La Casona del Elefante (Plaza San Jacinto 9)* has a few pleasant outdoor tables, and is not a bad value with a vegetarian *thali* plate at US$4 or chicken curry for US$3.50. You may have to wait a while for a table on Saturdays. Drinks include *lassi* for US$0.90. *Fonda San Ángel (Plaza San Jacinto 3)* has outdoor tables and is very popular on Saturday, but we haven't found the food to be anything outstanding. Most main dishes are US$6 or more.

Avenida La Paz between Revolución and Insurgentes is thick with places to eat. You can hardly choose better than the pancake house *Cluny (Avenida de la Paz 57)*, a cozy place with art nouveau glass and Toulouse Lautrec posters. Cluny has been serving up scrumptious and original crepas (savory US$5 to US$6, sweet around US$4) since the 1970s, and is as popular as ever. It's open 1 pm to midnight daily (to 11 pm Sunday) but you'll often have to wait for a table in the evening (put your name on the waiting list). Cluny also serves good salads, satay and burgers, and you can drink nice wine from US$3 a glass or US$12 a bottle. Across the street is Cluny's younger sibling, the bright *Le Petit Cluny (Avenida de la Paz 58)*, which is probably San Ángel's best and most popular Italian restaurant. Quality pizza and pasta costs around US$6 or US$7, and wine by the glass is US$4. It's open 8 am to midnight Tuesday to Saturday, 8 am to 10.30 pm Sunday. A take-away section sells, among other things, some of the city's most delicious bread.

The winner by a mile of our prize for Mexico city's best-decorated restaurant is the *Modern Art Café* in Plaza Opción, the mall neighboring Plaza Loreto between Altamirano and Río de la Magdalena. It's both a genuine art gallery and a genuine restaurant, with the walls covered in bright contemporary paintings, and quirky modern sculpture set among the tables. Even the chairs you sit on and the plates you eat off are art – and nearly everything's for sale. The food includes brick-oven pizzas, pasta, burgers, salads and meat, in the US$5 to US$9 range, and there's a bar, too. It's all open Sunday to Thursday 1 pm to midnight, Friday and Saturday 1 pm to 3 or 4 am.

Pabellón Altavista mall at Revolución and Camino al Desierto de los Leones houses plenty of eateries, including branches of *TGI Friday's*, *Taco Inn* and *Sushi Itto*, and the popular *Italianni's* (pasta and pizza US$4.50 to US$7.50).

Saks Natural (Insurgentes Sur 1641), at Damas, 2.5km north of the heart of San Ángel, is one of the city's best and most innovative vegetarian restaurants. The US$5.50 lunch buffet is popular; à la carte, the choice of salads is good and original main courses range from stuffed eggplant at US$3.50, through savory organic-flour crêpes (US$5), to cheese-stuffed artichoke hearts served on spinach purée (US$7.75). The setting, with its vaulted ceilings, is reminiscent of a monastery cellar, but there are big arched windows and colorful art on the walls. It's open 8 am to midnight daily (Map 1).

Top End

The liveliest place on Plaza San Jacinto, *La Camelia*, has people waiting in line to enjoy its seafood (US$7 to US$13) and trendy atmosphere.

Carnivores could head for Camino al Desierto de los Leones between Revoluciòn and Insurgentes, where among other eateries you'll encounter the popular *Carlos 'n Charlie's*, serving meat and fish dishes around US$8, and the *Angus Butcher House*, where fine steaks cost from US$9 to US$27. In the Pabellón Altavista mall at the Revolución end of this block, the good Argentine steak house *El Buen Bife* serves up hunks of meat from US$9 and set meals US$12 to US$15 between 1 and 10 pm or later daily.

To dine in style, head for the *San Ángel Inn* (☎ 5-616-14-02, *Diego Rivera 50*), at Avenida Altavista, 1km (a 15-minute walk) northwest of Plaza San Jacinto. This is an ex-hacienda with a lovely flowery courtyard, fountain and gardens, now transformed into a luxurious restaurant serving delicious traditional Mexican and European cuisine. If you order carefully you can eat two courses for US$9, but you could easily spend US$25 or more on a full meal. It's open 1 pm to 1 am daily. See San Ángel Inn in the Things to See & Do chapter for how to get there.

COYOACÁN
Budget

For inexpensive Mexican fare, leave Plaza Hidalgo along Higuera. The municipal building on the left is filled with *quesadilla stands* charging US$0.60 apiece for quesadillas with various tasty fillings. Or go half a block north from the plaza to the cheerful *El Tizoncito* (*Aguayo 3*), which serves up many varieties of taco at US$0.60 to US$1 each. Excellent choices here include

nopalqueso (cactus tips and cheese) and the fish and shrimp tacos. Less than one block south of the plaza, on Carrillo Puerto, colorful *La Casa de los Tacos* serves tacos from US$0.50 apiece, and also does four-course lunches from US$2.50 to US$3.25. There's a *Taco Inn* (see 'Chain Restaurants') at Carrillo Puerto and Carranza.

A good spot for breakfast, snacks or coffee is *Moheli*, a café-cum-gallery on Avenida Sosa a few steps west of Jardín del Centenario. A filled croissant or yogurt, fruit, granola and honey will cost you US$2, a bagel with salami or olive pâté US$2.50, or a Greek salad US$3.

The bright *Café Kowloon* (*Jardín del Centenario 6*) serves up Chinese set lunches for US$2.75 to US$4, 1 to 6 pm Monday to Friday. À la carte main dishes are US$3 to US$4. At *Café Chou Sou*, just south on Carrillo Puerto, you can get a fair Chinese lunch or dinner for US$2.50 to US$4. It also serves Mexican standards at good prices, and breakfasts for US$1.50 to US$2.

On the north side of the Jardín del Centenario are *El Hijo del Cuervo*, a fashionable café/bar with a young clientele (see the Entertainment chapter), and *Los Bigotes de Villa*, with outdoor and indoor tables, that serves enchiladas, quesadillas and chiles rellenos for US$2 to US$3, and meat or chicken dishes for US$3 to US$4. Los Bigotes de Villa's sign depicts a bushy Pancho Villa-style mustache in place of the word *bigotes* (mustache).

Mid-Range

Among the many pleasant sidewalk cafés around the Jardín del Centenario, *Café El Parnaso* is a fashionable place with a bookstore in the back. Good burritos, croissants, baguettes and *pan árabe* (pita bread) tacos, as well as breakfasts, all cost between US$2.50 and US$3.50. The coffee's good, too. It's open 9 am to 10 pm daily.

Restaurante Caballocalco (*Higuera 2*), facing the east side of Plaza Hidalgo, is relaxed and not too expensive, with good food. Soups are US$2.25 to US$3.25, meat and seafood US$4 to US$10. Hours are 8.30 am to 11 pm daily.

On the corner of Coyoacán's main market, on Allende 2½ blocks north of Plaza Hidalgo, is the excellent and busy *El Jardín del Pulpo* (The Octopus's Garden), serving fish platters at US$6.50 to US$7 and seafood cocktails or caldos (broths) at US$3 to US$5. Everyone sits on benches at long tables.

An enjoyable restaurant lies 700m west of the Jardín del Centenario on Plaza Santa Catarina, conveniently close to the Viveros (plant nurseries) if you're approaching or leaving Coyoacán that way. This is *Merendero Las Lupitas*, a friendly little place with chairs and cloths in bright primary colors, serving a variety of typical Mexican dishes with the home-cooked touch. Many of them are from the north of the country. All three meals are served; snacks and antojitos go for about US$3 to US$5, main courses for US$4 to US$8.

Entertainment

Mexico City's entertainment and nightlife scene is just as varied and lively as everything else about the city. A flick through *Tiempo Libre*, the city's fairly comprehensive what's-on magazine, is a good way to find out what's new and who's in town. It's a big city, so the locations of some events are far away and take some finding, but enough goes on in the central areas to keep you happy for a good while at least. Note that many bars and nightspots are closed on Sunday.

See Arts in the Facts about Mexico City chapter for background on Mexican music and dance.

LISTINGS

Tiempo Libre, published every Thursday, is sold at newsstands for US$0.70 and appears on the Internet at www.tiempolibre.com.mx. Even with limited Spanish, it's not too hard to decipher what's going on, from music and movies to exhibitions and lots of entertainment for children. Many of the nightlife listings – live music, bars and clubs, dance halls, cabaret – are in the *Espectáculos Nocturnos*, *Espectáculos Populares* and *Bares y Cantinas* sections.

The News and Mexican newspapers carry some what's-on information (the Saturday and Sunday *Cartelera* section of *La Jornada*, listing movies, theater, etc, is good). Ticketmaster (see Tickets, below) distributes a free monthly leaflet, *La Guía de Entretenimiento*, with information on events for which it sells tickets – including many of the major ones.

The Consejo Nacional para la Cultura y las Artes (National Council for Culture & the Arts) also has plenty of good what's-on information in the Cartelera section of its website (www.cnca.gob.mx).

TICKETS

Most concert halls, major sporting venues and theaters have box offices where you can buy tickets in advance if you wish. Another way to get tickets for main events is through Ticketmaster (☎ 5-325-90-00), which sells tickets for many major events at sales points called Centros Ticketmaster, around the city. You can also order tickets from Ticketmaster by phone or on the Internet (www.ticketmaster.com.mx) and pick them up at the venue. Centros Ticketmaster are at the following locations:

Mixup, Avenida Madero 51, Centro Histórico

Mixup, Génova 76, Zona Rosa

El Palacio de Hierro, Durango 230, Colonia Roma

Auditorio Nacional, Paseo de la Reforma 50, Bosque de Chapultepec

Mixup, Plaza Loreto, San Ángel

Mixup, Plaza Cuicuilco, Avenida Insurgentes Sur 3500 (Map 11)

Travel agencies and hotels can provide tickets for some events but mark up prices.

BARS & ANTROS

Antros – halfway between a bar and a dance club – are an innovation that has cropped up in Mexican cities in the past few years. They're basically bars with loud recorded music, maybe video screens, and enough space to dance if the mood takes you. Another name for them is 'disco-bars.' Some antros lean more toward the bar end of the spectrum, others are closer to a *discoteca*. The following is a very brief selection from Mexico City's hundreds of bars and antros. For bars with live music, see the various music headings, later in this chapter.

Centro Histórico

Bar Mata (☎ 5-518-02-37, *Mata 11, 4th floor*), on the corner of Avenida Cinco de Mayo, is one of the longest-running Centro antros, with a casual, hip atmosphere, good music and a roof terrace with great views. Most drinks are around US$2.75, and it's open 8 pm to 2 am, Wednesday to Saturday, with no cover charge (Ⓜ Bellas Artes).

La Ópera Bar (☎ 5-512-89-59, Avenida Cinco de Mayo 14) is an ornate early-20th-century watering hole that, after decades as a bastion of masculinity, opened its doors to women in the 1970s. Booths of dark wood and a massive bar are all original, and there's a hole in the ceiling said to have been made by a bullet from Pancho Villa. Drinks cost US$1.75 and up, lots of food is served at middling prices, and musicians serenade. It's a fun place to spend a couple of hours – open 1 pm to midnight Monday to Saturday, 1 to 6 pm Sunday (**Ⓜ** Allende).

Beer lovers should head for the no-frills **Salón Corona** (Bolívar 24). Amiable waiters serve up *tarros* (mugs) of light or dark *cerveza de barril* (draft beer) and bottles of almost every known Mexican beer for US$1.25 each. You can accompany your ale with all sorts of tacos for US$0.60 to US$0.80 each, or a bowl of *caldo de camarones* (shrimp soup, US$0.90). The Corona, going since 1928, is open 8 am to 11.30 pm daily.

La Casa de las Sirenas (Guatemala 32), in a 17th-century house just behind the cathedral, is both a restaurant (see the Places to Eat chapter) and a temple to tequila, serving up over 250 varieties of the national drink at between US$2 and US$13.50 a shot in its Salones Tequila – open 8 am to 11 pm Monday to Saturday, 8 am to 7 pm Sunday.

Juárez

The hub of a fun Mexico City scene of younger (20 to 40) expats, associated Mexicans and some travelers is a couple of cool bars a few blocks east of the Zona Rosa.

El Colmillo (☎ 5-592-61-14, Versalles 52) is a cool hangout run by a pair of British club impresarios. Downstairs there's loud dance music, a dance floor and a bar/lounge area; upstairs there's jazz Thursday to Saturday. Cover is US$4.50 for downstairs or upstairs, US$6.50 for both. A beer is US$2, cocktails – including frozen vodka concoctions that the club prides itself on – from US$4.50. It's open from 9 or 10 pm to 4 am Wednesday to Saturday. The door doesn't keep people waiting long (Map 5).

Bar Milán (☎ 5-592-00-31, Milán 18), owned by a well-known Mexican actor, Demian Bichir, plays great, varied music and gets packed by about midnight on Friday and Saturday. It's open 9 pm to 2 am nightly except Monday. A beer is US$2, cocktails are from US$2, and tequila from US$2.75 (Map 5).

Zona Rosa

In the Zona Rosa proper, **Cantina Las Bohemias**, on Londres west of Amberes, is a bright, jolly bar popular with women as well as men (it's not a *real* cantina). A beer is US$1 to US$1.50, spirits from US$1.25. **Freedom** (Copenhague 25) gets busy with a youngish after-work crowd. It has at least three bars on two levels, plays loud dance music, and is fun. A beer is US$2. There's just enough room to dance upstairs, and good food downstairs (see the Places to Eat chapter). Another popular but more expensive bar-cum-restaurant is the very American **Yuppie's Sports Café** (Génova 34), at Hamburgo (see the Places to Eat chapter).

Male pedestrians in this area should be prepared for aggressive invitations from numerous street-corner hustlers to 'ladies' bars' and 'table dance clubs.' The former offers 'desnudo de chicas,' and in the latter, women – for a fee – will dance with, and sit on the knees of, male customers.

Condesa & Roma

Condesa is known more for its restaurants and coffeehouses than its bars, but **Cantina El Centenario**, at the corner of Michoacán and Vicente Suárez, is a relaxed cantina with good free *botanas* (snacks). **Cantina Bar Tequila Maguey** (Nuevo León 92) is a bright, modern bar with backgammon and other board games to help you pass the time; free botanas are served after three drinks. It's open 1 pm to 2 am Monday to Saturday.

Ah...Men

Everyone knows about Mexican cantinas, those pits of wild drinking and even wilder displays of machismo. A Lonely Planet colleague was once in a Mexico City cantina where it was hardly noticed when a man drew his pistol and fired several rounds into the ceiling. Cantinas are generally loud, but not quite that loud.

Cantinas are usually for men only – no women or children are allowed. They don't usually have 'Cantina' signs outside, but can be identified by signs prohibiting minors, Wild West-type swinging half-doors, and a generally raucous atmosphere. Those who enter must be prepared to drink hard. You might be challenged to go one-on-one at a bottle of tequila, mezcal or brandy. If you're not up to this, excuse yourself and beat a retreat.

A few cantinas these days (including all those mentioned in this chapter) are much less forbidding and welcome women, but in others it's best to leave judgment of the situation up to a local.

Besides cantinas, Mexico City has lots of bars, lounges, 'pubs' and cafés in which all are welcome. You'll find some excellent drinking places recommended in this chapter.

Fixion (☎ 5-584-74-03, *Orizaba 146*) is a popular disco-bar in a big, old Roma house – open 11 pm to 4 am Thursday to Saturday. On Thursdays there's no cover charge and you pay for drinks; on Friday and Saturday men pay US$18, women get in free and drinks are free for both. Some nights live bands play.

San Ángel

In the evenings *La Camelia* restaurant on Plaza San Jacinto becomes a lively, sometimes rowdy antro for an 18-35 crowd, with beer at US$2 and cocktails and tequila from US$3.50.

Bar Grappa (☎ 5-616-45-04), upstairs in Pabellón Altavista mall at Avenida Revolu-

ción and Camino al Desierto de los Leones, is a fun antro with a youngish, chic-ish crowd. The space, not designed for quiet, intimate conversation, is long and dark, with a large video screen and loud mixed music. It's open from 9.30 pm Thursday to Saturday (men US$7, women free). *El Alebrije* (☎ 5-616-53-04, *Altamirano 46*), in Plaza Opción, is from a similar mold – open 10 pm to 3 or 4 am Thursday to Saturday (men US$5, women free).

Coyoacán

The central plazas are surrounded by cafés and bars. *El Hijo del Cuervo* (☎ 5-659-51-96, *Jardín del Centenario 17*), with a youngish crowd of Mexicans and foreigners, plays a mixture of recorded Mexican and gringo rock and stages occasional live music or theater. It gets busy most evenings (open 5 pm to midnight Monday, 1 pm to midnight Tuesday to Sunday). A beer is US$1.75, tequila from US$2.25.

La Guadalupana, on Higuera, is a great Spanish-style bar with *tapas* (Spanish snacks) and Mexican food. It closes about 10 pm.

El Ángel (*Tres Cruces 95*) is a funky little bar with good and varied music – rock, reggae, hip-hop – and a studenty, mainly Mexican crowd. It has just enough space for a bit of dancing. A beer is around US$1.25 and there's no cover. It's open till 2 am Wednesday to Sunday. There's no sign – the building is white and blue outside and black inside.

CLUBS
Centro Histórico

Dance clubs in marvelous old *palacios* and mansions are the chief nocturnal draw downtown. The crowd is mainly young, and Friday and Saturday nights, from about 10 pm, are the happening times. Places veer rapidly in and out of fashion. If you seek out some of the following, crowds on the street will guide you to others.

Altura (☎ 5-510-98-55, *Uruguay 87*), at 5 de Febrero – rooftop dancing Wednesday to Sunday from 9 pm atop a dramatically lit, medieval palace-like building; men pay around US$6, women free (Ⓜ Zócalo)

El Cirio (Carranza 73), in the 18th-century Antiguo Palacio de los Condes de Xala – latest cool spot at the time of research; clean casual is the look (**Ⓜ** Zócalo)

La Llorona (☎ 5-709-84-20, Mesones 87), at 5 de Febrero – one of the most popular Centro clubs; young, unexciting-looking crowd, men wearing collars; beautiful colonial mansion but bouncers like to keep crowds waiting outside; open Thursday to Saturday from 9.30 pm, entry US$13 (**Ⓜ** Pino Suárez)

Opulencia (☎ 5-512-04-17, Isabel la Católica 26), at Madero – a good street-corner upstairs location with big windows, lilac lighting and a young, average-Joe sort of crowd; open from 10 pm Friday and Saturday only; men pay US$17, women free, drinks free (**Ⓜ** Allende)

Pervert Lounge (☎ 5-518-09-76, Uruguay 70) – a different, more offbeat crowd; house, trip-hop, acid jazz; open Wednesday to Saturday from 11 pm, entry US$6 (**Ⓜ** Allende)

Zona Rosa

Caramba (☎ 5-553-55-31, Génova 44) attracts a youngish Mexican crowd with its varied music – open 9 pm to 4 am Thursday to Saturday (men US$15, women free till 10.30 pm, US$10 after 10.30 pm; drinks free). The *Carrousel Internacional* (see the Places to Eat chapter and Mariachi, later in this chapter) also has a loud and lively discoteca section with an entry charge of US$5. There are several more dance clubs around the Zona Rosa, especially on Niza and Avenida Florencia.

Insurgentes Sur

For dancing with a view, head up to the *Sky Club (☎ 5-488-07-00)* on the 46th floor of the World Trade Center at Insurgentes Sur and Filadelfia, Colonia Nápoles. It's open 9 pm to 3 am Wednesday to Saturday with music from salsa to techno – men can expect to pay around US$15, women will pay nothing (Map 1).

Polanco

This well-heeled neighborhood north of the Bosque de Chapultepec gets quite lively after dark. The thriving Italian restaurant *Mezzanotte (☎ 5-282-01-30, Avenida Presidente Masaryk 407)*, in Plaza Zentro, jumps

with a New York-club-style dance floor Thursday to Saturday nights.

In the west side of the Auditorio Nacional building off the south side of Reforma is the *Fashion Café (☎ 5-280-46-21)*, one of a small international chain of such places created by supermodels Elle MacPherson, Naomi Campbell and Claudia Schiffer. At the center of things is a catwalk where real fashion parades happen at 3.30 and 10.30 pm daily. By day there's a 'family ambiance,' by night the place becomes a fashionable dance club with the catwalk as dance floor (no cover charge). There are two bars, average food is served at slightly higher than average prices, and it's all open 1 pm to 1 am daily. A new discoteca section was being created downstairs when we visited.

San Ángel

The cavernous *Lhooqi* on Camino al Desierto de los Leones, with its pounding music and flashing lights, had people crowding around the door to get in when we last checked. A sister branch to the Italian restaurant-bar in Polanco, *Mezzanotte (☎ 5-550-29-48)*, in Plaza Opción, becomes a lively dance club from around 10 pm to 3 am (except on Sunday).

GAY & LESBIAN VENUES

Sergay magazine, available free in some of the clubs and bars mentioned below, has useful information on the Mexico City gay scene. It's on the Internet at www.sergay .com.mx. *Tiempo Libre* has long listings on its website. Also check *Don Pato's Gay Mexico City* (www.donpato.com/bars.html).

Zona Rosa

The Zona Rosa is the focus of the gay and lesbian scene. One of the longest-established spots is the relaxed bar *El Almacén (☎ 5-207-07-27, Avenida Florencia 37A)*, open daily from 4.30 pm and welcoming lesbians as well as gay men. Downstairs is the pounding, men-only disco-bar *El Taller (☎ 5-533-49-84)*, open 9 pm to 4 am daily except Monday (US$3 cover Thursday to Saturday), with a darkroom. The last Saturday of the month is usually a rave night, and on

Tuesday nights free men-only discussion sessions are held.

A fashionable disco, mainly for men, is *El Antro* (☎ 5-511-16-13, *Londres 77*), open Wednesday to Sunday nights with a piano bar, video lounge, darkroom, big dance floor and a variety of shows and strippers (cover US$3 to US$5).

Cabaré-Tito (☎ 5-514-94-55, *Local 20A Interior, Londres 161*), in Plaza del Ángel, is an innovative gay bar/disco/theater often featuring cabaret, drama or discussion sessions – open from 1 pm daily and attracting a wide range of people including some heterosexuals.

El Celo (☎ 5-514-47-66, *Londres 104*) is a gay music and dance bar and art gallery, open from 6 pm daily except Monday (US$3 cover Friday to Sunday). The music is mostly pop.

Other Areas

Butterfly (☎ 5-761-18-81, *Izazaga 5*) is a big, busy, high-tech gay dance club with great music, a few steps east of Eje Central Lázaro Cárdenas. It's open 9 pm to 4 am nightly, with transvestite shows Friday and Saturday. The US$3.50 cover includes two drinks (**Ⓜ** Salto del Agua; Map 4).

Enigma (☎ 5-207-73-67, *Morelia 111*) in Colonia Roma, is mainly a lesbian disco-bar but has regular transvestite shows. It's open 9 pm to 3.30 am Monday to Saturday, 6 pm to 2 am Sunday. The cost of admission ranges

---

Tropical Turns

Mexico City has a dozen or more clubs and large *salones de baile* (dance halls) devoted to *música tropical*. The city's many aficionados can go to a different hall each night of the week, some capable of holding thousands of people. You need to dress smart and know how to dance salsa, merengue, cumbia or danzón to really enjoy most of these places, and it's best to go in a group, or at least with someone to dance with. A good one is *Antillanos* (☎ 5-592-04-39, *Pimentel 78*), in Colonia San Rafael, 1.5km north of the Zona Rosa. Bands from Mexico, Cuba, Puerto Rico or Colombia grind out infectious rhythms 9 pm to 3 am Tuesday to Saturday. Tequila, rum and whisky are served by the bottle at around US$20; entry is US$5 (**Ⓜ** San Cosme; Map 5).

Meneo (☎ 5-523-94-48, *Nueva York 315*), just west of Insurgentes Sur, has salsa and merengue bands 9 pm to 3 am Thursday to Saturday. Entry costs around US$8 and men must wear a jacket. To get there, take a 'San Ángel' pesero 5km south from the Insurgentes metro station (Map 1). An interesting-sounding new place opened around the time of research for this book. It's *Salón 21* (☎ 5-255-14-96, *Andrómaco 17*), at the corner of Moliere in Polanco.

Neither flashy nor trendy, but a lot of fun, is the little *Restaurante-Bar León* (☎ 5-510-30-93, *Brasil 5*) in the Centro Histórico. Live salsa, merengue and rumba rhythms drive customers to the tightly packed dance floor 9 pm to 3 am Wednesday to Saturday – but no one will mind if you just sit, watch and listen. Cover charge is US$3.50 (women free on Thursday); drinks are US$2 and up (nearest **Ⓜ** Allende and Zócalo). Other major salones de baile include the following:

La Maraka (☎ 5-682-83-94, *Mitla 40*) in Colonia Narvarte at Avenida Eugenia; 9 pm to 3 am Friday and some Saturdays, with salsa and merengue bands; entry usually US$10 to US$15 (**Ⓜ** Eugenia; Map 1)

Salón México (☎ 5-518-09-31, *2° Callejón de San Juan de Dios 25*), north of the Alameda Central; 9 pm to 3 am Friday and Saturday for salsa and/or traditional danzón; entry US$4

Salón Riviera (☎ 5-575-40-36, *Avenida División del Norte 1157*), in Colonia Del Valle; 4 to 11 pm Wednesday for danzón with live bands (US$4, classes given until 6 pm); other dance nights staged here are advertised in *Tiempo Libre* and on posters (**Ⓜ** División del Norte; Map 1)

from free to US$3.50 (700m south of Ⓜ Cuauhtémoc; Map 7).

A recently fashionable spot is **Penelope** (☎ 5-566-14-72, *Antonio Caso 60*), in Colonia San Rafael about 1.5km northeast of the Zona Rosa. Frequented by some lesbians as well as gay men, it's open from 10 pm Thursday to Saturday, with strippers, go-go dancers and a show. There's usually a cover charge of US$3 Thursday, US$6 other nights, with one free drink (Map 5).

ROCK & POP

You need to watch the press and listings to find out who's playing.

Top Mexican and foreign performers tour at various venues in Mexico City including the **Auditorio Nacional** (☎ 5-280-92-50, *Paseo de La Reforma 50*) in Polanco (Ⓜ Auditorio); the **Teatro Metropólitan** (☎ 5-510-10-45, *Independencia 90*), near the Alameda Central (Ⓜ Juárez); the **Palacio de los Deportes** (☎ 5-237-99-99), at Avenida Río Churubusco and Calle Añil, Colonia Granjas México (Ⓜ Velódromo; Map 1); and the **Autódromo Hermanos Rodríguez**, on Viaducto Río de la Piedad (Ⓜ Ciudad Deportiva; Map 1).

The city is short on good smaller venues despite producing many bands. All the more reason, therefore, to be grateful for **Rockotitlán** (☎ 5-687-78-93, *Insurgentes Sur 953*), on Plaza Baja California, a time-honored stage for homegrown Mexican rock music. This graffiti-daubed, cavelike space presents live bands – usually up-and-coming outfits – nightly except Monday, usually at 10 pm. Entry is US$2 to US$10 depending who's on. There are also some Saturday and Sunday afternoon sessions at 3 pm, usually for US$5 with free beer (normally a beer is US$1.50). If you like this kind of thing, it's fun. You can drop by to pick up a schedule. About the easiest way to get there is by a 'San Ángel' pesero southbound on Insurgentes from the Insurgentes metro station for 4.5km (Map 1).

In the Zona Rosa, very raw and heavy live rock can be experienced from 6 pm to midnight nightly at **La Casa del Canto** (*Glorieta Insurgentes CC-04*), near the exit of the Insurgentes metro station. It's a small, no-frills place, which allows the decibels full effect (cover US$1.25).

In Polanco, **Circo** (☎ 5-282-27-29, *Avenida Presidente Masaryk 407*), in Plaza Zentro, is a popular bar with live music, usually rock-oriented, after 11 pm Wednesday to Sunday (cover US$3.50). Some of Mexico's best bands play at the **Hard Rock Café** (☎ 5-327-71-00, *Campos Elíseos 290*) but tickets are usually US$30 or so.

SON & MEXICAN MUSIC
Son

The place and time for hot, live Cuban son, with a bohemian atmosphere, is Thursday to Saturday nights at **Mama Rumba** (☎ 5-564-69-20, *Querétaro 230*), in Roma, south of the Zona Rosa. The music starts around 11 pm and cover is US$3.50 to US$4. The bar is small and tightly packed: you can't miss its bright neon lights. In Condesa, **La Bodega** (☎ 5-511-73-90, *Popocatépetl 25*) has son and/or rumba groups playing in its restaurant and/or bar most nights.

Barfly (☎ 5-282-26-56, *Avenida Presidente Masaryk 393*), in Plaza Mazarik, in Polanco, jumps to live Cuban sounds from 11.30 pm Tuesday to Saturday (cover US$6).

Mariachi

Plaza Garibaldi, five blocks north of the Palacio de Bellas Artes, is where the city's mariachi bands gather in the evenings. Often

considered the most 'typical' Mexican music of all, mariachi originated in the Guadalajara area, but Plaza Garibaldi is one of the country's main mariachi gathering spots (**M** Bellas Artes or Garibaldi).

The musicians, kitted out in their fancy costumes, tootle their trumpets, tune their guitars and stand around with drinks until approached by someone who's ready to pay for a song (about US$5) or whisk them away to entertain at a party. You can wander and listen to the mariachis in the plaza for free, and perhaps stay on in one of the bars or clubs around the plaza, some of which have live Latin dance music as a change from the mariachis. They usually have no entry fee but charge around US$2 for a shot of tequila or US$20 for a bottle – ask prices *before* you order drinks in these places. *El Tenampa* bar on the north side of the plaza has in-house mariachis and is decorated with murals of Mexican film stars. There are taquerías in the northeast corner of the plaza.

The plaza gets going by about 8 pm and stays busy until midnight or so.

In the Zona Rosa, the *Carrousel Internacional (Niza 33)* is a restaurant/bar that has mariachis singing energetically most of the time (see the Places to Eat chapter).

Banda & Grupera
The *Salón de Baile del Pacífico (☎ 5-592-27-78, Bucareli 43)* is a home for *banda*, *grupera* and similar Mexican music. Live bands play from about 11 pm to 4 am Thursday to Saturday. The cover charge is US$3 to US$6; a shot of tequila costs from US$1.50 (Map 5).

CANTO NUEVO & BALLADS
If your mood is romantic and you're not in need of alcohol, you could wander along to *La Hostería del Bohemio (Avenida Hidalgo 107)*, across Reforma from the Alameda Central. Lovey-dovey couples sit at tables around a leafy, candlelit courtyard, listening to *música romántica* by singers, groups or guitarists, and nibbling at ice cream or cakes or sipping nonalcoholic drinks, all at US$2 each. It's open 5 to 11 pm daily, with no cover charge (**M** Hidalgo).

Two small café-type venues in Colonia Roma for *canto nuevo* and contemporary *trova*, as well as other music such as blues or romantic ballads, are *El Café de Nadie (☎ 5-264-34-20, San Luis Potosí 121)*, with music Tuesday to Saturday, and *Café Arte (☎ 5-514-29-44, Obregón 225)*, Wednesday to Saturday. At both places the music gets going around 8.30 pm and there's an entry charge of about US$3.50. They may be bustling or empty, depending on the night and who's playing.

In Coyoacán, *El Trovador (☎ 5-554-72-47, Carranza 82)*, on the corner of Cinco de Febrero, is a *peña folklórica* (folk club) with live nueva trova, canto nuevo and similar forms from about 7 pm nightly except Sunday (no cover).

JAZZ
San Ángel's *New Orleans Jazz (☎ 5-550-19-08, Avenida Revolución 1655)* serves up good varied jazz from 8 or 9 pm Tuesday to Saturday. It's a restaurant, too (spaghetti, crêpes, chicken all US$3.50 to US$5). There's a cover charge of US$2.50 to US$5. Also in San Ángel, the Indian restaurant *La Casona del Elefante (☎ 5-616-22-08, Plaza San Jacinto 9)* usually has live jazz from 10 pm to 1 am Friday and Saturday (no cover). Also see El Colmillo under Bars & Antros, earlier in this chapter.

CLASSICAL MUSIC
The *Palacio de Bellas Artes* (see Dance Performances, later in this chapter) is home to the Orquesta Sinfónica Nacional (National Symphony Orchestra) and a main venue for classical music and opera in general. But the classical scene is a busy one and there are regular concerts at several other halls. They include the *Sala Nezahualcóyotl (☎ 5-622-71-11)* and *Sala Carlos Chávez (☎ 5-622-71-37)*, both in the *Centro Cultural Universitario (Avenida Insurgentes Sur 3000)* of the Ciudad Universitaria; the *Centro Cultural Ollin Yoliztli (☎ 5-606-81-91, Periférico Sur 5141)*, 700m east of Avenida Insurgentes Sur (Map 11); and the *Auditorio Blas Galindo* as well as other halls and theaters in the *Centro Nacional de*

las Artes (☎ *5-420-44-00*), on Avenida Río Churubusco just east of Calzada de Tlalpan, Colonia Country Club (Ⓜ General Anaya; Map 9).

Attractive old Centro Histórico venues such as the Museo de San Ildefonso, Museo Nacional de Arte and Pinacoteca Virreinal are also used for some concerts.

DANCE PERFORMANCES

A free and always entertaining spectacle is provided by the *conchero* dancers who gather informally every day in the Zócalo (and sometimes elsewhere) to carry out sweaty pre-Hispanic dances in feathered headdresses and *concha* (shell) anklets and bracelets, to the rhythm of big booming drums.

The *Palacio de Bellas Artes* (☎ *5-512-25-93*), beside the Alameda Central, stages the famous shows of the Ballet Folklórico de México, a two-hour festive blur of colored lights and regional costumes, music and dance from all over Mexico. This famous company has been doing shows like this since the 1950s and they are as spectacular and professional as ever. Tickets are not cheap, however, costing from US$12 to US$29. Performances are normally at 8.30 pm on Wednesday and 9.30 am and 8.30 pm on Sunday. Tickets are usually available on the day of the show or the day before at the ticket windows *(taquillas)* in the Bellas Artes lobby, open 11 am to 7 pm Monday to Saturday, 9 am to 7 pm Sunday. You can also get them from Ticketmaster.

Contemporary dance and ballet both have sizable followings here. Check *Tiempo Libre* for what's on. Venues are much the same as for classical music (see Classical Music, earlier). The national dance company dances *El Lago de los Cisnes (Swan Lake)* on islands in the Lago Chapultepec, in the first section of the Bosque de Chapultepec, usually at 8 pm Wednesday to Sunday from late February to early April.

THEATER & CABARET

Plenty of theater is staged in Mexico City: it's virtually all in Spanish. *Tiempo Libre* has full listings. A few bar/restaurant-type places

present varied cabaret-style or small-scale theater shows or offbeat musical performances that may be more accessible to non-fluent Spanish speakers – several are listed under 'Teatro Bar' in the *Espectáculos Nocturnos* section of *Tiempo Libre*. The admission charge at such places is usually US$10 to US$15. One top venue is *La Planta de Luz* (☎ *5-616-47-61*), in Plaza Loreto, San Ángel, with shows Thursday to Monday evenings. In Condesa, *La Bodega* (☎ *5-511-73-90, Popocatépetl 25)* puts on similar acts usually on Friday and Saturday in its *teatro-bar*. In Coyoacán, *El Hábito* (☎ *5-659-63-05, Madrid 13)* stages a varied program, mostly from Thursday to Saturday starting around 10 pm.

FLAMENCO

Mexico City is a minor home away from home for the song, dance and guitar arts of flamenco, from Andalucía, Spain. One of the more authentic venues is *Mesón Triana* (☎ *5-525-38-80, Oaxaca 90)*, in Colonia Roma, which is also a bar and restaurant. Shows get going around the suitably Andalucian hour of midnight Tuesday to Saturday. Cost is US$8, plus whatever you drink and eat.

CINEMAS

Foreign movies (except children's and educational films) are always shown in their original language, with Spanish subtitles. Cinema tickets are usually around US$2, half-price in most cinemas on Wednesday. Classic and art-house films are shown at the *Cineteca Nacional* (☎ *5-688-32-72, Avenida México-Coyoacán 389)*, 700m east of the Coyoacán metro station (Map 9); *Cinemanía* (☎ *5-616-48-36)*, in Plaza Loreto in San Ángel; the *Centro Cultural Universitario* (☎ *5-665-25-80, Avenida Insurgentes Sur 3000)* in the Ciudad Universitaria; and elsewhere. *Tiempo Libre* publishes full cinema listings. *The News* has partial cinema listings on Friday and Sunday. *Cinemex Casa de Arte* (*Avenida Presidente Masaryk 393)*, in the Plaza Mazarik in Polanco, is a multiscreen cinema showing some of the best current-release movies.

SPECTATOR SPORTS

Events such as soccer games, bullfights and wrestling can be fascinating: even if the action doesn't especially interest you, the crowd probably will.

Soccer (Football)

Fútbol is at least as popular in Mexico as bullfighting. The country has a national league with an 18-team *Primera División* (First Division), and Mexico City has several impressive stadiums, including the **Estadio Azteca** (☎ 5-617-80-80, *Calzada de Tlalpan 3465)*, which staged the World Cup final in 1970 and 1986.

The city stages two or three Primera División matches almost every weekend from August to May. Mexico's soccer calendar is divided into a *torneo de invierno* (winter season, August to December) and a *torneo de verano* (summer season, January to May), each ending in eight-team playoffs (La Liguilla) and eventually a two-leg final to decide the champion. *The News* and the Spanish-language press carry details on games.

The Mexico City team América, nicknamed Las Águilas (the Eagles), is the most popular in the country. Las Pumas, of UNAM, come second in popularity in the capital, with Cruz Azul (known as Los Cementeros) third. Other leading Mexico City teams include Atlante (Los Potros), Necaxa (Los Rayos) and Neza (Los Toros).

The biggest crowds flock to games between any pairing of América, Las Pumas, Cruz Azul and Guadalajara (Las Chivas), which is the biggest club outside the capital. The biggest match of all is 'El Clásico,' between América and Guadalajara, which fills the awesome Estadio Azteca with 100,000 flag-waving fans – an occasion surprising for the friendliness of the rivalry between the two bands of fans. This is about the only game of the year in the capital where you should get a ticket in advance. Crowds at other games range from a few thousand to around 70,000.

Most big matches are played at the Estadio Azteca. When games are on, peseros run to the stadium from the Tasqueña metro station; you can also get there by the Tren Ligero (streetcar) from the Tasqueña metro station to Estadio Azteca station (Map 1). The Pumas' home is the **Estadio Olímpico** (☎ 5-616-20-45) at the Ciudad Universitaria, and Cruz Azul's is the **Estadio Azul** (☎ 5-563-94-71, *Indiana 260)*, next door to the Monumental Plaza México bullring (see Bullfights; Map 1). Tickets for games are usually available at the gate right up to kickoff; prices range from less than US$1 to about US$10.

Bullfights

The **Monumental Plaza México** (☎ 5-563-39-61, *Rodin 241)*, a deep concrete bowl that can hold 48,000 spectators, is one of the largest bullrings in the world. If you're not put off by its very concept, a *corrida de toros* (bullfight) is quite a spectacle, from the milling throngs and hawkers outside the arena to the pageantry and drama in the ring itself and the crowd response it provokes. Six bulls are usually fought in an afternoon, two each by three matadors.

From October or November to March or April, professional fights are held at the Monumental most Sundays, starting at 4 pm. There are sometimes extra corridas – often with star Mexican and Spanish matadors – on holidays. The veteran Eloy Cavasos, from Monterrey, is often acclaimed as Mexico's best matador. Alfredo Lomeli and Eulalio 'Zotoluco' López are younger stars. Bullfights featuring star matadors from Spain such as Enrique Ponce, El Juli, José Tomás or El Cordobés have added spice. From June to October, junior matadors fight young bulls. *The News* runs a weekly bullfighting column, 'Blood on the Sand,' which will tell you what's in store.

The *taquillas* (ticket windows) by the bullring's main entrance on Rodin have printed lists of ticket prices. The cheapest seats, less than US$2, are in the Sol General section – the top tiers of seating on the sunny side of the arena. These are OK if the weather's not too hot – many of them fall into shade as the afternoon goes on, in any case. The Sombra General – the top tiers on the shady side – costs slightly more. The best seats are in the Barreras, the seven rows nearest the arena, and normally cost US$15 to US$25: the more expensive are in the *sombra* (shade), the cheaper are in the *sol* (sun). Between the Barreras and the

General sections are first the Primer (1er) Tendido, then the Segundo (2°) Tendido.

Except for the biggest corridas, tickets are available right up to the time the third bull is

La Corrida

It's said that Mexicans arrive on time for only two events – funerals and bullfights. To many gringo eyes, the corrida de toros (literally, running of the bulls) hardly seems to be sport or, for that matter, entertainment. Mexicans see it as both and more. As much a ritualistic dance as a fight, it originated in Spain and readily lends itself to a variety of symbolic interpretations, mostly related to machismo. It *is* also very dangerous for the matador.

The corrida, also known as the *fiesta brava* (wild festival), begins promptly. To the sound of music, usually a Spanish *paso doble*, the matador in his *traje de luces* (suit of lights) and his assistants *(toreros)* give the traditional *paseillo* (salute) to the fight authorities and the crowd. Then the first of the day's six bulls is released from its pen for the first of the ritual's three *suertes* (acts), or *tercios* (thirds).

The cape-waving toreros tire the bull by luring him around the ring. After a few minutes two *picadores*, on heavily padded horses, enter and jab long lances *(picas)* into the bull's shoulders to weaken him. Somehow this is often the most gruesome part of the whole process.

The band pipes up again, the picadores leave the ring, and the *suerte de banderillas* begins as the toreros attempt to stab three pairs of elongated darts (banderillas) into the bull's shoulders without getting impaled on his horns. After the band signals the end of this second suerte, the final *suerte de muleta* is the climax in which the matador has exactly 16 minutes to kill the bull. Starting with fancy cape work to tire the animal, the matador then exchanges his large cape for the smaller *muleta* and takes sword in hand, baiting the bull to charge before delivering the fatal *estocada* (lunge) with his sword. The matador must deliver the estocada between the shoulder blades from a position directly in front of the animal.

If the matador succeeds, and he usually does – if not always on the first attempt – the bull collapses and an assistant dashes into the ring to sever its jugular. If the applause from the crowd warrants, he will also cut off an ear or two and sometimes the tail for the matador. The dead bull is dragged from the ring to be butchered for sale.

A 'good' bullfight depends not only on the skill and courage of the matador but also the spirit of the bulls. Animals lacking heart for the fight bring shame on the ranch that bred them. Very occasionally, a bull that has fought outstandingly is *indultado* (spared) – an occasion for great celebration – and will then retire to stud.

Marionettes hanging around the Centro de Artesanías La Ciudadela

Fresh papier-mâché vegetables at the Centro de Artesanías La Ciudadela

Statue at Papalote Museo del Niño entrance

Sculpture at Museo Nacional de Antropología

Figura Obsena by José Luis Cuevas from Freedom in Bronze 2000 exhibit

killed, though the best seats may sell out early. You can buy advance tickets Thursday to Saturday from 9.30 am to 1 pm and 3.30 to 7 pm, and Sunday from 9.30 am onward. Most major hotels and many travel agencies sell tickets at a markup.

The Monumental is a few blocks west of Avenida Insurgentes Sur, 5.5km south of Paseo de la Reforma and a 10-minute walk eastward from San Antonio metro station (Map 1). 'Plaza México' peseros run along Insurgentes Sur on bullfight afternoons.

Baseball

Mexico City has two teams in the national league, called the Liga Mexicana de Béisbol. They are the Diablos Rojos (officially Club México) and the Tigres. Both play at the *Parque del Seguro Social (Avenida Cuauhtémoc 462)*, a block south of the Centro Médico metro station (Map 7). The season runs from March to August and crowds approach 10,000 when the two local teams play each other. Games usually start at 6.30 pm. Ticketmaster (see Tickets, earlier in this chapter) sells tickets for games and lists dates in its *La Guía de Entretenimiento*. The *Afición* sports paper also details upcoming games. The league's website is www.lmb.com.mx.

Charreadas

Charreada is the Mexican name for a rodeo, and Mexico City has a permanent, covered arena for this exciting spectacle. The *Rancho del Charro (☎ 5-277-87-06, Avenida Constituyentes 500)*, belonging to the Asociación Mexicana de Charros, is between the Panteón Civil de Dolores and the 3ª Sección of the Bosque de Chapultepec (Map 1). The major charreada season is from mid-May to early June. Entry is around US$2.50 for most events. See the Bosque de Chapultepec section in the Things to See & Do chapter for how to get there.

Jai Alai

This old Basque game is fast and elegant when played by experts – a bit like squash with a hard ball on a very long court, played with curved wicker baskets *(cestas)* attached

to the wrist. The ball travels at up to 160km/hour, which some say is the fastest ball in sport. Singles or doubles can be played. The ball must not bounce twice before being played (just as in squash and tennis), must strike the end wall of the court between an upper and a lower line, and must not go off the open side of the court. Only the server or serving pair can score a point. If they lose a rally, the opposition takes the next serve. The game ends when one side reaches 30 points.

Some of the best jai alai is played at the *Frontón México (☎ 5-546-32-40)*, in Plaza de la República. At this writing the Frontón had been closed for over two years by a strike of its workers. When it's in action, the attraction is not just the game but the chance to bet on it. Bookmakers call out changing odds as games progress.

Before the strike, games at the Frontón México were played nightly except Monday, almost all year, starting at 7 pm (5 pm on Sunday). Admission was around US$5. It's something of an upper-class sport: officially, formal dress is required (jacket and tie for men), but in practice visitors may get away with less (near Ⓜ Revolución; Map 5).

Boxing & Lucha Libre

Mexico has produced many world boxing champs and a big fight here is a big event, widely televised. As much showbiz as sport is *lucha libre*, wrestling. Participants give themselves silly names like Bestia Salvaje, Shocker, Los Karate Boy and Heavy Metal, then clown around in lurid masks and fancy dress. Two fairly central venues for both activities, with lucha libre on Friday and boxing on Saturday, are the *Arena Coliseo (☎ 5-588-02-66, Perú 73 and 77)*, near Plaza Santo Domingo (Ⓜ Allende; Map 4), and the *Arena México (Dr Río de la Loza 94)*, in Colonia Doctores (Ⓜ Balderas or Cuauhtémoc; Map 5).

Motor Racing

Events take place at the *Autódromo Hermanos Rodríguez* on Viaducto Río de la Piedad in the east of the city (Ⓜ Ciudad Deportiva; Map 1).

Shopping

Mexico City shopping ranges from modern boutiques, department stores and malls to street-side hawkers (who just might have exactly what you're looking for) and hole-in-the-wall purveyors of everything from shoelaces and nails to tortillas. This city is a good place to get things like shoe soles and cameras repaired – Mexicans prefer to mend things if they are mendable, rather than throw them away – and plenty of small street-corner workshops supply this need. The malls are full of designer clothing, shoe stores, toy stores, jewelers, cosmeticians and sometimes a music store. Most of them also have a range of places to eat and drink, often including food courts with a selection of inexpensive take-out counters surrounding a central area with tables and chairs. Shops are generally open Monday to Saturday from 9 or 10 am to 8 or 9 pm. A few big stores open Sunday, too.

Another characteristic Mexico City shopping experience is in the many markets *(mercados)* where the *capitalinos* themselves buy much of what they need. These are intriguing and lively places to browse even if you're not looking for anything in particular.

Mexico City has many bookstores, several with good ranges of English-language titles. Top-end hotels, Sanborns stores and major museums also often have stalls selling English-language books and other print media. For sources of maps, see Maps in the Facts for the Visitor chapter.

ARTESANÍAS

The most typically Mexican – and often the most attractive – purchases are the myriad *artesanías* (handicrafts). The term covers almost anything made mainly by hand. The best artesanías are often produced by Mexico's indigenous peoples, who have been expressing their creativity in this way for many centuries. Traditions of folk art go back a long, long way, and these arts are still very much alive. Mexico City has many shops and markets where you can see and buy fine artesanías from all over Mexico.

Pottery

As a visit to any archaeological museum will show, Mexicans have been making pottery of both simple and sophisticated designs for several millennia. A walk around almost any Mexican market or craft shop will reveal interesting contemporary pottery.

Many small-scale, often one-person, potters' workshops still turn out anything from the plain, everyday cooking or storage pots that you see in markets to elaborate decorative pieces that are really works of art.

One of the most distinctive forms you'll come across is the shiny, black, surprisingly light ware in hundreds of shapes and forms, from the small village of San Bartolo Coyotepec near Oaxaca in southern Mexico. Also very attractive is Talavera ware (named after a town in Spain whose pottery it resembles), made in Puebla, Dolores Hidalgo and elsewhere. Talavera comes in two main forms – tableware and tiles. Bright colors, with blue and yellow often prominent, and floral designs are typical – but tiles in particular may bear any kind of design.

One of Mexico's most unique pottery forms is the 'tree of life' *(árbol de la vida)*. These highly elaborate candelabra-like objects, often a meter or more high, are molded by hand and decorated with numerous tiny figures of people, animals, plants and so on. Packing one to take home would be a big challenge! Artisans in Acatlán and Izucar de Matamoros in Puebla state, east of Mexico City, and Metepec, near Toluca, to the west, make some of the best trees of life. Metepec also produces striking clay suns, often painted with very bright colors.

Masks

Like so many Mexican crafts, mask-making goes back to pre-Hispanic times. In authentic use, masks were and are worn for magical and religious purposes in dances, ceremonies and shamanistic rites. The wearer temporarily becomes the creature, person or deity depicted by the mask. The southern state of Guerrero has produced probably the most varied range of fine masks.

Wood is the usual basic material of masks but papier-mâché, clay, wax, leather and other materials are also used. A mask will often be painted and/or embellished with real feathers, hair or teeth. *Tigres* – jaguars or tigers – are fairly common masks, as are other animals and birds, actual and mythical. Christs and Devils are also numerous, as well as masks depicting 'Europeans,' whose pale, wide-eyed, usually mustachioed features may look as bizarre and comical to visitors today as the original Europeans in Mexico looked to the native Mexicans.

Today masks are also made for simple decoration, to hang on walls. Even miniature masks can be attractive.

Lacquerware & Woodwork

Gourds, the hard shells of certain squash-type vegetables, have been used since time immemorial in Mexico as bowls, cups and small storage vessels. Today they're also put to many other uses, including as children's rattles, maracas and even hats. The most eye-catching decorative technique is lacquering,

in which the outside of the gourd is coated with layers of paste or paint, then the artisan's chosen design is painted on and coated with oil or varnish to seal the lacquer.

Wood, too, can be lacquered, and today the majority of lacquerware you'll see in Mexico City is pine or a sweetly scented wood from the remote village of Olinalá in Guerrero state. Characteristic of Olinalá are boxes, trays, chests and furniture lacquered by the *rayado* method, in which designs are created by scraping off part of the top coat of paint to expose a different-colored layer below.

Another particularly attractive woodcraft is the brightly painted copal-wood animals and dragons and other imaginary beasts, produced by villagers around Oaxaca. You'll find these creatures, called *alebrijes*, arrayed in many Mexico City craft shops and markets. The craft emerged in the late 1980s from toys the local people had been carving for their children for generations.

Bark Paintings

Colorful paintings on *amate*, paper made from tree bark, are sold in countless souvenir shops. While many are humdrum productions for an undiscriminating tourist market, others depict village life skillfully and in some detail.

Bark paper has been made in Mexico since pre-Hispanic times, and has always been held sacred. The skill of making it survives only in one small remote area of central Mexico, in and around the Otomí village of San Pablito, in northern Veracruz state. Women boil the bark, then lay out the fibers and beat them with stones until they merge together. The resulting paper is dried in the sun. Much of it is then bought by Nahua villagers from Guerrero state, who have been doing bark paintings since the 1960s.

Leather

Leather belts, bags, sandals (*huaraches*), shoes, boots and clothes are often of good quality in Mexico, and usually much cheaper than in other countries. They're widely available in shops and markets.

In ritual use, the wearer becomes a tiger.

JOHN NOBLE

Silver

Some ancient Mexicans were expert metal-smiths and jewelers, as museum exhibits show. The Spanish fever for Mexico's gold and silver led to indigenous people being banned from working these metals for a time during the colonial period. But indigenous artisanship was revived in the 20th century – most famously in the town of Taxco by the American William Spratling, who initiated a silver-craft industry that now boasts more than 300 shops in the town. Silver is much more widely available than gold today, in all manner of styles and designs, and with artistry ranging from the dully imitative to the superb. It's quite possible to buy good pieces at sensible prices – see the Taxco section in the Excursions chapter for hints on judging and buying silver jewelry.

Baskets

Handmade baskets of multifarious shapes and sizes are common in Mexican markets. If you take a liking to one or two, at least you can use them to carry other souvenirs home. Materials used to make baskets include cane, bamboo and rush or palm-leaf strips. The latter may be wound around a filling of grasses. The more pliable materials enable a coiled construction, but weaving is more common. Many baskets are attractively patterned or colored.

Traditional Clothing

Traditional indigenous costume is not something you're often likely to buy for practical use, but many items might be purchased as works of art or for decorative purposes. Outstanding work doesn't come cheap: hundreds of dollars are asked for some of the very best *huipiles*, for instance.

Traditional clothing is now very rarely worn in Mexico City, but if you get out into some of Mexico's indigenous villages you won't fail to be intrigued by the variety of colorful costumes. Worn more often by women than men, these serve as a mark of the community to which their wearer belongs, and can also refer to a person's status in a community or to spiritual beliefs.

Much skilled work goes into creating such clothing. Many of the garment styles, techniques of production, and even some of the colorful, intricate designs woven or embroidered into the clothing, are little changed since before the Spanish reached Mexico.

Four important types of women's garment have been in use since long before the Spanish conquest:

Quechquémitl – a shoulder cape with an opening for the head, mainly worn in central and northern Mexico.

Huipil – a sleeveless tunic, often reaching as low as the thighs or ankles, though some are shorter and may be tucked into a skirt. The huipil is mainly used in southern Mexico.

Enredo – a wraparound skirt, almost invisible if worn beneath a long huipil.

Faja – a waist sash that holds the enredo in place.

Blouses, which were introduced by Spanish missionaries, are often embroidered with just as much care and detail as the more traditional garments. The *rebozo*, which also probably appeared in the Spanish era, is a long shawl that may cover the shoulders or head, or be used for carrying things. The male equivalent of the rebozo, also dating from the Spanish era, is the *sarape*, a blanket with an opening for the head.

The basic materials of indigenous weaving are cotton and wool, still sometimes home-produced and home-spun. Labor-saving factory yarn, including synthetic fibers, is increasingly common. Colors, too, are often synthetic – Mexicans use bright modern shades in some highly original combinations – but some natural dyes are still in use. Among these are deep blues from the indigo plant; reds and browns from various woods; and reds, pinks and purples from the cochineal insect (chiefly used in Oaxaca state). Textiles with more muted colors are less likely to have been made with synthetic dyes than some of the more garish offerings.

The traditional indigenous weaver's tool, used only by women, is the *telar de cintura* (backstrap loom). In simple terms, the warp (long) threads are stretched between two horizontal bars (one of which is fixed to a post or tree, the other being attached to a strap that goes around the weaver's lower back); the weft (cross) threads are then woven in. The length of a cloth woven on a backstrap loom is almost unlimited but the width is restricted to the weaver's arm-span.

The variety of color and pattern among the costumes of different indigenous peoples is immense. Some especially beautiful embroidered blouses and quechquémitls are created by Nahua women in Puebla state and the Mazahua in the west of México state. The Mazatecs, Triquis, Mixtecs, Zapotecs and Amuzgos of Oaxaca state, and the Tzotzils of Chiapas, create some of the finest, most colorful huipiles.

Other Textiles

One textile art practiced by men is weaving on the treadle loom, which is operated by foot pedals and tends to be used for blankets, rugs and wall hangings as well as rebozos, sarapes and skirt material. Probably Mexico's most famous blanket- and rug-weaving village is Teotitlán del Valle, near Oaxaca, which produces, among other things, fine textile versions of art by Picasso, Rivera, Escher and Miró, as well as pre-Hispanic-influenced geometric patterns.

The Huichol people of western Mexico make colorful and interesting 'yarn paintings' by pressing strands of wool or acrylic yarn onto wax-covered boards. The resulting scenes resemble visions experienced under the hallucinatory cactus peyote, which is sacred to the Huicholes. They also create more abstract patterns with beads pressed into beeswax on wooden bowls, animal skulls or masks.

Cloths embroidered with multitudes of bright birds, animals and insects by the Otomí people in and around San Pablito in northern Puebla state are found in many shops and markets in Mexico City.

SHOPS
Centro Histórico
& Alameda Central Area

For clothes and shoes, branches of the city's two top department stores, open daily, are conveniently placed within a block south of the Zócalo: El Palacio de Hierro on Cinco de Febrero, and Liverpool at Carranza 92. El Palacio de Hierro is the slightly classier and more expensive of the two.

For delicate Mexican sweets such as candied fruits, sugared almonds, crystallized strawberries, as well as honey and fruit jams, go directly to Dulcería de Celaya, Avenida Cinco de Mayo 39, near the Zócalo. These treats cost US$0.25 or more apiece, but anyone can afford at least one or two. The dulcería is open every day from 10.30 am to 7 pm.

Mixup, Avenida Madero 51, is a good place to find recorded music.

For specialty shops selling more everyday things, explore the streets around the Zócalo and the Alameda Central, where you'll find clusters of shops all offering one particular type of merchandise sometimes filling whole blocks or even two or three blocks. These can make a fascinating wander even if you don't want to buy. For example you'll find about a dozen shops selling wedding dresses on Chile between Tacuba and Perú. A similar number of places around the intersection of Brasil and Donceles sell film and cameras and do processing and camera repairs. Secondhand bookshops cluster on Donceles in the block west of Brasil. For sports gear and backpacks, Carranza between Bolívar and Eje Central Lázaro Cárdenas is the place: Deportes Rubens, Carranza 17, is a good stop for camping gear.

Fourteen shoe shops are strung along 16 de Septiembre between the Zócalo and the Eje Central, and many others are to be found on Tacuba, Pino Suárez, 20 de Noviembre and Bolívar south of Avenida Madero. Stationers congregate on El Salvador between Cinco de Febrero and Bolívar. About 50 computer stores huddle in the Plaza de la Computación y Electrónica on Eje Central Lázaro Cárdenas, south of Uruguay. Sound systems boom out all round the Bolívar's intersections with Uruguay and El Salvador. Calle Correo Mayor is chock-a-block with underwear. Electric-tool specialists cluster around the intersection of Artículo 123 and Revillagigedo. If you happen to need light fittings, shades or bulbs, Victoria, south of the Alameda, is the place.

Pasaje Catedral, between Tacuba and Donceles immediately north of the Catedral Metropolitana, has several religious goods shops full of chalices, crucifixes, and statues and pictures of Christ, the Virgin, saints, cherubim and so forth. Also here are a few stores devoted to medicinal plants.

These are the most interesting downtown bookstores:

American Bookstore
(☎ 5-512-03-06), Bolívar 23 – some novels and books on Mexico in English

Gandhi
Avenida Juárez 4 – good source of books about Mexico and Mexico City; novels in English, some Lonely Planet guides

Palacio de Bellas Artes
(☎ 5-521-92-51) – excellent arts bookstore, with some English-language titles on Mexico

Pórtico de la Ciudad de México
Eje Central Lázaro Cardenas 24 – excellent range of books in Spanish on Mexico, useful selection in English

Zona Rosa & Around

The Zona Rosa is full of often pricey boutiques and art and antique shops. Plaza La Rosa, an arcade between Hamburgo and Londres just west of Génova, is a good place to start if you're hunting for clothes. Plaza del Ángel, another arcade between Hamburgo and Londres, just west of Amberes, has a number of classy antique and art shops. A few more of the same can be found on Estocolmo as well as nearby on Hamburgo.

Mixup, Génova 76, and Tower Records (☎ 5-525-48-29), Niza 19, have two of the biggest ranges of recorded music in the city, both Mexican and international. Tower Records also has a book section with the city's best range of Lonely Planet guides. The sidewalk stalls that crowd the exit from the Insurgentes metro station to the Zona Rosa, on Génova, include many cheap music tape vendors (US$2 or so a tape) with long lists of the recordings available – but ask to try out any tape you're planning to buy as there are some defective or blank copies. La Bouquinerie is a small French bookshop in the Casa de Francia at Havre 15.

Librería Británica (☎ 5-705-24-74), Rosas Moreno 152, just north of the Jardín del Arte, has the city's best stock of English-language books, including novels and books on Mexico (Ⓜ San Cosme; Map 5).

Condesa & Roma

Condesa is beginning to sprout a few clever little clothes shops to go with its popular restaurants. One such 'sports fashion' boutique is Super Body Shop, Campeche 410. The Ollin Calli cultural center on Tamaulipas sells some interesting artesanías from the southern state of Chiapas.

In Roma, Librería Pegaso, in the Casa Lamm cultural center at Obregón 99, is an excellent arts, culture and history bookshop, with some titles in English. There's an El Palacio de Hierro department store at Durango 230.

Polanco

Polanco is a busy and classy shopping area, with many designer boutiques (women's and men's) lined up along Avenida Presidente Masaryk in the blocks between Aristóteles and Moliere – names like Versace, Armani, Hugo Boss, Hilfiger. Plaza Mazarik mall at the corner of Lafontaine includes María Isabel with some lovely women's clothes, and Scappino for men. Neighboring Plaza Zentro has Louis Vuitton handbags. Shops farther east on Masaryk, around Galileo and Newton, concentrate on furniture and fabrics for interior design.

The futuristic-looking Plaza Molière mall at Moliere and Horacio contains a branch of the classy El Palacio de Hierro department store dealing mainly in clothes, toys and cosmetics, plus a lot of other stores with clothes and shoes (Dockers, Zara, Original Levi's Store, etc). Fans of British marmalade and soap can stock up here at Crabtree & Evelyn! You'll find a similar range of clothing shops, including a Benetton, in the Pabellón Polanco mall farther west at Homero and Vázquez de Mella.

Fonart

Probably the biggest and best handicrafts store in the city is the government-run

Fonart (Fondo Nacional para el Fomento de las Artesanías, National Fund for the Promotion of Handicrafts, ☎ 5-563-40-60), out at Patriotismo 691, Colonia Mixcoac, between the Bosque de Chapultepec and San Ángel. The store holds a lot of beautiful wares from around the country, ranging from Olinalá lacquered boxes to Oaxacan alebrijes, blankets from Teotitlán del Valle, plenty of attractive pottery and a big variety of glassware. Prices are fixed and fair. Fonart is open 9 am to 8 pm Monday to Saturday, 10 am to 7 pm Sunday (600m north of Ⓜ Mixcoac; Map 1).

San Ángel

San Ángel has some attractive shops, as well as its bustling weekly Bazar Sábado (see Markets, later in this chapter). La Carreta, at Avenida Insurgentes and Avenida La Paz, has a large selection of crafts at lower prices than the Bazar Sábado, and there are some interesting boutiques and antique shops on Madero between Avenida Revolución and Plaza San Jacinto.

Plaza Loreto, an attractive mall-cum-entertainment space in an imaginatively converted old paper factory between Altamirano and Río de la Magdalena, has a smattering of boutiques, jewelers and furniture shops, and a branch of the Mixup music store.

Gandhi (☎ 5-661-09-11), Avenida MA de Quevedo 128 to 132, is a Mexico City literary institution with a big range of books on most subjects (mostly in Spanish), a worthwhile music section and a popular upstairs café. It's open 9 am to 11 pm Monday to Friday, 10 am to 10 pm Saturday and Sunday (Ⓜ MA de Quevedo).

La Bouquinerie (☎ 5-616-60-66), Camino al Desierto de los Leones 40, is the city's best French bookshop – open 10 am to 8 pm daily except Sunday.

Pabellón Altavista mall at Avenida Revolución and Camino al Desierto de los Leones contains a branch of Tower Records with a good selection of *rock en español* CDs and a few books in English (not on Mexican subjects). The rest of the mall is mostly given over to a typical collection of designer clothing stores (Hilfiger, Benetton, Armani, Scappino, Zara, Original Levi's Store, etc).

Coyoacán

Nalanda Libros (☎ 5-554-75-22), Centenario 16, specializes in books on religion and philosophy in English and Spanish, and also sells Lonely Planet titles.

Other Malls

Two of the city's biggest and glitziest malls are the Centro Comercial Santa Fe out west and Perisur in the southwest. Centro Comercial Santa Fe, Vasco de Quiroga 3800, about 18km southwest of the Zócalo, is a huge, three-story place. It has El Palacio de Hierro and Liverpool department stores and hosts of fashion, sportswear and cosmetics stores including Benetton, The Body Shop and another Crabtree & Evelyn. If you're out at Santa Fe a good place to eat or drink is the Rainforest Café at Local 421. A taxi is the easiest way to get there but 'Centro Comercial Santa Fe' buses and peseros do go from near Tacubaya metro station (exit the station and ask directions to the stop).

Perisur, at Periférico Sur 4690 by the intersection with Avenida Insurgentes Sur, includes Sears, El Palacio de Hierro, Liverpool and Suburbia department stores. A little farther south is the recently opened Plaza Cuicuilco, Insurgentes Sur 3500. It contains another of the excellent Mixup music stores as well as a place called Martí Soccer Soccer where you can buy yourself an Atletico Morelia, Cruz Azul, América, Pumas or any other Mexican soccer shirt – and even (is nowhere sacred?) a Manchester United one! These last two malls are both short walks from the Cuicuilco archaeological site – see Map 11 and the Cuicuilco section in the Things to See & Do chapter for how to get to them.

MARKETS

Many interesting markets dotted around the city offer the chance to buy – or just look at – all sorts of Mexican handicrafts, souvenirs and everyday goods.

La Lagunilla & Tepito

Two of the city's biggest markets, both open daily, merge into each other along Rayón and Héroe de Granaditas, about 1km north of the Zócalo. Both deal mainly in everyday things that Mexicans go shopping for, and are lively, crowded places.

La Lagunilla, the more westerly of the two markets, is centered on three large buildings. Building No 1 is full of clothes and fabrics, No 2 is given over to furniture, and No 3 is devoted to *comestibles* (food). Dozens of furniture shops are spread along the streets east of No 2, also. On Sunday, to all this is added a flea market with antiques, secondhand books and magazines, stamps, coins and more.

Tepito takes over where La Lagunilla ends and stretches several hundred meters east along Rayón and Héroe de Granaditas and deep into most of the side streets. Much of what's sold here is said to be *fayuca* (contraband), and the market has a reputation for pickpockets and thieves – so take care. It's mainly street-side stalls focusing on clothes (new and secondhand), antiques and leisure goods such as videos, CD players, TVs, roller blades and toys – which gives it a particularly fun atmosphere. The large building at Héroe de Granaditas and Aztecas is packed with every kind of shoe and boot you could imagine.

Garibaldi metro station is just west of La Lagunilla, Tepito station is just east of Tepito, and Lagunilla station is in the middle of it all. 'Tepito' and 'Lagunilla' buses and peseros seem to run from all over the city: you can pick them up near the Zócalo heading north on Isabel la Católica from Cinco de Mayo (Map 4).

La Merced & Sonora

Mercado La Merced, about 1km southeast of the Zócalo, occupies four whole blocks dedicated to the buying and selling of Mexicans' daily needs, such as food, clothes, crockery, cutlery, etc, which makes for an interesting wander. It's also worth straying a couple of blocks south to Mercado Sonora, on the south side of Fray Servando Teresa de Mier, which has four diverse specialties: toys, caged birds, herbs and folk medicine. Merced metro station is in the middle of La Merced Market (Map 4).

Alameda Central

A colorful little market with a mix of T-shirts, jewelry, toys, tapes, CDs, purses and so on sets up at the east end of the Alameda on Sunday.

La Ciudadela & San Juan

About 600m south of the Alameda, on Balderas at Dondé, the Centro de Artesanías La Ciudadela, open daily, is full of craft stalls with prices that are fair even before you try to bargain (some stalls will negotiate, some won't). You'll find brightly dyed sarapes, pretty lacquerware boxes and trays, masks, silver jewelry, pottery, Huichol bead masks, guitars, maracas and baskets of every shape and size. It's open every day (Ⓜ Balderas; Map 4).

The Mercado de Artesanías San Juan, four blocks east at Dolores and Ayuntamiento, has similar goods, and prices that are if anything a little cheaper. It's open 9 am to 7 pm Monday to Saturday, 9 am to 4 pm Sunday (Ⓜ San Juan de Letrán; Map 4).

Centro Artesanal Buenavista

Just east of the Buenavista train station, at Aldama 187, this large handicrafts 'market' is actually a huge fixed-price store. Much advertised and often visited by tour groups, it has a vast assortment of stuff. Some of it is quality – but bargains can be scarce. It's open 9 am to 6 pm daily (Map 1).

Tianguis Cultural del Chopo

This unusual little market is devoted mainly to punk and death metal music and fashions (and fans), but some stalls specialize in other musical genres such as rock, Cuban music, trova and Mexican regional sounds. It's held every Saturday from about 10 am to 4 pm on Hidalgo just north of the Centro Artesanal Buenavista (Map 1).

Mercado Insurgentes

This market stretches from Londres to Liverpool, just west of Amberes in the Zona

Rosa. It's packed with Mexican crafts – silver, textiles, pottery, leather, carved wood figures, etc. It's open 9 am to 7.30 pm Monday to Saturday, 10 am to 4 pm Sunday. Most prices are negotiable (**M** Insurgentes).

Tianguis del Oro

Saturday and Sunday (most of both days), Calle Oro off Insurgentes Sur, 500m south of Insurgentes metro station, becomes a lively market with clothes appealing to young Mexicans. A brilliant steak, salad and dessert stall run by the nearby Argentine restaurant Bariloche adds to the appeal (Map 7).

Mercado de Jamaica

The Jamaica market on Avenida Congreso de la Unión has specialties including fruit, vegetables, piñatas and potted plants, but most spectacular are its staggering quantities of cut flowers, piled up singly as well as in ready-made arrangements (**M** Jamaica; Map 1).

Bazar Sábado

The 'Saturday Bazaar,' Plaza San Jacinto 11, in the southern suburb San Ángel, is a showcase for some of Mexico's very best crafts including jewelry, woodwork, ceramics and textiles. Prices are high but so is quality. It's held 10 am to 7 pm every Saturday. At the same time, artists and artisans display work in Plaza San Jacinto itself and surrounding streets, and in nearby Plaza del Carmen. See the San Ángel section in the Things to See & Do chapter for how to reach San Ángel.

Coyoacán

On Saturday and Sunday a colorful informal jewelry and craft market spreads over much of Coyoacán's central Jardín del Centenario. Hippie jewelry, Mexican indigenous crafts, leatherwork and tie-dyed clothes are among the stocks-in-trade.

The Bazar Artesanal de Coyoacán on the west side of the adjoining Plaza Hidalgo (open Saturday and Sunday only), and Pasaje Coyoacán, 1½ blocks farther north at Aguayo and Cuauhtémoc (open 11 am to 8 pm daily except Monday), have more crafts. Coyoacán's regular market, on Allende 2½ blocks north of Plaza Hidalgo, is worth a look on the way to the Frida Kahlo and Leon Trotsky museums. See the Coyoacán section in the Things to See & Do chapter for how to get to Coyoacán.

Excursions

One of the best things about Mexico City is the many fascinating places within easy reach of it. Within a few hours' travel you can:

- explore many astounding pre-Hispanic sites – most notable among them Teotihuacán, with its awesome pyramids
- wander beautiful, historic colonial towns such as San Miguel de Allende, Guanajuato, Puebla, Tepoztlán, Cuernavaca and Taxco
- enjoy dramatic natural attractions such as the Desierto de los Leones, El Rosario monarch butterfly sanctuary, the Cacahuamilpa caves near Taxco and the 5286m volcano Iztaccíhuatl
- shop for silver in Taxco or crafts at Tequisquiapan, San Miguel de Allende, Puebla, Tepoztlán or Toluca
- cool off and relax around a pool at *balnearios* in and around Tequisquiapan or San Miguel de Allende

This chapter selects just a few of the best outings from the city. All can be done in a day or overnight – though many merit more time if you have it. Bus service to most of these places is frequent and good.

If you plan to travel widely in the country, Lonely Planet's *Mexico* guide has all the information you'll need.

Local telephone area codes are given at the start of each city or town section, where relevant.

Southwest Forest Rim

For the closest truly 'out-of-city' experience, head for the forested hills forming the southwestern rim of the Valle de México. A half-hour bus or *pesero* ride from the city will take you to several areas with walking trails amid fresh air and trees at altitudes of up to nearly 4000m – considerably higher, and often a lot cooler, than the city. A word of caution: robberies have been reported on these woodland paths, so it's advisable not to carry anything valuable. Opinion is divided over whether the risk is less at weekends, when more people visit these places, or during the week.

PARQUE NACIONAL DESIERTO DE LOS LEONES

Probably the most inviting area to head for is this 19-sq-km park of cool, fragrant, pine, fir and oak forests echoing to the sound of birdsong, some 23km southwest of downtown Mexico City – and up to 1600m higher. Its name means Desert of the Lions, but it's not a desert nor is it roamed by lions. The name comes from the Ex-Convento del Desierto de Santa Fe, the 17th-century former Carmelite monastery in the park. The Carmelites called their isolated monasteries 'deserts' to commemorate Elijah, who lived as a recluse in the desert near Mt Carmel. The Leones bit probably stems from José Manuel de León, who at one stage administered the monastery's finances.

The monastery and 10 *ermitas* (chapels) were originally built between 1606 and 1611. Most were ruined or damaged by an earthquake in 1711. The present monastery building was erected in 1722-23. The monks moved to Tenancingo in 1801 to escape the wet, cool climate and to reduce the frequency of visitors.

Today the restored ex-convento has exhibition halls, pretty patios within and lovely gardens around the buildings. Across the road is a path leading to three little stone chapels among the woods, the Ermita de la Soledad, Ermita de la Trinidad and Ermita Getsemani. The rest of the park has an extensive network of walking trails and is very popular with picnickers on weekends. The Vigilancia (park wardens) office in the ex-convento entrance has an aerial photo of the park with paths rather faintly marked. This is the nearest you'll come to any kind of map: the bookshop, also in the entrance, has nothing.

One good walk is from the spot known as Cruz Blanca (3130m) up to the chapel-crowned Cerro San Miguel (about 3800m). The route – 1½ to two hours one-way – follows part of the Barda de la Excomunión, the perimeter wall of the old monastery's property (so named, it's said, because any woman who crossed it was subject to excommunication).

The ex-convento is open 10 am to 5 pm – officially just Tuesday to Sunday but you may well find it open on Monday, too. It has a medium-to-expensive restaurant, and outside there are numerous *comedores*. The national park is open 6 am to 5 pm daily (US$1 per car, free for pedestrians).

Getting There & Away

On Saturday and Sunday peseros run to the ex-convento from near the Tacubaya metro station. Take the 'Av Jalisco Calle Manuel Dublan' exit from the station's line 9 platforms, cross the street outside and walk through to the far end of the market. We have been told, but have not confirmed, that Saturday and Sunday peseros also go from the corner of Madero and Avenida Revolución in San Ángel.

Any day, you can take a Flecha Roja 'Toluca Intermedio' bus from the Terminal Poniente bus station to La Venta on highway 15 to Toluca (US$0.70). The buses leave about every 20 minutes and the ride takes 15 to 20 minutes. Tell the driver you are going to the Desierto de los Leones and you should be dropped at a yellow footbridge over a tangle of merging highways just short of a toll station (*caseta de cobro*). Cross the footbridge and toward its far end you'll see, on your right, the Desierto de los Leones signposted on a side road to the east. At weekends peseros or taxis may wait here to take people up the 4km paved road to the ex-convento. Other days you'll probably have to walk but traffic will be light and it's a pleasant stroll, gently rising nearly all the way. About halfway to the ex-convento is a barrier where the charge on vehicles entering the park is collected. Immediately before the barrier, a dirt side road turns up to the right. It's about 4km by this road to Cruz

Blanca, where you should find a *vigilante* (forest warden) who can direct you to Cerro San Miguel.

Driving, you can also reach the park by following Avenida Altavista and the street named Desierto de los Leones west from San Ángel in the south of Mexico City (about 15km).

LA MARQUESA

La Marquesa is the common name for the 16-sq-km Parque Nacional Insurgente Miguel Hidalgo y Costilla, about 9km farther west along the Toluca road from the turnoff for the Desierto de los Leones. The forested area here, mainly on the north side of the road, is less extensive, but the flowers are pretty in winter and spring, and the area affords some good views and an interesting historical angle.

A 'Marqueza' pesero on Carlos Lazo, outside the 'Av Jalisco' exit of the Tacubaya metro station, will drop you at the main park entrance opposite the Restaurant Mesón del Tío Pepe on highway 15 (the free road). For a walk of about two hours, head initially for the rocky crags you can see up to the north-east. Walk up past the picnic tables (you can also rent horses here for about US$8 an hour) and through a tunnel under the westbound lanes of toll highway 15D, and take the path up to the right of the Centro de Información Turística (which you'll probably find closed). A web of paths winds up through the woods: follow your nose up to the crags, from which you'll enjoy some fine panoramas. From there head back along the ridge to the highest point of the area (with views to Mexico City, smog permitting) before descending back to the highway.

About 400 to 500m west of Restaurant Mesón del Tío Pepe along highway 15, in the small La Marquesa village, a left (southward) turn is signposted 'Malinalco, Chalma, Tianguistenco.' This road crosses the eastbound lanes of toll highway 15D after 250m, then winds onward in a generally southward direction. On a small rise to the east, just south of highway 15D, statues of three riders looking toward Mexico City commemorate the battle of Las Cruces, which took place

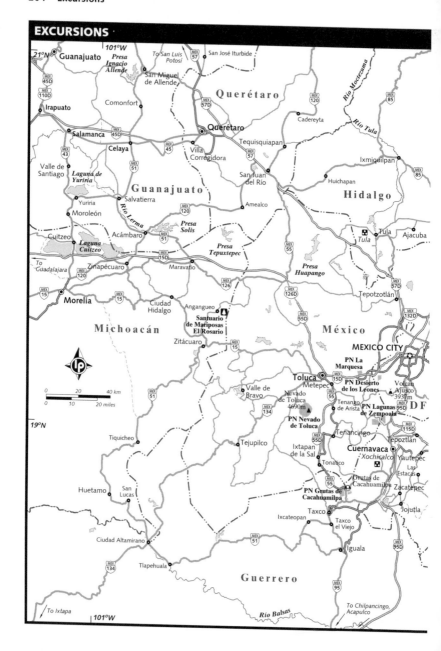

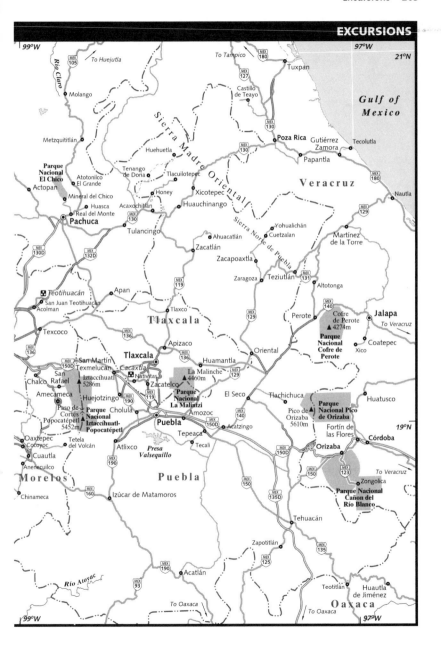

DESIERTO DE LOS LEONES, LA MARQUESA & AJUSCO

1 La Venta Toll Station
2 Centro de Información Turística
3 Restaurant Mesón del Tío Pepe
4 Battle of Las Cruces Monument
5 Cruz Blanca
6 Ex-Convento del Desierto de Santa Fe
7 'Ajusco' Peseros from Jardín Daniel Cosío Villegas
8 'Ajusco' Peseros from Reino Aventura
9 Entrance of Parque Ejidal San Nicolás Totolapan
10 Albergue Alpino Ajusco

here in October 1810. The riders are Miguel Hidalgo, Ignacio Allende and Mariano Jiménez, leaders of the Mexican independence rebels whose victory over Spanish loyalists in that battle put Mexico City at their mercy. For some reason, the rebels did not advance and occupy the capital – a decision that probably cost Hidalgo, Allende and Jiménez their lives and cost Mexico another decade of fighting before independence was gained.

A little over 1km along the Malinalco/ Chalma road, the Valle del Silencio opens out on the left (east). This shallow, grassy valley may once have been a place of silence, but today it's a major weekend getaway spot for the people of Mexico City, dotted with horse rental places, comedores offering rabbit and trout, picnic tables and several go-kart and *cuatrimoto* (four-wheeled motorcycle) tracks. Plenty of other comedores line up beside the free and toll highways at La Marquesa.

AJUSCO AREA
☎ 5

The **Parque Ejidal San Nicolás Totolapan** (☎ 630-89-35) is a mountainous, forested area of 23 sq km between altitudes of 2700 and 3740m to the southwest of the city. The park is crisscrossed by more than 50km of trails popular with local mountain bikers and also good for walking. The *ejidatarios* (communal landowners) set up the *parque ejidal* in the late 1990s chiefly to derive some benefit from their land's popularity.

The trails are not clearly signed, but with the aid of a rough map, sold for US$0.50 at the ticket office, you should be able to keep your bearings. If you head southwest and generally upward for 4km (about 1¾ hours and an ascent of 400m) you should come out at a line of comedores on the Circuito del Ajusco road, to the south of which rises Volcán Ajusco (3937m), an extinct volcano that is theoretically protected in the 9.2-sq-km Parque Nacional Cumbres de Ajusco.

Entry to the park is US$0.50 on foot and US$1 with a bike. There are currently no bikes for hire. A simple restaurant is at the park's entrance, which is at 2850m.

Places to Stay

About 250m up a track south from the road is the *Albergue Alpino Ajusco* (☎ 846-15-79, 846-26-92), where you can stay for US$5 per person in quite comfortable four-person bunk rooms (but you need to bring your own sleeping bag, sheets or blanket). The *albergue* (lodge) is open all year and has a kitchen and hot water in the mornings. At weekends you can eat at the roadside comedores, but during the week these may be shut.

Getting There & Away

Direct 'Ajusco' peseros reportedly run from the Huipulco *tren ligero* (streetcar) stop, but we haven't confirmed this. They certainly run from the Jardín Daniel Cosío Villegas, beside Carretera Picacho-Ajusco just south of the Anillo Periférico ring road, and from the Reino Aventura amusement park, 1.4km south up Carretera Picacho-Ajusco from there. From either place it's about a 25-minute ride, climbing through outlying southern barrios most of the way, to Parque Ejidal San Nicolás Totolapan. Ask for Las Llantas ('lahs YAHN-tahs,' the Tires), a

name that refers to lines of tires set in the ground at the parque ejidal's entrance to mark out a biking or riding track. The entrance is also marked by a parking lot and a '¡Bienvenido! Parque Ejidal San Nicolás Totolapan' sign.

You can reach the Jardín Cosío Villegas on a 'Ruta 87' pesero from the pesero terminus on Doctor Gálvez in San Ángel, and you can reach Reino Aventura on a 'Reino Aventura' pesero from the Universidad or MA de Quevedo metro stations. Allow an hour to the parque ejidal from any of these starting points.

North of Mexico City

TEOTIHUACÁN
● elev 2300m   ☎ 5

If there is one must-see attraction near Mexico City, it is the archaeological zone of Teotihuacán ('teh-oh-tih-wah-KAN'), 50km northeast of downtown. This is the site of the huge Pirámides del Sol y de la Luna (Pyramids of the Sun and Moon). A day here can be an awesome experience.

History

The building of a magnificent grid-plan city began about 2000 years ago. Most of the rest of the city was built between about 250 and 600 AD. Teotihuacán grew into one of Mexico's biggest pre-Hispanic cities, with an estimated 125,000 people at its peak around 400 AD. It may have controlled the southern two-thirds of Mexico, all of Guatemala and Belize and bits of Honduras and El Salvador – probably the biggest of all pre-Hispanic empires. Little is certain about Teotihuacán's inhabitants, however: no trace of a writing system has been found.

Its major buildings are typified by the *talud-tablero* style (see Architecture & Sculpture in the Facts about Mexico City chapter) and were often colorfully painted. Most of the city consisted of residential compounds about 50 or 60m square. Some of these, thought to be residences of nobility or priests, contain refined frescoes.

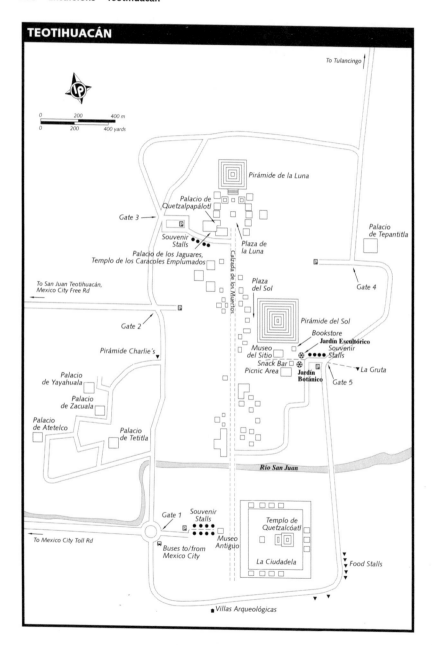

TEOTIHUACÁN

To Tulancingo

0   200   400 m
0   200   400 yards

Pirámide de la Luna

Palacio de Quetzalpapálotl

Gate 3

Souvenir Stalls

Palacio de los Jaguares,
Templo de los Caracoles Emplumados

Plaza de la Luna

Palacio de Tepantitla

Gate 4

To San Juan Teotihuacán,
Mexico City Free Rd

Plaza del Sol

Calzada de los Muertos

Gate 2

Pirámide Charlie's

Pirámide del Sol

Palacio de Yayahuala

Bookstore
Jardín Escultórico
Souvenir Stalls

Museo del Sitio
Snack Bar
Picnic Area

La Gruta

Palacio de Zacuala

Jardín Botánico
Gate 5

Palacio de Atetelco

Palacio de Tetitla

Río San Juan

Gate 1

Souvenir Stalls

Templo de Quetzalcóatl

To Mexico City Toll Rd

Buses to/from Mexico City

Museo Antiguo

La Ciudadela

Food Stalls

Villas Arqueológicas

In the 7th century Teotihuacán was burned, plundered and abandoned. It is likely that the state had already been weakened by the rise of rival powers in central Mexico or by environmental desiccation caused by the deforestation of the surrounding hillsides.

Teotihuacán's legacy was vast. Many of its gods – such as the feathered serpent Quetzalcóatl, an all-important symbol of fertility and life itself, and Tláloc, the water god – were still being worshipped by the Aztecs nearly a millennium later. Aztec royalty made pilgrimages to Teotihuacán, believing that all the gods had sacrificed themselves here to start the sun moving at the beginning of the 'fifth world,' which is what the Aztecs inhabited.

Orientation

Ancient Teotihuacán covered more than 20 sq km. The city was divided into quarters by two great avenues that met near the so-called Ciudadela (Citadel). One, running roughly north-south, is the famous Calzada de los Muertos (Avenue of the Dead) – so called because the later Aztecs believed the great buildings beside it were vast tombs, built by giants for Teotihuacán's first rulers.

Most of what there is to see lies along nearly 2km of the Calzada de los Muertos. Buses arrive at a traffic circle by the southwest entrance (Gate 1); four other entrances are reached by a road that circles the site. Ticket booths and parking lots are at all five entrances. The museum is just inside the main east entrance (Gate 5).

Information

Most of the year you should bring a hat and water; you may walk several kilometers and the midday sun can be brutal. Take your time exploring the expansive ruins and climbing the steep pyramids.

The ruins are open 7 am to 6 pm daily (US$2.75 plus US$3.25 for use of a video camera; free Sunday and holidays). Crowds are thickest from 10 am to 2 pm, and the site is busiest on Sunday and holidays.

An information booth inside the Museo Antiguo (Old Museum), near the southwest entrance (Gate 1), is staffed 9 am to 4 pm. Free site tours by authorized guides, in Spanish and English, depart from here.

The website 'Archaeology of Teotihuacán, Mexico' (http://archaeology.la.asu.edu/teo) has interesting reports on recent excavations and their significance.

Calzada de los Muertos

The Avenue of the Dead must have seemed incomparable to the ancient inhabitants, who would have seen its buildings at their best. Gate 1 brings you to the avenue in front of La Ciudadela. For 1.5km to the north the avenue is flanked by former palaces of Teotihuacán's elite and other major structures such as the Pirámide del Sol. At the northern end stands the Pirámide de la Luna. The original avenue extended 2km south of the Ciudadela.

La Ciudadela

The large square complex called The Citadel may have been the residence of the city's supreme ruler. It was built between 150 and 300 AD. Four broad walls, 390m long and topped by 15 pyramids, enclose a huge open space of which the main feature, toward the east side, is a pyramid called the Templo de Quetzalcóatl. The temple is flanked by two large ruined complexes of rooms and patios, which may have been the city's administrative center.

Templo de Quetzalcóatl The fascinating feature of this pyramidal temple is its west façade, which archaeologists revealed by excavating the later platform that had been built over it. The four surviving 'steps' of this façade are encrusted with striking carvings. In the upright tablero panels the sharp-fanged feathered serpent deity, its head emerging from a 'necklace' of 11 petals, alternates with a four-eyed, two-fanged creature often identified as Tláloc, the water god, but perhaps more authoritatively reckoned to be the fire serpent, bearer of the sun on its daily journey across the sky. On the sloping panels are side views of the plumed serpent, its body snaking along behind its head. Seashells, an important Teotihuacán motif,

RICHARD I'ANSON

Quetzalcóatl on his temple

form part of the background in both sets of panels.

Excavations beneath the pyramid in the late 1980s revealed more than 130 human skeletons, most of them soldiers who may have been captured in war and sacrificed.

Museo del Sitio
Farther north up the Calzada de los Muertos, a path to the right leads to the museum, which is just south of the Pirámide del Sol. The museum makes a refreshing stop midway through the site. Around it are a botanical garden, a lovely sculpture garden with Teotihuacán artifacts, a snack bar, picnic tables, a bookstore and restrooms.

The museum (free admission with site ticket) features excellent displays of artifacts, fresco panels, and an impressive large-scale model of the city set under a Plexiglas walkway. From the walkway you can view the real Pirámide del Sol, through a wall-size window. Explanatory matter is in Spanish, English and Náhuatl.

Pirámide del Sol
The Pyramid of the Sun – the world's third-largest pyramid – stands on the east side of the Calzada de los Muertos. It is surpassed in size only by the pyramid of Cholula and Egypt's Cheops. Reconstructed in 1908, it has a base about 225m square and is some 70m high (it originally had a wood and

thatch temple on top). The pyramid was built from 3 million tons of stone, brick and rubble without the use of metal tools, pack animals or the wheel!

The structure was enlarged at least twice from its original size, and the Aztec belief that it was dedicated to the sun god was substantiated in 1971, when archaeologists uncovered a 100m tunnel leading from near the pyramid's west side to a cave directly beneath its center, where they found religious artifacts. It is thought that the sun was worshiped here before the pyramid was built and that the city's ancient inhabitants traced the very origins of life to this grotto.

At Teotihuacán's height, the pyramid's plaster was painted bright red, which must have been a radiant sight at sunset. You can climb the pyramid's 248 steps for an overview of the entire ancient city.

Pirámide de la Luna
The Pyramid of the Moon, at the north end of Calzada de los Muertos, is not quite as big as the Pirámide del Sol but is more gracefully proportioned. Its summit is at virtually the same height, because it was built on higher ground.

Recent excavations beneath the Pirámide de la Luna have shown that it was layered with new pyramids several times following its initial construction, which was in probably the 1st century AD. Human, jaguar, wolf, puma, snake and bird skeletons and large jadeite (greenstone) and obsidian figurines were among the finds made in 1998 and 1999 by archaeologists from Mexico's Instituto Nacional de Antropología e Historia (INAH) and Arizona State University.

The Plaza de la Luna, in front of the pyramid, is a handsome arrangement of 12 temple platforms. The altar in the plaza's center is thought to have been the site of religious dancing.

Palacio del Quetzalpapálotl
Off the southwest corner of the Plaza de la Luna is the Palace of the Quetzal Butterfly, where it is thought a high priest lived. A flight of steps leads up to a roofed portico

with an abstract mural. Off the portico is a well-restored patio with thick columns carved with designs representing the quetzal bird or a hybrid quetzal-butterfly.

Palacio de los Jaguares & Templo de los Caracoles Emplumados

These structures lie behind and below the Palacio del Quetzalpapálotl. On the lower walls of several of the chambers off the patio of the Jaguar Palace are parts of murals showing the jaguar god in feathered head-dresses, blowing conch shells and apparently praying to Tláloc.

The Temple of the Plumed Conch Shells, entered from the Jaguar Palace patio, is a now-subterranean structure of the 2nd or 3rd century AD. Carvings on what was its façade show large shells – possibly used as musical instruments – decorated with feathers and flowers. The base on which the façade stands has a green, blue, red and yellow mural of birds with water streaming from their beaks.

Palacio de Tepantitla

Teotihuacán's most famous fresco, the worn *Paradise of Tláloc*, is in the Tepantitla Palace, a priest's residence about 500m northeast of the Pirámide del Sol. The mural flanks a doorway in the northeast corner of the building. Tláloc, attended by priests, is shown on both sides. Below, to the right of the doorway, appears his paradise, a garden-like place with tiny people, animals and fish swimming in a river flowing from a mountain. Left of the doorway, tiny human figures are engaged in a unique ball game. Frescoes in other rooms show priests with feathered headdresses.

Palacio de Tetitla & Palacio de Atetelco

Another group of palaces lies west of the main part of the site, several hundred meters from Gate 1. Many of their murals, discovered in the 1940s, are well preserved or restored and perfectly intelligible. The Tetitla Palace is a large complex, perhaps of several adjoining houses. No less than 120 walls have murals, with Tláloc, jaguars, serpents and eagles among the easiest figures to make out. Some 400m west is the Atetelco Palace, with vivid murals of what are either jaguar or coyote – a mixture of originals and restoration – in the so-called Patio Blanco in the northwest corner. Processions of these creatures in shades of red perhaps symbolize warrior orders. There are also crisscross designs of priests with Tláloc and coyote costumes.

Places to Stay & Eat

The *Villas Arqueológicas* (☎ 956-09-09), immediately south of the ancient city, has charming air-conditioned singles/doubles for US$39/49 Monday to Thursday, US$50/58 Friday to Sunday. It also has a pool, tennis court, billiards and a French-Mexican restaurant.

The town of San Juan Teotihuacán, 3km west of the Pirámide del Sol, features several less costly options. *Hotel Posada Sol y Luna* (☎ 956-23-68, Jiménez Cantú 13) has very comfortable rooms for US$17/20. *Hotel Pirámides Plaza* (☎ 956-01-67, Guerrero 12),

The Ball Game

As special H-shaped ball courts appear at archaeological sites all over the country, it is thought that all pre-Hispanic Mexican cultures probably played 'the ball game.' The game may have varied from place to place and era to era, but it had certain lasting features. It seems to have been played between two teams, and its essence was apparently to keep a rubber ball off the ground by flicking it with hips, thighs and possibly knees and elbows. The vertical or sloping walls around the courts were probably part of the playing area, not stands for spectators. The game had – at least sometimes – deep religious significance. Perhaps it served as an oracle, the outcome indicating which of two courses of action should be taken. Games could be followed by the sacrifice of one or more players – whether winners or losers, no one is sure!

a couple of blocks from the central plaza, offers clean, basic rooms with bathrooms for US$9.50/12.50.

Except for some dusty food stalls on the ring road on the southeast side of the archaeological site, meals around the ruins are pricey. The most convenient place to eat is the **Museo Antiguo**, where a relatively expensive restaurant has a great panorama of the site. The bar here has almost as good a view.

On the ring road south of Gate 2, **Pirámide Charlie's** serves savory but costly meals: US$2.75 for soup, chicken dishes from US$7.75, and beef and seafood dishes for around US$10.

An unusual place to dine is **La Gruta** (the Cave), 75m east of Gate 5. Meals have been served in this cool, wide-mouthed natural cave for a century. The food's just fine, and fairly priced: soups and salads are around US$3, meat and fish dishes about US$7. Try the *nopal* salad with tamarind dressing, or go for the chicken breast stuffed with squash blossoms and *xoconostle*, a tart cactus fruit.

Getting There & Away
The 2nd-class buses of Autobuses México-San Juan Teotihuacán run from Mexico City's Terminal Norte to the ruins every 15 minutes during the day (one hour, US$1.50). The ticket office is at the north end of the terminal. Make sure your bus is going to 'Los Pirámides,' not the nearby town of San Juan Teotihuacán.

Buses arrive and depart at the traffic circle near Gate 1, also making stops at Gates 2 and 3. Return buses are more frequent after 1 pm. The last bus back to the capital from the traffic circle leaves about 6.30 pm. Some terminate at the Indios Verdes metro station in the north of Mexico City, but most continue to Terminal Norte.

Combis to San Juan Teotihuacán stop at Gates 1, 2 and 3.

If you're driving, head north out of Mexico City on Avenida Insurgentes, which becomes highway 85D, the Autopista México-Pachuca. About 25km north of downtown, highway 132D veers off eastward to Teotihuacán.

Numerous tours from Mexico City go to the ruins.

TULA
• **pop 26,000** • **elev 2060m** ☎ 7
The ruins of the probable capital of the ancient Toltecs stand 65km north of Mexico City. Tula is best known for its fearsome telamones, 4.5m stone warrior figures. The modern town of Tula is unexciting.

History
It's hard to disentangle myth and history in the Tula/Toltec story, but a widely accepted version is that the Toltecs were one of several semicivilized tribes from the north who moved into central Mexico after the fall of Teotihuacán, and that Tula became their capital, probably in the 10th century, growing into a city of 30,000 or 40,000.

Later Aztec annals tell of a Toltec priest-king called Topiltzin (fair-skinned, long-haired, black-bearded...) who was dedicated to the peaceful worship of the feathered serpent god Quetzalcóatl. But Tula also housed devotees of Tezcatlipoca (Smoking

Telamon (stone warrior)

Mirror), god of warriors, witchcraft, life and death. The story goes that Tezcatlipoca appeared in various guises to provoke Topiltzin: as a naked chili-seller he aroused the lust of Topiltzin's daughter and eventually married her; as an old man he persuaded the sober Topiltzin to get drunk.

Eventually the humiliated Topiltzin left for the Gulf Coast and set sail eastward on a raft of snakes, promising one day to return and reclaim his throne. (When Hernán Cortés arrived on the Gulf Coast in 1519, the Aztec emperor Moctezuma suffered much consternation on account of this legend.) The conventional wisdom is that Topiltzin set up a new Toltec state at Chichén Itzá in Yucatán, while the Tula Toltecs built a brutal empire that dominated central Mexico, with warriors organized into orders dedicated to different animal-gods – the coyote, jaguar and eagle knights. Mass human sacrifice in Mexico may have started at Tula.

Tula was eventually abandoned around the beginning of the 13th century.

Zona Arqueológica

The ruins are on a hilltop on the north side of the town. Half a kilometer from the entrance you reach the site museum. From the museum it's 600m to the first large structure of the ancient ceremonial center, **Juego de Pelota No 1** (Ball Court No 1), 37m long.

The site's highlight is **Pirámide B** (Pyramid B), also known as the Temple of Quetzalcóatl or the Temple of Tlahuizcalpantecuhtli (the Morning Star). The four big basalt telamones *(atlantes* in Spanish) at the top, and the pillars behind, supported the roof of a temple. The left-hand telamon is a replica of the original, which is in the Museo Nacional de Antropología. These warriors symbolize Quetzalcóatl as the morning star. Their headdresses are vertical feathers set in what may be bands of stars; the breastplates are butterfly-shaped. Their short skirts, which leave the buttocks bare, are held in place at the back by disks representing the sun. The warriors' right hands hold spear-throwers; in their left hands are spears or arrows and incense bags. The columns

behind the telamones depict crocodile heads (which symbolize the earth), warriors, symbols of warrior orders, weapons and the head of Quetzalcóatl.

Near the north side of the pyramid stands the **Coatepantli** (Serpent Wall), carved with geometric patterns and a row of snakes devouring human skeletons. Traces remain of the bright colors with which most Tula structures were painted.

On the south side of the pyramid is the **Gran Vestíbulo** (Great Vestibule), a colonnaded hall with a stone bench carved with warriors, possibly for seating dignitaries observing ceremonies in the plaza.

The **Palacio Quemado** (Burnt Palace), immediately west of the pyramid, is a series of halls and courtyards with more low benches and relief carvings, one showing a procession of nobles.

The **Plaza** in front of Pirámide B was the scene of religious and military ceremonies. **Pirámide C**, on its east side, is largely unexcavated. To the west is **Juego de Pelota No 2**, the largest ball court in central Mexico, more than 100m long.

The ruins are open 9.30 am to 5 pm daily (US$2, free on Sunday). Signs at the site are in English, Spanish and Náhuatl.

Places to Stay & Eat

If you should want to stay, the best budget place is *Hotel Casa Blanca (☎ 732-11-86)* on Pasaje Hidalgo, a narrow street that starts beside the Singer store on Hidalgo. Its sparkling clean, bright and quiet singles/doubles are a great deal at US$7.50/10.50 (US$2 more with TV). *Hotel Lizbeth (☎ 732-00-45, Ocampo 200)* has clean, comfortable rooms with TV for US$21/24. The best place is *Hotel Sharon (☎ 732-09-76, Callejón de la Cruz 1)*, at the turnoff to the archaeological site, with rooms at US$26/32 and suites up to US$55.

The large, clean *Restaurant Casa Blanca* on Hidalgo serves decent, reasonably priced meals, with breakfasts and *antojitos* from around US$2. On Pasaje Hidalgo next door to Hotel Casa Blanca is the vegetarian *Restaurant Maná*, where at least half a dozen family members busily prepare veggie burgers, fruit salads, vegetable licuados and other meatless fare.

Getting There & Away

From Mexico City's Terminal Norte, 1st-class Ovnibus buses go to Tula every 40 minutes (1¼ hours, US$3.50). There are also frequent 2nd-class services. Tula's bus depot is on Xicoténcatl. The easiest way to the archaeological zone is a taxi from outside the depot (US$1.75). Microbuses labeled 'Actopan' ($0.30) depart from Cinco de Mayo and Zaragoza in the town center and will drop you 100m from the site entrance.

Motorists should leave Mexico City by highway 57D toward Querétaro. Turn off to Tula after about 45km; follow 'Parque Nacional Tula' and 'Zona Arqueológica' signs.

TEQUISQUIAPAN
● pop 24,000 ● elev 1880m ☎ 4

Tequisquiapan ('teh-kees-kee-AP-an'), a small town 185km northwest of Mexico City by road, is a quaint, pleasant retreat that has several attractive places to stay with courtyards, gardens and pools. One pleasure of the place is simply strolling the clean, colonial streets lined with brilliant purple bougainvillea.

The bus station is on the southwest outskirts, a 10-minute walk along Niños Héroes from the center. A town bus (US$0.25) heading to the Mercado will let you off on Carrizal, from which the central Plaza Principal is a two-minute walk to the southwest.

The tourist office (☎ 273-02-95), on the northeast side of the Plaza Principal, normally opens Wednesday to Sunday.

Things to See & Do

The wide, pretty, traffic-free **Plaza Principal** is surrounded by *portales* (arcades) in rich orange-pink hues, and overlooked by the 19th-century Templo de Santa María de la Asunción.

Hotel El Relox has two excellent spring-fed **swimming pools** in large, green, shady gardens. Nonguests can use these for US$12 a day, or use more expensive private pools.

The large, cool pool at the Hotel Neptuno, Juárez Oriente 5, two blocks east

of the plaza, is not quite as pleasant but costs only US$2.75 per person. It's open 8 am to 6 pm daily from Easter to October, just Saturday and Sunday in other months.

You can look for migratory birds at the **Santuario de Aves Migatorios La Palapa** at the north end of the lake just south of town. Other things you can do in or around Tequis include horse riding, tennis and golf.

Places to Stay

The best budget options are the posadas along Moctezuma, a couple of minutes' walk northwest of the Plaza Principal. *Posada Tequisquiapan* (☎ 273-00-10, *Moctezuma 6)* has pretty gardens and a splendid grottolike swimming pool. The spacious rooms have cable TV and start at US$17. *Posada San Francisco* (☎ 273-02-31, *Moctezuma 2)*, with a large garden and a pool overlooked by a statue of a ruminating nymph, and *Posada Los Arcos* (☎ 273-05-66, *Moctezuma 12)* are in the same price range.

Posada del Virrey (☎ 273-02-39, *Prieto Norte 9)*, in a pretty, courtyarded building one block west and two north of the Plaza Principal, has 22 rooms and a pool, with singles/doubles for US$42/46 including breakfast.

Hotel Maridelfi (☎ 273-00-52), on the Plaza Principal, is a lovely hotel around pleasant gardens. It's popular with Mexican families. It charges US$27 per person for a room, but from Thursday to Sunday it's US$50 per person, which includes three meals a day.

Hotel El Relox (☎ 273-00-06, *Morelos 8)*, entered from Montes, 1½ blocks north of the Plaza Principal, has 110 singles/doubles with TV, set in extensive gardens with pools, for around US$50.

Places to Eat

The cheapest place to eat is the rear of the main *mercado*, where many clean little *fondas* (food stalls) are open daily from around 8 am to 8 pm.

A good choice on the plaza is *K'puchinos*, with indoor and outdoor tables, where well-prepared main courses are around US$5 to US$7, and pasta and antojitos around US$4. It has an extensive choice of coffees. *La Casa de la Arrachera*, next door, does breakfasts for US$3 and comida for US$4.50. The restaurant at the *Hotel Maridelfi* on the plaza is very good but more expensive.

Shopping
Near the plaza are many artesanías shops with interesting crafts for sale. The main market, on Ezequiel Montes, and the Mercado de Artesanías (Crafts Market), on Carrizal, are just a couple of blocks away through little lanes.

Getting There & Away
Tequisquiapan is 20km northeast up highway 120 from the larger town of San Juan del Río on highway 57. Flecha Amarilla buses (2nd-class) go every 40 minutes, 6 am to 8 pm, to/from Mexico City's Terminal Norte (185km, 2¾ hours, US$8).

SAN MIGUEL DE ALLENDE
• pop 53,000 • elev 1840m ☎ 4
This charming colonial town 280km from Mexico City has attracted creative types of every persuasion from Mexico, the USA and farther afield since the 1940s, when David Alfaro Siqueiros taught mural-painting courses at the Escuela de Bellas Artes.

Many Americans seeking to escape the conformity of post-WWII USA gravitated to San Miguel, but once San Miguel was entrenched on the gringo circuit, it naturally lost some of its bohemian character. Today the town is home to several thousand foreigners. While many of them have retired here, others reside here only in winter. The town has lost none of the beauty of its hillside setting with vistas over the plains and distant hills, nor its lovely old buildings or cobbled streets. Its superbly clear light still attracts artists, and there are many art galleries and a thriving entertainment scene; many visitors are also attracted by the variety of language and arts courses available.

San Miguel's peak tourist period is from mid-December to the end of March, with a flurry again from June to August.

Orientation & Information
The Plaza Principal, called the Jardín, is San Miguel's pleasant focal point. The town slopes up from west to east. The bus station is a little over 1km west of the Jardín on Canal.

The tourist office (☎ 152-17-47), on the southeast corner of the Jardín, has maps and printed brochures, and can answer questions in English and Spanish. It's open 10 am to 5 pm Monday to Friday, 10 am to 2 pm Saturday and Sunday. The Asociación de Guias de Turistas (☎ 154-51-31) has an information booth on the corner of Canal and Hernández Macías – they have some printed information, answer questions and sell tours with the local guide association (open 10 am to 5 pm daily).

Banamex on the west side of the Jardín, and several banks on or near San Francisco in the couple of blocks east of the Jardín, have ATMs. Banks generally offer the best rates for changing money.

The post office is one block east of the Jardín at Correo and Corregidora. El Hormiguero, Juárez 7, offers Internet access for about US$5 an hour. The Biblioteca Pública (Public Library), Insurgentes 25, has more expensive Internet access but also an excellent collection of books in English and Spanish on Mexico. It's open 10 am to 2 pm and 4 to 7 pm Monday to Friday, 10 am to 2 pm Saturday.

Walking Tour
San Miguel has a fairly compact center, and a stroll around some of its fine colonial buildings, starting from the Jardín, is an enjoyable way to get the feel of the place. Virtually all the buildings date from the 18th century, when some of the wealth of the Guanajuato silver mines found its way to San Miguel.

The **Casa del Mayorazgo de Canal**, one of San Miguel's most imposing old residences, is closed to the public, but you can study the beautiful carved-wood doors at the entrance at Canal 4.

The **Templo de La Concepción**, a block down Canal, has a fine altar and several magnificent old oil paintings. A number of

SAN MIGUEL DE ALLENDE

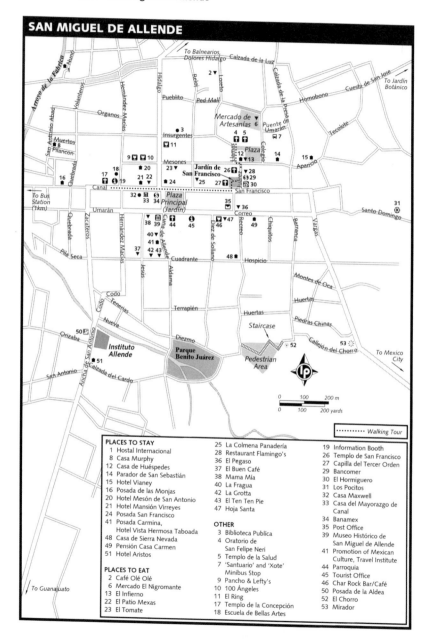

PLACES TO STAY
1 Hostal Internacional
8 Casa Murphy
12 Casa de Huéspedes
14 Parador de San Sebastián
15 Hotel Vianey
16 Posada de las Monjas
20 Hotel Mesón de San Antonio
21 Hotel Mansión Virreyes
24 Posada San Francisco
41 Posada Carmina,
   Hotel Vista Hermosa Taboada
48 Casa de Sierra Nevada
49 Pensión Casa Carmen
51 Hotel Aristos

PLACES TO EAT
2 Café Olé Olé
6 Mercado El Nigromante
13 El Infierno
22 El Patio Mexas
23 El Tomate

25 La Colmena Panadería
28 Restaurant Flamingo's
36 El Pegaso
37 El Buen Café
38 Mama Mía
40 La Fragua
42 La Grotta
43 El Ten Ten Pie
47 Hoja Santa

OTHER
3 Biblioteca Publica
4 Oratorio de
   San Felipe Neri
5 Templo de la Salud
7 'Santuario' and 'Xote'
   Minibus Stop
9 Pancho & Lefty's
10 100 Ángeles
11 El Ring
17 Templo de la Concepción
18 Escuela de Bellas Artes

19 Information Booth
26 Templo de San Francisco
27 Capilla del Tercer Orden
29 Bancomer
30 El Hormiguero
31 Los Pocitos
32 Casa Maxwell
33 Casa del Mayorazgo de
   Canal
34 Banamex
35 Post Office
39 Museo Histórico de
   San Miguel de Allende
41 Promotion of Mexican
   Culture, Travel Institute
44 Parroquia
45 Tourist Office
46 Char Rock Bar/Café
50 Posada de la Aldea
52 El Chorro
53 Mirador

wise sayings are painted on the interior doorway to give pause to those entering. The church was begun in the 18th century; its dome was added in the 19th century by Zeferino Gutiérrez, possibly inspired by pictures of Les Invalides in Paris. Next door at Hernández Macías 75, in the beautiful former monastery, which the church served, is the **Escuela de Bellas Artes**, an education and cultural center since 1938. One room is devoted to an unfinished mural by Siqueiros, done in 1948 as part of a course in mural painting for US war veterans. Its subject – apparently! – is the life and work of Ignacio Allende.

Back up the hill, the **Capilla del Tercer Orden** and the **Templo de San Francisco**, both on the small Jardín de San Francisco, at San Francisco and Juárez, were parts of one Franciscan monastery. The capilla's main façade shows San Francisco (St Francis) and symbols of the Franciscan order, while the church's façade is an elaborate late-18th-century Churrigueresque concoction.

The multitowered and domed **Oratorio de San Felipe Neri**, built in the early 18th century, stands at Insurgentes and Llamas. The pale-pink main façade is baroque with an indigenous influence. Inside are 33 oil paintings of scenes from the life of San Felipe Neri, the 16th-century Florentine who founded the Oratorio Catholic order. The east transept holds a painting of the Virgin of Guadalupe by Miguel Cabrera. In the west transept is a lavish chapel, the Santa Casa de Loreto, built in 1735, with tiles from Puebla, Valencia and China on the floor and walls, gilded cloth hangings and the tombs of chapel founder Conde Manuel de la Canal and his wife, María de Hervas de Flores.

The **Templo de La Salud**, just east of San Felipe Neri, has an early Churrigueresque façade and a blue and yellow tiled dome. Its paintings include one of San Javier by Miguel Cabrera.

Parroquia

The pink 'sugar-candy' pointed towers of the parish church dominate the Jardín. These strange, soaring pinnacles were designed by an untutored indigenous stone mason,

Zeferino Gutiérrez, in the late 19th century. Reputedly, he instructed the builders by scratching plans in the sand with a stick. Most of the rest of the church dates from the late 17th century.

Museo Histórico de San Miguel de Allende

Near the parroquia on Cuna de Allende stands the house where Mexican independence hero Ignacio Allende was born, now a museum. Exhibits relate the interesting history of the area, with special attention to Allende and his movement. The museum is open 10 am to 4 pm Tuesday to Sunday (US$2.25).

Mirador & Parque Juárez

One of the best views over the town and surrounding country is from the *mirador* (lookout point) up on Vargas, also known as the Salida a Querétaro, in the southeast of town. If you take Callejón del Chorro downhill from here, and turn left at the bottom, you reach El Chorro, the spring where the town was founded. Today it gushes out of a fountain built in 1960. A bit farther down the hill is the shady Parque Benito Juárez.

Botanical & Orchid Gardens

The large Jardín Botánico 'El Charco del Ingenio,' devoted mainly to cacti and other native plants of this semiarid area, is on the hilltop about 1.5km northeast of the town center. Though only a few years old, it's a lovely place for a walk, particularly in the early morning or late afternoon – though women alone should steer clear of its more secluded parts. It's open sunrise to sunset (US$1). A taxi from the center is US$1.75.

Los Pocitos, an orchid garden with 2000 plants covering 230 species, is at Santo Domingo 38.

Swimming

Several hotel pools are open to outsiders, including the one at the Posada de la Aldea, Ancha de San Antonio 15, Monday to Friday (US$2.25). Even nicer are some of the several balnearios at hot springs north of

Cradle of Independence

The states of Guanajuato and neighboring Querétaro make up one of Mexico's most fertile agricultural regions, known as the Bajío ('ba-HEE-o'). Historically they're known as La Cuna de la Independencia (The Cradle of Independence), for it was here that Mexico's movement for independence from Spain began in 1810.

One group of disaffected criollos plotting to free Mexico from Spanish rule met secretly in Querétaro city at the house of Doña Josefa Ortiz (La Corregidora), wife of a former *corregidor* (district administrator) of Querétaro. Among the conspirators were Ignacio Allende from San Miguel, 60km north of Querétaro, and Miguel Hidalgo, the priest of Dolores, 40km farther north. They had set December 8, 1810, as the date for armed uprising.

The colonial authorities got wind of the conspiracy and raided Doña Josefa's house on September 13, 1810. Though locked in a room in her house, Doña Josefa – the story goes – managed to whisper a warning through a keyhole to a coconspirator, Ignacio Pérez. Pérez rushed to San Miguel and gave the news to Juan de Aldama, another member of the coterie. Aldama sped north to Dolores where, in the early hours of September 16, he found Allende and Hidalgo at Hidalgo's house.

Deciding that immediate action was the only strategy, at 5 am on September 16, 1810, Hidalgo rang his church bells to summon the townspeople, and issued the Grito de Dolores, whose precise words have been lost to history but which boiled down to 'Viva Our Lady of Guadalupe! Death to bad government and the *gachupines*!' (Gachupines was the derisive name for Mexico's Spanish overlords.)

The rebels freed the prisoners in the Dolores jail, and, at the head of a growing band of criollo, mestizo and indigenous insurgents, Hidalgo and Allende set off for San Miguel. By that evening, San Miguel was in rebel hands, its local regiment having joined the insurgents. San Miguel's Spanish population was locked up, and Allende was only partly able to restrain the rebels from looting the town.

After San Miguel, the rebels won over Celaya and then, 20,000 strong, they marched on Guanajuato, where Spanish troops and loyalists barricaded themselves inside a big grain-and-seed

San Miguel, on or near the road to Dolores Hidalgo. All have swimming pools with mineral waters and pleasant surroundings. They're supposedly good for the skin, and definitely good for relaxation. Entry is US$4 to US$5 for a day. A taxi is around US$6 one-way (you can get it to come back later), or you can get within walking distance of any of the balnearios on a Dolores Hidalgo bus from San Miguel bus station (every 30 minutes in daytime by Flecha Amarilla and Herradura de Plata) or a 'Santuario' minibus (half-hourly) from the bus stop on Puente de Umarán, off Colegio, which is opposite the Mercado El Nigromante.

The most popular balneario is **Taboada** (☎ 152-08-50), 8km along the Dolores road then 3km west along a signposted side road. It has large lawns, one Olympic-size pool with warm water and two smaller pools that get quite hot. It's open 8 am to 5 pm daily except Tuesday. Minibuses to Xote (hourly from the Puente de Umarán bus stop mentioned above) will get you to within 1km of Taboada.

La Gruta (☎ 152-25-30), by the Dolores road 9km from San Miguel, has three small pools into which the waters of a thermal spring have been channeled. The hottest is in a cave entered through a tunnel, with hot water gushing from the roof. Another favorite is **Escondido Place**, about 1km down a dirt road, signposted on the highway, about 9km from San Miguel. It has two warm

Cradle of Independence

storehouse, the Alhóndiga de Granaditas. The defenders looked as if they would be able to hold out until, on September 28, a young indigenous miner, El Pípila, managed to set the Alhóndiga's gates ablaze before succumbing to a hail of bullets. While the Spaniards choked on smoke, the rebels moved in and took the Alhóndiga, killing most of those inside.

The rebels quickly captured other important towns in the region, and on October 30 their army, now numbering about 80,000, defeated loyalist forces at Las Cruces outside Mexico City. But Hidalgo hesitated to attack the capital, and the rebels occupied Guadalajara instead. Thereafter they were pushed north by their opponents, their numbers shrank, and in 1811 the leaders were captured in Chihuahua and executed.

When the Spaniards retook Guanajuato they conducted the infamous 'lottery of death,' in which names of Guanajuato citizens were drawn at random and the 'winners' were tortured and hanged. The heads of Aldama, Allende, Hidalgo and another rebel leader, Mariano Jiménez, were brought back to Guanajuato and hung in cages outside the Alhóndiga from 1811 until 1821, when Mexico finally achieved independence. (The cages were then removed and the heroes' skulls now reside in the Monumento a la Independencia in Mexico City.)

Dolores was renamed Dolores Hidalgo in 1824, and San Miguel became San Miguel de Allende in 1826. Today Hidalgo is Mexico's most revered hero, rivaled only by Benito Juárez in the number of streets, plazas and statues dedicated to him throughout the country. The Bajío is proud to have given birth to Mexico's most glorious moment and is visited almost as a place of pilgrimage by Mexicans from far and wide.

Freedom rebel Miguel Hidalgo

outdoor pools and three connected indoor pools, each progressively hotter. The picturesque grounds have plenty of space for picnicking.

Organized Tours

A tour visiting some of San Miguel's lovely houses and gardens that are otherwise closed to the public sets off by bus about noon every Sunday from the Biblioteca Pública. Tickets are on sale from 11 am. Cost is around US$15 for the two-hour tour, with three different houses visited each week. Promotion of Mexican Culture (PMC, ☎ 152-16-30), Cuna de Allende 11, and the Asociación de Guías de Turistas (see Orientation & Information, earlier), conduct walking tours of the town and bus tours that go farther afield.

Places to Stay

Some of the better-value places are often full; book ahead if you can, especially during the high seasons.

Budget The friendly *Hostal Internacional* (☎ 152-31-75, Nunó 28) has a good kitchen/dining area, seats outside in the courtyard and bunk beds in separate-sex dorms for US$6.50 (US$5.50 with a student or hostel card), including coffee, tea and continental breakfast. A few private singles/doubles are US$11/13.25. The hostel may move if a better building becomes available.

The **Casa de Huéspedes** (☎ 152-13-78, *Mesones 27*) is a clean, pleasant upstairs hostelry with six rooms, all with private bath. Singles/doubles cost US$13/19.50. **Parador de San Sebastián** (☎ 152-70-84, *Mesones 7*) is quiet and attractive, with 24 rooms, all with fireplace and bathroom, around a courtyard full of plants. Rooms are from US$13.50/15, up to US$27 for bigger rooms. If it's full, try **Hotel Vianey** (☎ 152-45-59, *Aparicio 18*), where a plant-filled courtyard is surrounded by small, plain rooms costing US$16.50 for one or two people.

Mid-Range San Miguel brims with good places in this range. **Posada Carmina** (☎ 152-04-58, *Cuna de Allende 7*), just off the Jardín, is a former colonial mansion with 12 large, attractive rooms costing from US$33/44 to US$62/71 for singles/doubles. In the same block, the less elegant **Hotel Vista Hermosa Taboada** (☎ 152-00-78, *Cuna de Allende 11*) has 17 rooms from US$26.

Half a block from the Jardín, **Hotel Mansión Virreyes** (☎ 152-08-51, *Canal 19*) is another colonial place with 22 rooms around two courtyards and a restaurant/bar in the rear patio. Singles/doubles are US$34/46.

The welcoming **Posada de las Monjas** (☎ 152-01-71, *Canal 37*) is a beautiful hotel in a former monastery. The 65 rooms are comfortable and well decorated: those in the new section out back are in better condition than those in the old section. Numerous terraces give lovely views, and the hotel offers a restaurant, bar and parking. Prices start at US$28/30. Larger rooms and those with fireplaces are more.

Hotel Mesón de San Antonio (☎ 152-05-80, *Mesones 80*) has an attractive courtyard with a lawn, a small swimming pool and rooms at US$49 single or double including breakfast.

Top End The **Posada San Francisco** (☎ 152-00-72, *Plaza Principal 2*) is a great value for its location on the Jardín and for its classic colonial style. Spacious, comfortable rooms cost US$57 for one or two people.

San Miguel has a slew of bed & breakfast places offering comfortable accommodations at quite high prices. One of the nicest is **Casa Murphy** (☎ 152-37-76, *San Antonio Abad 22*), off Canal, about 400m from the Jardín. Luxurious rooms in this colonial house cost US$70 for two people. More central is **Pensión Casa Carmen** (☎ 152-08-44, *Correo 31*), an old colonial home whose 12 rooms are set around a pleasant courtyard with a fountain, orange trees and flowers. The singles/doubles price of US$48/70 includes a delicious breakfast.

Down in the southwest of town about 750m from the Jardín, **Hotel Aristos** (☎ 152-03-92, 152-16-31, *Calzada del Cardo 2*) has a large garden with tennis courts and a big pool. Rooms, with terraces and parking, start at US$70 for one or two people.

The very luxurious and elegant **Casa de Sierra Nevada** (☎ 152-04-15, *Hospicio 35*) was converted from four colonial mansions. It has a swimming pool, fine restaurant, views over the town and superbly appointed rooms and suites from US$200 to US$410.

Places to Eat

Restaurants here cover an array of cuisines.

Budget Excellent bakeries such as **La Colmena Panadería** (*Reloj 21*), half a block north of the Jardín, offer quick, cheap eats. A few food stands on the east side of the Jardín have cheap, tasty Mexican fare like *elotes* (corn on the cob), fried chicken or tamales for around US$2.50.

Restaurant Flamingo's (*Juárez 15*), northeast of the Jardín, is a good, basic, family-run chicken restaurant, with birds turning on spits out front. It serves a good-value comida corrida (US$3.50) from 1 to 4 pm. Nearby on Mesones, **El Infierno** will do a full meal of soup, chicken, fries and vegetables for under US$4.

La Fragua (*Cuna de Allende 3*), just south of the Jardín, is a long-popular courtyard restaurant/bar with live music nightly and a happy hour from 6 to 8 pm. The menú del día is only US$3. On Cuna de Allende at Cuadrante, the little, family-run **El Ten Ten Pie** serves up home-style cooking with excellent chili sauces. Try the tasty cheese and mushroom tacos – under US$2 for a serving. The comida corrida is under US$4.

El Buen Café (Jesús 23) does economical breakfasts and snacks for around US$3.25. It's closed Sunday.

The daily food market, *Mercado El Nigromante*, is on Colegio.

Mid-Range & Top End Several lively but expensive places around the Jardín do good coffee, cakes and snacks. They're open from about 9 am to 10 pm.

The friendly *El Pegaso*, on Corregidora, is good for all meals (but closed Sunday). Head there for a not-too-expensive breakfast of fruit, eggs Benedict, fresh bread and coffee for under US$3.50, or try their fancy sandwiches such as smoked salmon with cream cheese (US$5). Main dishes, some Asian-inspired, start at US$4.75.

For a particularly imaginative menu, don't miss *Hoja Santa (Correo 19)*, serving *'nueva cocina Mexicana'* – typical Mexican ingredients in original combinations, creatively prepared and beautifully presented. Examples are nopal cactus with cream cheese and shrimp, and a pasta sauce made with six different types of chili pepper. The surroundings are comfortable and classy, and the prices very reasonable – starters are around US$3.50, and main courses of steak and seafood are all under US$6.

Mama Mía (Umarán 8), in a pleasant, cool courtyard near the Jardín, is a San Miguel favorite for its food and music (see Entertainment). Meats and seafoods cost from around US$6.50, pastas US$4 to US$6; their breakfasts are more economical.

Also near the Jardín, *La Grotta (Cuadrante 5)* is a small, intimate Italian restaurant with tasty food – the pizzas, from US$6, are excellent, and the homemade desserts delicious – but the bill quickly mounts up.

El Patio Mexas (Canal 15) is also on the expensive side, but it's a fun expats' restaurant/bar with excellent Tex-Mex specialties and Texas-size portions. Salads are from US$3, steaks around US$8.

The friendly, family-run *Café Olé Olé (Loreto 66)* is one of San Miguel's most popular eateries. It's brightly decorated with bullfighting memorabilia; the food is mainly char-grilled, with prices starting at US$5.50 for chicken and beef.

Vegetarians should head for *El Tomate (Mesones 62)*. Light meals such as pasta, sandwiches on whole wheat and salads (US$3.25 to US$4.50) all feature fantastically fresh and tasty ingredients – lettuce you can really taste. Freshly squeezed juices cost up to US$2, and the comida corrida is a great value at US$5. It's open 9.30 am to 3.30 pm Monday to Saturday.

Entertainment

Check the expat newspaper *Atención San Miguel* to find out what's on. The *Escuela de Bellas Artes (Hernández Macías 75)* hosts art exhibitions, concerts, readings and theater; check its notice board for the current schedule. Some events are in English.

Several restaurants double as drinking, dancing and entertainment venues. Most of the action is on Thursday, Friday and Saturday nights, but at holiday times some places will have live music and more any night of the week. The perennially popular *Mama Mía (Umarán 8)* has live South American music nightly from around 8 pm to late. There's a video bar at the front and a sometimes crowded dance floor, which usually gets going around 11 pm.

Pancho & Lefty's (Mesones 99) attracts a young crowd with live rock music and/or techno/dance on Wednesday, Friday and Saturday from around 10.30 pm to 3 am. Cover charge is about US$2.50 and drinks are inexpensive. *100 Ángeles* disco/dance club, right next door, is San Miguel's premier gay venue. *Char Rock Bar/Café*, upstairs at Correo and Diez de Sollano, has bands doing '60s and '70s covers – occasional cheap drink specials get the students in early, but later on it's mostly an older crowd.

The most popular dance club is *El Ring (Hidalgo 25)*, a flashy place blasting a mix of Latin, US, and Euro dance music. It opens around 10 pm Wednesday to Saturday, and from midnight it's usually full with young Mexicans and foreigners (cover US$4 to US$6).

Shopping

San Miguel has one of the biggest and best concentrations of craft shops in Mexico, selling handicrafts from all over the country. Prices are not low, but quality is high. Casa Maxwell on Canal, a few doors down from the Jardín, is one place with a huge range; there are many more within a few blocks, especially on Canal, San Francisco and Zacateros.

Getting There & Away

From Mexico City's Terminal Norte (280km, 3¼ to four hours) four deluxe ETN buses run daily to San Miguel (US$22), plus three 1st-class each by Primera Plus and Pegasso Plus (US$15.50) and around 30 2nd-class each by Flecha Amarilla and Herradura de Plata (US$14). Return services are similar.

Four daily 1st-class Primera Plus buses go from San Miguel to Guanajuato (82km, one to 1½ hours, US$6), plus about 10 2nd-class each by Flecha Amarilla and Servicios Coordinados (US$4.50).

San Miguel's Central de Autobuses is on Canal, a little over 1km west of the center. ETN, Primera Plus and Pegasso Plus tickets can be bought at the Travel Institute, Cuna de Allende 11.

Getting Around

'Central' buses (US$0.25) go every few minutes, 7 am to 9 pm, between the bus station and town center. They terminate on the corner of Mesones and Colegio. Heading out from the center, you can pick one up on Canal. A taxi between the center and the bus station costs US$1.75.

GUANAJUATO

• pop 70,000 • elev 2017m ☎ 4

Guanajuato ('gwah-nah-HWAH-toh') is a city crammed onto the steep slopes of a ravine, with underground tunnels acting as streets. This impossible topography was settled in 1559 after one of the hemisphere's richest veins of silver was uncovered at La Valenciana mine. For 250 years, the excavation of what is now the periphery above the city produced 20% of the world's silver. Many of the fine buildings paid for with Guanajuato silver remain intact, making the city a living monument to a prosperous, turbulent past.

Guanajuato's university, known for its arts programs, has over 21,000 students, adding a youthful vibrancy just as attractive as the colonial architecture and exotic setting. The city is a popular place for foreign students to study Spanish language and Latin American culture.

Orientation

Guanajuato's central area is quite compact. The main street, running roughly west-east, changes names from Juárez to Obregón and then to Sopeña. Pretty Jardín de la Unión, where Obregón becomes Sopeña, is the social heart of the city. People congregate here in the late afternoon and also in the evening, with street musicians serenading everyone.

Roughly parallel to Juárez-Obregón-Sopeña is another long street that goes through the names 28 de Septiembre, Galarza, Positos and Lascuraín de Retana. Paralleling Sopeña is another important street, Hidalgo – also called Cantarranas. Once you know these streets you can't get lost in the center. You can, however, have a great time getting lost among the city's callejones – the maze of narrow, crooked alleys winding up the hills from the center.

The underground streets are used only by vehicular traffic. Many were created along the dried-up bed of the Río Guanajuato, which was diverted in 1905.

Information

The tourist office (☎ 732-15-74) is at Plaza de la Paz 14, almost opposite the basílica – look for the 'Información Turística' sign. The friendly staff – mostly English-speaking – give out free city maps and brochures in Spanish and English. It's open 9 am to 8 pm Monday to Friday, 10 am to 4 pm Saturday and 10 am to 2 pm Sunday.

Banks along Juárez change cash and traveler's checks (some only until 2 pm), and most have ATMs. Bancentro, opposite the tourist office, is convenient and relatively quick. Divisas, at Juárez 33A, is a casa de

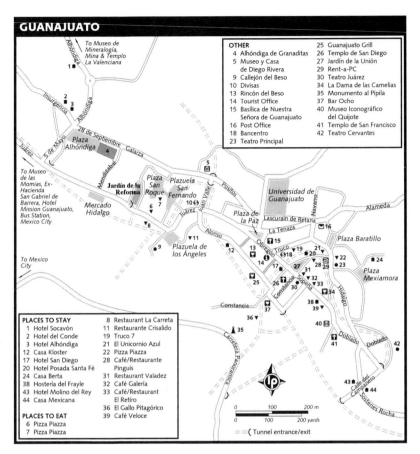

GUANAJUATO

To Museo de
Mineralogía,
Mina & Templo
La Valenciana

To Museo
de las
Momias, Ex-
Hacienda
San Gabriel de
Barrera, Hotel
Mission Guanajuato,
Bus Station,
Mexico City

To Mexico
City

Plaza
Alhóndiga

Jardín de la
Reforma

Mercado
Hidalgo

Plaza
San
Roque

Plazuela
San
Fernando

Plazuela de
los Ángeles

Universidad de
Guanajuato

Plaza de
la Paz

Plaza Baratillo

Plaza
Mexiamora

Constancia

OTHER
4 Alhóndiga de Granaditas
5 Museo y Casa
   de Diego Rivera
9 Callejón del Beso
10 Divisas
13 Rincón del Beso
14 Tourist Office
15 Basílica de Nuestra
   Señora de Guanajuato
16 Post Office
18 Bancentro
23 Teatro Principal

25 Guanajuato Grill
26 Templo de San Diego
27 Jardín de la Unión
29 Rent-a-PC
30 Teatro Juárez
34 La Dama de las Camelias
35 Monumento al Pípila
37 Bar Ocho
40 Museo Iconográfico
   del Quijote
41 Templo de San Francisco
42 Teatro Cervantes

PLACES TO STAY
1 Hotel Socavón
2 Hotel del Conde
3 Hotel Alhóndiga
12 Casa Kloster
17 Hotel San Diego
20 Hotel Posada Santa Fé
24 Casa Berta
38 Hostería del Frayle
43 Hotel Molino del Rey
44 Casa Mexicana

PLACES TO EAT
6 Pizza Piazza
7 Pizza Piazza

8 Restaurant La Carreta
11 Restaurante Crisalido
19 Truco 7
21 El Unicornio Azul
22 Pizza Piazza
28 Café/Restaurante
   Pinguis
31 Restaurant Valadez
32 Café Galería
33 Café/Restaurant
   El Retiro
36 El Gallo Pitagórico
39 Café Veloce

0   100   200 m
0   100   200 yards
==(Tunnel entrance/exit

cambio with reasonable rates, open 9 am to 3 pm and 4.30 to 7 pm Monday to Friday.

The main post office is at the east end of Lascuraín de Retana. There are pay phones in Pasaje de los Arcos, an alley off the south side of Obregón in the center.

The best place for Internet access is Rent-a-PC, upstairs at a kink in the road almost opposite the Teatro Principal, open daily (US$3 per hour).

Teatro Juárez

Just off the Jardín de la Unión stands the magnificent Teatro Juárez, built between 1873 and 1903 and inaugurated by the dictator Porfirio Díaz, whose lavish tastes it reflects. The outside is festooned with columns, lampposts and statues; inside, the impression is Moorish, with the bar and lobby gleaming with carved wood, stained glass and precious metals. The theater can be visited from 9 am to 1.45 pm and 5 to 7.45 pm daily, except Monday (US$0.60).

Basílica de Nuestra Señora de Guanajuato

This church, on Plaza de la Paz, one block west of the Jardín de la Unión, contains a jewel-covered image of the Virgin, patron of Guanajuato. The wooden statue was supposedly hidden from the Moors in a cave in Spain for 800 years. Felipe II of Spain gave it to Guanajuato in thanks for riches that accrued to the Crown. Plaza de la Paz is surrounded by the former homes of wealthy silver lords.

Universidad de Guanajuato

Guanajuato University, whose green ramparts are visible above much of the city, is on Lascuraín de Retana one block up the hill from the basílica. It is considered one of Mexico's finest schools for music, theater, mine engineering, industrial relations and law, and houses three art galleries plus the Museo de Historia Natural Alfredo Dugés, with a large collection of preserved fauna including freaks of nature such as a two-headed goat.

Museo y Casa de Diego Rivera

Diego Rivera was born in 1886 at Positos 46; the family moved to Mexico City when he was six. In conservative Guanajuato, where Catholic influence prevails, the socialist Rivera was persona non grata for years. The city now honors him with a collection of his work in the house where he was born. The 1st floor contains the Rivera family's 19th-century antiques and fine furniture. On the 2nd and 3rd floors are some 70 to 80 paintings and sketches by the master, including peasant portraits and a nude of Frida Kahlo. It's open 10 am to 6.30 pm Tuesday to Saturday, 10 am to 2.30 pm Sunday (US$0.90).

Alhóndiga de Granaditas

This structure, on 28 de Septiembre, was built between 1798 and 1808 as a massive grain-and-seed storehouse. It's famous as the site of the first major rebel victory in Mexico's independence struggle (see 'Cradle of Independence'). At the top of the four outer corners of the building you can see the long black hooks from which hung metal cages holding the heads of executed rebel leaders. The cages are now exhibited inside. The Alhóndiga became a history and art museum in 1967. The historical sections cover Guanajuato's pre-Hispanic past, its great flood of 1905, and modern times. Don't miss José Chávez Morado's dramatic murals of Guanajuato's history on the staircases.

It's open 10 am to 1.30 pm and 4 to 5.30 pm Tuesday to Saturday, 10 am to 2.30 pm Sunday (US$2.25, free on Sunday).

Callejón del Beso

The narrowest of the many narrow callejones climbing the hills from Guanajuato's main streets is Callejón del Beso, where the balconies on either side of the alley practically touch. In Guanajuatan legend, forbidden lovers living on opposite sides used to exchange furtive kisses from these balconies. From Plazuela de los Ángeles on Juárez, walk about 40m up Callejón del Patrocinio and you'll see Callejón del Beso taking off to your left.

Monumento al Pípila

The monument to El Pípila, with its torch raised high over the city, honors the hero who torched the Alhóndiga gates on September 28, 1810. On its base is the inscription 'Aún hay otras Alhóndigas por incendiar' ('There are still other Alhóndigas to burn').

It's worth going up to the statue for the magnificent view over the city. The walk from the center of town passes up steep, picturesque lanes. One route is up Callejón de Calvario from Sopeña (you'll see the 'Al Pípila' sign). If the climb is too much for you, the 'Pípila-ISSSTE' bus heading west on Juárez will let you off right by the statue.

Museo Iconográfico del Quijote

This excellent, surprisingly interesting museum is at Doblado 1, on the tiny plaza in front of the Templo de San Francisco. Every exhibit relates to Don Quijote de la Mancha, the famous hero of Spanish literature. It's fascinating to see the same subject depicted in so many different media by different artists in different styles – from room-size murals to a tiny picture on an eggshell. It's open 10 am to 6.30 pm Tuesday to Saturday, 10 am to 2.30 pm Sunday (free).

Teotihuacán's monstrous Pirámide del Sol – world's third-largest pyramid – was once bright red.

Colorful Guanajuato

Churrigueresque architecture: Taxco's beautiful Templo de Santa Prisca

Xochitécatl's Pirámide de las Flores was possibly the site of fertility rituals.

Ex-Hacienda San Gabriel de Barrera

Built at the end of the 17th century, this was the grand hacienda of Captain Gabriel de Barrera, descended from the first Count of Valenciana of the famous La Valenciana mine. Opened as a museum in 1979, the hacienda has been magnificently restored with period European furniture and art; in the chapel is an ornate gold-covered altar.

The large grounds, originally devoted to processing ore from La Valenciana, were converted in 1945 to beautiful terraced gardens with pavilions, pools, fountains and footpaths – a lovely, tranquil retreat from the city.

The museum, about 2km west of the city center, is open 9 am to 6 pm daily (US$1.25). Take one of the frequent 'Marfil' buses heading west on Juárez, and say you want to get off at Hotel Mission Guanajuato. From where they drop you, walk downhill past the hotel and the ex-hacienda will be on your right.

Museo de las Momias

The famous Museum of the Mummies, at the cemetery on the western outskirts of town, is a quintessential example of Mexico's obsession with death. Visitors from far and wide come to see scores of corpses disinterred from the public cemetery.

The first remains were dug up in 1865, when some bodies had to be moved to make room for more. What the authorities uncovered were not skeletons but flesh mummified in grotesque forms and facial expressions. The mineral content of the soil and dry conditions had combined to preserve the bodies in this unique way.

Today 119 mummies are displayed in the museum, including the smallest mummy in the world, a pregnant mummy and plenty more. Since space is still tight in the cemetery, mummies are still being found. It takes only five or six years for a body to become mummified here, though very few are considered 'display quality.' The others are cremated.

The museum is open 9 am to 6 pm daily (US$2.25). To get there take any 'Momias' or 'Panteón' bus west on Juárez.

Museo de Mineralogía

The Mineralogy Museum at the university's Escuela de Minas campus, northwest of the center, is among the world's foremost mineralogy museums. Over 20,000 specimens from around the world include some extremely rare minerals. The museum is open 9 am to 3 pm Monday to Friday (free). Take a 'Presa-San Javier' bus west on Juárez and ask to get off at the Escuela de Minas.

Mina & Templo La Valenciana

For 250 years La Valenciana mine, on a hill overlooking Guanajuato about 5km north of the center, produced 20% of the world's silver. Shut down after the revolution, it reopened in 1968 and is again in operation. Now cooperatively run, the mine still yields silver, gold, nickel and lead and can be visited any day from around 8 am to 7 pm (US$0.50). You can see the earth being extracted and miners descending an immense main shaft 9m wide and 500m deep.

Nearby is the magnificent Templo La Valenciana, also called the Iglesia de San Cayetano. One legend says that the silver baron of La Valenciana, the Conde de Rul, tried to atone for exploiting the miners by building the ultimate in Churrigueresque churches. Built between 1765 and 1788, the church has a spectacular façade and a dazzling interior with ornate golden altars, filigree carvings and giant paintings.

To get to La Valenciana, take a 'Cristo Rey' or 'Valenciana' bus (every 15 minutes) from the bus stop on Alhóndiga just north of 28 de Septiembre. Get off at Templo La Valenciana; the mine is about 300m down the dirt road opposite the church.

Special Events

Guanajuato's annual **Festival Internacional Cervantino** arts festival is dedicated to the pioneering Spanish novelist and creator of Don Quijote, Miguel Cervantes (1547-1616), and is one of the foremost arts extravaganzas in Latin America. Music, dance and theater groups converge on Guanajuato from around the world, performing work that may have nothing whatsoever to do with Cervantes. The festival lasts two to three weeks and is held in October.

Tickets and hotels should be booked in advance. Tickets normally go on sale around September 6. In Guanajuato they're sold on the left side of the Teatro Juárez; in Mexico City they can be bought at the Cervantino office at Obregón 273, Colonia Roma (☎ 5-533-41-21), or from Ticketmaster (☎ 5-325-90-00).

Among the most spectacular events are some of the *entremeses* (sketches), with galloping horses and medieval costumes, performed in the historic settings of Plaza San Roque and Plaza Alhóndiga.

Places to Stay

Prices given here are for the summer season, and may be higher at Christmas, Semana Santa and during the Cervantino festival, but lower in other months.

Budget The backpackers' favorite is *Casa Kloster* (☎ 732-00-88, Alonso 32), a short block down an alley from the basilica. Birds and flowers grace the sunny courtyard, and the well-cared-for rooms with shared bath are clean and comfortable. Cost is US$7.75 per person, slightly more for the larger rooms. It's a relaxed, friendly place and fills up early in the day.

Friendly *Casa Berta* (☎ 732-13-16, Tamboras 9), a few minutes east of the Jardín de la Unión, has four doubles at US$10 per person. It has modern bathrooms and is homey and well kept. Walk up the street

beside the Teatro Principal on Hidalgo to Plaza de Mexiamora. Head straight uphill, turn first right, then left and follow the path to the door directly ahead.

Casa Mexicana (☎ 732-50-05, Sostenes Rocha 28), about 300m southeast of the Jardín, offers smallish rooms around a central courtyard for US$5.50 per person with shared bathroom, or US$7.75 with private bath. It's a clean, friendly, family-run place.

Mid-Range Visible from Plaza Alhóndiga, *Hotel Alhóndiga* (☎ 732-05-25, Insurgencia 49) has clean, comfortable rooms with color TV, some with small private balconies; there's also parking. Hot water is sporadic. Single or double rooms are US$31.50. *Hotel del Conde* (☎ 732-14-65, Insurgencia 1), next door, is better, though its weekend disco is a recipe for lack of sleep. Spacious, bright singles/doubles cost US$25/30.

Hotel Socavón (☎ 732-48-85, Alhóndiga 41A) is a well-kept hostelry with attractive rooms around a courtyard. They cost US$27/31, possibly less at off-peak times.

A few minutes south, on Calle del Campanero opposite the Teatro Cervantes, *Hotel Molino del Rey* (☎ 732-22-23) is a good choice for its quietish location. Set around a pretty patio, the 35 rooms with bath are US$23/31. Its restaurant is inexpensive.

Top End Two old favorites stand right on Jardín de la Unión. *Hotel San Diego* (☎ 732-13-00/21, fax 732-56-26, Jardín de la Unión 1) has 55 elegant rooms and suites and a large roof terrace. Singles/doubles with a balcony over the plaza are US$88/93; other rooms are US$61 single or double. At the other end of the Jardín, *Hotel Posada Santa Fé* (☎ 732-00-84, fax 732-46-53) is a sumptuous hotel in an elegant 19th-century mansion. Singles/doubles are US$59/67; rooms with a plaza view are US$88. A block east of the Jardín, *Hostería del Frayle* (☎ 732-11-79, Sopeña 3) is a very attractive old building. All rooms have high wood-beamed ceilings, and though it's in the center of town, the building's thick adobe walls keep it quiet. Rooms are US$44/55.

Hotel Mission Guanajuato (☎/fax 732-39-80), in the west of the city beside the Ex-Hacienda San Gabriel de Barrera at Km 2.5 on the Camino Antiguo a Marfil, has a restaurant, bar, swimming pool, tennis courts and 160 luxury rooms from US$103.

Places to Eat

A popular standby is *Restaurant Valadez*, opposite the Teatro Juárez on the corner of the Jardín de la Unión, open 8 am to 11 pm daily, serving economical breakfasts for US$2.50 and comida corrida for US$3.50.

East along Sopeña there is a good selection of places for a snack, meal or drink. *Café Galería* is a lively, popular, mid-priced place with outdoor tables across the street. *Café/Restaurant El Retiro (Sopeña 12)*, a few doors down, has a similar menu and prices, and live music in the evenings. *Café Veloce* offers an excellent pasta selection (around US$3) and a 1950s motorcycle-racing theme.

On Jardín de la Unión itself, *Hotel San Diego* has an elegant upstairs restaurant with several balcony tables overlooking the plaza – the breakfast specials and the US$4 comida corrida are the best values here. At the tables outside *Hotel Posada Santa Fé*, well-prepared antojitos will cost US$3 to US$6, and steak dishes around US$7. You might allow extra for wandering musicians.

At the north end of the Jardín, *Café/Restaurante Pinguis* has no sign out front, but is one of the most popular places in town for its good prices: big sandwiches, egg dishes, enchiladas and the comida corrida all cost between US$1.50 and US$2.50.

Pizza Piazza has branches at *(Hidalgo 14)* just off the Jardín de la Unión, on *(Plazuela San Fernando)* and at *(Juárez 69A)*. All are open daily from 2 to 11 pm and have a relaxed student atmosphere and good pizza at good prices – a US$4 *chica* size is enough for one or two, while a US$5.75 *mediana* can fill four.

South of the Jardín, up the hill behind the Templo de San Diego, *El Gallo Pitagórico* is in a bright blue building with a wonderful view over the city. The fine Italian and Mexican fare includes assorted antipasti

from US$2 to US$4, rich minestrone for US$2.50 and pastas from US$3 to US$5. It's worth the walk.

Truco 7 (Truco 7), near the basilica, is an intimate, artsy café/restaurant/gallery with a great atmosphere and delicious food at reasonable prices. An à la carte breakfast will cost under US$3, the comida corrida is inexpensive and more imaginative than most, and for dinner it's hard to spend more than US$4 for a main course. It's open 8.30 am to 11.30 pm daily.

For delicious chicken try *Restaurant La Carreta (Juárez 96)*, down toward the Mercado Hidalgo. Served with plenty of rice and salad, a quarter grilled chicken costs US$2 and a half chicken US$3.25 – take away or eat on the spot.

For fresh produce and local sweets, head west on Juárez to the *Mercado Hidalgo*, an impressive construction from the Porfiriato.

For vegetarian try *El Unicornio Azul*, on Hidalgo near Truco, a health food store with a couple of tables where you can enjoy a yogurt and fruit breakfast (US$0.80) or a soyburger (US$1.25).

West of here, just uphill from Plazuela de los Ángeles, another vegetarian option is *Restaurante Crisalido (Callejón de Calixto 20)*, a peaceful place serving breakfast or a tasty comida corrida (US$3). It's open 8 am to 6 pm Tuesday to Sunday.

Entertainment

Every evening, the Jardín de la Unión comes alive with students, tourists and others congregating there; the restaurants along one side of the plaza are popular for having a drink, people-watching and listening to the strolling musicians. There are free band concerts some evenings around 7 to 8 pm and on Sunday around noon to 2 pm.

On Friday, Saturday and Sunday at about 8 or 8.30 pm, *callejoneadas* start in front of Templo de San Diego, the church on the Jardín de la Unión. A group of professional songsters and musicians, dressed in traditional costumes, starts up, a crowd gathers, and the whole mob takes off winding around through the old alleys of the city, playing and singing heartily. On special occasions they take along a donkey laden with wine – at other times wine is stashed midpoint on the route. Stories and jokes (in Spanish) are told between songs. It's one of Guanajuato's most enjoyable traditions. It's free except for a small charge for the wine you drink. Tour companies and others may try to sell you tickets for the callejoneadas, but you don't need them!

Bars & Clubs South of the Jardín, behind the Templo de San Diego, *Bar Ocho* is a studenty hangout with pool tables and drink specials. The *Guanajuato Grill (Alonso 20)* is a dance and drink spot frequented by more affluent students. It's open most nights till 3 am, but it's really packed after midnight on Friday and Saturday. A more mature crowd congregates at *Rincón del Beso (Alonso 21A)*. Sometimes, after 11 pm, the live music and the booze kick in and it really gets going. There's no cover charge, though the drinks are a bit expensive.

For Latin and Andean sounds in an artsy, gay-friendly atmosphere, check out *La Dama de las Camelias (Sopeña 34)*, which has a vintage cool clientele and live music until very late.

Performing Arts Guanajuato has three fine theaters, the *Teatro Juárez, Teatro Principal* and *Teatro Cervantes*, none far from the Jardín de la Unión. From Thursday to Saturday, March to September, Guanajuato's theaters stage a variety of music, dance and literary events in the Viva la Mágica program. Check theater posters and the tourist office to see what's on.

Getting There & Away
The Central de Autobuses is on the southwest outskirts of town. Around 20 deluxe and 1st-class buses a day run to/from Mexico City's Terminal Norte by various companies, including ETN and Primera Plus (380km, 4½ hours, US$20 to US$27). To San Miguel de Allende (82km, 1½ hours) there are five 1st-class Primera Plus (US$6) and nine 2nd-class by Flecha Amarilla (US$4.50).

Getting Around
'Central de Autobuses' buses run frequently between the bus station and city center up to midnight. From the center, you can catch them heading west on Juárez, or on the north side of the basilica. A taxi costs US$2.50.

East of Mexico City

TEXCOCO AREA
● pop 19,000 ● elev 2778m
An outing to the little-visited area around the town of Texcoco, a short distance east of Mexico City, will reward you with a selection of the best of all Diego Rivera art and a pair of interesting historical sites.

Diego Rivera Murals
Some of Rivera's very finest mural work can be found at the Universidad Autónoma de Chapingo, an agriculture school just outside Texcoco, 21km northeast of Mexico City airport. In the chapel of a former hacienda, now part of the university's administration building, sensual murals intertwine images of the Mexican struggle for agrarian reform and the earth's fertility cycles. One of the 24 panels covering the chapel's walls and ceiling depicts buried martyrs of reform symbolically fertilizing the land and thus the future. The chapel is open 9 am to 3 pm Monday to Friday, 10 am to 2 pm Saturday and Sunday.

Frequent buses go from Mexico City's Terminal Oriente (TAPO) to downtown Texcoco. The direct route for drivers is the Autopista Peñón Texcoco toll road, which passes between the artificial lakes constructed since the 1970s to conserve a small portion of the pre-Hispanic Lago de Texcoco. Chapingo is about 2.5km south of downtown Texcoco, at Km 38.5 on Carretera Federal México-Texcoco (highway 136). If you have a *Guía Roji Ciudad de México* street atlas, look up Profesores in the index of *colonias* and you'll find the Universidad Autónoma. 'Chapingo' combis run there from downtown Texcoco.

Parque Nacional Molino de Flores

Also worth visiting in this area is this park, 3km east of Texcoco. Established in 1585 as the first wheat mill in the region, the Molino de Flores later served as a pulque hacienda before being expropriated by the government in 1937. Many of its buildings are in ruins, but some have been partly restored and opened for the public to explore its nooks and crannies. Works of local artists are exhibited in the *tinacal* where pulque was processed. A walk past the main building will take you to an unusual little church built into the side of a gorge, accessible on one side by a hanging bridge.

To get to the park, take a 'Molino de Flores' combi from downtown Texcoco.

Baños de Nezahualcóyotl

This little known archaeological site, 8km east of Texcoco, contains the remains of temples, a palace, fountains, spring-fed aqueducts and baths built by Nezahualcóyotl, Texcoco's 15th-century poet-king. Nezahualcóyotl was perhaps the only Mesoamerican ruler to observe a type of monotheistic religion, worshiping an abstract god with feminine and masculine qualities. The site is on a hilltop with a view as far as Xochimilco when the pollution isn't bad.

To get there, take a 'Tlamincas' combi from downtown Texcoco or from the right fork just outside the entrance to the Parque Nacional Molino de Flores, and get off at the sign pointing to the site. From there, it's a 1km walk to the summit.

POPOCATÉPETL & IZTACCÍHUATL

Mexico's two most famous mountains ('poh-poh-kah-TEH-petl' and 'iss-tah-SEE-watl') rise on the eastern rim of the Valle de México, 70km southeast of Mexico City and above the town of Amecameca. While the craterless Iztaccíhuatl (5286m) remains dormant, the classic cone of Popocatépetl (5452m) has in recent years spouted plumes of gas and ash, forcing the evacuation of 25,000 people and spurring experts to issue warnings to the 30 million people who live within striking distance of the volcano. It's been more than a thousand years since 'Popo' delivered a really big blast, but experts don't discount the possibility of one now, and the Mexican authorities are not allowing anyone on the mountain except scientists monitoring its activity.

The Mexican federal agency Cenapred (National Disaster Prevention Center) provides updated Popo information on its website (www.cenapred.unam.mx).

Iztaccíhuatl, the 'White Woman,' 20km north of Popo summit to summit, remains open to climbers. At the time of research it was also quite possible for anyone to go up to the Paso de Cortés, the pass between the two mountains, for a ramble – a potentially enjoyable day's outing from Mexico City.

Legend has it that Popo was a warrior who was in love with Izta, an emperor's daughter. Izta died of grief while Popo was away at war. Upon his return, he created two mountains, laid her body on one and stood holding her funeral torch on the other. With some imagination, Izta does resemble a woman lying on her back. From the Mexico City side you can, if the sky is clear, make out four peaks from north to south known as the Cabeza (Head), Pecho (Breast), Rodillas (Knees) and Pies (Feet).

Paso de Cortés

The Paso de Cortés – where Cortés and his conquistadors first laid eyes on Aztec Tenochtitlán – is at 3650m altitude and is reached by a 25km paved road up from the town of Amecameca (population 28,000; altitude 2480m), which lies in the valley to the west. For US$20, taxis from Amecameca's main plaza will take you to the La Joya parking lot on the flank of Izta (a fairly gentle 8km north from the Paso), wait for three hours, then take you back. La Joya, at about 4000m, is where most Izta ascents start. Trails lead through pine forests and grassy meadows, some offering breathtaking glimpses of the nearby peaks. You can walk down to Amecameca in about six hours.

The *Altzomoni* lodge, by a microwave station roughly halfway between the Paso de Cortés visitor's center and La Joya, offers basic accommodation at US$2 per person per night. Bring bedding and drinking water. The **San Carlos** hotel on Amecameca plaza has 30 clean, comfortable singles/doubles for US$5.25/8.50, US$5 more with TV.

From Mexico City's Terminal Oriente (TAPO), the 2nd-class Volcanes bus line runs every few minutes to/from Amecameca (1¼ hours, US$1.50). From the Amecameca bus station, turn right and walk two blocks to the plaza.

Climbing Iztaccíhuatl

All routes to Izta's highest peak, El Pecho (5286m), require a night on the mountain. On average, it takes five hours from La Joya to a shelter hut before Las Rodillas, six hours from the hut to El Pecho, and six hours back down to La Joya. It can be windy and well below freezing on the upper slopes of Izta any time of year, and it's nearly always below freezing near the summit at night. The average snow line is 4200m. The best months for ascents are October to February, when there is hard snow for crampons. February and March are sometimes prone to storms and poor visibility. The rainy season, April to September, brings the threat of whiteouts, thunderstorms and avalanches.

An ascent should be attempted by experienced climbers only, and because of hidden crevices on the ice-covered upper slopes, a guide is highly recommended. Mexico City-based Mario Andrade has led many Izta ascents. His fee is US$140 per person including transportation from Mexico City to Izta and back, lodging, national park entry fees and the use of rope. Contact Andrade, who speaks Spanish and English, at his Mexico City home (☎ 5-875-01-05). His mailing address is PO Box M-10380, México DF, Mexico.

In Amecameca, José Luis Ariza (☎ 5-978-13-35), a member of the rescue squad Búsqueda y Salvamento, leads climbers to Izta's summit year-round, charging US$100 for one person, US$50 for each additional person.

Altitude Sickness Lack of oxygen at altitudes over 2500m affects most people to some extent. Acute Mountain Sickness (AMS) has been fatal at 3000m, although 3500m to 4500m is the usual problem range. Symptoms usually develop during the first 24 hours at altitude but may be delayed up to three weeks. Mild symptoms include headache, lethargy, dizziness, difficulty sleeping and loss of appetite. AMS may become more severe without warning and can be fatal. Severe symptoms include breathlessness, a dry, irritative cough (which may progress to production of pink, frothy sputum), severe headache, lack of coordination and balance, confusion, drowsiness, irrational behavior, vomiting and unconsciousness.

Treat mild symptoms by resting at the same altitude until recovery, usually a day or two. Paracetamol or aspirin can be taken for headaches. If symptoms persist or become worse, however, *immediate descent is necessary* – even 500m can help.

To prevent AMS, it helps to ascend slowly, ideally spending two to three nights at each rise of 1000m; drink extra fluids (but not alcohol) and eat light, high-carbohydrate meals for energy. It's wise to sleep at a lower altitude than the greatest height reached during the day.

Hypothermia Hypothermia occurs when the body loses heat faster than it can produce it and the core temperature of the body falls. It is surprisingly easy to progress from very cold to dangerously cold due to a combination of wind, wet clothing, fatigue and hunger, even if the air temperature is above freezing. It's best to dress in layers; silk, wool and some of the new artificial fibers are all good insulating materials. A hat is important, as a lot of heat is lost through the head. A strong, waterproof outer layer (and a 'space' blanket for emergencies) are essential. Carry basic supplies, including food containing simple sugars to generate heat quickly and fluid to drink.

Symptoms of hypothermia are exhaustion, numbness (particularly in toes and fingers), shivering, slurred speech, irrational or violent behavior, lethargy, stumbling, dizzy spells, muscle cramps and violent bursts of energy. Irrationality may take the form of sufferers claiming they are warm and trying to take off their clothes.

To treat mild hypothermia, get victims out of the wind and/or rain and replace wet clothing with dry, warm clothing. Give them hot liquids – not alcohol – and some high-calorie, easily digestible food. Do not rub victims; instead, allow them slowly to warm themselves. Early recognition and treatment of mild hypothermia are the only ways to prevent severe hypothermia, which is a critical condition.

PUEBLA

• pop 1.2 million • elev 2162m ☎ 2

Puebla, 130km east of Mexico City by road, is one of Mexico's best-preserved colonial cities. More than 70 churches and 1000 other colonial buildings cluster in the central area alone – many adorned with the hand-painted tiles for which the city is famous. The city is also a lively modern metropolis with a lot to see and do.

Founded by Spanish settlers in 1531, Puebla quickly grew into an important Catholic religious center. It was Mexico's second-biggest city until Guadalajara overtook it in the 19th century. In recent decades Puebla has seen huge industrial growth.

An earthquake on June 15, 1999 killed at least 20 people in Puebla and damaged many colonial buildings. Repairs will go on until at least mid-2001, and when you visit you may still find some buildings and museums closed for reconstruction.

Orientation & Information

Buses arrive at the modern Central de Autobuses de Puebla (CAPU), on the northern edge of the city. The city's heart is the spacious, shady zócalo, with the cathedral on its south side. Most places to stay, eat and visit are within a few blocks of here. Farther away, particularly to the north and west, you soon enter dirtier, poorer streets.

The helpful, English-speaking state tourist office (☎ 246-12-85) is at 5 Ote 3, facing the cathedral yard; it's open 9 am to 8.30 pm Monday to Saturday, 9 am to 2 pm

---

Puebla Pottery

Fine pottery has long been made from Puebla's local clay. At the time of the Spanish conquest, the colorful glazed Mixteca-Cholula-Puebla pottery was the finest in the land. The Aztec king Moctezuma, it was said, would eat off no other. After the Spanish colonists introduced new materials and techniques, Puebla pottery developed fast as an art and an industry. The city's colorful hand-painted ceramics, known as Talavera after a town in Spain, take many forms – plates, cups, vases, fountains, *azulejos* (tiles) – and designs show Asian, Spanish-Arabic and indigenous Mexican influences. Since the 17th century Puebla tiles have been used to fine effect on church domes and, with red brick, on building façades.

Quite a few shops along 18 Pte display and sell pretty Puebla ceramics. The big pieces are expensive and difficult to carry, but you could buy a small hand-painted Talavera tile for US$2 or US$3, or a plate for US$10. The Talavera Uriarte showroom, 4 Pte 911, has an on-site pottery factory, where tours are given Monday to Friday till 1 pm.

Sunday. The municipal tourist office (☎ 232-03-57), nearby on the corner of 2 Nte and Palafox y Mendoza, is open 9 am to 8 pm Monday to Friday, 9 am to 6 pm Saturday, 9 am to 3 pm Sunday.

Several city-center banks change money and traveler's checks, including Banamex, Bancomer and Bital (all with ATMs) on Reforma within two blocks west of the zócalo.

The main post office is on 16 de Septiembre, south of the cathedral. Cybercafé at 2 Sur 907 charges US$1.75 an hour for Internet access.

Museum Hours Nearly all Puebla museums are open 10 am to 5 pm daily except Monday. Admission prices vary; most are free on Sunday. The main exception to these rules is the Museo Amparo.

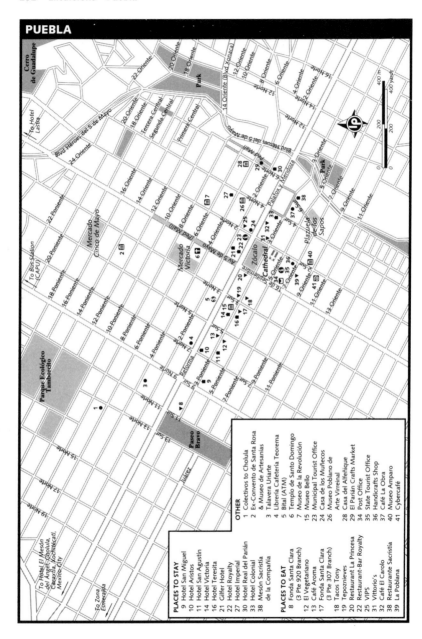

PUEBLA

PLACES TO STAY
9 Hotel San Miguel
10 Hotel Aristos
11 Hotel San Agustín
14 Hotel Victoria
16 Hotel Teresita
21 Gilfer Hotel
22 Hotel Royalty
27 Hotel Imperial
30 Hotel Real del Parián
33 Hotel Colonial
38 Mesón Sacristía
   de la Compañía

PLACES TO EAT
8 Fonda Santa Clara
   (3 Pte 920 Branch)
12 El Vegetariano
13 Café Aroma
17 Fonda Santa Clara
   (3 Pte 307 Branch)
18 Tacos Tony
19 Tepoznieves
20 Restaurant La Princesa
22 Restaurant-Bar Royalty
25 VIPS
31 Vittorio's
32 Café El Carolo
38 Restaurante Sacristía
39 La Poblana

OTHER
1 Colectivos a Cholula
2 Ex-Convento de Santa Rosa
   & Museo de Artesanías
3 Talavera Uriarte
4 Librería Cafetería Teorema
5 Bital (ATM)
6 Templo de Santo Domingo
7 Museo de la Revolución
15 Museo Bello
23 Municipal Tourist Office
24 Casa de los Muñecos
26 Museo Poblano de
   Arte Virreinal
28 Casa del Alfeñique
29 El Parián Crafts Market
34 Post Office
35 State Tourist Office
36 Handicrafts Shop
37 Café La Obra
40 Museo Amparo
41 Cybercafé

Zócalo

Puebla's arcaded central plaza was a marketplace before it acquired its current gardenlike appearance in 1854. The **cathedral** to its south, considered one of Mexico's best proportioned, was built between 1550 and 1650 and blends severe Herreresque Renaissance style with early baroque. Its bells are celebrated in the traditional rhyme *'Para mujeres y campanas, las poblanas'* – 'For women and bells, Puebla's (are best).'

South of the Zócalo

The excellent modern **Museo Amparo**, 2 Sur at 9 Ote, is a must-see. It's housed in two linked colonial buildings. The first has eight rooms with superb pre-Hispanic artifacts, well displayed with excellent explanations in English and Spanish. The second, a fascinating contrast, is rich with the finest art and furnishings from the colonial period. The museum is open daily except Tuesday, from 10 am to 6 pm (US$1.75, free on Monday) and has a cafeteria and a very good bookstore.

The **Museo Bello**, 3 Pte 302 at 3 Sur, is filled with the diverse art and crafts collection of 19th-century industrialist José Luis Bello and his son Mariano. It includes exquisite French, English, Japanese and Chinese porcelain, and a large collection of Pueblan Talavera. Cost is US$1.25 (free Tuesday). Tours are available in Spanish and English.

East of the Zócalo

The tiles on the **Casa de los Muñecos** (House of the Puppets) on 2 Nte, near the zócalo's northeast corner, caricature the city fathers who took its owner to court because his home was taller than theirs.

The **Museo Poblano de Arte Virreinal**, on 4 Nte, is a top-notch museum opened in 1999. Housed in the 17th-century Hospital de San Pedro, it displays a fascinating exhibit on the hospital's history and stages temporary shows of colonial-period art. The museum has an excellent bookstore (US$1.75).

The **Casa del Alfeñique**, at 6 Nte and 4 Ote, is an outstanding example of the 18th-century Puebla decorative style *alfeñique* – elaborate white stucco ornamentation named after a type of candy. Inside is the Museo del Estado with 18th- and 19th-century Puebla paraphernalia (US$1.50).

North of the Zócalo

The **Museo de la Revolución**, 6 Ote 206, was the scene of the first battle of the Mexican Revolution in 1910. Betrayed two days before the main uprising started, the Serdán family (Aquiles, Máximo, Carmen and Natalia) and 17 others fought 500 soldiers until only Aquiles, their leader, and Carmen were left alive. Aquiles, hidden under the floorboards, might have survived if a cough hadn't given him away. The house retains bullet holes, and the museum has memorabilia and a room dedicated to women of the revolution (US$1.50).

The **Templo de Santo Domingo** on Avenida 5 de Mayo is a fine church, but its Capilla del Rosario (Rosary Chapel), south of the main altar, is a gem. Built between 1680 and 1720, the chapel has a sumptuous baroque proliferation of gilded plaster and carved stone with angels and cherubim popping out from behind every leaf. See if you can spot the heavenly orchestra.

The **Ex-Convento de Santa Rosa & Museo de Artesanías**, on 14 Pte, is a 17th-century ex-nunnery housing an extensive collection of Puebla state handicrafts. You must take an English or Spanish tour with a guide, who may try to rush you through the fine displays of indigenous costumes, pottery, onyx, glass and metalwork (US$1.50).

Cerro de Guadalupe

This hilltop park, 2km northeast of the zócalo, was the site of a rare Mexican military triumph. On May 5, 1862, 2000 Mexicans under General Ignacio de Zaragoza defeated a frontal attack by 6000 French invaders, a lot of whom were suffering from a handicap experienced by many foreigners in Mexico, diarrhea. This victory is the excuse for annual Mexican national celebrations and hundreds of streets named in honor of Cinco de Mayo (May 5). Everyone quite conveniently forgets that the following year the reinforced French took Puebla and occupied the city until 1867.

Good views, relatively fresh air and eucalyptus groves add to the attractions of a visit. Take bus No 72 up Avenida 5 de Mayo (US$0.30).

The **Fuerte de Loreto** at the west end of the hilltop was one of the Mexican defense points in 1862. Today it houses the Museo de la No Intervención, with displays relating to the French occupation (US$2). A short walk east are the **Museo Regional de Puebla** (US$2.25), tracing human history in Puebla state, and the **Museo de Historia Natural** (US$1.25). At the east end of the hilltop is the **Fuerte de Guadalupe** (US$2), which also played a part in the Cinco de Mayo battle.

Places to Stay

Budget One and a half blocks west of the zócalo is the *Hotel Teresita* (☎ 232-70-72, 3 Pte 309). It has carpeted singles/doubles with tiled baths and good beds for US$12/19.

Hotel Victoria (☎ 232-89-92, 3 Pte 306), across the street, is gloomy and faded, but friendly enough and clean. Rooms with private bathrooms are US$7.50/13.

A block west, *Hotel San Agustín* (☎ 232-50-89, 3 Pte 531) is cleaner than the Victoria, with better beds, but pricier at US$15/19 for small, rather stuffy rooms with tiny TVs. Breakfast and parking are included in the price, however.

Just south of El Parián crafts market is the friendly *Hotel Real del Parián* (☎ 246-19-68, 2 Ote 601). At US$8.50/12.50, its freshly painted rooms are a good deal. If possible, choose one with a balcony.

Mid-Range Four blocks west of the zócalo, *Hotel San Miguel* (☎ 242-48-60, 3 Pte 721) has clean, respectably sized singles/doubles with private bath and TV for US$20/26. *Hotel Imperial* (☎ 242-49-80, 4 Ote 212) offers facilities such as voice mail, fax, photocopying, parking, gym, pool table and even *golfito* – a two-hole miniature golf course in the back patio – as well as 65 comfortable rooms from US$20/29 to US$22/36.

Some of the pricier mid-range places have lots of charm. *Hotel Colonial* (☎ 246-41-99, 4 Sur 105), a block east of the zócalo, offers lovely rooms for US$29/36 – an excellent value. Once part of a Jesuit monastery, it maintains a hearty colonial atmosphere despite modernization. It's often full, so reserve ahead.

The 45-room *Hotel Royalty* (☎ 242-47-40, Portal Hidalgo 8), on the zócalo, is another well-kept colonial-style place. Rooms, at US$31/40, are comfortable and colorful, though on the small side. The 92-room *Gilfer Hotel* (☎ 246-06-11, 2 Ote 11), one block off the zócalo, has comfortable modern rooms for US$29/36.

Top End At the *Hotel Aristos* (☎ 232-05-65, Reforma 533) there are 120 air-conditioned but not particularly spacious rooms. The normal price of US$65 drops to a very reasonable US$30 on weekends.

For a splurge, head for the *Mesón Sacristía de la Compañía* (☎ 242-35-54, 6 Sur 304) in an 18th-century building in the Barrio de los Sapos. The hotel combines modern comfort with colonial splendor – at a price. Rooms cost US$96, and two fabulous suites with canopied king-size beds are US$133.

The 51-room *Hotel Lastra* (☎ 235-97-55, Calzada de los Fuertes 2633), 2km northeast of the zócalo on the Cerro de Guadalupe, offers a peaceful location, good views, easy parking and a pleasing garden. Singles/doubles go for US$56/60 Monday to Thursday, US$46/49 Friday to Sunday. The basic rate at the 190-room *Hotel El Mesón del Ángel* (☎ 223-83-67, Hermanos Serdán 807, 6km northwest of the center, just off the Mexico City highway, is US$140.

Places to Eat

The zócalo's culinary highlight is the Italian-run *Vittorio's*, on the east side. Good individual-size pizzas are US$3 to US$6; *grande* (three- or four-person) pies are US$8 to US$15. The large *Restaurant La Princesa* (Portal Juárez 101), on the zócalo's west side, is packed at lunchtime for its five-course *cubiertos* (set meals) (US$4.25). On the plaza's north side, you can watch the world go by from the outdoor tables of the smart **Restaurant-Bar Royalty** for the price of a cappuccino (US$1.75). Fish and meat dishes run to US$10.

There's a **VIPS** in a beautiful 19th-century cast-iron building on the corner of 2 Ote and 2 Nte. **Café El Carolo** on Palafox y Mendoza, half a block east of the zócalo, serves fruit salad, yogurt and other healthy stuff cheap, and a comida corrida for only US$2.

Tepoznieves, on 3 Pte at 3 Sur, is Puebla's top ice creamery – it has lovely tables and chairs at which to enjoy many exotic flavors, including hibiscus and tequila.

El Vegetariano (3 Pte 525), open from 7.30 am to 9.30 pm, has a long menu of meat-less dishes such as *nopales rellenos* (stuffed cactus ears) and *enchiladas suizas*, all of which come with salad, soup and a drink for around US$3.50 (on their own for about US$2.50). **Café Aroma** (3 Pte 520), across the street, is the place to go for good coffee.

A *pan árabe* taco (made with pita bread instead of a tortilla) costs around US$0.75 at **Tacos Tony**, on 3 Pte a block west of the zócalo. Enormous cones of seasoned pork keep grilling till 9.30 pm.

Entertainment

A bookstore-cum-café, **Librería Cafetería Teorema**, Reforma at 7 Nte, fills up in the evenings with an arty/student crowd. Live music runs most nights from 9.30 pm to 1 am, with a cover charge averaging US$2.

At night mariachis lurk around the Callejón de los Sapos, a pedestrian section of 6 Sur, but they're being crowded out by the studenty bars on the nearby Plazuela de los Sapos, many of which become live music venues after dark. **Café La Obra**, nearby on 3 Ote, serves up live jazz and blues on Sunday afternoon.

A number of trendy dance clubs and *antros* (music bars) are spread around the 'Zona Esmeralda' on Juárez west of Paseo Bravo. Among them, usually with US$2 to US$3 cover charge, are **Corcores**, **Bar y Tono**, the disco **Tasaja** and **Portos Tropical** for salsa and merengue.

Shopping

Ceramics apart (see 'Puebla Pottery'), Puebla is a good place to look for crafts from elsewhere in Puebla state. Indigenous textiles and pottery can be found at the state-run handicrafts shop on 7 Ote near 2 Sur, and at the Centro Artesanal Segusino upstairs in the Mercado Victoria.

El Parián crafts market, between 2 and 4 Ote, east of 6 Norte, has a big variety of crafts – a lot of tacky souvenirs but also some good stuff, and prices are generally reasonable.

Antique shops dominate the Callejón de los Sapos, and on Sundays the Plazuela de los Sapos is the site of a lively outdoor antiques market.

Chocolate & Chicken

Mole poblano, found on almost every menu in Puebla and imitated Mexico-wide, is a spicy chocolate sauce, and it's usually served over turkey or chicken. Supposedly invented by Sor (Sister) Andrea de la Asunción of the Convento de Santa Rosa for a visit by the viceroy, it traditionally contains fresh chili, chipotle, pepper, peanuts, almonds, cinnamon, aniseed, tomato, onion, garlic and, of course, chocolate. If well prepared, it's a real taste sensation!

A super place to try *poblano* food, with two branches, is **Fonda Santa Clara** (3 Pte 307) and (3 Pte 920). No 307 is nearer to the zócalo but No 920 has a more festive atmosphere. The Santa Clara's delicious chicken mole costs US$7.50. Also tasty is the *mixiotes* – a stew of sliced mutton tied in a maguey-leaf bundle, served with guacamole (US$7.50). Another good option for poblano cuisine is the **Restaurant Sacristía** (6 Sur 304), in a delightful colonial patio. An average three-course meal is about US$10.

La Poblana (7 Ote 17), around the corner from the Museo Amparo, fixes authentic Puebla *cemitas*, sesame bread rolls filled with *chiles rellenos*, white cheese or ham and the herb *pápalo* (US$1).

Getting There & Away

Buses to/from Mexico City use the Terminal Oriente (TAPO) in the capital. The trip takes about two hours. Estrella Roja Pullman Plus (deluxe), Primera Más and ADO (1st-class) and Estrella Roja and AU (2nd-class) all run frequent services for US$5 to US$6.50. Puebla's bus station, the Central de Autobuses de Puebla (CAPU), is 4km north of the zócalo, by the corner of Boulevard Norte and Boulevard Carmen Serdán.

Tolls for cars from Mexico City on the fast highway 150D total US$8.50.

Getting Around

From the bus station to the center, you can take a taxi (US$2 ticket from the kiosk). Alternatively, leave the bus station at the 'Autobuses Urbanos' sign, take the ramp and cross the bridge over Boulevard Norte: on the far side, walk west to the Chedraui supermarket and catch a No 40 combi to 16 de Septiembre four blocks south of the zócalo. The ride takes 15 to 20 minutes.

From the city center to the bus station, get any 'CAPU' colectivo from 9 Sur or 9 Norte, four blocks west of the zócalo. All city buses, combis and colectivos cost US$0.30.

AROUND PUEBLA
Cholula

• pop 24,000 • elev 2170m ☎ 2

Ten kilometers west of Puebla stands the largest pyramid ever built, Pirámide Tepanapa – the Great Pyramid of Cholula. At 450 sq meters and 65m high it was even larger in volume than Egypt's Pyramid of Cheops. But because it's now overgrown and topped by a church, it's a bit hard to even recognize the huge mound as a pyramid at all.

Cholula, today a small, dusty sort of place, was one of central Mexico's largest cities in pre-Hispanic times. By 1519 it was under Aztec rule and had a population of 100,000, though the Great Pyramid was already overgrown. Aztec warriors set an ambush for Cortés here, but the Spaniards were tipped off and struck first, massacring 6000 Cholulans in one day.

Arriving buses and colectivos drop you two or three blocks north of Cholula's zócalo. Two long blocks east of there, the pyramid with its domed church on top is a clear landmark. Cholula has a helpful tourist office (☎ 247-18-97) at 4 Pte 103A, half a block northwest of the zócalo, open 10 am to 8 pm.

Zona Arqueológica You can climb to the church of **Nuestra Señora de los Remedios**, atop the **Great Pyramid**, by a path from the pyramid's northwest corner; there is no admission charge.

The Zona Arqueológica comprises the excavated areas around the pyramid and the tunnels underneath. Entry is via a tunnel on the north side, open 10 am to 6 pm daily (US$2, free on Sunday and holidays). The fee includes entry to a small **museum**, which is across the road from the ticket office and provides the best introduction to the site – a large cutaway model of the pyramid showing its many reconstructions.

More than 8km of **tunnels** have been dug beneath the pyramid by archaeologists, to penetrate each of its building stages. Guides at the entrance to the tourist access tunnel offer one-hour tours for US$4.25 (sometimes in English); they can be useful in explaining features of the site, as nothing is labeled.

The tunnel emerges on the east side of the pyramid, from where a path leads around to the **Patio de los Altares**, or Great Plaza, which is on the south side. This was the main approach to the pyramid, and it's ringed by platforms and unique diagonal stairways. At its south end is an Aztec-style altar in a pit: human bones indicate this was probably a sacrificial site. On the west side of the mound is a reconstructed section of the final pyramid, with two earlier layers exposed to view.

Zócalo The **Ex-Convento de San Gabriel** (former San Gabriel Monastery), along the east side of Cholula's wide zócalo, includes three fine churches. On the left, as you face the ex-convento, is the Arabic-style **Capilla Real**, dating from 1540, unique in Mexico because of its 49 domes. In the middle is the

17th-century **Capilla del Tercer Orden**, and on the right the **Templo de San Gabriel**, founded in 1530 on the site of a pyramid.

Places to Eat About the most popular place in town is the **Café Enamorada**, at the southwest corner of the zócalo. Sandwiches go for US$1.50 to US$3, and tostadas, quesadillas and tacos for about US$2.50. Underneath the zócalo's attractive portales, **Los Jarrones** serves set breakfasts at very fair prices: under US$3 gets you a plate of waffles, a dish of mixed fruit with yogurt and two cups of good coffee.

Restaurant Güero's (*Avenida Hidalgo 101*), across from the zócalo, is a cheerful spot decorated with antique photos of Cholula. Among its hearty Mexican favorites are *pozole*, *cemitas* and quesadillas served with a delicious *salsa roja* (US$1.50 for an order of three).

Getting There & Away Frequent colectivos to Cholula leave from the corner of 6 Pte and 13 Nte in Puebla (20 minutes, US$0.50). Frequent Estrella Roja buses between Mexico City's Terminal Oriente (TAPO) and Puebla stop in Cholula on 12 Pte.

Tonantzintla & Acatepec

The **Templo de Santa María** in Tonantzintla, 4km south of Cholula, has one of the most exuberant church interiors in Mexico. Every available surface under the dome is covered with colorful stucco saints, devils, flowers, fruit, birds and more – a great example of indigenous artisanship applied to Christian themes.

The **Templo de San Francisco** in Acatepec, 1.5km southeast of Tonantzintla, dates from about 1730. The exterior is brilliantly decorated with blue, green and yellow Puebla tiles set in red brick on an ornate Churrigueresque façade.

Both these small churches are open 10 am to 1 pm and 3 to 5 pm daily.

Autobuses Puebla-Cholula runs 'Chipilo' buses from the Puebla bus station to Tonantzintla and Acatepec. In Cholula you can pick them up on the corner of 7 Pte and Miguel Alemán.

Cacaxtla & Xochitécatl

The hilltop ruins at Cacaxtla, about 35km northwest of Puebla, discovered in 1975, feature vividly colored and well-preserved frescoes showing, among many other scenes, nearly life-size warriors engaged in battle. The older ruins at Xochitécatl, atop a higher hill 2km west, include an exceptionally wide pyramid as well as a circular pyramid. Excavations at Xochitécatl began in 1969 but the site was not opened to the public until 1994. Both these interesting sites are open 10 am to 5.30 pm daily (US$2.75, free on Sunday and holidays). One ticket is good for both. It is possible to hire a guide at the site Thursday to Sunday.

Cacaxtla was the capital of a group of Olmeca-Xicallanca or Putún Maya, who first arrived in central Mexico as early as 400 AD. It peaked from 650 to 900 AD. Many of the symbols in its murals display a unique combination of highland Mexican and Mayan influences that is the subject of much speculation.

Xochitécatl predated Christ by a millennium. Experts agree that whereas the

A peek of the Ex-Convento de San Gabriel

GREG ELMS

Cacaxtla site primarily served as living quarters for its ruling class, Xochitécatl was chiefly used for gory ceremonies to honor Quecholli, the fertility god. Which isn't to say that Cacaxtla didn't hold similar ceremonies; the skeletal remains of mutilated children attest to Cacaxtla's bloody past.

Cacaxtla From the parking lot, it's a 200m walk to the ticket office, museum, shop and restaurant. Then it's 300m more to the site's main feature, a natural platform 200m long and 25m high called the **Gran Basamento** (Great Base), now under a huge metal roof. Here stood Cacaxtla's main buildings and the residences of its ruling priests. At the top of the entry stairs is an open space called the **Plaza Norte**. Follow a clockwise path around the ruins until you reach the murals.

Before the first mural, you come to an **altar** fronted by a small square pit in which the remains of 218 mutilated children were found. They are thought to have been sacrificed to the water god Tláloc as an appeal for rain. Just beyond the altar is the **Templo de Venus**, with two figures in blue – a man and a woman, wearing short jaguar skins.

The **Templo Rojo** (named for the amount of red paint used), nearly opposite the Templo de Venus, contains four murals but only one is currently visible. Its weird imagery is dominated by a row of maize crops whose husks contain human heads.

Facing the north side of the Plaza Norte is the long **Mural de la Batalla** (Battle Mural), dating from before 700 AD. It shows two groups of warriors, one wearing jaguar skins and the other bird feathers, engaged in a battle. The Olmeca-Xicallanca (the jaguar-warriors, with round shields) are clearly repelling the invading Huastecs from northeast Mexico (the bird-warriors, with jade ornaments and deformed skulls).

At the end of the Mural de la Batalla, turn left and climb some steps to the second main **murals group**, to your right behind a fence. The two major murals, from about 750 AD, show a figure in jaguar costume and a black-painted figure in bird costume (who may be the Olmeca-Xicallanca priest-governor) standing on a plumed serpent.

Xochitécatl From the Xochitécatl parking lot a path leads around to the circular **Pirámide en Espiral**, topped by a cross placed by local villagers long before archaeologists confirmed the hill contained a pyramid. Archaeologists believe this circular pyramid was built between 1000 and 800 BC. Its form and hilltop location suggest it may have been an astronomical observation post or a temple to Ehecatl, the wind god.

The path then leads to the **Basamento de los Volcanes**, a two-phase pyramid of which only the base remains. In parts it's possible to see the original stone. Later, cut square stones were placed over the original stones and stuccoed over.

Next is the **Pirámide de la Serpiente**, which gets its name from a large piece of carved stone with part of the head of a snake at one end. The huge stone pot found at its center was carved from a single boulder hauled from another region. Scientists surmise it was used to hold water.

The last pyramid is the large **Pirámide de las Flores** (Pyramid of Flowers). Experts speculate that rituals honoring the fertility god were held here. Inside the pyramid there were several sculptures and the remains of 30 sacrificed infants found. Near the pyramid's base is a pool carved from a massive rock. It's thought that the infants were probably washed in the pool before being killed.

Getting There & Away The Cacaxtla site is 1.5km uphill from a back road between San Martín Texmelucan (near highway 190) and Zacatelco on highway 119, which is a secondary road between Puebla and Tlaxcala. A sign on the back road, 1.5km west of the village of Nativitas, points to Cacaxtla and the nearby village of San Miguel del Milagro. A 'Zacatelco-San Martín' bus from the Puebla bus station will drop you at this turnoff. They leave every 10 minutes; tickets are sold at the Flecha Azul desk. Or you can get a bus to Zacatelco, then a minibus to San Miguel del Milagro, which will drop you 300m from the site. From Cacaxtla to Xochitécatl, you can take a taxi (US$3) or hike the 2km.

By car, turn west off highway 119 at the 'Cacaxtla' sign just north of Zacatelco. From there it's 7.5km to the Cacaxtla turnoff.

South of Mexico City

TEPOZTLÁN
• pop 14,000 • elev 1701m ☎ 7

A few kilometers east of highway 95D, 80km from Mexico City, Tepoztlán (Place of Copper) sits in a valley surrounded by high, jagged cliffs. It's a magical place, the legendary birthplace more than 1200 years ago of Quetzalcóatl, the potent pre-Hispanic feathered serpent god. The town retains indigenous traditions, with many older people still speaking the Náhuatl language, and younger people now learning it in secondary school. It's well known for its *curanderos* (traditional healers). Also something of an international New Age venue, Tepoztlán attracts writers, artists and astrologers who feel the place has a creative energy, as well as many more conventional weekenders

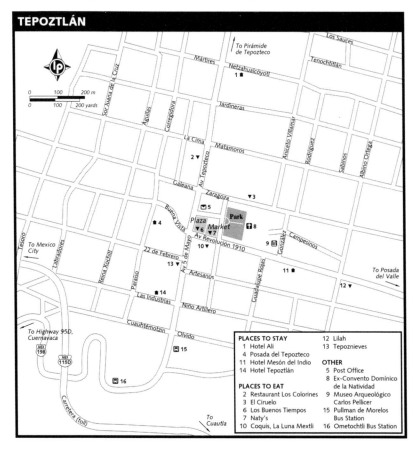

TEPOZTLÁN

PLACES TO STAY
1 Hotel Ali
4 Posada del Tepozteco
11 Hotel Mesón del Indio
14 Hotel Tepoztlán

PLACES TO EAT
2 Restaurant Los Colorines
3 El Ciruelo
6 Los Buenos Tiempos
7 Naty's
10 Coquis, La Luna Mextli

12 Lilah
13 Tepoznieves

OTHER
5 Post Office
8 Ex-Convento Domínico
   de la Natividad
9 Museo Arqueológico
   Carlos Pellicer
15 Pullman de Morelos
   Bus Station
16 Ometochtli Bus Station

from Mexico City. In the mid-1990s the locals successfully banded together to fight off a plan for a large golf club complex – planned by Jack Nicklaus, no less – which they feared would threaten their water supplies. Traces of the conflict are still visible in the form of widespread graffiti.

Just about everything here is accessible on foot.

Ex-Convento Domínico de la Natividad

This former monastery and the attached church were built for Dominican monks between 1560 and 1588 and are the dominant feature of the town. The plateresque church façade has Dominican seals interspersed with indigenous symbols, floral designs and various figures including the sun, moon and stars, animals, angels and the Virgin Mary.

The monastery section is undergoing major restoration. Some 4500 sq meters of murals from the 16th and 17th centuries have been meticulously restored. The cells of the west wing house a museum covering the region's natural history, economy, social organization and religion. The monastery is open 10 am to 5 pm Tuesday through Sunday (free).

Museo Arqueológico Carlos Pellicer

This museum, at González 2 (behind the Dominican church), has a small but interesting collection of pieces from many parts of Mexico, donated to the people of Tepoztlán by the scholar and poet Carlos Pellicer Cámara from Tabasco state. The pieces of pre-Hispanic art on display are lively and vibrant, with an emphasis on human figures but also some animals. The museum is open 10 am to 6 pm Tuesday to Sunday (US$0.50).

Pirámide de Tepozteco

The 10m-high Pyramid of Tepozteco is visible at the top of the cliffs north of Tepoztlán, 400m above the town. It honors Tepoztécatl, the Aztec god of the harvest, fertility and pulque and is accessible by a steep path from the end of Avenida Tepozteco – a strenuous climb of one to 1½ hours. At the top you may be rewarded with a panorama of Tepoztlán and the valley, depending on haze levels.

The site is open 9.30 am to 5.30 pm daily (US$1.50). It's best to climb early, when the air is clear and before it gets hot. Hiking boots or at least good tennis shoes are recommended.

Special Events

Tepoztlán is a festive place, where there are many Christian festivals superimposed on pagan celebrations. Carnaval, on the five days preceding Ash Wednesday, features the colorful Huehuenches and Chinelos dances, with feathered headdresses and beautifully embroidered costumes. El Reto del Tepozteco, an all-night festival on September 7, is celebrated on Tepozteco hill near the pyramid, with copious consumption of pulque and *ponche* in honor of the god Tepoztécatl.

Places to Stay

It can be difficult to find inexpensive accommodations on weekends. About the cheapest place is the *Hotel Mesón del Indio (☎ 395-02-38, Avenida Revolución 1910 No 44)*; its sign is barely larger than a loaf of bread. This is a friendly little place with eight small, moldy rooms beside a garden, each with private bath and hot water, costing US$12/13 for singles/doubles. *Hotel Ali (☎ 395-19-71, Netzahualcóyotl 2)*, north of the center, is a homey place featuring several large suites with king-size beds, spacious bathrooms and sitting rooms for US$40. A tiny room on the roof goes for US$26.

The better hotels cater to the weekend crowd from Mexico City, and are expensive. *Hotel Tepoztlán (☎ 395-05-22, Las Industrias 6)* is a health-resort-style hotel with 36 singles/doubles at US$49/66, a pool, restaurant and bar. *Posada del Tepozteco (☎ 395-00-10, Paraíso 3)*, only a short walk from the central plaza, was built as a hillside hacienda in the 1930s and has two pools, a restaurant/ bar and terraces with panoramic views of the town and valley. The 18 rooms cost from

US$82; suites with private spa baths start at US$104.

Posada del Valle (☎ 395-05-21, *Camino a Mextitla 5*) has a pool, majestic mountain views and quiet, romantic rooms for US$61. To get there take Avenida Revolución 1910 east for 2km, then follow signs the remaining 100m to the hotel.

Places to Eat
Many of the better restaurants close from Monday to Thursday. Avenida Revolución 1910 has a varied string of eateries, including *Naty's* at No 7, an inexpensive spot to breakfast and watch the action in the market. Fancier and more expensive places like *Coquis* at No 10 and *La Luna Mextli* at No 16 are combinations of restaurant, bar and art gallery.

For a bit of good traditional Mexican food, try **Restaurant Los Colorines** (*Avenida Tepozteco 13*). This popular restaurant with vibrant decor offers a variety of dishes from US$2 to US$5 and a large selection of tequilas served in tiny clay mugs.

Lilah, at the bottom of Avenida Revolución 1910 where the asphalt begins, offers wonderful organic salads from its own garden for around US$4, plus other veggie fare. *El Ciruelo* (*Zaragoza 17*) is an elegant restaurant/bar that hosts live jazz on Friday and Saturday nights.

An obligatory stop in Tepoztlán is the ice cream emporium **Tepoznieves**, scooping up 70 flavors, including cactus fruit and pineapple-chili. **Los Buenos Tiempos** is a cool stall at the edge of the market on Avenida Revolución 1910, serving perhaps Tepoztlán's finest coffee, espresso, cappuccino and homemade strudels from 8.30 am.

Shopping
On weekends, Tepoztlán's market stalls sell a melange of handicrafts, including sarapes, embroidery, weaving, carvings, baskets and pottery. There's some good stuff. Shops in the adjacent streets also have interesting wares (some from Bali and India) at upscale prices. A local craft is cute miniature houses and villages carved from the corklike spines of the *pochote* tree.

Getting There & Away
First-class Pullman de Morelos buses run hourly between Mexico City's Terminal Sur and Tepoztlán till 8 pm (1¼ hours, US$3.75). The Tepoztlán terminal (it's not exactly a bus station) is at Avenida 5 de Mayo 35 at the southern entrance to town. Ometochtli buses to Cuernavaca (23km, 30 minutes, US$1) go every 15 minutes, 5 am to 9 pm, from their terminal on the road south of town on the way to the autopista. Buses to Oaxtepec (15 minutes, US$0.75) can be picked up at the *caseta* (tollbooth) on the autopista outside town. Pullman de Morelos runs free combis between the 5 de Mayo terminal and the gas station near the autopista entrance; from there, walk down the left (exit) ramp to the caseta.

CUERNAVACA
● pop 311,000 ● elev 1480m ☎ 7

With a mild climate, once described as 'eternal spring,' Cuernavaca ('kwehr-nah-VAH-kah'), the capital of the state of Morelos, 90km south of Mexico City, has been a retreat from the big city since colonial times. Many wealthy and fashionable folk from Mexico and abroad stayed on to become semipermanent residents, and a number of their residences have become attractions in themselves, now housing museums, galleries, expensive restaurants and hotels. As the local population grows and more and more visitors come, especially on weekends, Cuernavaca is unfortunately losing some of its charm and acquiring the problems that people from the capital try to escape – crowds, traffic, smog and crime.

It's certainly a city whose elegance is best appreciated by those with money to spend. Try to save some pesos to enjoy the food and ambiance at some of the better restaurants. A lot of visitors stay longer to enroll in one of the many Spanish-language schools, and they find Cuernavaca a pleasant city with an enjoyable social life.

History
Pre-Hispanic settlers in the area around 1220 developed a highly productive agricultural society based at Cuauhnáhuac (Place

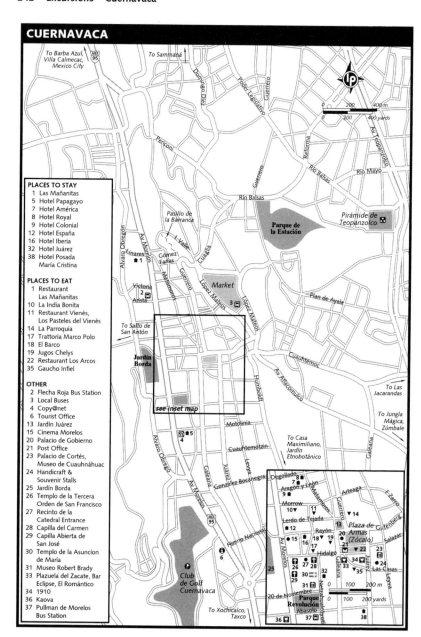

CUERNAVACA

To Barba Azul,
Villa Calmecac,
Mexico City

To Sammaná

PLACES TO STAY
1 Las Mañanitas
5 Hotel Papagayo
7 Hotel América
8 Hotel Royal
9 Hotel Colonial
12 Hotel España
16 Hotel Iberia
32 Hotel Juárez
38 Hotel Posada
María Cristina

PLACES TO EAT
1 Restaurant
Las Mañanitas
10 La India Bonita
11 Restaurant Vienés,
Los Pasteles del Vienés
14 La Parroquia
17 Trattoria Marco Polo
18 El Barco
19 Jugos Chelys
22 Restaurant Los Arcos
35 Gaucho Infiel

OTHER
2 Flecha Roja Bus Station
3 Local Buses
4 Copy@net
6 Tourist Office
13 Jardín Juárez
15 Cinema Morelos
20 Palacio de Gobierno
21 Post Office
23 Palacio de Cortés,
Museo de Cuauhnáhuac
24 Handicraft &
Souvenir Stalls
25 Jardín Borda
26 Templo de la Tercera
Orden de San Francisco
27 Recinto de la
Catedral Entrance
28 Capilla del Carmen
29 Capilla Abierta de
San José
30 Templo de la Asunción
de María
31 Museo Robert Brady
33 Plazuela del Zacate, Bar
Eclipse, El Romántico
34 1910
36 Kaova
37 Pullman de Morelos
Bus Station

Pasillo de
la Barranca

Río Balsas

Parque de
la Estación

Pirámide de
Teopanzolco

Market

Plan de Ayala

Victoria

Gómez
Fañas

Jardín
Borda

To Salto de
San Antón

see inset map

Cuauhtémoc

To Las
Jacarandas

To Jungla
Mágica,
Zúmbale

Motolinia

To Casa
Maximiliano,
Jardín
Etnobotánico

Cuauhtemotzin

Club
de Golf
Cuernavaca

To Xochicalco,
Taxco

Degollado
Aragón y León

Morrow

Lerdo de Tejada

Rayón

Plaza de
Armas
(Zócalo)

Hidalgo

Parque
Revolución

Abasolo

20 de Noviembre

at the Edge of the Forest). The Aztecs conquered Cuauhnáhuac in 1379 and called its people 'Tlahuica,' which means 'people who work the land.' The Tlahuica prospered under the Aztecs, and their city was a center of religion and learning. They resisted the Spanish fiercely, getting their city torched as a result. The Spanish city that replaced it became known as Cuernavaca, a Spanish version of Cuauhnáhuac.

In 1528 the Spanish Crown granted Hernán Cortés an estate in Mexico that covered 22 towns, including Cuernavaca, and a charge of 23,000 indigenous people. He introduced sugarcane and other crops, as well as new farming methods, which resulted in Cuernavaca becoming an agricultural center for the Spanish, as it had been before them.

With its pleasant climate, rural surroundings and colonial elite, Cuernavaca became a retreat for the rich and powerful. It also attracted artists and writers, and achieved literary fame as the setting for Malcolm Lowry's novel *Under the Volcano*. The very rich of Mexico City are now just as likely to go to Acapulco or Dallas for the weekend, but many still have magnificent properties in the suburbs of Cuernavaca.

Orientation & Information
The Plaza de Armas is the heart of the city. Most budget hotels, important sites and bus terminals are nearby.

The tourist office (☎ 314-38-72), inconveniently located at Avenida Morelos Sur 187, was understaffed and not very well informed on our last visit. It's supposedly open 8 am to 6 pm Monday to Friday, 10 am to 4 pm Saturday and Sunday, but phone ahead to be sure.

The post office is on the south side of the Plaza de Armas. Copy@net, at Avenida Morelos 178 on the corner of Motolonía, offers excellent Internet service for US$3.75 an hour.

Plaza de Armas & Jardín Juárez
The Plaza de Armas is flanked on the east by the Palacio de Cortés and on the west by the Palacio de Gobierno (the government building of Morelos state). The smaller Jardín Juárez adjoins the northwest corner of the Plaza de Armas and has a central gazebo designed by tower specialist Gustave Eiffel.

Numerous stalls and sidewalk restaurants around both plazas will serve you anything from breakfast to an after-dinner drink while you watch the world go by. It's quite a scene.

Palacio de Cortés & Museo de Cuauhnáhuac
Cortés' imposing two-story fortress-palace was built between 1522 and 1532, on the base of – and using stones from – the city pyramid that he destroyed. Cortés lived here until he departed for Spain in 1540. The palace remained in his family for most of the next century. Today it houses the Museo de Cuauhnáhuac, with two floors of exhibits highlighting the history and cultures of Mexico up to the present, including the pre-Hispanic Tlahuica. The base of the original pyramid can still be seen at various places around the ground floor.

On the upstairs balcony is a large, fascinating mural by Diego Rivera, commissioned in the 1920s as a gift to Cuernavaca by Dwight Morrow, the US ambassador to Mexico. The mural shows scenes from the Spanish conquest to the 1910 revolution, emphasizing the oppression and violence in Mexican history.

The museum is open 10 am to 5 pm Tuesday to Sunday (US$2, free on Sunday).

Jardín Borda
The Borda Garden was created in 1783 for Manuel de la Borda, as an addition to the stately residence built by his father, José de la Borda, the Taxco silver magnate. In the mid-1860s the house was the summer residence of Emperor Maximilian and Empress Carlota, who entertained courtiers in the gardens.

From the entrance on Avenida Morelos, you can tour the house and gardens to get an idea of how Mexico's aristocracy lived – open 10 am to 5.30 pm Tuesday to Sunday (US$1, free on Wednesday). In typical colonial style, the buildings are arranged around courtyards. In one wing, the **Museo de Sitio** has exhibits on daily life during the empire period – one famous painting depicts Maximilian in the garden and La India Bonita, 'the pretty Indian' who became his lover.

The formal gardens spread over a series of terraces, with steps and fountains. The vegetation is exuberant, though it lacks its original wide range of species – and the pretty pond you see in the painting now looks more like a dirty concrete swimming pool. Unfortunately, a water shortage in the city has led to the fountains being turned off.

Recinto de la Catedral

Cuernavaca's cathedral stands in a large walled compound *(recinto)* entered from Hidalgo near Avenida Morelos. Like the Palacio de Cortés, it was built from the rubble of Cuauhnáhuac, on a grand scale and in a fortresslike style, as a defense against the natives and to intimidate them. Franciscans started work under Cortés in 1526, using indigenous labor; it was one of the earliest Christian missions in Mexico. The first part to be built was the **Capilla Abierta de San José**, the open chapel on the west side of the cathedral.

The cathedral itself, the **Templo de la Asunción de María**, is plain and solid. The north-facing side door shows a mixture of indigenous and European features – the skull and crossbones above it is a symbol of the Franciscan order. Inside are frescoes said to show the persecution of Christian missionaries in Japan. They were supposedly painted by a 17th-century Japanese convert to Christianity.

Also in the cathedral compound is the **Templo de la Tercera Orden de San Francisco**, begun in 1723, with its exterior carved in 18th-century baroque style by indigenous artisans and its interior full of ornate, gilded decoration. And left as you enter is the 19th-century **Capilla del Carmen**, where believers seek cures for illness. Mass in English is given here at 9.30 am on Sunday.

Museo Robert Brady

Robert Brady (1928-86), a wealthy, well-traveled American artist and collector, lived in Cuernavaca for 24 years. His home, the Casa de la Torre at Netzahualcóyotl 4, a short walk from the Plaza de Armas, was originally part of the monastery within the Recinto de la Catedral. Brady acquired fine and applied art from around the world. The collection includes several paintings by well-known Mexican artists, including Rufino Tamayo and Frida Kahlo, but most impressive is its sheer diversity and the way it's arranged with delightful contrasts of styles, periods and places. One wall displays masks from Mexico, Bali and Central Africa. Elsewhere, New Guinean carvings stand next to a Mexican table on a Persian carpet.

The museum is open 10 am to 6 pm Tuesday to Saturday (US$2).

Salto de San Antón

For a pleasant walk less than 1km from the city center, follow the small streets west of the Jardín Borda to this 36m waterfall. A walkway is built into the cliff face right behind the falls. It's a picturesque place, with lush vegetation. San Antón village, which is above the falls, is a traditional pottery center.

Casa Maximiliano & Jardín Etnobotánico

This 1866 house, 1.5km southeast of the center, was once a rural retreat for Emperor Maximilian, where he would meet his lover La India Bonita. It was called La Casa del Olvido (The House of Forgetfulness), because Maximilian 'forgot' to include a room for his wife there. He did remember to include a small house in the back for his lover; it's now the **Museo de Medicina Tradicional**, a museum of traditional herbal medicine. Around the museum, the **Jardín Etnobotánico** has a collection of 455 herbs and medicinal plants from around the world. The museum and garden are open 9 am to 5 pm daily (free). Catch a Ruta 6 'Jardines' bus from the corner of Avenida Morelos and Degollado. The address is Matamoros 14 in Colonia Acapantzingo; it's 200m south of Tamayo.

Jungla Mágica

Magic Jungle (☎ 315-87-76), Bajada de Chapultepec 27, is a children's park with a jungle theme, a popular bird show and boating and picnicking facilities where you can swim with dolphins. It's open 10 am to 6 pm Thursday to Sunday (US$2 adults, US$1.50 kids). To get there, take a Ruta 17 bus and tell the driver you're going to La Luna, which is a traffic circle; walk two blocks along Chapultepec, and you'll come to the park entrance.

Pasillo de la Barranca

This is a 250m trail that follows a deep gorge bursting with flowers and butterflies, well below the roar of traffic. Along the way are a few waterfalls and no trash. It begins by the fountain at the base of Calle Guëmes, 1km north of the Plaza de Armas, and emerges by the arches at Guerrero and Gómez Farías.

Places to Stay

Accommodations in Cuernavaca don't offer great value. The cheap places tend to be depressingly basic, many mid-range ones are lacking in charm, and the top-end hotels are wonderful but very expensive. On weekends and holidays, however, the town fills up fast, so phone ahead or try to secure your room early in the day.

Budget One of the best in this bracket is *Hotel Juárez* (☎ 314-02-19, Netzahualcóyotl 19). Centrally located but quiet, with a swimming pool encircled by lawn, it offers 13 simple but airy rooms with 24-hour hot water at US$16/18 for singles/doubles. *Hotel Iberia* (☎ 312-60-40, Rayón 7) has long been patronized by travelers and foreign students. Its small, basic rooms around a tiled parking lot are a tad pricey at US$16.50/18.50, but it's only a short walk to the Plaza de Armas. The colonial *Hotel España* (☎ 318-67-44, Avenida Morelos 190) is nicer than the Iberia because it has toilet seats, shower curtains and better ventilation, but in other cities its fairly worn rooms (US$14/18) would cost less.

The cheapest places are on a section of Aragón y León worked by a handful of hookers. *Hotel América* (☎ 318-61-27, Aragón y León 14) is the best of these – basic but very clean rooms with bath and hot water are US$10.50/15. Around the corner, *Hotel Royal* (☎ 318-64-80, Matamoros 11) offers clean rooms with hot water and a central parking lot for US$11.50/14 (plus US$3.75 for TV).

Mid-Range The most attractive place in this price range is the *Hotel Papagayo* (☎ 314-17-11, Motolinía 13), with 77 modern rooms, two swimming pools and plenty of parking. The price of US$18/27 for singles/ doubles includes breakfast. *Hotel Colonial* (☎ 318-14-64, Aragón y León 19) charges US$12.50/20 for pleasant rooms, some facing a cute garden, with private bathrooms.

Villa Calmecac (☎ 313-21-46, Zacatecas 114), in Colonia Buenavista, is a hostel in the HI-affiliated REMAJ group. It's very pleasant though quite a distance from the center, 800m west of the Mexico City autopista. A bunk in one of its eight rustic-style rooms costs US$10.50 (US$12.75 with an all-natural buffet breakfast; 10% less with an HI card). The adobe-and-wood building is surrounded by organic gardens. It's a 20-minute ride on a Ruta 1, 2 or 3 bus from Avenida Morelos and Degollado in the center. Zacatecas is two blocks past the Zapata monument, on the left. Visitors must check in before 9 pm.

Top End One of the finest hotels in Mexico is *Las Mañanitas* (☎ 314-14-66, Linares 107), renowned for its large emerald-green garden where peacocks and flamingos stroll around while guests enjoy the pool. Prices run from US$125 for standard rooms to US$274 for gorgeous garden suites.

Hotel Posada María Cristina (☎ 318-57-67, Juárez 300) has tasteful rooms in a nicely restored colonial building with lovely hillside gardens and an inviting pool. Rooms start at US$67 (US$84 on Saturdays).

On the east side of the center in Colonia Chapultepec, *Las Jacarandas* (☎ 315-77-77,

Cuauhtémoc 133), set on rambling, verdant grounds, has three pools at varying temperatures and standard rooms (US$71). Buses run along Cuauhtémoc to the center.

Places to Eat

Budget For a simple snack or breakfast, you can get yogurt with fruit, *escamochas* (a kind of fruit salad), corn on the cob or ice cream from one of the booths at the *Jardín Juárez gazebo*, then eat your treat on one of the park's benches.

South on Galeana from the Jardín Juárez, *Jugos Chelys* has interesting fresh fruit juice combos for US$1.25, plus burgers and quesadillas.

The popular *El Barco (Rayón 5)*, near Comonfort, serves Guerrero-style *pozole* (shredded pork and hominy in delicious broth) for US$2/2.50 per small/large bowl, accompanied by oregano, chili, chopped onions and lime. Specify *'maciza'* unless you want your pozole to include bits of fat.

Mid-Range On the east side of Jardín Juárez, *La Parroquia*, open 7.30 am to midnight, is one of Cuernavaca's favorite restaurants. But you pay for the location – main meat dishes, for example, cost around US$7.

The parasol-shaded tables of *Restaurant Los Arcos* on the south side of the Plaza de Armas are a pleasant place for a meal or just to sip coffee or soda and watch the action on the plaza. The bilingual menu has something for everyone and is not too expensive.

Gaucho Infiel, on Las Casas, is a good Argentine steak place with a charcoal grill. Steaks are US$5 to US$7.50, the *parrillada* (an assortment of meats and sausages served on a carving board) costs US$10.50 for two.

La India Bonita (Morrow 106), northwest of Jardín Juárez, is a lovely courtyard restaurant with tasty, traditional Mexican food. The house specialties (US$5.50 to US$8.75) are chicken in *mole*, charcoal-grilled filet mignon, *huitlacoche* crepes and a Mexican platter with seven different selections. It closes at 7.30 pm (6.30 on Sunday) and all day Monday.

Restaurant Vienés (Lerdo de Tejada 4) offers central European dishes, such as *knackwurst* with sauerkraut and German fried potatoes, for an average of US$8 per main course. *Los Pasteles del Vienés*, next door and under the same ownership, serves the best cakes, cookies and chocolate-rum truffles you've tasted since the last time you were in Vienna. Their superb coffee comes with free refills.

Trattoria Marco Polo (Hidalgo 30), open till 11 pm, makes excellent pizzas, with one-person pies from US$2.75 and large ones from US$6. Balcony tables have a lovely view of the cathedral compound.

Top End At the hotel of the same name, *Restaurant Las Mañanitas (☎ 314-14-66, Linares 107)* is one of Mexico's best and most famous restaurants. It has tables both inside the mansion and on the gorgeous garden terrace. The menu, which waiters will show you on a large blackboard, features meals from around the world. Bring at least US$20 in cash per person, unless you have an American Express card. If you'd rather not spend all that cash, you may have a drink in the garden. Las Mañanitas is open 1 to 5 pm and 7 to 10.30 pm daily; reservations are recommended.

Entertainment

Hanging around the central plazas is always a popular pastime, especially on Sunday and Thursday from 6 pm, when open-air concerts are often held.

Plazuela del Zacate and adjacent Las Casas come alive at night with many bars featuring live music. *Bar Eclipse* has performers on two levels, folk below and rock above. *El Romántico* is a venue for balladeers.

The better dance clubs charge a cover of at least US$5; women are usually admitted free Friday and Saturday nights. Some places enforce dress codes, and the trendier places post style police at the door. *Barba Azul (Prado 10)* in Colonia San Gerónimo, and *Kaova*, near the corner of Abasolo and Avenida Morelos, are two of the most popular places. The revolutionary-themed *1910 (☎ 315-04-77)*, on Juárez 100m south of the Plaza de Armas, is so popular that you need to make a reservation well in advance to get in.

For live salsa dance music, try the very cool **Zúmbale** *(Bajada Chapultepec 13)*, near Glorieta La Luna, (US$10 cover), or the glitzy **Sammaná** *(☎ 313-47-27, Domingo Diez 1522)*, open Wednesday to Saturday.

Cinema Morelos, Avenida Morelos at Rayón, is the Morelos state theater, hosting quality film series, plays, dance and so on.

Shopping

Cuernavaca has no distinctive handicrafts, but if you want an onyx ashtray, a leather belt or some second-rate silver, try the stalls just south of the Palacio de Cortés. Assorted ceramic figurines of campesina women, animals and miniature buildings are sold on 3 de Mayo, south of the center, at prices far lower than what you'd find elsewhere.

Getting There & Away

Bus Frequent services of all classes by the Pullman de Morelos and Cuernavaca lines run from Mexico City's Terminal Sur to Cuernavaca (one to 1½ hours, US$4 to US$5). Returning, Pullman de Morelos deluxe buses depart from their downtown terminal at Abasolo and Netzahualcóyotl every 25 minutes (US$4), and Flecha Roja runs 33 daily buses from its station at Avenida Morelos 503, also for US$4. Fourteen daily Flecha Roja buses run to Taxco (80km, 1½ hours, US$3.50). Buses for Tepoztlán (23km, 30 minutes, US$1) depart every 15 minutes till 10 pm from the local bus terminal at the city market.

Car & Motorcycle Cuernavaca is a 1½-hour drive on highway 95 from Mexico City, or one hour on the toll highway 95D (US$5.25). The 95D skirts the east side of Cuernavaca: to enter the city take the Cuernavaca exit and cross to highway 95. Highway 95 becomes Boulevard Zapata as you go south into town, then Avenida Morelos; south of Avenida Matamoros, Avenida Morelos is one-way, northbound only. To reach the center, veer left and go down Matamoros.

Getting Around

You can walk to most places of interest in central Cuernavaca. The local buses (US$0.30) have the neighborhood they're going to marked on their windshields. Taxis will go to most places in town for under US$2.

XOCHICALCO

Atop a desolate plateau 15km southwest of Cuernavaca as the crow flies, but about 38km by road, is one of the most important archaeological sites in central Mexico, Xochicalco ('soh-chee-CAHL-coh').

The white stone ruins, many yet to be excavated, cover approximately 10 sq km and represent the various cultures – Olmec, Toltec, Aztec and others – for which Xochicalco was a commercial, cultural or religious center. Around 650 AD a congress of spiritual leaders from the Zapotec, Mayan and Gulf Coast peoples is believed to have met here to correlate their calendars. Xochicalco achieved its maximum splendor between 650 and 850 AD and declined around 1200.

The most famous monument is the Pirámide de Quetzalcóatl (Pyramid of the Plumed Serpent); from its well-preserved bas-reliefs archaeologists have surmised that astronomer-priests met here at the beginning and end of each 52-year cycle of the pre-Hispanic calendar. Signs at the site are in English and Spanish, but information at the impressive site museum 200m away is in Spanish only.

Getting There & Away

Flecha Roja and Autos Pullman de Morelos run hourly buses from Cuernavaca to within 4km of the site, from where you can walk (uphill) or catch a taxi (US$2). The site is open 10 am to 5 pm daily (US$2.75, free on Sunday).

TAXCO

• pop 95,000 • elev 1800m ☎ 7

Taxco ('TASS-co'), 170km southwest of Mexico City, is one of the most picturesque and pleasant places in Mexico. Clinging to a steep hillside, its narrow, cobbled streets twist and turn between well-worn buildings, open unexpectedly onto pretty plazas and reveal delightful vistas at every corner. Taxco has not surrounded itself with industrial suburbs, and few of its streetscapes are defaced with rows of parked cars, because there's simply no room for them.

Taxco is also famous for its hundreds of silver shops. The Spanish found tremendous lodes of silver here in 1534 but quickly emptied them, and it was not until 1743 that Don José de la Borda, who had come from France as a boy to work with his miner brother, uncovered another fabulously rich vein. According to a Taxco legend, Borda was riding near where the church of Santa Prisca now stands when his horse stumbled, dislodged a stone and exposed the silver. Borda went on to lose two fortunes but make three. A devout man, he reportedly treated his indigenous workers much better than those working in other colonial mines, and Santa Prisca was his gift to Taxco. He is remembered for the saying '*Dios da a Borda, Borda da a Dios*' ('God gives to Borda, Borda gives to God').

Borda's success attracted many more prospectors, and new veins of silver were found – and emptied. Taxco became a quiet, shrinking town until in 1929 an American professor and architect named William (Guillermo) Spratling set up a small silver workshop. The workshop became a factory and Spratling's apprentices began establishing their own shops. Today Taxco has more than 300 silver shops.

Orientation

Taxco's twisting streets may make you feel like a mouse in a maze, but it's a nice place to get lost. Plaza Borda, also called the zócalo, is the heart of the town, and its church, Santa Prisca, is a good landmark.

Highway 95 is called Avenida de los Plateros as it winds its way around the eastern side of central Taxco. Both bus stations are on Plateros. La Garita branches west from Plateros opposite the Pemex station, and – changing its name to Juárez on the way – follows a convoluted route, more or less southwest (one-way only), to Plaza Borda. Past the plaza, this main artery becomes

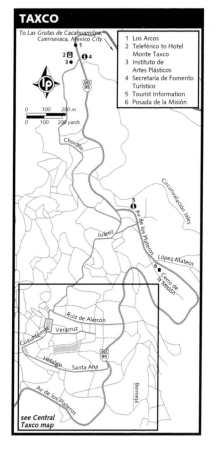

TAXCO

To Las Grutas de Cacahuamilpa, Cuernavaca, Mexico City

1 Los Arcos
2 Teleférico to Hotel Monte Taxco
3 Instituto de Artes Plásticos
4 Secretaría de Fomento Turístico
5 Tourist Information
6 Posada de la Misión

Chorrillo
Circunvalación Jales
Juárez
Av de los Plateros
López Mateos
Cerro de la Misión
Ruiz de Alarcón
Cuauhtémoc Veracruz
Hidalgo Santa Ana
Av de los Plateros
Bermeja

see Central Taxco map

Cuauhtémoc, and goes down to the Plazuela de San Juan. Most of the essentials are along this La Garita-Juárez-Cuauhtémoc route, or pretty close to it. Several side roads go east back to Plateros, which is the only way a vehicle can get back to the north end of town.

Information

The Secretaría de Fomento Turístico (☎ 622-66-16) has a helpful tourist office in the Centro de Convenciones de Taxco, on Plateros at the north end of town, open 9.30 am to 7 pm Monday to Saturday, 10 am to 5 pm Sunday. A non-government Tourist

Information Office (☎ 622-07-98) 1km farther south along Plateros functions primarily to arrange city tours, but its knowledgeable English (and French and German) speaking staff can answer most questions. The Flecha Roja bus station also has a tourist information booth.

There are several banks with ATMs around the main plazas. The post office is at Plateros 382, at the south end of town. Café Internet Azul, Hidalgo 7-1, offers web access till 11 pm daily for US$0.10 a minute (minimum 25 minutes). Arroba in Plaza Taxco is a little cheaper.

All Taxco's museums are open 10 am to 5 pm Tuesday to Sunday.

Templo de Santa Prisca

This church of rose-colored stone on Plaza Borda is a jewel of Churrigueresque architecture, its façade decorated with elaborately sculpted figures. The bas-relief over the doorway depicts Christ's baptism. Inside, the intricately sculpted altarpieces covered with gold are equally fine examples of Churrigueresque art. The building of Santa Prisca, to the designs of the Spanish architects Diego Durán and Juan Caballero between 1748 and 1758, almost bankrupted Don José de la Borda.

Museo Guillermo Spratling

This museum of archaeology and history is at Delgado 1, directly behind the Templo de Santa Prisca. Pre-Hispanic art on the two upper floors, mostly from William Spratling's private collection, includes jade statuettes and Olmec ceramics. The ground floor is devoted to temporary exhibits (US$2).

Museo de la Platería

This small museum of silverwork (US$1) exhibits some superb examples of the silversmiths' art, and outlines (in Spanish) its development in Taxco. Included are some classic Spratling designs. Notice the very colorful combinations of silver with semiprecious minerals such as jade, lapis lazuli, turquoise, malachite and obsidian – a feature of much of the silverwork for sale in

the town, and a link with pre-Hispanic stone-carving traditions.

The museum is at Plaza Borda 1, downstairs from the Patio de las Artesanías.

Museo de Arte Virreinal

Commonly known as Casa Humboldt, this is one of the oldest colonial homes in Taxco. It's on Ruiz de Alarcón, a couple of blocks down the hill from Plazuela de Bernal, and houses a small but well-displayed collection of colonial religious art, and an interesting exhibit on the restoration of the Templo de Santa Prisca, when some fabulous material was found in the basement (US$1).

Silver Shops

Even if you can't afford to buy the best, it's definitely worth looking in some of Taxco's best silver shops to see the finest work and most creative designs. Several are in the Patio de las Artesanías building on the corner of Plaza Borda, on your left as you face Santa Prisca. Pineda's, on the corner of the plaza and Muñoz, and Joyería Elena Ballesteros, a couple of doors down at Muñoz 4, are both famous shops. The tableware in the showroom of Emilia Castillo, at Ruiz de Alarcón 7, is a unique blend of porcelain and silver. See Shopping for more on silver.

Rancho Spratling

William Spratling died in 1967, but his former workshop, just south of Taxco el Viejo, which is 11km south of Taxco on highway 95, continues to produce some of the finest silver in Mexico. It employs the same handcrafted methods and classic designs that made Spratling pieces collectibles. The ranch has been proudly maintained, and a new generation of artisans adheres to Spratling's standards under the guidance of maestro Don Tomás, one of Spratling's principal workers for many years.

Visitors are encouraged to enter the workshop and see how fine silver is crafted. Also on the premises are showrooms displaying designs by Spratling and Tomás' apprentices. It's open 9 am to 1 pm and 2 to 5 pm Monday to Saturday (free).

From Taxco, catch any of the frequent 2nd-class Iguala-bound buses at the Flecha Roja terminal, and ask the driver to let you off at Rancho Spratling. Take any northbound bus or combi to return to Taxco.

Teleférico & Monte Taxco

From the northern end of Taxco, a Swiss-made cable car ascends 173m to the luxurious Monte Taxco resort hotel. The views from the cable car and resort are fantastic. The cable car runs 8 am to 7 pm daily (US$2.75 round-trip, half for children). To find it, walk uphill from Los Arcos (the arches that were once part of the aqueduct of Taxco's first silver mine), and turn right through the gate of the Instituto de Artes Plásticos; you can see the cable car terminal from the gate.

Special Events

During Semana Santa, visitors pour into Taxco to see its processions and events. Be sure to reserve a hotel room in advance. On Palm Sunday, Christ's triumphant entry into Jerusalem on a donkey is reenacted in the streets. On the following Thursday, processions of hooded penitents – some bearing

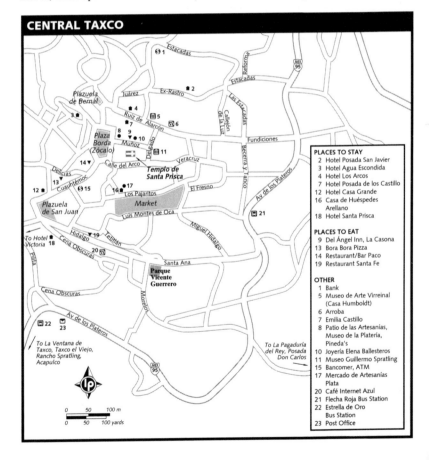

CENTRAL TAXCO

PLACES TO STAY
2 Hotel Posada San Javier
3 Hotel Agua Escondida
4 Hotel Los Arcos
7 Hotel Posada de los Castillo
12 Hotel Casa Grande
16 Casa de Huéspedes Arellano
18 Hotel Santa Prisca

PLACES TO EAT
9 Del Ángel Inn, La Casona
13 Bora Bora Pizza
14 Restaurant/Bar Paco
19 Restaurant Santa Fe

OTHER
1 Bank
5 Museo de Arte Virreinal (Casa Humboldt)
6 Arroba
7 Emilia Castillo
8 Patio de las Artesanías, Museo de la Platería, Pineda's
10 Joyería Elena Ballesteros
11 Museo Guillermo Spratling
15 Bancomer, ATM
17 Mercado de Artesanías Plata
20 Café Internet Azul
21 Flecha Roja Bus Station
22 Estrella de Oro Bus Station
23 Post Office

crosses or flagellating themselves with thorns – wind through town.

Another special Taxco event is *El Día del Jumil*, on the first Monday after November 2. Traditionally, the entire population of the town climbs Cerro de Huixteco (the hill behind Taxco), bringing picnics, sharing food and fellowship and collecting *jumiles*. These small beetles, about 1cm long, are found on the hill from about September to January and are considered a great delicacy. Taxco people eat them alone or mixed in salsa with tomatoes, garlic, onion, chilies and so on, or even *alive*, rolled into tortillas.

In the last week of November or the first week of December, Taxco stages the *Feria de la Plata*, a weeklong national silver fair with many associated frolics such as rodeos, donkey races, concerts and dances.

Places to Stay

Budget At the *Hotel Casa Grande* (☎ 622-09-69, Plazuela de San Juan 7) there are 12 clean, basic rooms around a courtyard; the rooftop rooms are the airiest but can be noisy. Singles/doubles are US$8.50/16 with private bath or US$6.50/9.50 with a tiny, dirty shared bathroom.

Casa de Huéspedes Arellano (☎ 622-02-15, Los Pajaritos 23) offers 10 simple, clean rooms for US$13/19 or US$8.50/13 with shared bath. It's a family-run place with terraces for sitting out. To find it, walk down the alley on the south side of Santa Prisca to a staircase going down to your right. Follow this down until you see a flight of steps down to your left: the *casa* is 30 steps down these, on the left.

Mid-Range One of the most attractive places in Taxco at any price is *Hotel Posada San Javier* (☎ 622-31-77, Ex-Rastro 6). It's peaceful, with a parking area and a lovely, large garden with a big swimming pool. The high-ceilinged rooms are clean and comfortable, and many have private terraces. Singles/doubles start at US$21/25.

Hotel Los Arcos (☎ 622-18-36, Ruiz de Alarcón 4) has 26 clean and spacious rooms at US$16/21. Once a monastery, it retains a

pleasant courtyard, a roof terrace and lots of character. *Hotel Posada de los Castillo* (☎ 622-13-96, Ruiz de Alarcón 7), across the road, is another place with colonial charm but even better prices – US$16/19.

Hotel Agua Escondida (☎ 622-07-26, Plaza Borda 4) has large and small swimming pools on a high terrace, and a basement parking lot. Comfy, airy rooms cost US$31/38.

The elegant *Hotel Santa Prisca* (☎ 622-09-80, Cena Obscuras 1), on Plazuela de San Juan, features a quiet interior patio and a pleasant restaurant. Rooms, most with private terraces, are US$20/31 (US$23/36 with breakfast).

Top End Out of the center, *Posada Don Carlos* (☎ 622-00-75, Calle del Consuelo 8) has eight tasteful rooms, most with balconies enjoying superb views of Taxco, for US$42/47. The hill to the Don Carlos is a tough climb – take a taxi for US$1.

The sprawling *Hotel Victoria* (☎ 622-00-04, Nibbi 14) dominates Taxco's southern hills. It's overpriced, with rooms starting at US$42, but it has character. It feels like a colonial village wrapped around a bend in the mountainside, complete with cobblestone streets and little overgrown nooks.

The luxurious *Posada de la Misión* (☎ 622-00-63), on Cerro de la Misión, has 120 big rooms, featuring private terraces with fine views of Taxco. Singles/doubles are US$67/74 including breakfast (more at weekends). There is a mosaic mural of the Aztec emperor Cuauhtémoc, created by Juan O'Gorman, overlooking the pool.

Places to Eat

A few doors downhill from Plazuela de San Juan, *Restaurant Santa Fe* (Hidalgo 2) serves good food at fair prices. Set breakfasts cost US$4.50 or less, and the US$4 comida corrida includes four courses.

Restaurant/Bar Paco, overlooking the Plaza Borda through large picture windows, is great for people-watching. The food is good, too, but you pay for the view – meat dishes start at US$8.50 and chicken at US$6. Try the delicious enchiladas with mole

(US$4.75). The Paco is open 1 to 10 pm daily.

Bora Bora Pizza *(Delicias 4)*, just off Cuauhtémoc near the Plaza Borda, serves the best pizza in Taxco (though some have complained of less-than-cordial service). Prices range from US$2.50 to US$9.

The **Del Ángel Inn** *(Muñoz 3)*, on the left side of Santa Prisca, has a spectacular roof terrace with bar. It's definitely tourist-oriented but the food isn't bad. A US$6.50 set lunch includes fresh bread with herbed butter, soup, a main course and dessert. Salads and pastas go for around US$4, Mexican dishes from US$5 to US$10. Next door, **La Casona** has similar fare a little cheaper, as well as an excellent balcony with a view of Taxco tumbling down the hillside.

The top two restaurants in Taxco are on hills facing the city center and are best reached by taxi. **La Ventana de Taxco**, south of town, specializes in Italian food; its *piccata Ventana* (veal sautéed in a lemon, butter and parsley sauce) is superb; expect to spend about US$25 for dinner. **La Pagaduría del Rey**, in the Barrio Bermeja, is equally fancy but less expensive, with salads and pastas from US$3.75 and Mexican dishes for around US$6. It's a great place simply to sip a drink and admire the view.

Shopping

Silver The selection is mind-boggling. It's a good idea to look at some of the best places first, to see what's available (see Silver Shops, earlier in this chapter), then try to focus on the things you're really interested in, and shop around for those. If you're careful and willing to bargain a bit, you can buy wonderful pieces at reasonable prices. The shops in and around the Plaza Borda tend to have higher prices than those farther from the center, but they also tend to have more interesting work. The shops on Avenida de los Plateros are often branches of downtown businesses, set up for the tourist buses, which can't make it through the narrow streets. The stalls in the Mercado de Artesanías Plata go for quantity rather than quality, but you may spot something special.

The price of a piece is determined principally by its weight, though items with exceptional artisanship can command a premium. If you're serious about buying silver, find out the current pesos-per-gram rate when you're in Taxco. All the silver shops have scales, mostly electronic devices that should be accurate. If a piece costs less than the going price per gram, it's not real silver. Don't buy anything that doesn't have the Mexican government '.925' stamp, which certifies that the piece is 92.5% sterling silver (most pieces also bear a set of initials identifying the workshop where they were made). If a piece is too small or delicate to stamp, a reputable shop will supply a certificate of its purity.

Other Crafts It's easy to overlook them among the silver, but Taxco offers other things to buy, too. Finely painted wood and papier-mâché trays and boxes are sold along Calle del Arco, on the south side of Santa Prisca. Quite a lot of shops sell semiprecious stones, fossils and mineral crystals, and some have good selections of masks, puppets and semi-antique carvings.

Getting There & Away

Estrella de Oro and the Cuernavaca line run a total of about 15 daily deluxe and 1st-class buses to Taxco from Mexico City's Terminal Sur (170km, three hours, US$7.75 to US$8.50).

In Taxco, 1st-class Flecha Roja and Futura buses and deluxe Turistar buses, as well as several 2nd-class bus lines, use the terminal at Avenida de los Plateros 104. Hourly buses leave here for Mexico City. The Estrella de Oro terminal is at the south end of town, with six daily buses to Mexico City. To Cuernavaca (80km, 1½ hours), Flecha Roja runs hourly buses until 7 pm (US$3.50). Book early for buses out of Taxco as it can be hard to get a seat.

Getting Around

Combis (white Volkswagen minibuses) are frequent and cheap (US$0.30) and operate from 7 am to 8 pm. The 'Zócalo' combi departs from Plaza Borda, goes down

Cuauhtémoc to Plazuela de San Juan, then heads down the hill on Hidalgo, turns right at San Miguel and left on Plateros, which it follows northward until La Garita, where it turns left and goes back to the zócalo. The 'Arcos/Zócalo' combi follows basically the same route except that it continues past La Garita to Los Arcos, where it does a U-turn and heads back to La Garita. Combis pass both bus terminals every few minutes: get one marked 'Zócalo' to head to the Plaza Borda. To reach the Estrella de Oro bus station from the center, take a 'PM' combi.

Taxis cost from US$1 to US$1.50 for trips in town.

LAS GRUTAS DE CACAHUAMILPA

The Cacahuamilpa caverns, 30km northeast of Taxco by road, are a beautiful natural wonder of stalactites, stalagmites and twisted rock formations, with huge chambers up to 82m high – well worth visiting.

From the visitor's center at the entrance, guided tours in Spanish (US$1.50) start every hour on the hour from 10 am to 5 pm. You are taken 2km along an illuminated walkway, with the commentary focusing on formations named for some fanciful resemblance to an elephant, champagne bottle, Dante's head and so on. Geological information is minimal. You then return to the entrance at your own pace. The entire tour takes two hours.

Outside the cave entrance, a path goes down a steep valley to the Río Dos Bocas, where two rivers emerge from the caves. The walk down and back takes 30 minutes if you do it slowly, and it's very pretty.

There are restaurants, snacks and souvenir shops at the visitor's center.

Getting There & Away

From Taxco, blue-striped combis to the visitor's center at the caves depart every two hours from opposite the Flecha Roja bus terminal (one hour, US$1.25). Alternatively, you can take any bus heading for Toluca or Ixtapan de la Sal, get off at the 'Grutas' crossroads and walk 1km down the road to the entrance, on your right. The last combis

leave the site at 6 pm Saturday and Sunday, 5 pm other days.

West of Mexico City

SANTUARIO DE MARIPOSAS EL ROSARIO

☎ 7 (Angangueo)

Every year many millions of large, beautiful monarch butterflies migrate from the USA and Canada to breed in the mountain coniferous forests around the borders of México and Michoacán states, some 200km west of Mexico City. The easiest to visit of their breeding grounds, which are officially protected, is the El Rosario Butterfly Sanctuary.

The monarchs (*mariposas monarcas* in Spanish) arrive, after a four-week journey, around late October or early November, and set off back northward around the beginning of March. When they are present, there are so many butterflies in the sanctuary that they cover the trees, turning them a flaming orange – it's a marvelous sight! Environmental threats to the butterflies include damage to these southern breeding grounds by fire and logging.

The sanctuary is open 9 am to 6 pm daily during the butterfly season. The entry fee of US$2 includes a guide who takes you through the sanctuary, explaining the insects' life cycle and so on. You can stay as long as you like, but it only takes two hours to tour. It's a good idea to get there early, when the butterflies are up in the trees. As the day warms up, many flutter to the ground, where it's more humid, and you can't avoid crushing some as you walk.

Places to Stay & Eat

The best base for visiting the sanctuary is Angangueo, a pretty former mining village at 2980m, 25km north of Zitácuaro, which is on highway 15 between Toluca and Morelia. Accommodations are along the single main street, called Nacional for most of its length. A few blocks down from the plaza at the uphill end of the street, the *Casa Huéspedes El Paso de la Monarca*

(☎ 156-01-87) has simple rooms around a tiered garden with views of the hills. Singles/doubles with private bath cost around US$11/13. *Casa Huéspedes Juárez* has rooms of a similar standard and price, centered on a rose-filled courtyard. Farther down the hill, the very appealing *Albergue Don Bruno* (☎ 156-00-26) is the first place to stay as you come into town, with attractive rooms from US$27/38. The Don Bruno's *Restaurant Los Geranios* has great views and does a fine comida corrida (US$2.75) and other meals. A few eateries on the plaza are also OK.

Getting There & Away

Autobuses de Occidente runs infrequent 2nd-class buses direct to Angangueo from Mexico City's Terminal Poniente (four hours, US$8). It's probably better to go first to Zitácuaro, then take one of the local buses from there to Angangueo – they leave every 15 minutes (1 hour, US$1.25). From Mexico City's Terminal Poniente, bus lines with frequent service to Zitácuaro (2¾ hours, US$7) include Autobuses de Occidente and México-Toluca-Zinacántepec y Ramales.

For the rugged, 9km, one-hour trip to the sanctuary, *camionetas* (vans) depart from the main road in Angangueo. You have to hire the whole 10-person van for about US$20 to US$30 (subject to negotiation), so the more people sharing the cost, the better. You'll have the best chance of finding other travelers to share the ride on weekends. The fee includes two hours waiting while you visit the sanctuary.

The walk from Angangueo to the sanctuary is a steep uphill hike of around three hours (the near-3000m altitude will make it tougher). After about an hour, you will come to a statue of the Virgin of Guadalupe; you should turn left here, and then stay on the middle track until you reach the entrance of the sanctuary.

Language

Pronunciation

Pronunciation of Spanish is not difficult, given that many Spanish sounds are similar to their English counterparts, and there is a clear and consistent relationship between pronunciation and spelling. Unless otherwise indicated, the English words used below to approximate Spanish sounds take standard American pronunciation.

Vowels Spanish has five vowels: **a**, **e**, **i**, **o** and **u**. They are pronounced something like the highlighted letters of the following English words:

a as in 'father'
e as in 'met'
i as in 'feet'
o as in the British 'hot'
u as in 'put'

Diphthongs A diphthong is one syllable made up of two vowels, each of which conserves its own sound. Here are some diphthongs in Spanish, and their approximate pronunciations:

ai as in 'hide'
au as in 'how'
ei as in 'hay'
ia as in 'yard'
ie as in 'yes'
oi as in 'boy'
ua as in 'wash'
ue as in 'well'

Consonants Many consonants are pronounced in much the same way as in English, but there are some exceptions:

c is pronounced like 's' in 'sit' when before 'e' or 'i'; elsewhere it is like 'k'
ch as in 'choose'
g as the 'g' in 'gate' before 'a,' 'o' and 'u'; before 'e' or 'i' it is a harsh, breathy sound like the 'h' in 'hit.' Note that when 'g' is followed by 'ue' or 'ui' the 'u' is silent, unless it has a dieresis (ü), in which case it functions much like the English 'w':
guerra 'GEH-rra'
güero 'GWEH-ro'
h always silent
j a harsh, guttural sound similar to the 'ch' in the Scottish 'loch'

ll as the 'y' in 'yellow'
ñ nasal sound like the 'ny' in 'canyon'
q as the 'k' in 'kick'; always followed by a silent 'u'
r a very short rolled 'r'
rr a longer rolled 'r'
x like the English 'h' when it comes after 'e' or 'i,' otherwise it is like English 'x' as in 'taxi'; in many Indian words (particularly Mayan ones) 'x' is pronounced like English 'sh'
z the same as the English 's'; under no circumstances should 's' or 'z' be pronounced like English 'z' – that sound does not exist in Spanish

There are a few other minor pronunciation differences, but the longer you stay in Mexico, the easier they will become. The letter ñ is considered a separate letter of the alphabet and follows 'n' in alphabetically organized lists and books, such as dictionaries and phone books.

Stress There are three general rules regarding stress:

- For words ending in a vowel, 'n' or 's,' the stress goes on the penultimate (next-to-the-last) syllable:

  naranja na-RAHN-ha   *joven* HO-ven   *zapatos* sa-PA-tos

- For words ending in a consonant other than 'n' or 's,' the stress is on the final syllable:

  estoy es-TOY   *ciudad* syoo-DAHD   *catedral* ka-teh-DRAL

- Any deviation from these rules is indicated by an accent:

  México MEH-hee-ko   *mudéjar* moo-DEH-har   *Cortés* cor-TESS

Gender

Nouns in Spanish are either masculine or feminine. Nouns ending in 'o,' 'e' or 'ma' are usually masculine. Nouns ending in 'a,' 'ión' or 'dad' are usually feminine. Some nouns take either a masculine or feminine form, depending on the ending; for example, *viajero* is a male traveler, *viajera* is a female traveler. An adjective usually comes after the noun it describes and must take the same gender as the noun.

Greetings & Civilities

Hello/Hi.	*Hola.*
Good morning/Good day.	*Buenos días.*
Good afternoon.	*Buenas tardes.*
Good evening/Good night.	*Buenas noches.*
See you.	*Hasta luego.*
Good-bye.	*Adiós.*
Pleased to meet you.	*Mucho gusto.*
How are you? (to one person)	*¿Como está?*
How are you? (to more than one person)	*¿Como están?*
I am fine.	*Estoy bien.*
Please.	*Por favor.*
Thank you.	*Gracias.*
You're welcome.	*De nada.*
Excuse me.	*Perdóneme.*

People

I	*yo*	they (f)	*ellas*
you (familiar)	*tú*	my wife	*mi esposa*
you (formal)	*usted*	my husband	*mi esposo, mi marido*
you (pl, formal)	*ustedes*	my sister	*mi hermana*
he/it	*el*	my brother	*mi hermano*
she/it	*ella*	Sir/Mr	*Señor*
we	*nosotros*	Madam/Mrs	*Señora*
they (m)	*ellos*	Miss	*Señorita*

Useful Words & Phrases

For words pertaining to food and restaurants, see the Food and Drinks sections of the Places to Eat chapter.

Yes.	*Sí.*	I am ...	*Estoy ...*
No.	*No.*	(location or temporary condition)	
What did you say?	*¿Mande?* (colloq)	here	*aquí*
	¿Cómo?	tired (m/f)	*cansado/a*
good/OK	*bueno*	sick/ill (m/f)	*enfermo/a*
bad	*malo*		
better	*mejor*	I am ...	*Soy ...*
best	*lo mejor*	(permanent state)	
more	*más*	a worker	*trabajador*
less	*menos*	married	*casado*
very little	*poco* or *poquito*		

Buying

How much?	*¿Cuánto?*
How much does it cost?	*¿Cuánto cuesta?* or *¿Cuánto se cobra?*
How much is it worth?	*¿Cuánto vale?*
I want ...	*Quiero ...*
I do not want ...	*No quiero ...*
I would like ...	*Quisiera ...*
Give me ...	*Deme ...*
What do you want?	*¿Qué quiere?*
Do you have ... ?	*¿Tiene ... ?*
Is/are there ... ?	*¿Hay ... ?*

Nationalities

American (m/f)	*(norte)americano/a*
Australian (m/f)	*australiano/a*
British (m/f)	*británico/a*
Canadian (m & f)	*canadiense*
English (m/f)	*inglés/inglesa*
French (m/f)	*francés/francesa*
German (m/f)	*alemán/alemana*

Languages

I speak ...	*Yo hablo ...*	I understand.	*Entiendo.*
I do not speak ...	*No hablo ...*	I do not understand.	*No entiendo.*
Do you speak ... ?	*¿Habla usted ... ?*	Do you understand?	*¿Entiende usted?*
Spanish	*español*	Please speak slowly.	*Por favor hable despacio.*
English	*inglés*		
German	*alemán*		
French	*francés*		

Crossing the Border

birth certificate	*certificado de nacimiento*	immigration	*inmigración*
		insurance	*seguro*
border (frontier)	*la frontera*	passport	*pasaporte*
car-owner's title	*título de propiedad*	temporary vehicle import permit	*permiso de importación temporal de vehículo*
car registration	*registración*		
customs	*aduana*		
driver's license	*licencia de manejar*	tourist card	*tarjeta de turista*
identification	*identificación*	visa	*visado*

Getting Around

street	*calle*	forward, ahead	*adelante*
boulevard	*bulevar, boulevard*	straight ahead	*todo recto* or *derecho*
avenue	*avenida*	this way	*por aquí*
road	*camino*	that way	*por allí*
highway	*carretera*	north	*norte (Nte)*
corner (of)	*esquina (de)*	south	*sur*
corner/bend	*vuelta*	east	*este*
block	*cuadra*	east (in an address)	*oriente (Ote)*
to the left	*a la izquierda*	west	*oeste*
to the right	*a la derecha*	west (in an address)	*poniente (Pte)*

Where is . . . ?	*¿Dónde está . . . ?*
the bus station	*el terminal de autobuses/central camionera*
the train station	*la estación del ferrocarril*
the airport	*el aeropuerto*
the post office	*el correo*
a long-distance phone	*un teléfono de larga distancia*
bus	*camión* or *autobús*
minibus	*colectivo*, *combi* or (in Mexico City) *pesero*
train	*tren*
taxi	*taxi*
ticket sales counter	*taquilla*
waiting room	*sala de espera*
baggage check-in	*(recibo de) equipaje*
toilet	*sanitario*
departure	*salida*
arrival	*llegada*
platform	*andén*
left-luggage room/checkroom	*guardería* (or *guarda*) *de equipaje*
How far is . . . ?	*¿A qué distancia está . . . ?*
How long? (How much time?)	*¿Cuánto tiempo?*
short route (usually a toll highway)	*vía corta*

Driving

gasoline	*gasolina*	full	*lleno* or '*ful*'
fuel station	*gasolinera*	oil	*aceite*
unleaded	*sin plomo*	tire	*llanta*
fill the tank	*llene el tanque; llenarlo*	puncture	*agujero*

How much is a liter of gasoline?	*¿Cuánto cuesta el litro de gasolina?*
My car has broken down.	*Se me ha descompuesto el carro.*
I need a tow truck.	*Necesito un remolque.*
Is there a garage near here?	*¿Hay un garaje cerca de aquí?*

Highway Signs

Though Mexico mostly uses the familiar international road signs, you should be prepared to encounter these other signs as well:

road repairs	*camino en reparación*
keep to the right	*conserve su derecha*
do not overtake	*no rebase*
dangerous curve	*curva peligrosa*
landslides or subsidence	*derrumbes*
slow	*despacio*
detour	*desviación*
slow down	*disminuya su velocidad*
school (zone)	*escuela (zona escolar)*
men working	*hombres trabajando*
road closed	*no hay paso*
danger	*peligro*
continuous white line	*raya continua*
speed bumps	*topes* or *vibradores*
road under repair	*tramo en reparación*
narrow bridge	*puente angosto*
toll highway	*vía cuota*
short route (often a toll road)	*vía corta*
have toll ready	*prepare su cuota*
one-lane road 100 meters ahead	*un solo carril a 100 m*

Accommodations

hotel	*hotel*	shower	*ducha* or *regadera*
guesthouse	*casa de huéspedes*	hot water	*agua caliente*
inn	*posada*	air-conditioning	*aire acondicionado*
room	*cuarto, habitación*	blanket	*manta, cobija*
room with one bed	*cuarto sencillo*	towel	*toalla*
room with two beds	*cuarto doble*	soap	*jabón*
room for one person	*cuarto para una persona*	toilet paper	*papel higiénico*
		the check (bill)	*la cuenta*
room for two people	*cuarto para dos personas*	What is the price?	*¿Cuál es el precio?*
double bed	*cama matrimonial*	Does that include taxes?	
		¿Están incluidos los impuestos?	
twin beds	*camas gemelas*	Does that include service?	
with bath	*con baño*	*¿Está incluido el servicio?*	

Money

money	*dinero*
traveler's checks	*cheques de viajero*
bank	*banco*
exchange bureau	*casa de cambio*
credit card	*tarjeta de crédito*
exchange rate	*tipo de cambio*
ATM	*caja permanente* or *cajero automático*
I want/would like to change some money.	*Quiero/quisiera cambiar dinero.*
What is the exchange rate?	*¿Cuál es el tipo de cambio?*
Is there a commission?	*¿Hay comisión?*

Telephones

telephone	teléfono
telephone call	llamada
telephone number	número telefónico
telephone card	tarjeta telefónica
area or city code	clave
prefix for long-distance call	prefijo
local call	llamada local
long-distance call	llamada de larga distancia
long-distance telephone	teléfono de larga distancia
coin-operated telephone	teléfono de monedas
card-operated telephone	teléfono de tarjetas telefónicas
long-distance telephone office	caseta de larga distancia
tone	tono
operator	operador(a)
person to person	persona a persona
collect (reverse charges)	por cobrar
dial the number	marque el número
please wait	favor de esperar
busy	ocupado
toll/cost (of call)	cuota/costo
time & charges	tiempo y costo
don't hang up	no cuelgue

Times & Dates

Monday	lunes		Saturday	sábado
Tuesday	martes		Sunday	domingo
Wednesday	miércoles		yesterday	ayer
Thursday	jueves		today	hoy
Friday	viernes			

tomorrow (also at some point, or maybe)	mañana
right now (meaning in a few minutes)	horita, ahorita
already	ya
morning	mañana
tomorrow morning	mañana por la mañana
afternoon	tarde
night	noche
What time is it?	¿Qué hora es?

Numbers

0	cero	9	nueve	18	dieciocho
1	un, uno (m), una (f)	10	diez	19	diecinueve
2	dos	11	once	20	veinte
3	tres	12	doce	21	veintiuno
4	cuatro	13	trece	22	veintidós
5	cinco	14	catorce	30	treinta
6	seis	15	quince	31	treinta y uno
7	siete	16	dieciséis	32	treinta y dos
8	ocho	17	diecisiete	40	cuarenta

50	cincuenta	100	cien	700	setecientos
60	sesenta	101	ciento uno	900	novecientos
70	setenta	143	ciento cuarenta y tres	1000	mil
80	ochenta	200	doscientos	2000	dos mil
90	noventa	500	quinientos		

Mexican Slang

Pepper your conversations with a few slang expressions! You'll hear many of these slang words and phrases all around Mexico, but others are particular to Mexico City.

¡Quiúbole!	Hello!
¿Qué onda?	What's up?, What's happening?
¿Qué pex?	What's up?
¿Qué pasión? (Mexico City only)	What's up?, What's going on?
¡Qué padre!	How cool!
fregón	really good at something, way cool, awesome
Este club está fregón.	This club is way cool.
El cantante es un fregón.	The singer is really awesome.
ser muy buena onda	to be really cool, nice
Mi novio es muy buena onda.	My boyfriend is really cool.
Eres muy buena onda.	You are really cool (nice).
estar de pelos	to be super, awesome
La música está de pelos.	The music is awesome.
unas serpientes bien elodias	some ice-cold beers (sounds like *unas cervezas bien heladas*)
pomo (in the south)	booze
pisto (in the north)	booze
alipús	booze
echarse un alipús, echarse un trago	to go get a drink
Echamos un alipús/trago.	Let's go have a drink.
dar un voltión	go cruising, drive around
tirar la onda	try to pick someone up, flirt
ligar	to flirt
irse de reventón	go partying
¡Vámonos de reventón!	Let's go party!
reven	a 'rave' – huge party, lots of loud music and wild atmosphere
un toquín	an informal party with live music
un desmadre	a mess
Simón.	Yes.
Nel.	No.
Naranjas Dulces.	No.
No hay tos.	No problem. (literally 'there's no cough.')
¡Órale! – positive	Sounds great! (responding to an invitation)
¡Órale! – negative	What the *#*!? (taunting exclamation)
¡Caray!	Shit!
¿Te cae?	Are you serious?
Me late.	Sounds really good to me.
Me vale.	I don't care, 'Whatever.'

Sale y vale.	I agree, Sounds good.
¡Paso sin ver!	I can't stand it!, No thank you!
¡Guácatelas! ¡Guácala!	How gross! That's disgusting!
¡Bájale!	Don't exaggerate!, Come on!
¡¿Chale?! (Mexico City only)	Really?! No way!
¡Te sales! ¡Te pasas!	That's it! You've gone too far!
¿Le agarraste?	Did you understand?, Do you get it?
un resto	a lot
lana	money, dough
carnal	brother
cuate, cuaderno	buddy
chavo	guy, dude
chava	girl, gal
jefe	father
jefa	mother
la tira, la julia	the police
chapusero	a cheater (at cards, for example)

Glossary

For food and drink terms, see the Food and Drinks sections in the Places to Eat chapter; for bus and train terms, see the Getting There & Away chapter; for general terms, see the Language chapter.

AC – *antes de Cristo* (before Christ); equivalent to BC

adobe – sun-dried mud brick used for building

aduana – customs

agave – type of *maguey* from which tequila is made

aguardiente – literally 'burning water'; strong liquor usually made from sugarcane

Alameda – name of formal parks in several Mexican cities

albergue de juventud – youth hostel

alfarería – potter's workshop

alfiz – rectangular frame around a curved arch; an Arabic influence on Spanish and Mexican buildings

amate – paper made from tree bark

Ángeles Verdes – Green Angels: government-funded mechanics who patrol Mexico's major highways in green vehicles; they help stranded motorists with fuel, spare parts and service

antro – bar with (often loud) recorded music and usually some space to dance

Apdo – abbreviation for *Apartado* (Box) in addresses; hence Apdo Postal means Post Office Box

arroyo – brook, stream

artesanías – handicrafts, folk arts

atlas (s), **atlantes** (pl) – sculpted male figure(s) used instead of a pillar to support a roof or frieze; a *telamon*

atrium – churchyard, usually a big one

autopista – expressway, freeway

azulejo – painted ceramic tile

bahía – bay

balneario – bathing-place, often a natural hot spring

baluarte – bulwark, defensive wall

barrio – neighborhood of a town or city, often a poor neighborhood

billete – bank note

boleto – ticket

brujo, -a – witch doctor, shaman; similar to *curandero, -a*

burro – donkey

caballeros – literally 'horsemen,' but corresponds to 'gentlemen' in English; look for it on toilet doors

cabaña – cabin, simple shelter

cacique – regional warlord or political strongman

cafetería – a snack bar or coffeehouse

calle – street

callejón – alley

callejoneada – originally a Spanish tradition, still enjoyed in cities such as Guanajuato and Zacatecas, in which musicians lead a crowd of revellers through the streets, singing and telling stories as they parade along

calzada – grand boulevard or avenue

calzones – long baggy shorts worn by indigenous men

camarín – chapel beside the main altar in a church; contains ceremonial clothing for images of saints or the Virgin

camión – truck or bus

camioneta – pickup truck

campesino, -a – country person, peasant

capilla abierta – open chapel; used in early Mexican monasteries for preaching to large crowds of indigenous people

casa de cambio – exchange house; place where currency is exchanged, faster to use than a bank

caseta de larga distancia, caseta de teléfono, caseta telefónica – public telephone call station, often in a shop

cazuela – clay cooking pot; usually sold in a nested set

central camionera – bus terminal

cerro – hill

Chac – Mayan rain god

chac-mool – pre-Hispanic stone sculpture of a hunched, belly-up figure; the stomach may have been used as a sacrificial altar

charreada – Mexican rodeo

charro – Mexican cowboy

chilango, -a – citizen of Mexico City

chinampas – Aztec gardens built from lake mud and vegetation; versions still exist at Xochimilco, Mexico City

chingar – literally 'to fuck'; it has a wide range of colloquial usages in Mexican Spanish equivalent to those in English

Churrigueresque – Spanish late-baroque architectural style; found on many Mexican churches

cigarro – cigarette

Coatlicue – mother of the Aztec gods

colectivo – minibus or car that picks up and drops off passengers along a predetermined route; can also refer to other types of transport, such as boats, where passengers share the total fare

coleto, -a – citizen of San Cristóbal de Las Casas

colonia – neighborhood of a city, often a wealthy residential area

comedor – literally 'eating place,' usually a sit-down stall in a market or a small, cheap restaurant

comida corrida – fixed-price menu with several courses; cheaper than eating á la carte

completo – no vacancy, literally 'full up'; a sign you may see at hotel desks

conasupo – government-owned store that sells many everyday basics at subsidized prices

conde – count (nobleman)

conquistador – early Spanish explorer-conqueror

cordillera – mountain range

correos – post office

coyote – person who smuggles Mexican immigrants into the USA

criollo, -a – Mexican-born person of Spanish parentage; in colonial times considered inferior by peninsular Spaniards (see *gachupines, peninsulares*)

Cristeros – Roman Catholic rebels of the late 1920s

cuota – toll; a *vía cuota* is a toll road

curandero, -a – literally 'curer'; a medicine man or woman who uses herbal and/or magical methods and often emphasizes spiritual aspects of disease

damas – ladies; the sign on toilet doors

DC – *después de Cristo* (after Christ); equivalent to AD

de lujo – deluxe; often used with some license

delegación – a large urban governmental subdivision in Mexico City comprising numerous *colonias*

de paso – a bus that began its route somewhere else, but stops to let passenger on or off at various points – often arriving late; a *local* bus is preferable

descompuesto – broken, out of order

DF – Distrito Federal (Federal District); about half of Mexico City lies in the DF

edificio – building

ejido – communal landholding

embarcadero – jetty, boat landing

encomienda – a grant made to a *conquistador* of labor by or tribute from a group of indigenous people; the conquistador was supposed to protect and convert them, but usually treated them as little more than slaves

enramada – literally an arbor or bower, but often refers to a thatch-covered, open-air restaurant

enredo – wraparound skirt

entremeses – hors d'oeuvres; also theatrical sketches, such as those performed during the Cervantino festival in Guanajuato

escuela – school

esq – abbreviation of *esquina* (corner) in addresses

estación de ferrocarril – train station

estípite – long, narrow, pyramid-shaped, upside-down pilaster; the hallmark of Churrigueresque architecture

ex-convento – former convent or monastery

excusado – toilet

faja – waist sash used in traditional indigenous costume

feria – fair or carnival, typically occurring during a religious holiday

ferrocarril – railway
ficha – locker token available at bus terminals
fonda – eating stall in market; small restaurant
fraccionamiento – subdivision, housing development; similar to a *colonia*, often modern
frontera – border between political entities

gachupines – derogatory term for the colonial *peninsulares*
giro – money order
gringo, -a – US or Canadian (and sometimes European, Australasian, etc) visitor to Latin America; can be used derogatorily
grito – literally 'shout'; the Grito de Dolores was the 1810 call to independence by parish priest Miguel Hidalgo, which sparked the struggle for independence from Spain
gruta – cave, grotto
guarache – also *huarache*; woven leather sandal, often with tire tread as the sole
guardería de equipaje – room for storing luggage, eg, in a bus station
guayabera – also *guayabarra*; man's shirt with pockets and appliquéd designs up the front, over the shoulders and down the back; worn in place of a jacket and tie in hot regions
güero, -a – fair-haired, fair-complexioned person; a more polite alternative to *gringo*

hacendado – *hacienda* owner
hacienda – estate; Hacienda (capitalized) is the Treasury Department
hay – there is, there are; you're equally likely to hear *no hay* (there isn't, there aren't)
hombres – men; sign on toilet doors
huarache – see *guarache*
huevos – eggs; also slang for testicles
huipil, -es – indigenous woman's sleeveless tunic, usually highly decorated; can be thigh-length or reach the ankles
Huizilopochtli – Aztec tribal god

iglesia – church
INAH – Instituto Nacional de Antropología e Historia; the body in charge of most ancient sites and some museums

indígena – indigenous, pertaining to the original inhabitants of Latin America; can also refer to the people themselves
INI – Instituto Nacional Indígenista; set up in 1948 to improve the lot of indigenous Mexicans and to integrate them into society; sometimes accused of paternalism and trying to stifle protest
ISH – *impuesto sobre hospedaje*; lodging tax on the price of hotel rooms
isla – island
IVA – *impuesto de valor agregado*, or 'EE-bah'; a 15% sales tax added to the price of many items
ixtle – *maguey* fiber

jaguar – jaguar, a panther native to southern Mexico and Central America; principal symbol of the Olmec civilization
jai alai – the Basque game *pelota*, brought to Mexico by the Spanish; a bit like squash, played on a long court with curved baskets attached to the arm
jarocho, -a – citizen of Veracruz
jefe – boss or leader, especially a political one
jorongo – small poncho worn by men

Kukulcán – Mayan name for the plumed serpent god Quetzalcóatl

lada – short for *larga distancia*
Ladatel – the long-distance telephone system operated by the former monopoly Telmex
ladino, -a – more or less the same as *mestizo*
larga distancia – long-distance; usually refers to telephones
latifundio – large landholding; these sprang up after Mexico's independence from Spain
latifundista – powerful landowner who usurped communally owned land to form a *latifundio*
libramiento – road, highway
licenciado – university graduate, abbreviated as Lic and used as an honorific before a person's name; a status claimed by many who don't actually possess a degree
licuado – drink made from fruit juice, water or milk, and sugar

lista de correos – literally 'mail list,' a list displayed at a post office of people for whom letters are waiting; similar to General Delivery or Poste Restante

lleno – full, as with a car's fuel tank

local – can mean premises, such as a numbered shop or office in a mall or block, or can mean local; a *local* bus is one whose route starts at the bus station you are in

machismo – Mexican masculine bravura

madre – literally 'mother'; but the term can be used colloquially with an astonishing array of meanings

maguey – a type of agave, with thick pointed leaves growing straight out of the ground; *tequila* and *mezcal* are made from its sap

mañana – literally 'tomorrow' or 'morning'; in some contexts it may just mean 'some time in the future'

maquiladora – assembly-plant operation usually in northern Mexico and owned, at least in part, by foreigners; allowed to import equipment, raw materials and parts duty-free for finishing or assembly by Mexican labor

mariachi – small ensemble of street musicians playing traditional ballads on guitars and trumpets

marimba – wooden xylophone-type instrument, popular in Veracruz and the south

mercado – market; often a building near the center of a town, with shops and open-air stalls in the surrounding streets

Mesoamerica – the region inhabited by the ancient Mexican and Mayan cultures

mestizaje – 'mixedness,' Mexico's mixed-blood heritage; officially an object of pride

mestizo – person of mixed (usually indigenous and Spanish) ancestry, ie, most Mexicans

metate – shallow stone bowl with legs, for grinding maize and other foods

Mexican Hat Dance – a courtship dance in which a girl and boy dance around the boy's hat

mezcal – strong alcoholic drink produced from *maguey* sap

microbus – small bus – in Mexico City, the most common type of *pesero*

milpa – peasant's small cornfield, often cultivated by the slash-and-burn method

mirador, -es – lookout point(s)

mole – a spicy sauce usually made with chilies and usually chocolate and served with meat

Montezuma's revenge – Mexican version of Delhi-belly or travelers' diarrhea

mordida – literally 'little bite'; a small bribe to keep the wheels of bureaucracy turning; giving a mordida to a traffic policeman may ensure that you won't have to pay a bigger fine later

moreno, -a – dark, especially a dark-complexioned or dark-haired person

mota – marijuana

Mudéjar – Moorish architectural style, imported to Mexico by the Spanish

mujeres – women; seen on toilet doors

municipio – small local-government area; Mexico is divided into 2394 of them

na – Mayan thatched hut

NAFTA – North American Free Trade Agreement (see TLC)

Nahuatl – language of the Nahua people, descendants of the Aztecs

naos – Spanish trading galleons

norteamericanos – North Americans; people from north of the US-Mexican border

Nte – abbreviation for *norte* (north); used in street names

Ote – abbreviation for *oriente* (east); used in street names

paceño, -a – person from La Paz, Baja California Sur

palacio de gobierno – state capitol, state government headquarters

palacio municipal – town or city hall, headquarters of the municipal corporation

palapa – thatched-roof shelter, usually on a beach

panadería – bakery, pastry shop

parada – bus stop, usually for city buses

parado – standing up, as you often are on 2nd-class buses

parque nacional – national park; an environmentally protected area in which human exploitation is supposedly banned or restricted

parroquia – parish church

paseo – boulevard, walkway or pedestrian street; also the tradition of strolling in a circle around the plaza in the evening, men and women moving in opposite directions

Pemex – government-owned petroleum extraction, refining and retailing monopoly

peña – evening of Latin-American folk songs, often with a political protest theme

peninsulares – those born in Spain and sent by the Spanish government to rule the colony in Mexico (see *criollo, gachupines)*

periférico – ring road

pesero – Mexico City's word for *colectivo*

petate – mat, usually made of palm or reed

peyote – a hallucinogenic cactus

pinacoteca – art gallery

piñata – clay pot or papier-mâché mold decorated to resemble an animal, pineapple, star, etc; filled with sweets and gifts and smashed open at fiestas, particularly children's birthdays and Christmas

playa – beach

plaza de toros – bullring

plazuela – small plaza

poblano, -a – person from Puebla, or something in the style of Puebla

pollero – same as a *coyote*

Porfiriato – Porfirio Díaz's reign as president-dictator of Mexico for 30 years, until the 1910 revolution

portales – arcades

potosino – from the city or state of San Luis Potosí

presidio – fort or fort's garrison

PRI – Partido Revolucionario Institucional (Institutional Revolutionary Party); the political party that ruled Mexico for most of the 20th century

propina – tip; different from a *mordida*, which is closer to a bribe

Pte – abbreviation for *poniente* (west); used in street names

puerto – port

pulque – thick, milky, alcoholic drink of fermented *maguey* juice

quechquémitl – indigenous woman's shoulder cape with an opening for the head;

usually colorfully embroidered, often diamond-shaped

quetzal – crested bird with brilliant green, red and white plumage, native to southern Mexico, Central America and northern South America; quetzal feathers were highly prized in pre-Hispanic Mexico

Quetzalcóatl – plumed serpent god of pre-Hispanic Mexico

rebozo – long woolen or linen shawl covering the head or shoulders

refugio – a very basic cabin for shelter in the mountains – usually free, and available on a first-come basis

regiomontano, -a – person from Monterrey

reja – wrought-iron window grille

reserva de la biósfera – biosphere reserve; an environmentally protected area where human exploitation is steered toward ecologically unharmful activities

retablo – altarpiece; or small painting on wood, tin, cardboard, glass, etc, placed in a church to give thanks for miracles, answered prayers, etc

río – river

s/n – *sin número* (without number); used in street addresses

sacbe (s), **sacbeob** (pl) – ceremonial avenue(s) between great Mayan cities

sanatorio – hospital, particularly a small private one

sanitario(s) – toilet(s), literally 'sanitary place'

sarape – blanket with opening for the head, worn as a cloak

Semana Santa – Holy Week, the week from Palm Sunday to Easter Sunday; Mexico's major holiday period, when accommodations and transport get very busy

servicios – toilets

sierra – mountain range

sitio – taxi stand

stele, -es – standing stone monument(s), usually carved

supermercado – supermarket; anything from a small corner store to a large, US-style supermarket

Sur – south; often seen in street names

taller – shop or workshop; a *taller mecánico* is a mechanic's shop, usually for cars; a *taller de llantas* is a tire-repair shop

talud-tablero – stepped building style typical of Teotihuacán, with alternating vertical *(tablero)* and sloping *(talud)* sections

tapatío, -a – person born in the state of Jalisco

taquería – place where you buy tacos

taquilla – ticket window

telamon – statue of a male figure, used instead of a pillar to hold up the roof of a temple; see also *atlas*

telar de cintura – backstrap loom; the warp (lengthwise) threads are stretched between two horizontal bars, one of which is attached to a post or tree, the other to a strap around the weaver's lower back, and the weft (crosswise) threads are then woven in

teleférico – cable car

templo – church; anything from a wayside chapel to a cathedral

teocalli – Aztec sacred precinct

tequila – vaguely vodka-like liquor produced, like *pulque* and *mezcal*, from the *maguey* plant

Tex-Mex – an Americanized version of Mexican food

Tezcatlipoca – multifaceted pre-Hispanic god, lord of life and death and protector of warriors; as a smoking mirror he could see into hearts, as the sun god he needed the blood of sacrificed warriors to ensure he would rise again

tezontle – light-red, porous volcanic rock used for buildings by the Aztecs and *conquistadors*

tianguis – indigenous people's market

tienda – store

típico, -a – characteristic of a region; particularly used to describe food

Tláloc – pre-Hispanic water god

TLC – Tratado de Libre Comercio, the North American Free Trade Agreement (NAFTA)

topes – speed bumps; found on the outskirts of many towns and villages; they are only sometimes marked by signs

trajinera – gondola-like boat punted along the canals of Xochimilco

tzompantli – rack for the skulls of Aztec sacrificial victims

UNAM – Universidad Nacional Autónoma de México (National Autonomous University of Mexico)

universidad – university

viajero, -a – traveler

villa juvenil – youth sports center, often the location of an *albergue de juventud*

voladores – literally 'fliers,' the Totonac ritual in which men, suspended by their ankles, whirl around a tall pole

were-jaguar – half-human, half-jaguar being, portrayed in Olmec art

zaguán – vestibule or foyer, sometimes a porch

zócalo – main plaza or square; a term used in some (but by no means all) Mexican towns

Zona Rosa – literally 'Pink Zone'; an area of expensive shops, hotels and restaurants in Mexico City frequented by the wealthy and tourists; by extension, a similar area in another city

Acknowledgments

THANKS
Many readers wrote with helpful information and suggestions, including:

Jan Brugard, Raul Calderon, Kate Elliott, Roger Henderson, Pamela King, Irving Levinson, Stefan Schirmer, Barbara Whyte and Kay Yip Wong.

Guides by Region

Lonely Planet is known worldwide for publishing practical, reliable and no-nonsense travel information in our guides and on our web site. The Lonely Planet list covers just about every accessible region of the world. Currently there are fifteen series: travel guides, Shoestrings, Condensed, Phrasebooks, Read This First, Healthy Travel, Walking guides, Cycling guides, Pisces Diving & Snorkeling guides, City Maps, Travel Atlases, Out to Eat, World Food, Journeys travel literature and Pictorials.

AFRICA Africa on a shoestring • Africa – the South • Arabic (Egyptian) phrasebook • Arabic (Moroccan) phrasebook • Cairo • Cape Town • Cape Town city map • Central Africa • East Africa • Egypt • Egypt travel atlas • Ethiopian (Amharic) phrasebook • The Gambia & Senegal • Healthy Travel Africa • Kenya • Kenya travel atlas • Malawi, Mozambique & Zambia • Morocco • North Africa • Read This First Africa • South Africa, Lesotho & Swaziland • South Africa, Lesotho & Swaziland travel atlas • Swahili phrasebook • Tanzania, Zanzibar & Pemba • Trekking in East Africa • Tunisia • West Africa • Zimbabwe, Botswana & Namibia • Zimbabwe, Botswana & Namibia travel atlas • World Food Morocco

Travel Literature: The Rainbird: A Central African Journey • Songs to an African Sunset: A Zimbabwean Story • Mali Blues: Traveling to an African Beat

AUSTRALIA & THE PACIFIC Auckland • Australia • Australian phrasebook • Bushwalking in Australia • Bushwalking in Papua New Guinea • Fiji • Fijian phrasebook • Healthy Travel Australia, NZ and the Pacific • Islands of Australia's Great Barrier Reef • Melbourne • Melbourne city map • Micronesia • New Caledonia • New South Wales & the ACT • New Zealand • Northern Territory • Outback Australia • Out to Eat – Melbourne • Out to Eat – Sydney • Papua New Guinea • Pidgin phrasebook • Queensland • Rarotonga & the Cook Islands • Samoa • Solomon Islands • South Australia • South Pacific • South Pacific Languages phrasebook • Sydney • Sydney city map • Sydney condensed • Tahiti & French Polynesia • Tasmania • Tonga • Tramping in New Zealand • Vanuatu • Victoria • Western Australia

Travel Literature: Islands in the Clouds • Kiwi Tracks: A New Zealand Journey • Sean & David's Long Drive

CENTRAL AMERICA & THE CARIBBEAN Bahamas, Turks & Caicos • Bermuda • Central America on a shoestring • Costa Rica • Cuba • Dominican Republic & Haiti • Eastern Caribbean • Guatemala, Belize & Yucatán: La Ruta Maya • Jamaica • Mexico • Mexico City • Panama • Puerto Rico • Read This First Central & South America • World Food Mexico • Yucatán

Travel Literature: Green Dreams: Travels in Central America

EUROPE Amsterdam • Amsterdam city map • Andalucía • Austria • Baltic States phrasebook • Barcelona • Berlin • Berlin city map• Britain • British phrasebook • Brussels, Bruges & Antwerp • Budapest city map • Canary Islands • Central Europe • Central Europe phrasebook • Corfu & Ionians • Corsica • Crete • Crete condensed • Croatia • Cyprus • Czech & Slovak Republics • Denmark • Dublin • Eastern Europe • Eastern Europe phrasebook • Edinburgh • Estonia, Latvia & Lithuania • Europe on a shoestring • Finland • Florence • France • French phrasebook • Germany • German phrasebook • Greece • Greek Islands • Greek phrasebook • Hungary • Iceland, Greenland & the Faroe Islands • Istanbul city map • Ireland • Italian phrasebook • Italy • Krakow • Lisbon • London • London city map • London condensed • Mediterranean Europe • Mediterranean Europe phrasebook • Munich • Norway • Paris • Paris city map • Paris condensed • Poland • Portugal • Portugese phrasebook • Portugal travel atlas • Prague • Prague city map • Provence & the Côte d'Azur • Read This First Europe • Romania & Moldova • Rome • Russia, Ukraine & Belarus • Russian phrasebook • Scandinavian & Baltic Europe • Scandinavian Europe phrasebook • Scotland • Slovenia • Spain • Spanish phrasebook • St Petersburg • Switzerland • Trekking in Spain • Ukrainian phrasebook • Venice • Vienna • Walking in Britain • Walking in Ireland • Walking in Italy • Walking in Spain • Walking in Switzerland • Western Europe • Western Europe phrasebook • World Food Italy • World Food Spain

Travel Literature: The Olive Grove: Travels in Greece

Mail Order

Lonely Planet products are distributed worldwide. They are also available by mail order from Lonely Planet, so if you have difficulty finding a title please write to us. North and South American residents should write to 150 Linden St, Oakland, CA 94607, USA; European and African residents should write to 10a Spring Place, London, NW5 3BH; and residents of other countries to PO Box 617, Hawthorn, Victoria 3122, Australia.

INDIAN SUBCONTINENT Bangladesh • Bengali phrasebook • Bhutan • Delhi • Goa • Hindi/Urdu phrasebook • India • India & Bangladesh travel atlas • Indian Himalaya • Karakoram Highway • Kerala • Mumbai • Nepal • Nepali phrasebook • Pakistan • Rajasthan • Read This First: Asia & India • South India • Sri Lanka • Sri Lanka phrasebook • Trekking in the Indian Himalaya • Trekking in the Karakoram & Hindukush • Trekking in the Nepal Himalaya
Travel Literature: In Rajasthan • Shopping for Buddhas • The Age of Kali

ISLANDS OF THE INDIAN OCEAN Madagascar & Comoros • Maldives • Mauritius, Réunion & Seychelles

MIDDLE EAST & CENTRAL ASIA Bahrain, Kuwait & Qatar • Central Asia • Central Asia phrasebook • Dubai • Hebrew phrasebook • Iran • Israel & the Palestinian Territories • Israel & the Palestinian Territories travel atlas • Istanbul • Istanbul city map • Istanbul to Cairo on a shoestring • Jerusalem • Jerusalem city map • Jordan • Jordan, Syria & Lebanon travel atlas • Lebanon • Middle East • Oman & the United Arab Emirates • Syria • Turkey • Turkey travel atlas • Turkish phrasebook •Yemen
Travel Literature: The Gates of Damascus • Kingdom of the Film Stars: Journey into Jordan • Black on Black: Iran Revisited

NORTH AMERICA Alaska • Backpacking in Alaska • Baja California • Boston • California & Nevada • California condensed • Canada • Chicago • Chicago city map • Deep South • Florida • Hawaii • Las Vegas • Los Angeles • Miami • New England • New Orleans • New York City • New York city map • New York condensed • New York, New Jersey & Pennsylvania • Oahu • Pacific Northwest USA • Puerto Rico • Rocky Mountain States • San Francisco • San Francisco city map • Seattle • Southwest USA • Texas • USA • USA phrasebook • Vancouver • Washington, DC & the Capital Region • Washington, DC city map
Travel Literature: Drive Thru America

NORTH-EAST ASIA Beijing • Cantonese phrasebook • China • Hong Kong • Hong Kong city map • Hong Kong, Macau & Guangzhou • Japan • Japanese phrasebook • Japanese audio pack • Korea • Korean phrasebook • Kyoto • Mandarin phrasebook • Mongolia • Mongolian phrasebook • North-East Asia on a shoestring • Seoul • South-West China • Taiwan • Tibet • Tibetan phrasebook • Tokyo
Travel Literature: Lost Japan • In Xanadu

SOUTH AMERICA Argentina, Uruguay & Paraguay • Bolivia • Brazil • Brazilian phrasebook • Buenos Aires • Chile & Easter Island • Chile & Easter Island travel atlas • Colombia • Ecuador & the Galapagos Islands • Healthy Travel Central & South America • Latin American Spanish phrasebook • Peru • Quechua phrasebook • Rio de Janeiro • Rio de Janeiro city map • South America on a shoestring • Trekking in the Patagonian Andes • Venezuela
Travel Literature: Full Circle: A South American Journey

SOUTH-EAST ASIA Bali & Lombok • Bangkok • Bangkok city map • Burmese phrasebook • Cambodia • Hanoi • Healthy Travel Asia & India • Hill Tribes phrasebook • Ho Chi Minh City • Indonesia • Indonesia's Eastern Islands • Indonesian phrasebook • Indonesian audio pack • Jakarta • Java • Laos • Lao phrasebook • Laos travel atlas • Malay phrasebook • Malaysia, Singapore & Brunei • Myanmar (Burma) • Philippines • Pilipino (Tagalog) phrasebook • Read This First Asia & India • Singapore • South-East Asia on a shoestring • South-East Asia phrasebook • Thailand • Thailand's Islands & Beaches • Thailand travel atlas • Thai phrasebook • Thai audio pack • Vietnam • Vietnamese phrasebook • Vietnam travel atlas • World Food Thailand • World Food Vietnam

ALSO AVAILABLE: Antarctica • The Arctic • Brief Encounters: Stories of Love, Sex & Travel • Chasing Rickshaws • Lonely Planet Unpacked • Not the Only Planet: Travel Stories from Science Fiction • Sacred India • Travel with Children • Traveller's Tales

Index

Bold indicates maps.

Bold indicates maps.

Bold indicates maps.

Boxed Text

Ah…Men 185
Air Travel Glossary 86
Airline Offices 90-1
The Art Scene 30-1
Aztec Culture & Religion 13
The Ball Game 211
Bonds for All? 98
Chain Restaurants 168
Chocolate & Chicken 235
Cradle of Independence 218-9
Diego & Frida 140-1
Embassy Websites 50
An Environmental Success Story 22
Have Bra, Can Bust 105
How to Drink Tequila Like a Pro 166
La Corrida 192
La Lotería 120

Little Whims 161
Mexico City Hostels 148
Mexico City on Foot 107
Mexico's Area Code & Phone Number
   Changes 56
Puebla Pottery 231
Ready for Take-Off 158
Retablos 130
Shantytowns 41
Square Meals: Food with a Zócalo View 170
TAESA 87
Tropical Turns 187
The UNAM Strike 136
A Vivid Production 75
Voladores 126
What's in a Name? 37

Bold indicates maps.

Mexico City Map Section

DALE BUCKTON

MAP 1 MEXICO CITY

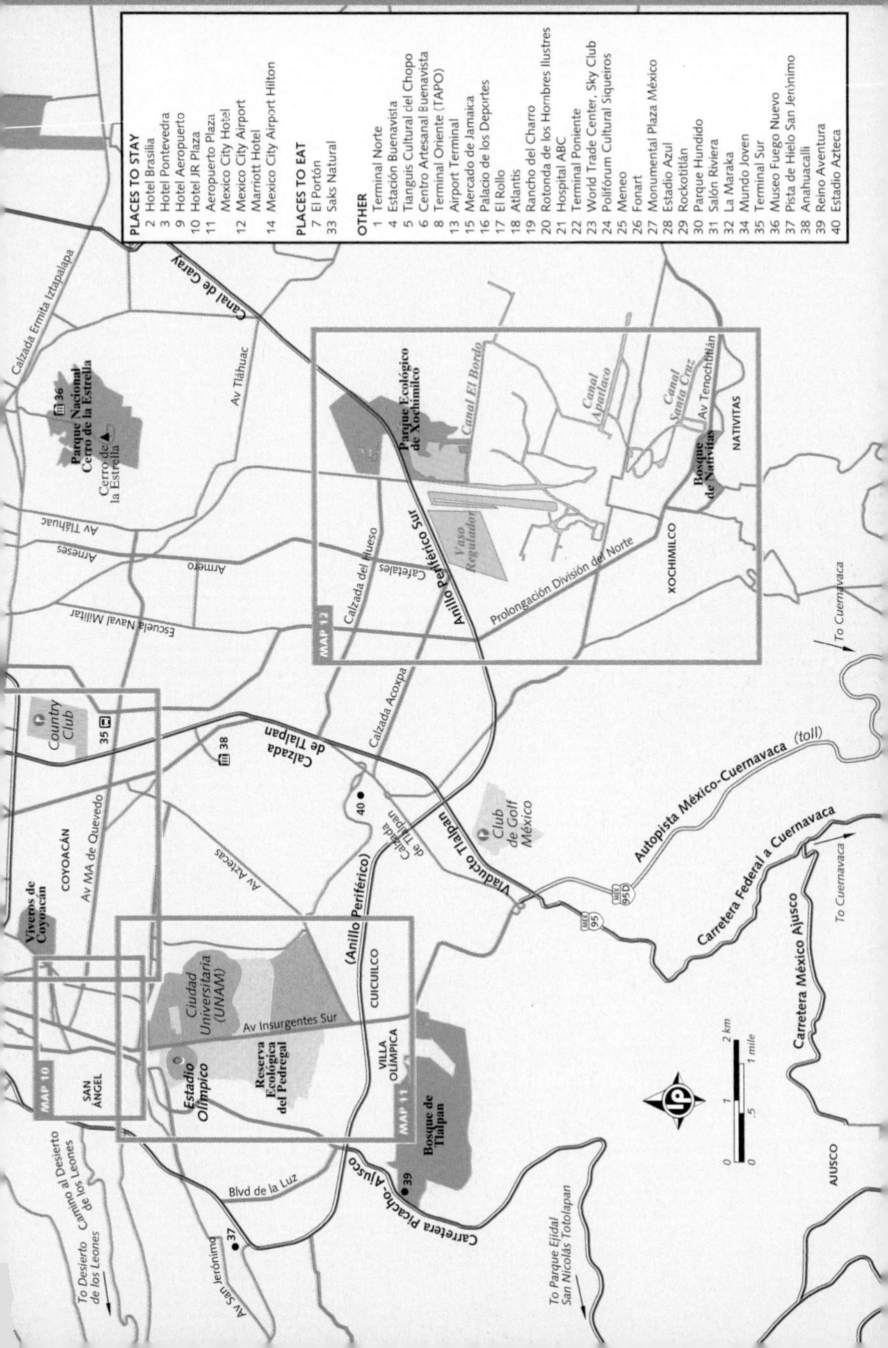

PLACES TO STAY
2 Hotel Brasilia
3 Hotel Pontevedra
9 Hotel Aeropuerto
10 Hotel JR Plaza
11 Aeropuerto Plaza
12 Mexico City Hotel
  Mexico City Airport
  Marriott Hotel
14 Mexico City Airport Hilton

PLACES TO EAT
7 El Portón
33 Saks Natural

OTHER
1 Terminal Norte
4 Estación Buenavista
5 Tianguis Cultural del Chopo
6 Centro Artesanal Buenavista
8 Terminal Oriente (TAPO)
13 Airport Terminal
15 Mercado de Jamaica
16 Palacio de los Deportes
17 El Rollo
18 Atlantis
19 Rancho del Charro
20 Rotonda de los Hombres Ilustres
21 Hospital ABC
22 Terminal Poniente
23 World Trade Center, Sky Club
24 Polifórum Cultural Siqueiros
25 Meneo
26 Fonart
27 Monumental Plaza México
28 Estadio Azul
29 Rockotitlán
30 Parque Hundido
31 Salón Riviera
32 La Maraka
34 Mundo Joven
35 Terminal Sur
36 Museo Fuego Nuevo
37 Pista de Hielo San Jerónimo
38 Anahuacalli
39 Reino Aventura
40 Estadio Azteca

Calzada Ermita Iztapalapa
Canal de Garay
Av Tláhuac
Av Tláhuac
Parque Nacional Cerro de la Estrella
Cerro de la Estrella
Ameres
Armero
Escuela Naval Militar
Calzada del Hueso
Cartales
Anillo Periférico Sur
Vaso Regulador
Parque Ecológico de Xochimilco
Canal El Bondo
Canal Apatlaco
Canal Santa Cruz
Av Tenochtitlán
Bosque de Nativitas
NATIVITAS
XOCHIMILCO
MAP 12
Prolongación División del Norte
To Cuernavaca
Calzada Acoxpa
Country Club
COYOACÁN
Av MA de Quevedo
Viveros de Coyoacán
Calzada de Tlalpan
Club de Golf México
Av Aztecas
Av Tulpan
Viaducto Tlalpan
Autopista México-Cuernavaca (toll)
Carretera Federal a Cuernavaca
To Cuernavaca
Ciudad Universitaria (UNAM)
MAP 10
SAN ÁNGEL
Estadio Olímpico
Reserva Ecológica del Pedregal
Av Insurgentes Sur
CUICUILCO
(Anillo Periférico)
VILLA OLÍMPICA
MAP 11
Bosque de Tlalpan
Blvd de la Luz
Carretera Picacho-Ajusco
Av San Jerónimo
To Desierto de los Leones
Camino al Desierto de los Leones
To Parque Ejidal San Nicolás Totolapan
AJUSCO
Carretera México Ajusco
To Cuernavaca
0 2 km
0 1 mile

MAP 2 METRO

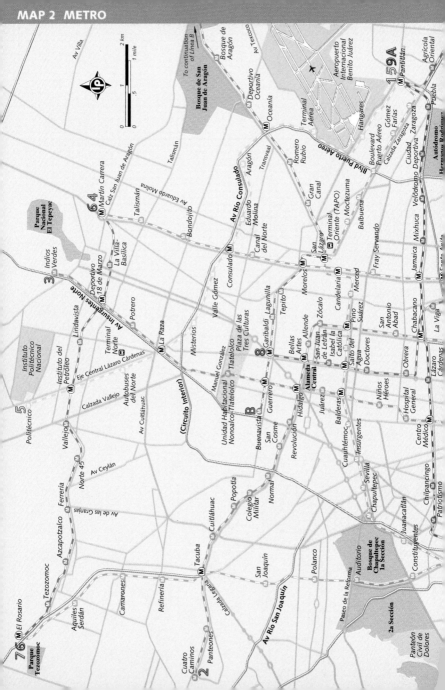

Continuation of Linea A

see inset map below for continuation of Linea A

Av Rio Churubusco (Circuito Interior)

Coyuya
Iztacalco
Apatlaco
Aculco
Escuadrón 201
Atlalilco
Iztapalapa
Cerro de la Estrella
Av Jalisco
Leyes de Reforma
Rojo Gómez
Oriente 253
Purísima
Constitución de 1917

Parque Nacional Cerro de la Estrella

Calzada Ermita Iztapalapa

Calzada de la Viga
Viaducto
Xola
Villa de Cortés
Nativitas
Portales
Ermita
Av Molina Enríquez

Calzada de Tlalpan
Av Presidente Calles
General Anaya
Country Club
Tasqueña
Terminal Sur
Las Torres
Ciudad Jardín
La Virgen
Xotepingo
Nezahualpilli
Registro Federal
Textitlán
El Vergel

to continuation of Linea A, see Map 12 for end of line

Etiopía
Eugenia
División del Norte
Zapata
Av Cuauhtémoc
Av División del Norte
Coyoacán
Av Universidad
Viveros de Coyoacán
Av Coyoacán
Av MA de Quevedo
MA de Quevedo
Henríquez Ureña
Copilco
Universidad
Av Aztecas

Ciudad Universitaria (UNAM)
Av Insurgentes Sur
Reserva Ecológica del Pedregal

Viaducto Presidente Alemán
Tacubaya
Observatorio
Terminal Poniente
San Pedro de los Pinos
San Antonio
Mixcoac
Barranca del Muerto
Av Insurgentes Sur
Paseo del Pedregal
Blvd López Mateos (Anillo Periférico)

Continuation of Linea A

0   .5   1 mile
0   1   2 km

La Paz
Los Reyes
Santa Marta
Acatitla
Peñón Viejo
Guelatao
Tepalcates
Calzada Zaragoza
Canal de San Juan
Oriente 253
Parque Santa Cruz Meyehualco

Legend:
- Terminus
- Metro Transfer Station
- Metro Station
- Tren Ligero Station

A Metro Line Terminus
M Metro Transfer Station
● Metro Station
○ Tren Ligero Station

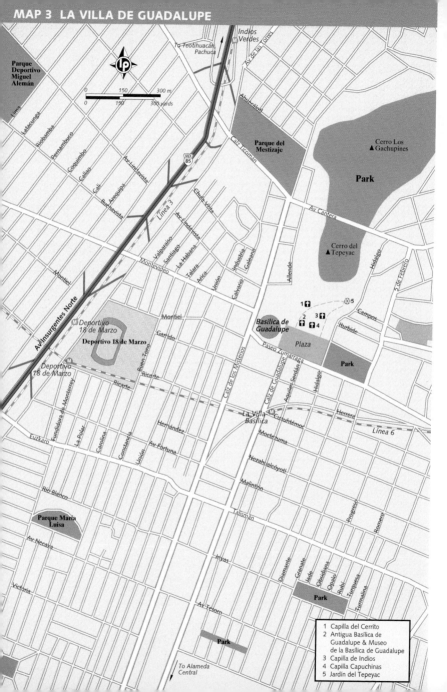

MAP 3 LA VILLA DE GUADALUPE

To Teotihuacán
Pachuca

Indios
Verdes

Av las Torres

Parque
Deportivo
Miguel
Alemán

Ahtíxotatl

150   300 m
150   300 yards

Lima

Latacunga

Riobamba

Fernambuco

Coquimbo

Callao

Av Limbarde

Calz Acequia

Buehavista

Parque del
Mestizaje

Cerro Los
▲ Gachupines

Park

MEX
85

Linea 3

Chdz Vita

Av Industria

Av Cantera

Cerro del
▲ Tepeyac

Montiel

Valparaiso

Santiago

La Habana

Montevideo

Talara

Arica

Unión

Galveston

Industria

Galeana

Gallardo

5 de Febrero

Hidalgo

Allende

Av Insurgentes Norte

🏛 Deportivo
18 de Marzo

Montiel

Deportivo 18 de Marzo

Garrido

Buen Tono

Ricarte

1 🏛
2 🏛 3 🏛
        4 🏛

⚬ 5

Basílica de
Guadalupe

Campos

Iturbide

Calz de los Misterios

Paseo Zumárraga

Plaza

Park

Deportivo
18 de Marzo

Ricarte

Fundidora de Monterrey

Euzkaro

La Polar

Catolina

Constanela

Unión

Hernández

Av Fortuna

Calz de Guadalupe

Aquiles Serdán

Hidalgo

La Villa
Basílica

Cuauhtémoc

Moctezuma

Nezahualcóyotl

Herrera

Línea 6

Malintzin

Río Blanco

Parque María
Luisa

Av Necaxa

Talismán

Victoria

Jnyas

Av Tesoro

Diamante

Granate

Jade

Obsidiana

Opalo

Rubí

Turquesa

Turmalina

Progreso

Monterrey

Park

Park

To Alameda
Central

1 Capilla del Cerrito
2 Antigua Basílica de
   Guadalupe & Museo
   de la Basílica de Guadalupe
3 Capilla de Indios
4 Capilla Capuchinas
5 Jardín del Tepeyac

Ceremonious opening parade at Monumental Plaza México bullring

Still stylish!

Sombreros for sale

MAP 4 CENTRO HISTÓRICO & ALAMEDA CENTRAL

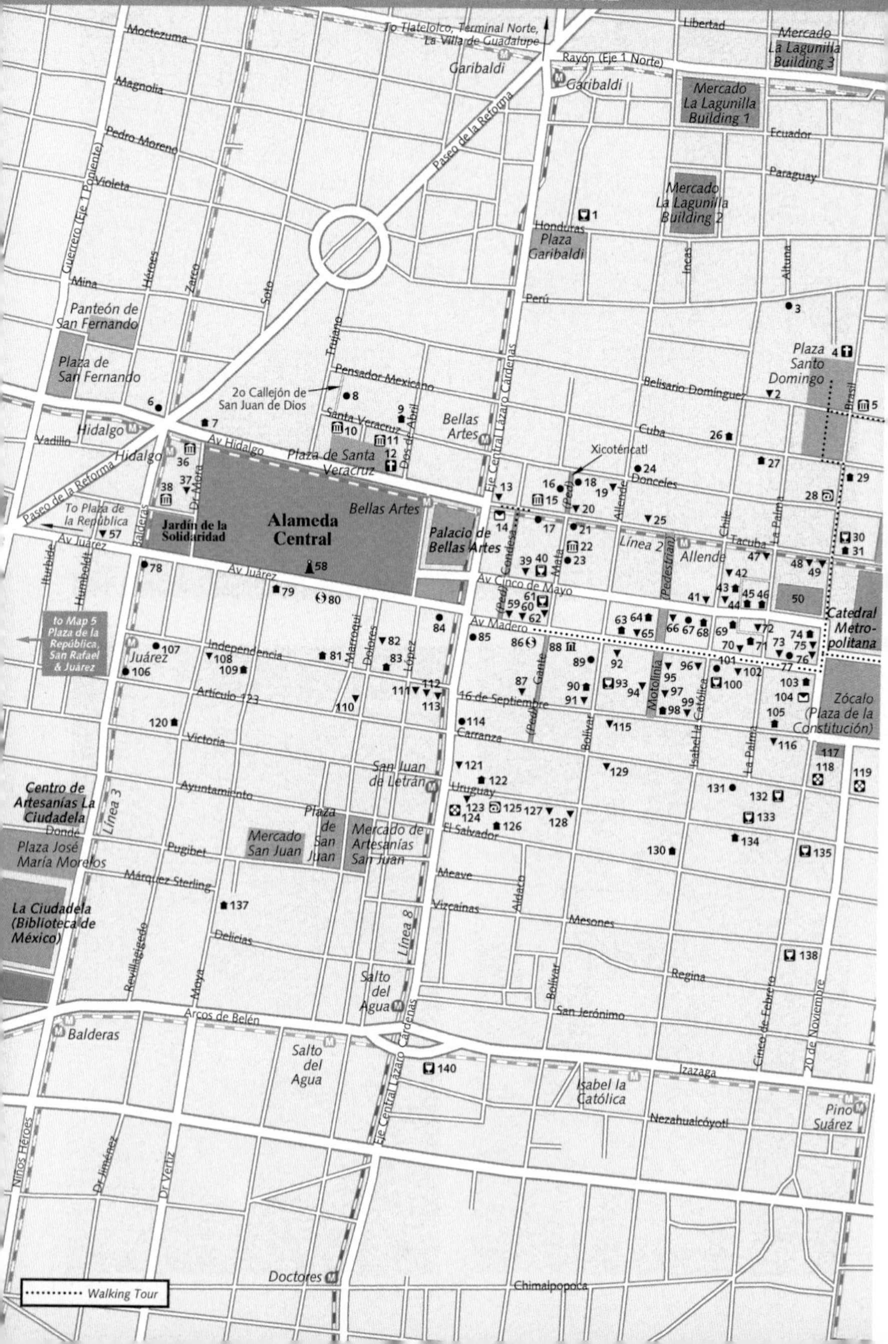

Moctezuma

To Tlatelolco, Terminal Norte,
La Villa de Guadalupe

Libertad

Mercado
La Lagunilla
Building 3

Magnolia

Garibaldi

Rayón (Eje 1 Norte)

Mercado
La Lagunilla
Building 1

Pedro Moreno

Garibaldi

Ecuador

Violeta

Paseo de la Reforma

Honduras

Paraguay

1

Mercado
La Lagunilla
Building 2

Plaza
Garibaldi

Perú

Incas

Altuna

Mina

3

Panteón de
San Fernando

Plaza Santo
Domingo

4

Plaza de
San Fernando

Belisario Domínguez

2

5

6

8

Santa Veracruz

9

Bellas
Artes

Cuba

26

27

7

2o Callejón de
San Juan de Dios

Pensador Mexicano

Av Hidalgo

10

11

Plaza de Santa
Veracruz

12

Xicoténcatl

24

Donceles

28

29

Hidalgo

36

13

16

18

19

30

Vadillo

37

38

14

15

17

20

21

22

23

25

Línea 2

Allende

Tacuba

47

31

Jardín de la
Solidaridad

57

Alameda
Central

Bellas Artes

Palacio de
Bellas Artes

39

40

42

48

49

Catedral
Metro-
politana

78

58

Av Juárez

79

59

60

61

62

41

43

44

45

46

50

to Map 5
Plaza de
la República,
San Rafael
& Juárez

80

Av Madero

84

85

86

88

89

90

91

63

64

65

66

67

68

69

70

71

72

73

74

75

76

77

Zócalo
(Plaza de la
Constitución)

107

108

109

Independencia

82

83

81

92

93

94

95

96

97

98

99

100

101

102

103

104

105

Juárez

106

Dolores

López

87

116

Artículo 123

110

111

112

113

115

117

118

120

Victoria

114

Carranza

129

131

132

119

Centro de
Artesanías La
Ciudadela

San Juan
de Letrán

121

122

Línea 3

Ayuntamiento

Plaza
de
San Juan

123

124

125

126

127

128

133

134

Plaza José
María Morelos

Pugibet

Mercado
San Juan

Mercado de
Artesanías
San Juan

El Salvador

130

135

La Ciudadela
(Biblioteca de
México)

Márquez Sterling

137

Meave

Vizcaínas

Mesones

138

Delicias

Línea 8

Balderas

Arcos de Belén

Salto
del
Agua

Regina

San Jerónimo

Salto
del
Agua

140

Isabel la
Católica

Izazaga

Pino
Suárez

Doctores

Chimalpopoca

Nezahualcóyotl

Isabel la Católica

.... Walking Tour

Mercado Tepito

Lagunilla

Mercado Tepito
Shoes Building

Héroe de Granaditas

Línea B

Tepito

Costa Rica

0   150   300 m
0   150   300 yards

Aztecas

Florida

Nicaragua

Av. de Trabajo

Bolivia

Morelos

Morelos

To Airport

Colombia

Albañiles

Argentina

Venezuela

Carmen

Secretaría de
Educación Pública

San Ildefonso

Pasaje Catedral

▼33

32

Plaza
Loreto

35

Sierra

34
▼

Templo Mayor
(Ped)

Guatemala

Loreto

Alcocer

Seminario

51

52   53

55

Santísima

56

Moneda

Correo Mayor

Academia

54

Zócalo

Palacio
Nacional

Zapata

La Soledad

Suprema
Corte de
Justicia

Corregidora

Línea 4

To TAPO

Correo Mayor

136

Las Cruces

Jesús María

Talavera

Roldán

Manzanares

Parque
Guadalupe
Victoria

Palacio Legislativo

Santo Tomás

Santa Escuela

El Rosario

Candelaria

Candelaria

139

Pino Suárez

General Anaya

Cabaña

Candelaria

Av. Congreso de la Unión (Eje 1 Oriente)

Anillo de Circunvalación (Eje 1 Oriente)

Mercado
La Merced

Deportivo
Venustiano
Carranza

San Pablo

Línea 1

Olvera

Carretones

Merced

San Ciprián

Jardín Chiapas

Gurrión

Cuamatzin

Fray Servando Teresa de Mier (Eje 1 Sur)

Mercado
Sonora

Fray Servando

MAP 4 CENTRO HISTÓRICO & ALAMEDA CENTRAL

PLACES TO STAY

7 Hotel de Cortés
9 Hotel Hidalgo
26 Pensión del Centro
27 Hotel Habana
29 Hotel Azores
31 Hostel Catedral
32 Hotel Catedral
43 Hotel Juárez
45 Hotel Zamora
46 Hotel Washington
53 Hostal Moneda
63 Hotel Ritz
64 Hotel Buenos Aires
68 Hotel Gillow
69 Hotel Canadá
71 Hotel San Antonio
74 Holiday Inn Select
79 Hotel Bamer
81 Hotel Del Valle
83 Hotel Marlowe
90 Hotel Principal
98 Hotel Lafayette
103 Hotel Majestic
105 Gran Hotel Ciudad de México
109 Hotel Metropol
120 Hotel Fleming
122 Hotel Capitol
126 Hotel El Salvador
130 Hotel Isabel
134 Hotel Montecarlo
136 Hotel Roble
137 Hotel San Diego

PLACES TO EAT

2 Hostería de Santo Domingo
10 Cafetería del Claustro
13 Sanborns
19 Wings
20 Los Girasoles, Taco Inn
25 Café de Tacuba
33 Café del Centro
34 La Casa de las Sirenas
37 Café Trevi
39 Café El Popular
41 Café La Blanca
42 Tacos Beguis
44 Taquería Tlaquepaque
45 Café El Popular
47 La Vasconia
48 Los Bisquets Bisquets Obregón
49 Restaurante México Viejo
57 Sanborns
59 Sanborns Casa de Azulejos
60 The Coffee Factory
62 Restaurante El Vegetariano
65 VIPS
66 Potzollcalli
69 Jugos Canadá
70 Restaurante El Vegetariano

72 Pizza Hut
73 Bertico Café
74 Restaurante El Campanario,
    Cafetería El Invernadero
75 Flash Taco
76 Shakey's Pizza y Pollo
82 Centro Naturista de México
87 Pastelería Ideal
91 Super Soya
92 Los Bisquets Bisquets Obregón
94 Comedor Vegetariano
95 McDonald's
96 KFC
97 La Casa del Pavo
99 Sanborns
102 VIPS
103 Restaurante Terraza
105 Cafetería Mirador, Restaurante
    del Centro
108 Restaurante Continental
110 Hong King
111 La Pizza
112 Fonda Santa Rita
113 Taquería Tlaquepaque
115 El Molino
116 Super Soya
121 Churrería El Moro
123 Restaurante Danubio
127 Rincón Mexicano, Antojitos Tere
128 La Esquina del Pibe
129 Santa Clara
130 Restaurant Isabel
136 Restaurante-Bar Maple

OTHER

1 El Tenampa
3 Arena Coliseo
4 Iglesia de Santo Domingo
5 Museo de la Medicina Mexicana
6 La Hostería del Bohemio
8 Salón México
10 Museo Franz Mayer
11 Museo de la Estampa
12 Iglesia de la Santa Veracruz
14 Correo Mayor (Central Post
    Office)
15 Museo Nacional de Arte
16 Central de Telégrafos
17 Colegio de Minería
18 Cámara de Senadores
21 Jardín de la Triple Alianza
22 Museo del Ejército y Fuerza
    Aérea
23 La Torre del Papel
24 Asamblea Legislativa del Distrito
    Federal
28 Centro de Estudios Superiores
    Lafoel
30 Restaurante-Bar León
35 Museo de San Ildefonso

36 Pinacoteca Virreinal
38 Museo Mural Diego Rivera
40 La Ópera Bar
50 Nacional Monte de Piedad
51 Fuente de Tenochtitlán
52 Museo de la Secretaría de
    Hacienda y Crédito Público
53 Ecogrupos de México
54 Museo Nacional de las Culturas
55 Museo José Luis Cuevas
56 Templo de la Santísima
58 Hemiciclo a Juárez
59 Casa de Azulejos
61 Bar Mata
67 Dulcería de Celaya
77 DHL
78 Mexicana Airlines
80 Casa de Cambio Plus
84 Gandhi
85 Torre Latinoamericana
86 Cambios Exchange
88 Palacio de Iturbide
89 American Bookstore
93 Salón Corona
100 Opulencia
101 Mixup
104 Post Office
106 Elektra
107 Teatro Metropólitan
114 Pórtico de la Ciudad de México
117 Gobierno del Distrito Federal
118 El Palacio de Hierro
119 Liverpool
124 NETFM, Plaza de la
    Computación y Electrónica
125 Ultra Byte
131 Turismo Zócalo
132 El Cirio
133 Pervert Lounge
135 Altura
138 La Llorona
139 Elektra
140 Butterfly

MAP 5 PLAZA DE LA REPÚBLICA, SAN RAFAEL & JUÁREZ

PLACES TO STAY
3 Hotel Lepanto
9 Hotel Texas
12 Casa de los Amigos
13 Hotel Édison
15 Hotel Ibiza
17 Hotel Carlton
18 Hotel Oxford
20 Hotel New York
23 Hotel Jena
24 Hotel Frimont
27 Palace Hotel
28 Hotel Corinto
31 Hotel Mayaland
32 Hotel Casa Blanca
34 Hotel Crowne Plaza
43 Hotel Mallorca
44 Hotel Compostela
45 Hotel Sevilla
51 Hotel Regente
53 Hotel Sevilla Palace
56 Hotel Imperial
60 Fiesta Americana
67 Hotel María Cristina
72 Hotel El Ejecutivo
73 Mi Casa

PLACES TO EAT
2 Sanborns
7 El Tigre
8 Super Cocina Los Arcos

10 Potzollcalli
19 Restaurant Cahuich
21 Seafood Cocktail Stand
22 Restaurante Samy
29 VIPS
30 Tacos El Caminero
33 Sanborns
47 Café Gran Premio
48 VIPS
50 Sanborns
51 Restaurant Korinto
57 Toks
58 Wings
59 Café Vendôme
64 Café La Habana
68 Restaurante Nucleo

OTHER
1 Museo Universitario del Chopo
4 Iglesia de San Fernando
5 Antillanos
6 ACE Gallery
11 Post Office
14 Lavandería Automática Édison
16 Museo de San Carlos
25 Torre Caballito
26 Monumento a la Revolución,
    Museo Nacional de la Revolución
35 Mexico City National Chamber of
    Commerce
36 Dryclean USA

37 TAESA
38 Iberia, Aerolíneas Argentinas
39 Viajes Universales
40 El Universal, Sala Internet
41 Consejo Británico
42 Librería Británica
46 Lavandería Las Artes
49 Penelope
52 Telecomm
54 Post Office
55 Monumento a Cristóbal Colón
61 Aeroméxico, Aerolitoral
62 DHL
63 Salón de Baile del Pacífico
65 National Confederation of
    Industrial Chambers
66 Institut Français d'Amérique
    Latine
69 Monumento a Cuauhtémoc
70 Bital Bank
71 American Chamber of Commerce
    Mexico
74 Bar Milán
75 El Colmillo
76 Biblioteca Benjamín Franklin,
    Institute of International
    Education
77 US Trade Center, American
    Business Information Center
78 Arena México

NEIL SETCHFIELD

VW taxi whooshing by – be cautious!

MAP 5 PLAZA DE LA REPÚBLICA, SAN RAFAEL & JUÁREZ

San Cosme

Ribera de San Cosme

Dr González Martínez

1 ▥

Herrera

Delegación Miguel Hidalgo (Circuito Interior)

Pimentel

SAN RAFAEL

Prieto

5 ▣

● 6

Covarrubias

Gómez Farías

0   150   300 m
0   150   300 yards

Lorenzana

Velázquez de León

Martín Contreras

Barreda

Aldamirano

Río Usuri

Río Amur

Río Amoy

Villalongín

Av Parque Vía

Rosas-Moreno

Schultz

41 ●

Antonio Caso

46 ● 47 ▼

49 ▣

▼ 50

65 ●

● 42

43 ▮

51 ▮

Río Balsas

Río Éufrates

Serapio Rendón

44 ●   ● 45

52 ●

Madrid

Perlit

66 ●

Jardín del Arte

48 ●
▼

Sadi Carnot

Sullivan

Plaza
Villalongín

Río Sena

Río Nilo

Río Marne

Río Támesis

Río Nazas

Río Tigris

Río Pánuco

Plaza
Necaxa

▼ 68

67 ●

Río Nexa

Río Guadiana

Paseo de la Reforma

73 ▮

● 72

74
▼

Río Po

Río Danubio

Río Rhin

Río Amazonas

69 ●

● 70

71 ●   Lucerna

Río Lerma

to Map 8
Bosque de
Chapultepec
& Polanco

see Map 6
Zona Rosa

Roma

Viena

Milán

Río Tíber

Río Papaloapan

Hamburgo

JUÁREZ

Río Volga

María Isabel-
Sheraton Hotel

Av Insurgentes Centro

Londres

● 76

Berlín

Río Guadalquivir

Bucareli

Ramberes

Liverpool

Dinamarca

77 ●

Marsella

Av Florencia

Lieja

Abraham

Estocolmo

Estrasburgo

Copenhague

Niza

Havre

Nápoles

to Map 7
Condesa
& Roma

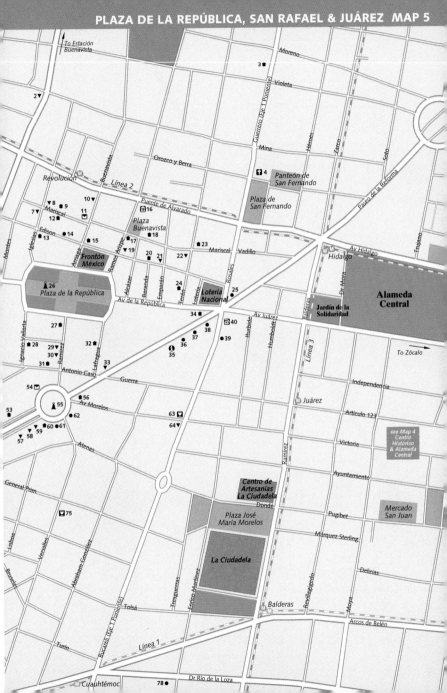

MAP 6 ZONA ROSA

ANZURES

CUAUHTÉMOC

ZONA ROSA

ROMA NORTE

Plaza
Grijalva

Plaza
Necaxa

María Isabel-
Sheraton Hotel

Plaza
del Ángel

Mercado
Insurgentes

see Map 8
Bosque de
Chapultepec
& Polanco

Calzada Melchor Ocampo (Circuito Interior)

Paseo de la Reforma

Bosque de
Chapultepec
1a Sección

(Pedestrian)

Chapultepec
M

Sevilla
M

Av Ejército Nacional

Av Chapultepec

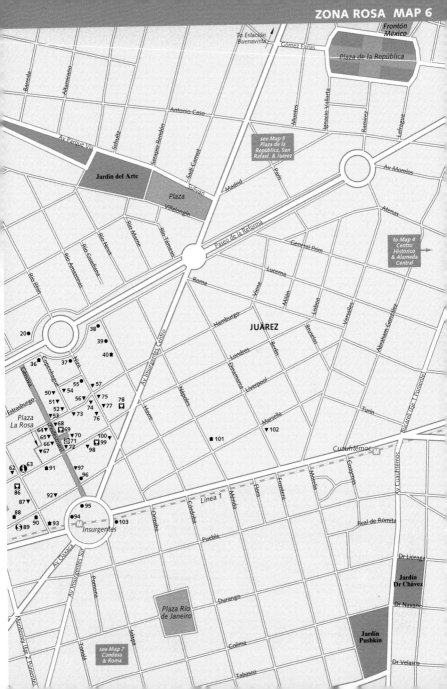

Frontón México

Plaza de la República

To Estación Buenavista

Gómez Farías

Antonio Caso

Av Parque Via

*see Map 5
Plaza de la
República, San
Rafael, & Juárez*

Jardín del Arte

Plaza
Villalongín

Madrid

Av Morelos

Atenas

Paseo de la Reforma

to Map 4
Centro
Histórico
& Alameda
Central

General Prim

Roma

Lucerna

20●

38●

39●

40■

37▼

36●

JUÁREZ

Hamburgo

Londres

Dinamarca

Liverpool

Havre

Berlín

Biarritz

Versalles

Río Neva

Río Marne

Río Tamesis

Río Guadiana

Río Amazonas

Río Rhin

Copenhague

Amberes

Hamburgo

Viena

Milán

Lisboa

Génova

Estrasburgo

Plaza
La Rosa

55▼
54▼

57▼

50▼

51▼

52▼

53▼

56▼

75▼

77▼

78▣

74▼

73▼

76▼

Nápoles

Marsella

Turín

68▼
69▣

64▼
65▼
66▼
67▼

70▼
71▣
72▼

100▣
99▣

98▣

101■

102▼

Cuauhtémoc

62■
63▤

91■

97▼
96

86▣

87▼

92▼

88■

89⊕

90

93▼

94Ⓜ

95●

103●

Insurgentes

Línea 1

Orizaba

Córdoba

Puebla

Mérida

Frontera

Morelia

Jalapa

Guaymas

Av Cuauhtémoc

Real de Romita

Av Oaxaca

Av Insurgentes Sur

Pomona

Monterrey (Eje 1 Poniente)

Tonalá

Durango

Dr Liceaga

Jardín
Dr Chávez

Dr Navarro

Plaza Río
de Janeiro

Jardín
Pushkin

*see Map 7
Condesa
& Roma*

Colima

Tabasco

Dr Velasco

MAP 6 ZONA ROSA

PLACES TO STAY
1 Hotel Bristol
· 5 San Marino Hotel-Suites
10 Casa González
14 Hotel Marquis Reforma
21 Four Seasons Hotel
36 Hotel Aristos
40 Hotel Internacional Havre
42 Hotel Westin Galería Plaza
46 Hotel Marco Polo
83 Hotel Plaza Florencia
88 Hotel Krystal Rosa
90 Hotel Century
91 Calinda Geneve & Spa
93 Hotel Royal
101 Hotel Misión Zona Rosa

PLACES TO EAT
2 Restaurante Vegetariano Las Fuentes
3 Fuji
12 Les Moustaches
17 Sanborns
21 Restaurant La Jolla
25 Anderson's de Reforma
26 Restaurante Vegetariano Yug
31 Restaurant Champs Elysées
42 Ile de France
45 Auseba
46 Il Caffe Milano
47 Restaurante Passy
48 Sushi Itto
50 Freedom
51 El Perro d'Enfrente
52 Angus Butcher House
53 Yuppie's Sports Café
54 Mesón del Perro Andaluz
56 Focolare
57 Pizza Hut
60 Parri Pollo Restaurante

62 Sanborns
64 Dunkin' Donuts
65 Burger King
66 Konditori
67 El Mariachi Tacos, Los Bisquets Bisquets Obregón, Massangui, Oscar's Seafood
68 Häagen-Dazs
70 Comedor
72 McDonald's
73 Taco Inn
74 Carrousel Internacional
75 Sanborns
76 Luaú
77 Chalet Suizo
81 La Beatricita
84 Ricocina
87 Harry's Bar
91 Café Jardín
92 Sanborns
93 Restaurante Tezka
97 KFC
98 Coffee House
100 VIPS
102 Restaurant El Asado Argentino

OTHER
4 America West, Alitalia
6 Jiffy
7 Casa de Cambio Tíber
8 Lavandería Automática
9 Tony Pérez
11 UK Embassy
13 British Chamber of Commerce
15 Aeroméxico, Aerolitoral
16 Canadian Airlines
18 US Embassy
19 Japan Airlines
20 Centro Bursátil
22 La Diana Cazadora

23 Japanese Chamber of Commerce
24 UPS
27 Monumento a la Independencia (El Ángel)
28 Money Exchange
29 Casa de Cambio Bancomer
30 Aero California
32 American Airlines
33 Mexicana
34 FedEx
35 Impulsora Cambiaria
37 DHL
38 American Express
39 Casa de Francia, La Bouquinerie, Mundo Joven
41 Alaska Airlines, United Airlines
43 Police Office
44 Café Internet
49 La Casa de la Prensa
55 Tower Records
58 Gray Line
59 El Taller, El Almacén
61 Cabaré-Tito
63 Oficina de Turismo de la Ciudad de México
69 Caramba
71 Java Chat
78 El Antro
79 Casanova Chapultepec
80 Post Office
82 La Casa de la Prensa
85 Grey Line
86 Cantina Las Bohemias
89 Money Exchange
94 INEGI Map Shop
95 La Casa del Canto
96 Mixup
99 El Celo
103 Instituto Nacional de Migración

RICHARD NEBESKY

Stone replica of a *tzompantli* (rack for the skulls of sacrifice victims), Templo Mayor

MAP 7 CONDESA & ROMA

The glorious Palacio de Bellas Artes

RICHARD I'ANSON

MAP 7 CONDESA & ROMA

Paseo de la Reforma

ZONA ROSA

Av Colegio Militar

(Pedestrian)

Hamburgo

Londres

Línea 1

Sevilla

Av Chapultepec

Chapultepec

Bosque de
Chapultepec
1a Sección

M

ROMA NORTE

Melgar

Durango

1

2

Av Oaxaca

3

Av Sonora

Colima

4

Tobasco

Veracruz

5

Obregón

Barrera

Solá

Parque
España

19

Calaya

CONDESA

18

Parque
México

25

Vasconcelos (Circuito Interior)

Escutia (Eje 2 Sur)

Montes de Oca

Av Mazatlán

Ámsterdam

27

Sonora

35   36   37 38

28

32

34   30

Michoacán

46

48

33   39   40 41

49

Campeche

42

47

51

43

44

52

45

50

Franklin

53

Patriotismo   M

Chilpancingo   M

Baja California

54

To San Ángel

0   150   300 m
0   150   300 yards

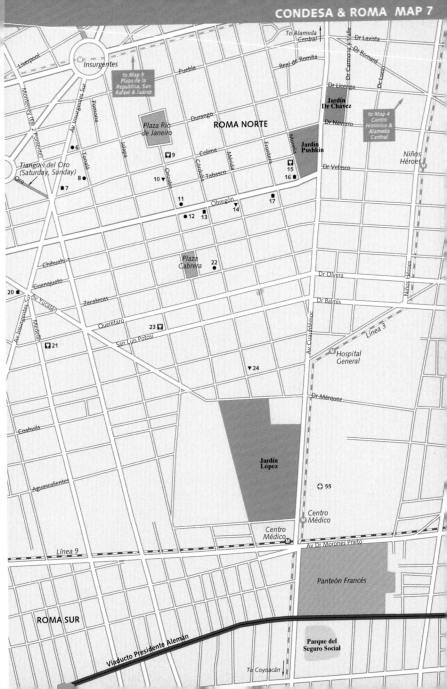

To Alameda Central
Dr Lavista
Dr Carmona y Valle
Dr Bernard
Liverpool
Insurgentes
Puebla
Real de Romita
Dr Lucio
Dr Licenga
Monterey (El 2 poniente)
Av Insurgentes Sur
Pomona
Plaza de la República, San Rafael & Juárez to Map 5
Durango
ROMA NORTE
Dr Navarro
Jardín Dr Chávez
to Map 4 Centro Histórico & Alameda Central
Plaza Río de Janeiro
6
Tonalá
Jalapa
9
Colima
Oaxaca
Mérida
Tabasco
Córdoba
Frontera
Morelia
Jardín Pushkin
15
16
Dr Velasco
Niños Héroes
Tianguis del Oro (Saturday, Sunday)
Oro
8
7
10
11
12 13
Obregón
14
17
Chihuahua
Plaza Cabrera
22
Dr Olvera
20
Guanajuato
Av Yucatán
Zacatecas
Dr Balmis
Niños Héroes
Medellín
Querétaro
23
San Luis Potosí
Línea 3
Av Cuauhtémoc
Hospital General
21
24
Dr Márquez
Coahuila
Jardín López
Aguascalientes
55
Centro Médico
Av Insurgentes Sur
Centro Médico
Av Dr Morones Prieto
Línea 9
Panteón Francés
ROMA SUR
Viaducto Presidente Alemán
Parque del Seguro Social
To Coyoacán

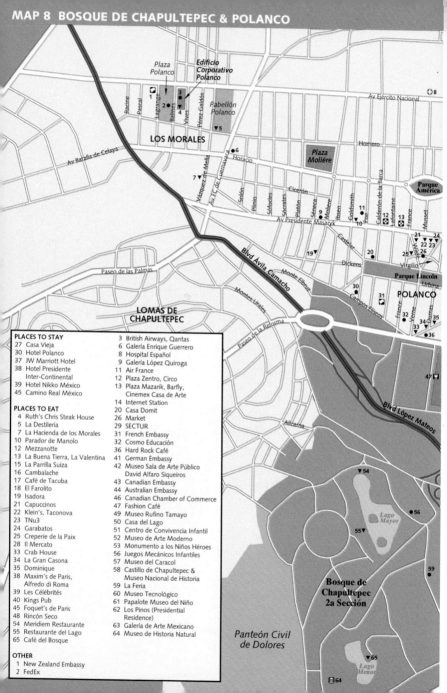

MAP 8 BOSQUE DE CHAPULTEPEC & POLANCO

PLACES TO STAY
27 Casa Vieja
30 Hotel Polanco
37 JW Marriott Hotel
38 Hotel Presidente
   Inter-Continental
39 Hotel Nikko México
45 Camino Real México

PLACES TO EAT
4 Ruth's Chris Steak House
5 La Destilería
7 La Hacienda de los Morales
10 Parador de Manolo
12 Mezzanotte
13 La Buena Tierra, La Valentina
15 La Parrilla Suiza
16 Cambalache
17 Café de Tacuba
18 El Farolito
19 Isadora
21 Capuccinos
22 Klein's, Taconova
23 TNu3
24 Garabatos
25 Creperie de la Paix
28 Il Mercato
33 Crab House
34 La Gran Casona
35 Dominique
38 Maxim's de Paris,
   Alfredo di Roma
39 Les Célébrités
40 Kings Pub
42 Foquet's de Paris
48 Rincón Seco
54 Meridiem Restaurante
55 Restaurante del Lago
65 Café del Bosque

OTHER
1 New Zealand Embassy
2 FedEx
3 British Airways, Qantas
6 Galería Enrique Guerrero
8 Hospital Español
9 Galería López Quiroga
11 Air France
12 Plaza Zentro, Circo
13 Plaza Mazarik, Barfly,
   Cinemex Casa de Arte
14 Internet Station
20 Casa Domit
26 Market
29 SECTUR
31 French Embassy
32 Cosmo Educación
36 Hard Rock Café
41 German Embassy
42 Museo Sala de Arte Público
   David Alfaro Siqueiros
43 Canadian Embassy
44 Australian Embassy
46 Canadian Chamber of Commerce
47 Fashion Café
49 Museo Rufino Tamayo
50 Casa del Lago
51 Centro de Convivencia Infantil
52 Museo de Arte Moderno
53 Monumento a los Niños Héroes
56 Juegos Mecánicos Infantiles
57 Museo del Caracol
58 Castillo de Chapultepec &
   Museo Nacional de Historia
59 La Feria
60 Museo Tecnológico
61 Papalote Museo del Niño
62 Los Pinos (Presidential
   Residence)
63 Galería de Arte Mexicano
64 Museo de Historia Natural

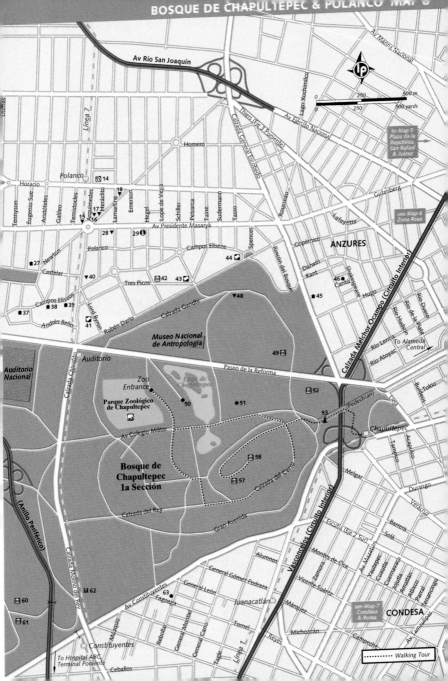

Av Marina Nacional

Av Río San Joaquín

Lago Xochimilco

Thiers (Eje 3 Poniente)

Calzada Central Escorado

Av Ejército Nacional

0   250   500 m

250   500 yards

See Map 5
Plaza de la
República,
San Rafael
& Juárez

Linea 7

Homero

Polanco

Horacio

See Map 6
Zona Rosa

Tennyson
Eugenio Sue
Aristóteles
Galileo
Temístocles
Arquímedes
Heráclito
Lamartine
Emerson
Hegel
Lope de Vega
Schiller
Petrarca
Taine
Sudermann
Tasso

Rousseau

Lafayette

Gutenberg

14

18

15
16
17

Av Presidente Masaryk

Spencer

Copérnico

ANZURES

28   29

Polanco

Campos Elíseos

Rincón del Bosque

Darwin
Kant

27
Castelar

Newton

44

Tres Picos

42   43

Shakespeare
Cantú
46

Huxley

Campos Elíseos
38   39

Lord Byron

Calzada Gandhi

48

45

Calzada Melchor Ocampo (Circuito Interior)

Río Duero

37

Andrés Bello

Rubén Darío

Río de la Plata
Río Hudson

40

41

Museo Nacional
de Antropología

49

Río Lerma

To Alameda
Central

Río Atoyac

Auditorio
Nacional

Auditorio

Calzada Chivatito

Paseo de la Reforma

Lieja

Buffalo Tokio

Zoo
Entrance

Lago de
Chapultepec

52

(Pedestrian)

Tampico

Acapulco

50

51

53

Chapultepec

Parque Zoológico
de Chapultepec

Durango

Veracruz

Av Colegio Militar

Melgar

(Anillo Periférico)

Bosque de
Chapultepec
1a Sección

58

Barrera
Solá

Calzada del Cerro

57

Calzada del Rey

Av Mazatlán

Gran Avenida

Escutia (Eje 2 Sur)

Vasconcelos (Circuito Interior)

Alumnos

Montes de Oca

Calzada Molino del Rey

General Gómez Pedraza

General León

Vicente Suárez

Zamora

Cuauhtémoc

Saltillo

Ometusco

Amatlán

Atlixco

Parral

Pachuca

See Map 7
Condesa
& Roma

CONDESA

62

Av Constituyentes
Fagoaga

63

Juanacatlán

Márquez

Michoacán

Campeche

Tamaulipas

60

Constituyentes

Mazatlán

Rébsamen

General Cano

Tornel

Linea 1

Reyes

Walking Tour

61

To Hospital ABC
Terminal Poniente

Ceballos

General Mártir

Tlapa

Enjoying lunch outdoors in San Ángel

Aztec dancer in the Zócalo

Ballet Folklórico dancers

Mosaic by Francisco Eppens on the UNAM Facultad de Medicina building

Local craftwork

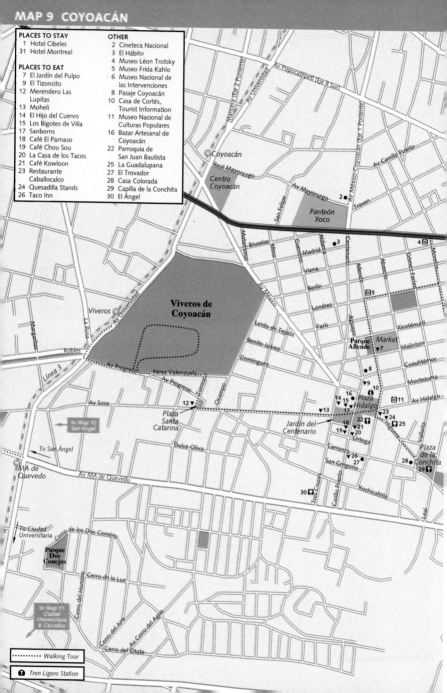

MAP 9 COYOACÁN

MAP 10 SAN ÁNGEL

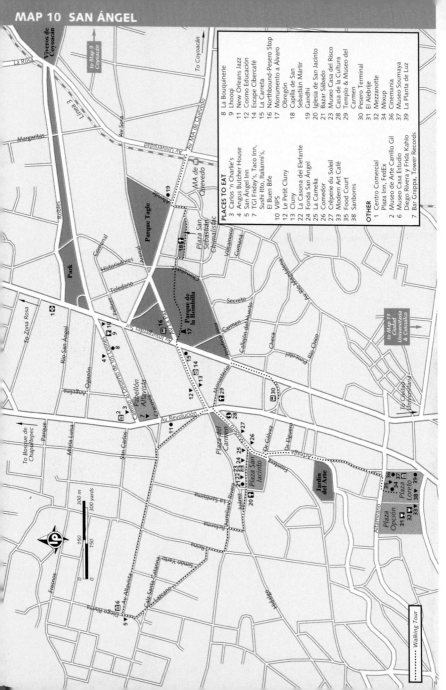

PLACES TO EAT

3 Carlos 'n Charlie's
4 Angus Butcher House
5 San Ángel Inn
7 TGI Friday's, Taco Inn, Sushi Itto, Italianni's, El Buen Bife
10 VIPS
12 Le Petit Cluny
13 Cluny
22 La Casona del Elefante
24 Fonda San Ángel
25 La Camelia
26 Comedor
27 Crêperie du Soleil
33 Modern Art Café
35 Food Court
38 Sanborns

8 La Bouquinerie
9 Lhooqi
11 New Orleans Jazz
12 Cosmo Educación
14 Escape Cibercafé
15 La Carreta
16 Northbound-Pesero Stop
17 Monumento a Álvaro Obregón
18 Capilla de San Sebastián Mártir
19 Gandhi
20 Iglesia de San Jacinto
21 Bazar Sábado
23 Museo Casa del Risco
28 Casa de la Cultura
29 Templo & Museo del Carmen
30 Pesero Terminal
31 El Alebrije
32 Mezzanotte
34 Mixup
36 Cinemanía
37 Museo Soumaya
39 La Planta de Luz

OTHER

1 Centro Comercial Plaza Inn, FedEx
2 Museo de Arte Carrillo Gil
6 Museo Casa Estudio Diego Rivera y Frida Kahlo
7 Bar Grappa, Tower Records

Walking Tour

Exterior detail on the Casa de Azulejos (House of Tiles)

The Casa Vieja hotel: quaint and colonial on the outside with modern luxuries on the inside

MAP 11 CIUDAD UNIVERSITARIA & CUICUILCO

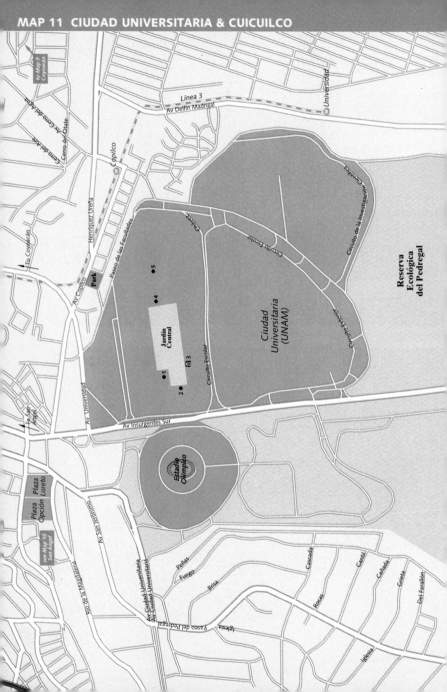

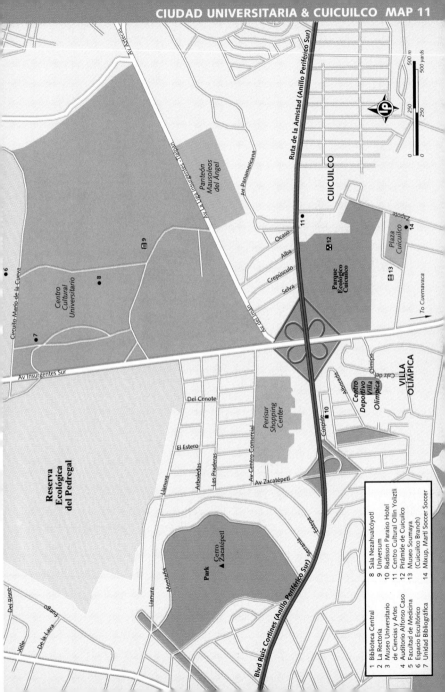

1 Biblioteca Central
2 La Rectoría
3 Museo Universitario
   de Ciencias y Artes
4 Auditorio Alfonso Caso
5 Facultad de Medicina
6 Espacio Escultórico
7 Unidad Bibliográfica

8 Sala Nezahualcóyotl
9 Universum
10 Radisson Paraíso Hotel
11 Centro Cultural Ollin Yoliztli
12 Pirámide de Cuicuilco
13 Museo Soumaya
   (Cuicuilco Branch)
14 Mixup, Martí Soccer Soccer

MAP 12 XOCHIMILCO

Canal Tlithuil

Canal El Bordo

Calle 24

Av Canal de Chalco

Anillo Periférico

Parque Ecológico de Xochimilco

Mercado de Flores, Plantas y Hortalizas

Lago Huetzalin

Canal Nacional

Av Canal Nacional

Antiguo Canal de Cuemanco

2

Pista Olímpica de Canotaje Virgilio Uribe

Hacienda de las Morales

Park

Calzada del Hueso

Canal Cuemanco

Canal Toltenco

Av Sauzales

Anáhuac

Rancho La Estanzuela

Park

Park

Vaso Regulador

Rancho Vista Hermosa

Park

Acatitales

Av Moyoguarda

Cuchatitlán

Pilastra

Camino a las Cánteras

Villa de Ayala

Alameda del Sur

Calzada de los Tenorios

Calzada del Hueso

Anillo Periférico Sur

Prolongación División del Norte

Park

Av Canal de Miramontes

Calzada Acoxpa

500 m
500 yards
250
250
0
0

Canal Apatlaco

Canal Ampampilco

Canal Santa Cruz

NATIVITAS

Av Mexico

Av Tenochtitlan

10
Embarcadero

Canal de Acromulco

11

Mercado Central

Gardenias

Bosque de Nativitas

Cemetery

Carr Xochimilco-Tulyehualco

Camino Vieja a Nativitas

8
Av Nuevo León

Parroquia de San
Bernardino de Siena

Av Nuevo León

7
Violeta

Hidalgo

Madero

9

Camino a Nativitas

Carretera Xochimilco-Tulyehualco

Prol Division del Norte

5
Pino

6
Av Morelos

Nezahualcoyotl

Embarcadero

Cuauhtémoc

Cuauhtémoc

16 de Mayo

Cadena

Ramino del Conejo

5 de Mayo

Cuauhtémoc

Coulia

16 de Septiembre

Prolongación 16 de Septiembre

Circunvalación

XOCHIMILCO

Gladiolas

Margaritas

Av Morelos

Xochimilco

Prolongación División del Norte

Av Mexico

Citlaltépetl

Centro Deportivo
Xochimilco

Vaso Regulador
San Lucas

Av la Presa San Lucas

Camino

Matiz

Río Santiago

Park

Acceso Oriente

Patios

Av Tepotzotlán

Av Nezahualcóyotl

Ahuéuetes

Prolongación Acueducto

Av 20 de Noviembre

10

Huichapan

Clavel

Av Guadalupe Ramírez

La Noria

Panteón
Jilotepec

3

Calzada San Bernardino

Martires del Río Blanco

Carretera Xochimilco San Pablo Toplejo

Prolongación-Acueducto

Carretera Xochimilco San Pablo

Antiguo Camino a Xochimilco

Av Mexico

12

MAP LEGEND

BOUNDARIES

- ·•·■·•·■·•· International
- ·•··■·•··■·•· Province

HYDROGRAPHY

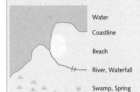

- Water
- Coastline
- Beach
- River, Waterfall
- Swamp, Spring

ROUTES & TRANSPORT

- Freeway
- Toll Freeway
- Primary Road
- Secondary Road
- Tertiary Road
- Unpaved Road
- Pedestrian Mall
- Trail
- Walking Tour
- Ferry Route
- Railway, Train Station
- Metro Line, Metro Station

ROUTE SHIELDS

- 95 Mexico Highway
- 95D Mexico Toll Highway

AREA FEATURES

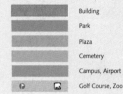

- Building
- Park
- Plaza
- Cemetery
- Campus, Airport
- Golf Course, Zoo

MAP SYMBOLS

- ○ NATIONAL CAPITAL
- ◉ State, Provincial Capital
- ● LARGE CITY
- ● Medium City
- ● Small City
- ● Town, Village
- ● Point of Interest

- ⬛ Place to Stay
- ⬛ Campground
- ⬛ RV Park

- ▼ Place to Eat
- ⬛ Bar (Place to Drink), Nightclub

- ✝ Airfield
- ✈ Airport
- ⬛ Archaeological Site, Ruins
- ⬛ Bank
- ⬛ Baseball Diamond
- ⬛ Beach
- ⬛ Border Crossing
- ⬛ Bus Station
- ⬛ Bus Stop
- ⬛ Cable Car
- ⬛ Cathedral
- ⬛ Cave
- ⬛ Church
- ⬛ Embassy, Consulate
- ⬛ Fish Hatchery
- ⟩⟨ Footbridge
- ⬛ Garden
- ⬛ Gas Station
- ⬛ Hospital, Clinic
- ⬛ Information
- ⬛ Internet Access

- ⬛ Lighthouse
- ⬛ Lookout
- ▲ Monument
- ▲ Mountain
- ⬛ Museum
- ⬛ Observatory
- ⬛ Park
- ⬛ Parking
- ⟩⟨ Pass
- ⬛ Picnic Area
- ⬛ Police Station
- ⬛ Pool
- ⬛ Post Office
- ⬛ Shopping Mall
- ⬛ Skiing (Alpine)
- ⬛ Skiing (Nordic)
- ⬛ Stately Home
- ⬛ Trailhead
- ⟩ Tunnel
- ▲ Volcano
- ⬛ Winery

Note: Not all symbols displayed above appear in this book.

LONELY PLANET OFFICES

Australia
PO Box 617, Hawthorn 3122, Victoria
☎ 03 9819 1877 fax 03 9819 6459
email talk2us@lonelyplanet.com.au

USA
150 Linden Street, Oakland, California 94607
☎ 510 893 8555, TOLL FREE 800 275 8555
fax 510 893 8572
email info@lonelyplanet.com

UK
10A Spring Place, London NW5 3BH
☎ 020 7428 4800 fax 020 7428 4828
email go@lonelyplanet.co.uk

France
1 rue du Dahomey, 75011 Paris
☎ 01 55 25 33 00 fax 01 55 25 33 01
www.lonelyplanet.fr

World Wide Web: www.lonelyplanet.com *or* AOL keyword: lp
Lonely Planet Images: lpi@lonelyplanet.com.au